London

"All you've got to do is decide to go
and the hardest part is over.

So go!"

TONY WHEELER, COFOUNDER – LONELY PLANET

Damian Harper, Peter Dragicevich, Steve Fallon, Emilie Filou

Contents

(left) **Brixton village p296** Multicultural London at its best.

(above) **Houses of Parliament p85** Your London postcard view.

(right) **Claridge's Foyer & Reading Room p120** Treat yourself to the perfect afternoon tea.

Welcome to London

One of the world's most visited cities, London has something for everyone: from history and culture to fine food and good times.

Time Travel

Immersed in history, London's rich seams of eye-opening antiquity are everywhere. The city's buildings are striking milestones in a unique and beguiling biography, and a great many of them – the Tower of London, Westminster Abbey, Big Ben – are instantly recognisable landmarks. There's more than enough innovation (the Shard, the Tate Modern extension, the planned Garden Bridge) to put a crackle in the air, but it never drowns out London's seasoned, centuries-old narrative. Architectural grandeur rises all around you in the West End, ancient remains dot the City, and charming pubs punctuate the historic quarters, leafy suburbs and river banks. Take your pick.

Art & Culture

A tireless innovator of art and culture, London is a city of ideas and imagination. Londoners have always been fiercely independent thinkers (and critics), but until not so long ago people were suspicious of anything they considered avant-garde. That's in the past now, and the city's creative milieu is streaked with left-field attitude, whether it's theatrical innovation, contemporary art, music, writing, poetry, architecture or design. Food is another creative arena that has become a tireless obsession in certain circles.

Diversity

This city is deeply multicultural, with one in three Londoners foreign-born, representing 270 nationalities and 300 tongues. Britain may have voted for Brexit (although the majority of Londoners didn't), but for now London remains one of the world's most cosmopolitan cities, and diversity infuses daily life, food, music and fashion. It even penetrates intrinsically British institutions; the British Museum and Victoria & Albert Museum have collections as varied as they are magnificent, while the flavours at centuries-old Borough Market run the full global gourmet spectrum.

A Tale of Two Cities

London is as much about wide-open vistas and leafy landscape escapes as it is high-density, sight-packed urban exploration. Central London is where the major museums, galleries and most iconic sights congregate, but visit Hampstead Heath or the Queen Elizabeth Olympic Park to flee the crowds and frolic in wide open green expanses. You can also venture further out to Kew Gardens, Richmond or Hampton Court Palace for beautiful panoramas of riverside London followed by a pint in a quiet waterside pub.

Why I Love London

By Emilie Filou, Writer

London has been my adopted home for nearly 15 years and I still marvel at its energy and diversity. Living here is a constant discovery: new restaurants and bars, outstanding museum extensions or refurbishments (and yet many remain free), once-derelict but now trendy neighbourhoods, and four distinct seasons that each bring unique pleasures. The spectre of Brexit may be looming over the city's famed cultural diversity but I take heart in the fact that London always seems to buck the trend. I, for one, ain't going anywhere.

For more about our writers, see p480

Top: View of Tower Bridge (p146) and City Hall

London's
Top 16

British Museum (p79)

1 With more than six million visitors trooping through its doors annually, the British Museum in Bloomsbury is Britain's most visited attraction. You could spend a lifetime in this vast and hallowed collection of artefacts, art and age-old antiquity, and still make daily discoveries. If you're not sure where to start, join one of the highlights or eye-opener tours for a precis of the museum's treasures. Whatever your approach, make sure you glimpse the Rosetta Stone, key to deciphering hieroglyphics, and the other-worldly mummies.

◉ *The West End*

Tate Modern (p160)

2 The favourite museum of Londoners (and quite possibly the world), this contemporary art collection enjoys a triumphant position right on the River Thames. Housed in the former Bankside Power Station, the Tate Modern is a vigorous statement of modernity, architectural renewal and accessibility. The permanent collection is free, and the gallery's ziggurat extension, opened in 2016, provides 60% more exhibition space and a new (and free) vantage point in London. Exhibition spaces are pushing the conceptual envelope too, with installation and performance art.

◉ *The South Bank*

ANNA LEVAN/SHUTTERSTOCK ©

MATT MUNRO/LONELY PLANET ©

ENTRY TO THE TRAITORS GATE

National Gallery

(p87)

3 This superlative collection of (largely premodern) art in the heart of London is one of the largest anywhere, and provides a roll-call of some of the world's most outstanding artistic compositions. With highlights including works by Leonardo da Vinci, Michelangelo, Gainsborough, Constable, Turner, Monet, Renoir and Van Gogh, it's a bravura performance and one not to be missed. The on-site restaurant is also exceptional, rounding out a terrific experience and putting the icing on an already eye-catching cake.

⊙ *The West End*

Tower of London

(p137)

4 Few parts of the UK are as steeped in history or as impregnated with legend and superstition as the titanic stonework of this fabulous fortress. Not only is the tower an architectural odyssey but there's also one of the world's largest diamonds, free tours from magnificently attired 'Beefeaters', a dazzling array of armour and weaponry, and a palpable sense of ancient history at every turn. Because there is simply so much to see, it's well worth getting here early – you will need at least half a day for exploration.

⊙ *The City*

Culinary London

(p44)

5 Don't let anybody tell you that the food in England is a let-down: London has long been a shining light in culinary excellence, with a kaleidoscope of cuisines unrivalled in Europe. The capital is particularly strong in Indian and other Asian flavours, but don't miss the opportunity of trying traditional or Modern British cuisine, either in a good gastropub or one of the finer restaurants, such as Dinner. For those with a sweet tooth, an afternoon tea or a treat from the capital's many cake shops is a must.

✗ *Eating*

Victoria & Albert Museum (p178)

6 You could spend a whole day in the huge Victoria & Albert Museum and still be astounded at its variety and depth. Located in stylish South Kensington, the world's leading collection of decorative arts has something for everyone, from Islamic textiles to antique Chinese ceramics, photography, fashion, works by Raphael and modern design classics from iMacs to Nike shoes. And don't overlook the fabulous architecture of the museum, which is a major attraction in itself.

◉ *Kensington & Hyde Park*

London Pubs (p52)

7 London minus its pubs such as Lamb & Flag would be like Paris sans cafes. Pub culture is a part of London's DNA and the pub is best place to see local people in their hop-scented element. Longer opening hours have cemented them as the cornerstone for a good night out across the capital. They're also a favourite for family-friendly long weekend lunches. Once no-go zones for discerning foodies, pubs have long upped their game: standout gastropubs dot London's culinary cosmos and rival great restaurants.

🍷 *Drinking & Nightlife*

London Eye (p165)

8 You may have eyeballed London from altitude as you descended into Heathrow, but your pilot won't have lingered over the supreme views that extend in every direction from London's great riverside Ferris wheel. The queues move as slowly as the Eye rotates (though there are ways to fast-track admission), but you're rewarded once you've lifted off and London unfurls beneath you. Avoid grey days – if possible! If you've limited time, make this the first stop on your visit so you can at least say you've seen the sights.

◉ *The South Bank*

Natural History Museum (p182)

9 With its thunderous, animatronic *Tyrannosaurus rex*, riveting displays about planet Earth, the outstanding Darwin Centre and architecture straight from a Gothic fairy tale, the Natural History Museum is quite simply a work of great curatorial imagination. Kids are the target audience but, looking around, you'll see adults equally mesmerised. Unveiled in 2017 the new-look Hintze Hall, with its diving blue whale and new exhibits, keeps the museum looking fresh. Winter brings its own magic, when the glittering ice rink by the east lawn swarms with skaters.

⊙ *Kensington & Hyde Park*

Westminster Abbey (p76)

10 Adorers of medieval ecclesiastic architecture will be in seventh heaven at this sublime abbey, hallowed place of coronation for England's sovereigns. Almost every nook and cranny has a story attached to it. Among the highlights, you will find the oldest door in the UK, Poet's Corner, the Coronation Chair, 14th-century cloisters, a 900-year-old garden, royal sarcophagi and much more. Be warned that the crowds are almost as solid as the abbey's unshakeable stonework, so aim to join the queue first thing in the morning.

⊙ *The West End*

Kew Gardens (p314)

11 Where else in London can you size up an 18th-century 10-storey Chinese pagoda and a Japanese gateway while finding yourself among one of the world's most outstanding botanical collections? Kew Gardens is loved by Londoners for its 19th-century Palm House and other Victorian glasshouses, its conservatories, tree canopy walkway, architectural follies and mind-boggling variety of plants. Kids will have a ball in the play areas. You could easily spend the day here, but the Kew Explorer train will help you tick the main sights in half that time.

⊙ *Richmond, Kew & Hampton Court*

Hampton Court Palace *(p310)*

12 It may no longer be a royal residence but Hampton Court hasn't lost its splendour – inside or out. The magnificent Tudor palace, so coveted by Henry VIII that he coaxed it from Cardinal Thomas Wolsey in 1515, was extended in the 17th century by Christopher Wren, and visitors can delight in the different architectural styles. Don't miss the Tudor kitchens, which once churned out meals for up to 1200 people for Henry's court, and make sure you leave time for the sumptuous gardens – you might get lost in the maze...

⊙ Richmond, Kew & Hampton Court

West End Performances (p126)

13 The West End is synonymous with musicals; no trip to London would be complete without an evening of *Mama Mia!*, *Les Misérables* or *Phantom of the Opera*. But if musicals aren't to your taste, there are more alternatives than you'll have evenings to fill: theatre, dance, opera, small gigs, big-ticket concerts or live jazz at venues such as Ronnie Scott's. London truly is the capital of the arts. The trick is to book either far in advance for a particular show or last minute for bargains. APOLLO VICTORIA THEATRE

⭐ *Entertainment*

Camden Town (p253)

14 A foray into trendy North London, away from the central sights, is a crucial part of the London experience. Camden's market – actually three markets in one great melange – may be a hectic and tourist-oriented attraction, but snacking on the go from its international food stalls is a great way to enjoy browsing the merchandise. At night Camden's terrific music scene, throbbing nightlife and well-seasoned pub culture are magnets pulling in night owls from across the city. CAMDEN LOCK

⊙ *Hampstead & North London*

Shakespeare's Globe (p162)

15 Few London experiences can beat a Bard's-eye view of the stage at the re-created Globe. Get a standing ticket as one of the all-weather 'groundlings' who watch from the open-air yard before the stage for an unusual Elizabethan-style experience. Otherwise pay extra for a seat in the gallery. The theatre is a triumph of authenticity, right down to the nail-less construction, English-oak beams, original joinery and thatching (sprinklers are a modern touch). If you've a soft spot for Shakespeare, you'll have an absolute ball here.

👁 *The South Bank*

Hyde Park & Kensington Gardens (p184)

16 London's urban parkland is virtually second to none and is *the* place to see locals at ease and in their element. Hyde Park alone ranges across a mighty 142 hectares; throw in Kensington Gardens and you have even more space to roam and everything you could want: a central London setting, a royal palace, extravagant Victoriana, boating opportunities, open-air concerts, art galleries, magnificent trees, and a tasteful granite memorial to Princess Diana, as well as a magnificently overblown memorial to Prince Albert facing the grand form of the Albert Hall. HYDE PARK

👁 *Kensington & Hyde Park*

What's New

Tate Modern Extension

At long last the Tate Modern can spread its expansive collection into Switch House. The views from the 10th floor are second to none (and free). (p160)

Fourth Plinth gets Geopolitical

In 2018 artist Michael Rakowitz will take over the Fourth Plinth on Trafalgar Sq with *The Invisible Enemy Should Not Exist*, a re-creation of a sculpture destroyed by so-called Islamic State. (p102)

All Aboard Crossrail

The capital's most ambitious transport project in a generation has started operating between London Liverpool St and Shenfield in the east; the Paddington to Heathrow branch in the west is scheduled to open in May 2018.

Southbank Facelift

The brutalist wing of the Southbank Centre, which contains the Hayward Gallery and the Queen Elizabeth Hall, has been given a 21st-century makeover, scheduled for unveiling in early 2018. (p168)

Architecture for Science

The Science Museum has unveiled its new Mathematics gallery; the stunning look is courtesy of the late and much acclaimed architect Zaha Hadid. (p186)

Bigger & Better Design Museum

The Design Museum moved to its new premises in Holland Park, West London, in November 2016. The building itself is a 1960s design icon and the museum has three times more space than in its previous location by the Thames. (p273)

Natural History Museum Newcomers

In summer 2017 the Natural History Museum unveiled its new look Hintze Hall, the heart of the gallery, which is now spectacularly adorned by the plunging skeleton of a blue whale and features new displays too. (p182)

West Ham Move In

East London's West Ham United football club has a new home at the Olympic Stadium after protracted negotiations and a long refurbishment of the ground. (p232)

Regeneration in King's Cross

The redevelopment of once derelict King's Cross continues apace, with the opening of the stunning Gasholder Park, an artisan food market, and a smattering of new restaurants and bars. (p251)

A Giant Slide

Carsten Höller's giant slide opened in 2016. It corkscrews 12 times around Anish Kapoor's famous Queen Elizabeth Olympic Park landmark ArcelorMittal Orbit tower and has proved a hit. (p232)

For more recommendations and reviews, see **lonelyplanet. com/london**

Need to Know

For more information, see Survival Guide (p409)

Currency
Pound sterling (£)

Language
English (and more than 300 others)

Visas
Not required for Australian, Canadian, New Zealand and US visitors, as well as several other nations, for stays of up to six months.

Money
ATMs are widespread. Major credit cards are accepted everywhere. The best place to change money is in post-office branches, which do not charge a commission.

Mobile Phones
Buy local SIM cards for European and Australian phones, or a pay-as-you-go phone. Set other phones to international roaming.

Time
London is on GMT/UTC; during British Summer Time (BST; late March to late October), London clocks are one hour ahead of GMT/UTC.

Tourist Information
Visit London (www.visitlondon.com) can fill you in on everything from attractions and events to tours and accommodation. Kiosks are dotted about the city and can also provide maps and brochures; some branches are able to book theatre tickets.

Daily Costs

Budget: Less than £85
➡ Dorm bed: £12–30
➡ Market-stall lunch or supermarket sandwich: £3.50–5
➡ Many museums: free
➡ Standby theatre tickets: £5–25
➡ Santander Cycles daily rental fee: £2

Midrange: £85–200
➡ Double room: £100–200
➡ Two-course dinner with glass of wine: £35
➡ Temporary exhibitions: £12–18
➡ Theatre tickets: £15–60

Top end: More than £200
➡ Four-star or boutique hotel room: more than £200
➡ Three-course dinner in top restaurant with wine: £60–90
➡ Black cab trip: £30
➡ Top theatre tickets: £65

Advance Planning
Three months before Book performances for top shows; make dinner reservations at renowned restaurants; snap up tickets for must-see temporary exhibitions; book accommodation.

One month before Check listings on entertainment sites such as *Time Out* (www.timeout.com/london) for fringe theatre, live music and festivals, and book tickets.

A few days before Check the weather online through the **Met Office** (www.metoffice.gov.uk).

Useful Websites

Lonely Planet (www.lonelyplanet.com /england/london) Destination information, hotel bookings, traveller forum and more.)

Time Out London (www.timeout.com/london) Up-to-date and comprehensive entertainment listings distributed for free every Tuesday.

Londonist (www.londonist.com) A website about London and everything that happens in it.

Transport for London (www.tfl.gov.uk) Essential tool for staying mobile in the capital.

London Evening Standard (www.standard.co.uk) The capital's main newspaper, distributed free at every tube station.

WHEN TO GO

Summer is peak season: days are long and festivals are afoot, but expect crowds. Spring and autumn are cooler, but delightful. Winter is cold, with short days.

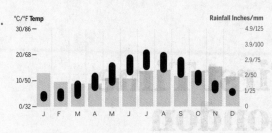

°C/°F Temp
30/86 —
20/68 —
10/50 —
0/32 —

J F M A M J J A S O N D

Rainfall Inches/mm
4.9/125
3.9/100
2.9/75
2/50
1/25
0

Arriving in London

Heathrow Airport Trains, the tube and buses to London from just after 5am to before midnight (night buses run later and 24-hour tube runs Friday and Saturday) cost £5.70–21.50; taxi £46–87. From 2018 express trains run along the Elizabeth Line (Crossrail).

Gatwick Airport Trains to London from 4.30am to 1.35am cost £10–20; hourly buses to London 24/7, from £5; taxi £100.

Stansted Airport Trains to London from 5.30am to 1.30am cost £23.40; 24/7 buses to London from £12; taxi from £130.

Luton Airport Trains to London from 7am to 10pm from £14; buses 24/7 to London, £10; taxi £110.

London City Airport DLR trains to central London from 5.30am to 12.30am Monday to Saturday, 7am to 11.15pm Sunday from £2.80; taxi around £30.

St Pancras International Train Station In Central London (for Eurostar train arrivals from Europe) and connected by many underground lines to other parts of the city.

For much more on **arrival** see p410

Digital London

There are scores of cool apps for travellers. Here are some of our favourite free ones – from inspirational to downright practical. Many museums and attractions also have their own.

Streetmuseum Historical images (photographs, paintings, drawings etc) superimposed on modern-day locations.

Street Art Tours London Hand-picked graffiti and other street-art locations.

CityMapper Great app giving you all the options for getting from A to B (on foot, by public transport, bike or cab).

TubeMap Features a tube map offline, and a full interactive route service when connected.

Hailo Summons the nearest black cab right to the curb.

Uber A taxi, private car or ride-share at competitive prices.

London Bus Live Real-time route finder and bus arrivals for a stop of your choice.

Santander Cycles Find a 'Boris Bike', a route and a place to return it.

For much more on **getting around** see p22

Sleeping

Hanging your hat (or anything else you care to remove) in London can be painfully expensive, and you'll almost always need to book well in advance. Decent hostels are easy to find but aren't as cheap as you might hope for. Hotels range from no-frills chains through to the world's most ritzy establishments, such as the Ritz itself. B&Bs are often better value and more atmospheric than hotels.

Useful Websites

Visit London (www.visitlondon. com) Huge range of listings from the city's official tourism portal.

London Town (www.london town.com) Excellent last-minute offers on boutique hotels and B&Bs.

Alastair Sawdays (www. sawdays.co.uk) Hand-picked selection of boltholes in the capital.

Lonely Planet (www.lonely planet.com /london)

For much more on **sleeping** see p342

First Time London

For more information, see Survival Guide (p409)

Checklist

➡ Make sure your passport is valid for at least six months past your arrival date.

➡ Check the latest visa requirements.

➡ Arrange travel insurance and inform your debit-/credit-card company of your travel plans.

➡ Book tickets for popular plays, shows or festivals to avoid disappointment.

➡ Reserve hotel rooms well in advance.

What to Pack

➡ An umbrella (yes, the rumours about the weather are true)

➡ Good walking shoes – the city is best explored on foot

➡ UK plug adaptor

➡ A few extra layers – it can be cool, even in summer

➡ A small day pack

Top Tips for Your Trip

➡ London is huge – organise your visit by neighbourhood to avoid wasting time (and money) on transport.

➡ An Oyster Card is a cheaper and convenient way to use public transport, but you can also pay by credit or debit card provided it has a contactless function indicated by a wi-fi-like symbol.

➡ Walk – it's cheaper, and the best way to discover central London.

➡ For West End performances at bargain prices, opt for standby tickets or last-minute tickets from the booths on Leicester Sq.

➡ To treat yourself to fine dining without breaking the bank, opt for lunch rather than dinner, or try for pre- or post-theatre dinner deals.

➡ Book online for ticketed attractions to save money and skip queues.

What to Wear

Fashion is big in London but very eclectic so you're unlikely to stand out, whatever your sartorial choice. Many top-end restaurants, bars and clubs will insist on smart attire, especially shoes. Style is pretty relaxed elsewhere, although Londoners usually make an effort in the evenings.

The weather has a mind of its own, regardless of the season: always carry an umbrella or a jacket that can repel a shower or two. And do wrap up warm in winter: the wind can be punishing.

Be Forewarned

London is a fairly safe city, so exercising common sense should keep you secure.

➡ A number of high-profile terrorist attacks have taken place in London, but the risk of an incident affecting individual visitors is remote. If you see anything suspicious, contact the police by calling 999 (emergency) or 101 (non-emergency).

➡ Pickpocketing does happen, so keep an eye on your valuables

➡ Be discreet with your tablet/smartphone – snatching happens.

➡ If you're getting a cab after a night's clubbing, make sure you go for a black taxi or a licensed minicab firm.

Money

ATMs are widespread. Major credit cards are accepted everywhere. The best place to change money is in post-office branches, which do not charge a commission.
For more information, see p419.

Taxes & Refunds

Value-added tax (VAT) is a 20% sales tax levied on most goods and services. Restaurants must always include VAT in their prices, but the same requirement does not apply to hotel room prices, so double-check when booking.

It's sometimes possible for visitors to claim a refund of VAT (p420) paid on goods.

Tipping

➡ **Hotels** Pay a porter £1 per bag; gratuity for room staff is at your discretion.

➡ **Pubs** Not expected unless table service is provided, then £1 for a round of drinks is sufficient. Do not tip at the bar.

➡ **Restaurants** Service charge often included in the bill. If not, 10% for decent service, up to 15% if exceptional.

➡ **Taxis** Londoners generally round fare up to nearest pound only.

Tower Bridge (p146)

Etiquette

Although largely informal in their everyday dealings, Londoners do observe some (unspoken) rules of etiquette.

➡ **Strangers** Unless asking for directions, British people generally won't start a conversation at bus stops or on tube platforms. More latitude is given to non-British people.

➡ **Queues** The British don't tolerate queue jumping. Any attempt to do so will receive tutting and protest.

➡ **Tube** Stand on the right and pass on the left while riding an Underground escalator.

➡ **Bargaining** Haggling over the price of goods (but not food) is okay in markets, but non-existent in shops.

➡ **Apologise** The British love apologising. If you bump into someone on the tube, say sorry.

Staying Connected

➡ Virtually every hotel in London now provides wi-fi free of charge.

➡ A huge number of cafes, restaurants and cultural centres offer free wi-fi to customers

➡ Open-air and street wi-fi access is available in areas across London, including Oxford St, Trafalgar Sq, Piccadilly Circus, the City of London and Islington's Upper St.

➡ Most major train stations, airport terminals and even some Underground stations also have wi-fi, but access isn't always free.

➡ See Time Out's Free Wi-fi Map (www.timeout.com/london/things-to-do/where-to-find-free-wi-fi-in-london-9) for more locations.

Getting Around

For more information, see Transport (p410)

The cheapest way to get around London is with an Oyster Card or a UK contactless card (foreign cardholders should check for contactless charges first).

Tube (London Underground) The fastest and most efficient way of getting around town. First/last trains operate from around 5.30am/12.30am and 24 hours on Friday and Saturday on five lines.

Train The DLR and Overground network are ideal for zooming across more distant parts of the city. Trains run from a number of stations to more distant destinations in and around London.

Bus The London bus network is very extensive and efficient; while bus lanes free up traffic, buses can still be slow going.

Taxis Black cabs are ubiquitous, but not cheap. Available around the clock.

Rideshare Apps such as Uber or Kabbee allow you to book a ride in double-quick time and can save you money.

Bicycle Santander Cycles are great for shorter journeys around central London.

Key Phrases

Black cab London's signature taxi. Despite the name, they're not all black!

Boris bike A colloquialism that has stuck for the red Santander-branded bikes for hire all across London. Nicknamed after former mayor – and current Foreign Secretary – Boris Johnson.

Contactless Payment card (debit or credit) that can be used to make quick (and reduced fare) payments without signature or chip and pin; used in the same way as an Oyster Card.

DLR Docklands Light Railway, an overground, driver-less train in East London.

Minicab A taxi that cannot be hailed in the street and must be pre-booked over the phone, in person with the dispatcher (offices generally have an orange flashing light) or through apps such as Uber.

Oyster Card Smart-card ticket for London's transport network.

Night tube London's underground all-night service, running 24 hours on Friday and Saturday across five lines.

The tube London's underground metro system.

Key Routes

Bus Route 15 This 'heritage' bus route uses the classic Routemaster double-decker buses and takes in the Tower of London, St Paul's, the Strand and Trafalgar Sq.

Bus Route 9 Another 'heritage' classic Routemaster double-decker bus passing through the West End to Kensington High St.

Bus Route RV1 Links the sights along the South Bank with Covent Garden across the river.

DLR: Bank to Greenwich Bag the seats at the front for an amazing sightseeing trip through the Docklands and Canary Wharf.

Tube: Piccadilly Line This tube line stops at some of London's key sights and neighbourhoods and also runs from all Heathrow airport terminals.

How to Hail a Taxi

➡ To hail a black cab, look for a stationary or approaching cab with its 'For Hire' sign lit up.

➡ If the car is approaching, stand in a prominent place on the side of the road and stick out your arm.

➡ Alternatively find them at the numerous taxi ranks dotting the city

➡ Use a smartphone app such as mytaxi (https://uk.mytaxi.com/hailo), which uses your phone's GPS to find the nearest available black cab.

TOP TIPS

➡ As a general rule, eschew the tube within Zone 1 unless going from one end to the other: cycling, walking or the bus will be cheaper/quicker.

➡ Check www.tfl.gov.uk or advanced notices in tube stations for engineering works and line closures at weekends.

➡ Get an Oyster Card – and return it when you leave to get the £5 deposit back, along with any remaining credit.

➡ Santander Cycles (p415) are good for short trips. Get a rental bike for longer trips.

➡ Hail black cabs in the street and book ahead for a minicab.

When to Travel

➡ Rush hour is between 6.30am and 9.30am and from 4pm to 7pm.

➡ Travelling at these times can be uncomfortably crowded: think seat races, face-in-armpit standing, toe-treading and frayed nerves.

➡ Tube fares are more expensive at rush hour.

➡ Weekends are notorious for engineering works, when entire tube lines or sections shut down. Replacement bus services are usually in place, but they take longer so try to plan ahead.

➡ On Sunday to Thursday nights, the tube stops running around 12.30am. The Night Tube operates a 24-hour service on Friday and Saturday nights, covering the Central, Jubilee, Victoria, Northern and Piccadilly lines, with trains running roughly every eight to 10 minutes. Night Tube fares are standard off-peak.

➡ Night buses cover all of London, but some services only run every half-hour. Check times before leaving.

Travel Etiquette

➡ Have your ticket or card ready before you go through the gate. Londoners are well practised at moving through ticket barriers without breaking stride.

➡ On escalators, stand on the right-hand side and use the left if you want to walk down. Failure to observe this can cause consternation and tutting among other users, especially during rush hour.

➡ Take your rucksack off at rush hour to avoid sweeping off somebody's newspaper, tablet or child.

➡ Give up your seat for people less able to stand than you – people with reduced mobility have priority over the seats closest to the doors on the tube.

➡ Cars will almost always stop for pedestrians at zebra crossings without a traffic light; remember to look right first!

Tickets & Passes

➡ The cheapest and most convenient way to pay for public transport is to buy an Oyster Card, a smart card on which you can store credit. The card works on the entire transport network and can be purchased from all tube and train stations and some shops.

➡ Oyster Cards will work out whether to charge you per journey, for a return or for a day Travelcard.

➡ You need to pay a £5 deposit per Oyster Card, which you will get back when you return the card, along with any remaining credit.

➡ If you're staying for more than just a few days, consider getting a weekly or monthly pass (which can be loaded on to the Oyster Card).

➡ Paper tickets are still available but are more expensive than Oyster Card fares.

➡ Contactless cards can be used instead of Oyster Cards (they benefit from the same 'smart-fare' system); just check for international fees with your card issuer.

For much more on **getting around** see ➡ p413

Top Itineraries

Day One

The West End (p74)

 First stop, **Westminster Abbey** for an easy intro to the city's (and nation's) history and then to **Buckingham Palace** for the **Changing of the Guard**. Walk up the Mall to **Trafalgar Square** for its architectural grandeur and photo-op views of **Big Ben** down Whitehall. Art lovers will make a beeline for the **National Gallery** and its outstanding collection of European paintings.

> ✕ **Lunch** Portrait (p117) for excellent set lunches and unparalleled views.

The South Bank (p158)

With your pre-booked ticket for the **London Eye**, walk across pedestrian Hungerford Bridge to the South Bank and enjoy a 30-minute revolution in the city skies and superb views, notably of the **Houses of Parliament**. Afterwards stroll along the river and head into the bowels of the **Tate Modern** for some grade-A art. Aim your camera at **St Paul's Cathedral** on the far side of the elegant **Millennium Bridge**.

> ✕ **Dinner** Grills or more complex dishes at Skylon (p169).

The South Bank (p158)

 Depending on what mood you're in, you might catch a performance at **Shakespeare's Globe**. 'Groundling' (standing) tickets can be bought last minute but book ahead for seats. Otherwise, join the post-work crowds in the **pubs** around London Bridge for real ales and historical surrounds.

Day Two

The City (p135)

 London's finance-driven Square Mile is home to the sprawling and ancient **Tower of London**. Spend the morning watching the Beefeaters and resident ravens preen and strut, and then marvel at the **Crown Jewels**. When you're finished, admire the iconic **Tower Bridge** from the banks of the Thames or through the glass floors of the walkways connecting the two towers.

> ✕ **Lunch** Perkin Reveller (p153), a glassed-in pub at the northern end of the bridge.

The West End (p74)

Hop on a double-decker bus for city views and head to the **British Museum** for a shot of world culture. Choose one of the excellent introductory tours or rent an audio guide so as not to feel overwhelmed. Round off the afternoon with a recuperative pint at a local such as the **Museum Tavern**.

> ✕ **Dinner** Head to Asadal (p118) for excellent Korean cuisine.

The West End (p74)

 If you fancy soaking up the atmosphere, stroll through **Chinatown** and **Soho** and make your way to **Leicester Sq** for some people-watching. There are literally dozens of pubs, bars and cocktail bars along the way from which to choose.

Day Three

Greenwich & South London (p287)

 Hop on a boat from any central London pier and make your way down to Greenwich with its world-renowned architecture and links to time, the stars and space. Start your visit at the legendary **Cutty Sark**, a star clipper during the tea-trade years, and have a look into the **National Maritime Museum**.

 Lunch Goddards at Greenwich (p300) for traditional English pie and mash.

Greenwich & South London (p287)

Stroll up through **Greenwich Park** all the way to the **Royal Observatory**. The views of **Canary Wharf**, the business district across the river, are stunning. Inside the observatory, straddle the **Greenwich Meridian** and find out about the incredible quest to solve the longitude problem. At the **planetarium**, join another quest: finding extra-terrestrial life. Walk back down to Greenwich and settle down for a pint at the **Trafalgar Tavern**.

 Dinner Polpo (p208) for tasty Italian-style tapas in a picturesque street.

Clerkenwell, Shoreditch & Spitalfields (p202)

Head back to central London on the DLR from Greenwich and treat yourself to dinner in one of the fine restaurants dotting this part of town. Clubs abound if you fancy a boogie after dinner, otherwise opt for a beautifully crafted cocktail at **Zetter Townhouse Cocktail Lounge** or **Worship St Whistling Shop**.

Day Four

Kew, Richmond & Hampton Court (p308)

 Head to **Kew Gardens** bright and early to make the most of the morning: this is so much more than a botanical garden that it warrants extra time! Families shouldn't miss the treetop walkway, while plant lovers will go weak at the knees in the **Victorian Palm House** and **Princess of Wales Conservatory**.

 Lunch Glasshouse (p321) for fine gastronomy.

Kensington & Hyde Park (p176)

Hop on the tube to **Knightsbridge**. Keen shoppers will want to stroll down Old Brompton Rd and pop into **Harrods**, the famous department store. Culture vultures should save their energy for the nearby **Victoria & Albert Museum**, the **Natural History Museum** or the **Science Museum**.

 Dinner Zuma (p193) for robata (Japanese chargrilled) dishes and sushi.

West London (p271)

If the pubs around Knightsbridge and South Kensington tube stations are too staid for you, hop over to **Notting Hill** where the crowds are livelier and the nightlife more eclectic. If you just fancy sitting down with a good film, you're in luck: Notting Hill has some of the coolest independent cinemas in London, including the iconic **Electric Cinema**.

If You Like...

Royalty

Tower of London Castle, tower, prison, medieval execution site and home of the dazzling Crown Jewels. (p137)

Buckingham Palace The Queen Mother of all London's royal palaces, with lovely gardens and – the popular draw – the Changing of the Guard. (p83)

Hampton Court Palace Magnificent Tudor palace located within beautiful grounds on the Thames. (p310)

Kensington Palace Princess Diana's former home, this stately and stunning royal palace is the highlight of Kensington Gardens. (p188)

Windsor Castle Magnificent and ancient royal fortress within easy reach of London. (p326)

Westminster Abbey Virtually every monarch has been crowned here; many are buried here; and future king Prince William was married here. (p76)

History

Tower of London Spanning almost 1000 years of history, from fortress to home of the Crown Jewels. (p137)

Churchill War Rooms Ground zero of London's war effort during WWII, left pretty much as it was in 1945. (p93)

Museum of London Traces the history of the capital, from Anglo-Saxon village to 21st-century metropolis. (p151)

St George Chapel, Windsor Castle (p326)

Museum of London Docklands
See how the Thames and the Docklands have shaped London's history. (p229)

Geffrye Museum A fascinating insight into the daily lives of London residents through the ages. (p206)

British Museum Millennia of human history on display, conveniently summarised through a 'History of the World in 100 objects'. (p79)

Views

London Eye For gently rotating, tip-top views of London – but choose a fair-weather day. (p165)

Shard The highest – but most expensive – views in London. (p166)

Parliament Hill Skyscraping views across London from Hampstead Heath. (p254)

Greenwich Park Clamber up to the statue of General Wolfe for superlative views of Canary Wharf, the Thames and the O2 Arena. (p195)

Sky Pod Phenomenal views of London, a roof garden and no sight of the awkward Walkie Talkie building – because you're in it! (p146)

Tate Modern Head up to Level 10 of Switch House, the Tate Modern extension, for free, panoramic views of London. (p160)

Parks & Gardens

Hampstead Heath Woods, hills, meadows and top scenic views, all rolled into one sublime sprawl. (p254)

Richmond Park Europe's largest urban parkland has everything from herds of deer to tranquil pockets of woodland,

seemingly infinite wild tracts and beautiful vistas. (p316)

St James's Park Feast on some sublime views in one of London's most attractive royal parks. (p98)

Kew Gardens A botanist's paradise, a huge expanse of greenery and a great day out with the kids. (p195)

Chelsea Physic Garden A tranquil and particularly tidy botanical enclave just a stone's throw from the Thames. (p190)

Greenwich Park A delightful mix of views, expansive lawns, beautiful trees in the home of the Meridian. (p195)

Squares

Trafalgar Square London's iconic central square, lorded over by Lord Nelson – and four magnificent felines. (p92)

Soho Square Serene spot for a sandwich in the sun in the heart of the West End. (p100)

Trinity Square Gardens Picturesque and well-tended one-time location of the notorious Tower Hill scaffold. (p150)

Squares of Bloomsbury Elegant, historic and tranquil squares dotted around literary Bloomsbury.

Covent Garden Piazza Fine-looking West End square originally laid out in the 17th century, and now popular with street performers. (p102)

Leicester Square Unbeatable for people-watching and celebrity-spotting on film premiere nights. (p103)

Modern Architecture

30 St Mary Axe Colloquially dubbed 'the Gherkin', this is

For more top London spots, see the following:
→ Eating (p44)
→ Drinking & Nightlife (p52)
→ Entertainment (p56)
→ Shopping (p60)
→ Sports & Activities (p63)

the City's most iconic modern edifice. (p152)

Shard A crystalline spike dominating the South Bank, with to-die-for views of the city. (p166)

London Eye Unsurprisingly, it's visible from many remote parts of town. (p165)

City Hall Does it look like a woodlouse or Darth Vader's helmet? Your call.

Serpentine Sackler Gallery A former 19th-century gunpowder depot, with an undulating modern extension by late architect Zaha Hadid. (p185)

20 Fenchurch St Love it or loathe it from the outside, you can't help marvelling at the Walkie Talkie's amazing roof gardens. (p146)

Music

Ronnie Scott's Legendary jazz den in the heart of Soho. (p127)

O2 Academy Brixton A stalwart of the gig circuit for all touring bands, and just the right size too. (p305)

Royal Opera House London's world-famous opera in Covent Garden is second to none for lavish opera productions. (p126)

Royal Festival Hall Fantastic acoustics and an excellent program of music across the aural spectrum. (p174)

Wigmore Hall One of the best and most active classical music concert venues in the capital. (p126)

Free church recitals Take a pew at St-Martin-in-the-Fields for free lunchtime concerts (p103)

Cultural Diversity

Chinatown At the heart of London, and the place to be for dim sum dining or Chinese New Year. (p100)

Brick Lane Take a wander do some shopping around this vibrant neighbourhood, shaped by migration over the centuries. (p207)

Brixton Village Great dining and shopping converge in South London's most famous multicultural neighbourhood. (p296)

Whitechapel Road Lively, vibrant and cacophonous tangle of cultures and languages. (p224)

Churches

St Paul's Cathedral Sir Christopher Wren's 300-year-old domed masterpiece and London's most iconic historic church. (p143)

Westminster Abbey Ancient and sublime site of coronation for English monarchs since William the Conqueror. (p76)

Westminster Cathedral The gaunt interior sparkles fitfully with dazzling Byzantine mosaics. (p95)

All Saints An extraordinarily beautiful example of lavish High Victorian Gothic architecture. (p96)

St Stephen Walbrook Sir Christopher Wren's finest City church, and his first experience

with a dome – a precursor to St Paul's. (p147)

Cemeteries

Highgate Cemetery Gothic and sublimely overgrown 20-hectare Victorian place of the dead, including Karl Marx and George Michael. (p256)

Brompton Cemetery Some of this cemetery's dead found immortality in the names of Beatrix Potter's animal characters. (p275)

Abney Park Cemetery Tangled with weeds and reclaimed by nature, with moments of magic. (p263)

Kensal Green Cemetery Distinctive Greek Revival architecture and illustrious residents including Isambard Kingdom Brunel and Charles Babbage. (p275)

Rivers & Canals

Regent's Canal Amble along the historic trade route and take a shortcut across North London at the same time. (p251)

Little Venice Flower-decked narrow boats and tree-lined towpaths: London canals at their most picturesque. (p275)

Petersham Meadows A slice of English countryside nestled in a bend of the river at Richmond. (p317)

Cutty Sark Tavern Pop into this Greenwich riverside pub and toast the fine river views with a pint. (p303)

Thames Rockets Add some thrill to your sightseeing with this adrenaline-infused boat ride. (p63)

Hampton Court Palace Take a riverboat up the Thames to Henry VIII's spectacular palace. (p310)

Animals & Wildlife

London Wetland Centre Birds, bats, dragonflies, otters and much more – this is proper wildlife in the heart of London. (p318)

London Zoo One of the world's oldest and most famous zoos, with tiger cubs and gorilla babies to coo at. (p248)

Mudchute A lovely city farm on the Isle of Dogs: cows, sheep and llamas with a Canary Wharf backdrop. (p230)

London Sea Life Aquarium A tremendous collection of creatures from the world's saltwater depths on display next to the Thames. (p164)

Walking

Hampstead Heath Wild, hilly, carefree heathland and woodland, with some excellent views from London's highest open space. (p254)

Regent's Canal Take a canalside hike across North London. (p251)

Thames Path Amble along the delightful riverside stretch between Putney and Barnes. (p319)

Wimbledon Common Head off in any direction for woodland, heath, grassland and bracing exploration. (p319)

Month By Month

January

The new year in London kicks off with a big bang at midnight. London is in the throes of winter, with short days: light appears at 8am and is all but gone by 4pm.

✪ London International Mime Festival

Held over the month of January, this festival (www.mimelondon.com) is a must for lovers of originality, playfulness, physical talent and the unexpected.

✪ London Art Fair

More than 100 major galleries participate in this contemporary art fair (www.londonartfair.co.uk), now one of the largest in Europe, with thematic exhibitions, special events and the best emerging artists.

February

February is usually chilly and wet (sometimes even snow-encrusted). The Chinese New Year (Spring Festival) is fun, and Londoners lark about with pancakes on Shrove Tuesday.

✪ Chinese New Year

In late January or early February, Chinatown fizzes, crackles and pops in this colourful street festival, which includes a Golden Dragon parade, feasting and partying.

✪ BAFTAs

The British Academy of Film and Television Arts (BAFTA; www.bafta.org) rolls out the red carpet mid-February to hand out its annual cinema awards. It's the British Oscars, if you will. Expect plenty of celebrity glamour.

March

March sees spring in the air, with trees beginning to flower and daffodils emerging across parks and gardens. London is getting in the mood to head outdoors again.

✪ Head of the River Race

Some 400 crews take part in this colourful annual boat race (p317), held over a 7km course on the Thames, from Mortlake to Putney.

✪ St Patrick's Day Parade & Festival

Top festival for the Irish in London, held on the Sunday closest to 17 March, with a colourful parade through central London and other festivities in and around Trafalgar Sq.

✪ Flare

This LGBTQI film festival, organised by the British Film Institute (www.bfi.org.uk/flare), runs a packed program of film screenings, along with club nights, talks and events.

April

London is in bloom, with warmer days and a lighthearted vibe. British Summer Time starts late March, moving clocks forward an hour, so it's now light until 7pm. Some

sights previously shut for winter reopen.

🏃 Oxford & Cambridge Boat Race

Crowds line the banks of the Thames for the country's two most famous universities going oar-to-oar from Putney to Mortlake. Dates vary, due to each university's Easter breaks, so check the website (www. theboatraces.org).

🏃 London Marathon

Some 35,000 runners – most running for charity – pound through London in one of the world's biggest road races (www.virgin moneylondonmarathon. com), heading from Blackheath to the Mall.

☆ Udderbelly Festival

Housed in a temporary venue in the shape of a purple upside-down cow on the South Bank, this festival of comedy, circus and general family fun (www.udder belly.co.uk) has become a spring favourite. Events run from April to July.

May

A delightful time to be in London: days are warming up and Londoners begin to start lounging around in parks, popping on their sunglasses and enjoying two bank holiday weekends (the first and the last in May).

🏃 Museums at Night

For one weekend in May, numerous museums across London open after-hours (http://museumsatnight. org.uk), with candlelit tours, spooky atmospheres, sleep-overs and special events such as talks and concerts.

🌺 Chelsea Flower Show

The world's most renowned horticultural event (p190) attracts London's green-fingered and flower-mad gardeners. Expect talks, presentations and spectacular displays from the cream of the gardening world.

June

The peak season begins with long, warm days (it's light until 10pm), the arrival of Wimbledon and other alfresco events.

🌺 Trooping the Colour

The Queen's official birthday (www.trooping-the-colour.co.uk) is celebrated with much flag-waving, parades, pageantry and noisy flyovers. The royal family usually attends in force.

🌺 London Festival of Architecture

This month-long celebration of London's built environment (www.london festivalofarchitecture.org) explores the significance of architecture and design and how London has become a centre for innovation in these fields.

☆ Meltdown

The Southbank Centre hands over the curatorial reins to a legend of contemporary music (eg Morrissey, Patti Smith or Guy Garvey) to pull together a full program of concerts, talks and films mid-June (www. southbankcentre.co.uk).

🌺 Royal Academy Summer Exhibition

Beginning in June and running through August, this exhibition at the Royal Academy of Arts (p106) showcases works submitted by artists from all over Britain, distilled to a thousand or so pieces.

🌺 Open Garden Squares Weekend

Over one weekend, more than 200 gardens in London that are usually inaccessible to the public fling open their gates for exploration (www.opensquares. org).

🏃 Wimbledon Lawn Tennis Championships

For two weeks a year, the quiet South London village of Wimbledon falls under a sporting spotlight as the world's best tennis players gather to battle for the championships (p323).

July

This is the time to munch on strawberries, drink in beer gardens and join in the numerous outdoor activities, including big music festivals.

🌺 Pride London

The gay community paints the town pink in this annual extravaganza (www. prideinlondon.org), featuring a smorgasbord of experiences, from talks to live events and culminating in a huge parade across London.

☆ Wireless

One of London's top music festivals, with an emphasis on dance and R&B, Wireless (www.wirelessfestival.co.uk)

(Top) Marin Čilić at the Wimbledon Lawn Tennis Championships (p323)
(Bottom) Royal Albert Hall (p187)

SHAUN BOTTERILL/STAFF/GETTY IMAGES ©

I WEI HUANG/SHUTTERSTOCK ©

takes place in Finsbury Park in northeast London. It is extremely popular, so book in advance.

☆ BBC Promenade Concert (the Proms)

Starting in mid-July and ending in early September, the Proms offers two months of outstanding classical concerts (www.bbc.co.uk/proms) at various prestigious venues, centred on the Royal Albert Hall.

☆ Lovebox

This two-day music extravaganza (www.loveboxfestival.com) in Victoria Park, East London, was created by dance duo Groove Armada. Its raison d'être is dance music, but there are plenty of other genres too, including indie, pop and hip hop.

August

School's out for summer, families are holidaying and the hugely popular annual Caribbean carnival dances into Notting Hill. The last weekend brings a bank holiday.

☆ Summer Screen at Somerset House

For a fortnight every summer, Somerset House turns its stunning courtyard into an open-air cinema (p107) screening an eclectic mix of film premieres, cult classics and popular requests.

☆ Great British Beer Festival

Organised by CAMRA (Campaign for Real Ale), this boozy festival (www.gbbf.org.uk) cheerfully cracks open casks of ale from the UK and abroad at Olympia exhibition centre.

✿ Notting Hill Carnival

Europe's biggest – and London's most vibrant – outdoor carnival (p275) is a celebration of Caribbean London, featuring music, dancing and costumes over the summer bank-holiday weekend.

September

The end of summer and start of autumn is a lovely time to be in town, with comedy festivals and a chance to look at London properties normally shut to the public.

✿ The Mayor's Thames Festival

Celebrating the River Thames, this cosmopolitan festival (www.totally thames.org) brings fairs, street theatre, music, food stalls, fireworks and river races, culminating in the superb Night Procession.

☆ Greenwich Comedy Festival

This week-long laugh fest – London's largest comedy festival – brings big names and emerging acts to the National Maritime Museum.

✿ Open House London

For a weekend in mid-September the public is invited in to see more than 700 heritage buildings throughout the capital that are normally off-limits (www. openhouselondon.org.uk).

🏃 Great Gorilla Run

It looks bananas, but this gorilla-costume charity run (www.greatgorillarun.org) along an 8km route from the City to Bankside and back again is all in aid of gorilla conservation.

October

The weather is getting colder, but London's parklands are splashed with gorgeous autumnal colours. Clocks go back to winter time the last weekend of the month.

☆ London Film Festival

The city's premier film event (www.bfi.org.uk/lff) attracts big overseas names and show more than 100 British and international films before their cinema release. Masterclasses are given by world-famous directors.

☆ Dance Umbrella

London's annual festival of contemporary dance (www.danceumbrella. co.uk) features two weeks of performances by British and international dance companies at venues across London.

November

London nights are getting longer. It's the last of the parks' autumn colours – enjoy them on a walk and relax by an open fire in a pub afterwards.

✿ Guy Fawkes Night (Bonfire Night)

Bonfire Night commemorates Guy Fawkes' foiled attempt to blow up Parliament in 1605. Bonfires and fireworks light up the night on 5 November. Primrose Hill, Highbury Fields, Alexandra Palace, Clapham Common and Blackheath have some of the best firework displays.

✿ Lord Mayor's Show

In accordance with the Magna Carta of 1215, the newly elected Lord Mayor of the City of London travels in a state coach from Mansion House to the Royal Courts of Justice to take an oath of allegiance to the Crown – nowadays with floats, bands and fireworks (www.lord mayorsshow.london).

☆ London Jazz Festival

Musicians from around the world swing into town for 10 days of jazz (www.efg londonjazzfestival.org.uk). World influences are well represented, as are more conventional styles.

December

A festive mood reigns as Christmas approaches and shops are decorated. Days are increasingly shorter. Christmas Day is the quietest day of the year, with all shops and museums closed and the tube network shut.

◉ Christmas Tree Lighting & Lights

A celebrity is called up to switch on all the festive lights that line Oxford, Regent and Bond Streets, and a towering Norwegian spruce is set up in Trafalgar Sq.

🏃 Ice-skating

From mid-November until January, open-air ice-rinks pop up across the city, including one in the exquisite courtyard of Somerset House (p107) and another one in the grounds of the Natural History Museum (p182).

With Kids

London is a fantastic place for children. The city's museums will fascinate all ages, and you'll find theatre, dance and music performances ideal for older kids. Playgrounds and parks, city farms and nature reserves are perfect for either toddler energy-busting or relaxation.

Natural History Museum (p182)

Museums

London's museums are nothing if not child friendly. There are dedicated children or family trails in virtually every museum. Additionally, you'll find plenty of activities such as storytelling at the National Gallery (p87), thematic backpacks to explore the British Museum (p79), pop-up performances at the Victoria & Albert Museum (p178), family audio guides at the Tate Modern (p160), and art and crafts workshops at Somerset House (p107), where kids can dance through the fountains in the courtyard in summer. The Science Museum (p186) has a marvellous interactive area downstairs called the Garden, where tots can splash around with water; however, some kids never get past the fantastic shop at the museum. Older kids will be thrilled with the flight simulators at the Science Museum too.

In winter (November to January), a section by the East Lawn of the Natural History Museum (p182) is transformed into a glittering and highly popular ice rink; book your slot well ahead (www.ticket master.co.uk). Somerset House also sparkles with a fantastic ice rink in winter.

Remember, many activities are free (check websites for details).

Museum & Attraction Sleepovers

What better fun than sleeping at the feet of a dinosaur? Museum sleepovers are very popular and must be booked at least a couple of months in advance.

Natural History Museum

Snooze under the watchful eye of the Blue Whale in the Hintze Hall, having first explored the museum's darkest nooks and crannies with only a torch to light your way. Monthly; adults welcome too! (p182)

Science Museum

Each month kids aged seven to 13 get the chance to experience a night of

hands-on workshops, science shows and an IMAX 3D film. (p186)

British Museum
Sleepovers give kids the chance to bed down next to Egyptian sculpture. (p79)

ZSL London Zoo
Don't let the bedbugs bite! Sleepovers for kids aged to 11. (p248)

Best for Kids
There is so much to see and do that you won't know where to start.

V&A Museum of Childhood
Dressing-up boxes, toys from times gone-by and interactive play areas. (p226)

Natural History Museum
Dinosaurs, animals, more dinosaurs, Planet Earth and the role of scientific research – all fascinating stuff at this museum. (p182)

London Transport Museum
Twenty London Transport buses and trains are on display and available for touching, climbing on and general child-handling at this museum. (p102)

Royal Observatory & Greenwich Park
First there is the park (p99), which you need to gambol through to get to the Observatory (p289); then there are the Astronomy galleries and the Planetarium, which kids will marvel at, as well as the Camera Obscura.

ZSL London Zoo
Want to see your kids saucer-eyed with wonder in London's largest menagerie? Well, they can do that here. (p248)

Golden Hinde
Kids go wild for the treasure hunts (p165), the tall tales of pirates and mutinies, and the incredibly evocative interior of this 16th-century galleon.

Horniman Museum
An aquarium, a hands-on music room, natural history galleries and huge grounds – this museum (p296) offers endless fun.

Best for Teenagers
London punches above its weight when it comes to entertaining blasé teenagers.

Science Museum
The sensational displays about space, information technology, flying and more will have teenagers enthralled at the Science Museum. (p186)

Tate Modern
The Drawing Bar at Bloomberg Connects at the modern art museum (p160) has digital sketch pads where teens can express their inner Rothko.

Madame Tussauds
With its celebrity waxworks this museum (p106) is selfie heaven, be it with Luke Skywalker, David Beckham or Benedict Cumberbatch.

London Film Museum
The James Bond car collection steals the show, but there is plenty more film memorabilia (p102) to enjoy.

Changing of the Guard (p84)

with amazing displays to bring those history lessons to life.

Changing of the Guard

Soldiers in bearskin hats, red uniforms, military orders and all the pomp at the Changing of the Guard (p84) – everyone will gape.

Best for Rainy Days

Plans rain-checked by London's famously unpredictable weather? As well as myriad museums and galleries, here are some ideas to stay warm and dry.

BFI IMAX Cinema

Documentaries and blockbusters in 3D for a different cinema (p175) experience.

Queens Ice & Bowl

Get your skates on and go spinning around the rink (p286), or have they kids aim for a strike in the bowling alley.

West End matinee show

The West End (p126) has plenty of plays and musicals children will love, from *Matilda* to *The Curious Incident of the Dog in the Night Time*. Tickets are often available on the day.

London Transport Museum

The A to Zs and nuts and bolts of London transport (p102) told in fun fashion. The museum also stages Hidden London tours (from 14 years) taking you down into secret shelters and disused tunnels across London (book early).

HMS Belfast

HMS Belfast (p166) was a real light cruiser that served in WWII and the Korean War,

Best for Outdoor Fun

Treetop Walkway

Go underground and then up 18m into the canopy for an unforgettable encounter with nature at Kew Gardens (p314).

Mayfield Lavender

Wander among the lavender flowers in a magically beautiful landscape (☏07503-877 707; www.mayfieldlavender.com; admission free; ☉9am-6pm early June to mid-Sep) 🅵FREE.

Thames River Cruise

These river cruises (p295) may be less thrilling than a high-speed boat, but there will definitely be more sightseeing.

Hampton Court Palace Maze

It takes the average visitor 20 minutes to find the centre of the maze (p311) – can your kids beat that? Look out for summer events such as jousting and falconry too.

NEED TO KNOW

Public transport Under-16s travel free on buses, under-11s travel free on the tube and under-5s go free on trains. Steps and escalators mean some stations are hard to access with buggies (strollers) – buses are a safer bet. TfL has detail on accessible transport options (www.tfl.gov.uk/transport-accessibility/).

Babysitter Get a babysitter or nanny at Sitters (www.sitters.co.uk).

Walking The best way to see London is to walk – public transport can be crowded and hot in summer.

Like a Local

Local life envelops you in London, but you might notice it only in snatches. London being a big city, its residents are pragmatic about crowds: Londoners will wait for late-opening nights before slipping into museums or galleries to avoid the worst of the rush, but swarm en masse to parks as soon as the sun pops out to make the most of every ray of sunshine.

Notting Hill (p271)

Drinking Like a Local

Londoners, and the British in general, get bad press for binge drinking. But most drinking in London is actually warmly sociable, gregarious and harmless fun. Londoners drink at the 'local' – shorthand for the 'pub around the corner'. Prices may be high but generosity is commonplace and drinkers always step up to buy a round. Despite the fickle weather, alfresco drinking is commonplace, be it in beer gardens, on patios or along pavements.

Dining Like a Local

As a rule of thumb, Londoners will dine at their local fish and chip shop or enjoy Sunday roast at their local gastropub rather than trek across town for dinner, but they'll readily go out for a meal further afield for special occasions. You'll also find them piling on the peri-peri sauce at Nando's, enjoying a fry-up (full English breakfast) at a 'greasy spoon' (a no-frills cafe), grabbing a sandwich from Marks & Spencer to lunch outside in Hyde Park or, increasingly, queuing outside the numerous food trucks dotting the city for a hot takeaway lunch. Food markets are incredibly popular, be they the gourmet kind such as Borough Market (p163) or smaller farmers markets across town.

Idiosyncratic delicacies you'll find Londoners tucking in include chip butty (fries in a sandwich), marmite (a yeast extract spread) on toast and jellied eel (often served with pies).

Shopping Like a Local

They are on home turf, so Londoners know precisely where to shop. They'll be in charity shops hunting for overlooked first editions and cheap clothing, skimming market stalls for vintage togs at the Sunday UpMarket (p219) off Brick Lane, browsing along Portobello Rd (p274), rifling through Brixton Village (p296) or retreating to small, independent bookshops for peace, quiet and old-school service. But you'll also find them in their droves in high-street franchises in Kensington High St and Oxford St, or shiny malls such as Westfield (p285).

Taking to the Park

London has some of the world's most beautiful urban green spaces and locals swarm en masse to the park the minute the sun pops out to read a book, play football, rule over a picnic or barbeue, or just chat with friends on the grass. Join them at lunchtime when office workers come out for their fix of sunlight or at weekends for fun and games.

Sightseeing Like a Local

Londoners habitually head off the beaten track, taking the back route into their local park, exploring London's wilder fringes or making short cuts such as following Regent's Canal (p251) across North London. Go exploring in zones 2 and 3 and see what you find. Many Londoners bide their time till late-night openings for central London museums, when there are smaller crowds, and save 'regular hour' visits for special exhibitions.

Londoners are also well tuned to special events such as Open House London (p417) and Museums at Night (p30), which shine a new light on familiar attractions and buildings.

Local Obsessions

Property

Owning a property is a national obsession in the UK, but is made particularly difficult in London, where prices are stratospheric. Talks of unaffordable housing, renting versus buying, mortgage deals, putting an offer and being gazumped, DIY and grand renovations are classic Sunday lunch fodder.

North vs South

The existential divide between 'Norff' and 'Saff' of the river remains as wide as ever. Each camp swears by its side. For Londoners, the main difference is that South London is less accessible by tube (which means that house prices are generally lower, although this is about to change with the extension of the northern line). But for visitors, the debate is moot: London is London, with the same amazing array of sights, restaurants, bars and markets.

NEED TO KNOW

Santander Cycles (p415) Bike-sharing is fun, cheap, practical and definitively local, and there are docking stations everywhere.

Oyster Cards (p414) Londoners who travel by public transport use this contactless card, which nets excellent discounts and avoids queues for tickets.

Routemaster heritage bus 15 This bus line is excellent for sightseeing, so grab a seat upstairs.

The Weather (& Whether It'll Hold Out for Saturday's barbecue)

More than wet, cold or grey, London's weather is unpredictable. This causes Londoners any amount of angst about their barbecue/picnic/beer garden plans from April to September, when it's supposed to be spring/summer but you may still get hit by unseasonal showers/cold snaps/high winds.

Public Transport

London has a world-class public transport network, but Londoners like nothing more than to moan about their commute to work. Grievances range from delays due to improbably long red lights/signal failure/leaves on track/the wrong kind of snow (all real-life examples) to the horribly high fares. Londoners can also argue endlessly about the definitive route from A to B.

Politics

Britain has a tradition of rabble-rousing – see the rather combative style of debate in the House of Commons. While Londoners may be reticent at first, once their teeth are stuck in they won't let a political debate go; so if you like politics, you'll find company.

Football

Passions run high when it comes to the beautiful game, and rivalries between London's three major teams (Arsenal, Chelsea and Tottenham Hotspur) are real. The capital has other clubs in the Premier League, including West Ham and Crystal Palace, each with equally devoted supporters.

For Free

London may be one of the world's most expensive cities, but it doesn't have to cost the Earth. Many sights and experiences are free or cost next to nothing.

Foot Guard, Buckingham Palace (p83)

ALEXANDER CHAIKIN/SHUTTERSTOCK ©

Sights

It costs nothing to visit the Houses of Parliament (p85) and watch debates. Another institution of public life, the Changing of the Guard (p84), is free to watch. For one weekend in September, Open House London (p417) opens 850 buildings for free.

Museums & Galleries

The permanent collections of all state-funded museums and galleries are open to the public free of charge. They include the V&A (p178), Tate Modern (p160), British Museum (p79) and National Gallery (p87). The Saatchi Gallery (p190) is also free.

Views

Why pay good money when some of the finest viewpoints in London are free? Head to Level 10 of Switch House at Tate Modern (p160) or the Sky Garden atop the Walkie Talkie (p146).

Concerts

A number of churches offer free lunchtime classical music concerts. Try St Martin-in-the-Fields (p103), St James's Piccadilly (p99), Temple Church (p104) and St Alfege Church (p293).

Walks

Walking around town is possibly the best way to get a sense of the city and its history. Roam through Hampstead Heath (p254) in North London, follow the Thames along the South Bank, or just walk from A to B in the compact West End.

Low-Cost Transport

Bike-share your way around through Santander Cycles (p415) – the access fee is £2 for 24 hours; bike hire is then free for the first 30 minutes. Travel as much as you like on London Transport with a one-day Travelcard or an Oyster Card.

NEED TO KNOW

Websites Click on London for Free (www.londonforfree.net) for ideas.

Discount cards The **London Pass** (p418) can be a good investment **Wi-fi access** Many cafes and bars offer free wi-fi to customers.

Newspapers The *Evening Standard* and *Metro* are both free.

Children Under-11s travel free on buses and the tube, under-5s go free on trains.

Above: City Hall;
Right: Tate Modern (p160)

Earth Hall entrance, Natural History Museum (p182)

Museums & Galleries

London's museums and galleries are some of the city's most unmissable attractions – and not just for rainy days. Many display incomparable collections that make them acknowledged leaders in their field. A trinity of top-name museums awaits in South Kensington, and there is a similar concentration in the West End, especially around Trafalgar Square.

The Heavy Hitters

London's most famous museums are all central, easy to get to and – best of all – free. The National Gallery (p87) on Trafalgar Sq displays masterpieces of Western European art from the 13th to the early 20th centuries, with everyone represented from Leonardo da Vinci and Rembrandt to Turner and Van Gogh. Just behind the gallery, the National Portrait Gallery (p91) celebrates famous British faces through a staggering collection of 4000 paintings, sculptures and photographs from the 16th century to the present day. A 15-minute walk to the north is the British Museum (p79) in Bloomsbury, housing an astonishing assembly of antiquities representing 7000 years of human civilisation.

South Kensington is the home of three of London's leading museums: the Victoria & Albert Museum (p178), with its vast range of historical exhibits from the decorative arts, and the kid-friendly Natural History (p182) and Science Museums (p186).

Modern and contemporary art lovers will enjoy the Tate Modern (p160) on the South Bank. The Tate Britain (p90), venue of the annual Turner Prize, is home to British artworks across the centuries.

Private Galleries

London's vibrant artistic scene finds expression in around 1500 private galleries – more than any other city in the world. Mayfair has long been strong in the more highbrow, traditional schools of art, while more cutting-edge art finds its way into spaces in Spitalfields, Hoxton and Hackney Wick.

AVOIDING CROWDS

Unfortunately, queues, crowds and bag searches are all too common at London's most popular attractions. The busiest times tend to be on weekend afternoons and during school holidays. Even during these times, though, you can duck the worst of the crowds by arriving right on opening time or during the late evening sessions. Weekday afternoons are best at the Natural History Museum, as school groups tend to visit in the mornings.

NEED TO KNOW

Tickets

➡ Permanent collections at national museums (eg British Museum, National Gallery, Victoria & Albert Museum) are free; temporary exhibitions cost extra and should be booked ahead.

➡ Smaller museums will charge an entrance fee, typically £5 to £8.

➡ Private galleries are usually free or have a small admission fee.

Opening Hours

National collections are generally open 10am to about 6pm, with one or two late nights a week; evenings are an excellent time to visit museums as there are far fewer visitors.

Dining

Many of the top museums also have fantastic restaurants (eg National Portrait Gallery, Wallace Collection. Royal Academy), worthy of a visit in their own right.

Useful Websites

Most London museums – especially the most visited ones such as the British Museum, the National Gallery and the Victoria & Albert Museum – have sophisticated and comprehensive websites.

Culture 24 (www.culture24.org.uk) Reams of museum and gallery info.

London Galleries (www.london-galleries.co.uk) A to Z of all London's galleries, with web links.

A Night at the Museum

Many museums open late once or even twice a week, but several museums organise special nocturnal events to extend their range of activities and to present the collection in a different light. Some museums arrange night events only once a year, in May.

Museums with special nocturnal events or late-night opening hours:

British Museum (p79) Open to 8.30pm on Friday.

British Library (p246) Galleries open to 8pm Tuesday to Thursday.

National Portrait Gallery (p91) Open to 9pm Thursday and Friday.

Sir John Soane's Museum (p94) Evenings (6pm to 9pm) of the first Tuesday of each month are illuminated by candlelight.

Tate Britain (p90) Open to 10pm on select Fridays.

Tate Modern (p160) Open to 10pm Friday and Saturday.

Courses, Talks & Lectures

Museums and galleries are excellent places to pick up specialist skills from qualified experts in their field. If you'd like to learn a new skill, brush up on an old one, or attend a fascinating lecture, there are many to choose from. Venues include the British Library (p246), British Museum (p79), Courtauld Gallery (p107), Dulwich Picture Gallery (p298), National Gallery (p87), National Portrait Gallery (p91), Tate Britain (p90), Tate Modern (p160) and Victoria & Albert Museum (p178).

Museums and Galleries by Neighbourhood

The West End (p74) British Museum, National Gallery, National Portrait Gallery, Tate Britain, Churchill War Rooms and many others.

The City (p135) Museum of London, Guildhall Art Gallery, Barbican, Bank of England Museum and Dr Johnson's House.

The South Bank (p158) Tate Modern, Hayward Gallery, Fashion & Textile Museum and other smaller museums and galleries.

Kensington & Hyde Park (p176) Victoria & Albert Museum, Natural History Museum, Science Museum, Saatchi Gallery, Serpentine Gallery and others.

Clerkenwell, Shoreditch & Spitalfields (p202) Geffrye Museum, Dennis Severs House and St John's Gate.

East London (p222) Museum of London Docklands, Ragged School Museum, V&A Museum of Childhood, Whitechapel Gallery and others.

Hampstead & North London (p244) Wellcome Collection, London Canal Museum, Kenwood House, British Library, Freud Museum, Jewish Museum and others.

Notting Hill & West London (p271) Design Museum, Museum of Brands, Leighton House and William Morris Society.

Greenwich & South London (p287) National Maritime Museum, Royal Observatory, Ranger's

Above: Imperial War Museum (p294); Below: National Gallery (p87)

House, Imperial War Museum, Horniman Museum and others.

Richmond, Kew & Hampton Court (p308) The Cumberland Art Gallery at Hampton Court Palace and the Wimbledon Lawn Tennis Museum.

Best Museums

British Museum (p79) Supreme collection of international artefacts and an inspiring testament to human creativity over seven millennia.

Tate Modern (p160) A feast of modern and contemporary art, housed within a transformed riverside power station.

National Gallery (p87) One of the world's great art collections.

Natural History Museum (p182) A cathedral to the natural world.

Victoria & Albert Museum (p178) Eclectic collection of decorative arts in what is affectionately known as 'the nation's attic'.

Museum of London (p151) The history of the city entertainingly explained and on display.

Best Small Museums

Geffrye Museum (p206) A fascinating journey through British living rooms from the 17th century onwards.

Sir John Soane's Museum (p94) The atmospheric home of the 19th-century architect showcasing his collection of art and antiquities.

Shakespeare's Globe (p162) As much as you'll ever need to know about the Bard and his work.

London Transport Museum (p102) Everything from horse-drawn omnibuses to the still-under-construction Crossrail project.

Viktor Wynd Museum of Curiosities, Fine Art & Natural History (p227) Highly eclectic collection of strange and disturbing ephemera.

Old Operating Theatre Museum & Herb Garret (p166) Delve into the pre-anaesthetic, pre-antiseptic days of medicine.

Best Small Galleries

Kenwood (p255) Spectacular collection of art from the 17th to 19th century in an equally wonderful setting.

Guildhall Art Gallery (p148) Eclectic City of London collection above a Roman amphitheatre.

Courtauld Gallery (p107) Arguably the best collection of Impressionist art in London.

Whitechapel Gallery (p225) A groundbreaking gallery that continues to challenge with excellent exhibitions.

Saatchi Gallery (p190) Cutting-edge, ultra-cool shrine to contemporary art.

The Photographers' Gallery (p101) Photography as an art form in a splendid building.

Best House Museums

Dennis Severs' House (p204) A quirky time capsule that sends you back to an 18th-century Huguenot house.

Charles Dickens Museum (p96) The Victorian novelist's only London house.

18 Stafford Terrace (p273) A comfortable middle-class Victorian family brought back to life.

Apsley House (p189) No 1 London: home to the Iron Duke of Wellington for 35 years.

Leighton House (p273) Byzantine gem on the cusp of Holland Park.

Red House (p298) Arts and Crafts designer William Morris' charmingly decorated home.

Best Specialist Museums

Imperial War Museum (p294) Devoted to Britain's military history, with a must-see WWI section.

Churchill War Rooms (p93) The nerve centre of Britain's war effort during WWII.

Science Museum (p186) Spellbinding A to Z of gizmos, devices, contraptions and thingamabobs.

Design Museum (p273) Devoted to the role of design in everyday life.

Museum of London Docklands (p229) The story of the river and the trade that made London prosper.

Fan Museum (p294) Tortoiseshell, ivory, bony, feather and paper fans in all their glory.

English breakfast

 # Eating

Once the butt of many a culinary joke, London has transformed itself over the last few decades and today is a global dining destination. World-famous chefs can be found at the helm of several top-tier restaurants, but it is the sheer diversity on offer that is head-spinning: from Afghan to Zambian, London delivers an A to Z of world cuisine.

Specialities
ENGLISH FOOD

England might have given the world baked beans on toast, mushy peas and chip butties (fried potatoes between slices of buttered white bread), but that's hardly the whole story. When well prepared – be it a Sunday lunch of roast beef and Yorkshire pudding (batter baked until fluffy, eaten with gravy) or a cornet of fish and chips sprinkled with salt and malt vinegar – English food can be excellent. And nothing beats a full English breakfast the morning after a big night out.

Modern British food has become a cuisine in its own right, championing traditional (and sometimes underrated) ingredients such as root vegetables, smoked fish, shellfish, game, salt-marsh lamb, sausages, black pudding (a kind of sausage stuffed with oatmeal, spices and blood), offal, secondary cuts of meat and bone marrow.

WINE & CHEESE

If English cuisine was once sniggered at, English wine had them rolling in the aisles. However, this too is changing. Locally produced sparkling wine has garnered much international attention and it is now served at state banquets in Buckingham Palace and in first class on British Airways. Even the Champagne house Taittinger has gotten in on the act, acquiring a vineyard in Kent in 2015. Producers to look out for include Wiston Estate, Furleigh Estate, Theale Vineyard, Ridgeview, Bolney Estate and Hambledon.

The cold and wet climate lends itself to particular hardy white grape varieties, many of which are quite obscure. Alongside Chardonnay you'll see the likes of Bacchus, Madeleine Angevine, Seyval Blanc, Pinot Blanc, Reichensteiner and Müller-Thurgau. Some good Pinot Noir is also being produced.

British cheese doesn't have such an image problem. For a nation that has traditionally held its nose in response to strong flavours, it makes the exception for some particularly pungent blue cheeses. Stilton is the most famous, but look out for Stinking Bishop and the blues from Wensleydale, Derby, Dorset and Shropshire. The king of the crumbly hard cheeses is aged cheddar, but Cheshire, Lancashire and Caerphilly all have their own distinctive varieties.

Great places to sample British wine and cheese in London include the Wine Pantry (p157), Neal's Yard Dairy (p132), Rippon Cheese (p201), Teddington Cheese (p323), Borough Market (p163) and La Fromagerie (☏020-7935 0341; www.lafromagerie.co.uk; 2-6 Moxon St, W1; mains £7-18; ☺8am-7.30pm Mon-Fri, 9am-7pm Sat, 10am-6pm Sun; ☏; ⊖Baker St) ✦.

SEAFOOD

Many visitors to England comment that for islanders, Brits seem to make surprisingly little of their seafood, with the exception of the ubiquitous – and institutionalised – fish and chips. But modern British restaurants have started to cast their nets wider and many offer local specialities such as Dover sole, Cornish oysters, Scottish scallops, smoked Norfolk eel, Atlantic herring, and mackerel. Top-of-the-line restaurants specialising in seafood abound and fish-and-chips counters trading in battered cod, haddock and plaice are everywhere.

DESSERTS

England does a mean dessert, and establishments serving British cuisine revel in these indulgent treats. Favourites include bread-and-butter pudding, sticky toffee pudding (steamed pudding with dates, topped with a caramel sauce), the alarmingly named spotted dick (steamed suet pudding with currants and raisins), Eton mess (meringue, cream and strawberries mixed into a gooey mess), and seasonal musts such as Christmas pudding (a steamed pudding with candied fruit and brandy) and fruity crumbles (rhubarb, apple etc).

BREAKFAST

The Brits have always been big on breakfast – and they even invented one, the Full English. It's something of a protein overload but there's nothing quite like it to mop up the excesses of a night on the tiles. A typical plate will include bacon, sausages, baked beans in tomato sauce, eggs (fried or scrambled), mushrooms, tomatoes and toast (maybe with Marmite). You'll find countless brightly lit, grotty caffs (cafes) – nicknamed 'greasy spoons' – serving these monster plates. They're also a must at gastropubs.

Making a comeback on the breakfast table is porridge (boiled oats in water or milk, served hot), sweet or savoury. Top-end restaurants serving breakfast, such as Balthazar (p117), have played a big part in glamming up what was essentially poor folk's food. It's great with banana and honey, fruit compote or even plain with some chocolate powder.

WORLD FOOD

One of the joys of eating out in London is the profusion of choice. For historical reasons Indian cuisine is widely available (curry has been labelled a national dish), but Asian cuisines in general are very popular. You'll find dozens of Chinese, Thai, Vietnamese Japanese and Korean restaurants, as well as elaborate fusion establishments blending flavours from different parts of Asia. Middle Eastern cuisine is also well covered. Continental Europe cuisines – French, Italian, Spanish, Greek, Scandinavian etc – are well represented, with many excellent modern European establishments.

Restaurants serving ethnic cuisines tend to congregate where their home community is based: Eastern European in Shepherd's Bush, Turkish in Dalston, Korean in New Malden, Bengali in Brick Lane, African Caribbean in Brixton, Vietnamese around Kingsland Rd etc.

Eating by Neighbourhood

The West End (p108) Avoid the tourist traps and you'll find some of London's best and most eclectic restaurants.

The City (p152) Lunch bars and some signature restaurants cater to a be-suited crowd; quiet at weekends.

The South Bank (p169) Dodge the riverside chains and seek out foodie markets and back-street gems.

Kensington & Hyde Park (p192) Some of London's finest and most famous restaurants, at sweat-inducing prices.

Clerkenwell, Shoreditch & Spitalfields (p208) Well-priced Vietnamese, lots of street food and some world-class restaurants.

East London (p233) An eclectic mix of ethnic cuisines and hip joints pushing the boundaries of British cooking.

Hampstead & North London (p258) Gastropubs, upmarket cafes and London's best variety for vegetarians.

Notting Hill & West London (p277) Affordable eats from a diverse range of ethnic cuisines.

Greenwich & South London (p298) Cheap international bites in Brixton and good midrange brasseries in Clapham and Greenwich.

Richmond, Kew & Hampton Court (p321) Gastropubs, gelato shops and some destination restaurants.

Gastropubs

While not so long ago the pub was where you went for a drink, with maybe a packet of potato crisps to soak up the alcohol, the birth of the gastropub in the 1990s means that today just about every establishment serves full meals. The quality varies widely, from defrosted-on-the-premises to Michelin-star-worthy.

Vegetarians & Vegans

London has been one of the best places for vegetarians to dine out since the 1970s, initially due mostly to its many Indian restaurants, which have always catered for people who don't eat meat for religious reasons. A number of dedicated vegetarian restaurants have since cropped up, offering imaginative, filling and truly delicious meals. Most nonvegetarian places generally offer a couple of veggie dishes, and some top-end places offer full vegetarian degustation menus. Vegans, however, will find it harder outside of Indian or dedicated vegan establishments, although these have been growing in number in recent years.

Celebrity Chefs

London's food renaissance was partly led by a group of telegenic chefs who built culinary empires around their names, made famous by their TV shows. Gordon Ramsay is the most (in)famous of the lot and his London venues are still standard-bearers for top-quality cuisine. Other big names include Jamie Oliver, whose restaurant Fifteen (p221) trains disadvantaged young people, and Heston Blumenthal, whose mad-professor-like experiments with food have earned him rave reviews.

Cafes

Tea is the quintessential English beverage, but until very recently, the quality of coffee in the capital was abysmal. The situation has rapidly turned around and London now has an incredibly vibrant and varied coffee scene, due in large part to the influence of Australians and New Zealanders living in the city, bringing their coffee culture with them.

The large chains are typically mediocre, but now most neighbourhoods have at least

Eating by Neighbourhood

North London
Gastropubs, cafes and
great vegetarian options
(p258)

**Clerkenwell, Shoreditch
& Spitalfields**
Vietnamese, street food and
world-class restaurants
(p208)

**East End &
Docklands**
Curry houses,
traditional caffs,
cool restaurants
(p233)

West London
Affordable eats from
diverse ethnic cuisines
(p277)
(1mi)

The City
Geared towards the
business lunch
(p152)

The West End
True standouts among
the tourist traps
(p108)

(1mi)

Kensington & Hyde Park
London's most famous
and priciest restaurants
(p192)

*London
Eye*

The South Bank
Chains on the river,
culinary gems 'inland'
(p169)

**Richmond, Kew &
Hampton Court**
Gastropubs, gelato and
some destination restaurants
(p321)
(2mi)

**Greenwich &
South London**
Cheap eats and good
midrange brasseries
(p298)

---

a few independent cafes that know how to
make a decent white coffee without burning or bubbling the milk. To catch London's
new-found coffee obsession in full swing,
pitch up during the London Coffee Festival
in spring. And if it's just coffee beans you're
after, swing by the fantastic Algerian Coffee
Stores (p131) or Monmouth Coffee Company (p132).

Food Markets

The boom in London's eating scene has extended to its markets, which come in three
broad categories: food stalls that are part
of a broader market and appeal to visitors
keen to soak up the atmosphere (Spitalfields, p220 and Camden, p253); specialist
food and farmers markets, which sell pricey
local and/or organic produce and artisanal
products (Borough, p163, Broadway, p242
and **Marylebone** www.lfm.org.uk/markets/
marylebone; Cranmer St Carpark, Cramer St, W1;
◷10am-2pm Sun; ⊖Baker St; see www.lfm.
org.uk for others); and the many colourful
general markets, where the oranges and
lemons come from who knows where and
the barrow boys and girls speak with perfect Cockney or Caribbean accents (Brixton,
p307, Ridley Road, p227, Portobello Road,
p274, and **Berwick Street** (www.berwickstreet
london.co.uk/market; Berwick St, W1; ◷9am-6pm
Mon-Sat; ⊖Piccadilly Circus, Oxford Circus).

Food Trends

Just like with fashion and music, Londoners like to keep up with the Joneses when it
comes to eating. Here are some of the current food obsessions in the capital:

Food trucks Whether part of a market or just
occupying a chain-free corner, food trucks have
become a feature of the capital's eating scene.
You'll find them all over the place.

NEED TO KNOW

Opening Hours

As a rule, most restaurants serve lunch between noon and 2.30pm and dinner between 6pm and 11pm. Brasserie-type establishments and chains tend to have continuous service from noon to 11pm.

Price Ranges

The following price ranges refer to a main course.

£ less than £12

££ £12–25

£££ more than £25

Reservations

In London it always pays to make a reservation, but it's absolutely essential at weekends or if you're in a group of more than four people. Top-end restaurants often run multiple sittings, with allocated time slots (generally two hours); pick a late slot if you don't want to be rushed.

Tipping

Most restaurants automatically tack a 'discretionary' service charge (usually 12.5%) onto the bill; this should be clearly advertised. If you feel the service wasn't adequate, you can ask for it to be removed. If there is no service charge on your bill and you would like to tip, 10% is about right.

Haute Cuisine, Low Prices

➡ Many top-end restaurants offer set lunch menus that are great value. À la carte prices are also sometimes cheaper for lunch than dinner.

➡ Many West End restaurants offer good-value pre- or post-theatre menus.

➡ The reliable internet booking service Open Table (www.opentable.co.uk) offers substantial discounts (up to 50% off the food bill) at selected restaurants.

BYO

BYO (bring your own) is common among budget establishments; some charge corkage (£1 to £5 per bottle of wine).

Going regional It's no longer plain old Chinese but Dōngběi or Xīnjiāng; Indian is now Gujarati, Goan or Punjabi.

Smokehouse The growing fad for flame-seared flavours, glowing charcoals and red coals has hatched a host of restaurants across town.

Burgers London remains fixated with gourmet meat-and-bun combos (or vegetarian alternatives) from both independents and mushrooming local chains.

Ramen Still satisfying the slurping masses, the Japanese noodle broth is quickly served, swiftly consumed and perfect for snackers on the move.

Queuing Whether its waiting in line for the tastiest street food or at trendy restaurants that maintain wait lists rather than taking bookings, the British propensity for orderly queuing is being tested to its limits in the capital's eateries.

Chain Gang

While all the usual lacklustre international chain restaurants are to be found all over the capital, London also boasts some excellent homegrown chains. They're good value and made even cheaper by regular voucher offers: check out www.vouchercodes.co.uk and www.myvouchercodes.co.uk for the latest offers.

The following are some of the better offerings; check individual websites for a full list of outlets.

Busaba Eathai (www.busaba.com) Thai food served without fuss among beautiful, modern Asian decor.

Franco Manca (www.francomanca.co.uk) Wood-fired sourdough pizza.

Giraffe (www.giraffe.net) Family-friendly world cuisine.

Honest Burgers (www.honestburgers.co.uk) Hamburgers made with quality British produce.

Le Pain Quotidien (www.lepainquotidien.com) Simple, French-style cafes that serve salads, baguettes and cakes.

Masala Zone (www.masalazone.com) Indian chain that specialises in *thalis* (a meal made up of several small dishes).

Nando's (www.nandos.co.uk) Ever-popular for its peri-peri chicken and off-the-scale trademark spicy sauces; order at the till.

Pret a Manger (www.pret.co.uk) Affordable sandwich chain with a good selection of fillings; they've recently launched dedicated Veggie Pret shops.

Maltby Street Market (p171)

Real Greek (www.therealgreek.com) Beautifully presented mezze and souvlaki, perfect for sharing between friends.

Tas (www.tasrestaurants.co.uk) Established chain of Turkish restaurants with a roll-call of stews, grills and mezze.

Wagamama (www.wagamama.com) Japanese noodle place with rapid turnover, ideal for a quick meal.

Wahaca (www.wahaca.com) Working the Mexican street-food angle in fresh, colourful settings.

Wasabi (www.wasabi.uk.com) Sushi and bento chain, with fantastic rice sets, noodles, rolls and salads.

Food Festivals

Because just eating never seems enough, London has whole festivals dedicated to food and related beverages. They generally have tastings galore and are always good for inspiration.

London Coffee Festival If you know your robusta from your arabica, this is the place for you.

Taste of London This festival turns Regent's Park into a haze of Michelin stars, with top chefs competing for your palate's attention.

BBC Good Food Show Masterclasses, recipes, tastings – these events are very hands-on and very delicious.

Lonely Planet's Top Choices

Clove Club (p213) From Dalston supper club to stupendous Michelin-starred restaurant.

City Social (p154) The best of Modern British, with unforgettable views.

Glasshouse (p321) Kew stalwart serving exemplary contemporary European cuisine.

Koi Ramen Bar (p298) Cheap and delicious Japanese noodles in Brixton.

May the Fifteenth (p300) Smart Clapham brasserie with a modern sensibility.

Best by Budget

£

Koi Ramen Bar (p298) Brixton-based Japanese noodle bar full of happy slurpers.

Padella (p170) Handmade pasta specialists in Borough Market.

Hook Camden Town (p261) Sustainable fish and chips with homemade sauces.

Talli Joe (p112) West End specialists in lesser-known regional Indian dishes.

Towpath (p235) Sunny-day canalside cafe with tasty food and great coffee.

££

Glasshouse (p321) Michelin-starred Modern European restaurant in Kew.

May the Fifteenth (p300) Clapham brasserie serving contemporary British and European fare.

Palomar (p114) Excellent Jerusalem-style dishes for sharing in Soho.

Smoking Goat (p114) Filling the West End with the aroma of Thai barbecue.

Ottolenghi (p263) Islington's legendary Mediterranean cafe and bakery.

£££

Clove Club (p213) Adventurous Shoreditch restaurant rated among the very best in the world.

City Social (p154) Jason Atherton's contemporary dishes do well to compete with the extraordinary views.

Ledbury (p279) French fine dining at its most elegant, in Notting Hill.

Five Fields (p197) Chelsea restaurant serving inventive British fare.

Dinner by Heston Blumenthal (p192) A supreme fusion of perfect British food, eye-catching design and celeb stature.

Best by Cuisine

British

Dinner by Heston Blumenthal (p192) Seriously good-looking Knightsbridge choice putting fresh spins on British culinary history.

Trinity (p301) Clapham fine diner serving the best of British cuisine.

Launceston Place (p196) Magnificent food, presentation and service.

Rabbit (p197) Hop to King's Rd for seasonal British cuisine.

Hook Camden Town (p261) What sort of British list would it be without fish and chips?

French

Ledbury (p279) Still causing a gastronomic stir in Notting Hill.

Gordon Ramsay (p197) The scary chef's signature restaurant; one of only two in London with three Michelin stars.

Chez Bruce (p301) Timeless elegance on the edge of Wandsworth Common.

Club Gascon (p153) City restaurant showcasing the cuisine of France's southwest.

Chez Lindsay (p321) A bit of Brittany in Richmond.

Italian

Padella (p170) Cheap and flavourful homemade pasta in Borough Market.

Locanda Locatelli (p118) London's most renowned Italian restaurant.

Polpo (p113) Serves *ciccheti* like the Venetians make it.

Trullo (p263) Italian-style charcoal grills in Islington.

River Cafe (p280) Another famous name, drawing legions of loyal fans to Fulham.

Indian

Quilon (p109) London's most inventive Indian cuisine.

Talli Joe (p112) A great place to sample some more unusual regional specialities.

Café Spice Namasté (p233) The best of the East End's celebrated subcontinental restaurants.

Gymkhana (p120) Splendid club-style Raj environment and top cuisine.

Potli (p279) Steeping Hammersmith in authentic Indian aromas.

Chinese

Hakkasan Hanway Place (p110) Superlative subterranean Cantonese den in the West End.

Yauatcha (p113) Glamorous dim sum and great for people-watching.

Mamalan (p298) Beijing street food in Brixton.

Bar Shu (p114) Authentic Sichuan that will sear your taste buds.

Min Jiang (p196) Peking duck meets glorious views.

Vegetarian

Gate Hammersmith (p280) Offers an inventive meat-free, flavour-filled menu.

Gate Islington (p210) Another branch, with plenty of Indian and Middle Eastern influences.

Mildreds (p112) Soho stalwart with vegan dishes too.

Manna (p259) Upmarket restaurant for vegetarians and vegans on date nights.

Sagar (p110) South Indian vegetarian food as light as it is tasty.

Best Gastropubs

Anchor & Hope (p170) Flying the gastropub flag on the South Bank for over a decade.

Empress (p235) Choice East End spot with an excellent modern British menu.

Wells Tavern (p262) Posh English pub grub in leafy Hampstead.

Lots Road Pub & Dining Room (p196) Swish West London establishment serving the classics.

Garrison Public House (p173) Bermondsey boozer with top-notch food.

Best for Views

City Social (p154) Wow-factor views from the City to the Shard and beyond.

Skylon (p169) The same views in reverse, from the South Bank to the City skyline.

Portrait (p117) Classic views over Nelson's Column and down Whitehall to Big Ben.

Min Jiang (p196) Breathtaking panoramas over Kensington Gardens.

Duck & Waffle (p153) Hearty British dishes round the clock at the top of Heron Tower.

Best Afternoon Teas

Claridge's Foyer & Reading Room (p120) The last word in classic art-deco elegance.

Portrait (p117) The tea and accompaniments compete with the views.

The Delaunay (p116) Viennese-style afternoon teas complete with *gugelhupfs* (fruit scones) and Sachertorte.

Orangery (p193) Sit with tea and cake in the shadow of Kensington Palace.

Oscar Wilde Bar (p115) Take tea in one of London's most over-the-top rooms.

Best Food Markets

Borough Market (p163) Foodscapes, free tastings and glorious takeaways.

Broadway Market (p242) The East End foodies' weekly event.

Portobello Road Market (p274) A global atlas of street food.

Maltby Street Market (p171) Perfect for lazing an afternoon away at quirky food stalls.

Marylebone Farmers Market (p47) A posh offering reflecting the neighbourhood's make-up.

Best Gourmet Shops

Fortnum & Mason (p128) Elegant Piccadilly shop with no end of fine comestibles.

Harrods (p199) The Food Hall is an epicurean paradise.

Algerian Coffee Stores (p131) Beans and more beans for sale at this historic Soho shop.

Lina Stores (p131) Yummy-looking prewar delicatessen selling Italian goods.

Chinese Tea Company (p284) Just like it says on the tea tin.

Best Celebrity Chef Restaurants

Dinner by Heston Blumenthal (p192) Molecular gastronomy at its very best.

Gordon Ramsay (p197) Where Ramsay's culinary credentials reside.

Tom's Kitchen (p196) Tom Aiken's relaxed Chelsea brasserie remains ever popular.

Nobu (p120) London outpost of Nobuyuki Matsuhisa's famous Japanese restaurant brand.

Fifteen (p211) Product of Jamie Oliver's popular television show, providing jobs to disadvantaged youth.

Spring (p118) Skye Gyngel's delightfully flowery eatery in Somerset House looks onto Waterloo Bridge.

Best Ice Cream

Gelateria Danieli (p321) Hand-made ice cream with seasonal flavours, such as Christmas pudding.

Ruby Violet (p258) Next-level flavours.

Chin Chin Labs (p261) Liquid nitrogen ice cream: weird and utterly wonderful.

Gelupo (p113) All natural ingredients, right in central London.

♟ Drinking & Nightlife

You need only glance at William Hogarth's Gin Lane prints from 1751 to realise that Londoners and alcohol have had more than a passing acquaintance. The metropolis offers a huge variety of venues to wet your whistle in – from cosy neighbourhood pubs to glitzy all-night clubs, and everything in between.

The Pub

The pub (public house) is at the heart of London life and is one of the capital's great social levellers. Virtually every Londoner has a 'local' and looking for your own is a fun part of any visit to the capital.

Pubs in the City and other central areas are mostly after-work drinking dens, busy from 5pm onwards with the post-work crowd during the week. But in more residential areas, pubs come into their own at weekends, when long lunches turn into sloshy afternoons and groups of friends settle in for the night. Many also run popular quizzes on week nights and host live music or comedy. Some have developed such a reputation for the quality of their food that they've been dubbed gastropubs (p46).

You can order almost any beverage you like in a pub: beer, wine, soft drinks, spirits and sometimes hot drinks too. Some specialise in craft beer, offering drinks from local microbreweries, including real ale, fruit beers, organic ciders and other rarer beverages. Others, particularly the gastropubs, invest in a good wine list.

In winter, some pubs offer mulled wine; in summer the must-have drink is Pimms and lemonade (if it's properly done it should have fresh mint leaves, citrus, strawberries and cucumber).

BEER

The raison d'être of a pub is first and foremost to serve beer – be it lager, ale or stout, in a glass or a bottle. On draught (drawn from the cask), it is served by the pint (570mL) or half-pint (285mL) and, more occasionally, third-of-a-pint for real ale tasting.

Pubs generally serve a good selection of lager (highly carbonated and drunk cool or cold) and a smaller selection of real ales or 'bitter' (still or only slightly gassy, drunk at room temperature, with strong flavours). The best-known British lager brand is Carling, though you'll find everything from Fosters to San Miguel.

Among the multitude of ales on offer in London pubs, London Pride, Courage Best, Burton Ale, Adnam's, Theakston (in particular Old Peculiar) and Old Speckled Hen are among the best. Once considered something of an old man's drink, real ale has enjoyed a renaissance among young Londoners, riding tandem with the current fashion for craft beer (small-batch beers from independent brewers). Staff at bars serving good selections are often hugely knowledgeable, just like a sommelier in a restaurant, so ask them for recommendations if you're not sure what to order.

Stout, the best known of which is Irish Guinness, is a slightly sweet, dark beer with a distinct flavour that comes from malt that is roasted before fermentation.

Numerous microbreweries have sprouted throughout London in recent years. Names to look out for include Meantime, Sambrooks, Camden Town Brewery, London Fields Brewery, the Five Points Brewing Co, Redchurch, Beavertown, Crate Brewery, Hackney Brewery, Pressure Drop, Anspach & Hobday, Partizan, the Kernel, London Brewing Co,

Howling Hops, One Mile End, Wild Card Brewery and Brew By Numbers.

Bars

In the large party space left between pubs and clubs, bars are a popular alternative for a London night out. Generally staying open later than pubs but closing earlier than clubs, they tempt those keen to skip bedtime at 11pm but not keen enough to pay a hefty cover charge and stay out all night. Many have DJs on weekends and sometimes a small dance floor too. Drinks tend to be more expensive than pub prices, and some dance bars charge a small cover charge.

Cocktail bars are undergoing a renaissance, so you'll find lots of upmarket options serving increasingly interesting concoctions. Specialist wine, whisky, craft beer and cider bars have also been sprouting in profusion. A romantic attachment to the US prohibition era has seen a scattering of speakeasies hiding in basements and down back lanes.

Clubbing

When it comes to clubbing, London is up there with the best of them. You'll probably know what you want to experience – it might be big clubs such as Fabric (p215) or Ministry of Sound (p306), or sweaty shoebox clubs with the freshest DJ talent – but there's plenty to tempt you to branch out from your usual tastes and try something new. Whether thumping techno, indie rock, Latin, ska, pop, dubstep, grime, minimal electro, R&B or hip hop, there's something going on every night.

Thursdays are loved by those who want to have their fun before the office workers mob the streets on Friday. Saturdays are the busiest and best if you're a serious clubber, and Sundays often see surprisingly good events throughout London, popular with hospitality workers who traditionally have Mondays off.

There are clubs across town, though it has to be said that the best of them are moving further out of the centre every year, so be prepared to take a hike on a night bus. The East End is the top area for cutting-edge clubs, especially Shoreditch. Dalston and Hackney are popular for makeshift clubs in restaurant basements and former shops – so it's great for night-fun hunters. Camden Town still favours the indie crowd, while King's Cross has a bit of everything. The gay party crowd mainly gravitates south of the river, especially Vauxhall, although they still maintain a toehold in the West and East End.

Cabaret

After years of low-profile parties with high-glitter gowns, the cabaret scene burst into the mainstream in the noughties, showering London with nipple tassels, top hats, sexy lingerie and some of the best parties in town. Subsequently, the 'alternative' cabaret scene became overwhelmingly mainstream, and some club-night organisers raised prices to ward off those who wouldn't buck up and dress up. So prepare to pay up to £25 for some (but not all) of the city's best cabaret nights, and make sure you look like a million dollars.

NEED TO KNOW

Opening Hours

Pubs traditionally open at 11am or midday and close at 11pm, with earlier closing on Sunday. Some open later and remain open until around 2am or 3am on weekends. Clubs generally open at 10pm on the weekend and close between 3am and 7am.

Costs

Many clubs are free or cheaper midweek. If you want to go to a famous club on a Saturday night (*the* night for clubbing), expect to pay up to £25. Some places are considerably cheaper if you arrive earlier in the night.

Tickets & Guest Lists

Queuing in the cold at 11pm can be frustrating; arrive early and/or book tickets for bigger events if you can't bear being left in limbo. Some clubs allow you to sign up on their guest list beforehand; check ahead on their websites.

Dress Code

London's clubs are generally relaxed. Posh clubs in areas such as Kensington will want a glam look, so dress to impress (that means no jeans or trainers). The further east you go, the more laid-back and edgy the fashion.

What's On

Check the listings in *Time Out* (www.time-out.com/london) or the *Evening Standard*. London's nightlife is always changing, so keep your eyes peeled.

Drinking by Neighbourhood

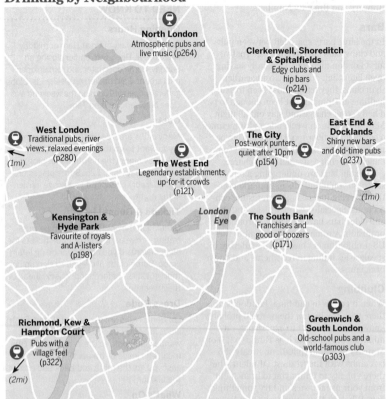

North London
Atmospheric pubs and
live music (p264)

**Clerkenwell, Shoreditch
& Spitalfields**
Edgy clubs and
hip bars
(p214)

West London
Traditional pubs, river
views, relaxed evenings
(p280)
(1mi)

**East End &
Docklands**
Shiny new bars
and old-time pubs
(p237)

The City
Post-work punters,
quiet after 10pm
(p154)

The West End
Legendary establishments,
up-for-it crowds
(p121)

(1mi)

**Kensington &
Hyde Park**
Favourite of royals
and A-listers
(p198)

*London
Eye*

The South Bank
Franchises and
good ol' boozers
(p171)

**Richmond, Kew &
Hampton Court**
Pubs with a
village feel
(p322)
(2mi)

**Greenwich &
South London**
Old-school pubs and a
world-famous club
(p303)

Expect anything from male burlesque contests to girls on roller skates hosting tea parties. Bethnal Green Working Men's Club (p238) is a true working men's club that nonetheless hosts quirky cabaret nights. RVT (p304) is the kooky kingpin of London's queer cabaret scene and home to the legendary Duckie and Sunday Social. Soho Theatre (p128), meanwhile, is an acclaimed comedy venue that lets the freaks off the leash in their Downstairs bar.

Drinking & Nightlife by Neighbourhood

The West End (p121) Soho is the traditional heart of London's nightlife, with pubs, bars, clubs and music venues.

The City (p154) Historic pubs busy after work, quiet after dark and dead on the weekends.

The South Bank (p171) An engaging mix of great

old pubs and swanky modern bars.

Kensington & Hyde Park (p197) Characterful pubs catering to a well-heeled crowd.

Clerkenwell, Shoreditch & Spitalfields (p214) Shoreditch has the capital's most happening nightlife, with dozens of bars, pubs and clubs.

East London (p237) Dalston and Hackney are London's newest hip 'hoods, with interesting and eclectic venues galore.

Hampstead & North London (p264) Amped-up guitars in Camden Town and cosy pubs all around.

Notting Hill & West London (p280) Riverside pubs, smart bars and a rooftop garden club.

Greenwich & South London (p303) Everything from world-famous nightclubs to historic pubs by the river.

Richmond, Kew & Hampton Court (p322) Richmond has some of London's most charming riverside pubs.

Lonely Planet's Top Choices

Holly Bush (p266) Cosy Georgian pub tucked away in genteel Hampstead.

American Bar (p126) Age-old elegance in Mayfair's Beaumont Hotel.

Netil360 (p240) Hip East Enders head to this rooftop eyrie for expansive views and rounds of croquet.

White Cross (p322) Richmond pub set so close to the river you might literally get your feet wet.

Little Bird Gin (p173) South London distillery serving daytime cocktails to Maltby Street Market goers.

Best Pubs

Holly Bush (p266) Antique Georgian interiors and a roaring fire in winter.

White Cross (p322) Great old riverside pub in Richmond.

Lamb & Flag (p124) Just about everyone's West End favourite, so expect a scrum.

Cat & Mutton (p239) Simultaneously traditional and hip, and always up for a party.

Mayflower (p173) Venerable riverside pub with an American connection.

Best Cocktail Bars

Dukes London (p121) Bond-worthy martinis in Ian Fleming's favourite St James's bar.

Zetter Townhouse Cocktail Lounge (p215) Louche, antique-filled lounge tucked away in Clerkenwell.

High Water (p238) Welcoming Dalston bar devising its own delectable concoctions.

Satan's Whiskers (p238) Friendly crew swizzling up a storm in Bethnal Green.

Swift (p122) Pre-dinner or post-theatre tipples in Soho.

Best Bars

American Bar (p126) Mayfair hotel bar with an art-deco ambience.

Queen of Hoxton (p216) Industrial-chic space with regular events and a rooftop bar.

Bar Pepito (p264) Pocket-sized Andalucian bar dedicated to lovers of sherry.

Proud Camden (p265) Rock bar with a snazzy garden terrace.

Paradise by Way of Kensal Green (p281) Eclectically furnished West London bar-club.

Best Clubs

Fabric (p215) Massive club with a global reputation.

Roof Gardens (p281) Party in large gardens with resident flamingos.

Ministry of Sound (p306) The original superclub is in top form.

XOYO (p216) Excellent and varied gigs, club nights and art events.

Egg LDN (p265) Flit between indoor and outdoor spaces at this multistorey megaclub.

Best Views

Netil360 (p240) Uber-hip rooftop bar gazing over the East End to the City skyline.

Oblix (p172) It's not even half-way up the Shard, but the views are legendary.

Galvin at Windows (p126) Fabulous cocktails and views west across Hyde Park.

Sky Pod (p156) Sip a cocktail on a terrace, 35 floors above the city.

Madison (p156) Gaze directly at the dome of St Paul's from One New Change's terrace.

Best Beer Gardens

Windsor Castle (p280) Come summer, regulars abandon the Windsor's historic interior for the chilled-out garden.

Earl of Lonsdale (p280) Old-time Notting Hill pub with a large and leafy beer garden.

Edinboro Castle (p265) A festive place to stretch out on a summer evening.

Garden Gate (p266) Sip on a Pimms amid the greenery.

Greenwich Union (p303) Work your way through the Meantime brews from a garden table.

Entertainment

Whatever it is that sets your spirits soaring or your booty shaking, you'll find it in London. The city's been a world leader in theatre ever since a young man from Stratford-upon-Avon set up shop here in the 16th century. And if London started swinging in the 1960s, its live rock and pop scene has barely let up since.

Theatre

A night out at the theatre is as much a must-do London experience as a trip on the top deck of a double-decker bus. London's Theatreland in the dazzling West End – from Aldwych in the east, past Shaftesbury Ave to Regent St in the west – has a concentration of theatres only rivalled by New York's Broadway. It's a thrillingly diverse scene, encompassing Shakespeare's classics performed with old-school precision, edgy new works, raise-the-roof musicals and some of the world's longest-running shows.

London's cosmopolitan DNA and multicultural roots nourish a great flowering of theatrical creativity. Even Hollywood stars are willing to abandon their pampered lives for a season treading the boards in London.

There are around 40 theatres in the West End alone, but Theatreland is just the brightest facet of London's sparkling theatre world, where off–West End venues range from highbrow theatrical institutions to tiny fringe stages tucked away above pubs. The newest addition is Sir Nicholas Hytner's Bridge Theatre (www.bridgetheatre.co.uk), which opened in Borough in 2017.

The celebrated National Theatre (p174) is the regular home of innovative new shows, creative directing and much-loved classics that often migrate to West End theatres. The Barbican Centre (p157) hosts foreign drama companies to massive acclaim. Traditional stagecraft is also on offer, particularly at the re-creation of Shakespeare's Globe (p174), a

wonderful venue where the focus is on the authentic Shakespearean experience.

The theatrical fringes are busy with peripheral, subsidised shows from experimental groups, where conceptual ideas find expression to sometimes bewildered audiences. In summer, open-air theatres avail themselves of balmy days (sometimes punctuated with sudden showers) to entertain crowds, most famously in Regent's Park.

Classical Music

With multiple world-class orchestras and ensembles, quality venues, reasonable ticket prices and performances covering the whole musical gamut from traditional crowd-pleasers to innovative compositions, London will satisfy even the fussiest classical music buff. The Southbank Centre (p174), Barbican Centre (p157), Royal Albert Hall (p199) and the new King's Place (www.kingsplace.co.uk) all maintain an alluring roster of performances, further gilding London's outstanding reputation as a cosmopolitan centre for classical music. The Proms is the year's biggest event; the hugely famous orchestral festival runs for eight weeks at the Royal Albert Hall (p199) and Cadogan Hall (p199).

Opera

With one of the world's leading opera companies at the Royal Opera House (p126) in Covent Garden, the English National Opera (p127) based at the London Coliseum and plenty of other smaller players and events, London will keep opera lovers busy. It's not just the classics that get attention, as new productions are regularly staged which grapple with a host of contemporary themes. In summer, Holland Park (p273) is the venue for opera under the stars. Opera is expensive to produce and, consequently, tickets can be pricey.

Dance

London is home to five major dance companies and a host of small and experimental ones. The Royal Ballet (p128), the best classical ballet company in the land, is based at the Royal Opera House in Covent Garden. The English National Ballet (p393) often performs at the London Coliseum, especially at Christmas and in summer. Sadler's Wells (p219) is excellent for experimental dance. Also worth investigating is the Laban Theatre (p306), which features performances by students of the Trinity Laban Conservatoire of Music & Dance.

Dance Umbrella (www.danceumbrella.co.uk; ☉mid-Oct) is a contemporary dance festival that takes place in late October.

Live Rock, Pop, Jazz & Blues

Musically diverse and defiantly different, London is a hot spot of musical innovation and talent. It leads the world in articulate indie rock, in particular, and tomorrow's guitar heroes are right-this-minute paying their dues on sticky-floored stages in Camden Town, Shoreditch and Dalston.

Monster international acts see London as an essential stop on their transglobal stomps, but be prepared for tickets selling out faster than you can find your credit card. The city's beautiful old theatres and music halls play host to a constant roster of well-known names in more intimate settings. In summer, giant festivals take over the city's parks, while smaller, more localised events such as the **Dalston Music Festival** (www.dalstonmusicfestival. com) showcase up-and-comers in multiple spaces.

Londoners are more musically aware than most – perhaps it's got something to do with all that time spent on the tube with their headphones on. The beauty about catching a gig in London is that its sheer size means that there's always enough totally devoted fans who know all the words to all the songs to fill any venue – whether it's Blur at Hyde Park or Kate Tempest at the Brixton Academy.If jazz or blues are

PLAN YOUR TRIP ENTERTAINMENT

NEED TO KNOW

Purchasing Tickets

➡ Book well ahead for live performances and, if you can, buy directly from the venue.

➡ Enquire at the theatre's own box office about cut-price standby tickets or limited late releases for otherwise sold-out shows.

➡ At gigs, be wary of touts outside the venue on the night. Tickets may be counterfeit or stolen.

Student Discounts

➡ Student standby tickets are sometimes available one hour or so before performances start.

➡ Some theatres have cheap tickets or cheap student/youth tickets on certain days.

Standing Tickets

➡ Shakespeare's Globe (p174) offers 700 standing tickets (£5) for each performance.

➡ Limited 10p standing tickets are available for performances at the Jerwood Theatre Downstairs at the Royal Court Theatre (p199).

Cheaper Sessions

➡ Midweek matinees at such venues as the Royal Opera House are usually cheaper than evening performances.

➡ Most cinemas offer discounts on Monday (or Tuesday) and most weekday afternoon screenings.

➡ On the day of performance, you can buy discounted tickets for West End productions from **Tkts Leicester Square** (http://www.tkts.co.uk/leicester-square/).

Useful Magazines & Websites

Time Out (www.timeout.com/london) Free weekly magazine with up-to-date theatre and entertainment listings.

London Theatre (www.londontheatre.co.uk) Listings for musicals, plays, drama and fringe theatre in London.

London Dance (www.londondance.com) Listings of dance performances.

your thing, London has some truly excellent clubs and pubs where you can catch classics and contemporary tunes. The city's major jazz event is the **London Jazz Festival** (www.efglondonjazzfestival.org.uk; ☉Nov) in November.

Comedy

They may look a miserable bunch on the tube – and the winter drizzle and summer wash-outs don't help – but Londoners have a solid sense of humour and comedy is flourishing in the capital. On any given night, you can pitch up at any one of the 20-plus major comedy clubs or countless other venues (including pubs) to roll in the aisles or snort your drink down the wrong way.

Most acts have both eyes on the critical Edinburgh Festival season. From April to July, new material is being tried out on audiences. August is the cruellest month for comedy in London because everyone's shifted up north for the festival itself. Come winter, London's stages are full of comedians performing the stuff that went down well in Edinburgh. Check the winners list of the **Edinburgh Comedy Awards** (www. comedyawards.co.uk) for the brightest new stars.

Some of the world's most famous modern comedians hail from, or made their names in, London, including Ben Elton, Kathy Burke, Julian Clary, Jo Brand, Sacha Baron Cohen, Sue Perkins, James Corden, Catherine Tate, Matt Lucas, David Walliams, Tracey Ullman, Jack Whitehall and Russell Brand.

Film

Londoners have a passion for film, with movie buffs filling venues large and small all across the city. For eclectic tastes, shorts and foreign cinema, as well as mainstream movies, London's independent cinemas allow you to put your feet up, sip a glass of wine and feel right at home. You can often catch monthly seasons and premieres, as well as actors and directors chatting about their work and answering questions. Cinemas such as the Prince Charles (p127)

have cheap tickets, run mini-festivals and screen popular singalong classics. For back-catalogue classics, turn to the BFI Southbank (p175). The BFI (British Film Institute) also runs the biggest film event of the year, the **London Film Festival** (www.bfi.org.uk/ lff; ☉Oct).

Many major premieres are held in Leicester Sq, the priciest part of London for cinema tickets. Look out also for the Summer Screen at Somerset House (p107), and the Luna Cinema (www.thelunacinema. com), which screens movies under the stars at famous London venues including Kew Gardens, Hampton Court Palace, Fulham Palace, Alexandra Palace and Regent's Park.

Entertainment by Neighbourhood

The West End (p74) Packed with theatres, opera houses, classical music concert halls, small live-music venues, comedy clubs and cinemas.

The City (p135) Barbican Centre and church concerts.

The South Bank (p56) A major concentration of some of London's best-known and most prestigious theatres.

Kensington & Hyde Park (p176) Royal Albert Hall, the Royal Court Theatre and some smaller music venues.

Clerkenwell, Shoreditch & Spitalfields (p202) Sadler's Wells, live music bars and comedy.

East London (p222) Theatres, independent cinemas and live music venues.

North London (p244) The works: indie rock, jazz, blues, traditional music, folk dancing, comedy and theatre.

Notting Hill & West London (p271) Tremendous independent cinemas, live music and summer opera.

Greenwich & South London (p287) Live music, dance, theatre and cinema.

Richmond, Kew & Hampton Court (p308) Live jazz, open-air concerts and live-music pubs.

Lonely Planet's Top Choices

Royal Opera House (p126) London's pre-eminent stage for opera and classical dance.

Shakespeare's Globe (p174) Experience the Bard's work as it was first performed.

Southbank Centre (p174) Concerts, recitals, musicals – you name it – the Southbank Centre has it.

Barbican Centre (p157) A powerhouse of culture, from music and dance to theatre and film.

Wilton's (p241) The Victorian music hall tradition lives on in the East End.

Sadler's Wells (p219) Modern dance at its most immediate.

Best Theatre

Shakespeare's Globe (p174) Shakespeare, as it would have been 400 years ago.

National Theatre (p174) Contemporary theatre on the South Bank.

Old Vic (p175) A heavy hitter in London's theatrical scene.

Donmar Warehouse (p128) Consistently delivers thought-provoking productions.

Royal Court Theatre (p199) Forward-thinking, promoting new voices.

Best Classical Music

Royal Opera House (p126) One of the world's great opera venues, with classical ballet too.

Royal Albert Hall (p199) The Grand Dame of classical music venues.

Wigmore Hall (p126) London's most important chamber music venue.

Southbank Centre (p174) Classical music from around the world in the wonderful Royal Festival Hall.

Cadogan Hall (p199) Chelsea home of the Royal Philharmonic Orchestra.

Best Music in Churches

St Martin-in-the-Fields (p103) Excellent classical music concerts, many by candlelight.

Westminster Abbey (p76) Evensong and the city's finest organ concerts.

St Paul's Cathedral (p143) Evensong at its most evocative.

St Alfege Church (p293) Free lunchtime concerts on Thursday.

St Lawrence Jewry (p151) Weekly piano and organ concerts.

Best Dance

Sadler's Wells (p219) Top-drawer international and UK contemporary dance.

Royal Ballet (p128) The nation's largest ballet company, based at the Royal Opera House.

English National Ballet (p393) Touring company based at the London Coliseum.

Southbank Centre (p174) From Bollywood to break-dancing, and all things in between.

The Place (p127) The very birthplace of modern English dance.

Best Live Rock & Pop Venues

Royal Albert Hall (p199) Gorgeous, grand and spacious, yet strangely intimate.

Union Chapel (p269) One of London's most atmospheric venues.

O2 Arena (p305) A massive venue for the biggest gigs.

KOKO (p267) Fabulously glitzy venue, showcasing original indie rock.

Eventim Apollo (p283) Formerly the Hammersmith Apollo, this is the legendary venue where David Bowie retired Ziggy Stardust.

Best Live Jazz

606 Club (p198) Legendary Chelsea basement jazz outfit.

Pizza Express Jazz Club (p126) Top-class jazz in the basement of a chain restaurant.

Ronnie Scott's (p127) Britain's most famous jazz club.

Vortex Jazz Club (p241) Tiny but packing a punch with superb programming.

Jazz Cafe (p267) Much more than just jazz these days, but still staging some of London's best jams.

Best Comedy

Soho Theatre (p128) Stages local and foreign talent.

Comedy Store (p127) Hosts the most famous improvisation outfit in town.

Angel Comedy (p268) Free shows every night of the week.

Union Chapel (p269) Giggle in church at the monthly Live at the Chapel.

Up the Creek (p306) Long-standing comedy favourite south of the river.

 # Shopping

From charity-shop finds to designer bags, there are thousands of ways to spend your hard-earned cash in London. Many of the big-name shopping attractions, such as Harrods, Hamleys, Camden Market and Old Spitalfields Market, have become must-sees in their own right. Chances are that with so many temptations, you'll give your wallet a full workout.

Markets

Perhaps the biggest draw for visitors is the capital's famed markets. A treasure trove of small designers, unique jewellery pieces, original framed photographs and posters, colourful vintage pieces and bric-a-brac, they are the antidote to impersonal, carbon-copy shopping centres.

The most popular markets are Camden (p253), Old Spitalfields (p220) and Portobello Road (p274), which operate most days, but there are dozens of others, such as Brick Lane's excellent Sunday UpMarket (p219), which only pop up on the weekend. Camden and Old Spitalfields are both mainly covered, but even the outdoor markets are busy, rain or shine.

Designers

London-based designers are well established in the fashion world and a visit to Stella Mc-Cartney, Vivienne Westwood, Paul Smith or Burberry is an experience in its own right. The fashion house started by the late Alexander McQueen is now under the creative direction of Sarah Burton, perhaps most famous as the designer of Princess Catherine's wedding dress. Other names to watch out for include Molly Goddard (available at Browns (p129)), Christopher Kane and Mimi Wade (both available at Selfridges (p133)).

Vintage Fashion

The realm of vintage apparel has moved from being sought out by those looking for something off-beat and original, to an all-out mainstream shopping habit. Vintage designer garments and odd bits and pieces from the 1920s to the 1980s are all gracing the rails in some surprisingly upmarket boutique vintage shops.

The less self-conscious charity shops – especially those in areas such as Chelsea, Kensington and Islington – are your best bets for real bargains on designer wear (usually, the richer the area, the better the secondhand shops).

Chain Stores

Many bemoan the fact that chains have taken over the main shopping centres, leaving independent shops struggling to balance the books. But since they're cheap, fashionable and always conveniently located, Londoners (and others) keep going back for more. As well as familiar overseas retailers, such as Gap, H&M, Urban Outfitters and Zara, you'll find plenty of home-grown chains, including luxury womenswear brand **Karen Millen** (☎020-7836 5355; www.karenmillen.com; 2-3 James St, WC2; ⊙10am-8pm Mon-Sat, 11am-6pm Sun; ⊖Covent Garden) and global giant Topshop (p131).

Shopping by Neighbourhood

North London
It's all about Camden Market
(p269)

**Clerkenwell, Shoreditch &
Spitalfields**
Vintage, vintage, vintage,
fashion and jewellery
(p219)

West London
Famous market, vintage stores
and lovely boutiques
(p283)

(1mi)

The City
Good for suits but
little else
(p157)

**East End &
Docklands**
Wonderful markets,
discounted fashion
(p242)

(1mi)

The West End
Shopping galore,
from franchises to
boutiques
(p128)

Kensington & Hyde Park
High fashion and
glamorous shopping
(p199)

*London
Eye*

The South Bank
Fabulous food and
small designer shops
(p175)

**Greenwich &
South London**
Eclectic markets, handicrafts
and antiques
(p306)

Need to Know

OPENING HOURS

➡ Shops generally open from 9am or 10am to
6pm or 7pm Monday to Saturday.

➡ Most stores in popular strips open on Sunday,
typically from noon to 6pm but sometimes 10am
to 4pm.

➡ West End stores open to 9pm on Thursday;
those in Chelsea, Knightsbridge and Kensington
open late on Wednesday.

➡ Sales Tax

➡ A 20% value-added tax (VAT) is included in
the advertised prices of most goods, excluding

some categories such as children's clothing and
food.

➡ Tax Refunds

➡ In stores displaying a 'tax free' sign, visitors
from non-EU countries are entitled to claim back
the VAT on purchases.

➡ The retailer should provide a VAT 407 form,
which needs to be completed and presented at
Customs when leaving the country, along with
the receipt and goods. See www.gov.uk/tax-on-
shopping/taxfree-shopping.

Lonely Planet's Top Choices

Sunday UpMarket (p219) Up-and-coming designers, cool tees and terrific food.

Fortnum & Mason (p128) The world's most glamorous grocery store?

Camden Market (p253) Every shade of exotic and alternative: steampunk fashion, navel jewellery, Moroccan lamps.

Harrods (p199) Garish and kitsch yet perennially popular department store.

Portobello Road Market (p274) A colourful clash of fashion, vintage clothing, antiques and exotic food.

Best Fashion Shops

Selfridges (p133) Everything from streetwear to high fashion under one roof.

Collectif (p219) Spitalfields store taking inspiration from the 1940s and '50s.

Hackney Walk (p242) Big-brand outlet shopping at its very best.

Folk (p130) Simple but striking Scandinavian style for men and women.

Browns (p129) Great for up-and-coming designers.

Best Markets

Sunday UpMarket (p219) Load up on delicious food before tackling the designer stalls.

Camden Market (p253) From authentic antiques to tourist tat – and everything in between.

Portobello Road Market (p274) Classic Notting Hill sprawl, perfect for vintage everything.

Broadway Market (p242) Local market known for its food but with plenty else besides.

Old Spitalfields Market (p220) One of London's best for young fashion designers.

Best Vintage

Annie's Vintage Costume & Textiles (p269) High-end Islington boutique specialising in recycled glamour.

Traid (p243) Dalston not-for-profit selling both top-notch vintage duds and new clothes made from offcuts.

Blitz London (p220) A massive selection of just about everything.

Beyond Retro (p242) London vintage empire with a rock 'n' roll heart.

Rellik (p285) Classic designer cast-offs from the 1920s to the 1980s.

Best Bookshops

John Sandoe Books (p199) Gorgeous bookshop full of gems.

Peter Harrington (p200) First editions and rare books.

Lutyens & Rubinstein (p284) Curated selections of exceptional writing.

Foyles (p130) Stocks a brilliant selection covering most bases and incorporates the Grant & Cutler foreign-language bookshop.

Hatchards (p129) London's oldest bookshop, selling the good stuff since 1797.

Best Music Shops

Rough Trade East (p219) Excellent selection of vinyl and CDs, plus in-store gigs.

Casbah Records (p307) Classic vinyl and memorabilia.

Honest Jon's (p285) For reggae, jazz, funk, soul, dance and blues junkies.

Sounds of the Universe (p131) Soul, reggae, funk and dub CDs and vinyl and some original 45s.

Phonica (p131) Dance music specialist but more besides.

Best Department Stores

Fortnum & Mason (p128) A world of food in luxurious historic surroundings.

Harrods (p199) Enormous, overwhelming and indulgent, with a world-famous food hall.

Liberty (p130) Fabric, fashion and much, much more.

Selfridges (p133) Over 100 years of retail innovation.

Harvey Nichols (p200) Fashion, food, beauty and lifestyle over eight floors.

Sports & Activities

London boasts a well-developed infrastructure for participatory and spectator sports, with world-famous venues scattered around the city and a surprisingly large amount of green space for weekend warriors to work up a sweat in.

Cycling

London is criss-crossed by dedicated cycle paths, from breezy canalside towpaths to routes through parks and commons. Central London is flat and surprisingly compact, making two-wheeled exploration a great way to experience the city. The easiest way to do this is to take advantage of the many Santander Cycles (p415) self-service docking stations scattered around the city.

Cycling enthusiasts should consider heading to the Lee Valley VeloPark (p243) for the experience of riding on the Olympic velodrome and BMX park.

Swimming

With two 50m pools and a 25m diving pool, the London Aquatics Centre (p243) at Queen Elizabeth Olympic Park is a magnet for swimmers. London also has some lovely 1930s art-deco lidos (public outdoor swimming pools) and famous swimming ponds in Hampstead Heath (p270) and Hyde Park (p201).

Boating, Rafting & Kayaking

Options range from gentle cruises on the Thames to white-water rafting, kayaking, hydrospeeding and tubing sessions at the Lee Valley White Water Centre (www.gowhitewater.co.uk), built for the 2012 Olympics. Kayaking London (www.kayakinglondon.com) offers river and canal expeditions, or if that sounds too much like hard work, Alfred Le Roy (p243) is a booze-filled narrowboat taking to the canals around Hackney Wick. For a faster pace, there's **Thames Rockets**

(020-7928 8933; www.thamesrockets.com; Boarding Gate 1, London Eye, Waterloo Millennium Pier, Westminster Bridge Rd, SE1; adult/child £43.50/29.50; 10am-6pm;), or you can hire a rowboat from the Richmond Bridge Boathouses (p324) and paddle about at your leisure.

Cricket

On a long summer's day, there's no more of an English thing to do than to pack a picnic and enjoy the thwack of leather on willow. The English Cricket Board (www.ecb.co.uk) website has complete details of match schedules and tickets. International test matches are played at Lord's (p268) and the Oval (p287).

Football

Football is at the very heart of English sporting culture, with about a dozen league teams in London. At the time of writing five London teams were in the Premier League (www.premierleague.com): Arsenal, Chelsea, Crystal Palace, Tottenham Hotspur and West Ham United. The competition runs from August to May, although it's extremely difficult for visitors to secure tickets to matches (they are usually all snapped up by season-ticket holders). Consider taking a tour at **Wembley** (0800 169 9933; www.wembleystadium.com; tours adult/child £20/12; Wembley Park), London Stadium (p232) or Arsenal Emirates Stadium (p255) instead.

NEED TO KNOW

Opening Hours

As a rule, most gyms open very early, usually from 6.30am, to ensure early risers get their workouts in before work, and stay open until at least 9pm. Parks are generally open from dawn to dusk. Most swimming pools are open year-round, including the Hampstead Heath Ponds.

Tickets

Finding tickets for Premier League matches during the August to mid-May football season in London is more or less impossible, as seats are snapped up by season-ticket holders. Tickets for all other sporting events need to be booked well in advance; check the websites for the individual teams, venues and events for details.

Ice Skating

A combined ice rink and bowling venue, Queens Ice & Bowl (p286) has skating year-round and disco nights on ice. In winter months, outside ice rinks sparkle at Somerset House (p107), the Natural History Museum (p182), the Tower of London (p137), Hyde Park's Winter Wonderland (p201) and other venues.

Tennis

Wimbledon (p323) becomes the centre of the sporting universe for a fortnight in June/July when the world's most famous tennis tournament gets underway, but obtaining tickets (p323) is far from straightforward. To view or visit Centre Court at other times of the year, head to the Wimbledon Lawn Tennis Museum (p319). Numerous parks around London have tennis courts, many free.

Queen Elizabeth Olympic Park (p232)

Sports & Activities by Neighbourhood

The West End (p74) Ice climbing at Vertical Chill.

Kensington & Hyde Park (p176) Jogging, horse riding, cycling, swimming, boating and tennis in Hyde Park itself.

Clerkenwell, Shoreditch & Spitalfields (p202) Playing minigolf in the Old Truman Brewery.

East London (p222) Myriad activities in Queen Elizabeth Olympic Park, climbing in Mile End and horse riding in Mudchute.

Hampstead & North London (p244) Home to Lord's, Arsenal Emirates Stadium and sporting facilities in Hampstead Heath and Regent's Park.

Notting Hill & West London (p271) Chelsea Football Club, Queens Ice & Bowl and kayaking in Little Venice.

Greenwich & South London (287) Cricket at the Oval and thrillseeking with Go Ape Battersea and Up at the O2.

Richmond, Kew & Hampton Court (p308) World-famous Wimbledon tennis centre and Twickenham rugby stadium, plus boating at Richmond.

Lonely Planet's Top Choices

Wimbledon (p323) Enter the ballot and cross your fingers to secure a ticket to the word's greatest tennis clashes.

Lee Valley VeloPark (p243) Tear around the actual Olympic velodrome and BMX course.

Vertical Chill (p134) Ice isn't just for cocktail glasses in the West End.

London Aquatics Centre (p243) Channel your inner Michael Phelps or Shiwen Ye in the actual Olympic pool.

Lord's (p252) Tour the venerable stadium or settle in for a few days of bat-on-ball action.

Best Stadium Tours

Lord's (p252) The hallowed 'home of cricket', with a fascinating museum.

Wembley Stadium (p63) The city's landmark national stadium, used for football test matches and mega concerts.

Twickenham Stadium (p319) London's famous rugby union stadium, used for international test matches.

London Stadium (p232) Built as the centrepiece stadium for the 2012 Olympics and now home to West Ham United FC.

Arsenal Emirates Stadium (p255) Offers both self-guided tours or tours led by former Arsenal players.

Stamford Bridge (p275) Home of Chelsea FC.

Best Swimming

London Aquatics Centre (p243) Actual Olympic pools encased in a beautiful shell.

London Fields Lido (p243) Restored East End complex with 1930s charm.

Hampstead Heath Ponds (p270) Single-sex and mixed bathing ponds for murky freshwater dips.

Serpentine Lido (p201) Cordoned-off swimming in Hyde Park's lake.

BeachEast (p232) Large paddling pools for toddler splash-about in Queen Elizabeth Olympic Park's artificial beach.

Best for Adrenaline

ArcelorMittal Orbit (p232) Free-fall abseil off the tower or take a 178m slide to the ground.

Thames Rockets (p63) Blast along the Thames, James Bond–style, in a rigid inflatable speedboat.

Go Ape Battersea (p307) Zipline and high-wire course in Battersea Park.

Up at the O2 (p307) Scale the heights of the O2 arena.

◉ LGBT+

The city of Oscar Wilde, Virginia Woolf and Elton John does not disappoint its queer visitors, proffering a fantastic mix of highbrow culture and brash parties year-round. It's a world gay capital on par with New York and San Francisco, with visible gay, lesbian and transgender communities and enlightened laws to protect them.

Legal Rights

Protection from discrimination is enshrined in law and same-sex couples have the right to marry. That's not to say that homophobia does not exist, and anti-gay violence still occurs with some regularity. However, it would be extremely surprising (not to mention illegal) for same-gender couples to strike any problems when booking a double bed in a hotel or, indeed, dealing with any service provider.

Gay Bars & Clubs

Several famous venues have closed their doors in recent years – due, in part, to gentrification of traditionally gay neighbourhoods. That said, London still has a widely varied bar scene with venues spread across the city, not just in the traditional Soho heartland. Whether you fancy a quiet pint in an old-fashioned boozer that just happens to be gay, or a pumping place to wet your whistle before going out dancing, plenty of options remain.

Clubbing in London, and on the gay scene in particular, is less about specific clubs than it is about promoters staging specialist nights at established venues. This means that a club that was full of shirtless gay dudes one night might well be full of straight goths the next.

Lesbian Hang-outs

The lesbian scene has few venues of its own – She Soho (p123) on Old Compton St being a notable exception – and most gay bars are overwhelmingly male. That said, the hipper, younger venues (such as the Glory, Dalston Superstore and Her Upstairs) tend to be much more mixed, and there are regular women's nights held at establishments straight and gay, especially in the East End.

Gay & Lesbian by Neighbourhood

The West End Centred on Old Compton St, Soho's gay village still has London's greatest concentration of venues.

East London Dalston has an alternative, diverse and mixed scene, while Limehouse has some old-school gay venues.

Greenwich & South London Vauxhall has a good-natured but somewhat blokey scene, leavened by the kooky RVT.

Best Events

BFI Flare: London LGBT Film Festival (p406) Renowned film festival, hosted by the British Film Institute, with screenings, premieres, awards and talks.

Pride (www.prideinlondon. com) One of the world's largest LGBTQI parades, complete with floats, stalls and performers.

Fringe! (www.fringefilmfest. com) Queer film and arts festival, held in various venues in November.

Best Bars & Pubs

Yard (p122) A rare indoor-outdoor venue in the middle of gay Soho.

Glory (p216) One of London's most eclectic venues, where weird is a term of genuine endearment.

Two Brewers (p305) Long-standing Clapham bar serving a local South London crowd.

Duke of Wellington (p123) Unpretentious gay boozer attracting a beardy crowd.

Old Ship (p241) Unassuming and cosy corner pub in Limehouse.

Best For Lesbians

She Soho (p123) London's only dedicated lesbian bar, in the heart of the gay strip.

Ku Klub (p124) Party girls head down the stairs for the weekly Ruby Tuesdays takeover.

Dalston Superstore (p239) Regular women's nights readjust the gender balance of this female-friendly hispter hang-out.

RVT (p304) Monthly *Butch, Please!* nights, plus a whole host of drag kings and other lesbian performers.

Best Clubs

Heaven (p125) London's most famous gay club has been reeling them in since the late 1970s.

Dalston Superstore (p239) Diner by day, subterranean nightclub after dark.

Eagle (p304) Blokey, beardy and a bit beary, this is a cracker of a late-night venue.

RVT (p304) Themed nights, cabaret, drag shows, open stage and all kinds of shenanigans.

Best Club Nights

Popcorn at Heaven (p125) A fun and cheap Monday night out, with a great selection of music.

G-A-Y at Heaven (p125) Love it or hate it, G-A-Y is where half of Soho heads on Saturday.

Duckie at the RVT (p304) Tagged London's 'flagship rock 'n' roll honky-tonk', this is the club's legendary queer performance night.

Pop Horror at the RVT (p304) If you like pop and you like horror, combine them in a monthly disco bloodbath.

Best Best Historical & Cultural Sites

Gay's the Word (p130) Bookshop that's been a bastion of gay culture since 1979.

Hampstead Heath (p254) Legendary cruising ground, with popular single-sex bathing ponds immortalised in Hollinghurst's *The Line of Beauty*.

Cadogan Hotel, Sloane St, Knightsbridge Site of Oscar Wilde's arrest in 1895; due to reopen in 2018.

Admiral Duncan, 54 Old Compton St, Soho Gay pub that was the site of a homophobic bombing in 1999, killing three patrons.

NEED TO KNOW

Free Press

London has a lively gay press charting the ever-changing scene. Check out any of these publications, their listings are the most up-to-date available.

Boyz (www.boyz.co.uk) Weekly magazine covering the bar and club scenes.

QX (www.qxmaga zine.com) Another weekly mag devoted mainly to men's venues.

Pride Life (www.pridelife. com) Quarterly lifestyle magazine.

Magazines

The following magazines are for sale at newsagents.

Gay Times (www. gaytimes.co.uk) Long-standing monthly gay men's mag.

Diva (www.divamag. co.uk) Monthly lesbian magazine.

Attitude (www.atti tude.co.uk) Monthly gay men's lifestyle glossy.

Blogs & Resources

60by80 (www.60by80. com/london) Gay travel information.

Time Out London LGBT (www.timeout.com/ london/lgbt) Bar, club and events listings.

Help

Always report homophobic crimes to the police (p418).

Switchboard LGTB & Helpline (https://switch board.lgbt/)

Explore London

Left: Big Ben (p85)

Neighbourhoods at a Glance

① The West End p74

With many of London's poshest neighbourhoods and superlative restaurants, hotels and shops, the West End should be your first port of call. Iconic sights (Trafalgar Sq, Piccadilly Circus), buildings and museums (Buckingham Palace, Westminster Abbey, British Museum), nightlife (Soho), shopping (Oxford St, Covent Garden, Bond Sts), parks (St James's Park) and theatres – they are all in the West End.

② The City p135

London's historic core is a tale of two cities: packed during the week and eerily quiet at weekends. For most of its history, the entire city was enclosed by walls that were only dismantled in the 18th century. A profusion of daring skyscrapers sprout from the City's fringes, but the essential sights have been standing for hundreds of years: St Paul's Cathedral and the Tower of London.

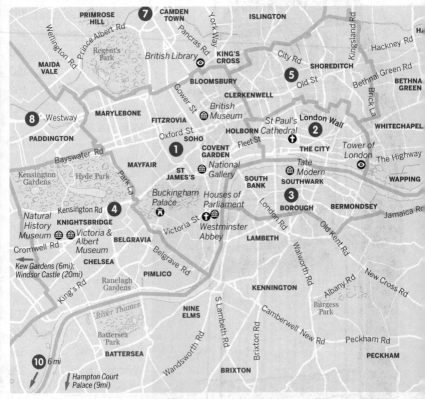

❸ The South Bank p158

The South Bank is a must-visit area for art lovers, theatre-goers and culture hounds, and has been significantly re-energised by the renowned Tate Modern. Come for iconic Thames views, great food markets, first-rate pubs, dollops of history, striking examples of modern architecture, and a sprinkling of fine bars and restaurants.

❹ Kensington & Hyde Park p176

Splendidly well groomed, Kensington is one of London's most handsome neighbourhoods. You'll find three fine museums here – the V&A, the Natural History Museum and the Science Museum – as well as excellent dining and shopping, graceful parklands and elegant streets of grand period architecture.

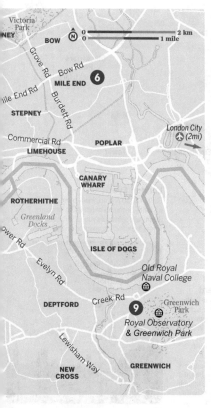

❺ Clerkenwell, Shoreditch & Spitalfields p202

These historic city-fringe neighbourhoods contain a few significant sights, but is best known for its nightlife. Shoreditch and Hoxton long ago replaced Soho and Camden as the hippest, most alternative parts of London, and they're still holding their own.

❻ East London & Docklands p222

Anyone with an interest in multicultural London needs to visit the East End. There's standout ethnic cuisine, museums and galleries, excellent pubs, canal-side eating and drinking, hip neighbourhoods, and the vast Queen Elizabeth Olympic Park to explore.

❼ North London p244

North London houses Camden's eponymous market, and unrivalled music and pub scene. King's Cross is has transformed, and is now a destination in its own right. There's plenty for quiet enjoyment too – green spaces, overgrown Victorian cemeteries and canal walks.

❽ Notting Hill & West London p271

This large and fairly spread out neighbourhood has several interesting museums including the new Design Museum, recently relocated. Portobello Road Market is the main draw to Notting Hill for most visitors.

❾ Greenwich & South London p287

Regal riverside Greenwich complements its village feel with some grand architecture, grassy parkland and riverside pubs. Brixton has the creative edge in its glorious food-and-shop The villages are full of hidden gems, and tranquil, leafy charm.

❿ Richmond, Kew & Hampton Court p308

Flee London's concrete urban interior and get a look at the city's leafy, riverside complexion – where the air is cleaner and the landscapes increasingly pastoral. Wander by the river, explore haunted palaces, get lost in beautiful Kew Gardens, go deer-spotting and down a pint at sunset.

The River Thames

A FLOATING TOUR

London's history has always been determined by the Thames. The city was founded as a Roman port nearly 2000 years ago and over the centuries since then many of the capital's landmarks have lined the river's banks. A boat trip is a great way to experience the attractions.

There are piers dotted along both banks at regular intervals where you can hop on and hop off the regular services to visit

places of interest. The best place to board is Westminster Pier, from where boats head downstream, taking you from the City of Westminster, the seat of government, to the original City of London, now the financial district and dominated by a growing band of skyscrapers. Across the river, the once shabby and neglected South Bank now bristles with as many top attractions as its northern counterpart, including the slender Shard.

In our illustration we've concentrated on the top highlights you'll enjoy from a waterborne

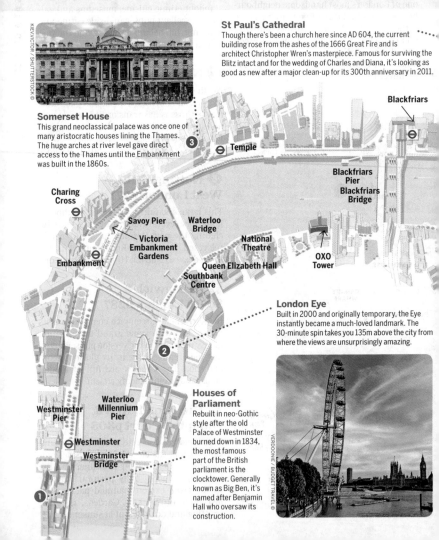

St Paul's Cathedral
Though there's been a church here since AD 604, the current building rose from the ashes of the 1666 Great Fire and is architect Christopher Wren's masterpiece. Famous for surviving the Blitz intact and for the wedding of Charles and Diana, it's looking as good as new after a major clean-up for its 300th anniversary in 2011.

KIEV.VICTOR / SHUTTERSTOCK ©

Blackfriars

Somerset House
This grand neoclassical palace was once one of many aristocratic houses lining the Thames. The huge arches at river level gave direct access to the Thames until the Embankment was built in the 1860s.

3 Temple

Blackfriars Pier
Blackfriars Bridge

Charing Cross

Savoy Pier   **Waterloo Bridge**

Victoria Embankment Gardens   **National Theatre**

Embankment   **OXO Tower**

Queen Elizabeth Hall
Southbank Centre

London Eye
Built in 2000 and originally temporary, the Eye instantly became a much-loved landmark. The 30-minute spin takes you 135m above the city from where the views are unsurprisingly amazing.

Westminster Pier   **Waterloo Millennium Pier**

Houses of Parliament
Rebuilt in neo-Gothic style after the old Palace of Westminster burned down in 1834, the most famous part of the British parliament is the clocktower. Generally known as Big Ben, it's named after Benjamin Hall who oversaw its construction.

1   **Westminster**
Westminster Bridge

VERDOONE / BUDGET TRAVEL ©

vessel. These are, from west to east, the **1 Houses of Parliament**, the **2 London Eye**, **3 Somerset House**, **4 St Paul's Cathedral**, the **5 Tate Modern**, **6 Shakespeare's Globe**, the **7 Tower of London** and **8 Tower Bridge**.

In addition to covering this central section of the Thames, boats can also be taken upstream as far as Kew Gardens and Hampton Court Palace, and downstream as far as Greenwich and the Thames Barrier.

BOAT HOPPING

Thames Clippers hop-on/hop-off services are aimed at commuters but are equally useful for visitors, operating every 15 minutes on a loop from piers at Westminster, Embankment, Waterloo, Blackfriars, Bankside, London Bridge and the Tower. Oyster cardholders get a discount off the boat ticket price.

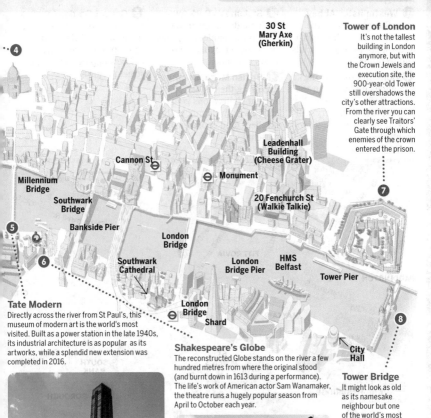

Tower of London
It's not the tallest building in London anymore, but with the Crown Jewels and execution site, the 900-year-old Tower still overshadows the city's other attractions. From the river you can clearly see Traitors' Gate through which enemies of the crown entered the prison.

30 St Mary Axe (Gherkin)

Leadenhall Building (Cheese Grater)

Cannon St

Monument

Millennium Bridge

20 Fenchurch St (Walkie Talkie)

Southwark Bridge

Bankside Pier

London Bridge

HMS Belfast

Southwark Cathedral

London Bridge Pier

Tower Pier

London Bridge

Shard

City Hall

Tate Modern
Directly across the river from St Paul's, this museum of modern art is the world's most visited. Built as a power station in the late 1940s, its industrial architecture is as popular as its artworks, while a splendid new extension was completed in 2016.

Shakespeare's Globe
The reconstructed Globe stands on the river a few hundred metres from where the original stood (and burnt down in 1613 during a performance). The life's work of American actor Sam Wanamaker, the theatre runs a hugely popular season from April to October each year.

Tower Bridge
It might look as old as its namesake neighbour but one of the world's most iconic bridges was only completed in 1894. Not to be confused with London Bridge upstream, this one's famous raising bascules allowed tall ships to dock at the old wharves to the west and are still lifted up to 1000 times a year.

CLAUDIO DIVIZIA / SHUTTERSTOCK ©

PRES PANAYOTOV / SHUTTERSTOCK ©

West End

WESTMINSTER | BLOOMSBURY & FITZROVIA | ST JAMES'S | SOHO & CHINATOWN | COVENT GARDEN
& LEICESTER SQUARE | WHITEHALL | HOLBORN & THE STRAND | MARYLEBONE | MAYFAIR | WESTMINSTER
& ST JAMES'S | BLOOMSBURY | FITZROVIA | HOLBORN

Neighbourhood Top Five

❶ Westminster Abbey
(p76) Stepping on to 'the
nation's stage' – the church
of coronations, royal burials
and weddings.

❷ Soho (p100) Enjoying
a fabulous night out on the
dance floor or at the bar
in what is still the city's all
singin', all dancin' centre of
nightlife.

❸ St James's Park (p98)
Hiring a deckchair in the
city's most manicured green
space and enjoying regal
views of London.

❹ British Museum (p79)
Exploring the history of
ancient civilisations going
back seven millennia at this
excellent (and enormous)
museum.

❺ Covent Garden (p102)
Hitting shops and bou-
tiques like Ted Baker in
this vibrant neighbourhood
before stopping to watch the
street performers.

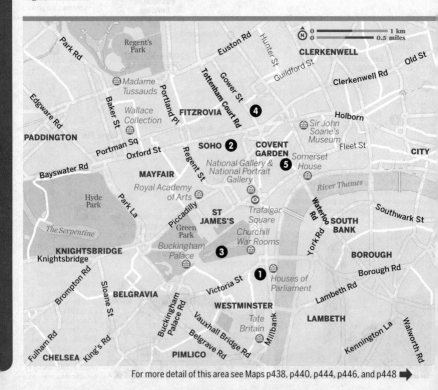

For more detail of this area see Maps p438, p440, p444, p446, and p448 ➡

Explore West End

It may be a compact area, but the West End packs in a lot when it comes to sights. You'll need to allow up to a half-day for each of the big museums (the British Museum, p79; and the National Gallery, p87), and at least a couple of hours for places like Westminster Abbey (p76) and Buckingham Palace (p83), when it opens in summer.

One of the delights of the West End is its energy, and there is no better way to enjoy it than by walking around and taking it all in. Atmospheric places for a breather include Covent Garden, Trafalgar Sq, St James's Park (p98), Marylebone and Soho (p100) – even by day.

Westminster and Whitehall are quiet in the evenings, with little in the way of bars and restaurants to tempt you. It's a similar story in St James's. Instead, head for vibrant Soho for fantastic bars and restaurants, or the streets surrounding Covent Garden.

Local Life

➡ **Eating out** Soho is unrivalled when it comes to eating out. Andrew Edmunds (p115) and **Gay Hussar** (☎020-7437 0973; www.gayhussar.co.uk; 2 Greek St, W1; mains £13.50-19; ⊙12.15-2.30pm & 5.30-10.45pm Mon-Sat; ☉Tottenham Court Rd) never seem to go out of fashion, while hip new places such as Polpo (p113), Kricket Soho (p114) and Palomar (p114) open all the time.

➡ **Late-night openings** Be it catching the latest exhibition or simply enjoying the permanent collections without the weekend crowds, many Londoners make the best of late-night openings at the National Gallery (p87), the National Portrait Gallery (p91) and the British Museum (p79), and the less-frequent ones at the Tate Britain (p90) and Sir John Soane's Museum (p94).

➡ **Shopping** Love it or loathe it, most Londoners will hit crowded Oxford St at some stage to shop; it's smack bang in the centre of town and has every franchise under the sun, as well as such good department stores as Selfridges (p133) and John Lewis (p133).

Getting There & Away

➡ **Underground** Almost every tube line goes through the West End, so wherever you're staying in London, you'll have no difficulty getting here. The tube is also good for getting from one end of the West End to the other.

➡ **Walking** The West End is relatively compact, so it'll be cheaper and generally more enjoyable to walk from one place to another rather than take public transport.

➡ **Bicycle** Cycling is your best bet for short journeys, and there are Santander Cycles docking stations everywhere within the West End.

Lonely Planet's Top Tip

The West End is paradise for budget travellers as many of London's most important and best-known museums are here (British Museum, National Galley, Tate Britain) as well as many of its lesser known ones (Sir John Soane's Museum, Wallace Collection) and all of them offer free entry. Here you'll also find two of the city's verdant royal parks, including the smallest (Green Park) and the prettiest (St James's Park). The West End is compact, so walk whenever possible.

✕ Best Places to Eat

➡ Balthazar (p117)
➡ Palomar (p114)
➡ Quilon (p109)
➡ Smoking Goat (p114)
➡ Bar Shu (p114)

For reviews, see p108. ➡

🍷 Best Places to Drink

➡ American Bar (p126)
➡ Dukes London (p121)
➡ Lamb & Flag (p124)
➡ Swift (p122)
➡ Queen's Larder (p122)

For reviews, see p121. ➡

⊙ Best Entertainment

➡ Donmar Warehouse (p128)
➡ Royal Opera House (p126)
➡ Prince Charles Cinema (p127)
➡ Wigmore Hall (p126)
➡ Ronnie Scott's (p127)

For reviews, see p126. ➡

TOP SIGHT
WESTMINSTER ABBEY

Westminster Abbey is such an important commemoration site that it's hard to overstress its symbolic value or imagine its equivalent anywhere else in the world. Except for Edward V (murdered) and Edward VIII (abdicated), every English sovereign has been crowned here since William the Conqueror in 1066, many were married here and a total of 17 are buried here.

A Regal History

Though a mixture of architectural styles, the Abbey is considered the finest example of Early English Gothic (1190–1300). The original church was built in the 11th century by King (later St) Edward the Confessor, who is buried in the chapel behind the sanctuary and the main altar. Henry III (r 1216–72) began work on the new building but didn't complete it; the Gothic nave was finished by Richard II in 1388. Henry VII's huge and magnificent Lady Chapel was added in 1519.

The Abbey was initially a monastery for a dozen Benedictine monks, and many of the building's features attest to this collegial past (the octagonal Chapter House, the Quire and the four cloisters). In 1536 Henry VIII separated the Catholic Church in England from Rome and dissolved the monasteries. The king became head of the Church of England and the Abbey acquired its 'royal peculiar' status, meaning it is administered directly by the Crown and exempt from any ecclesiastical jurisdiction.

DON'T MISS

- ➡ Coronation Chair
- ➡ Henry VII's Lady Chapel
- ➡ Cosmati pavement
- ➡ Tomb of the Unknown Warrior
- ➡ Chapter House
- ➡ Queen's Diamond Jubilee Galleries
- ➡ College Garden

PRACTICALITIES

- ➡ Map p448, D4
- ➡ ☏020-7222 5152
- ➡ www.westminster-abbey.org
- ➡ 20 Dean's Yard, SW1
- ➡ adult/child £20/9, cloister & gardens free
- ➡ ⊙9.30am-4.30pm Mon, Tue, Thu & Fri, to 7pm Wed, to 2.30pm Sat
- ➡ ⊖Westminster

North Transept, Sanctuary & Quire

Entrance to the Abbey for individuals is via the Great North Door. The North Transept is often referred to as **Statesmen's Aisle**: politicians (notably prime ministers) and eminent public figures are commemorated by large marble statues and imposing marble plaques here.

At the heart of the Abbey is the beautifully tiled **sanctuary** (or sacrarium), a stage for coronations, royal weddings and funerals. George Gilbert Scott designed the ornate **high altar** in 1873. In front of the altar is the marble **Cosmati pavement** dating back to 1268. It has intricate designs of small pieces of marble inlaid into plain marble, which predicts the end of the world in AD 19,693! At the entrance to the lovely **Chapel of St John the Baptist** is a sublime alabaster Virgin and Child bathed in candlelight.

The **Quire**, a magnificent structure of gold, blue and red Victorian Gothic by Edward Blore, dates from the mid-19th century. It sits where the original choir for the monks' worship would have been, but bears no resemblance to the original. Nowadays the quire is still used for singing, but its regular occupants are the Westminster Choir – 22 boys and 12 'lay vicars' (men) who sing the daily services and evensong (5pm weekdays, 3pm weekends).

Chapels & Chair

The sanctuary is surrounded by chapels. Henry VII's magnificent Perpendicular Gothic-style **Lady Chapel**, in the easternmost part of the Abbey, is the most spectacular with its fan vaulting on the ceiling, colourful banners of the Order of the Bath and dramatic oak stalls with carved misericord seats. Behind the chapel's altar is the elaborate sarcophagus of Henry VII and his queen, Elizabeth of York.

Beyond the chapel's altar is the **Royal Air Force Chapel**, with a stained-glass window commemorating the force's finest hour, the Battle of Britain (1940), and 1500 RAF pilots who died fighting. A stone plaque on the floor marks the spot where Oliver Cromwell's body lay for two years from 1658 until the Restoration, when it was disinterred, hanged and beheaded.

There are two small chapels on either side of the Lady Chapel with the tombs of famous monarchs: on the left (north) is where **Elizabeth I** and her half-sister **Mary I** (or 'Bloody Mary') rest. Two bodies, believed to be those of the so-called **Princes in the Tower** allegedly murdered there by their uncle Richard III in 1483, were buried here almost two

A ROYAL WEDDING

On 29 April 2011, Prince William married his fiancée, Catherine Middleton, at Westminster Abbey. (William's parents, Prince Charles and Princess Diana, had been married in St Paul's Cathedral for reasons that remain unclear.) Unusually, the couple decided to decorate the Abbey with trees; less controversial was the bride's decision to opt for a gown by a British designer, Sarah Burton of Alexander McQueen. And in a tradition started by the future Queen Mother at her wedding in 1923, Kate left her bridal bouquet on the Tomb of the Unknown Warrior.

A NEW ABBEY MUSEWUM

Scheduled for completion in 2018 are the **Queen's Diamond Jubilee Galleries**, a new museum and gallery space located in the medieval triforium, the arched gallery above the nave. Its exhibits will include the death masks of generations of royalty, wax effigies representing Charles II and William III (who is on a stool to make him as tall as his wife, Mary II), armour and stained glass. Highlights are the graffiti-inscribed Mary Chair (used for the coronation of Mary II) and the Westminster Retable, England's oldest altarpiece, from the 13th century.

centuries later in 1674. On the right (south) is the tomb of **Mary Queen of Scots**, beheaded on the orders of her cousin Elizabeth in 1587.

Shrine of St Edward the Confessor

The most sacred spot in the Abbey lies behind the high altar; access is generally restricted for worship twice a day to protect the 13th-century marble flooring. St Edward was the founder of the Abbey and the original building was consecrated a few weeks before his death. His tomb was slightly altered after the original was destroyed during the Reformation, but it still contains Edward's remains – the only complete saint's body in Britain. **Verger-led tours** (£5 plus admission) of the Abbey lasting 1½ hours include a visit to the shrine.

South Transept & Nave

The south transept contains **Poets' Corner**, where many of England's finest writers are buried and/or commemorated (including most recently the poet Philip Larkin) by monuments or memorials.

In the nave's northern aisle is **Scientists' Corner**, where you will find **Sir Isaac Newton's tomb** and monument with its celestial globe. Just ahead of it is the northern aisle of the quire, known as **Musicians' Aisle**, where baroque composer Henry Purcell is buried, as well as more modern music-makers Benjamin Britten and Edward Elgar.

At the western end of the nave, near the **Tomb of the Unknown Warrior** killed in northern France during in WWI and laid to rest here in 1920, is **St George's Chapel**, which contains the rather ordinary-looking **Coronation Chair**. Every monarch since the early 14th century has been crowned on this wooden throne (apart from joint-monarchs Mary II and William III, who had their own seats fashioned for the event).

The two towers above the **West Front** were designed by Christopher Wren's disciple Nicholas Hawksmoor and completed in 1745. Just above the door outside, perched in 15th-century niches, are additions to the Abbey unveiled in 1998: 10 stone statues of **20th-century Martyrs** who died around the world for their Christian faith. These include American pacifist Dr Martin Luther King, the Polish priest St Maximilian Kolbe, who was murdered by the Nazis at Auschwitz, and Wang Zhiming, publicly executed during the Chinese Cultural Revolution.

Outer Buildings & Gardens

The oldest part of the cloister is the **East Cloister** (or East Walk), dating from the 13th century. Off the cloister is the octagonal **Chapter House** with one of Europe's best-preserved medieval tile floors and religious murals on the walls. It was used as a meeting place by the House of Commons in the second half of the 14th century. To the right of the entrance to Chapter House is what is claimed to be the oldest door in Britain – it's been there since the 1050s.

The adjacent **Pyx Chamber** is one of the few remaining relics of the original Abbey, including the 10th-century **Altar of St Dunstan**. The chamber contains the pyx, a chest with standard gold and silver pieces for testing coinage weights in a ceremony called the Trial of the Pyx, which nowadays takes place in Goldsmiths' Hall in the City of London.

To reach the 900-year-old **College Garden**, enter Dean's Yard and the Little Cloisters off Great College St.

TOP SIGHT
BRITISH MUSEUM

Britain's most visited attraction for a decade, the British Museum draws in 6.5 million visitors each year. It's an exhaustive and exhilarating stampede through world cultures over 7000 years, with 90 galleries of seven million exhibits devoted to ancient civilisations, from Egypt to western Asia, the Middle East, Rome and Greece, India, Africa, prehistoric and Roman Britain, and medieval antiquities.

History & the Great Court

The museum was founded in 1753 when royal physician Hans Sloane sold his 'cabinet of curiosities' for the then-princely sum of £20,000, raised by national lottery. The collection opened to the public for free in 1759, and the museum has since kept expanding its collection through judicious acquisitions, bequests and the controversial imperial plundering.

The first thing you'll see on entry is the Great Court covered with a spectacular glass-and-steel roof designed by Norman Foster in 2000. It is the largest covered public square in Europe. In its centre is the celebrated **Reading Room**, once part of the British Library, which has been frequented by the big brains of history, from Mahatma Gandhi to Karl Marx. It is now used for temporary exhibits.

Ancient Egypt, Middle East & Greece

The most prized item in the museum (and the most popular postcard in the shop) is the **Rosetta Stone** (room 4), the key to deciphering Egyptian hieroglyphics. In the same gallery is the enormous bust of the pharaoh **Ramesses II** (room 4).

DON'T MISS

➡ Rosetta Stone
➡ Mummy of Katebet
➡ Parthenon Sculptures
➡ Winged Bulls from Khorsabad
➡ Sutton Hoo Ship Burial artefacts
➡ Mildenhall Treasure
➡ Lewis Chessmen

PRACTICALITIES

➡ Map p444, E6
➡ ☎020-7323 8299
➡ www.britishmuseum.org
➡ Great Russell St & Montague Pl, WC1
➡ admission free
➡ ⏰10am-5.30pm Sat-Thu, to 8.30pm Fri
➡ ⊜Russell Sq, Tottenham Court Rd

The British Museum

A HALF-DAY TOUR

The British Museum, with almost eight million items in its permanent collection, is so vast and comprehensive that it can be daunting for the first-time visitor. To avoid a frustrating trip – and getting lost on the way to the Egyptian mummies – set out on this half-day exploration, which takes in some of the museum's most important sights. If you want to see and learn more, join a tour or grab an audioguide (£5).

A good starting point is the ❶ **Rosetta Stone**, the key that cracked the code to ancient Egypt's writing system. Nearby treasures from Assyria – an ancient civilisation centred in Mesopotamia between the Tigris and Euphrates Rivers – including the colossal ❷ **Winged Bulls from Khorsabad**, give way to the ❸ **Parthenon Sculptures**, highpoints of classical Greek art that continue to influence us today. Be sure to see both the sculptures and the monumental frieze celebrating the

Winged Bulls from Khorsabad
This awesome pair of alabaster winged bulls with human heads once guarded the entrance to the palace of Assyrian King Sargon II at Khorsabad in Mesopotamia, a cradle of civilisation in present-day Iraq.

Parthenon Sculptures
The Parthenon, a white marble temple dedicated to Athena, was part of a fortified citadel on the Acropolis in Athens. There are dozens of sculptures and friezes with models and interactive displays explaining how they all once fitted together.

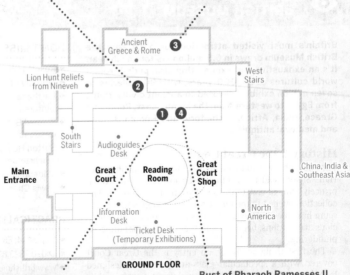

Ancient Greece & Rome ❸

Lion Hunt Reliefs from Nineveh ❷

West Stairs

❶ ❹

South Stairs

Audioguides Desk

Main Entrance

Great Court

Reading Room

Great Court Shop

China, India & Southeast Asia

Information Desk

North America

Ticket Desk (Temporary Exhibitions)

GROUND FLOOR

Rosetta Stone
Written in hieroglyphic, demotic (cursive ancient Egyptian script used for everyday use) and Greek, the 762kg stone contains a decree exempting priests from tax on the first anniversary of young Ptolemy V's coronation.

Bust of Pharaoh Ramesses II
The most impressive sculpture in the Egyptian galleries, this 725kg bust portrays Ramesses the Great, scourge of the Israelites in the Book of Exodus, as great benefactor.

birth of Athena. En route to the West Stairs is a huge ❹ **Bust of Pharaoh Ramesses II**, just a hint of the large collection of ❺ **Egyptian mummies** upstairs. (The earliest, affectionately called Ginger because of wispy reddish hair, was preserved simply by hot sand.) The Romans introduce visitors to the early Britain galleries via the rich ❻ **Mildenhall Treasure**. The Anglo-Saxon ❼ **Sutton Hoo Ship Burial** and the medieval ❽ **Lewis Chessmen** follow.

EATING OPTIONS

Court Cafe At the northern end of the Great Court; takeaway counters with salads and sandwiches; communal tables.

Gallery Cafe Slightly out of the way off Room 12; quieter; offers hot dishes.

Great Court Restaurant Upstairs overlooking the former Reading Room; sit-down meals.

Lewis Chessmen
The much-loved 78 chess pieces portray faceless pawns, worried-looking queens, bishops with their mitres turned sideways and rooks (or castles) as 'warders', gnawing away at their shields.

ILEANA_BT / SHUTTERSTOCK ©

Egyptian Mummies
Among the rich collection of mummies and funerary objects is 'Ginger', who was buried at the site of Gebelein, in Upper Egypt, almost 5500 years ago, and Katebet, a one-time chantress (ritual performer) at the Amun temple in Karnak.

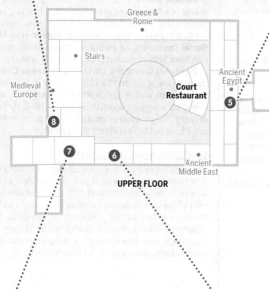

UPPER FLOOR

Sutton Hoo Ship Burial
This unique grave of an important (but unidentified) Anglo-Saxon royal has yielded drinking horns, gold buckles and a stunning helmet with face mask.

Mildenhall Treasure
Roman gods such as Neptune and Bacchus share space with early Christian symbols like the *chi-rho* (short for 'Christ') on the find's almost three dozen silver bowls, plates and spoons.

CONQUERING THE MUSEUM

The British Museum is enormous, so make a few judiciously focused visits if you have time, and consider taking one of the free tours. There are up to 15 free Eye-opener tours of individual galleries each day lasting 30 to 40 minutes. The museum also has free 45-minute lunchtime gallery talks (1.15pm Tuesday to Saturday), a 1½-hour highlights tour (£12, 11.30am and 2pm Friday, Saturday and Sunday) and free 20-minute spotlight tours on Friday evenings. Audio and family guides (adult/ child £6/5.50) in 10 languages are available from the audio-guide desk in the Great Court.

MUSEUM EXTENSIONS

The British Museum's long-awaited extension, the £135 million World Conservation & Exhibitions Centre, opened in 2014, in the same year as the Sainsbury Exhibitions Gallery, which hosts high-profile exhibitions.

Assyrian treasures from ancient Mesopotamia include the **Winged Bulls from Khorsabad** (room 10), at 16 tonnes the heaviest object in the museum. Behind it are the exquisite **Lion Hunt Reliefs from Ninevah** (room 10) dating from the 7th century BC, which influenced Greek sculpture. Such antiquities are all the more significant after the so-called Islamic State's bulldozing of Nimrud in 2015.

A major highlight of the museum is the **Parthenon sculptures** (room 18). The 80m-long marble frieze is thought to be of the Great Panathenaea, a blow-out version of a festival in honour of Athena held every four years.

The star of the show is the **Ancient Egypt** collection upstairs. It comprises sculptures, fine jewellery, papyrus texts, coffins and mummies, including the beautiful and intriguing **Mummy of Katebet** (room 63).

Roman & Medieval Britain

Also upstairs are finds from Britain and the rest of Europe (rooms 40 to 51). Many go back to Roman times, when the empire spread across much of the continent, including the **Mildenhall Treasure** (room 49), a collection of almost three-dozen pieces of 4th-century-AD Roman silverware unearthed in Suffolk with both pagan and early-Christian motifs.

Lindow Man (room 50) is the well-preserved remains of a 1st-century man discovered in a bog near Manchester in northern England in 1984. Equally fascinating are artefacts from the **Sutton Hoo Ship Burial** (room 41), an elaborate Anglo-Saxon burial site from Suffolk dating back to the 7th century.

Perennial favourites are the lovely **Lewis Chessmen** (room 40), some 78 12th-century game pieces carved from walrus tusk and whale teeth that were found on a remote Scottish island in the early 19th century. They served as models for the game of Wizard Chess in the first Harry Potter film.

Enlightenment Galleries

Formerly known as the King's Library, this stunning neoclassical space (room 1) just off the Great Court was built between 1823 and 1827 and was the first part of the new museum building as it is seen today. Through a fascinating collection of artefacts, the collection traces how such disciplines as biology, archaeology, linguistics and geography emerged during the Enlightenment of the 18th century.

 TOP SIGHT
BUCKINGHAM PALACE

Built in 1705 for the Duke of Buckingham and then purchased by George III, the palace has been the Royal Family's London lodgings since 1837 when Queen Victoria moved in. Commoners can now get a peek of the State Rooms, a mere 19 of the palace's 775 rooms, from late July to September when HRH (Her Royal Highness) takes her holidays in Scotland.

State Rooms

The tour starts in the **Grand Hall** at the foot of the monumental **Grand Staircase**, commissioned by George IV in 1828. It takes in John Nash's Italianate **Green Drawing Room**, the **State Dining Room** (all red damask and Regency furnishings), the **Blue Drawing Room** (which has a gorgeous fluted ceiling by Nash) and the **White Drawing Room**, where foreign ambassadors are received.

Admission includes entry to a themed special exhibition (eg royal couture during the Queen's reign, growing up at the palace etc) in the enormous **Ballroom**, built between 1853 and 1855. The **Throne Room** is rather anticlimactic, with his-and-her pink chairs monogrammed 'ER' and 'P'.

Picture Gallery & Gardens

The most interesting part of the tour is the 47m-long **Picture Gallery**, featuring splendid works by such artists as Van Dyck, Rembrandt, Canaletto, Poussin, Rubens, Canova and Vermeer.

Wandering the 18 hectares of **gardens** at the end of the tour is another highlight – as well as admiring some of the 350 or so species of flowers and plants and listening to the

DON'T MISS

➡ Changing of the Guard
➡ Picture Gallery
➡ Royal Mews
➡ Palace Gardens
➡ Queen's Gallery
➡ Throne Room

PRACTICALITIES

➡ Map p448, A4
➡ ☏0303 123 7300
➡ www.royalcollection.org.uk/visit/the-state-rooms-buckingham-palace
➡ Buckingham Palace Rd, SW1
➡ adult/child/under 5yr £23/13/free, evening tour £80
➡ ⏱5.30pm & 6pm late Mar-Apr, 9.30am-7.30pm late Jul-Aug, to 6.30pm Sep
➡ ⊖Green Park, St James's Park

CHANGING OF THE GUARD

A London 'must see', this is when the Old Guard (Foot Guards of the Household Regiment) comes off duty to be replaced by the New Guard on the forecourt of palace. Tourists gape – sometimes from behind as many as 10 people – at the bright-red uniforms, bearskin hats and full-on pageantry. The official name for the ceremony is Guard Mounting and it lasts for around 45 minutes. The ceremony (http:// changing-guard.com) usually takes place daily at 11am in June and July, and on Sunday, Monday, Wednesday and Friday, weather permitting, during the rest of the year, but be sure to check the website before setting out.

THE MUSIC ROOM

At the centre of Royal Family life is the palace's Music Room, where four royal babies have been christened – the Prince of Wales (Prince Charles), the Princess Royal (Princess Anne), the Duke of York (Prince Andrew) and the Duke of Cambridge (Prince William) – with water brought from the River Jordan.

many birds, you'll get beautiful views of the palace and a peek of its famous lake.

Queen's Gallery

Since the reign of Charles I – a bad king but one with exquisite taste – the Royal Family has amassed a priceless collection of paintings, sculpture, ceramics, furniture and jewellery. The splendid **Queen's Gallery** showcases some of the palace's treasures on a rotating basis.

The gallery, in the South Wing of the palace, was originally designed as a conservatory by John Nash. It was converted into a chapel for Queen Victoria in 1843, destroyed in a 1940 air raid and reopened as a gallery in 1962. A £20 million renovation for Elizabeth II's Golden Jubilee in 2002 added three times more display space.

Royal Mews

Southwest of the palace, the **Royal Mews** started life as a falconry but is now a working stable looking after the royals' immaculately groomed horses, along with the opulent vehicles the monarch uses for transport. The Queen is well known for her passion for horses; she names every horse that resides at the mews. Nash's 1820 stables are stunning.

Highlights for visitors include the enormous and opulent Gold State Coach of 1762, which has been used for every coronation since that of George IV in 1821; the 1911 Glass Coach used for royal weddings (Prince William and Catherine Middleton actually used the 1902 State Landau to make the best of the good weather); and a Rolls-Royce Phantom VI from the royal fleet.

TOP SIGHT
HOUSES OF PARLIAMENT

Both the elected House of Commons and the House of Lords, who are appointed or hereditary, sit in the sumptuous Palace of Westminster, a neo-Gothic confection dating from the mid-19th century (with a few sections that survived a catastrophic fire in 1834). A visit here is a journey to the very heart of British democracy.

Towers

The most famous feature of the Houses of Parliament is the Clock Tower, officially named the Elizabeth Tower to mark the Queen's Diamond Jubilee in 2012 but commonly known as **Big Ben**. Big Ben is actually the 13.5-tonne bell hanging inside and is named after Benjamin Hall, the rather large first Commissioner of Works when the tower was completed in 1858. At the base of the taller **Victoria Tower** at the southern end is the Sovereign's Entrance, which is used by the Queen.

Westminster Hall

One of the most interesting features of the Palace of Westminster, seat of the English monarchy from the 11th to the early 16th centuries, is Westminster Hall. Originally built at the end of the 11th century, it is the oldest surviving part of the complex; the awesome hammer-beam roof was added between 1394 and 1401. It has been described as 'the greatest surviving achievement of medieval English carpentry'. The only other part of the original palace to survive the devastating 1834 fire is the **Jewel Tower** (www.english-heritage.org.uk/visit/places/jewel-tower; adult/child £5/3; ⏱10am-5pm daily Apr-Oct, 10am-4pm Sat & Sun Nov-Mar), built in 1365 and used to store the monarch's valuables.

Westminster Hall was used for coronation banquets in medieval times and also served as a courthouse until the 19th century. The trials of William Wallace (1305), Thomas More

DON'T MISS

➡ Westminster Hall's hammerbeam roof
➡ The 'Tudor Gothic' interior
➡ Sovereign's Entrance
➡ Jewel Tower

PRACTICALITIES

➡ Palace of Westminster
➡ Map p448, E4
➡ www.parliament.uk
➡ Parliament Sq, SW1
➡ admission free
➡ ⊖Westminster

PARLIAMENTARY DEBATES

When Parliament is in session, visitors are welcome to attend the debates in the House of Commons and the House of Lords. Enter via Cromwell Green Entrance. It's not unusual to have to wait up to two hours to access the chambers (though waiting times have improved in recent years). The best (and busiest) time to watch a debate is during Prime Minister's Question Time at noon on Wednesday. The debating style in the Commons is quite combative, but not all debates are flamboyant argumentative duelling matches. In fact, many are rather boring and long-winded.

RIFLE CLUB

Astonishingly, until 2015 the Houses of Parliament was home to the Palace of Westminster Rifle Club, a shooting range. The club was open to club members from Monday to Thursday when the House of Commons was sitting. Before 1997, handguns could be discharged, but this was changed to only permit the use of .22 calibre rifles.

(1535), Guy Fawkes (1606) and Charles I (1649) all took place here. In the 20th century, monarchs and Sir Winston Churchill lay in state here after their deaths.

House of Commons

The **House of Commons** (www.parliament.uk/business/commons; ⊘2.30-10pm Mon & Tue, 11.30am-7.30pm Wed, 10.30am-6.30pm Thu, 9.30am-3pm Fri) is where Members of Parliament (MPs) meet to propose and discuss new legislation and to grill the prime minister and other ministers. The chamber, designed by Giles Gilbert Scott, replaced the one destroyed by a 1941 bomb.

Although the Commons is a national assembly of 650 MPs, the chamber only has seating for 437. Government members sit to the right of the Speaker and Opposition members to the left.

House of Lords

The **House of Lords** (www.parliament.uk/business/lords;⊘2.30-10pm Mon & Tue, 3-10pm Wed, 11am-7.30pm Thu, 10am-close of session Fri) is visited via the amusingly named Strangers' Gallery. The intricate 'Tudor Gothic' interior led its architect, Auguste Pugin (1812–52), to an early death from overwork and nervous strain.

The House of Lords contains Lords Spiritual, linked to the established church, and Lords Temporal, who are both appointed and hereditary.

Most – in fact 85% – of the more than 800 lords are life peers (appointed for their lifetime by the monarch); among them are 146 'crossbench' members not affiliated to the main political parties. Some 75% of the members of the House of Lords are men.

Tours

Visitors are welcome on Saturdays year-round and on most weekdays during parliamentary recesses (which include Easter, summer and Christmas). You can choose either a self-guided audio tour (adult/child £18.50/7.50) in one of eight languages lasting about 75 minutes or a much more comprehensive 1½-hour **guided tour** (☑020-7219 4114; www.parliament.uk/visiting/visiting-and-tours; adult/child £25.50/11) of both chambers, Westminster Hall and other historic buildings conducted by qualified Blue Badge Tourist Guides in a myriad of tongues.

Buy tickets from the office in Portcullis House on Victoria Embankment. Tour schedules change and are subject to variation or cancellation, so check ahead and book.

ANDERSPHOTO/SHUTTERSTOCK ©

TOP SIGHT
NATIONAL GALLERY

With some 2300 European paintings on display, this is one of the world's richest art collections, with seminal paintings from the mid-13th to the early 20th century, including works by Leonardo da Vinci, Michelangelo, Titian, Van Gogh and Renoir.

The modern Sainsbury Wing on the gallery's western side, the newest part of the gallery, houses the oldest paintings, dating from 1250 to 1500. Here you will find largely religious works commissioned for private devotion such as the stunning *Wilton Diptych* (room 53), as well more unusual masterpieces such as Botticelli's *Venus & Mars* (room 58) and Van Eyck's *Arnolfini Portrait* (room 56). Leonardo Da Vinci's *Virgin of the Rocks* (room 66) is a visual and technical masterpiece.

Works from the High Renaissance (1500–1600) embellish the West Wing where Michelangelo, Titian, Raphael, Correggio, El Greco and Bronzino hold court; Rubens, Rembrandt and Caravaggio grace the North Wing (1600–1700). Notable here are two self-portraits of Rembrandt (at age 34 in room 24 and at 63 in room 23) and the beautiful *Rokeby Venus* by Velázquez in room 30.

Many visitors flock to the East Wing (1700–1900), where works by 18th-century British artists such as Gainsborough, Constable and Turner, and seminal Impressionist and post-Impressionist masterpieces by Van Gogh, Renoir and Monet await. Don't, however, overlook the astonishing floor mosaics in the main vestibule inside the main entrance to the gallery.

DON'T MISS

➡ *Venus & Mars* by Botticelli

➡ *Arnolfini Portrait* by Van Eyck

➡ *Wilton Diptych*

➡ *Rokeby Venus* by Velázquez

➡ *Sunflowers* by Van Gogh

➡ *The Hay Wain* by Constable

PRACTICALITIES

➡ Map p438, B7

➡ ☎020-7747 2885

➡ www.nationalgallery.org.uk

➡ Trafalgar Sq, WC2

➡ admission free

➡ ⊙10am-6pm Sat-Thu, to 9pm Fri

➡ ⊖Charing Cross

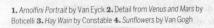

1. *Arnolfini Portrait* by Van Eyck **2.** Detail from *Venus and Mars* by Boticelli **3.** *Hay Wain* by Constable **4.** *Sunflowers* by Van Gogh

ARTEPICS/AGE FOTOSTOCK/FOTOSTOCK ©

National Gallery Masterpieces

The National Gallery's collection spans seven centuries of European painting in a whirl of 2300-odd tableaux displayed in sumptuous, airy galleries. All are masterpieces, but some stand out for their sheer beauty and brilliance.

Venus and Mars, Botticelli

Venus, goddess of love, upright and alert, stares intently at Mars, god of war, fast asleep after they've made love. The message: make love not war because love conquers all.

Sunflowers, Van Gogh

This instantly recognisable masterpiece, one of four by the great Dutch Post Impressionist, depicts 14 sunflowers at different stages of life. The main colour – yellow – is applied thickly, a bold new 'sculptural' approach to painting.

Rockeby Venus, Velázquez

A rare subject during the Spanish Inquisition, a self-absorbed Venus is gazing at herself – and us – in a mirror held by her son Cupid.

Arnolfini Portrait, Van Eyck

This is history's first bourgeois portrait, an early example of the use of oils and a revolutionary way to create space by painting light. It shows a rich Bruges merchant and his wife, who, despite looking pregnant, is actually making a fashion statement with her voluminous attire.

Hay Wain, Constable

A horse-drawn wagon in the middle of a river is a romantic portrayal of England on the eve of the Industrial Revolution. Flecks of white paint ('Constable snow') reflect and create movement – a foretaste of Impressionism.

Fighting Temeraire, Turner

Painted by JMW Turner in his 60s, this magnificent painting shows the ghostly ship Temeraire, a hero of Trafalgar, being towed to a ship-breaking yard in Rotherhithe. The sun goes down, the moon comes up; her world is ending and the age of steam and industrialisation approaches.

TOP SIGHT
TATE BRITAIN

The older and more venerable of the two Tate siblings celebrates British works from 1500 to the present, including those from Blake, Hogarth, Gainsborough, Barbara Hepworth, Whistler, Constable and Turner, as well as vibrant modern and contemporary pieces from Lucian Freud, Francis Bacon and Henry Moore.

The stars of the show at Tate Britain are, however, the light infused visions of JMW Turner – 300 oil paintings and about 30,000 sketches and drawings bequeathed to the nation. The collection at the Tate Britain constitutes a sweeping celebration of his work, including such classics as *The Scarlet Sunset* and *Norham Castle, Sunrise*.

There are also seminal works from Constable, Gainsborough and Reynolds, as well as the pre-Rahaelites, including William Holman Hunt's *The Awakening Conscience*, John William Waterhouse's *The Lady of Shalott*, *Ophelia* by John Everett Millais and Edward Burne-Jones's *The Golden Stairs*. Look out also for Francis Bacon's *Three Studies for Figures at the Base of a Crucifixion*.

Tate Britain hosts the prestigious and often controversial Turner Prize for contemporary art from October to early December every year.

DON'T MISS

➜ *The Scarlet Sunset* by JMW Turner

➜ *Three Studies for Figures at the Base of a Crucifixion* by Francis Bacon

➜ *Ophelia* by John Everett Millais

➜ *The Awakening Conscience* by William Holman Hunt

PRACTICALITIES

➜ Map p448, E7

➜ 📞020-7887 8888

➜ www.tate.org.uk/visit/tate-britain

➜ Millbank, SW1

➜ admission free

➜ ⊙10am-6pm, to 10pm on selected Fri

➜ 🚇Pimlico

TOP SIGHT
NATIONAL PORTRAIT GALLERY

What makes the National Portrait Gallery, the only such museum in Europe, so compelling is its familiarity; in many cases you'll have heard of the subject (royals, scientists, politicians, celebrities) or the artist (Andy Warhol, Annie Leibovitz, Sam Taylor-Wood) but not necessarily recognise the face.

The collection is organised chronologically (starting with the early Tudors on the 2nd floor), and then by theme. Highlights here include the 'Chandos portrait' of William Shakespeare, believed to be the only one to have been painted during the playwright's lifetime; the 'Ditchley' portrait of Queen Elizabeth I displaying her might by standing on a map of England; and a touching sketch of novelist Jane Austen by her sister.

The 1st-floor portraits illustrate the rise and fall of the British Empire through the Victorian era and the 20th century. Don't miss the high-kitsch statue of Victoria and Albert in Anglo-Saxon dress in room 21.

The ground floor is dedicated to modern figures, using a variety of media (sculpture, photography, video etc). Among the most popular have been the iconic Blur portraits by Julian Opie, Sam Taylor-Johnson's *David,* a (low-res by today's standards) video-portrait of David Beckham asleep after football training, and Michael Craig-Martin's *Dame Zaha Hadid.*

DON'T MISS

➡ Shakespeare 'Chandos Portrait' attributed to John Taylor

➡ *Jane Austen* by Cassandra Austen

➡ *Queen Elizabeth I* by Marcus Gheeraerts the Younger

➡ Victoria and Albert in Anglo-Saxon dress

➡ Michael Craig-Martin's *Dame Zaha Hadid*

PRACTICALITIES

➡ Map p438, B6

➡ ☏ 020-7321 0055

➡ www.npg.org.uk

➡ St Martin's Pl, WC2

➡ admission free

➡ ⊙ 10am-6pm Sat-Wed, to 9pm Thu & Fri

➡ ⊖ Charing Cross, Leicester Sq

 TOP SIGHT
TRAFALGAR SQUARE

Trafalgar Square is the true centre of London, where rallies and marches take place, tens of thousands of revellers usher in the New Year, and locals congregate for anything from communal open-air cinema and Christmas celebrations to political protests. It is dominated by the 52m-high Nelson's Column, which honours Admiral Lord Horatio Nelson, who led the fleet's heroic victory over Napoleon in 1805, and is ringed by many large bronze lions and many splendid buildings, including the National Gallery (p87) and St Martin-in-the-Fields (p103) church. Here, too, is the latest (and no doubt zany) Fourth Plinth Commission (p102) of art and the Admiralty Arch (1910), from where the ceremonial Mall leads to Buckingham Palace.

For decades the great square was ringed with traffic and given over to flocks of pigeons fed by tourists and locals alike. In 2000 a scheme was launched to transform the square into the kind of space John Nash had intended it to be when he designed it in the early 19th century. Traffic was banished from the northern flank in front of the National Gallery, the pigeons were sent packing (with the help of a team of Harris hawks) and a new pedestrian plaza built, making way for cohorts of living statues, gravity-defying Yodas and other street artistes.

DON'T MISS

➡ Nelson's Column
➡ Bronze lions
➡ Fourth Plinth
➡ Admiralty Arch

PRACTICALITIES

➡ Map p438, B7
➡ ⊖ Charing Cross

TOP SIGHT
CHURCHILL WAR ROOMS

In late August 1939, with war appearing imminent, the British cabinet and chiefs of the armed forces decided to move underground into a converted basement below what is now the Treasury. On 3 September Britain was at war.

The bunker served as nerve centre of the war cabinet until the end of WWII in 1945: here chiefs of staff ate, slept and plotted Hitler's downfall, believing they were protected from Luftwaffe bombs (it turns out the 3m slab of concrete above them would have crumpled had the area taken a direct hit).

The **Cabinet War Rooms** have been left much as they were on 15 August 1945. Many rooms have been preserved, including the room where the War Cabinet met 115 times; the Transatlantic Telegraph Room, with a hotline to US President Roosevelt; the converted broom cupboard that was Churchill's office-bedroom (though he slept here only three times); and the all-important Map Room, which was the operational centre.

The superb multimedia **Churchill Museum** in the centre doesn't shy away from its hero's foibles – it portrays the heavy-drinking Churchill as having a legendary temper, being a bit of a maverick and, on the whole, a pretty lousy peace-time politician. It does focus on his strongest suit: his stirring speeches.

DON'T MISS

➡ Map Room
➡ Anecdotes from former War Rooms staff
➡ Extracts from Churchill's famous speeches
➡ Churchill's office-bedroom
➡ The film footage of Churchill's funeral

PRACTICALITIES

➡ Map p448, D3
➡ www.iwm.org.uk/visits/churchill-war-rooms
➡ Clive Steps, King Charles St, SW1
➡ adult/child £17.25/8.60
➡ ⊘9.30am-6pm
➡ ⊜Westminster

TOP SIGHT
SIR JOHN SOANE'S MUSEUM

This little museum is one of the most atmospheric and fascinating in London. The building is the bewitching home of architect Sir John Soane (1753–1837), which he left brimming with surprising personal effects and curiosities.

A professor of architecture at the Royal Academy, Soane designed the Bank of England, among other buildings. In his work, he drew on classical ideas picked up while on an 18th-century grand tour of Italy. After his marriage, Soane built his house-museum at No 13 Lincoln's Inn Sq, and eventually bought the one next door at No 12.

The heritage-listed house is itself a main part of the attraction. It has a canopy dome that brings light right down to the crypt, a colonnade filled with statuary and a picture gallery. This is where Soane's choicest artwork is displayed, including paintings by Canaletto and the original *A Rake's Progress,* William Hogarth's set of satirical cartoons of late-8th-century London lowlife. Among Soane's more unusual acquisitions are the sarcophagus of the Egyptian Pharaoh Seti I and his precious Model Room, located in his private apartment at the 2nd floor of the house.

Tours (£10) of the house, including the private apartment and Model Room, leave at 11am Tuesday and Saturday and at noon Tuesday, Thursday, Friday and Saturday.

DON'T MISS

➤ *A Rake's Progress* by William Hogarth

➤ Sarcophagus of King Seti I

➤ *Riva degli Schiavoni, Looking West* by Canaletto

➤ The Model Room

PRACTICALITIES

➤ Map p438, E2

➤ ☎ 020-7405 2107

➤ www.soane.org

➤ 12 Lincoln's Inn Fields, WC2

➤ admission free

➤ ⏰10am-5pm Tue-Sat, plus 6-9pm 1st Tue of month

➤ ⊖Holborn

◉ SIGHTS

◉ Westminster

WESTMINSTER ABBEY   CHURCH
See p76.

HOUSES OF PARLIAMENT   HISTORIC BUILDING
See p85.

ST MARGARET'S CHURCH   CHURCH
Map p448 (☑020-7654 4840; www.westminster-
abbey.org/st-margarets-church;   ◉9.30am-
3.30pm Mon-Fri, to 1.30pm Sat, 2-4.30pm Sun;
◉Westminster) Adjacent to Westminster
Abbey is St Margaret's Church, the House
of Commons' place of worship since 1614,
where windows commemorate churchgo-
ers Caxton and Milton, and Sir Walter
Raleigh is buried by the altar. It can look
insubstantial alongside the vast abbey, but
it was constructed next to the abbey run by
Benedictine monks to serve the spiritual
needs of the common people. It is the third
church dedicated to St Margaret to stand at
this spot since the end of the 11th century.

WESTMINSTER CATHEDRAL   CHURCH
Map p448 (☑020-7798 9055; www.westminster
cathedral.org.uk; Victoria St, SW1; adult/child
tower £6/3, treasury £5/2.40, combined £9/4.50;
◉church 7am-7pm Mon-Fri, 8am-7pm Sat & Sun,
tower & treasury 9.30am-5pm Mon-Fri, to 6pm Sat
& Sun; ◉Victoria) With its distinctive candy-
striped red-brick and white-stone tower features, John Francis Bentley's 19th-century
Cathedral of the Most Precious Blood, the
mother church of Roman Catholicism in
England and Wales, is a splendid example
of neo-Byzantine architecture. Although
construction started here in 1895 and worshippers began attending services seven
years later, the church ran out of money
and the sparse interior remains largely un-
finished, although some radiant mosaics
dazzle from the altar and side chapels.

The Chapel of the Blessed Sacrament, to
the left of the main altar, is ablaze with Eastern Rite mosaics and ornamented with 100
types of marble; the arched ceiling of the
Lady Chapel in the other side of the main
altar is also richly presented. Some other
areas of the church remain unfaced brick.

The highly regarded stone bas-reliefs of
the Stations of the Cross (1918) by Eric Gill
and the marvellously sombre atmosphere
make this a welcome haven from the traffic
outside. The views from viewing gallery
64m (210ft) up in the 83m (272ft) bell tower
– thankfully, accessible by lift – are impressive. The church plate and ecclesiastical
objects on display in the Treasury are a delight and there's a cafe near the Baptistery
to the right as you enter. Several Masses are
held daily, including one in Latin (usually
at 10.30am), and one accompanied by the
cathedral's choir (at 5.30 or 6pm); check the
website for the details.

ST JOHN'S, SMITH SQUARE   CHURCH
Map p448 (☑020-7222 1061; www.sjss.org.uk;
Smith Sq, SW1; ◉Westminster, St James's Park)
In the heart of Westminster, this eye-catching church was built by Thomas Archer in
1728 under Queen Anne's *New Churches in
London and Westminster Act* (1710), which
aimed to build 50 new churches for London's rapidly growing metropolitan area.
After receiving a direct hit during WWII,
it was rebuilt in the 1960s as a classical music venue and is renowned for its excellent
acoustics. Check the website for upcoming
concerts and other events.

SUPREME COURT   LANDMARK
Map p448 (☑020-7960 1900; www.supreme
court.uk; Parliament Sq, SW1; ◉9.30am-4.30pm
Mon-Fri; ◉Westminster) **FREE** The Supreme
Court, the highest court in the UK, was the
Appellate Committee of the House of Lords
until 2009. It is now housed in the neo-
Gothic Middlesex Guildhall (1913) on Parliament Sq. There's a permanent exhibition
looking at the work and history of the court
as well as the building's history on the lower ground floor. There's a self-guided tour
booklet (£1) or guided tours (adult/child £7/
free) at 11am, 2pm and 3pm on Friday.

During the Supreme Court's summer re-
cess (August to early September), there are
also tours at 11am and 2pm on most weekdays. Members of the public are welcome
to observe cases when the court is sitting
(11am to 4pm Monday, 10.30am to 4pm
Tuesday to Thursday). For who or what's
on trial, ask for a list at reception, or go to
the 'Current Cases' section of the Supreme
Court website.

◉ Bloomsbury & Fitzrovia

BRITISH MUSEUM   MUSEUM
See p79.

NEW LONDON ARCHITECTURE MUSEUM

Map p444 (☑020-7692 4000; www.newlondon architecture.org; Bldg Centre, 26 Store St, WC1; ⏱9am-6pm Mon-Fri, 10am-5pm Sat; ⊖Goodge St) FREE A large, constantly updated scale model of the capital highlights planned and new buildings, as well as various neighbourhood regeneration programs. It's an excellent place to see which way London's architectural development is going, and the frequently changing exhibitions will capture the imagination. There's a good cafe here too.

ALL SAINTS CHURCH

Map p444 (☑020-7636 1788; www.allsaintsmar garetstreet.org.uk; 7 Margaret St, W1; ⏱7am-7pm; ⊖Oxford Circus) In 1859 architect William Butterfield completed one of the country's most supreme examples of Victorian Gothic Revival architecture, enclosing the 65ft-long nave with extraordinary tiling and sumptuous stained glass. All Saints was selected by the head of English Heritage in 2014 as one of the top 10 buildings in the UK that have changed the face of the nation, a list that included Westminster Abbey and Christ Church in Oxford.

CHARLES DICKENS MUSEUM MUSEUM

Map p444 (☑020-7405 2127; www.dickens museum.com; 48 Doughty St, WC1; adult/child £9/4; ⏱10am-5pm Tue-Sun; 🐾; ⊖Chancery Lane, Russell Sq) A £3.5 million renovation funded by the Heritage Lottery Fund has made this museum – located in a handsome four-storey house that is the beloved Victorian novelist's sole surviving residence in London – bigger and better than ever. A period kitchen in the basement and a nursery in the attic were added, and newly acquired 49 Doughty St increased the exhibition space substantially.

Not that the prolific writer stayed here very long – a mere 2½ years (1837–39). But this is where his work really flourished: he dashed off *The Pickwick Papers, Nicholas Nickleby* and *Oliver Twist*, despite anxiety over debts, the death of his beloved sister-in-law, Mary Hogarth, and his ever-growing family.

The house was saved from demolition and the museum opened in 1925, showcasing the family drawing room (restored to its original condition) and a dozen rooms containing various memorabilia, including the study where you'll find the desk at which Dickens wrote *Great Expectations*.

The charming **Garden Cafe** (open 10am to 4.30pm Tuesday to Sunday) is free to visit, without requiring admission to the museum. Audio guides are £3 (or download the free app to your smartphone). One night a month, the museum is open till 8pm (check the calendar on the website).

ST GEORGE'S HANOVER SQUARE CHURCH

Map p444 (☑020-7629 9874; www.stgeorges hanoversquare.org; St George St, W1; ⏱8am-4pm Mon, Tue, Thu & Fri, to 6pm Wed, to noon Sun; ⊖Oxford St) Built in 1724 as one of 50 churches projected by Queen Anne's Act of 1710, St George's has hosted more than a few society weddings over the years; among those married here were Lady Hamilton, Shelley, Disraeli, George Eliot and, in 1886, the 26th president of the USA, Theodore Roosevelt. It's also the church referred to in the song 'Get Me to the Church on Time' in the musical *My Fair Lady*.

POLLOCK'S TOY MUSEUM MUSEUM

Map p444 (☑020-7636 3452; www.pollocks toys.com; 1 Scala St, enter from 41 Whitfield St, W1; adult/child £6/3; ⏱10am-5pm Mon-Sat; ⊖Goodge St) Aimed at adults as much as kids, this museum is simultaneously creepy and mesmerising. You walk in through its shop, laden with excellent wooden toys and various games, and start your exploration by climbing up a rickety narrow staircase, where displays begin with mechanical toys, puppets and framed dolls from Latin America, Africa, India and Europe.

PETRIE MUSEUM OF EGYPTIAN ARCHAEOLOGY MUSEUM

Map p444 (UCL; ☑020-7679 2884; www.ucl. ac.uk/culture/petrie-museum; University College London, Malet Pl, WC1; ⏱1-5pm Tue-Sat; ⊖Goodge St) FREE With some 80,000 artefacts, this is one of the most impressive collections of Egyptian and Sudanese archaeology in the world. The old-fashioned displays in glass cases and outdated presentation don't really do much to highlight them, though. Torches are available to pierce the gloomier recesses of the collection.

ST GEORGE'S BLOOMSBURY CHURCH

Map p444 (☑020-7242 1979; www.stgeorges bloomsbury.org.uk; Bloomsbury Way, WC1; ⏱1-4pm; ⊖Holborn, Tottenham Court Rd) One of a half-dozen designed by Nicholas Hawksmoor, this superbly restored church (1730) is distinguished by its classical portico of

Corinthian capitals and a steeple (visible in William Hogarth's satirical painting *Gin Lane*) inspired by the Mausoleum of Halicarnassus (now Bodrum in Turkey). The statue atop the steeple is of King George I in Roman dress, while lions and unicorns scamper about its base.

Phone ahead, as the church relies on volunteers and may not be open. Guided tours of the church (£5) also should be booked ahead.

MARBLE ARCH   MONUMENT
Map p444 (⊖Marble Arch) Designed by John Nash in 1828, this huge white arch was moved here from its original spot in front of Buckingham Palace in 1851, when adjudged too unimposing an entrance to the royal manor. If you're feeling anarchic, walk through the central portal, a privilege reserved by (unenforced) law for the Royal Family and the ceremonial King's Troop Royal Horse Artillery.

Lending its name to the neighbourhood, the arch contains three rooms (inaccessible to the public) and was a police station from 1851 to 1968 (two doors access the interior), large enough to accommodate 100 policemen who could rush to nearby Speaker's Corner if trouble was a-brewing.

A ground **plaque** on the traffic island between Bayswater and Edgware Rds indicates the spot where the infamous Tyburn Tree, a three-legged gallows, once stood. An estimated 50,000 people were executed here between 1571 and 1783, many having been dragged from the Tower of London. During the 16th century many Catholics were executed for their faith, and it later became a place of Catholic pilgrimage.

To the west of the arch stands a magnificent outsized bronze sculpture of a horse's head called *Still Water,* created by Nic Fiddian-Green in 2011.

FOUNDLING MUSEUM   MUSEUM
Map p444 (✆020-7841 3600; http://foundling museum.org.uk; 40 Brunswick Sq, WC1; adult/ child £8.25/free; ⊙10am-5pm Tue-Sat, 11am-5pm Sun; ⊖Russell Sq) Thomas Coram established the Foundling Hospital in 1739 for children abandoned or handed over by their mothers; when it closed in 1953 it had been the home of 27,000 children. The museum in its place traces the history of the hospital and the children who lived here; particularly moving is the collection of amulets left behind by mothers for their children to

remember them by. The Georgian interior also contains a wonderful art gallery.

ST PANCRAS NEW CHURCH   CHURCH
Map p444 (✆020-7388 1461; www.stpancras church.org; cnr Euston Rd & Upper Woburn Place, WC1; ⊙8am-6pm Mon-Fri, 7.30-11.30am & 5.30-7pm Sun; ⊖Euston) The striking Greek Revival St Pancras New Church has a tower designed to imitate the Temple of the Winds in Athens, a portico with six Ionic columns and a wing decorated with caryatids like the Erechtheion on the Acropolis. When it was completed in 1822 this was the most expensive new church to have been built in London since St Paul's Cathedral. Art exhibitions take place in the Crypt Gallery.

WIENER LIBRARY   MUSEUM
Map p444 (✆020-7636 7247; www.wienerlibrary. co.uk; 29 Russell Sq, WC1; ⊙10am-5pm Mon & Wed-Fri, to 7.30pm Tue; ⊖Russell Square) FREE The Wiener Library was established by a German Jew called Alfred Wiener in 1933 to document the rise of anti-Semitism in his home country, from which he had fled in the face of Nazi persecution. It's the world's oldest institution dedicated to the study of the Holocaust. Now a public library and research institute, it contains over a million items relating to one of history's darkest periods.

GRANT MUSEUM OF ZOOLOGY   MUSEUM
Map p444 (www.ucl.ac.uk/culture/grant-museum -zoology; Rockefeller Bldg, University College London, 21 University St, WC1; ⊙1-5pm Mon-Sat; ⊖Euston Sq) FREE This fascinating and little-known museum contains 68,000 specimens from the animal kingdom, including many that are extinct or critically endangered. Items of particular interest include the very rare skeleton of a quagga (an extinct South African zebra), the bones of a dodo and a Tasmanian tiger (an extinct dog-like striped marsupial), plus a riveting collection of bisected animal heads. The Micrarium displays backlit microscope slides framing over some 20,000 tiny objects, including the hair of a woolly mammoth.

BROADCASTING HOUSE   HISTORIC BUILDING
Map p444 (✆0370 901 1227; www.bbc.co.uk/ showsandtours; Portland Pl, W1; ⊙cafe & shop 9.30am-5.30pm Mon-Sat, from 10am Sun; ⊖Oxford Circus) The iconic building from which the BBC began radio broadcasting in 1932 and from where all TV and radio broadcasting in London has taken place since 2013 no

LITERARY BLOOMSBURY

Bloomsbury's beautiful squares were once colonised by the so-called Bloomsbury Group, a coterie of artists and writers that included Virginia Woolf and EM Forster, whose intricate love affairs (heterosexual, bisexual and homosexual) were as fascinating as their books. Charles Dickens, Charles Darwin, William Butler Yeats and George Bernard Shaw also lived in this district, as attested by the many blue plaques that speckle the neighbourhood.

Bedford Square (⊖Tottenham Court Rd) was home to many London publishing houses until the 1990s, when they were swallowed up by multinational conglomerates, and relocated. They included Jonathan Cape, Chatto and the Bodley Head (set up by Woolf and her husband Leonard), and were largely responsible for perpetuating interest in the Bloomsbury Group by churning out seemingly endless collections of associated letters, memoirs and biographies.

Today Bloomsbury contains some excellent bookshops and cafes, while remaining relatively uncommercial.

longer offers tours to the public, but you can have a look at the restored art-deco foyer and peer down into the newsroom through floor-to-ceiling windows by visiting the shop that sells BBC-branded gifts and souvenirs or the 450-seat Media Cafe.

⊙ St James's

BUCKINGHAM PALACE PALACE
See p83.

TATE BRITAIN GALLERY
See p90.

ST JAMES'S PARK PARK
Map p448 (www.royalparks.org.uk/parks/st-jamess-park; The Mall, SW1; ⊙5am-midnight; ⊖St James's Park, Green Park) At just 23 hectares, St James's is the second smallest of the eight royal parks after Green Park (p99). But what it lacks in size it makes up for in grooming as it is the most manicured green space in London. It has brilliant views of the London Eye, Westminster, St James's Palace, Carlton Tce and the Horse Guards Parade; the photo-perfect sight of Buckingham Palace from the footbridge spanning the central lake is the best you'll find.

The lake brims with ducks, geese, swans and other waterfowl, and the rocks on its southern side serve as a rest stop for a half-dozen pelicans (fed at 2.30pm daily). Some of the technicolour flower beds were modelled on John Nash's original 'floriferous' beds of mixed shrubs, flowers and trees. You can rent deckchairs (£1.50/7 per hour/day) to make lounging around more comfortable during daylight hours from March to October.

At the junction of Horse Guards Rd and the Mall stands the **National Police Memorial** (Map p448; ⊖Charing Cross), one column of marble and another of glass. Conceived by film director Michael Winner (Death Wish) and designed by architect Norman Foster and artist Per Arnoldi, it pays tribute to around 4000 policemen and women who have lost their lives in the line of duty. Note also the ivy-covered concrete bastion nearby, the **Admiralty Citadel** (Map p448; Horse Guards Rd, SW1; ⊖Charing Cross), a heavily fortified, bomb-proof command and control fortress built for the Royal Navy in 1941 to prepare for a German land invasion. Sitting over a network of tunnels, the building has 20ft-thick concrete and steel walls (making it impossible to demolish) and a lawn roof to render it invisible to overhead reconnaissance.

BURLINGTON ARCADE HISTORIC BUILDING
Map p448 (www.burlington-arcade.co.uk; 51 Piccadilly, W1; ⊙8am-8pm Mon-Fri, 9am-8pm Sat, 11am-6pm Sun; ⊖Green Park) Flanking Burlington House, which is home to the Royal Academy of Arts (p106), is this delightful arcade, built in 1819. Today it is a shopping precinct for the wealthy, and is most famous for the Burlington Berties, uniformed guards who patrol the area keeping an eye out for such offences as running, chewing gum, whistling, opening umbrellas or anything else that could lower the tone. (The fact that the arcade once served as a brothel is kept quiet.)

Running perpendicular to it between Old Bond and Albermarle streets is the more recent 1880 **Royal Arcade** (btwn 28 Old Bond & 12 Albemarle Sts, W1).

ST JAMES'S PICCADILLY   CHURCH

Map p448 (☑020-7734 4511; www.sjp.org.uk; 197 Piccadilly, W1; ⊙8am-8pm; ⊜Piccadilly Circus) The only church (1684) Christopher Wren built from scratch and one of a handful established on a new site (most of the other London churches are replacements for those destroyed in the Great Fire), this simple building substitutes what some might call the pompous flourishes of Wren's most famous churches with a warm and elegant accessibility. The baptismal font portraying Adam and Eve on the shaft and the altar reredos are by Grinling Gibbons.

This is a wonderfully sociable and charitable church; it houses a counselling service, provides a night shelter for the homeless in winter (they can sleep in the pews), stages lunchtime and evening concerts, and hosts a food market (10am to 3.30pm Monday and Tuesday) and an arts and crafts fair (10am to 6pm Wednesday to Saturday) in the forecourt. Note the arresting bronze Statue of Peace in the garden. It costs £1800 per day to run this generous church. Consider leaving a donation, however small.

ST JAMES'S PALACE   PALACE

Map p448 (www.royal.gov.uk; Cleveland Row, SW1; ⊜Green Park) The striking Tudor gatehouse of St James's Palace is the only surviving part of a building initiated by the palace-mad Henry VIII in 1531 on the grounds of a famous leper hospital. While it's not open to the public, you can admire it from the outside; it's best approached from St James's St to the north of St James's Park (p98). The official residence of kings and queens for more than three centuries, St James's is the most senior royal palace in the UK.

CLARENCE HOUSE   PALACE

Map p448 (☑0303 123 7300; www.royalcollection.org.uk/visit/clarence-house; Cleveland Row, SW1; adult/child £10/6; ⊙10am-4.30pm Mon-Fri, to 5.30pm Sat & Sun Aug; ⊜Green Park) Five ground-floor rooms of Clarence House, the official residence of Charles, the Prince of Wales and his consort, Camilla, the Duchess of Cornwall, are open to the public on 45-minute guided tours for one month in summer. The highlight is the late Queen Mother's small art collection, including one painting by playwright Noël Coward and others by WS Sickert and Sir James Gunn. The house was originally designed by John Nash in the early 19th century but has been modified much since.

Exclusive 90-minute after-hours tours (£35) departing at 4.30pm on Wednesday, Thursday and Friday also explore the Cornwall Room, inaccessible on the standard tour, where you can see two-dozen of the Prince of Wales's watercolours and sip a glass of Champagne. All tours need to be booked in advance.

SPENCER HOUSE   HISTORIC BUILDING

Map p448 (☑020-7499 8620; www.spencerhouse.co.uk; 27 St James's Pl, SW1; adult/child £12/10; ⊙10.30am-5.45pm Sun Feb-Jul & Sep-Dec; ⊜Green Park) Just outside the borders of Green Park is Spencer House, completed in the Palladian style in 1766 for the first Earl Spencer, an ancestor of the late Princess Diana. The Spencers moved out in 1927 and their grand family home was used as an office, until Lord Rothschild stepped in and returned it to its former glory in 1987 with an £18 million restoration. Visits to the eight lavishly furnished state rooms designed by John Vardy and James 'Athenian' Stuart are by guided tour only.

The 18th-century gardens are open only between 2pm and 5pm on a couple of Sundays in summer; consult the 'What's On' section of the website for details.

QUEEN'S CHAPEL   CHURCH

Map p448 (Marlborough Rd, SW1; ⊙services 8.30am & 11.15am Sun Easter-Jul; ⊜Green Park) This small chapel (1625) is where royals such as Princess Diana and the Queen Mother have lain in their coffins in the days before their funerals. The church was originally built by Inigo Jones in the Palladian style for the French wife of Charles I and was the first post-Reformation Roman Catholic church erected in England.

GREEN PARK   PARK

Map p448 (www.royalparks.org.uk/parks/green-park; ⊙5am-midnight; ⊜Green Park) At 19 hectares Green Park is the smallest of the eight royal parks. Still, it has huge plane and oak trees and undulating meadows, and it's never as crowded as its neighbour, the more manicured St James's Park (p98). It was once a duelling ground and, like Hyde Park (p184), served as a vegetable garden during WWII.

FARADAY MUSEUM   MUSEUM

Map p448 (☑020-7409 2992; www.rigb.org/visit-us/faraday-museum; Royal Institution, 21 Albemarle St, W1; ⊙9am-6pm Mon-Fri; ⊜Green Park) **FREE** Housed for the most part in the basement of the Royal Institution of Great Britain, this low-key and neon-lit museum is a tranquil escape from the bustle of Mayfair at street level. The exhibits themselves commemorate the work of scientist Michael Faraday, the 'Father of Electricity', including his isolation of benzene, his 'condenser' to prove electricity is a force, and a glass 'egg' for electric experiments.

GUARDS MUSEUM
MUSEUM

Map p448 (☑020-7414 3428; www.theguardsmuseum.com; Wellington Barracks, Birdcage Walk, SW1; adult/child £6/free; ☺10am-4pm; ☺St James's Park) Take stock of the history of the five regiments of foot guards (Grenadier, Coldstream, Scots, Irish and Welsh Guards) and their role in military campaigns from Waterloo onwards at this little museum in Wellington Barracks. There are uniforms, oil paintings, medals, curios and memorabilia that belonged to the soldiers. Perhaps the biggest draw is the huge collection of toy soldiers for sale in the shop. Don't miss the adjoining Royal Military Chapel flattened by a flying bomb in June 1944.

If you found the crowds at the Changing of the Guard (p84) overwhelming and didn't see much, get here 10.30am on any day of the change to see the soldiers of the New Guard muster and get into formation outside the museum, be inspected 20 minutes later, and depart just before 11am for their march over to Buckingham Palace to relieve the Old Guard.

INSTITUTE OF
CONTEMPORARY ARTS
ARTS CENTRE

Map p448 (ICA; ☑020-7930 3647; www.ica.org.uk; Nash House, The Mall, SW1; day admission £1; ☺11am-11pm Tue-Sun, exhibitions 11am-6pm Tue, Wed & Fri-Sun, to 9pm Thu; ☎; ☺Charing Cross) FREE Housed in a Regency building designed by John Nash along the Mall, the untraditional ICA is where Picasso and Henry Moore had their first UK shows. Since then the ICA has been on the cutting (and controversial) edge of the British arts world, with an excellent range of experimental and progressive films, music nights, photography, art, lectures, multimedia works and book readings.

◉ Soho & Chinatown

SOHO
AREA

Map p440 (☺Tottenham Court Rd, Leicester Sq) In a district that was once pastureland, the name Soho is thought to have evolved from a hunting cry. While the centre of London nightlife has shifted east, and Soho has recently seen landmark clubs and music venues shut down, the neighbourhood definitely comes into its own in the evenings and remains a proud gay district. During the day you'll be charmed by the area's bohemian side and its sheer vitality.

At Soho's northern end, leafy **Soho Square** (Map p440) is the area's back garden. It was laid out in 1681 and originally called King's Square; a statue of Charles II stands in its northern half. In the centre is a tiny half-timbered mock-Tudor cottage built as a gardener's shed in the 1870s. The space below it was used as an underground bomb shelter during WWII.

South of the square is **Dean Street**, lined with bars and restaurants. No 28 was the home of Karl Marx and his family from 1851 to 1856; they lived here in extreme poverty as Marx researched and wrote *Das Kapital* in the Reading Room of the British Museum.

Old Compton Street is the epicentre of Soho's gay village. It's a street loved by all, gay or other, for its great bars, risqué shops and general good vibes.

Seducer and heart-breaker Casanova and opium-addicted writer Thomas de Quincey lived on nearby **Greek Street**, while the parallel **Frith Street** housed Mozart at No 20 for a year from 1764.

CHINATOWN
AREA

Map p440 (www.chinatownlondon.org) Immediately north of Leicester Sq – but a world away in atmosphere – are Lisle and Gerrard streets, focal points for London's growing Chinese community. Although not as big as Chinatowns in many other world-class cities – it's just two streets really – this is a lively quarter with Oriental gates, street signs in Chinese characters, red lanterns, restaurants and noodle shops, great Asian supermarkets and gift shops. The quality of food varies enormously, but there's a good choice of places for dim sum and other cuisines from across China and other parts of Asia.

PICCADILLY CIRCUS
SQUARE

Map p440 (☺Piccadilly Circus) Architect John Nash had originally designed Regent St and Piccadilly in the 1820s to be the two most elegant streets in London but, restrained by city planners, he couldn't realise his dream to the full. He may be disappointed, but suitably astonished, by Piccadilly Circus

SEX, DRUGS & ROCK 'N' ROLL: THE HISTORY OF SOHO

Soho's character was moulded by successive waves of immigration. Residential development started in the 17th century, after the Great Fire of 1666 had levelled much of the city. Greek and Huguenot refugees, and later the 18th-century influx of Italian, Chinese and other artisans and radicals into Soho, replaced the bourgeois residents, who moved into neighbouring Mayfair. During the following century, Soho was little more than a slum, beset by cholera and squalor. Despite its difficulties, the cosmopolitan vibe attracted writers and artists, and the overcrowded area became a centre for entertainment, with restaurants, taverns and coffee houses springing up. The squalor also helped incubate radical ideas: Karl Marx lived in shocking poverty at 28 Dean St between 1851 and 1856.

The 20th century was even more raucous, when a fresh wave of European immigrants settled in, making Soho a bona-fide bohemian enclave for the two decades after WWII. Ronnie Scott's famous jazz club, originally in Gerrard St, provided Soho's soundtrack from the 1950s, while the likes of Jimi Hendrix, the Rolling Stones and Pink Floyd had early gigs at the legendary Marquee club, which used to be on Wardour St. Soho had long been known for its seediness, but when the hundreds of prostitutes who served the Square Mile were forced off the streets and into shop windows, it became the city's red-light district and a centre for porn, strip joints and bawdy drinking clubs. Gay liberation soon followed, and by the 1980s Soho was the hub of London's gay scene, as it remains today. The neighbourhood has a real sense of community, best absorbed on a weekend morning when Soho almost feels like a village.

today: a traffic maelstrom, deluged by visitors and flanked by flashing advertisement panels.

Piccadilly Circus has become a postcard for the city, buzzing with the liveliness that makes it exciting to be in London. 'Piccadilly' was named in the 17th century for piccadills, the stiff collars were the must-have accessory at the time (and were the making of a nearby tailor's fortune), while 'Circus' comes from the Latin word meaning ring or circle.

At the centre of the circus stands the famous aluminium statue mistakenly called **Eros** (Map p440) as it actually portrays his twin brother, Anteros. To add to the confusion, the figure is officially the 'Angel of Christian Charity' and dedicated to the philanthropist and social reformer Lord Shaftesbury. The sculpture was at first cast in gold but later replaced by newfangled aluminium, the first outdoor statue in that lightweight metal.

REGENT STREET STREET
Map p440 (🚇Piccadilly Circus, Oxford St) The handsome border dividing trainer-clad clubbers of Soho from the Gucci-heeled hedge-fund managers of Mayfair, Regent St was designed by John Nash as a ceremonial route linking Carlton House, the Prince Regent's long-demolished town residence, with the 'wilds' of Regent's Park. Nash had

to downsize his plan and build the thoroughfare on a curve, but Regent St is today a well-subscribed shopping street lined with some lovely listed buildings.

PHOTOGRAPHERS' GALLERY GALLERY
Map p440 (📞020-7087 9300; www.thephoto graphersgallery.org.uk; 16-18 Ramillies St, W1; adult/child £4/free; ⏰10am-6pm Mon-Sat, to 8pm Thu, 11am-6pm Sun; 🚇Oxford Circus) FREE With six galleries over five floors, an excellent cafe and a shop brimming with prints and photography books, the Photographers' Gallery is London's largest public gallery devoted to photography. It has awarded the prestigious Deutsche Börse Photography Prize, which is of major importance for contemporary photographers, annually since 1997. Admission is free to all before noon.

☉ Covent Garden & Leicester Square

NATIONAL GALLERY GALLERY
See p87.

NATIONAL PORTRAIT GALLERY GALLERY
See p91.

TRAFALGAR SQUARE SQUARE
See p92.

LONDON TRANSPORT MUSEUM MUSEUM

Map p438 (✆020-7379 6344; www.ltmuseum.co.uk; Covent Garden Piazza, WC2; adult/child £17.50/free; ⏰10am-6pm Sat-Thu, 11am-6pm Fri; ⊖Covent Garden) This entertaining and informative museum looks at how London developed as a result of better transport and contains horse-drawn omnibuses, early taxis, underground trains you can drive yourself, a detailed look at Crossrail (a new high-frequency 75-mile rail service linking Reading with Essex), and everything in between, including signage. Start on Level 2 and don't miss the museum shop for imaginative souvenirs, including historical tube posters, 'Mind the Gap' socks and 'Way Out' T-shirts.

Hard-core transport enthusiasts can sign up for one of several popular tours (from £5) of the museum's depot in Acton where more than 370,000 other items are stored. There are also 'Hidden London' tours (£77.50, 1½ hours) to parts of the underground network and disused stations such as Down St station once used as a wartime bunker by Winston Churchill. See the website for details.

COVENT GARDEN PIAZZA SQUARE

Map p438 (✆020-7836 5221; ⊖Covent Garden) London's fruit-and-vegetable wholesale market until 1974 is now mostly the preserve of visitors, who flock here to shop among the quaint old arcades, eat and drink in any of the myriad cafes and restaurants, browse through eclectic market stalls, toss coins at street performers pretending to be statues and traipse through the fun **London Transport Museum**. On the square's western side is handsome **St Paul's Church**, built in 1633.

ST PAUL'S CHURCH CHURCH

Map p438 (✆020-7836 5221; www.actorschurch.org; Bedford St, WC2; ⏰8.30am-5pm Mon-Fri, 9am-1pm Sun, hours vary Sat; ⊖Covent Garden) When the Earl of Bedford commissioned Inigo Jones to design **Covent Garden Piazza**, he asked for a simple church 'not much better than a barn'; the architect responded by producing 'the handsomest barn in England'. Completed in 1633, St Paul's Church has long been regarded as the actors' church for its associations with all the nearby theatres.

LONDON FILM MUSEUM MUSEUM

Map p438 (✆020-7836 4913; www.londonfilmmuseum.com; 45 Wellington St, WC2; adult/child £14.50/9.50; ⏰10am-6pm Sun-Fri, to 7pm Sat; ⊖Covent Garden) This museum's star – in fact, only – attraction is its signature Bond in Motion exhibition. Get shaken and stirred

---

FOURTH PLINTH

Three of the four plinths at Trafalgar Square's corners are occupied by notables: King George IV on horseback, and military men General Sir Charles Napier and Major General Sir Henry Havelock. The other, originally intended for a statue of William IV, remained largely vacant for more than a century and a half. The Royal Society of Arts conceived what is now called the **Fourth Plinth Commission** (Map p438; www.london.gov.uk/what-we-do/arts-and-culture/art-and-design/fourth-plinth; ⊖Charing Cross) in 1999, deciding to use the empty space for works by contemporary artists.

Works exhibited for 18 months in 'the smallest sculpture park in the world' are invariably both fun and challenging, creating a sense of dissonance with the grand surrounds of Trafalgar Sq. Pieces have included *Ecce Homo* by Mark Wallinger, a life-size statue of Jesus, which appeared tiny in contrast to the enormous plinth, while Rachel Whiteread's *Monument* was clear resin copy of the plinth turned upside down. Antony Gormley's *One & Other* featured no inanimate object but simply a space for individuals to occupy (each person spent an hour on the plinth, addressing the crowds on any chosen subject, performing or simply sitting quietly).

More recently Michael Elmgreen's and Ingar Dragset's *Powerless Structures, Fig 101* (a playful boy on a rocking horse) contrasted amusingly with the haughty grandeur of nearby equestrian statues. Another horse – Hans Haacke's *Gift Horse*, an equine in skeletal form – was on the plinth in 2015–16. The 2017 work is David Shrigley's *Really Good,* a giant hand in a thumbs-up gesture with an elongated digit. The 2018-20 work will be *The Invisible Enemy Should Not Exist,* a reconstruction in tin cans of one of the Winged Bulls at Nineveh (now in Iraq) destroyed by so-called Islamic State in 2015.

at the largest official collection of 007 vehicles, with over two dozen on display, including Bond's submersible Lotus Esprit (*The Spy Who Loved Me*), the iconic Aston Martin DB5, Goldfinger's Rolls Royce Phantom III, Timothy Dalton's Aston Martin V8 (*The Living Daylights*) and several of Daniel Craig's cars from *Spectre*.

Film clips, costumes and other props associated with the Bond films increase the excitement. The audio tour costs £5.

LEICESTER SQUARE   SQUARE
Map p438 (⊖Leicester Sq) Although Leicester Sq was very fashionable in the 19th century, in more recent times it was associated with antisocial behaviour, rampant pickpocketing, outrageous cinema-ticket prices and the nickname 'Fester Sq' during the 1979 Winter of Discontent strikes, when it was filled with refuse. As part of the Diamond Jubilee and 2012 Olympics celebrations, the square was given an extensive £15.5 million makeover to turn it once again into a lively plaza. Today a sleek, open-plan design has replaced the once-dingy little park.

ST MARTIN-IN-THE-FIELDS   CHURCH
Map p438 (☑020-7766 1100; www.stmartin-in-the-fields.org; Trafalgar Sq, WC2; ⊘8.30am-1pm & 2-6pm Mon, Tue, Thu & Fri, 8.30am-1pm & 2-5pm Wed, 9.30am-6pm Sat, 3.30-5pm Sun; ⊖Charing Cross) This parish church to the royal family is a delightful fusion of neoclassical and baroque styles. It was designed by James Gibbs, completed in 1726 and served as a model for many wooden churches in New England. The church is well known for its excellent classical music concerts, many by candlelight, and its links to the Chinese community (with services in English, Mandarin and Cantonese).

The wonderful **Cafe in the Crypt** hosts two-hour jazz evenings at 8pm on Wednesday; there's also free lunchtime concerts at 1pm on Monday, Tuesday and Friday, and the shop offers brass rubbing for kids. Refurbishment excavations in the last decade unearthed a 1.5-tonne limestone Roman sarcophagus in the churchyard.

ST GILES-IN-THE-FIELDS   CHURCH
Map p438 (☑020-7240 2532; www.stgilesonline.org; 60 St Giles High St, WC2; ⊘9am-4.30pm Mon-Fri; ⊖Tottenham Court Rd) Built in what used to be countryside between the City of London and Westminster, St Giles-in-the-Fields isn't much to look at but its history

is a chronicle of London's most miserable inhabitants. The current structure (1733) is the third to stand on the site of an original chapel built in the 12th century to serve as a hospital for lepers.

⊙ Whitehall

CHURCHILL WAR ROOMS   MUSEUM
See p93.

NO 10 DOWNING STREET   HISTORIC BUILDING
Map p448 (www.number10.gov.uk; ⊖Westminster) The official office of British leaders since 1732, when George II presented No 10 to 'First Lord of the Treasury' Robert Walpole, this has also been the prime minister's London residence since refurbishment in 1902. For such a famous address, No 10 is a small-looking Georgian building on a plain-looking street, hardly warranting comparison with the White House, for example. Yet it is actually three houses joined into one and boasts roughly 100 rooms plus a 2000-sq-metre garden.

BANQUETING HOUSE   PALACE
Map p448 (☑020-3166 6000; www.hrp.org.uk/banquetinghouse; Whitehall, SW1; adult/child £6.50/free; ⊘10am-5pm; ⊖Westminster) Banqueting House is the sole surviving section of the Tudor Whitehall Palace (1532) that once stretched most of the way down Whitehall before burning to the ground in a 1698 conflagration. Designed by Inigo Jones in 1622 and refaced in Portland stone in the 19th century, Banqueting House was England's first purely Renaissance building and resembled no other structure in the country at the time. The English apparently loathed it for over a century.

In a huge, virtually unfurnished hall on the 1st floor there are nine ceiling panels painted by Peter Paul Rubens in 1635. They were commissioned by Charles I and celebrate the 'benefits of wise rule' and the *Union of England and Scotland Act* (1603).

A bust outside commemorates the date 30 January 1649, when Charles I, accused of treason by Oliver Cromwell during the Civil War, was executed on a scaffold built against a 1st-floor window here. When the monarchy was reinstated with his son crowned as Charles II, it became something of a royalist shrine. Look to the clock tower opposite at Horse Guards Parade. The

WEST END SIGHTS

number 2 (the time of the execution) has a black background.

Tickets are cheaper if you buy online. Call ahead or check the closure schedule on the website as Banqueting House occasionally shuts at 1pm for functions.

HORSE GUARDS PARADE
HISTORIC SITE

Map p448 (http://changing-guard.com/queens-life-guard.html; Horse Guards Parade, off Whitehall, SW1; ⏰11am Mon-Sat, 10am Sun; ⓔWestminster, Charing Cross, Embankment) In a more accessible version of Buckingham Palace's Changing of the Guard (p84), the mounted troops of the Household Cavalry's two regiments, the Life Guards and the Blues & Royals, change guard here daily, at what is the official vehicular entrance to the royal palaces. A slightly less ceremonial version takes place at 4pm when the dismounted guards are changed. On the Queen's official birthday in June, the Trooping the Colour (www.trooping-the-colour.co.uk; ⏰Jun) takes place here.

During the reigns of Henry VIII and his daughter Elizabeth I, jousting tournaments were staged here. The parade ground and its buildings were built in 1745 to house the Queen's so-called Life Guards. Here you'll also find the **Household Cavalry Museum** (Map p448 ☎020-7930 3070; adult/child £7/5; ⏰10am-6pm Apr-Oct, to 5pm Nov-Mar).

THE CENOTAPH
MEMORIAL

Map p448 (Whitehall, SW1; ⓔWestminster, Charing Cross) The Cenotaph, completed in 1920 by Edwin Lutyens and fashioned from Portland stone, is Britain's most important memorial to the men and women of Britain and the Commonwealth killed during the two world wars. The Queen and other public figures lay poppies at its base on Remembrance Sunday, the second Sunday in November. The word 'cenotaph' derives from the Greek words 'kenos' ('empty') and 'taphos' ('tomb').

⊙ Holborn & The Strand

SIR JOHN SOANE'S MUSEUM
MUSEUM

See p94.

TEMPLE CHURCH
CHURCH

Map p438 (☎020-7353 3470; www.templechurch.com; adult/child £5/3; ⏰10am-4pm Mon, Tue, Thu & Fri, 2-4pm Wed, hours & days vary; ⓔTemple) This magnificent church was built by the secretive Knights Templar, an order of crusading monks founded in the 12th century to protect pilgrims travelling to and from Jerusalem. Today the sprawling oasis of fine buildings and pleasant, traffic-free green space is home to two Inns of Court: Inner Temple and Middle Temple. A key scene of *The Da Vinci Code* by Dan Brown was set here.

INNS OF COURT

Clustered around Holborn and just off Fleet St are the Inns of Court, with quiet alleys, open spaces and a serene atmosphere. All London barristers must work from within one of the four inns, and a roll-call of former members includes the likes of Oliver Cromwell, Charles Dickens, Mahatma Gandhi and Margaret Thatcher. It would take a lifetime working here to grasp all the intricacies of their arcane protocols, most of which originated in the 13th century. It's best just to soak up the dreamy ambience of the alleys and open spaces.

Lincoln's Inn (Map p438 ☎020-7405 1393; www.lincolnsinn.org.uk; Lincoln's Inn Fields, Serle St, WC2; ⏰grounds 7am-7pm Mon-Fri, chapel 9am-5pm Mon-Fri; ⓔHolborn) still has some original 15th-century buildings. It's the oldest and most attractive of the bunch, with a 17th-century chapel and pretty landscaped gardens.

Gray's Inn (Map p438 ☎020-7458 7800; www.graysinn.org.uk; Gray's Inn Rd, WC1; ⏰grounds 6am-8pm Mon-Fri, chapel 10am-6pm Mon-Fri; ⓔChancery Lane) was largely rebuilt after German bombs levelled it during WWII.

Middle Temple and **Inner Temple** both sit between Fleet St and Victoria Embankment. The former is the better preserved, while the latter is home to the intriguing 12th-century **Temple Church**, built by the Knights Templar and featuring nine stone effigies of knights lying on the floor of its round chapel. Check the church's website or call ahead for opening times.

The Temple Church has a distinctive design and is in two parts: the Round (consecrated in 1185 and believed to have been modelled after the Church of the Holy Sepulchre in Jerusalem) adjoins the Chancel (built in 1240), which is the heart of the modern church. Both parts were badly damaged by a bomb in 1941. The church's most obvious points of interest are the life-size stone effigies of nine 13th-century knights lying on the floor of the Round. Some of them are cross-legged, but contrary to popular belief this doesn't necessarily mean they were crusaders. It's one of just four round churches left in England.

THE STRAND   STREET

Map p438 (●Charing Cross or Temple) In the late 12th century, nobles built houses of stone with gardens along the 'shore' (ie strand) of the Thames. The Strand linked Westminster, the seat of political power, with the City, London's centre of trade, and became one of the most prestigious places in London in which to live; in the 19th century Disraeli pronounced it the finest street in Europe. Some of these buildings are now fine hotels and restaurants; modern times have added offices and souvenir shops.

Other interesting addresses include **Twinings** (Map p438 ☑020-7353 3511; www. twinings.co.uk; 216 The Strand; ⊙9.30am-7pm Mon-Fri, 10am-5pm Sat, 11am-5pm Sun; ●Temple) at No 216 – a teashop opened by Thomas Twining in 1706 and thought to be the oldest company in the capital still trading on the same site – and the stamp- and coin-collectors' titan **Stanley Gibbons** (Map p438 ☑020-7836 8444; www.stanleygibbons.com; 339 The Strand; ⊙9am-5.30pm Mon-Fri, 9.30am-5.30pm Sat; ●Covent Garden, Embankment).

ROYAL COURTS OF JUSTICE   HISTORIC BUILDING

Map p438 (☑020-7947 6000; www.justice.gov. uk; 460 The Strand, WC2; ⊙9am-4.30pm Mon-Fri; ●Temple) `FREE` Where the Strand joins Fleet St, you'll see the entrance to this gargantuan melange of Gothic spires, pinnacles and burnished Portland stone, built in 1874. It is a public building and you're allowed to sit in on court proceedings; the daily 'cause list' of cases to be heard is both on the website and posted on signboards in the reception of the Great Hall.

MIDDLE TEMPLE   HISTORIC BUILDING

Map p438 (☑020-7427 4800; www.middletemple. org.uk; Middle Temple Lane, EC4; ⊙grounds 10-4pm Mon-Fri; ●Temple) From the Strand, look for a studded black door labelled 'Middle Temple Lane', opposite Bell Yard and the Royal Courts building, and you'll find yourself in the sprawling complex surrounding the Temple Church and the Elizabethan Middle Temple Hall. The church was originally planned and built by the secretive Knights Templar in the mid-12th century; the hall was pieced together bit by bit after being blown to smithereens during WWII. There are wonderful gardens and courtyards at every turn.

On weekends enter from Tudor St to the east. Tours of the Middle Temple are available (£8 to £12), but you will need to book ahead.

INNER TEMPLE   HISTORIC BUILDING

Map p438 (☑020-7797 8208; www.innertemple. org.uk; King's Bench Walk, EC4; ⊙grounds 6am-8pm, gardens 12.30-3pm Mon-Fri; ●Temple) Duck under the archway at Old Mitre Court (47 Fleet St EC4) and you'll find yourself in the Inner Temple, a sprawling complex of some of the finest buildings on the river, including 17th-century terrace houses and Temple Church. Forty-five-minute guided tours (£12) of the Inner Temple depart on alternating Wednesdays at 10.30am and Fridays at 2.30pm. Check the website for changes to the schedule.

ST CLEMENT DANES   CHURCH

(Map p438 ☑020-7242 8282; www.raf.mod.uk/ stclementdanes; The Strand, WC2; ⊙9am-4pm Mon-Fri, to 3pm Sat, 9.30am-3pm Sun; ●Temple) Christopher Wren designed the original church here in 1682, but only the walls and a steeple added by James Gibbs in 1719 survived bombing in 1941; the church was subsequently rebuilt as a memorial to Allied airmen. An 'island church' named after the Danes who colonized Aldwych in the 9th century, St Clement Danes today is the chapel of the Royal Air Force (RAF), and there are some 800 slate badges of different squadrons set into the nave pavement.

★TWO TEMPLE PLACE   GALLERY

(Map p438 ☑020-7836 3715; www.twotemple place.org; 2 Temple Pl, WC2; ⊙10am-4.30pm Mon & Thu-Sat, to 9pm Wed, 11am-4.30pm Sun mid-Jan–mid-Apr; ●Temple) `FREE` This neo-Gothic

TOP SIGHT
ROYAL ACADEMY OF ARTS

Britain's oldest society devoted to fine arts was founded in 1768 and the organisation moved to Burlington House exactly a century later. The collection contains drawings, paintings, architectural designs, photographs and sculptures by past and present academicians such as Joshua Reynolds, John Constable, Thomas Gainsborough, JMW Turner, David Hockney and Norman Foster. Highlights of the permanent collection are displayed in the **John Madejski Fine Rooms** on the 1st floor, which are accessible on free **guided tours** (◷noon-1pm Tue-Fri, 1-4pm Sat, 1-2pm Sun) only.

The famous **Summer Exhibition** (◷ Jun–mid-Aug), has showcased contemporary art for sale for nearly 250 years, and is the academy's biggest annual event.

Burlington House's courtyard features a stone-paved piazza with lights and fountains arranged to display the astrological star chart of Joshua Reynolds, the RA first president, on his birthday. The courtyard also hosts temporarily installed statues and outdoor works by contemporary artists.

The academy has now expanded magnificently into 6 Burlington Gardens behind the museum, which will provide more space in which to exhibit its permanent collection.

DON'T MISS

➡ Summer Exhibition
➡ John Madejski Fine Rooms
➡ Forecourt piazza

PRACTICALITIES

➡ Map p448, B1
➡ ☎020-7300 8000;
➡ www.royalacademy.org.uk
➡ Burlington House, Piccadilly, W1
➡ adult/child from £13.50/free, exhibition prices vary
➡ ◷10am-6pm Sat-Thu, to 10pm Fri
➡ ⊖Green Park

---

house built in the late 1890s for William Waldorf Astor, of hotel fame and once the richest man in America, showcases art from UK museum collections outside the capital. Visit as much to see the opulent house (it's astonishing) as the collections on display, but note it's only open for a few months each year for the Winter Exhibition Programme (see the website). Check out the bronze *putti* (cherubs) chatting on old telephones on the steps!

STAPLE INN   HISTORIC BUILDING
Map p438 (www.stapleinn.co.uk; Staple Inn, off Holborn, WC1; ⊖Chancery Lane) The half-timbered shopfront facade is the main interest at Staple Inn (1580), the last of eight Inns of Chancery whose functions were superseded by the Inns of Court (p104) in the 18th century. The buildings, mostly post-war reconstructions, are now occupied by offices and law chambers and aren't open to the public, though you can have a look around the courtyard.

◉ Marylebone

★**MADAME TUSSAUDS**   MUSEUM
Map p446 (☎0870 400 3000; www.madame-tussauds.com/london; Marylebone Rd, NW1; adult/child 4-15yr £35/30; ◷10am-6pm; ⊖Baker St) It may be kitschy and pricey, but Madame Tussauds makes for a fun-filled day. There are photo ops with your dream celebrity (be it Daniel Craig, Lady Gaga, Benedict Cumberbatch, Audrey Hepburn or the Beckhams), the Bollywood gathering (sparring studs Hrithik Roshan and Salman Khan) and the Royal Appointment (the Queen, Harry, William and Kate). Book online for much cheaper rates and check the website for seasonal opening hours.

If you're into politics, get up close and personal with Donald Trump who stands uncomfortably close to Vladimir Putin, while Luke Skywalker and Han Solo enthusiasts can turn to the Star Wars experience, which features a host of its key heroes and villains in iconic settings.

The whole place is pretty commercial, with shops and spending opportunities in every one of the dozen rooms. But the Spirit of London taxi ride through the city's history is great, educational fun, and the new Search for Sherlock Holmes (£5 extra) is theatrical.

The museum has a long and interesting history, which started when the French artist and model-maker Marie Tussaud (1761–1850) made death masks of people guillotined during the French Revolution. She came to London in 1803 and exhibited around 30 wax models in nearby Baker St, providing visitors with their only glimpse of the famous and infamous before photography became widespread.

SHERLOCK HOLMES MUSEUM   MUSEUM
Map p446 (☑020-7935 8866; www.sherlock-holmes.co.uk; 221b Baker St, NW1; adult/child £15/10; ⊗9.30am-6pm; ⊜Baker St) Thanks to the ongoing crime drama television series Sherlock, more than a few fans of Arthur Conan Doyle's classic detective novels will make the trek here to elbow their way over three floors of fusty, reconstructed Victoriana, complete with deerstalkers, costumed staff and flickering grates. But just as many would-be visitors balk at the tiring queues

and the extortionate entry fee, which was increased by 50% in the space of just a year.

◎ Mayfair

HANDEL & HENDRIX IN LONDON   MUSEUM
Map p446 (☑020-7399 1953; http://handel hendrix.org; 25 Brook St, W1; adult/child £10/5; ⊗11am-6pm Mon-Sat; ⊜Bond St) George Frederick Handel lived in this 18th-century Mayfair building for 36 years until his death in 1759. This is where he composed some of his finest works, including *Water Music, The Messiah, Zadok the Priest* and *Fireworks Music.* The house at No 23, now incorporated into the museum, was home to American guitarist Jimi Hendrix (1942–70), who lived there for less than a year from 1968.

Early editions of Handel's operas and oratorios, portraits of musicians and singers who worked with Handel, and musical instruments are in the composer's music and composition rooms on the 1st floor; musicians regularly come to practise so you may be treated to a free concert. On the 2nd floor are Handel's bedroom (where he died) and dressing room; there's also a shop here. The staff attending the rooms are all

TOP SIGHT
SOMERSET HOUSE

Passing beneath the arched entrance fronting this splendid Palladian masterpiece, it's hard to believe that the magnificent **Edmond J Safra Fountain Court**, with its 55 dancing fountains, was a car park for tax collectors until a spectacular refurbishment in 2000. William Chambers designed the house in 1775 for royal societies and it now contains two galleries.

In the North Wing the **Courtauld Gallery** (http://courtauld.ac.uk; adult/child £7/free, temporary exhibitions vary) displays a wealth of 14th- to 20th-century art, including masterpieces by Rubens, Botticelli, Cézanne, Degas, Renoir, Seurat, Manet, Monet, Leger and others. Works to look out for include Manet's *Le Déjeuner sur l'herbe* and his *Bar at the Folies-Bergère;* Seurat's pointillist-style *The Bridge at Courbevoie;* Gaugin's *Nevermore;* and a delightful collection of medieval and Renaissance art on the ground floor. The **Embankment Galleries** in the South Wing are devoted to temporary (mostly photographic, design and fashion) exhibitions.

The Fountain Court hosts open-air live performances and **Summer Screen** (tickets from £20) films in summer, and ice skating in winter.

DON'T MISS

➡ Courtauld Gallery

➡ Skating in winter

➡ Films in summer

➡ South Wing riverside terrace

PRACTICALITIES

➡ Map p438, E5

➡ ☑020-7845 4600

➡ www.somerset house.org.uk

➡ The Strand, WC2

➡ ⊗galleries 10am-6pm, courtyard 7.30am-11pm, terrace 8am-11pm

➡ ⊜Temple, Covent Garden

TOP SIGHT
WALLACE COLLECTION

Arguably London's finest smaller gallery, the Wallace Collection is an enthralling glimpse into 18th-century aristocratic life. The sumptuously restored Italianate mansion – worth the visit in itself – houses a treasure-trove of 17th- and 18th-century paintings, porcelain, artefacts and furniture collected by generations of the same family and bequeathed to the nation by the widow of Sir Richard Wallace (1818–90) on the condition it remain displayed in the same fashion.

Among the many highlights are paintings by Rembrandt, Delacroix, Titian, Rubens, Poussin, Velázquez and Gainsborough in the stunning Great Gallery; look out for the *Laughing Cavalier* by Frans Hals. Particularly rich is its collection of rococo paintings, such as the strangely titillating *The Swing* by Jean-Honoré Fragonard, and furniture, paintings and porcelain that belonged to French Queen Marie-Antoinette. There's also an astonishing array of armour and weapons, both medieval and Renaissance and from Europe and Asia. The sweeping staircase is deemed one of the best examples of French interior architecture anywhere in the world.

DON'T MISS
→ Great Gallery
→ Marie-Antoinette's furniture, paintings and porcelain
→ The *Laughing Cavalier* by Frans Hals
→ Medieval and Renaissance armour
→ *The Swing* by Jean-Honoré Fragonard

PRACTICALITIES
→ Map p446
→ ☑020-7563 9500
→ www.wallacecollection.org
→ Hertford House, Manchester Sq, W1
→ ⊙10am-5pm
→ ⊖Bond St

Handel enthusiasts and very knowledgeable. Ticketed events at the house include plays, concerts and recitals.

The 3rd floor is devoted to Hendrix, with a brief but comprehensive exhibition, photo gallery and record room. Most fetching is the fully restored 1960s-style bedroom Hendrix shared with his girlfriend Kathy Etchingham, complete with vintage turntable and television set, overflowing ashtrays and an overhead canopy made from an Indian shawl. Groovy.

Blue Plaques on the exterior attest to the residencies of both these great musicians.

EATING

With neighbourhoods as diverse as Soho, Mayfair, Bloomsbury and Marylebone, the West End is a difficult area to encapsulate, but many of the city's most eclectic, fashionable and, quite simply, best restaurants are dotted around this area. As with most things in London, it pays to be in the know: while there's a huge concentration of mediocre places to eat along the main tourist drags, the best eating experiences are frequently tucked away on back streets and are not at all obvious. You'll find everything here, from Hungarian to vegetarian. Chinatown, as you might guess, is a great spot for inexpensive Chinese and other Asian food.

✗ Westminster & St James's

KAHVE DÜNYASI   CAFE $
Map p448 (Coffee World; ☑020-7287 9063; http://kahvedunyasi.co.uk; Unit 3, 200 Piccadilly, W1; cakes £3.85-4.95; ⊙7.30am-10pm Mon-Fri, to 10.30pm Sat, to 9.30pm Sun; ⊖Piccadilly) As lovers of all things Turkic, we were (and remain) over the moon that a branch of our favourite Turkish cafe chain has opened in central London, with pistachio-based desserts, real *lokum* (Turkish delight) and mastic ice cream. Oh, and Turkish coffee – the best in the world. Stunning service. Eat-off-the-floor clean.

WEST END EATING

VINCENT ROOMS MODERN EUROPEAN $
Map p448 (☎020-7802 8391; www.westking.
ac.uk/about-us/vincent-rooms-restaurant; Westminster Kingsway College, Vincent Sq, SW1; mains
£9-13; ⊖noon-3pm Mon-Fri, 6-9pm Tue-Thu;
⊜Victoria) Care to be a guinea pig for student
chefs at Westminster Kingsway College,
where such celebrity chefs as Jamie Oliver
and Ainsley Harriott were trained? Service
is eager to please, the atmosphere in both
the Brasserie and the Escoffier Room smarter than expected, and the food (including
veggie options) ranges from wonderful to
exquisite – at very affordable prices.

THE OTHER NAUGHTY PIGLET BISTRO $$
Map p448 (☎020-7592 0322; www.naughty
piglets.co.uk; The Other Palace Theatre, Palace St,
SW1; meals £8-16; ⊖noon-2.30pm Tue-Sat, plus
5.15-9.15pm Mon-Sat; ⊜Victoria) Located in
the Other Palace Theatre and offering far
more elbow room than its titchy Brixton
sibling, this unpretentious restaurant is a
pleasure, tempting with dishes such as bur-
rata, confit onions and dukkah, or barbe-
cued pork belly, sesame and Korean spices,
all prepared in the open kitchen. For pud-
ding try the delicious vanilla panna cotta
or Yorkshire rhubarb. There's a long list of
natural, 'low intervention' wines. Two-hour
sittings are the rule.

CAFE MURANO ITALIAN $$
Map p448 (☎020-3371 5559; www.cafemurano.
co.uk; 33 St James's St, SW1; mains £18-25,
2-3-course set meal £19/23; ⊖noon-3pm & 5.30-
11pm Mon-Sat, 11.30am-4pm Sun; ⊜Green Park)
The setting may seem somewhat demure
at this superb and busy restaurant, but
with such a sublime North Italian menu on
o   ffer, it sees no need to be flashy and
of-the-moment. You get what you come for,
and the lobster linguini, pork belly and cod
with mussels and samphire are as close to
culinary perfection as you'll get.

5TH VIEW INTERNATIONAL $$
Map p448 (☎020-7851 2433; www.5thview.co.uk;
5th fl, Waterstone's Piccadilly, 203-206 Piccadilly,
W1; mains from £8.50; ⊖9am-9.30pm Mon-Sat,
noon-5pm Sun; ⊜Piccadilly Circus) The views
of Westminster from the top floor of Water-
stones on Piccadilly are just the start. Add
a relaxed, sophisticated dining room and
some lovely food, and it's a gem. We love the
Greek mezze and antipasti platters (£15.50)
to share and the prix fixe lunch (two/three
courses £16.95/19.95, with glass of vino).

Afternoon tea (one/two people £15.95/
29.95) is served from 3pm to 6pm Monday
to Saturday and noon to 5pm Sunday.

QUILON INDIAN $$$
Map p448 (☎020-7821 1899; www.quilon.co.uk;
41 Buckingham Gate, SW1; mains £18-35; ⊖noon-
2.30pm & 6-11pm Mon-Fri, 12.30-3.30pm &
6-11pm Sat, 12.30-3.30pm & 6-10.30pm Sun; ⊜St
James's Park) This award-winning, Michelin-
starred restaurant probably serves the best
and most inventive Indian food in London. While the restaurant itself in posh St
James's is nothing to write home about, the
dishes themselves demand not postcards
but missives: pink pepper chilli prawns,
Malabar lamb biryani, stuffed quail legs.
The menu is very vegetarian friendly, with
up to a dozen unique choices.

✖ Bloomsbury

LADY OTTOLINE GASTROPUB $$
Map p444 (☎020-7831 0008; www.theladyottoline.
com; 11a Northington St, WC1; mains £14-17;
⊖noon-11pm Mon-Sat, to 5pm Sun; ⊜Chancery
Lane) Bloomsbury can sometimes seem a bit
of a culinary wasteland, but this gastropub
(named after a patron of the Bloomsbury
Set) is a pleasant exception. You can eat in
the buzzy pub downstairs, but the cosy din-
ing room above is more tempting. Favour-
ites such as beer-battered fish and chips
and pork with apple ketchup are excellent.

Some 95 gins are on offer as well as Lady
Ottoline's own in-house vermouth.

BON VIVANT FRENCH $$
Map p444 (☎020-7713 6111; http://bonvivant
restaurant.co.uk; mains £14-14; ⊖8am-10.30pm;
⊜Russell Sq) A welcome addition to the dining scene in 'Upper Bloomsbury' is this oh-
so-Gallic bistro with a menu chock-a-block
with the real deal: *bavette, poulet farci*
(stuffed chicken), *magret de canard*. Surrounds are classy – a nice mix of blues and
greys and natural wood – and service très
correct. Open for breakfast too.

**NORTH SEA FISH
RESTAURANT** FISH & CHIPS $$
Map p444 (☎020-7387 5892; www.northsea
fishrestaurant.co.uk; 7-8 Leigh St, WC1; mains
£9.95-24.95; ⊖noon-2.30pm & 5-10pm Mon-Sat,
5-9.30pm Sun; ⊜Russell Sq) The North Sea
sets out to cook fresh fish and potatoes –
a simple ambition in which it succeeds

admirably. Look forward to jumbo-sized plaice or halibut fillets, deep-fried or grilled, and a huge serving of chips. There's takeaway next door with similar hours if you can't face the rather austere dining room and faceless service.

TEA & TATTLE
BRITISH $$

Map p444 (☎07722 192703; www.apandtea. co.uk; 41 Great Russell St, WC1; afternoon tea for one/two £17/33.50; ☺9am-6.30pm Mon-Fri, noon-4pm Sat; ☎; ⊖Tottenham Court Rd) After legging it around the British Museum, this six-table tearoom in the basement of a bookshop with Asian and African titles is a convenient spot to recuperate with some afternoon tea, sandwiches, cake and scones with clotted cream and jam.

✖ Fitzrovia

SAGAR
VEGETARIAN $

Map p444 (☎020-7631 3319; www.sagarveg. co.uk; 17a Percy St, W1; mains £5.50-9.45; ☺noon-3pm & 5.30-10.45pm Mon-Thu, noon-11pm Fri & Sat, noon-10pm Sun; ☑; ⊖Tottenham Court Rd) This branch of a mini-chain specialises in vegetarian dishes from the southern Indian state of Karnataka. It's cheap, filling and of a fine standard. Try the paper masala dosa, an enormous lentil pancake with spicy potato filling. Thalis – steel trays with a selection of small dishes – are £15.95 to £17.95.

FRANCO MANCA
PIZZA $

Map p444 (☎020-7580 1913; www.francomanca. co.uk; 98 Tottenham Court Rd, W1; mains £4.95-8.25; ☺11.30am-11pm Mon-Thu, to 11.30pm Fri & Sat, noon-11pm Sun; ☎; ⊖Goodge St) It's first come, first served at Franco Manca, which has come a long way since first feeding Brixton on slow-rise sourdough pizzas a decade ago. The six-pizza menu with an additional two daily specials may seem lightweight, but you really don't need to look any further as it's the real deal.

RAGAM
SOUTH INDIAN $

Map p444 (☎020-7636 9098; www.ragamindian. co.uk; 57 Cleveland St, W1; mains £7.50-9.95; ☺noon-3pm & 6-11pm; ⊖Goodge St) If it ain't broke, don't fix it, and tiny Ragam hasn't been messing with the fundamentals – affordable, excellent dishes – for three decades. It hardly merits a glance from the outside, suggesting a rather uninspiring

hole-in-the-wall with a rather cheesy interior, which it is, but never judge a book by its cover: the dosas (£5.95 to £6.95) are supreme.

ROKA
JAPANESE $$

Mapp444(☎020-75806464;www.rokarestaurant .com; 37 Charlotte St, W1; mains £9-37; ☺noon-3.30pm & 5.30-11.30pm Mon-Fri, noon-4pm & 6-11.30pm Sat, to 10.30pm Sun; ☎; ⊖Goodge St) This stunner of a Japanese restaurant mixes casual dining on wooden benches with savoury titbits from the *robatayaki* (grill) kitchen in the centre. It has modern decor, dominated by grey steel glass, with floor-to-ceiling windows.

PIED-À-TERRE
FRENCH $$$

Map p444 (☎020-7636 1178; www.pied-a-terre. co.uk; 34 Charlotte St, W1; 2-course lunch/dinner £29.50/65, 10-course tasting menu £105; ☺noon-2.30pm Mon-Fri, plus 6-10.45pm Mon-Sat; ☎; ⊖Goodge St) Gratifying diners since 1991, this petite and elegant Michelin-starred gourmet French choice pins its long-standing and ever-popular success to a much-applauded menu, with sensationally presented dishes from award-winning chef Andy McFadden.

LIMA
PERUVIAN $$$

Map p444 (☎020-3002 2640; www.limalondon. com; 31 Rathbone Pl, W1; mains £22-30; ☺5.30-10.30pm Mon, noon-3pm & 5.30-10.30pm Tue-Sat, noon-2.45pm & 5.30-9.30pm Sun; ☎; ⊖Tottenham Court Rd) Sublimely zestful and piquant Peruvian flavours percolate at the heart of this fantastic restaurant with large colourful mural. The stunningly presented cuisine has pulled a Michelin star, while helpful staff take pride in their work. Express lunch with a glass of wine is a snip at £19.

HAKKASAN HANWAY PLACE
CANTONESE $$$

Map p444 (☎020-7927 7000; www.hakkasan. com; 8 Hanway Pl, W1; mains £12-63.50; ☺noon-3.15pm & 5.30-11pm Mon-Wed, noon-3.15pm & 5.30pm-12.15am Thu & Fri, noon-4pm & 5.30pm-12.15am Sat, noon-11pm Sun; ☎; ⊖Tottenham Court Rd) This basement Michelin-starred restaurant – hidden down a back alleyway – successfully combines celebrity status, stunning design, persuasive cocktails and sophisticated Cantonese-style food. The low, nightclub-style lighting makes it a good spot for a date or a night out with friends; the bar serves seriously creative

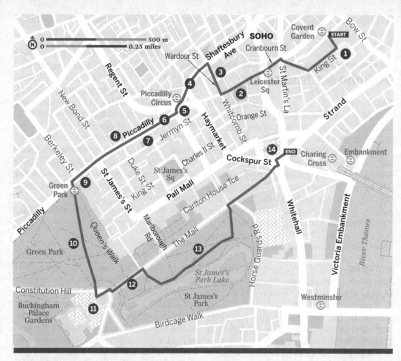

Neighbourhood Walk
The West End

START COVENT GARDEN TUBE STATION
END TRAFALGAR SQ
LENGTH 2.5 MILES; 1½ HOURS

This walk takes you through the heart of the West End, from Covent Garden's chic shopping streets to Trafalgar Sq, via Chinatown and leafy St James's Park.

First, head south to busy **① Covent Garden Piazza** (p102) and enjoy the street performers along James St and opposite St Paul's Church. Follow King and Garrick streets west; turn left onto Cranbourn St and you'll arrive at **② Leicester Square** (p103), where many international blockbuster films premiere. At the western end of the square turn right into Wardour St; you'll soon come to the Oriental gates of **③ Chinatown** (p100) on your right. The area is especially attractive around Chinese New Year, when hundreds of lanterns adorn the streets. Turn left on **④ Shaftesbury Ave**, where you'll find some of the West End's most prestigious theatres. At the end of the avenue is buzzy **⑤ Piccadilly Circus** (p100), full of shops, tourists and traffic.

Make your way west along **⑥ Piccadilly**; this avenue gives just a hint of the aristocratic St James's and Mayfair neighbourhoods. Pop into **⑦ St James's Piccadilly** (p99), the only church Wren built from scratch. Further along on the right, you'll see stately Burlington House, home of the **⑧ Royal Academy of Arts** (p106), while on the southern side of the road is the very ritzy **⑨ Ritz** (p346) hotel.

Turn left into **⑩ Green Park** (p99), a quiet space with stunning oak trees and old-style street lamps. **⑪ Buckingham Palace** (p83) is at the bottom of the park, past the beautiful Canada Gates.

Walk down the grandiose red-asphalt **⑫ Mall**; on the right is lovely (and well-manicured) **⑬ St James's Park** (p98). Views of Buckingham Palace and the Horse Guards Parade are stunning from the pedestrian Green Bridge over the lake. At the end of the Mall is **⑭ Trafalgar Square** (p92), dominated by Nelson's Column and the National Gallery. There are also great views of Big Ben and the Houses of Parliament from its southern side.

cocktails. Book far in advance or come for lunch (three courses £30, also available from 6pm to 7pm).

✕ Soho & Chinatown

TALLI JOE   INDIAN $

Map p438 (⌨020-7836 5400; www.tallijoe.com; 152-156 Shaftesbury Ave, WC2; dishes £4-11.50; ⊘noon-10.30pm Mon-Sat, to 4pm Sun; ⊖Leicester Sq, Tottenham Court Rd) Talli Joe is a colourful and very new breed of Indian restaurants serving 'half plates' (meaning share portions). The menu has been composed by the legendary Joe, who has travelled the length and breadth of India for regional dishes. So expect the unexpected: from Keralan-style fish curry and Bohri chicken from Gujarat, to a Kolkatta street snack of five-spiced potatoes.

HOPPERS   SRI LANKAN $

Map p440 (www.hopperslondon.com; 49 Frith St, W1; dishes £4.50-21; ⊘noon-2.30 & 5.30-10.30pm Mon-Thu, noon-10.30pm Fri & Sat; ⊖Tottenham Court Rd, Leicester Sq) This pint-sized and enormously popular place specialises in hoppers, the Sri Lankan national dish that is a thin pancake of rice flour and coconut milk with spices. Eat them (or dosas) with various types of *kari* (curry) or *kothu*, a dish of chopped roti with spices and meat, shellfish or vegetables. The decor here is Old Ceylon, and the service swift but personable.

KOYA BAR   JAPANESE $

Map p440 (www.koyabar.co.uk; 50 Frith St, W1; mains £7-15; ⊘8.30am-10.30pm Mon-Wed, to 11pm Thu & Fri, 9.30am-11pm Sat, to 10.30 Sun; ⊖Tottenham Court Rd, Leicester Sq) Arrive early if you don't want to queue at this informal but excellent Japanese eatery with counter seating. Londoners come here for their fill of authentic udon noodles (served hot or cold, in soup or with a cold sauce), efficient service and very reasonable prices. The saba udon noodles with chunks of smoked mackerel and watercress is excellent.

PIZZA PILGRIMS   PIZZA $

Map p440 (⌨020-7287 8964; http://pizza pilgrims.co.uk; 11 Dean St, W1; pizza £5.50-10; ⊘11.30am-10.30pm Mon-Sat, noon-9.30pm Sun; ⊘; ⊖Tottenham Court Rd) One of our favourite places for pizza in the very heart of Soho, PP serves 12in Neapolitan-style pizzas with delectably crispy crusts. There are a half-dozen on offer with a guest pizza

introduced each month. Very vegetarian friendly.

NORDIC BAKERY   SCANDINAVIAN $

Map p440 (⌨020-3230 1077; www.nordicbakery. com; 14a Golden Sq, W1; snacks £4-6; ⊘7.30am-8pm Mon-Fri, 8.30am-7pm Sat, 9am-7pm Sun; ⊘; ⊖Piccadilly Circus) This is the perfect place to escape the chaos that is Soho and relax in the dark-wood-panelled space on the southern side of a delightful 'undiscovered' square. Lunch on Scandinavian smoked-fish or meatball sandwiches (£4.50) or goat's cheese and beetroot salad, or have an afternoon break with tea/coffee and rustic oatmeal cookies.

Get inspired by co-owner Miisa Mink's *Nordic Bakery Cookbook*.

MILDREDS   VEGETARIAN $

Map p440 (⌨020-7484 1634; www.mildreds.co.uk; 45 Lexington St, W1; mains £7-12; ⊘noon-11pm Mon-Sat; ⊘⌨; ⊖Oxford Circus, Piccadilly Circus) Central London's most inventive vegetarian restaurant, Mildreds is crammed at lunchtime so don't be shy about sharing a table in the sky-lit dining room. Expect the likes of Sri Lankan sweet-potato and cashew-nut curry, ricotta and truffle tortellini, Middle Eastern mezze, wonderfully exotic (and filling) salads and delicious stir-fries. There are also vegan and gluten-free options.

CEVICHE   PERUVIAN $

Map p440 (⌨020-7292 2040; www.cevicheuk. com; 17 Frith St, W1; mains £6-13; ⊘noon-11.15pm Mon-Sat, to 10.15pm Sun; ⌨; ⊖Leicester Sq) This colourfully decorated bodega serves some of the most authentic Peruvian food in town. Start with cancha (large crunchy corn kernels) and move on to one of the signature dishes of ceviche (fish or shellfish marinated in lime juice with chillies, onion and coriander) or lomo saltado (steak stir-fry). Salads with quinoa and palm hearts are excellent.

SPUNTINO   AMERICAN $

Map p440 (www.spuntino.co.uk; 61 Rupert St, W1; mains £6-12.50; ⊘11.30am-midnight Mon-Wed, to 1am Thu-Sat, to 11pm Sun; ⌨; ⊖Piccadilly Circus) Offering an unusual mix of speakeasy decor and surprisingly creative American food, Spuntino is a delight at every turn. Try old favourites such as macaroni cheese (from £6), cheeseburger with jalapeño peppers (£8) and, as a dessert, a peanut butter and jelly sandwich. Seating is at the bar or counters at the back with two dozen stools.

BONE DADDIES RAMEN BAR NOODLES $
Map p440 (☎020-7287 8581; www.bonedaddies ramen.com; 21 Peter St, W1; dishes £10-13; ⏰noon-10pm Mon, to 11pm Tue-Wed, to 11.30pm Thu-Sat, to 9.30pm Sun; 🖥; ⊖Tottenham Court Rd) For a bowl of sustaining ramen noodles, you couldn't do better than Bone Daddies on Peter St, the original of an ever-expanding chain. Choose your 'foundation' – be it noodles in broth or a salad – and then add a topping or two (chashu pork, pulled chicken, bean sprouts etc).

THE BREAKFAST CLUB BREAKFAST $
Map p440 (☎020-7434 2571; www.thebreakfast clubcafes.com; 33 D'Arblay St, W1; mains £5-12.50; ⏰8am-10pm Mon-Sat, to 7pm Sun; 🖥; ⊖Oxford Circus) This fun and friendly original branch of The Breakfast Club chain has been successfully frying up since 2005. Full Monty or All American brekkies are the natural inclination, but chorizo hash browns, pancakes and delights of the El Butty also await (once you reach the front of the queue). You can bring your own booze after 6pm Monday to Saturday.

POLPO ITALIAN $
Map p440 (☎020-7734 4479; www.polpo.co.uk; 41 Beak St, W1; mains £6.80-12; ⏰11.30am-11pm Mon-Sat, to 10.30pm Sun; ⊖Oxford Circus, Piccadilly Circus) *Cichèti* – Italian tapas, for lack of a better word – are all the rage in backstreet *bàcari* (wine bars) in Venice, and rustic Polpo serves a lovely selection. More substantial are the half-dozen types of flavourful meatballs, the mini pizzas and the small plates of fish, pork or steak.

As coincidental as it may seem, the Venetian painter Canaletto lived at this very address for two years from 1749.

GELUPO ICE CREAM $
Map p440 (☎020-7287 5555; www.gelupo.com; 7 Archer St, W1; 1/2/3 scoops £3/4/5; ⏰11am-11pm Mon-Thu, to midnight Fri & Sat, noon-11pm Sun; ⊖Piccadilly Circus) The queue outside Gelupo can stretch down the street on warm summer weekend evenings, and it's no wonder: this is central London's most authentic *gelateria*. All the ingredients are natural and the servings are generous. Go for traditional flavours such as pistachio or bitter chocolate or try original creations such as bergamot, ricotta or fig and walnut.

JEN CAFE DUMPLINGS $
Map p440 (4-8 Newport Pl, WC2; mains £5-10; ⏰11.30am-9pm Mon-Wed, to 9.30pm Thu-Sun; ⊖Leicester Sq) This is a good choice for cheap, homemade wonton soup and dumplings. And you can be assured of their freshness by looking through the plate-glass window where they're in the process of being made, hour after hour...

YAUATCHA CHINESE $
Map p440 (☎020-7494 8888; www.yauatcha. com; 15 Broadwick St, W1; dishes £5-30; ⏰noon-11.30pm Mon-Sat, to 10.30pm Sun; ⊖Piccadilly Circus, Oxford Circus) London's most glamorous dim-sum restaurant has a Michelin star and is divided into two: the ground-floor dining room offers a delightful blue-bathed oasis of calm from the chaos of Berwick St Market, while downstairs has a smarter feel, with constellations of 'star' lights. Both serve exquisite dim sum and have a fabulous range of teas. Cakes here are creations to die for.

BAOZI INN CHINESE $
Map p440 (☎020-7287 6877; http://baoziinnlon don.com; 25 Newport Ct, WC2; mains £7.90-9.50; ⏰noon-10.30pm; ⊖Leicester Sq) Decorated in a vintage style that plays at kitsch communist pop, Baozi Inn serves quality Beijing- and Chengdu-style street food, such as *dan dan* noodles with spicy pork and *baozi* (steamed buns with stuffing) handmade daily. It's authentic, delicious and cheap food in often-unreliable Chinatown.

FERNANDEZ & WELLS SPANISH $
Map p438 (☎020-3302 9799; www.fernan dezandwells.com; 1-2 Denmark St, WC2; dishes £7.50-12.50; ⏰8am-9pm Mon & Tue, to 11pm Wed-Fri, 9am-10pm Sat, 10am-6pm Sun; 🖥; ⊖Tottenham Court Rd) A wonderful taste of Spain in Soho, Fernandez serves simple lunches of jamón (ham) and cured meats and cheese platters. The grilled chorizo sandwiches are perfect for quick bites. After 5pm F&W reinvents itself as an informal wine and tapas bar. Great post-industrial surrounds, huge windows and seating on two levels.

HONEST BURGERS BURGERS $
Map p440 (www.honestburgers.co.uk; 4a Meard St, W1; mains £7.50-10.75; ⏰11.30am-11pm Mon-Sat, to 10pm Sun; 🖥; ⊖Tottenham Court Rd, Piccadilly Circus) It's the burgers – made from Turner & George of Clerkenwell dry-aged beef – rather than the ambience that's

the pull at this hard-to-find branch of the much-mushrooming Honest Burgers empire. Served in glazed buns on white enamel plates with a side of rosemary salted chips, the burgers (or ribs) are just about worth the long wait for a table. No reservations.

★**PALOMAR**   ISRAELI **$$**
Map p440 (☑020-7439 8777; http://thepalomar. co.uk; 34 Rupert St, W1; mains £7-16.50; ⊙noon-2.30pm & 5.30-11pm Mon-Sat, 12.30-3.30pm & 6-9pm Sun; ☎; ⊖Piccadilly Circus) The buzzing vibe at this good-looking celebration of modern-day Jerusalem cuisine (in all its permutations) is infectious, but the noise in the back dining room might drive you mad. Choose instead the counter seats at the front. The 'Yiddish-style' chopped chicken liver pâté, the Jerusalem-style polenta and the 'octo-hummus' are all fantastic, but portions are smallish, so you'll need to share.

SMOKING GOAT   THAI **$$**
Map p440 (www.smokinggoatsoho.com; 7 Denmark St, WC2; mains £7-17; ⊙noon-3pm & 5-11pm Mon-Fri, noon-11pm Sat, to 10pm Sun; ⊖Tottenham Court Rd) This warren of a restaurant in Tin Pan Alley serves a type of food long overlooked outside its national borders – Thai barbecue – and we celebrate its arrival in London. Dishes come in small and large sizes for sharing; try the pungent fish-sauce wings, the spicy barbecue beef short-rib massaman and the classic gai yang (grilled chicken) with red chillies. Parties over six can book for dinner. Otherwise, you'll just have to wait in the queue like everybody else.

BAR SHU   SICHUAN **$$**
Map p440 (☑020-7287 6688; www.barshu restaurant.co.uk; 28 Frith St, W1; mains £12.90-28.90; ⊙noon-11pm Sun-Thu, to 11.30pm Fri & Sat; ⊖Piccadilly Circus, Leicester Sq) The restaurant that introduced London to the joys of spicy Szechuan (or Sichuan) cuisine remains more authentic than much of the competition. Dishes are steeped in the flavours of smoked chillies and the all-important huajiao peppercorn. Service can be a little brusque, but the food is good.

BRASSERIE ZÉDEL   FRENCH **$$**
Map p440 (☑020-7734 4888; www.brasserie zedel.com; 20 Sherwood St, W1; mains £13.50-25.75; ⊙11.30am-midnight Mon-Sat, to 11pm Sun; ☎; ⊖Piccadilly Circus) This brasserie in the renovated art deco ballroom of a former hotel is the Frenchest eatery west of Calais. Favourites include *choucroute alsacienne* (sauerkraut with sausages and charcuterie, £15.50) or a straight-up *steak haché* (chopped steak) with pepper sauce and *frites* (£9.95). Set menus (£9.75/12.75 for two/three courses) and plats du jour (£15.50) offer excellent value in a terrific setting. Also here, the **Bar Américain** is a classic art deco spot for a pre-dinner cocktail (from £12.25).

KRICKET SOHO   INDIAN **$$**
Map p440 (☑020-7734 5612; www.kricket.co.uk; 12 Denman St, W1; small dishes £4.20-11.50; ⊙noon-2.30pm & 5.30-10.30pm Mon-Sat; ⊖Piccadilly Circus) Inspired by Indian subcontinental street food, Kricket serves up unusual small sharing dishes like Karnatakan mussel and Keralan fried chicken using British ingredients only. Spread over two floors, Kricket has an open kitchen, with counter seating and large communal tables for groups.

BARRAFINA   SPANISH **$$**
Map p438 (☑020-7440 1456; www.barrafina. co.uk; 10 Adelaide St, WC2; tapas £6.50-15.80; ⊙noon-3pm & 5-11pm Mon-Sat, 1-3.30pm & 5.30-10pm Sun; ⊖Embankment, Leicester Sq) With no reservations, you may need to get in line for an hour or so at this restaurant that does a brisk trade in some of the best tapas in town. Divine mouthfuls are served on each plate, from the stuffed courgette flower (£7.80) to the suckling pig's ears (£6.80) and crab on toast (£8), so would-be diners prepare to wait.

There's a maximum group size of four. There are a couple of tables on the pavement.

10 GREEK ST   MODERN EUROPEAN **$$**
Map p440 (☑020-7734 4677; www.10greekstreet. com; 10 Greek St, W1; mains £9-22; ⊙noon-2.30pm & 5-10.15pm Mon & Tue, noon-2.30pm & 5-10.45pm Wed-Sat; ☎; ⊖Tottenham Court Rd) This understated bistro is making quite a splash with a menu that takes top-quality British produce and puts a Mediterranean spin on it (mackerel, fennel, anchovy and botarga, or leek tarte Tatin with wild mushrooms and burrata). Desserts are especially fine and service is seamless. Bookings are taken for lunch but not dinner.

GAUTHIER SOHO   FRENCH **$$**
Map p440 (☑020-7494 3111; www.gauthiersoho. co.uk; 21 Romilly St, W1; 2-/3-course set lunch £24/30, with wine £32/38; ⊙6.30-10pm Mon,

noon-2.30pm & 6.30-9.30pm Tue-Thu, noon-2.30pm & 6.30-10pm Fri & Sat; ⊜Leicester Sq) Alexis Gauthier's temple of gastronomy is housed over two floors of a discreet Georgian town house where you have to buzz to be let in. Evening meals are a delight but pricey at £50/60/70 for three/four/70 courses. Do what we do and treat yourself to a luxurious weekday lunch for half the price.

ANDREW EDMUNDS BRITISH $$

Map p440 (⌁020-7437 5708; www.andrew edmunds.com; 46 Lexington St, W1; mains £14.30-19.20; ⊙noon-3.30pm & 5.30-10.45pm Mon-Fri, 12.30-3.30pm & 5.30-10.45pm Sat, 1-4pm & 6-10.30pm Sun; ⊜Oxford Circus, Piccadilly Circus) This cosy little place, in situ since 1986, is exactly the sort of restaurant you wish you could find everywhere in Soho. Two floors of wood-panelled bohemia, with a hand-written menu of Modern British cooking (Galloway beef mince with swede and kale, smoked haddock and leek). It's a real find and reservations are essential.

POLLEN STREET
SOCIAL MODERN EUROPEAN $$$

Map p440 (⌁020-7290 7600; www.pollenstreet social.com; 8-10 Pollen St, W1; mains £33-38; ⊙noon-2.45pm & 6-10.45pm Mon-Sat; ⊜Oxford Circus) Jason Atherton's cathedral to haute cuisine would be beyond reach of many people not on a hefty expense account, but the excellent-value set lunch (£32/37 for two/three courses) makes it fairly accessible to all. A generous two-hour slot allows ample time to linger over such delights as lime-cured salmon, braised West Country ox cheek and your choice from the dessert bar.

OSCAR WILDE BAR BRITISH $$$

Map p440 (⌁020-74063310; www.hotelcaferoyal. com/afternoontea; 68 Regent St, W1; afternoon tea £42, with Champagne £55; ⊙noon-6.30pm Mon-Fri, noon-6.30pm Sat & Sun; ⊜Piccadilly Circus) The jewellery box of the luxury Hotel Café Royal, the Oscar Wilde Bar – dating from 1865 and named after its most famous habitué – is one of the most extravagant rooms in London, and a brilliant spot for afternoon tea. The gold decor and mirror-covered walls are dizzying to the senses – it's not unlike sitting inside a kaleidoscope.

✖ Covent Garden & Leicester Square

★SHORYU NOODLES $

Map p440 (www.shoryuramen.com; 9 Regent St, SW1; mains £9.50-14.90; ⊙11.15am-midnight Mon-Sat, to 10.30pm Sun; ⊜Piccadilly Circus) Compact, well-mannered and central noodle-parlour Shoryu draws in reams of noodle diners to feast at its wooden counters and small tables. It's busy, friendly and efficient, with helpful and informative staff. Fantastic *tonkotsu* pork-broth ramen is the name of the game here, sprinkled with *nori* (dried, pressed seaweed), spring onion, *nitamago* (soft-boiled eggs) and sesame seeds. No bookings. Veggie and gluten-free ramen is available to,o as well as a range of sake, Korean soju, Japanese whisky and beer.

DISHOOM INDIAN $

Map p438 (⌁020-7420 9320; www.dishoom. com; 12 Upper St Martin's Lane, WC2; mains £4.50-16.50; ⊙8am-11pm Mon-Thu, to midnight Fri, 9am-midnight Sat, to 11pm Sun; 🕾; ⊜Covent Garden) This branch of a highly successful mini-chain takes the fast-disappearing Iranian cafe of Bombay and gives it new life. Distressed with a modern twist (all ceiling fans, stained mirrors and sepia photos), you'll find yummy favourites like *sheekh kabab* and spicy chicken ruby, okra fries and snack foods such as *bhel* (Bombay mix and puffed rice with pomegranate, onion, lime and mint).

Booking rules are complicated: groups under six only till 5.45pm and over six after that. No same-day bookings accepted.

BATTERSEA PIE STATION BRITISH $

Map p438 (⌁020-7240 9566; www.battersea piestation.co.uk; lower ground fl, 28 The Market, Covent Garden, WC2; mains £5.50-6.50; ⊙11am-7.30pm Mon-Fri, 10am-7.30pm Sat, 11am-6.30pm Sun; ⊜Covent Garden) Just what Covent Garden needs, this small, white-tiled cafe has a terrific choice of pies (baby or big) to satisfy all levels of hunger, from careful nibblers to voracious teens. Meat is all free-range, flavours are classic and rich (lamb and mint, fish, steak and stout, chicken and mushroom, butternut squash and goat's cheese), and each comes with a dollop of mashed potatoes.

LONDON'S BEWILDERING POSTCODES

Just take a look at the 20 *arrondissements* in Paris that spiral clockwise from the centre in such a lovely – and logical – fashion. If you've got a letter for someone in the 5th, you simply write 75005. Now take a look at London's codes on a map. How on Earth can SE23 border SE6? If there's a north (N), a west (W) and an east (E), why isn't there a south (S)? And what happened to the northeast (NE)?

When they were introduced in 1858, the postcodes were fairly clear, with all the compass points represented, along with an east and west central (EC and WC). But not long afterwards NE was merged with E and S with SE and SW, and the problems began. The real convolution came during WWI when a numbering system was introduced for inexperienced sorters (regular employees were off fighting in 'the war to end all wars'). No 1 was the centre of each zone, but other numbers related to the alphabetical order of the postal districts' names. Thus anything starting with a letter near the beginning of the alphabet, like Chingford in East London, would get a low number (E4), even though it was miles from the centre at Whitechapel (E1), while Poplar, which borders Whitechapel, got E14. It's still mind-boggling.

COUNTER AT THE DELAUNAY   DELI $

Map p438 (☏020-7499 8558; www.thedelaunay. com; 55 Aldwych, WC2; soups & sandwiches £4.5-10; ⏱7am-8pm Mon-Wed, to 10.30pm Thu & Fri, 10.30am-10.30pm Sat, 11am-5.30pm Sun; ☻Temple, Covent Garden) Drop in to the relaxed Counter for a nosh of chicken noodle soup and a New York–style hot dog. The entrance is just east of the Delaunay.

WAHACA   MEXICAN $

Map p438 (☏020-7240 1883; www.wahaca.com; 66 Chandos Pl, WC2; mains £8.95-12.25; ⏱noon-11pm Mon-Sat, to 10.30pm Sun; ☏; ☻Covent Garden) 🍃 This delightful but frequently busy carbon-neutral cantina, which is part of an ever-expanding and ever-popular chain, styles itself as a 'Mexican-market eating' experience. Choose to share a selection of street snacks (tacos, tostadas, *quesadillas*) or aim for a more traditional main such as chargrilled chicken breast marinated in spices from Yucatan. Wash it down with one of a dozen tequilas.

Sharing places for two with a half-dozen items cost £23 to £36.

ROCK & SOLE PLAICE   FISH & CHIPS $

Map p438 (☏020-7836 3785; www.rockand soleplaice.com; 47 Endell St, WC2; mains £11-13; ⏱11.30am-10.30pm; ☻Covent Garden) This no-nonsense chippie dating back to 1871 (but surely without the overwrought cutesy name) is simplicity itself: basic wooden tables under the trees in summer, simple decor inside in three separate seating areas, and delicious cod, haddock or skate in batter served with a generous portion of chips.

Eat in or take away. Ichthyphobes can choose from a range of pies and sausages.

THE DELAUNAY   BRASSERIE $$

Map p438 (☏020-7499 8558; www.thedelaunay. com; 55 Aldwych, WC2; mains £7.50-35; ⏱7am-11.30pm Mon-Fri, 8am-midnight Sat, 9am-11pm Sun; ☏; ☻Temple, Covent Garden) This smart brasserie southeast of Covent Garden is a kind of Franco-German hybrid, where schnitzels and wieners sit happily beside croque-monsieurs and *choucroute alsacienne* (Alsace-style sauerkraut). Even more relaxed is the adjacent Counter at the Delaunay (p116).

Brunch is from 11am to 5pm at the weekend and afternoon tea (£19.75, or £29.75 with Champagne) is available daily from 3pm.

GREAT QUEEN STREET   BRITISH $$

Map p438 (☏020-7242 0622; www.greatqueen streetrestaurant.co.uk; 32 Great Queen St, WC2; mains £15.80-19.80; ⏱noon-2.30pm & 5.30-10.30pm Mon-Sat, noon-3.30pm Sun; ☻Holborn) The menu at one of Covent Garden's best places to eat is seasonal (and changes daily), with an emphasis on quality, hearty dishes and fine ingredients – there are always delicious stews, roasts and simple fish dishes. The atmosphere is lively, with the small **Cellar Bar** (5pm to 11pm Tuesday to Saturday) open for cocktails and drinks. Booking is essential. The weekday 'worker's lunch' menu is £20/22 for two/three courses.

ENCANT   TAPAS $$

Map p438 (☏020-7836 5635; www.encant london.com; 16 Maiden Lane, WC2; tapas £6-14; ⏱noon-11.30pm; ☻Covent Garden) Some of

London's finest (and arguably priciest) tapas can be had at this hole in the wall with counter seating and a copper bar just south of Covent Garden. Choose from the likes of velveted hake, grilled octopus, fried oysters, roasted quail with foie gras and Galician seaweed salad. There's a lunch-tasting menu with a bit of everything for £24.

IVY MARKET GRILL
INTERNATIONAL $$

Map p438 (☑020-3301 0200; www.theivymarket grill.com; 1 Henrietta St, WC2; mains £13.50-34, 2-/3-course theatre menu £16.50/21; ☉8am-midnight Mon-Sat, to 11pm Sun; ⊖Covent Garden) Spawn of what was once London's premier celeb-spotting venue, this welcome addition to the southern side of Covent Garden has a lovely front terrace full of greenery, traditional interior with lots of wood and brass lanterns, and high-end comfort food like shepherd's pie, fish and chips and steak tartare. It's also a fine and convenient place for afternoon tea served daily from 3pm to 5pm.

NATIONAL CAFE
MODERN EUROPEAN $$

Map p438 (☑020-7747 5942; www.national gallery.org.uk/visiting/eat-and-drink; ground fl, National Gallery, Trafalgar Sq, WC2; 2-/3-course set lunch £17/21; ☉8am-11pm Mon-Fri, 9am-11pm Sat, to 6pm Sun; ⊖Charing Cross) Our favourite place for a meal at the National Gallery, this cafeteria-cum-cafe-restaurant offers both self-serve light meals for those on the go and a proper sit-down bistro that is as popular with locals as museum-goers thanks to its extended opening hours. Enter from within the National Gallery or St Martin's Pl. Come for breakfast, lunch, tea (3pm to 5.30pm daily) or dinner.

★PORTRAIT
MODERN EUROPEAN $$$

Map p438 (☑020-7312 2490; www.npg.org.uk/ visit/shop-eat-drink.php; 3rd fl, National Portrait Gallery, St Martin's Pl, WC2; mains £19.50-26, 2-3-course menu £27.50/31.50; ☉10-11am, 11.45am-3pm & 3.30-4.30pm daily, 6.30-8.30pm Thu, Fri & Sat; 🛜; ⊖Charing Cross) This stunningly located restaurant above the excellent National Portrait Gallery (p91) comes with dramatic views over Trafalgar Sq and Westminster. It's a fine choice for tantalising food and the chance to relax after a morning or afternoon of picture-gazing at the gallery. The breakfast/brunch (10am to 11am) and afternoon tea (3.30pm to 4.30pm) come highly recommended. Booking is advisable.

J SHEEKEY
SEAFOOD $$$

Map p438 (☑020-7240 2565; www.j-sheekey. co.uk; 28-32 St Martin's Ct, WC2; mains £17.50-44; ☉noon-3pm & 5.30pm-midnight Mon-Sat, noon-3pm & 5.30-10.30pm Sun; 🛜; ⊖Leicester Sq) A jewel of the local dining scene, this incredibly smart restaurant, whose pedigree stretches back to the closing years of the 19th century, has four elegant, discreet and spacious wood-panelled rooms in which to savour the riches of the sea, cooked simply and exquisitely. The three-course weekend lunch is £28.75.

The **Atlantic Bar** (noon to midnight Monday to Saturday, from 5pm Sunday), popular with pre- and post-theatre goers for its oysters and shellfish, is another highlight.

BALTHAZAR
BRASSERIE $$$

Map p438 (☑020-3301 1155; www.balthazar. com; 8 Russell St, WC2; mains £18-43; ☉7.30am-11.30pm Mon-Thu, 9am-midnight Fri & Sat, 9am-11pm Sun; 🛜; ⊖Covent Garden, Temple) Few diners have been disappointed by the mostly French fare on offer – mussels, bouillabaisse, duck confit – at this handsome brasserie, where there's the odd nod to *les rosbifs* ('roast beefs', or Britons) in the way of shepherd's pie (though it's made with duck). Fabulous zinc bar and yummy bakery treats on offer at the adjacent *boulangerie*.

The excellent-value two-/three-course weekday set lunch for £19.50/22.50 is also available from 5pm to 6.30pm and from 10pm till closing Monday to Saturday.

RULES
BRITISH $$$

Map p438 (☑020-7836 5314; www.rules.co.uk; 35 Maiden Lane, WC2; mains £18.95-31.50; ☉noon-11.30pm Mon-Sat, to 10.30pm Sun; 🛜; ⊖Covent Garden) Established in 1798, this posh and very British establishment lays claim to being London's oldest restaurant. The menu is inevitably meat-oriented – Rules specialises in classic game cookery, serving up tens of thousands of birds between mid-August and January from its own estate in the High Pennines of northwest England – but fish dishes are also available. Puddings are traditional: tarts, crumbles, sticky toffees and treacles with lashings of custard.

✖ Holborn

KANADA-YA
NOODLES $

Map p438 (☑020-7240 0232; www.kanada-ya. com; 64 St Giles High St, WC2; mains £10.50-14;

⊗noon-3pm & 5-10pm Mon-Sat; ⊖Tottenham Court Rd) With no reservations taken, queues can get impressive outside this tiny and enormously popular canteen, where ramen cooked in *tonkotsu* (pork bone broth) draws in diners for its three types of noodles delivered in steaming bowls, steeped in a delectable broth and highly authentic flavours. The restaurant also serves up *onigiri* (dried seaweed-wrapped rice balls; £2).

SUSHI HIROBA
JAPANESE $

Map p438 (⌕020-7430 1888; www.sushihiroba. co.uk; 50-54 Kingsway, WC2; sushi £2.80-5.20, rice & noodle dishes £7-15; ⊗noon-3pm Mon-Fri, plus 6-11pm Mon-Thu & Sat, to 11.30 Fri, to 10.30pm Sun; ⊖Holborn) One of the more attractive and very central places for conveyor-belt sushi, Sushi Hiroba has seating on two levels done up in traditional decor. On the menu is a wide choice of *udon* and *soba* dishes, tempura and sushi and sashimi set menus (£12 to £35).

ASADAL
KOREAN $$

Map p438 (⌕020-7430 9006; http://asadal. co.uk; 227 High Holborn, WC1; mains £8.50-20; ⊗noon-3pm & 6-11pm Mon-Sat, to 10.30pm Sun; ⊖Holborn) If you fancy Korean but want a bit more style thrown into the act, head for this spacious basement restaurant conveniently located next to the Holborn tube station. The kimchi (pickled Chinese cabbage with chillies) is searing and the barbecues are done at your table. The bibimbap is the best in town.

HOLBORN DINING ROOM
MODERN BRITISH $$

Map p438 (⌕020-3747 8633; www.holborndining room.com; 252 High Holborn, WC1; mains £16-26; ⊗7am-11.30pm Mon-Sat, to 10.30am Sun; ⊖Holborn) This masculine-feeling brasserie attached to the Rosewood London (p346) – all reclaimed oak, antique mirrors and leather banquettes – serves up such delights as roast Suffolk pork belly, curried mutton pie and shrimp burger. But you'd be forgiven for making an appearance at the huge copper-topped bar to try one of their 425 gins combined with any of the 30 tonics on offer.

SPRING
INTERNATIONAL $$$

Map p438 (⌕020-3011 0115; www.spring restaurant.co.uk; New Wing, Somerset House, Lancaster Pl, WC2; mains £18-31, 2-/3-course lunch £27.50/31.50; ⊗noon-2.30pm & 5.30-10.30pm Mon-Sat; ⊖Temple, Covent Garden) The white walls, ball chandeliers and columns are offset only by the odd blossom in this favourite feminine eatery in Somerset House that looks onto Waterloo Bridge. Award-winning chef Skye Gyngel is at the helm. Try her Guinea fowl with parsnip purée, or monkfish and clams with roasted almonds. Desserts are legendary here.

✖ Marylebone

GOLDEN HIND
FISH & CHIPS $

Map p446 (⌕020-7486 3644; www.facebook. com/thegoldenhindmarylebone; 73 Marylebone Lane, W1; mains £7.90-11.90; ⊗noon-3pm Mon-Fri, 6-10pm Mon-Sat; ⊖Bond St) This 100-year-old chippie offers a classic interior, vintage fryer and chunky wooden tables, plus builders sitting elbow-to-elbow with folks in suits, tucking into ace fish and chips. It recently procured a liquor licence so now you can really make a meal of it here.

ROTI CHAI
INDIAN $

Map p446 (⌕020-7408 0101; www.rotichai.com; 3 Portman Mews S, W1; mains from £5-16; ⊗noon-10.30pm Mon-Sat, 12.30-9pm Sun; ☎; ⊖Marble Arch) With a refreshing street-kitchen menu from India, colourful Roti Chai does a roaring trade in Bombay-style *bhel puri* (puffed rice with tamarind), *aloo papri chaat* (wheat crisps, potato and sweet yoghurt) and 'railway' lamb curries (lamb and potato) for upstairs snackers, with a more expansive menu in the basement dining room (5.30pm to 10.30pm Monday to Saturday).

LOCANDA LOCATELLI
ITALIAN $$

Map p446 (⌕020-7935 9088; www.locanda locatelli.com; 8 Seymour St, W1; mains £17-34.50; ⊗noon-3pm daily, 6-11pm Mon-Thu, to 11.30pm Fri & Sat, to 10.15pm Sun; ☎; ⊖Marble Arch) This quietly glamorous restaurant in an otherwise unremarkable Marble Arch hotel remains one of London's most established tables, and you're likely to see some famous faces being greeted by chef Giorgio Locatelli. The restaurant is renowned for its pasta dishes, and the mains include five fish dishes and five meat ones. Booking is essential.

WALLACE
MODERN EUROPEAN $$

Map p446 (⌕020-7563 9505; www.wallace collection.org/visiting/thewallacerestaurant; Hertford House, Manchester Sq, W1; mains £14-22.50; ⊗10am-5pm Sun-Thu, to 11pm Fri & Sat; ⊖Bond St) There are few more idyllically placed restaurants than this spot in the enclosed courtyard of the Wallace Collection (p108). The emphasis is on seasonal French-inspired dishes, with the daily menu offering two- or three-course meals for £22.50/25.50. Afternoon tea is £18.50.

28-50 INTERNATIONAL $$

Map p446# (☑020-7486 7922; www.2850. co.uk/marylebone; 15-17 Marylebone Lane, W1; mains £15.50-21.50; ☺noon-10.30pm Mon-Wed, to 11pm Thu-Sat; ☻Bond St) This intimate, triangular-shaped wine bar and restaurant with floor-to-ceiling windows just north of Oxford St is a favourite of clued-in shoppers and concert-goers (Wigmore Hall (p126) is around the corner). Dishes are unfussy but always excellent: barbecued pulled-pork burger, Cornish cod, Icelandic fish pie. If solo, sit at the long bar and commune with the friendly staff.

FISHWORKS SEAFOOD $$

Map p446 (☑020-7935 9796; www.fishworks. co.uk; 89 Marylebone High St, W1; mains £15-40, 2-/3-course set lunch £19/22; ☺noon-10.30pm; ☻Baker St) The emphasis is on the freshest seafood and, to get that across, you enter the restaurant via the fishmongers. There are some nice English specialities to try such as Dover sole, Devon scallops, Dartmouth crab and Colchester oysters, but you'll also find seafood delights from across the pond or the Mediterranean, including lobster, tuna steak and Italian-style fish soup.

ETHOS VEGETARIAN $$

Map p444 (☑020-3581 1538; www.ethosfoods. com; 48 Eastcastle St, W1; lunch/dinner per 100g £2.30/2.50; ☺9am-10pm Mon-Fri, 11.30am-10pm Sat, 10am-5pm Sun; ☻🖉; ☻Oxford Circus) 🌿 Busy, self-service Ethos sells creative, meat-free food chosen from the buffet and then priced by weight. Doors open for breakfast (smashed avocado on toast, gluten-free porridge with almond milk etc), moving through lunch and dinner (guacamole, chickpea and coconut curry, Japanese-miso aubergine etc) via afternoon tea (£20, with prosecco £26) and brunch on Sunday.

Dairy-free, vegan, gluten-free and refined-sugar-free diets are all covered on the menu. Food can be bought to take away too.

YALLA YALLA LEBANESE $$

Map p444 (☑020-7637 4748; www.yalla-yalla. co.uk; 12 Winsley St, W1; mains £10.50-14.50; ☺11am-11pm Mon-Sat; 🖉; ☻Oxford Circus) A funky pit stop for lunch, this bright, buzzing and brisk restaurant specialises in Beirut street food, welcoming droves of customers who fill the communal counters and individual tables. Dishes are delightful, from the hummus drizzled with olive oil to the delish *arayes* (grilled pitta filled with minced lamb), grills, lunch platters and great pastries and desserts.

CHILTERN FIREHOUSE MODERN EUROPEAN $$$

Map p446 (☑020-7073 7676; www.chilternfire house.com; 1 Chiltern St, W1; mains £19-44; ☺7-10.30am Mon-Fri, 8-10am Sat & Sun, noon-2.30pm Mon-Wed, noon-3pm Thu & Fri, 11am-3pm Sat & Sun, 5.30-10.30pm Mon-Wed, 6-10.30pm Thu-Sun; 🖉; ☻Baker St, Bond St) When they can secure a table, diners come to this splendidly dapper eatery to celeb-spot and bask in its glorious setting as much as to dine. Chef Nuno Mendes has worked some considerable culinary flair into his menu, but the hype and overarching trendiness guarantee an outlay almost as high as the red-brick chimneys aloft. The covered front terrace is delightful.

TEXTURE SCANDINAVIAN $$$

Map p446 (☑020-7224 0028; www.texture-restaurant.com; 34 Portman Sq, W1; mains £29.90-43.50; ☺noon-2.30pm Wed-Sat, 6-10.30pm Tue-Sat; ☻Marble Arch) Housed in one of the finest Georgian buildings in London, this Michelin-starred restaurant can be found by following the birch trees that lead (literally) inside. The menu uses mostly fresh Scandinavian ingredients (Icelandic cod and lamb, Norwegian crab) in quite an imaginative way. The crab, for example, is in a coconut soup with lime leaf and lemongrass. Bookings essential.

The two-/three-course set lunch is a budgeter's delight at just £29/33.50. A multicourse meat/fish tasting menu is £95/85 with an additional £65 for wine pairings.

✖ Mayfair

BRICIOLE ITALIAN $

Map p446 (☑020-7723 0040; www.briciole. co.uk; 20 Homer St, W1; mains £7-19; ☺11am-11pm Mon-Sat, to 10.30pm Sun; ☻Edgware Rd) This trattoria fronted by a cafe and a deli is tiny but perfectly formed. It serves pretty basic stuff: Palermo-style sweet-and-sour meatballs, Tuscan barbecue and all kinds of pasta. But it's very tasty and excellent value, especially for this part of London.

★GYMKHANA   INDIAN $$

Map p448 (☑020-3011 5900; www.gymkhana
london.com; 42 Albemarle St, W1; mains £10-38,
2-/3-course lunch £25/30; ☺noon-2.30pm &
5.30-10.30pm Mon-Sat; ☎; ⊖Green Park) The
rather sombre setting is all British Raj: ceiling fans, oak ceiling, period cricket photos
and hunting trophies, but the menu is lively,
bright and inspiring. For lovers of variety, the six-course tasting meat/vegetarian
menu (£70/65). The bar is open to 1am.

MOMO   MOROCCAN $$

Map p440 (☑020-7434 4040; www.momoresto.
com; 25 Heddon St, W1; mains £13.50-29.50,
2-/3-course set lunch £18.50/22.50; ☺noon-
2.30pm Mon-Fri, 11am-3pm Sat & Sun, plus 6pm-
1am Mon-Sat, 6pm-midnight Sun; ☎; ⊖Picca-
dilly Circus) Overflowing with cushions and
lamps, and staffed by tambourine-playing
waiters, this atmospheric Moroccan restaurant has warm service and dishes as
exciting as you dare to be. After the mezze,
eschew the traditional and ordinary *tagine*
(stew cooked in a clay pot) and couscous,
and tuck into the splendid Moroccan speciality *pastilla* (wood pigeon pie).

There's outside seating on this quiet
backstreet in the warmer months.

EL PIRATA   SPANISH $$

Map p446 (☑020-7491 3810; www.elpirata.co.uk;
5-6 Down St, W1; tapas £4.95-8.95; ☺noon-
11.30pm Mon-Fri, 6pm-11.30pm Sat; ⊖Green
Park) Its silly name notwithstanding, this
is a good Spanish restaurant with a great
list of tapas and traditional mains such as
paella (from £21). There are two set menus (£18.50 and £23.50) if you can't decide
which tapas to choose. The selection of
Spanish wines is among the best in London.
Seating is on two levels.

EMBER YARD   TAPAS $$

Map p440 (☑020-7439 8057; http://emberyard.
co.uk; 60 Berwick St, W1; mains £7-11; ☺noon-
midnight Mon-Sat, to 10pm Sun; ⊖Oxford Circus) Infused with beautiful flavours that
capture the culinary aromas of the Basque
country, many of Ember Yard's tapas are
fired up on an imported Basque-style
grill. The atmosphere is lively, warm and
buzzing, while staff are thoughtful and
informed. Expect dishes such as steamed,
chargrilled octopus and Iberico presa with
whipped jamon butter. Weekend brunch is
served from 11am to 4pm.

★CLARIDGE'S FOYER & READING ROOM   BRITISH $$$

Map p446 (☑020-7107 8886; www.claridges.
co.uk; 49-53 Brook St, W1; afternoon tea £68, with
Champagne £79; ☺afternoon tea 2.45-5.30pm;
☎; ⊖Bond St) Extend that pinkie finger to
partake in afternoon tea within the classic art-deco foyer and Reading Room of
this landmark hotel, where the gentle clink
of fine porcelain and champagne glasses
could be a defining memory of your trip to
London. The setting is gorgeous and dress
is elegant, smart casual (ripped jeans and
baseball caps won't get served).

GREENHOUSE   MODERN EUROPEAN $$$

Map p446 (☑020-7499 3331; www.facebook.
com/thegreenhousemayfair; 27a Hay's Mews, W1;
2-/3-course set lunch £35/40, dinner £75/100;
☺noon-2.30pm Mon-Fri, 6.30-11pm Mon-Sat; ☎;
⊖Green Park) Located at the end of a wonderful garden filled with sculptures, the
Greenhouse offers some of the best food in
Mayfair. The tasting menu (£125) is only
for the intrepid and truly hungry. Bear in
mind that this place doles out so many extras – from *amuses-gueule* (appetisers) and
inter-course sorbets to petits fours – you'll
never get up.

NOBU   JAPANESE $$$

Map p446 (☑020-7447 4747; www.nobu
restaurants.com; 1st fl, Metropolitan Hotel, 19
Old Park Lane, W1; mains £15-52.50; ☺noon-
2.30pm daily, 6-10.30pm Mon-Wed, 6-11pm Thu-
Sat, 6-10pm Sun; ☎; ⊖Hyde Park Corner) You'll
have to book a month in advance to eat here
(or resign yourself to a 6pm or 10pm sitting
– maybe – if you book just a few days before), but you'll get to chew at and view one
of the greatest celebrity restaurant magnets
in town. Signature dishes include the black
cod with miso and the wagyu sukiyaki.

SEXY FISH   JAPANESE $$$

Map p446 (☑020-3764 2000; www.sexyfish.
com; Berkeley Sq House, Berkeley Sq, W1; mains
£20-45; ☺noon-11pm Mon-Sat, to 10pm Sun;
⊖Green Park) The interior of this flamboyant place with the in-your-face name will
blow you away, with artful fish and alliga-
tors by the likes of Damien Hirst and Frank
Gehry climbing the walls and an enormous
aquarium. But keep your eyes on the menu,
with sushi and sashimi sharing space with
tempura and robata grills. The late-night
bar apparently contains the second-largest
Japanese whisky collection in the world.

KITTY FISHER'S
MODERN BRITISH $$$

Map p446 (☑020-3302 1661; www.kittyfishers.
com; 10 Shepherd Market, W1; mains £28-31;
☉noon-2.30pm & 6-9.30pm Mon-Sat; ⊖Green
Park) Taking pride of place in Mayfair's historic Shepherd Market (which was in fact once London's red-light district), this cosy dining room is aptly named after the 18th-century courtesan painted by Joshua Reynolds. But come here now for delights of the tummy – Cornish pollock, Iberico pork and Anjou pigeon. It can be a devil to get in, but like Kitty herself, worth the wait.

TAMARIND
INDIAN $$$

Map p446 (☑020-7629 3561; www.tamarind
restaurant.com; 20 Queen St, W1; mains £20.75-
25.75; ☉noon-2.45pm daily, 5.30-10.45pm Mon-
Sat, 6-10.15pm Sun; ⊖Green Park) A mix of spicy Moghul classics and new creations have earned this northwest Indian restaurant plaudits and a loyal clientele. The set lunches are a good deal at £21.50/24.50 for two/three courses, and with wine £31.50/34.50.

PARK CHINOIS
CHINESE $$$

Map p446(☑020-33278888;https://parkchinois.
com; 17 Berkeley St, W1; mains £25-42; ☉noon-
11.30pm; ⊖Green Park) This opulent restaurant and club just south of posh Berkeley Sq serves dim sum lunch and dinner daily in the ground-floor **Salon de Chine**. Dining moves downstairs to the **Club Chinois** from Wednesday to Saturday, where there is live music and dancing as well. Think 1930s Shanghai – and the still before the storm.

LE BOUDIN BLANC
FRENCH $$$

Map p446 (☑020-7499 3292; www.boudinblanc.
co.uk; 5 Trebeck St, W1; mains £17-31.50; ☉noon-
3pm & 6-11pm Mon-Sat, to 10.30pm Sun; ☎;
⊖Green Park) Surely one of the best French bistros in the capital, with meat dishes such as pork cheek or chicken leg confit cooked to perfection, sauces mouth-watering and portions huge. The *frites* (chips) are the best you'll find this side of La Manche. And with a whopping 600 wines to choose from, no wonder it's always full.

🍷 DRINKING & NIGHTLIFE

Over the last decade or so, the East End has trumped the West End as the coolest place in town. But this is still a wonderful place for a night out – Friday and Saturday nights buzz with excitement and decadence, particularly the areas around Soho, Leicester Sq and Covent Garden where people, booze and rickshaws fill the streets till the early hours. Bars and clubs range from the skanky to the swanky – with everything in between.

🍷 St James's

RIVOLI BAR
COCKTAIL BAR

Map p448 (☑020-7300 2340; www.theritz
london.com/rivoli-bar; Ritz London, 150 Piccadilly,
W1; ☉11.30am-11.30pm Mon-Sat, noon-10.30pm
Sun; ☎; ⊖Green Park) You may not quite need a diamond as big as the Ritz (p346) to drink at this art-deco marvel, but it might help. All camphor wood, illuminated Lalique glass, golden ceiling domes and stunning cocktails, the bar is a gem. Unlike in some other parts of the Ritz, dress code here is smart casual.

★DUKES LONDON
COCKTAIL BAR

Map p448 (☑020-7491 4840; www.dukeshotel.
com/dukes-bar; Dukes Hotel, 35 St James's Pl,
SW1; ☉2-11pm Mon-Sat, 4-10.30pm Sun; ☎;
⊖Green Park) Sip to-die-for martinis like royalty in a gentleman's-club-like ambience at this tucked-away classic bar where white-jacketed masters mix up some awesomely good preparations. Ian Fleming used to frequent the place, perhaps perfecting his 'shaken, not stirred' James Bond maxim. Smokers can ease into the secluded Cognac and Cigar Garden to light up cigars purchased here.

🍷 Bloomsbury & Fitzrovia

LAMB
PUB

Map p444 (☑020-7405 0713; www.thelamb
london.com; 94 Lamb's Conduit St, WC1; ☉11am-
11pm Mon-Wed, to midnight Thu-Sat, noon-
10.30pm Sun; ⊖Russell Sq) The Lamb's central mahogany bar with beautiful Victorian 'snob screens' (so-called as they allowed the well-to-do to drink in private) has been a favourite with locals since 1729. Nearly three centuries later, its popularity hasn't waned, so come early to bag a booth and sample its good selection of Young's bitters and genial atmosphere.

QUEEN'S LARDER
PUB

Map p444 (☎020-7837 5627; www.queenslarder.
co.uk; 1 Queen Sq, WC1; ◷11.30am-11pm Mon-Fri,
noon-11pm Sat, noon-10.30pm Sun; ◉Russell Sq)
In a lovely square southeast of Russell Sq
is this cosy pub, so called because Queen
Charlotte, wife of 'Mad' King George III,
rented part of the pub's cellar to store special foods for her husband while he was being treated nearby for what is now believed
to have the genetic disease porphyria.
There are benches outside and a dining
room upstairs. American poet Sylvia Plath
married Ted Hughes on Bloomsday (16
June) 1956 in the Church of St George the
Martyr, Holborn, just opposite.

MUSEUM TAVERN
PUB

Map p444 (☎020-7242 8987; www.taylor-walker.
co.uk/pub/museum-tavern-bloomsbury/c0747;
49 Great Russell St, WC1; ◷11am-11.30pm Mon-
Thu, to midnight Fri & Sat, noon-10.30pm Sun;
☎; ◉Holborn, Tottenham Court Rd) Karl Marx
used to tarry here for a well-earned pint after a hard day inventing communism in the
British Museum's Reading Room; George
Orwell also boozed here, as did Sir Arthur
Conan Doyle and JB Priestley. A lovely traditional pub set around a long bar, it has
friendly staff and period features, and is
popular with academics and students alike.

LONDON COCKTAIL CLUB
COCKTAIL BAR

Map p444 (☎020-7580 1960; www.london
cocktailclub.co.uk; 61 Goodge St, W1; ◷4.30-
11.30pm Mon-Thu, to midnight Fri & Sat; ◉Goodge
St) There are cocktails and then there are
cocktails. The guys in this slightly tatty
('kitsch punk') subterranean bar will shake,
stir, blend and smoke (yes, smoke) you some
of the most inventive, colourful and punchy
concoctions in creation. Try the bacon and
egg martini or the smoked Manhattan. And
relax. You'll be staying a lot longer than you
thunk (err, make that thought).

Cocktails are two for £12 at happy hour
(4.30pm to 7.30pm).

🍺 Soho & Chinatown

SWIFT
COCKTAIL BAR

Map p440 (☎020-7437 7820; www.barswift.com;
12 Old Compton St, W1; ◷3pm-midnight Mon-
Sat, to 10.30pm Sun; ◉Leicester Sq, Tottenham
Court Rd) Our favourite new place for cocktails, Swift (as in the bird) has a black-and-
white, candlelit **Upstairs Bar** designed for

those who want a quick tipple before dinner or the theatre, while the **Downstairs
Bar** (open from 5pm), with its sit-down bar
and art-deco sofas, is a place to hang out.
There's live jazz and blues at the weekend.
Cocktails are £10 to £12 and light meals
(oysters, steak tartare, baguettes) £5 to £9.
Swift's whisky collection numbered 235 at
last count.

EXPERIMENTAL COCKTAIL
CLUB
COCKTAIL BAR

Map p440 (☎07825 215877; www.experimental
cocktailclublondon.com; 13a Gerrard St, W1;
◷6pm-3am Mon-Sat, to midnight Sun; ☎;
◉Leicester Sq, Piccadilly Circus) The three-floor
ECC is a sensational cocktail bar in Chinatown with an unmarked, shabby green door
(it's next to the Four Seasons restaurant).
The interior, with its soft lighting, mirrors,
bare brick wall and distressed furnishings,
matches the sophistication of the cocktails:
rare and original spirits, vintage Champagne and homemade fruit syrups. Reservations not essential, but there's a £5 cover
charge after 11pm.

YARD
GAY

Map p440 (☎020-7437 2652; www.yardbar.
co.uk; 57 Rupert St, W1; ◷4-11.30pm Mon & Tue,
noon-11.30pm Wed & Thu, noon-midnight Fri &
Sat, 1-10.30pm Sun; ◉Piccadilly Circus) This
Soho favourite attracts a cross-section of
the great and the good. It's fairly attitude-
free, perfect for pre-club drinks or just an
evening out. There are DJs upstairs in the
renovated **Loft Bar** most nights as well as
a friendly crowd in the open-air (heated in
season) **Courtyard Bar** below.

BAR TERMINI
BAR

Map p440 (☎07860 945018; www.bar-termini.
com; 7 Old Compton St, W1; ◷10am-11.30pm Mon-
Thu, to 1am Fri & Sat, to 10.30pm Sun; ◉Leices-
ter Sq, Tottenham Court Rd) Cool and assured,
this tiny Soho cafe-bar is a neat choice for a
Negroni (the speciality) or a house cocktail
(from £9), but you won't need long to ponder
the wine list (three varieties) or beer choice
(one – piccolo Peroni). Staff are attentive
and helpful, but it's recommended that you
book a table (one-hour slots) as it's generally
seating only. The coffee here is tip-top too,
as is the cheese and charcuterie menu.

JEWEL PICCADILLY
COCKTAIL BAR

Map p440 (☎020-74394990; www.jewelpiccadilly.
co.uk; 4-6 Glasshouse St, W1; ◷noon-1am;

Piccadilly Circus) Quite a find, this multi-room oasis of a cocktail bar with distressed brick walls and chandeliers is just off Piccadilly Circus. There's bar food (£5 to £12), cocktails (from £9.50) and a post-work happy hour weekdays from 4pm to 8pm. DJs take up residence later in the evening. Good fun!

TWO FLOORS
BAR

Map p440 (020-7439 1007; www.twofloors. com; 3 Kingly St, W1; ☺noon-11.30pm Mon-Thu, to midnight Fri & Sat, to 10.30pm Sun; ☻Oxford Circus, Piccadilly Circus) It's not surprising that this chilled spot has managed to stay off the lager-lout radar screen without a sign outside. The Pacific bar on the main floor has a cool bar and tables but, as suckers for anything Polynesian (grass skirts, poi, aloha), we head straight downstairs to the Tiki bar for a maitai or a zombie (£7.50 to £9). Enter from Kingly St or Kingly Court.

G-A-Y LATE
CLUB

Map p440 (020-7437 0479; www.facebook. com/G.A.Y.late.Bar; 5 Goslett Yard, WC2; ☺11pm-3am Mon-Thu, 10.30pm-3am Fri-Sun; ☻Tottenham Court Rd) This hugely popular lesbian and gay bar and club with a late licence plays pop and other nonsense (Donna Summer's' Last Dance') till the wee hours.

CAHOOTS
COCKTAIL BAR

Map p440 (020-7352 6200; www.cahoots-london.com; 13 Kingly Street, W1; ☺5pm-1am Mon-Wed, 4pm-2am Thu, 4pm-3am Fri, 1pm-3am Sat, 3pm-midnight Sun; ☻Oxford Street) All aboard the nostalgia train, and mind the gap: Cahoots is a retro cocktail bar in the Kingly Court shopping and foodie centre themed on the Underground and wartime London. The cocktails come in teacup and saucer and the bar snacks – crisps and salad cream sandwich, anyone? – in ration trays. It is madly popular, so book in advance.

Cahoots is not the easiest place to find; you can also enter from Beak St.

APE & BIRD
PUB

Map p438 (020-7836 3119; www.apeandbird.com; 142 Shaftesbury Ave, WC2; ☺11.30am-11.30pm Mon-Fri, 10am-11.30pm Sat, 10am-10.30pm Sun; ☎; ☻Leicester Sq) This excellent pub right on Cambridge Circus, where Covent Garden abuts Soho, has teamed up with Polpo (p113) and offers that chain's full range of Italian 'tapas'. But punters still come for the comprehensive craft beer, spirit and wine selection. Ranged around a large copper bar, Ape & Bird has artfully distressed walls and exposed pipes, with large windows giving on to Shaftesbury Ave. For cocktails head for the dive bar downstairs.

VILLAGE
GAY

Map p440 (020-7478 0530; www.village-soho. co.uk; 81 Wardour St, W1; ☺5pm-1am Mon & Tue, to 2am Wed-Sat, to 11.30pm Sun; ☻Piccadilly Circus) The Village is always up for a party, whatever the night of the week. There are karaoke nights, 'discolicious' nights, go-go-dancer nights – take your pick. And if you can't wait until the clubs open to strut your stuff, there's a dance floor downstairs, complete with pole, of course. Open till 3am on the last weekend of the month.

DOG & DUCK
PUB

Map p440 (020-7494 0697; www.nicholsons pubs.co.uk/restaurants/london/thedoganddduck-soholondon; 18 Bateman St, W1; ☺11am-11pm Mon-Sat, noon-10pm Sun; ☻Tottenham Court Rd) With a fine array of real ales, some stunning Victorian glazed tiling and garrulous crowds spilling onto the pavement, the Dog & Duck has attracted a host of famous regulars, including painters John Constable and pre-Raphaelite Dante Gabrielle Rossetti, dystopian writer George Orwell and musician Madonna.

SHE SOHO
LESBIAN

Map p438 (020-7287 5041; www.she-soho. com; 23a Old Compton St, W1D; ☺4-11.30pm Mon-Thu, noon-midnight Fri & Sat, noon-10.30pm Sun; ☻Leicester Sq) This intimate and dimly lit basement bar has DJs, comedy, cabaret, burlesque, live music and party nights. Open till 3am on the last Friday and Saturday of the month. Everybody is welcome at this friendly place.

FRENCH HOUSE SOHO
PUB

Map p440 (020-7437 2477; www.french housesoho.com; 49 Dean St, W1; ☺noon-11pm Mon-Sat, to 10.30pm Sun; ☻Leicester Sq) French House is Soho's legendary boho boozer with a history to match: this was the meeting place of the Free French Forces during WWII, and de Gaulle is said to have drunk here often, while Dylan Thomas, Peter O'Toole and Francis Bacon all ended up on the wooden floor at least once.

DUKE OF WELLINGTON   GAY

Map p440 (☑020-7439 1274; www.facebook.com/Duke.Of.Welly; 77 Wardour St, W1; ⊘noon-midnight Mon & Wed-Sat, 11am-11pm Tue, noon-11.30pm Sun; ◉Leicester Sq) This seasoned pub off Old Compton St is often busy but has few pretensions, attracting a more beardy, fun-loving gay crowd, many of whom gather outside in warmer months.

🍷 Covent Garden & Leicester Square

★LAMB & FLAG   PUB

Map p438 (☑020-7497 9504; www.lambandflag coventgarden.co.uk; 33 Rose St, WC2; ⊘11am-11pm Mon-Sat, noon-10.30pm Sun; ◉Covent Garden) Everybody's favourite pub in central London, pint-sized Lamb & Flag is full of charm and history, and is on the site of a pub that dates from at least 1772. Rain or shine, you'll have to elbow your way to the bar through the merry crowd drinking outside. Inside are brass fittings and creaky wooden floors.

A few centuries ago, the pub was called The Bucket of Blood for its bare-knuckle fighting; indeed the poet John Dryden was mugged in the adjoining alleyway in December 1679. The main entrance is at the top of tiny, cobbled Rose St, but you can also reach it from the backstreet donkey path called Lazenby Ct that'll transport you back to Dickensian London.

TERROIRS   WINE BAR

Map p438 (☑020-7036 0660; www.terroirswine bar.com; 5 William IV St, WC2; ⊘noon-11pm Mon-Sat; 🛜; ◉Charing Cross Rd) A fab two-floor spot for a pre-theatre glass and some expertly created charcuterie, with informative staff, tempting and affordable lunch specials (£10), a lively, convivial atmosphere and a breathtaking list of organic, natural and biodynamic wines.

SALISBURY   PUB

Map p438 (☑020-7836 5863; www.taylor-walker. co.uk/pub/salisbury-covent-garden/c3111; 90 St Martin's Lane, WC2; ⊘11am-12.30pm Mon-Sat, noon-11pm Sun; ◉Leicester Sq) Brave the crowds at this centrally located pub established in 1898 just to see the beautifully etched and engraved windows and other Victorian features that have somehow escaped the developer's hand. It has a vast range of beers, including lots of cask ales and some rarer continental lagers.

KU KLUB LISLE ST   GAY

Map p440 (☑020-7437 4303; www.ku-bar.co.uk; 30 Lisle St, WC2; ⊘noon-3am Mon-Sat, to midnight Sun; ◉Leicester Sq) With its smart interior and busy events schedule (disco, cabaret, DJ sets etc) in the club basement, the Lisle St branch of this gay mini-chain attracts a young, fun-loving crowd. Sunday is retro night.

🍷 Holborn & The Strand

★AMERICAN BAR   COCKTAIL BAR

Map p438 (☑020-7836 4343; www.fairmont. com/savoy-london/dining/americanbar; Savoy, The Strand, WC2; ⊘11.30am-midnight Mon-Sat, noon-midnight Sun; ◉Covent Garden) Home of the Hanky Panky, White Lady and other classic infusions created en situ, the seriously dishy and elegant American Bar is an icon of London, with soft blue and rust art-deco lines and live piano music. Cocktails start at £16.50 and peak at a stupefying £5000 (the Original Sazerac, containing Sazerac de Forge cognac from 1857).

Fabulous celebrity photos and memorabilia adorn the walls.

CRAFT BEER COMPANY   CRAFT BEER

Map p438 (☑020-7240 0431; www.thecraft beerco.com/covent-garden; 168 High Holborn, WC1; ⊘noon-midnight Sun-Wed, to 1am Thu-Sat; ◉Tottenham Court Rd) Probably the best place to go in London to enjoy craft beer, this branch of a six-strong chain boasts 15 cask pumps of UK-sourced beers as well as 30 keg lines and 200-plus bottles and cans of beers from around the world. Most pints are under £5.

RADIO ROOFTOP BAR   ROOFTOP BAR

Map p438 (☑020-7395 3440; ME London, 10th fl, 336-337 The Strand, WC2; ⊘noon-1am Mon-Wed, to 2am Thu-Sat, noon-midnight Sun; ◉Temple, Covent Garden) This stunner of an art-deco cocktail bar (drinks from £13) offers gorgeous views, especially of the Thames, South Bank and Trafalgar Sq, from the terrace on the 10th floor of the ME London (p347).

HOLBORN WHIPPET   PUB

Map p438 (www.holbornwhippet.com; 25-29 Sicilian Ave, WC1; ⊘noon-11.30pm Mon-Sat, to 10.30pm Sun; ◉Holborn) Tiny, all wood and at the end of a pedestrian-only street, this hideaway stocks a commendable range of ales and lagers from small craft breweries (we counted 15 from the keg and the tap). Staff are more than keen to offer a taste from the spouts on the 'brick wall' to help you decide.

PRINCESS LOUISE
PUB

Map p438 (☑020-7405 8816; http://princess louisepub.co.uk; 208 High Holborn, WC1; ⓧ11am-11pm Mon-Fri, noon-11pm Sat, noon-6.45pm Sun; ⊜Holborn) The ground-floor saloon of this pub dating from 1872 is spectacularly decorated with a riot of fine tiles, etched mirrors, plasterwork and a stunning central horseshoe bar. The old Victorian wood partitions give drinkers plenty of nooks and alcoves to hide in, and the frosted-glass 'snob screens' add further period allure.

The Princess Louise is a tied house owned by Samuel Smith Brewery.

GORDON'S WINE BAR
BAR

Map p438 (☑020-7930 1408; www.gordonswine bar.com; 47 Villiers St, WC2; ⓧ11am-11pm Mon-Sat, noon-10pm Sun; ⊜Embankment, Charing Cross) Cavernous, candlelit and atmospheric, Gordon's (founded in 1890) is a victim of its own success – it's relentlessly busy and unless you arrive before the office crowd does (around 6pm), forget about landing a table. The French and New World wines are heady and reasonably priced; buy by the glass, the beaker (12CL), the schooner (15CL) or the bottle.

You can nibble on bread, cheese and olives, and there's outside garden seating in the warmer months.

SEVEN STARS
PUB

Map p438 (☑020-7242 8521; 53-54 Carey St, WC2; ⓧ11am-11pm Mon-Fri, noon-11pm Sat, to 10.30pm Sun; ⊜Holborn, Temple) Even though it's packed with lawyers in the after-office booze rush hour, the tiny Seven Stars is still a relative secret to many Londoners. Sitting between Lincoln's Inn Fields and the Royal Courts of Justice, and originally a sailors' hang-out, this is the place to come for real ale and ravishing game dishes like guinea fowl (£12) and Irish stew (£11.50).

The eccentric landlady and chef, Roxy Beaujolais, is a former TV chef and raconteur.

HEAVEN
CLUB, GAY

Map p438 (http://heaven-live.co.uk; Villiers St, WC2; ⓧ11pm-5am Mon, Thu & Fri, 10pm-5am Sat; ⊜Embankment, Charing Cross) This perennially popular gay club under the arches beneath Charing Cross station is host to excellent live gigs and club nights. Monday's Popcorn (mixed dance party, with an all-welcome door policy) offers one of the best weeknight's clubbing in the capital. The celebrated G-A-Y takes place here on Thursday (G-A-Y Porn Idol), Friday (G-A-Y Camp Attack) and Saturday (plain ol' G-A-Y).

POLSKI BAR
BAR

Map p438 (☑020-7831 9679; www.facebook.com/barpolskilondon; 11 Little Turnstile, WC1; ⓧ4-11pm Mon, 12.30-11pm Tue-Thu, 12.30-11.30pm Fri, 6-11pm Sat; ⊜Holborn) With around 60 different types of vodka – from hazelnut to wheat-flavoured, and simple old *slivowica* (plum brandy) to kosher – everyone should find something that tickles their taste buds. There's also great Polish food like *bigos* (hunter's stew) and *pierogis* (dumplings), but the bare, cold interior leaves something to be desired.

🍸 Marylebone

ARTESIAN
BAR

Map p446 (☑020-7636 1000; www.artesian-bar.co.uk; Langham Hotel, 1c Portland Pl, W1; ⓧ11am-2am Mon-Sat, to midnight Sun; ⊜Oxford Circus) For a dose of colonial glamour with a touch of Oriental elegance, the sumptuous bar at the Langham hits the mark, though it's often packed. Its cocktails (£17) have won multiple awards.

PURL
COCKTAIL BAR

Map p446 (☑020-7935 0835; www.purl-london.com; 50-54 Blandford St, W1; ⓧ5-11.30pm Mon-Thu, to midnight Fri & Sat; ⊜Baker St, Bond St) Purl is a fabulous underground drinking den. Decked out in vintage furniture, it serves original and intriguingly named cocktails and a punch of the day. It's all subdued lighting and hushed-tone conversations, which only adds to the mysterious air. Bookings recommended. Sounds come from the jazz/blues stable, while live jazz is on the cards Wednesday night.

GOLDEN EAGLE
PUB

Map p446 (☑020-7935 3228; 59 Marylebone Lane, W1; ⓧ11am-11pm Mon-Sat, noon-10.30pm Sun; ⊜Bond St, Baker St) If you are seriously into singalongs, head for this attractive freehouse in Marylebone, where the keys of the honky-tonk piano get tickled by Tony 'Fingers' Pearson from 8.30pm to 10.30pm on Tuesday and to 11pm Thursday and Friday. Usually attracts a fun (if boisterous) crowd.

📍 Mayfair

★ AMERICAN BAR   BAR

Map p446 (www.thebeaumont.com/dining/ameri can-bar; The Beaumont, Brown Hart Gardens, W1; ⊙11.30am-midnight Mon-Sat, to 11pm Sun; 🛜; ☻Bond St) Sip a bourbon or a classic cocktail in the classic 1930s art-deco ambience of this stylish bar at the hallmark Beaumont (p346) hotel. It's central, period and like a gentleman's club, but far from stuffy. Only a few years old, the American Bar feels like it's been pouring drinks since the days of the flapper and jazz age.

GALVIN AT WINDOWS   BAR

Map p446 (📞020-7208 4021; www.galvinat windows.com; London Hilton on Park Lane, 28th fl, 22 Park Lane, W1; ⊙11am-1am Mon-Wed, to 2am Thu & Fri, 3pm-2am Sat, 11am-10.30pm Sun; 🛜; ☻Hyde Park Corner) From the 28th floor of the London Hilton on Park Lane, this swish bar gazes on to awesome views, especially come dusk. Cocktail prices reach similar heights (£10 to £18), but the leather seats are inviting and the marble bar is gorgeous. The one-Michelin-star restaurant (same views) offers a giveaway weekday lunch menu (two/three courses £30/35). Dress code is smart casual.

CONNAUGHT BAR   COCKTAIL BAR

Map p446 (📞020-7314 3419; www.the-connaught. co.uk/mayfair-bars/connaught-bar; Connaught Hotel, Carlos Pl, W1; ⊙11am-1am Mon-Sat, to midnight Sun; ☻Bond St) Drinkers who know their stuff single out the travelling Martini trolley for particular praise, but almost everything at this sumptuous bar at the exclusive and very British Connaught Hotel gets the nod: lavish art-deco-inspired lines, faultless and cheerful service, and some of the best drinks in town. Cocktails, classic and those given a thoroughly contemporary twist, start at £18. Dress at the Connaught Bar is smart casual.

PUNCH BOWL   PUB

Map p446 (📞020-7493 6841; www.punchbowl london.com; 41 Farm St, W1; ⊙noon-11pm Mon-Sat, to 10.30pm Sun; ☻Green Park) The Grade II–listed Punch Bowl attracts a young and happening crowd sipping cask ales, fine wines and whisky rather than run-of-the-mill pints. The pub retains many of its original 18th-century features (wood panels, cornicing etc), although the dining room at the back (mains £14 to £19.50) has a more modern feel to it.

☆ ENTERTAINMENT

The West End is not only where you'll find the lion's share of London's theatres – 40 out of 215 – but also the city's two opera houses. Cinemas and comedy clubs abound, and the doyen of jazz clubs, Ronnie Scott' s (p127), is also here.

★ WIGMORE HALL   CLASSICAL MUSIC

Map p446 (www.wigmore-hall.org.uk; 36 Wigmore St, W1; ☻Bond St) This is one of the best and most active (more than 400 concerts a year) classical-music venues in town, not only because of its fantastic acoustics, beautiful art nouveau hall and great variety of concerts and recitals, but also because of the sheer standard of the performances. Built in 1901, it has remained one of the world's top places for chamber music.

★ PIZZA EXPRESS JAZZ CLUB   JAZZ

Map p440 (📞020-7439 4962; www.pizzaexpress live.com/venues/soho-jazz-club; 10 Dean St, W1; tickets £15-40; ☻Tottenham Court Rd) Pizza Express has been one of the best jazz venues in London since opening in 1969. It may be a strange arrangement, in a basement beneath a branch of the chain restaurant, but it's highly popular. Lots of big names perform here and promising artists such as Norah Jones, Gregory Porter and the late Amy Winehouse played here in their early days.

Times vary according to the day but doors are usually open at 7pm, with shows starting at 8.30pm. Check the website.

ROYAL OPERA HOUSE   OPERA

Map p438 (📞020-7304 4000; www.roh.org.uk; Bow St, WC2; tickets £4-270; ☻Covent Garden) Classic opera in London has a fantastic setting on Covent Garden Piazza and coming here for a night is a sumptuous – if pricey – affair. Although the program has been fluffed up by modern influences, the main attractions are still the opera and classical ballet – all are wonderful productions and feature world-class performers.

Midweek matinees are usually cheaper than evening performances, and restricted-view seats cost as little as £4. Discounted tickets for each day of the week (two per customer available to the first 49 people in the queue) priced from £4 to £68 go on sale on Friday at 1pm; students must apply for special standby tickets (£10) by email. Half-price standby tickets four hours before the performance are very occasionally available. Free lunchtime recitals are held on Mondays, when possible, in the Crush Room or Paul Hamlyn Hall, depending on the program, though ongoing building works have recently seen the venue moved to the nearby Swiss Church London at 79 Endell St.

THE PLACE
DANCE

Map p444 (☑020-7121 1100; www.theplace.org. uk; 17 Duke's Rd, WC1; ⊜Euston Sq) The birthplace of modern British dance is one of London's most exciting cultural venues, still concentrating on challenging and experimental choreography. Behind the late-Victorian terracotta facade you'll find a 300-seat theatre, an arty, creative cafe atmosphere and a dozen training studios. Tickets usually cost from £15.

PRINCE CHARLES CINEMA
CINEMA

Map p440 (www.princecharlescinema.com; 7 Leicester Pl, WC2; tickets £8-16; ⊜Leicester Sq) Leicester Sq cinema-ticket prices are very high, so wait until the first-runs have moved to the Prince Charles, central London's cheapest cinema, where non-members pay only £9 to £11.50 for new releases. Also on the cards are mini-festivals, Q&As with film directors, classics, sleepover movie marathons and exuberant sing-along screenings of films like *Frozen*, *The Sound of Music* and *Rocky Horror Picture Show* (£16).

ENGLISH NATIONAL OPERA
OPERA

Map p438 (ENO; ☑020-7845 9300; www.eno.org; St Martin's Lane, WC2; ⊜Leicester Sq) The English National Opera is celebrated for making opera modern and more relevant, as all productions are sung in English. It's based at the impressive London Coliseum, built in 1904 and lovingly restored a century later. The English National Ballet also does regular performances at the Coliseum. Tickets range from £12 to £125.

POETRY CAFÉ
PERFORMING ARTS

Map p438 (☑020-7420 9888; www.poetry society.org.uk; 22 Betterton St, WC2; ⊜11am-11pm Mon-Fri, from 7pm Sat; ⊜Covent Garden) Covent Garden's renovated Poetry Café is a favourite for lovers of verse. It has almost daily readings and performances by established poets, open-mic evenings and writing workshops.

RONNIE SCOTT'S
JAZZ

Map p440 (☑020-7439 0747; www.ronniescotts. co.uk; 47 Frith St, W1; ⊜7pm-3am Mon-Sat, 1-4pm & 8pm-midnight Sun; ⊜Leicester Sq, Tottenham Court Rd) Ronnie Scott's jazz club opened at this address in 1965 and became widely known as Britain's best. Support acts are at 7pm, with main gigs at 8.15pm (8pm Sunday) and a second house at 11.15pm Friday and Saturday (check ahead though). The more informal Late, Late Show runs from 1am to 3am. Expect to pay from £25 upwards; the Late, Late Show and Sunday lunch shows are just £10.

Ronnie Scott's has hosted such luminaries as Miles Davis, Charlie Parker, Thelonious Monk, Ella Fitzgerald, Count Basie and Sarah Vaughan. The club continues to build upon its formidable reputation by hosting a range of big names and new talent. The atmosphere is great, but talking during music is a big no-no.

COMEDY STORE
COMEDY

Map p440 (☑0844 871 7699; www.thecomedy store.co.uk; 1a Oxendon St, SW1; tickets £8-22.50; ⊜Piccadilly Circus) This is one of the first (and still one of the best) comedy clubs in London. Wednesday and Sunday night's Comedy Store Players are the most famous improvisation outfit in town, with the wonderful Josie Lawrence, now a veteran of two decades. On Thursdays, Fridays and Saturdays, Best in Stand Up features the best on London's comedy circuit.

BORDERLINE
LIVE MUSIC

Map p440 (☑020-7734 5547; http://border line.london; Orange Yard, off Manette St, W1; ⊜Tottenham Court Rd) Through the hard-to-find entrance off Orange Yard and down into the basement you'll find a packed, 275-capacity venue that really punches above its weight. Read the gig list: Ed Sheeran, REM, Blur, Counting Crows, PJ Harvey, Lenny Kravitz and Pearl Jam, plus anonymous indie outfits, have all played here. The crowd's equally diverse but can contain music journos and record-company talent spotters.

100 CLUB
LIVE MUSIC

Map p444 (📞020-7636 0933; www.the100club. co.uk; 100 Oxford St, W1; tickets £8-20; ⊖check website for gig times; ⊖Oxford Circus, Tottenham Court Rd) This heritage London venue at the same address for over a half-century started off as a jazz club but now leans towards rock. Back in the day it showcased Chris Barber, BB King and the Rolling Stones, and it was at the centre of the punk revolution and the '90s indie scene. It hosts dancing gigs, the occasional big name, where-are-they-now bands and top-league tributes.

AMUSED MOOSE SOHO
COMEDY

Map p440 (📞box office 020-7287 3727; www. amusedmoose.com; Sanctum Soho Hotel, 20 Warwick St, W1; ⊖Piccadilly Circus, Oxford Circus) One of the city's best clubs, the peripatetic Amused Moose (the cinema in the Sanctum Soho Hotel is just one of its hosting venues) is popular with audiences and comedians alike, perhaps helped along by the fact that heckling is 'unacceptable' and all the acts are 'first-date friendly' (ie unlikely to humiliate the front row). Shows are usually at 8.15pm on Saturday.

ROYAL BALLET
BALLET

Map p438 (www.roh.org.uk; ⊖Covent Garden) Although the Royal Ballet's program has been altered by modern influences, classical ballet is still its bread and butter. This is where to head if you want to see traditional performances such as *Giselle* or *Romeo & Juliet* performed by established dancers. They're based at the Royal Opera House (p134).

DONMAR WAREHOUSE
THEATRE

Map p438 (📞0844 871 7624; www.donmarware house.com; 41 Earlham St, WC2; ⊖Covent Garden) The cosy Donmar Warehouse is London's 'thinking person's theatre'. Current artistic director Josie Rourke has staged some intriguing and successful productions, including the well-received comedy *My Night with Reg*, George Bernard Shaw's *St Joan* and the political drama *Limehouse* by Steve Waters.

ICA CINEMA
CINEMA

Map 448# (📞020-7930 3647; www.ica.art/ whats-on/films; Nash House, The Mall, SW1; ⊖Charing Cross, Piccadilly Circus) The Institute of Contemporary Arts (ICA) is a treasure for lovers of indie cinema – its program always has material no one else is showing, such as the latest independents from the developing world, films showing out of season, all-night screenings and rare documentaries. The two cinemas are quite small, but comfortable enough. Tickets usually cost £6 to £11.

CURZON SOHO
CINEMA

Map p440 (www.curzoncinemas.com; 99 Shaftesbury Ave, W1; tickets £8-15; ⊖Leicester Sq, Piccadilly Circus) The Curzon Soho is one of London's best cinemas. It has a fantastic program line-up with the best of British, European, US and world indie films; regular Q&As with directors; shorts and mini festivals; a cafe on the ground floor with cakes to die for; and an ultra-comfortable bar upstairs.

SOHO THEATRE
COMEDY

Map p440 (📞020-7478 0100; www.sohotheatre. com; 21 Dean St, W1; tickets £8-25; ⊖Tottenham Court Rd) The Soho Theatre has developed a superb reputation for showcasing new comedy-writing talent and comedians. It's also hosted some top-notch stand-up or sketch-based comedians including Alexei Sayle and Doctor Brown, plus cabaret. Staff don't always seem to get the joke.

🛍 SHOPPING

The West End's shopping scene hardly needs a formal introduction. Oxford St is heaven or hell, depending on what you're after. It's all about chains, from Marks & Spencer to H&M, Top Shop to Gap. Covent Garden is also beset by run-of-the-mill outlets, but they tend to be smaller and counterbalanced by independent boutiques, vintage ones in particular. As well as fashion, the West End is big on music and books, with some great independent shops specialising in both.

🏛 Westminster & St James's

⭐ FORTNUM & MASON
DEPARTMENT STORE

Map p448 (📞020-7734 8040; www.fortnumand mason.com; 181 Piccadilly, W1; ⊙10am-8pm Mon-Sat, 11.30am-6pm Sun; ⊖Piccadilly Circus) With its classic eau-de-nil (pale green) colour scheme, 'the Queen's grocery store' established in 1707 refuses to yield to modern times. Its staff – men and women – still wear old-fashioned tailcoats and its glamorous food hall is supplied with hampers, cut marmalade, speciality teas, superior fruitcakes and so forth. Fortnum & Mason remains the quintessential London shopping experience.

HATCHARDS
BOOKS

Map p448 (☏020-7439 9921; www.hatchards.co.uk; 187 Piccadilly, W1; ⊗9.30am-8pm Mon-Sat, noon-6.30pm Sun; ⊖Green Park, Piccadilly Circus) London's oldest bookshop dates back to 1797. Holding three royal warrants, it's a stupendous bookshop now in the Waterstones stable, with a solid supply of signed editions and bursting at its smart seams with very browsable stock. There's a strong selection of first editions on the ground floor and regularly scheduled literary events.

WATERSTONES PICCADILLY
BOOKS

Map p448 (☏020-7851 2433; www.waterstones.com; 203-206 Piccadilly, W1; ⊗9am-9.30pm Mon-Sat, noon-5pm Sun; ⊖Piccadilly Circus) The chain's megastore is the largest bookshop in Europe, with helpful, knowledgeable staff and regular author readings, signings and discussions. The store spreads across eight floors, with a fabulous rooftop bar–restaurant, 5th View (p109), and Cafe W in the basement.

PENHALIGON'S
PERFUME

Map p448 (☏020-7629 1416; www.penhaligons.com; 16-17 Burlington Arcade, W1; ⊗10am-6pm Mon-Fri, 9.30am-6.30pm Sat, 11.30am-5.30pm Sun; ⊖Piccadilly Circus, Green Park) Located in the historic Burlington Arcade (p98), Penhaligon's is a classic British perfumery. Attendants enquire about your favourite smells, take you on an exploratory tour of the shop's signature range and help you discover new scents in their traditional perfumes, home fragrances and bath and body products. Everything is produced in England.

PAXTON & WHITFIELD
FOOD & DRINKS

Map p448 (☏020-7930 0259; www.paxtonandwhitfield.co.uk; 93 Jermyn St, W1; ⊗10am-6.30pm Mon-Sat, 11am-5pm Sun; ⊖Piccadilly Circus, Green Park) With modest beginnings as an Aldwych stall in 1742 and purveying a dizzying range of fine cheeses, this black- and gold-fronted shop holds two royal warrants. Whatever your cheese leanings, you'll find the shop well supplied with

hard and soft cheeses as well as blue and washed-rind examples.

TAYLOR OF OLD BOND STREET
COSMETICS

Map p448 (☏020-7930 5321; www.tayloroldbondst.co.uk; 74 Jermyn St, SW1; ⊗8.30am-6pm Mon-Sat; ⊖Green Park, Piccadilly Circus) Plying its trade since the mid-19th century, this shop supplies the 'well-groomed gentleman' with every sort of razor, shaving brush and scent of shaving soap imaginable – not to mention oils, soaps and other bath products.

BROWNS
CLOTHING

Map p446 (☏020-7629 1416; www.brownsfashion.com; 23-27 South Molton St, W1; ⊗10am-7pm Mon-Wed & Sat, to 8pm Thu & Fri, noon-6pm Sun; ⊖Bond St) Edgy and exciting, this parade of shops on upmarket South Molton St is full of natty and individual clothing ideas and shoes from Ashish, Stella Jean, Natasha Zinko and other creative designers.

🏠 Bloomsbury & Fitzrovia

JAMES SMITH & SONS
FASHION & ACCESSORIES

Map p444 (☏020-7836 4731; www.james-smith.co.uk; 53 New Oxford St, WC1; ⊗10am-5.45pm Mon, Tue, Thu & Fri, 10.30am-5.45pm Wed, 10am-5.15pm Sat; ⊖Tottenham Court Rd) Nobody makes and stocks such elegant umbrellas (not to mention walking sticks and canes) as this place. It's been fighting the British weather from the same address since 1857 and, thanks to London's ever-present downpours, will hopefully do great business for years to come. Prices start at around £40 for a pocket umbrella.

SCANDINAVIAN KITCHEN
FOOD

Map p444 (☏020-7580 7161; www.scandikitchen.co.uk; 61 Great Titchfield St, W1; ⊗8am-7pm Mon-Fri, 10am-6pm Sat, 10am-4pm Sun; ⊖Oxford Circus) Scandinavian Kitchen was established by a homesick Dane and Swede who couldn't find authentic Scandinavian food in London. The small shop, which specialises in Nordic cuisine, doubles as a cafe and serves some of the best open sandwiches (£5.95 to £8.50) in the city.

JARNDYCE
BOOKS

Map p444 (☏020-7631 4220; www.jarndyce.co.uk; 46 Great Russell St, WC1; ⊗11am-5.30pm Mon-Fri; ⊖Tottenham Court Rd) Named after a court case in Charles Dickens' *Bleak House*, this antiquarian bookshop is opposite the

British Museum in a building dating from the early 18th century. It specialises in literature from around that period – particularly Dickens – but is packed with other affordable curiosities.

LONDON REVIEW BOOKSHOP BOOKS

Map p444 (☎020-7269 9030; www.london reviewbookshop.co.uk; 14 Bury Pl, WC1; ☺10am-6.30pm Mon-Sat, noon-6pm Sun; ⊖Holborn) The flagship bookshop of the *London Review of Books* fortnightly literary journal doesn't put faith in towering piles of books and slabs on shelves, but offers a wide range of titles in a handful of copies only. It often hosts high-profile author talks (tickets usually £10), and there's a charming cafe where you can leaf through your new purchases.

FORBIDDEN PLANET COMICS

Map p438 (☎020-7420 3666; www.forbidden planet.com; 179 Shaftesbury Ave, WC2; ☺10am-7pm Mon & Tue, to 7.30pm Wed, Fri & Sat, to 8pm Thu, noon-6pm Sun; ⊖Tottenham Court Rd) Forbidden Planet is a trove of comics, sci-fi, horror and fantasy literature, as well as action figures and toys, spread over two floors. It's an absolute dream for anyone into manga comics, off-beat genre titles, and sci-fi and fantasy memorabilia.

FOLK FASHION & ACCESSORIES

Map p444 (☎men's 020-7404 6458, women's 020-8616 4191; www.folkclothing.com; 49 Lamb's Conduit St, WC1; ☺11am-7pm Mon-Fri, 10am-6pm Sat, noon-5pm Sun; ⊖Holborn) Offers simple but strikingly styled casual clothes, often in bold colours and with a handcrafted feel. Head for No 49 for Folk's own line of menswear and to nearby No 53 for womenswear.

GAY'S THE WORD BOOKS

Map p444 (☎020-7278 7654; www.gaystheword. co.uk; 66 Marmont St, WC1; ☺10am-6.30pm Mon-Sat, 2-6pm Sun; ⊖Russell Sq) This London gay institution has been selling books nobody else stocks since 1979, with a superb range of gay- and lesbian-interest books and magazines plus a real community spirit. Used books available as well.

PERSEPHONE BOOKS BOOKS

Map p444 (☎020-7242 9292; www.persephone books.co.uk; 59 Lamb's Conduit St, WC1; ☺10am-6pm Mon-Fri, noon-5pm Sat; ⊖Russell Sq) This charming and very low-key bookshop sells works published by independent Bloomsbury publishers, most of which are reprints

of neglected fiction and nonfiction by early to mid-20th-century women writers. There are some lovely gift items here, including porcelain repros of London Blue Plaques.

BLADE RUBBER STAMPS ARTS & CRAFTS

Map 444# (☎020-7831 4242; www.bladerubber stamps.co.uk; 12 Bury Pl, WC1; ☺10.30am-6pm Mon-Sat, 11.30am-4.30pm Sun; ⊖Holborn) Just south of the British Museum, this specialist shop stocks just about every wooden-handled rubber stamp you care to imagine: from London icons like phone boxes, Beefeaters and the Houses of Parliament to landscapes, planets, rockets and Christmas stamps. They can make you one to your design or you can have a go yourself with a stamp-making kit.

🏠 Soho & Chinatown

HAMLEYS TOYS

Map p440 (☎0371 704 1977; www.hamleys.com; 188-196 Regent St, W1; ☺10am-9pm Mon-Fri, 9.30am-9pm Sat, noon-6pm Sun; ⊖Oxford Circus) Claiming to be the world's oldest (and some say, the largest) toy store, Hamleys moved to its address on Regent St in 1881. From the basement's Star Wars Collection and ground floor where staff blow bubbles and glide foam boomerangs through the air with practised nonchalance to Lego World and a cafe on the 5th floor, it's a rich layer cake of playthings.

LIBERTY DEPARTMENT STORE

Map p440 (☎020-7734 1234; www.liberty.co.uk; Great Marlborough St, W1; ☺10am-8pm Mon-Sat, noon-6pm Sun; ⊖Oxford Circus) An irresistible blend of contemporary styles in an old-fashioned mock-Tudor atmosphere (1875), Liberty has a huge cosmetics department and an accessories floor, along with a breathtaking lingerie section, all at sky-high prices. A classic London gift or souvenir is a Liberty fabric print, especially in the form of a scarf.

GRANT & CUTLER BOOKS

Map p440 (☎020-3206 2640; www.grantand cutler.com; 4th fl, 107 Charing Cross Rd, WC2; ☺9.30am-9pm Mon-Sat, 11.30am-6pm Sun; ⊖Oxford Circus) The UK's largest foreign-language bookseller with titles representing more than 100 languages is located on the 4th floor of Foyles.

FOYLES
BOOKS

Map p440 (☑020-7434 1574; www.foyles.co.uk; 107 Charing Cross Rd, WC2; ⊙9.30am-9pm Mon-Sat, 11.30am-6pm Sun; ⊖Tottenham Court Rd) This is London's most legendary bookshop, where you can bet on finding even the most obscure of titles. Once synonymous with chaos, Foyles got its act together and in 2014 moved just down the road into the spacious former home of Central St Martins art school. Thoroughly redesigned, its stunning new home is a joy to explore.

The cafe is on the 5th floor, where you can also find the Gallery at Foyles for art exhibitions. **Grant & Cutler**, the UK's largest foreign-language bookseller, is on the 4th floor while **Ray's Jazz** is on the 2nd floor.

WE BUILT THIS CITY
GIFTS & SOUVENIRS

Map p440 (☑020-3642 9650; www.webuiltthiscity.com; 56-57 Carnaby St, W1; ⊙10am-7pm Mon-Wed, to 8pm Thu-Sat, noon-6pm Sun; ⊖Oxford Circus) Taking a commendable stand against Union Jack hats and black cab key rings, We Built This City is a shop selling London-themed souvenirs that the recipient might actually want. The products are artistic and thoughtful, and celebrate the city's creative side.

PHONICA
MUSIC

Map p440 (☑020-7025 6070; www.phonica records.co.uk; 51 Poland St, W1; ⊙11.30am-7.30pm Mon-Wed & Sat, to 8pm Thu & Fri, noon-6pm Sun; ⊖Tottenham Court Rd, Oxford Circus) A cool and relaxed shop that stocks a lot of house, electro, hip hop and punk funk mostly on vinyl. You'll also find just about anything from reggae to dub, jazz and rock.

SOUNDS OF THE UNIVERSE
MUSIC

Map p440 (☑020-7734 3430; www.sounds oftheuniverse.com; 7 Broadwick St, W1; ⊙10am-7.30pm Sat, 11.30am-5.30pm Sun; ⊖Oxford Circus, Tottenham Court Rd) Outlet of the Soul Jazz Records label (responsible for many great soul, reggae, funk and electronic albums), this place stocks CDs and vinyl plus some original 45s.

LINA STORES
FOOD

Map p440 (☑020-7437 6482; www.linastores. co.uk; 18 Brewer St, W1; ⊙8.30am-7.30pm Mon & Tue, to 8.30pm Wed-Fri, 9am-7.30pm Sat, 11am-5pm Sun; ⊖Piccadilly Circus) This delightful Italian delicatessen in the heart of Soho, here since 1944, is so gorgeous in its cream and pastel green that you could almost imagine eating it. Come here for picnic cheeses, charcuterie, bread and olives. In fine weather tables line the adjacent alleyway appropriately named Green's Court.

URBAN OUTFITTERS
FASHION & ACCESSORIES

Map p440 (☑020-7907 0800; www.urbanoutfitters.co.uk; 200 Oxford St, W1; ⊙9am-9pm Mon-Sat, noon-6pm Sun; ⊖Oxford Circus) Probably the trendiest of all chains, this cool Philadelphia-based store serves both men and women and has the best young designer T-shirts, an excellent designer area (stocking Angel Chan, MM6, Peter Jensen and Something Else, among others), 'renewed' secondhand pieces, saucy underwear, records, fun homewares and quirky gadgets.

AGENT PROVOCATEUR
CLOTHING

Map p440 (☑020-7439 0229; www.agentprovo cateur.com; 6 Broadwick St, W1; ⊙11am-7pm Mon-Wed, Fri & Sat, 11am-8pm Thu, noon-5pm Sun; ⊖Oxford Circus) For women's lingerie designed to be worn and seen, and certainly *not* hidden, pull up to wonderful Agent Provocateur, originally set up by Joseph Corré, son of Vivienne Westwood. Its sexy and saucy corsets, and bras and nighties for all shapes and sizes, exude confident and positive sexuality. Lovely staff too.

ALGERIAN COFFEE STORES
COFFEE

Map p440 (☑020-7437 2480; www.algcoffee. co.uk; 52 Old Compton St, W1; ⊙9am-7pm Mon-Wed, to 9pm Thu & Fri, to 8pm Sat; ⊖Leicester Sq) Stop for a shot of espresso (£1) or cappuccino (£1.20) while choosing your freshly ground beans from over 80 varieties of coffee and 120 teas at this fantastic shop, caffeinating Soho since 1887.fashion to the youth market affordably and quickly.

TOPSHOP
CLOTHING

Map p440 (☑020-7927 0000; www.topshop. co.uk; 214 Oxford St, W1; ⊙9am-9pm Mon-Sat, 11.30am-6pm Sun; ⊖Oxford Circus) The 'It' store when it comes to clothes and accessories, venturing boldly into couture in recent years, Topshop encapsulates London's supreme skill at bringing catwalk fashion to the youth market affordably and quickly.

🔒 Covent Garden & Leicester Square

STANFORD'S
BOOKS, MAPS

Map p438 (📞020-7836 1321; www.stanfords. co.uk; 12-14 Long Acre, WC2; ⊗9am-8pm Mon-Sat, 11.30am-6pm Sun; ⊜Leicester Sq, Covent Garden) Trading from this address since 1853, this granddaddy of travel bookshops and seasoned seller of maps, guides, globes and literature is a destination in its own right. Ernest Shackleton and David Livingstone and, more recently, Michael Palin and Brad Pitt have all popped in and shopped here.

NEAL'S YARD DAIRY
FOOD

Map p438 (📞020-7240 5700; www.nealsyard dairy.co.uk; 17 Shorts Gardens, WC2; ⊗10am-7pm Mon-Sat; ⊜Covent Garden) A fabulous, fragrant cheese house that would fit in in rural England, this place is proof that Britain can produce top-quality world-class cheeses in most classes. There are more than 70 varieties of English and Irish cheeses that the shopkeepers will let you taste, including independent farmhouse brands. Condiments, pickles, jams and chutneys are also on sale.

CAMBRIDGE SATCHEL COMPANY
FASHION & ACCESSORIES

Map p438 (📞020-3077 1100; www.cambridge satchel.com; 31 James St, WC2; ⊗10am-7pm Mon-Sat, 11am-6pm Sun; ⊜Covent Garden) The classic British leather satchel concept has morphed into a trendy and colourful array of backpacks, totes, clutches, bags, mini satchels and more for men and women.

MOLTON BROWN
COSMETICS

Map p438 (📞020-7240 8383; www.moltonbrown. co.uk; 18 Russell St, WC2; ⊗10am-7pm Mon-Sat, 11am-6pm Sun; ⊜Covent Garden) A fabulously fragrant British natural beauty range, Molton Brown is *the* choice for boutique hotel, posh restaurant and 1st-class airline bathrooms. Its skincare products offer plenty of pampering for both men and women. In this store you can also pick up home accessories.

WATKINS
BOOKS

Map p438 (📞020-7836 2182; www.watkinsbooks. com; 19-21 Cecil Court, WC2; ⊗10.30am-6.30pm Mon-Wed & Fri, 11am-7.30pm Thu & Sat, noon-7pm Sun; ⊜Leicester Sq) More books than you can shake a dreamcatcher at on subjects as wide-ranging as the afterlife, taijiquan, divination, fairies, tarot, the Kabbalah, shamanism, religious spirituality, astrology, Indian philosophy, Tibetan Buddhism, conspiracy theories and more. If you've even the mildest interest in the occult, you could find yourself here for hours.

MONMOUTH COFFEE COMPANY
FOOD & DRINKS

Map p438 (📞020-7232 3010; www.monmouth coffee.co.uk; 27 Monmouth St, WC2; pastry & cakes from £2.50; ⊗8am-6.30pm Mon-Sat; ⊜Tottenham Court Rd, Leicester Sq) Essentially a shop selling beans from just about every coffee-growing country, Monmouth, here since 1978, has wooden alcoves at the back where you can squeeze in and savour blends from around the world as well as cakes from local patisseries.

TED BAKER
FASHION & ACCESSORIES

Map p438 (📞020-7836 7808; www.tedbaker.com; 9-10 Floral St, WC2; ⊗10.30am-7.30pm Mon-Fri, 10am-7pm Sat, noon-6pm Sun; ⊜Covent Garden) The one-time Glasgow-based tailor shop has grown into a superb brand of clothing for both men and women. Ted's forte is its formal wear, with beautiful dresses for women (lots of daring prints and exquisite material) and sharp tailoring for men. The casual collections (denim, beachwear etc) are excellent too.

RECKLESS RECORDS
MUSIC

Map p440 (📞020-7437 4271; www.reckless. co.uk; 30 Berwick St, W1; ⊗10am-7pm; ⊜Oxford Circus, Tottenham Court Rd) This outfit hasn't really changed in spirit since it first opened its doors in 1984. It still stocks secondhand records and CDs, from punk, soul, dance and independent to mainstream.

SISTER RAY
MUSIC

Map p440 (📞020-7734 3297; www.sisterray. co.uk; 75 Berwick St, W1; ⊗10am-8pm Mon-Sat, noon-6pm Sun; ⊜Oxford Circus, Tottenham Court Rd) If you were a fan of the late John Peel on the BBC, this specialist in innovative, experimental and indie music is just right for you. Those of you who have never heard of him will probably also like the shop that 'sells music to the masses'.

🏛 Marylebone

DAUNT BOOKS
BOOKS

Map p446 (⌨020-7224 2295; www.dauntbooks.
co.uk; 83 Marylebone High St, W1; ☺9am-7.30pm
Mon-Sat, 11am-6pm Sun; ☻Baker St) An original
Edwardian bookshop, with oak panels, galleries and gorgeous skylights, Daunt is one
of London's loveliest travel bookshops. It has
two floors and stocks general fiction and
nonfiction titles as well. Helpful, informed
staff.

CATH KIDSTON
FASHION & ACCESSORIES

Map p446 (⌨020-7935 6555; www.cathkidston.
com; 51 Marylebone High St, W1; ☺10am-7pm Mon-
Sat, 11am-5pm Sun; ☻Baker St) If you favour the
preppy look, you'll love Cath Kidston's signature floral prints and vintage-inspired fashion. There's also a range of homewares and
some delightful London-branded gift items.

ABERCROMBIE &
FITCH
FASHION & ACCESSORIES

Map p440 (⌨0844 412 5750; www.abercrombie.
com; 7 Burlington Gardens, W1; ☺10am-8pm
Mon-Sat, noon-6pm Sun; ☻Piccadilly Circus)
All tall wood doors, hip sounds, low lighting and two floors of stylish casual wear
staffed by over-sized lads, A&F is one cool
customer that hasn't waned in popularity.
The shop is busy from the minute it opens
its doors, and at weekends there are sometimes queues through the ground floor.

BUTTON QUEEN
ARTS & CRAFTS

Map p446 (⌨020-7935 1505; www.thebutton
queen.co.uk; 76 Marylebone Lane, W1; ☺10am-
5.30pm Mon-Fri, to 3pm Sat; ☻Bond St) Make a
beeline to this place for all your fastening
needs. It's been in business for more than
60 years and is creaking under the weight
of an absurd variety of buttons, including
ones old enough to qualify as antiques.

POSTCARD TEAS
FOOD & DRINKS

Map p446 (⌨020-7629 3654; www.postcardteas.
com; 9 Dering St, W1; ☺10.30am-6.30pm Mon-Fri,
11am-6.30pm Sat; ☻Bond St) If you know your
longjing from your *pu'er,* or your Nokcha
from your Lotus Lake Green – or wish to
know the differences – Postcard Teas could
be, well, your cup of tea. This small shop specialises in carefully sourced teas and small
producers (15 acres or less) from China, Japan, Vietnam, Korea, Taiwan and India.

SELFRIDGES
DEPARTMENT STORE

Map p446 (⌨0800 123 400; www.selfridges.
com; 400 Oxford St, W1; ☺9.30am-9pm Mon-Sat,
11.30am-6pm Sun; ☻Bond St) Selfridges loves
innovation – it's famed for its inventive window displays by international artists, gala
shows and, above all, its amazing range
of products. It's the trendiest of London's
one-stop shops, with labels such as Alexander McQueen, Tom Ford, Missoni, Victoria
Beckham and so on; an unparalleled food
hall; and Europe's largest cosmetics department.

MULBERRY
FASHION & ACCESSORIES

Map p446 (⌨020-7491 3900; www.mulberry.
com; 50 New Bond St, W1; ☺10am-7pm Mon-Sat,
noon-6pm Sun; ☻Bond St) Mulberry bags are
voluptuous and a massive style statement.
The brand has followed in the footsteps of its
other British design titans like Burberry and
Pringle and modernised itself in recent years.

BURBERRY
FASHION & ACCESSORIES

Map p440 (⌨020-3402 1500; www.burberry.
com; 21-23 New Bond St, SW1; ☺10am-7pm Mon-
Sat, noon-6.30pm Sun; ☻Bond St) The first traditional British brand to reach the heights
of fashion, Burberry is known for its innovative take on classic pieces (eg brightly
coloured trench coat and khaki pants with
large and unusual pockets), its brand check
pattern, and a tailored, groomed look.

JOHN LEWIS
DEPARTMENT STORE

Map p446 (⌨0345 604 9049; www.johnlewis.
co.uk; 300 Oxford St, W1; ☺9.30am-8pm Mon-
Wed, Fri & Sat, to 9pm Thu, 11.30am-6pm Sun;
☻Oxford Circus) 'Never knowingly undersold'
is the motto of this store, whose range of
household goods, fashion and luggage is
better described as reliable rather than cutting edge. And for that reason it's some people's favourite store in the whole wide world.

BEATLES STORE
GIFTS & SOUVENIRS

Map p446 (⌨020-7935 4464; www.beatles
storelondon.co.uk; 230 Baker St, NW1; ☺10am-
6.30pm; ☻Baker St) Fab Four guitar picks,
Abbey Road fridge magnets, Ringo T-shirts,
mop top mugs, Magical Mystery Tour bags,
Yellow Submarine Christmas lights, Help!
posters, alarm clocks...the whole Beatles
shebang. Other artistes (from Bowie and
Queen to Nirvana and Jimi Hendrix) are
represented in their sister shop **It's Only
Rock 'n' Roll** across the street.

STELLA MCCARTNEY
FASHION & ACCESSORIES

Map p446 (020-7518 3100; www.stellamc cartney.com; 30 Bruton St, W1; 10am-7pm Mon-Sat; Bond St, Green Park) Stella McCartney's sharp tailoring, floaty designs, accessible style and 'ethical' approach to fashion (no leather or fur) is very of-the-moment. This three-storey terraced Victorian home is a minimalist showcase for the designer's current collections. Depending on your devotion and wallet, you'll feel at ease or like a trespasser.

MONOCLE SHOP
FASHION & ACCESSORIES

Map p446 (020-7486 8770; www.monocle.com; 2a George St, W1; 11am-7pm Mon-Sat, noon-5pm Sun; Bond St) Run by the people behind the design and international current affairs magazine *Monocle,* this tiny (and attitudy) shop stocks very costly clothing, bags, umbrellas and books (including their own guides). But if you are a fan of minimalist quality design, you'll want to stop by. There's the **Monocle Cafe** not far away too, on Chiltern St.

🔒 Mayfair

VIVIENNE WESTWOOD
FASHION & ACCESSORIES

Map p440 (020-7439 1109; www.vivienne westwood.com; 44 Conduit St, W1; 10am-6pm Mon-Wed, Fri & Sat, to 7pm Thu, noon-5pm Sun; Bond St, Oxford Circus) The designer who created the punk look has always had a reputation for being controversial (she flashed her privates at the paparazzi after receiving her OBE). Thankfully, though, La Westwood continues to design clothes as bold, innovative and provocative as ever, featuring 19th-century-inspired bustiers, wedge shoes, tartan and sharp tailoring.

GINA
SHOES

Map p446 (020-7499 7539; www.gina.com; 119 Mount St, W1; 10am-6pm Mon-Sat, to 7pm Thu, noon-5pm Sun; Bond St) Beyond the quality of leathers and fabrics and gorgeously chic styling, a frequent motif of these beautifully made and elegant British couture women's sling backs, stilettos, court shoes, flat sandals, peep toes and platforms is their glittering Swarovski crystals. Prices start from around £485.

GRAYS ANTIQUES
ANTIQUES

Map p446 (www.graysantiques.com; 58 Davies St, W1; 10am-6pm Mon-Fri, 11am-5pm Sat; Bond St) Some 200 specialist stallholders selling antique jewellery, costumes, military collectables, Oriental works and much more can be found in two buildings, the main one on Davies St and an adjoining one on Davies Mews. Make sure you head to the basement of the Mews Building where the Tyburn River still runs through a channel in the floor. Not all dealers open on Saturday.

🏃 SPORTS & ACTIVITIES

ROYAL OPERA HOUSE
TOUR

Map p438 (020-7304 4000; www.roh.org. uk; Bow St, WC2; adult/child general tours £9.50/7.50, backstage tours £12/8.50; general tour 4pm daily, backstage tour 10.30am, 12.30pm & 2.30pm Mon-Fri, 10.30am, 11.30am, 12.30pm & 1.30pm Sat; Covent Garden) On the northeastern side of Covent Garden Piazza is the gleaming Royal Opera House. The Velvet, Gilt & Glamour Tour is a general, 45-minute twirl around the auditorium; more distinctive is the 1¼-hour backstage tour taking you through the venue. The latter is a much better way to experience the preparation, excitement and histrionics before a performance.

VERTICAL CHILL
ADVENTURE SPORTS

Map p438 (020-7395 1010; www.vertical-chill. com/location-london; 10-12 Southampton St, WC2; climb £25, incl gear £35, incl tuition & gear £50; 11.30am-6.30pm Tue-Fri, 10am-6pm Sat, noon-5pm Sun; Covent Garden) 'Ice climbing' and 'Central London' aren't usually seen in the same sentence, but Vertical Chill, the company responsible for an 8m wall of ice complete with overhang, have made it a reality. You can hire equipment and tuition for an added fee. Find it located inside a giant freezer in the basement of Covent Garden's Ellis Brigham Mountain Sports shop.

The City

Neighbourhood Top Five

❶ Tower of London (p137) Walking through a treasury of history, past the colourful Yeoman Warders (or Beefeaters), the spectacular Crown Jewels, the soothsaying ravens and armour fit for a *very* large king.

❷ St Paul's Cathedral (p143) Listening in on whispering strangers in the dome before enjoying its far-reaching views.

❸ Museum of London (p151) Exploring the city's many and varying incarnations through artefacts, interactive displays and recreated streetscapes.

❹ The Monument (p149) Imagining the tragedy of medieval London ablaze as you climb the column commemorating the Great Fire of 1666.

❺ Sky Garden (p146) Marvelling at the City's ultramodern new buildings from what is perhaps its least admired building, 20 Fenchurch St, aka the 'Walkie Talkie'.

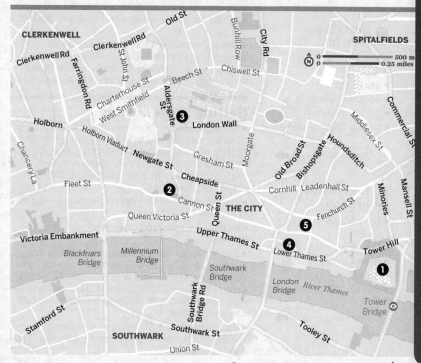

For more detail of this area see Map p450 ➡

Lonely Planet's Top Tip

Designed by Jean Nouvel, One New Change (p157) – called the 'Stealth Bomber' by some because of its distinctive shape – is a shopping mall housing mainly high-street brands, but take the lift to its 6th floor and an open viewing platform will reward you with up-close views of the dome of St Paul's Cathedral and out over London.

✗ Best Places to Eat

➡ City Social (p154)
➡ Sauterelle (p154)
➡ Miyama (p153)
➡ Club Gascon (p152)
➡ City Càphê (p152)

For reviews, see p152. ➡

🍷 Best Places to Drink

➡ Jamaica Wine House (p154)
➡ Sky Pod (p154)
➡ Madison (p156)
➡ Counting House (p156)
➡ Ye Olde Cheshire Cheese (p156)

For reviews, see p154. ➡

🔒 Best Places to Shop

➡ London Silver Vaults (p157)
➡ One New Change (p157)
➡ Royal Exchange (p150)
➡ Wine Pantry (p156)
➡ City of London Distillery (p156)

For reviews, see p157. ➡

Explore the City

For its size – just over 1 sq mile (nearly 3 sq km) – the City punches well above its weight for attractions. Start with the heavyweights – the Tower of London and St Paul's – allowing at least a half-day for each. It's worth arriving early to avoid the queues in season. You can combine the other big attractions with explorations of the City's lesser-known delights and quieter corners – Christopher Wren's dozens of churches make peaceful stops along the way.

While more than 350,000 people work in the City of London, fewer than 8000 actually live here. To appreciate its frantic industry and buzz, come during the week, when you'll find everything open. It largely empties in the evening as its workers retreat to the suburbs, and weekends have traditionally been quiet. But in recent years, the One New Change shopping mall and the new bars and restaurants atop the City's flashiest skyscrapers have begun attracting people outside of regular business hours.

Local Life

➡ **Culture vulture nest** A powerhouse of culture (though arguably not the prettiest kid in class), people flock to the Barbican (p150) for its innovative dance, theatre, music, films and art.

➡ **Meals with a view** There's nothing like getting a taste of the high life, trying to spot your hotel and watching the sun go down over the capital at Tower 42's City Social (p154).

➡ **Old-style drinking** Though they tend to keep bankers' hours, the City's pubs are some of the most atmospheric and historic – the Jamaica Wine House (p154) once did time as London's first coffee house.

Getting There & Away

➡ **Underground** The City is served by seven tube lines (Hammersmith & City, Circle, Metropolitan, Central, District, Northern and Waterloo & City) and 11 stations (Blackfriars, Barbican, St Paul's, Mansion House, Cannon St, Monument, Bank, Moorgate, Liverpool St, Aldgate and Tower Hill).

➡ **Overground** From Liverpool St, trains head east to Bethnal Green and Hackney.

➡ **DLR** Bank and Tower Gateway both connect east to the Docklands.

➡ **Bus** Numerous bus routes pass through the City, including Nos 4 (Waterloo to Archway), 8 (Oxford St to Bow Church), 11 (Liverpool St to Fulham), 15 (Charing Cross to Blackwall), 26 (Waterloo to Hackney Wick), 56 (City to Stratford), 76 (Waterloo to Tottenham) and 172 (City to Brockley).

➡ **Train** Network Rail services head to Moorgate, Liverpool St, Fenchurch St, Cannon St, Blackfriars and City Thameslink.

TOP SIGHT
TOWER OF LONDON

With a history as bloody as it is fascinating, the Tower deserves to top the list of London sights. Begun during the reign of William the Conqueror, the Tower is in fact a castle containing 22 towers, and has served as a palace, an observatory, an armoury, a mint, a zoo, a prison and a site of execution.

Tower Green

The buildings to the west and the south of this verdant patch have always accommodated Tower officials. Indeed, the current constable has a flat in Queen's House, built in 1540. But what looks at first glance like a peaceful, almost village-like slice of the Tower's inner ward is actually one of its bloodiest.

Scaffold Site

Those 'lucky' enough to have met their fate here (rather than suffering the embarrassment of execution on Tower Hill observed by thousands of jeering and cheering onlookers) included two of Henry VIII's wives, Anne Boleyn and Catherine Howard; 16-year-old Lady Jane Grey, who fell foul of Henry's daughter Mary I after her family attempted to have her crowned queen; and Robert Devereux, Earl of Essex, once a favourite of Elizabeth I. Just west of the scaffold site is **Beauchamp Tower** (1280), where high-ranking prisoners left behind unhappy inscriptions and other graffiti. In total, 22 people are known to have been executed within the Tower grounds, including 11 German spies killed by firing squad during WWI and WWII.

DON'T MISS

- Crown Jewels
- Scaffold Site
- White Tower and its armour collection
- A Yeoman Warder's tour
- The ravens

PRACTICALITIES

- Map p450, G4
- ☑0844 482 7777
- www.hrp.org.uk/tow-eroflondon
- Petty Wales, EC3
- adult/child £25/12, audio guide £4/3
- ⊙9.30am-5pm
- ⊖Tower Hill

YEOMAN WARDERS

A true icon of the Tower, the Yeoman Warders have been guarding the fortress since the 15th century. There can be up to 40 and, in order to qualify for the job, they must have served a minimum of 22 years in any branch of the British Armed Forces. In 2007 the first woman was appointed to the post. While officially they guard the Tower, their main role these days is as tour guides. Free hour-long tours leave from the Middle Tower every 30 minutes until 3.30pm (2.30pm in winter).

THE BEEF ABOUT 'BEEFEATERS'

The Yeoman Warders may seem jovial, but don't go calling them Beefeaters – it's a nickname they're said to despise. The name has been around since at least the 17th century and its origins are unknown, although it's thought to be due to the rations of beef – then a luxury – given to them in the past. Lessening the offence somewhat, each warder receives a bottle of Beefeater Gin on their birthday as part of an old arrangement with its producers for use of their image on the bottle.

Chapel Royal of St Peter ad Vincula

On the northern edge of Tower Green is the 16th-century Chapel Royal of St Peter ad Vincula (St Peter in Chains), a rare surviving example of ecclesiastical Tudor architecture. Those buried here include three saints (Thomas More, John Fisher and Philip Howard, although the latter's body was subsequently moved to Arundel) and three queens (Anne Boleyn, Catherine Howard and Jane Grey). The church can be visited on a Yeoman Warder tour, or during the first and last hour of normal opening times.

Crown Jewels

To the east of the Chapel Royal and north of the White Tower is **Waterloo Barracks**, the home of the Crown Jewels, which are in a very real sense priceless. Visitors to the barracks file past film clips of the jewels and their role through history (including fascinating footage of Queen Elizabeth II's coronation in 1953) before reaching the vault itself.

Once inside you'll be dazzled by lavishly bejewelled sceptres, orbs and, naturally, crowns. A moving walkway takes you past the dozen or so crowns and other coronation regalia, including the platinum crown of the late Queen Mother, Elizabeth, which is set with the 106-carat Koh-i-Nûr (Persian for 'Mountain of Light') diamond, and the State Sceptre with Cross topped with the 530-carat First Star of Africa (or Cullinan I) diamond. A bit further on, exhibited on its own, is the centrepiece: the Imperial State Crown, set with 2868 diamonds (including the 317-carat Second Star of Africa, or Cullinan II), sapphires, emeralds, rubies and pearls. It's worn by the Queen at the State Opening of Parliament in May/June. Note the bizarrely shaped boxes at the exit used to transport the baubles from the Tower to state functions.

White Tower

Built in stone as a fortress in 1078, this was the original 'Tower of London' – its name arose after Henry III whitewashed it in the 13th century. Standing just 30m high, it's not exactly a skyscraper by modern standards, but in the the Middle Ages it would have dwarfed the wooden huts surrounding the castle walls and intimidated the peasantry.

Apart from St John's Chapel, most of its interior is given over to a **Royal Armouries** collection of cannons, guns and suits of mail and armour for men and horses. Among the most remarkable exhibits on the entrance floor are Henry VIII's two suits of armour, one made for him when he was a dashing 24-year-old and the other when he was a bloated 50-year-old with a waist measuring 129cm. You won't miss the oversized codpiece. Also here is the **Line of Kings**, a late-17th-century parade of carved wooden horses and heads of historic kings. Look out for the 2m suit of armour once thought to have been made for the giant-like John of Gaunt and, alongside it, a tiny child's suit of armour designed for James I's young son, the future Charles I.

Up on the top floor you'll find the block and axe used to execute Simon Fraser at the last public beheading on Tower Hill in 1747; hangings continued here until 1780. You can also try your hand at various interactive displays, including archery.

St John's Chapel

This unadorned chapel (1080), with its vaulted ceiling, rounded archways and 12 stone pillars, is a fine example of Norman architecture and the oldest place of Christian worship still standing in London. Elizabeth of York, wife of the grief-stricken Henry VII, lay in state here for 12 days, surrounded by candles, having died after complications in childbirth on her 37th birthday in 1503.

Bloody Tower

Directly opposite the Traitors' Gate, through which prisoners were transported by boat, is the huge portcullis of the Bloody Tower (1225). It takes its nickname from the 'princes in the Tower' – Edward V and his younger brother, Richard – who were held here 'for their own safety' and later murdered to annul their claims to the throne. The blame is usually laid (notably by Shakespeare) at the feet of their uncle, Richard III, but is open to debate. An exhibition inside looks at the life and times of Elizabethan adventurer Sir Walter Raleigh, who was imprisoned here three times by the capricious Elizabeth I and her successor James I.

Medieval Palace

The Medieval Palace complex is composed of three towers. The entrance is via **St Thomas's Tower** (built 1275–81), where there's a reconstructed hall and bedchamber from the time of Edward I. Adjoining **Wakefield Tower** (1220–40) was built by Edward's father, Henry III. It has been furnished with a replica throne and other decor to give an impression of how it might have looked. During the 15th-century Wars of the Roses between the Houses of York and Lancaster, Henry VI is said to have been murdered as he knelt in prayer in this tower. A plaque on the chapel floor commemorates this Lancastrian king. There's a display on torture in the basement of this tower, but it's accessed from a separate entrance. The main Palace route, however, continues through **Lanthorn Tower** (1220–1238), residence of medieval queens.

THE RAVENS

Common ravens have been scavenging here for centuries, snacking on scraps chucked from the Tower's windows and feasting on the corpses of beheaded traitors displayed as a deterrent. Tower tradition tells us that when it was proposed they be culled after the Restoration, someone remembered the old legend that should the ravens depart, both the Tower and the kingdom would fall. Having lived through the plague, the Great Fire *and* the execution of his father, Charles II clearly wasn't going to take any chances and he let the birds remain in residence. There are always at least six ravens in residence at the Tower, and their wing feathers are clipped to keep them around. The birds all have names and live charmed, well-fed lives – 170g of raw beef, biscuits soaked in blood, the odd egg and so on. Even so, mind your fingers.

Tower of London

TACKLING THE TOWER

Although it's usually less busy in the late afternoon, don't leave your assault on the Tower until too late in the day. You could easily spend hours here and not see it all. Start by getting your bearings on one of the Yeoman Warder (Beefeater) tours; they are included in the cost of admission, entertaining and the easiest way to access the ❶ **Chapel Royal of St Peter ad Vincula**, which is where they finish up.

When you leave the chapel, the ❷ **Scaffold Site** is directly in front. The building immediately to your left is Waterloo Barracks, where the ❸ **Crown Jewels** are housed. These are the absolute highlight of a Tower visit, so keep an eye on the entrance and pick a time to visit when it looks relatively quiet. Once inside, take things at your own pace. Slow-moving travelators shunt you past the dozen or so crowns that are the treasury's centrepieces, but feel free to double-back for a second or even third pass.

Allow plenty of time for the ❹ **White Tower**, the core of the whole complex, starting with the exhibition of royal armour. As you continue onto the 1st floor, keep an eye out for ❺ **St John's Chapel**.

The famous ❻ **ravens** can be seen in the courtyard south of the White Tower. Next, visit the ❼ **Bloody Tower** and the torture displays in the dungeon of the Wakefield Tower. Head next through the towers that formed the ❽ **Medieval Palace**, then take the ❾ **East Wall Walk** to get a feel for the castle's mighty battlements. Spend the rest of your time poking around the many other fascinating nooks and crannies of the Tower complex.

BEAT THE QUEUES

➡ Buy tickets online, avoid weekends and aim to be at the Tower first thing in the morning, when queues are shortest.

➡ An annual Historic Royal Palaces membership allows you to jump the queues and visit the Tower (and four other London palaces) as often as you like.

Chapel Royal of St Peter ad Vincula
This chapel serves as the resting place for the royals and other members of the aristocracy who were executed on the small green out front. Several other historical figures are buried here too, including St Thomas More.

Scaffold Site
Seven people, including three queens (Anne Boleyn, Catherine Howard and Jane Grey), lost their heads here during Tudor times, saving the monarch the embarrassment of public executions on Tower Hill. The site features a rather odd 'pillow' sculpture by Brian Catling.
Above: Execution Site Memorial, by Brian Catling

Dry Moat

Beauchamp Tower

Coins & Kings display

Main Entrance

Middle Tower

Byward Tower

Bell Tower

White Tower
Much of the White Tower is taken up with an exhibition on 500 years of royal armour. Look for the virtually cuboid suit made to match Henry VIII's bloated 49-year-old body, complete with an oversized armoured codpiece to protect, ahem, the crown jewels.

St John's Chapel
The White Tower's unadorned chapel dates from 1080, making it the oldest surviving Christian place of worship in London.

JOSEPH M. ARSENEAU / SHUTTERSTOCK ©

Crown Jewels
When they're not being worn for ceremonies of state, Her Majesty's bling is kept here. Among the 23,578 gems, look out for the 530-carat 1st Star of Africa diamond at the top of the Sovereign's Sceptre with cross, the largest part of what was then the largest diamond ever found.

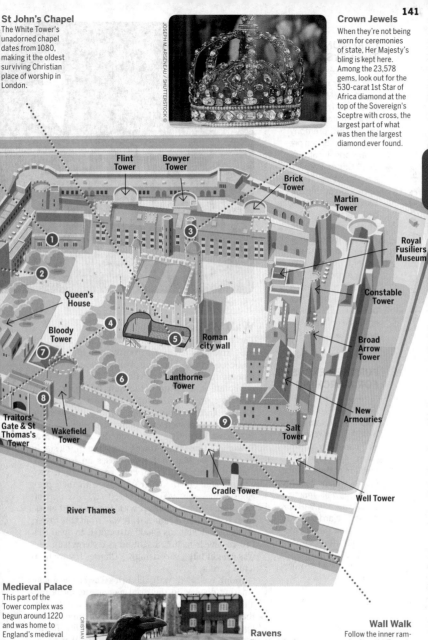

Flint Tower
Bowyer Tower
Brick Tower
Martin Tower
Royal Fusiliers Museum
Queen's House
Constable Tower
Bloody Tower
Roman city wall
Broad Arrow Tower
Lanthorne Tower
New Armouries
Traitors' Gate & St Thomas's Tower
Wakefield Tower
Salt Tower
Cradle Tower
Well Tower

River Thames

Medieval Palace
This part of the Tower complex was begun around 1220 and was home to England's medieval monarchs. Look for the recreations of the bedchamber of Edward I (1272–1307) in St Thomas's Tower and the throne room of his father, Henry III (1216–72) in the Wakefield Tower.

CRISTIAN SANTINON / SHUTTERSTOCK ©

Ravens
This stretch of green is where the Tower's half-dozen ravens are kept, fed on raw meat and blood-soaked biscuits. According to legend, if the ravens depart the fortress, the Tower will fall.

Wall Walk
Follow the inner ramparts along the Tower's eastern and northern fortifications. Each of the seven towers along the way has themed displays, covering everything from the royal menagerie to the Tower during WWI.

CEREMONY OF THE KEYS

The elaborate locking of the main gates has been performed daily without fail for more than 700 years. The ceremony begins at 9.53pm precisely, and it's all over by 10.05pm. Even when a bomb hit the Tower of London during the Blitz, the ceremony was only delayed by 30 minutes – some say that displays the essence of the famed British stiff upper lip, others their sheer lunacy. Entry to the ceremony begins at 9.30pm and is free, but you must book in advance online (www.hrp.org.uk).

FURTHER EXCUSES FOR MARCHING

The Tower is officially unlocked at 9am daily by a Yeoman Warder accompanied by a military guard. At 2.45pm daily, soldiers of the Queen's Guard, who protect the Crown Jewels, march from Waterloo Barracks to the Byward Tower to collect the secret password for after-hours entry to the Tower from the Chief Yeoman Warder.

VULTURE LABS/GETTY IMAGES ©

St John's Chapel (p139)

Wall Walk

The huge inner wall of the Tower was added to the fortress by Henry III from 1220 to improve the castle's defences. The Wall Walk allows you to tour its eastern and northern edge and the towers that punctuate it. First up is the **Salt Tower**, probably built to store saltpetre for gunpowder but, as the historic graffiti demonstrates, it was also used to house prisoners such as St Henry Walpole.

The walk continues through the **Broad Arrow Tower** and **Constable Tower**, each containing small displays. The **Martin Tower** houses an exhibition about the original coronation regalia. Here you can see some of the older crowns, with their precious stones removed. The oldest (1715) is that of George I, which is topped with the ball and cross from the crown of James II. It was from this tower that Colonel Thomas Blood attempted to steal the Crown Jewels in 1671 disguised as a clergyman. He was caught but – surprisingly – Charles II gave him a full pardon.

Along the north wall, the **Brick Tower** has a fascinating display on the royal menagerie, including a tethered polar bear that used to swim and fish in the Thames. The **Bowyer Tower** has exhibits relating to the Duke of Wellington, while the **Flint Tower** is devoted to the role of the castle during WWI.

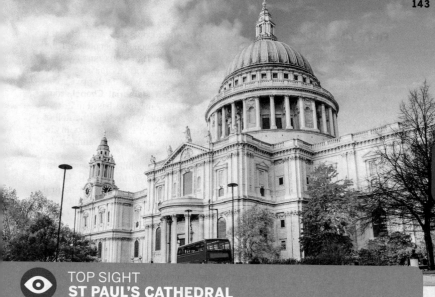

ZEPART/SHUTTERSTOCK ©

TOP SIGHT
ST PAUL'S CATHEDRAL

Towering over diminutive Ludgate Hill in a position that's been a place of Christian worship for over 1400 years (and pagan before that), St Paul's is the City's most magnificent building. Built between 1675 and 1710 after the Great Fire destroyed its predecessor, Sir Christopher Wren's gleaming white-domed masterpiece became the very symbol of London's resistance and pride during WWII.

Interior

At a time of anti-Catholic fervour, it was controversial to build a Roman-style basilica rather than using the more familiar Gothic style. The interiors were more reflective of Protestant mores, though, being relatively unadorned, with large clear windows. The statues and mosaics that are now visible followed much later.

In the north aisle of the vast nave you'll find the grandiose **Duke of Wellington Memorial** (1912), which took 54 years to complete – the Iron Duke's horse Copenhagen originally faced the other way, but it was deemed unfitting that a horse's rear end should face the altar. In contrast, just beneath the dome is an elegant epitaph written for Wren by his son: *Lector, si monumentum requiris, circumspice* (Reader, if you seek his monument, look around you).

In the north transept chapel is William Holman Hunt's celebrated painting, **The Light of the World** (1851–53), which depicts Christ knocking at a weed-covered door that, symbolically, can only be opened from within. Beyond, in the cathedral's heart, you'll find the spectacular **quire** (or chancel) – its ceilings and arches dazzling with colourful mosaics – and the **high altar**. The ornately carved **choir stalls** by Dutch-British sculptor Grinling Gibbons on either side of the quire are exquisite, as are

DON'T MISS

➡ Climbing the dome

➡ Quire ceiling mosaics

➡ Tombs of Admiral Nelson and Duke of Wellington

➡ American Memorial Chapel

➡ *Martyrs (Earth, Air, Fire, Water)* video installation

PRACTICALITIES

➡ Map p450, C2

➡ ☏020-7246 8357

➡ www.stpauls.co.uk

➡ St Paul's Churchyard, EC4

➡ adult/child £18/8

➡ ⊖St Paul's

FIFTH TIME LUCKY

London's mother church has stood on this site since 604. Wren's cathedral is the fifth incarnation, built to replace the soaring Gothic-style Old St Paul's after it was destroyed in the Great Fire. The pre-Fire cathedral was both longer and taller than Wren's version.

ST PAUL'S FACIAL

As part of its 300th-anniversary celebrations in 2011, St Paul's underwent a £40-million, decade-long renovation project that cleaned the cathedral inside and out – a painstakingly slow process that has been likened to carefully applying and removing a face mask. To the right as you face the enormous Great West Door from inside, there's a section of unrestored wall under glass that shows the effects of centuries of pollution and failed past restoration attempts.

the ornamental **wrought-iron gates**, separating the aisles from the altar, by French Huguenot Jean Tijou (both men also worked on Hampton Court Palace).

Walk around the altar, with its massive gilded oak **baldacchino** (canopy) with barley-twist columns, to the **American Memorial Chapel**, commemorating the 28,000 Americans based in Britain who lost their lives during WWII. Note the Roll of Honour book (turned daily), the state flags in the stained glass and American flora and fauna in the carved wood panelling.

In the south quire aisle, Bill Viola's poignant video installation *Martyrs (Earth, Air, Fire, Water)* depicts four figures being overwhelmed by natural forces. A bit further on is an **effigy of John Donne** (1573–1631), metaphysical poet and one-time cathedral dean, that survived the Great Fire.

Dome

Wren wanted to construct a dome that was imposing on the outside but not overbearingly large on the inside. The solution was to build it in three parts: a plastered brick inner dome, a nonstructural lead outer dome and a brick cone between them holding it all together, one inside the other. This unique structure, second only in size to St Peter's in the Vatican, made the cathedral Wren's tour de force. He originally wanted mosaics to decorate the interior of the dome, but the sober *grisaille* tones of Sir James Thornhill's scenes from St Paul's life were deemed more appropriately Protestant.

Some 528 stairs take you to the top, but it's a three-stage journey. Enter through the door on the western side of the southern transept, where 257 steps lead to the interior walkway around the dome's base, 30m above the floor. This is the **Whispering Gallery**, so called because if you talk close to the wall it carries your words around to the opposite side, 32m away.

Climbing another 119 steps brings you to the **Stone Gallery**, an exterior viewing platform 53m above the ground, obscured by pillars and other suicide-preventing measures. The remaining 152 iron steps to the **Golden Gallery** are steeper and narrower than below but are really worth the effort. From here, 85m above London, you can enjoy superb 360-degree views of the city.

Crypt

On the eastern side of both the north and south transepts are stairs leading down to the crypt and the **OBE Chapel**, where services are held for members of the Order of the British Empire.

ST PAUL'S CATHEDRAL

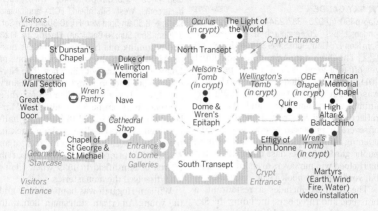

Cathedral Floor & Crypt

The crypt has memorials to around 300 of Britain's great and good, including Florence Nightingale, TE Lawrence (of Arabia) and Sir Winston Churchill. Those actually buried here include the Duke of Wellington, Vice Admiral Horatio Nelson, Sir Christopher Wren and the painters Sir Joshua Reynolds, Sir John Everett Millais, JMW Turner and William Holman Hunt. On the surrounding walls are plaques in memory of those from the Commonwealth who died in various conflicts during the last century.

The **Oculus** projects images onto the walls of the former treasury. If you're not up to climbing the dome, experience it here audiovisually.

Also in the crypt is the cathedral's cafe and gift shop.

Churchyard & Surrounds

Just outside the north transept, there's a simple, squat, round **monument to the people of London**, honouring the 32,000 civilians killed (and another 50,000 seriously injured) during WWII. Nearby is **St Paul's Cross**, topped by a gilded statue of the saint – an Edwardian replacement for the original preaching cross that was removed in 1643. Another returnee is **Temple Bar**, the only surviving gateway to the old City. This stone archway once straddled Fleet St but was removed in 1877. It was placed at the entrance to Paternoster Sq in 2004.

◉ SIGHTS

ST PAUL'S CATHEDRAL　　　CATHEDRAL
See p143.

TOWER OF LONDON　　　CASTLE
See p137.

★ SKY GARDEN　　　VIEWPOINT
Map p450 (☎020-7337 2344; www.skygarden.
london; L35-37, 20 Fenchurch St, EC3; ⊙10am-
6pm Mon-Fri, 11am-9pm Sat & Sun; ⊜Monument)
FREE The City's sixth-tallest building didn't
get off to a good start when it opened in
2014. Officially called 20 Fenchurch St it
was quickly dubbed the 'Walkie Talkie' by
unimpressed Londoners, and its highly
reflective windows melted the bodywork
of several cars parked below. However, the
opening of this 155m-high, three-storey,
public garden in the glass dome at the top
has helped win naysayers over. Entry is free,
but you'll need to book a slot in advance.

The complex includes a restaurant, a
brasserie and three bars, including the Sky
Pod (p154) cafe-bar, which doesn't require
a separate reservation for garden-ticket
holders.

The building's top-heavy design helps
maximise upper-floor office space, where
rents are highest, but it's overbearing shape
earned it the Carbuncle Cup for the worst
new building in the UK in 2015.

ST BARTHOLOMEW-THE-GREAT　　　CHURCH
Map p450 (☎020-7600 0440; www.greatst
barts.com; West Smithfield, EC1; adult/child
£5/3; ⊙8.30am-5pm Mon-Fri, 10.30am-4pm Sat,
8.30am-8pm Sun; ⊜Barbican) Dating to 1123
and adjoining one of London's oldest hos-
pitals, St Bartholomew-the-Great is one of
London's most ancient churches. The Norman arches and profound sense of history
lend this holy space an ancient calm, while
approaching from nearby Smithfield Market through the restored 13th-century half-
timbered archway is like walking back in
time. The church was originally part of an
Augustinian priory; but became the parish
church of Smithfield in 1539 when Henry
VIII dissolved the monasteries.

William Hogarth was baptised here and
the young American statesman Benjamin
Franklin worked in what is now the Lady
Chapel as an apprentice printer. The church
has been used as a setting for many films

◉ TOP SIGHT
TOWER BRIDGE

One of London's most recognisable sights, familiar from
dozens of movies, Tower Bridge doesn't disappoint in
real life. Its neo-Gothic towers and sky-blue suspension
struts add extraordinary elegance to what is a supremely functional structure. London was a thriving port in
1894 when it was built as a much-needed crossing point
in the east, equipped with a then-revolutionary steam-
driven bascule (counter-balance) mechanism that could
raise the roadway to make way for oncoming ships in
just three minutes.

A lift leads up from the northern tower to the Tower
Bridge Exhibition (p147), where the story of its building
is recounted within the two walkways at the top, 42m
above the river. A wow-inducing, 11m-long glass floor
provides views plunging to the road and river below.
The exhibition continues in the Victorian Engine Rooms,
which provide the real mechanical detail and also house
interactive exhibits and a couple of short films.

The bridge is still operational, although these days it's
electrically powered and rises mainly for pleasure craft.
It does so around 1000 times a year and as often as 10
times a day in summer; consult the Exhibition website
for times to watch it in action.

DON'T MISS

➡ View from the top
➡ Glass floor
➡ Victorian Engine
Rooms
➡ Bridge lifting

PRACTICALITIES

➡ Map p450, G4
➡ ⊜Tower Hill

and TV productions, including *Four Weddings and a Funeral, Shakespeare in Love, Sherlock Holmes* and a very funny mobile-phone advertisement satirising the royal wedding of Prince William and Kate Middleton in 2011. Look out for the astonishingly macabre Damien Hirst gilded statue of St Bartholomew with his flayed skin (2006).

ALL HALLOWS BY THE TOWER   CHURCH

Map p450 (☑020-7481 2928; www.ahbtt.org.uk; Byward St, EC3; ☺8am-5pm Mon-Fri, 10am-5pm Sat & Sun; ☻Tower Hill) All Hallows (meaning 'all saints'), which dates from AD 675, survived virtually unscathed by the Great Fire, only to be hit by German bombs in 1940. Come to see the church itself, by all means, but the best bits are in the atmospheric undercroft (crypt), where you'll discover a pavement of 2nd-century Roman tiles and the walls of the 7th-century Saxon church.

Free 20-minute tours are available between 2pm and 4pm most weekdays from April to October.

In the nave, note the pulpit taken from a Wren church on Cannon St that was destroyed in WWII and, by the south door, a Saxon archway and a beautiful 17th-century font cover decorated by the master woodcarver Grinling Gibbons. The church has two strong American connections: William Penn, founder of Pennsylvania, was baptised here in 1644 and schooled in what is now the Parish Room; and John Quincy Adams, sixth president of the USA, was married here in 1797.

ST OLAVE'S   CHURCH

Map p450 (☑020-7488 4318; www.sanctuary inthecity.net; 8 Hart St, EC3; ☺9am-5pm Mon-Fri Sep-Jul; ☻Tower Hill) St Olave's was built in the mid-15th century and is one of the few churches to have survived the Great Fire. However, it was badly damaged by a bomb in 1941 and substantially restored in 1954. The diarist Samuel Pepys was a parishioner and is buried here – see the elaborately carved memorial high up on the south wall. Dickens called the place 'St Ghastly Grim' because of the skulls above the gate to the peaceful little churchyard garden.

ST MARY-LE-BOW   CHURCH

Map p450 (☑020-7248 5139; www.stmarylebow. co.uk; Cheapside, EC2; ☺7.30am-6pm Mon-Thu, to 4pm Fri; ☻St Paul's, Bank) One of Wren's great churches, St Mary-le-Bow (1673) is famous as the church with the bells that still dictate who is – and who is not – a cockney; it's said that a true cockney has to have been born within earshot of Bow Bells. Those bells ring out from a delicate steeple that is considered one of Wren's finest works. The church was badly damaged during WWII and didn't reopen until 1964. The beautiful stained glass windows date from that time.

ST STEPHEN WALBROOK   CHURCH

Map p450 (☑020-7626 9000; www.ststephen walbrook.net; 39 Walbrook, EC4; ☺10am-4pm Mon-Fri; ☻Bank) Just south of Mansion House, St Stephen Walbrook (1679) is considered to be the finest of Wren's parish churches and, as it was his first experiment with a dome, a forerunner to St Paul's Cathedral. Sixteen pillars with Corinthian capitals support the dome, and the modern travertine marble altar, nicknamed 'the Camembert', is by sculptor Henry Moore.

TOWER BRIDGE EXHIBITION   BRIDGE

Map p450 (☑020-7403 3761; www.towerbridge. org.uk; Tower Bridge, SE1; adult/child £9.80/3.90, incl the Monument £12/5.50; ☺10am-5.30pm; ☻Tower Hill) This fascinating exhibition explains the nuts and bolts of Tower Bridge. If you're not technically minded, it's still fascinating to get inside the bridge and look along the Thames from its two walkways. A lift takes you to the top, 42m above the river, where you can walk along each of the walkways, which are lined with information boards. A wow-inducing 11m-long glass floor provides views plunging to the road and river below.

There are a couple of stops on the way down before you exit and continue on to the **Victorian Engine Rooms**, which provide the real mechanical detail and also house a few interactive exhibits and a couple of short films.

GUILDHALL   HISTORIC BUILDING

Map p450 (☑020-7332 1313; www.cityoflondon. gov.uk/guildhallgalleries; Gresham St, EC2; ☺10am-4.30pm daily May-Sep, Mon-Sat Oct-Apr; ☻Bank) **FREE** Guildhall has been the City's seat of government for more than 800 years. At its centre, the Great Hall dates from the early 15th century and is positively Hogwartsian in its Gothic grandeur. It's the only remaining secular stone structure to have survived the Great Fire of 1666, although it was severely damaged both then and during the Blitz of 1940.

THE CITY SIGHTS

Inside it's hung with the banners and shields of London's 12 principal livery companies, or guilds, which used to wield immense power throughout the city. The lord mayor and two sheriffs are still elected annually in the vast open hall. Among the monuments to look out for are statues of Winston Churchill, Admiral Nelson, the Duke of Wellington and both Prime Ministers William Pitt (the Elder and the Younger).

In the upper gallery, at the western end, are statues of the biblical giants **Gog and Magog**, traditionally considered to be guardians of the City – today's figures replaced similar 18th-century statues destroyed in the Blitz. The Guildhall's stained glass was also blown out during the bombing, but a modern window in the southwestern corner depicts the city's history – look for London's most famous lord mayor, Richard 'Dick' Whittington, with his famous cat, a scene of the Great Fire and even the Lloyd's of London building.

To visit the Great Hall, enter through the reception of the City's modern administration block.

GUILDHALL ART GALLERY   GALLERY

Map p450 (020-7332 3700; www.cityoflondon. gov.uk/guildhallgalleries; Guildhall Yard, EC2; 10am-5pm Mon-Sat, noon-4pm Sun; Bank) FREE The City of London has had centuries to acquire a tasty art collection, which has been shown off in a building near its Guildhall headquarters since 1886. It was only after the original gallery was destroyed during the Blitz that beneath it was discovered a long-sought-after archaeological prize: Londinium's **Roman amphitheatre** (c AD70). It's foundations are now displayed in the lower floors, alongside a **Heritage Gallery** devoted to important historic documents.

The collection is particularly strong on Victorian art, including significant pre-Raphaelite works by the likes of John Everett Millais and Dante Gabriel Rossetti. Taking pride of place is American artist John Singleton Copley's *Defeat of the Floating Batteries at Gibraltar* (1791), which depicts a 1782 British victory. This immense oil painting was removed to safety just three weeks before the gallery was hit by a German bomb in 1941; it spent 50 years rolled up before undergoing a spectacular restoration in 1999.

London landscapes include the great Venetian painter Canaletto's *The Monument from Gracechurch St* and 1960s visions of Smithfield and Leadenhall by Jacqueline Stanley. New works continue to be purchased on the themes of money, trade and capitalism – historically the City's chief concerns.

While only a few remnants of the stone walls lining the eastern entrance of the Roman amphitheatre still stand, they're imaginatively fleshed out with a black-and-fluorescent-green outline of the missing seating, and computer-meshed images of spectators and gladiators. Markings on the square outside the Guildhall indicate the original extent and scale of the stadium, which could seat up to 6000 spectators.

DR JOHNSON'S HOUSE   MUSEUM

Map p450 (020-7353 3745; www.drjohnsons house.org; 17 Gough Sq, EC4; adult/child £6/2.50, audio guide £2; 11am-5pm Mon-Sat; Chancery Lane) Built in 1700, this Georgian house is one of very few to survive in the City. It was the home of the great wit Samuel Johnson, the author of the first serious dictionary of the English language and the man who famously proclaimed, 'When a man is tired of London, he is tired of life'.

The house contains antique furniture and artefacts from Dr Johnson's life, including a chair from his local pub, the Cock Tavern on Fleet St, and numerous paintings and engravings of the lexicographer and his associates, including his black manservant and eventual heir, Francis Barber, and his clerk and biographer, James Boswell.

On the upper floors there are leaflets describing how Dr Johnson and six clerks developed the first English dictionary in the house's attic from 1748 to 1759, as well as a copy of the first edition of the dictionary from 1755. Children will love the Georgian dress-up clothes.

LEADENHALL MARKET   MARKET

Map p450 (www.cityoflondon.gov.uk/things-to-do/leadenhall-market; Whittington Ave, EC3; public areas 24hr; Bank) The Romans had their Forum on this site, but a visit to this covered shopping strip off Gracechurch St is a step back to the Victorian era, with cobblestones underfoot and late-19th-century Victorian ironwork linking its shops and bars. It appears as Diagon Alley in *Harry Potter and the Philosopher's Stone* and an optician's shop was used for the entrance to the Leaky Cauldron wizarding pub in *Harry Potter and the Goblet of Fire*.

BANK OF ENGLAND MUSEUM MUSEUM

Map p450 (📷020-76015545; www.bankofengland.co.uk/museum; Bartholomew Lane, EC2; ⏰10am-5pm Mon-Fri; 🚇Bank) **FREE** The centrepiece of this museum, which explores the evolution of money and the history of the venerable Bank of England (founded in 1694 by a Scotsman), is a reconstruction of architect John Soane's original Bank Stock Office. A series of rooms leading off the office are packed with exhibits including displays of coins and banknotes, and a hefty 13kg solid gold bar you can lift up.

POSTMAN'S PARK PARK

Map p450 (www.postmanspark.org.uk; King Edward St, EC1; 🚇St Paul's) This peaceful patch of greenery, just north of what was once London's General Post Office, contains the unusual **Memorial to Heroic Self-Sacrifice**, a loggia with 54 ceramic plaques describing deeds of bravery by ordinary people who died saving the lives of others and who might otherwise have been forgotten.

SMITHFIELD MARKET MARKET

Map p450 (📷020-7248 3151; www.smithfieldmarket.com; Charterhouse St, EC1; ⏰2-10am Mon-Fri; 🚇Farringdon) Smithfield is central London's last surviving meat market. Its name derives from 'smooth field', where animals could graze, although its history is far from pastoral as this was once a place where public executions were held. The market has been here since the Middle Ages, but the current colourful building was designed in 1868 by Horace Jones, who also designed Leadenhall Market and Tower Bridge. Visit by 7am at the latest to see it in full swing.

Described in terms of pure horror by Dickens in *Oliver Twist*, this was once the armpit of London, where animal excrement and entrails combined in a sea of filth. However, the area's bloody history goes back far further than Dickens, as this was the site of the notorious St Bartholomew's Fair, where witches were burned at the stake. Scottish independence leader William Wallace was executed here in 1305 (he's remembered by a plaque on the wall of St Bart's Hospital, south of the market, ending with the Gaelic words *Bas agus Buaidh* or 'Death and Victory'), as was Peasants' Revolt leader Wat Tyler in 1381.

Part of the vast market complex is now abandoned; the Museum of London (p151) is planning to relocate to the semi-derelict General Market section by 2022.

TOP SIGHT
THE MONUMENT

Designed by Sir Christopher Wren and Dr Robert Hooke in 1677, this huge column, known simply as the Monument, is a memorial to the Great Fire of London. The impact of the 1666 fire on London's history cannot be overstated. Much of medieval London was destroyed, with 13,200 houses reduced to rubble and an estimated 70,000 people made homeless (though only a half-dozen died).

An immense Doric column made of Portland stone, the Monument is 4.5m wide and 60.6m tall – the exact distance it stands from the bakery in Pudding Lane where the fire is thought to have started. It's topped with a gilded bronze urn of flames that some think resembles a big gold pincushion. An earlier design had in its place a phoenix rising from the ashes, while another featured a large statue of Charles II.

If you're wondering about the chiselled-out section of the Latin inscription on the side, text erroneously blaming Catholics for the fire was erased in 1830.

Although Lilliputian by today's standards, the Monument towered over London when it was built. Climbing up the column's 311 spiral steps still rewards you with great views, due to its location as much as its height.

DON'T MISS

➤ Views from the top
➤ Relief of Charles II on the front

PRACTICALITIES

➤ Map p450, E3
➤ 📷020-7403 3761
➤ www.themonument.org.uk
➤ Fish St Hill, EC3
➤ adult/child £5/2.50, incl Tower Bridge Exhibition £12/5.50
➤ ⏰9.30am-5.30pm
➤ 🚇Monument

BARBICAN
ARCHITECTURE

Map p450 (📞020-7638 4141; www.barbican.org.uk; Silk St, EC2; tours adult/child £12.50/10; ⏰9am-11pm Mon-Sat, 11am-11pm Sun; 📷; 🚇Barbican) Londoners remain fairly divided about the architectural value of this vast complex built after WWII, but the Barbican remains the City's pre-eminent cultural centre, with the main Barbican Hall, two theatres, a state-of-the-art cinema complex and two well-regarded art galleries: the 3rd-floor Barbican Art Gallery and the **Curve** (Map p450; L1 Barbican Centre; ⏰11am-8pm) FREE on the ground floor. There's also a large conservatory (p150), filled with tropical plants.

Built on a huge bomb site abandoned since WWII and opened progressively between 1969 and 1982, the vast housing and cultural complex is named after a Roman fortification built to protect ancient Londinium, the remains of which can still be seen. It incorporates John Milton's parish church, **St Giles' Cripplegate** (Map p450; 📞020-7638 1997; www.stgilescripplegate.com; St Giles' Terrace, EC2; ⏰11am-4pm Mon-Fri; 🚇Barbican), into its avant-garde (for the time) design and embellishes its public areas with lakes and ponds ringed with benches. Apartments in the three high-rise towers that surround the cultural centre are some of the city's most sought-after living spaces. Guided architectural tours are fascinating and the best way to make sense of the purpose and beauty of the estate.

Getting around the Barbican can be frustratingly difficult. There are stairs from Barbican tube station that take you up onto the elevated walkways where a yellow line on the floor guides you to the arts complex. More straightforward is to walk through the Beech St road tunnel to the Silk St entrance.

CONSERVATORY
GARDENS

Map p450 (📞020-7638 4141; www.barbican.org.uk; L3 Barbican Centre, Upper Frobisher Cres, EC2; ⏰noon-5pm Sun; 🚇Barbican) This cavernous tropical oasis touts itself as the second largest conservatory in London after Kew Gardens (p314) and is home to over 2000 species of plants, along with fish, birds and terrapins. It's a truly impressive venue and seems a rather defiant statement, surrounded as it is by the concrete Brutalism of the Barbican.

ST DUNSTAN-IN-THE-EAST
GARDENS

Map p450 (St Dunstan's Hill, EC3; 🚇Monument) Set amid the atmospheric ruins of the 12th-century St Dunstan Church, which was destroyed first in the Great Fire in 1666 and again in the Blitz in 1941, this utterly lovely garden is an oasis of tranquillity in the sometimes hectic City.

BARBICAN ART GALLERY
GALLERY

Map p450 (www.barbican.org.uk/artgallery; L3 Barbican Centre, Silk St, EC2; ⏰10am-6pm Sat-Wed, to 9pm Thu & Fri; 📷; 🚇Barbican) The larger of the Barbican's two art galleries, with cutting-edge temporary exhibitions.

TRINITY SQUARE GARDENS
GARDENS

Map p450 (Trinity Sq, EC3; ⏰8am-dusk; 🚇Tower Hill) This pleasant little park was the site of the Tower Hill scaffold, where a confirmed 125 people met their fate, including St Thomas More, St John Fisher and Thomas Cromwell. Now it's a much more peaceful place, ringed by important buildings and bits of London's ancient Roman wall. Within the park is Edwin Lutyens' **Tower Hill Memorial** (1928), dedicated to the almost 24,000 merchant sailors who died in both world wars and have no known grave.

ROYAL EXCHANGE
HISTORIC BUILDING

Map p450 (📞020-7283 8935; www.theroyalexchange.co.uk; Threadneedle St, EC3; 🚇Bank) The Royal Exchange was founded by 16th-century merchant Thomas Gresham as a centre for commerce and trade, with its original building officially opened by Elizabeth I in 1570. The imposing, colonnaded, neoclassical building that stands here today is the third on the site, built in 1844. It ceased functioning as a financial institution in the 1980s and now houses upmarket shops, cafes and restaurants.

ROMAN WALL
RUINS

Map p450 (Noble St; 🚇St Paul's) London's roots lie in the walled Roman settlement of Londinium, established in AD 43 on the northern banks of the River Thames, roughly echoing the dimensions of today's City. Few traces of the 2nd-century Roman wall survive, although post-Blitz demolitions uncovered a section running along Noble St. You can glimpse the remains of a bastion between the Museum of London and the Barbican, and other sections near Tower Hill tube stop and within the grounds of the Tower of London.

TOP SIGHT
MUSEUM OF LONDON

As entertaining as it is educational, the Museum of London meanders through the various incarnations of the city before eventually ending up in the 21st-century metropolis. Interesting objects and interactive displays bring each era to life, without ever getting too whizz-bang, making this one of the capital's best museums.

The first gallery, **London Before London**, sheds light on the ancient settlements that predated the capital and is followed by **Roman London**, which is full of engrossing displays, models and archaeological finds. After a glimpse of the real Roman wall from the window, head into **Medieval London** and then **War, Plague & Fire**, where a six-minute film covers the great 1666 conflagration that completely altered the city's face.

The story continues downstairs, starting with **Expanding City**. After a quick spin through the re-created Vauxhall Pleasure Gardens, you'll emerge into **People's City** where highlights include a 1908 taxi cab, a 1928 art-deco lift from Selfridges, and a fascinating multimedia display on the Suffragettes. This section ends with WWII, where the testimonies of ordinary people are particularly moving. **World City** brings things up to date with Beatles memorabilia, race riots and gay-rights marches.

DON'T MISS

➡ Lord Mayor's coach
➡ Victorian walk
➡ Roman-era Bucklersbury mosaic
➡ *Rhinebeck Panorama* of 1806 London
➡ 1750 prison cell

PRACTICALITIES

➡ Map p450, D1
➡ ☑020-7001 9844
➡ www.museumof london.org.uk
➡ 150 London Wall, EC2
➡ admission free
➡ ⊙10am-6pm
➡ ☎
➡ ⊜Barbican

CENTRAL CRIMINAL COURT
HISTORIC BUILDING

Map p450 (Old Bailey; ☑020-7248 3277; www.cityoflondon.gov.uk; cnr Newgate St & Old Bailey, EC4; ⊙9.45am-1pm & 2-4pm Mon-Fri; ⊜St Paul's) **FREE** Taking in a trial in what's nicknamed the Old Bailey leaves watching a TV courtroom drama for dust. Even if you end up sitting in on a fairly run-of-the-mill case, simply being in the court where such people as the Kray brothers and Oscar Wilde (in an earlier building on this site) once appeared is memorable.

ST BRIDE'S, FLEET STREET
CHURCH

Map p450 (☑020-7427 0133; www.stbrides.com; St Bride's Ave, EC4; tours £6; ⊙8am-6pm Mon-Fri, 10am-3.30pm Sat; ⊜Blackfriars) Printing presses fell silent on Fleet St in the 1980s, but St Bride's is still referred to as the 'journalists' church' and there's a moving chapel in the north aisle honouring journalists who've died in the course of their work. Designed by Christopher Wren in 1672, St Bride's was his tallest and most expensive church after St Paul's Cathedral. The spire, added in 1703, is said to have inspired the design of the tiered wedding cake.

The church was hit by bombs in December 1940, and the interior layout is wood-panelled, modern and not particularly attractive. In the 11th-century crypt, however, there's a well-presented history of the church, its surrounding areas and the printing industry – plus a section of Roman pavement from AD 180. Ninety-minute guided tours depart at 2.15pm on Tuesday.

ST LAWRENCE JEWRY
CHURCH

Map p450 (☑020-7600 9478; www.stlawrencejewry.org.uk; Guildhall Yard, EC2; ⊙9am-5pm Mon-Fri; ⊜St Paul's) The Corporation of London's official church was built by Christopher Wren in 1677, but almost completely destroyed during WWII bombing. Its immaculate alabaster walls and gilt trimmings do its restorers proud. Free piano recitals are held each Monday at 1pm; organ recitals are at the same time on Tuesday.

The first part of the church's name refers to a 3rd-century Christian martyr executed on a sizzling gridiron (see a copy of same atop the church spire). The second part tells us that this was once part of the Jewish quarter – the centre being Old Jewry, the street to the southeast. The Jews were expelled from England by Edward I in 1290 and were not permitted to return until the late 17th century.

30 ST MARY AXE
NOTABLE BUILDING

Map p450 (www.30stmaryaxe.info; 30 St Mary Axe, EC3; ⊖Aldgate) Nicknamed 'the Gherkin' for its unusual shape, 30 St Mary Axe is the City's most distinctive skyscraper, dominating its skyline despite actually being only the fourth tallest. Built in 2003 by award-winning Norman Foster, the Gherkin's futuristic exterior has become an emblem of modern London – as recognisable as Big Ben. The building is closed to the public, though in the past it has opened its doors over the Open House London (p417) weekend in September.

LEADENHALL BUILDING
NOTABLE BUILDING

Map p450 (www.theleadenhallbuilding.com; 122 Leadenhall St, EC3; ⊖Bank) More commonly known as the Cheese Grater, this wedge-shaped skyscraper is angled at 10 degrees and is the second-tallest tower in the City (the fourth tallest in London).

GOLDEN BOY OF PYE CORNER
STATUE

Map p450 (cnr Cock Lane & Giltspur St, EC1; ⊖St Paul's) This small statue of a podgy naked boy has a strange dedication: 'In memmory [sic] put up for the late fire of London occasion'd by the sin of gluttony 1666'. All becomes clear, however, when you realise the Great Fire started in a bakery on Pudding Lane and burned itself out in what was once called Pye (Pie) Corner. This was interpreted as a sign the fire was an act of God as punishment for the gluttony of Londoners.

TEMPLE OF MITHRAS
RUINS

Map p450 (3 Queen Victoria St, EC4; ⊖Bank) A 3rd-century Roman temple, uncovered in the 1950s, has gone back into hiding again at present but it's due to reappear at some point in the basement of the new Bloomsberg building. In the meantime if you're interested in this Persian god, artefacts found in the temple are on display at the Museum of London (p151).

LLOYD'S BUILDING
NOTABLE BUILDING

Map p450 (www.lloyds.com/lloyds/about-us/the-lloyds-building; 1 Lime St, EC3; ⊖Bank) While the world's leading insurance brokers are inside underwriting everything from astronauts' lives to Taylor Swift's legs, people

outside still stop to gawp at this famous inside-out building designed by Richard Rogers, one of the architects of Paris' Pompidou Centre. Completed in 1986, the stainless-steel ducting, vents and staircases are exposed on the outside for all to see. It's not open to the public.

EATING

The financial heart of London unsurprisingly caters for a well-heeled crowd and it can be a tough place to find a meal at the weekend, and even on a weekday evening. You'll find plenty of places to choose from, however, in One New Change (p157). During the week, Leadenhall Market (p148) stalls offer a delicious array of food, from steaming noodles to mountains of sarnies (sandwiches) at lunchtime.

CITY CÀPHÊ
VIETNAMESE $

Map p450 (www.citycaphe.com; 17 Ironmonger Lane, EC2; mains £4.45-7.25; ☺11.30am-4.30pm Mon-Fri; ☑; ⊖Bank) Don't be put off by the lunchtime queue of office workers stretching out the door; these Vietnamese street food specialists dispense steaming bowls of *phở* and *bún bò Huế* (noodle soups) and tasty *bánh mì* (filled baguettes) as efficiently as a Hanoi hawker.

BEA'S OF BLOOMSBURY
CAFE $

Map p450 (☎020-7242 8330; www.beas.london; 83 Watling St, EC4; snacks £3.50-10; ☺7.30am-7pm Mon-Fri, 10am-7pm Sat & Sun; ⊖St Paul's) Bea's made its name with its signature cupcakes, so it was only natural for it to offer a full afternoon tea (£27) too. This branch of the Bloomsbury institution is tiny, with a few tables spilling onto the street.

WREN'S PANTRY
CAFE $

Map p450 (☎020-7248 1574; www.searcysstpauls.co.uk; Crypt, St Paul's Cathedral, EC4; mains £9.50; ☺9am-4.30pm; ⊖St Paul's) In the Crypt of St Paul's, this cafe offers a selection of cakes, pastries and cooked meals kept warm under heat lamps.

★CLUB GASCON
FRENCH $$

Map p450 (☎020-7600 6144; www.clubgascon.com; 57 West Smithfield, EC1; mains £16-28; ☺noon-2pm & 6-10pm Tue-Fri, 6-10pm Sat; ⊖Barbican) Marble walls, white linen and exceedingly professional staff lend an old-fashioned gentlemen's-club feel to this Michelin-starred restaurant. Dishes from France's southwest are given a contemporary work over and while it's not cheap, Gascon does offer an excellent two-course 'express lunch' (£25). Don't be shy about requesting the 'express' menu as it's not always proffered automatically.

★MIYAMA   JAPANESE $$

Map p450 (📞020-7489 1937; www.miyama-restaurant.co.uk; 17 Godliman St, EC4; mains £8-26; ⊙11.30am-2.30pm & 5.45pm-9.30pm Mon-Fri; ⊜St Paul's) There's the sense of a well-kept secret about this friendly Japanese restaurant, tucked away in a basement of a nondescript building (enter from Knightrider St). Miyama offers something for everyone, from soba and udon noodles to sushi and bento boxes. Sit at the sushi or teppanyaki bar for culinary drama, or opt for the more discreet main restaurant.

HAWKSMOOR   STEAK $$

Map p450 (📞020-7397 8120; www.thehawks moor.com; 10 Basinghall St, EC2; breakfast £6-22, mains £13-36; ⊙7-10am, noon-3pm & 5-10.30pm Mon-Fri; ⊜Moorgate) Parquet floors, maroon leather and wood panelling create a clubby vibe in this subterranean steakhouse, patronised mainly by people in suits. Despite a good-value set lunch menu (two/three courses £25/28), we prefer to head here for the City's best cooked breakfasts. They're not all meaty either – the wild mushrooms with hollandaise on toast is particularly good.

WINE LIBRARY   BUFFET $$

Map p450 (📞020-7481 0415; www.winelibrary. co.uk; 43 Trinity Sq, EC3; buffet £18; ⊙buffet noon-3.30pm, shop 10am-6pm Mon, to 8pm Tue-Fri; ⊜Tower Hill) This is a great place for a light but boozy lunch opposite the Tower. Buy a bottle of wine at retail price from the large selection (£9.50 corkage fee) and then head into the vaulted cellar to snack as much as you like from the selection of delicious pâtés, charcuterie, cheeses, bread and salads.

PERKIN REVELLER   BRITISH $$

Map p450 (📞020-3166 6949; www.perkin reveller.co.uk; the Wharf, Tower of London, EC3; mains £13-20; ⊙10am-9pm Mon-Sat, to 5pm Sun Apr-Sep, 11am-6pm Tue-Sat, to 4pm Sun Oct-Mar; ⊜Tower Hill) The location of this minimalist new build beneath the walls of the Tower of London is hard to beat – indeed, it actually spreads under an arch of Tower Bridge. The food – mostly classic British (Cumberland sausage, fish and chips, fish pie) – matches the location admirably. The unusual name comes from a character in Chaucer's *The Canterbury Tales.*

DUCK & WAFFLE   MODERN BRITISH $$

Map p450 (📞020-3640 7310; www.duckand waffle.com; L40, 110 Bishopsgate, EC2; mains £19-20; ⊙24hr; 🤚; ⊜Liverpool St) If you like your views with sustenance round the clock, this is the place for you. Perched atop Heron Tower, it serves a well-waffled breakfast menu, hearty all-day sharing plates (confit duck, roast chicken, miso-glazed rabbit) and round-the-clocktails.

CAMINO   TAPAS $$

Map p450 (📞020-7841 7335; www.camino. uk.com; 15 Mincing Lane, EC3; tapas £4-16; ⊙noon-11pm Mon-Sat; 🍴; ⊜Monument) With an enormous map of the Iberian peninsula on one wall, there's no doubt you're in a Spanish restaurant. All the usual tapas classics are present and accounted for, and a few more besides.

CAFÉ BELOW   CAFE $$

Map p450 (📞020-7329 0789; www.cafebelow. co.uk; Cheapside, EC2; mains £11-16; ⊙7.30am-2.30pm Mon-Fri; ⊜Mansion House) This very atmospheric cafe-restaurant in the crypt of St Mary-le-Bow church offers a tasty range of international dishes. Summer sees tables set up outside in the shady courtyard.

SWEETING'S   SEAFOOD $$

Map p450 (📞020-7248 3062; www.sweetings restaurant.co.uk; 39 Queen Victoria St, EC4; mains £16-30; ⊙11.30am-3pm Mon-Fri; ⊜Mansion House) 🍴 A City institution, Sweeting's dates from 1889. It hasn't changed much, with its small sit-down dining area, terrazzo floor and narrow counters, behind which stand waiters in white aprons. Dishes include sustainably sourced fish of all kinds (grilled, fried or poached), potted shrimps, eels and Sweeting's famous fish pie (£16). Round it all off with a plate of steamed pudding.

WHITE SWAN   GASTROPUB $$

Map p450 (📞020-7242 9696; www.thewhiteswan london.com; 108 Fetter Lane, EC4; mains £17-19; ⊙11am-midnight Mon-Fri; ⊜Chancery Lane) Though it may look like just another City pub from the street, the White Swan is anything but typical. The smart downstairs bar serves excellent pub food (mains £10) under the watchful eyes of bird prints and trophies, while the upstairs dining room offers a classic, meaty and fishy British menu (two-/three-course meal £29/34).

ROYAL EXCHANGE GRAND CAFÉ CAFE $$

Map p450 (☑020-76182480; www.royalexchange-grandcafe.co.uk; Royal Exchange, Threadneedle St, EC3; mains £10-23; ⊗8am-10pm Mon-Fri; ⊖Bank) This lovely cafe sits in the middle of the covered courtyard of the beautiful Royal Exchange (p150) building. The food runs the gamut from breakfast, salads and sandwiches to oysters and a daily selection of cooked mains.

★SAUTERELLE EUROPEAN $$$

Map p450 (☑020-76182480; www.royalexchange-grandcafe.co.uk; Royal Exchange, Threadneedle St, EC3; mains £26-30; ⊗noon-11pm Mon-Fri; ⊖Bank) Take a seat on the elegant mezzanine of the Royal Exchange (p150) and prepare to be pampered with professional service and a menu of sophisticated British, French and Italian fare. Prices befit the sumptuous surroundings, but they also offer an excellent-value set menu (two/three courses £20/25), although you may need to ask to be shown it.

★CITY SOCIAL MODERN BRITISH $$$

Map p450 (☑020-7877 7703; www.citysocial-london.com; L24, 25 Old Broad St, EC2; mains £26-38; ⊗noon-3.30pm & 6-11.30pm Mon-Fri, 5-11.30pm Sat; ⊖Bank) Should you need to impress someone – even yourself – bring him, her and/or said self to this glamour puss on the 24th floor of Tower 42. Come for the extraordinary views (even from the toilets!), the art-deco decor and, especially, Jason Atherton's Michelin-starred meals. Excellent pasta and fish dishes sit alongside the likes of Lancashire rabbit and Romney Marsh lamb.

ANGLER SEAFOOD $$$

Map p450 (☑020-3215 1260; www.anglerres-taurant.com; L7, 3 South Pl, EC2; mains £32-38; ⊗noon-2.30pm & 6-10pm Mon-Sat, 6-10pm Sun; ⊖Moorgate) As the name suggests, fish is definitely on the menu of the South Place Hotel's Michelin-starred restaurant – but so are game meats such as duck and guinea

fowl. Expect elegant, precisely prepared and perfectly cooked dishes, whatever you choose. Despite being on the 7th floor there are no views to speak of, but there is some summertime terrace seating.

BREAD STREET KITCHEN BRITISH $$$

Map p450 (☑020-3030 4050; www.gordon ramsayrestaurants.com/bread-street-kitchen; 10 Bread St, EC4; mains £15-37; ⊗7am-midnight Mon-Fri, 11am-midnight Sat, 11am-10pm Sun; ☎; ⊖St Paul's) Gordon Ramsay's foray into the City makes us wonder whether he thinks he's in hipster East London. It's a huge warehouse-like space in One New Change with a raw bar, wine balcony and open kitchen that produces cooked breakfasts and British favourites such as sausages and roasted cod.

🍷 DRINKING & NIGHTLIFE

Traditionally a dead zone after dark, things in the City have improved in recent years with the opening of destination bars on the roofs of some of the newer skyscrapers. The other area in which the City excels is in historic pubs, although mostly these are daytime and early-evening affairs, and many shut completely on the weekends.

★JAMAICA WINE HOUSE PUB

Map p450 (☑020-7929 6972; www.jamaicawine house.co.uk; 12 St Michael's Alley, EC3; ⊗11am-11pm Mon-Fri; ⊖Bank) Not a wine bar at all, the 'Jam Pot' is a historic wood-lined pub that stands on the site of what was London's first coffee house (1652). Reached by a narrow alley, it's slightly tricky to find but well worth seeking out for the age-old ambience of its darkened rooms.

BY APPOINTMENT ONLY COCKTAIL BAR

Map p450 (☑020-3617 9944; www.victorianbath house.co.uk/bao/; Bishopsgate Churchyard, EC2; ⊗5pm-midnight Fri; ⊖Liverpool Street) Set in a kooky Victorian-era Turkish bathhouse, this subterranean wonderland is one of the most flamboyant cocktail bars in the city. It's mainly used for private functions, but on Fridays you can book ahead to sip on Victorian-inspired cocktails within its tiled confines.

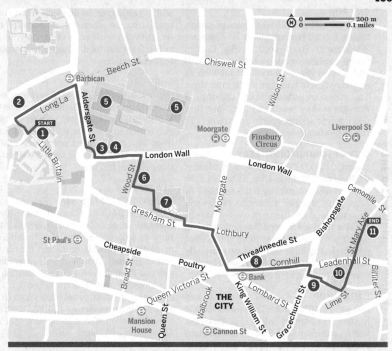

🏃 Neighbourhood Walk
A Taste of the City

START ST BARTHOLOMEW-THE-GREAT
END 30 ST MARY AXE (THE GHERKIN)
LENGTH 1.5 MILES; THREE HOURS

The City of London has as much history in its square mile as the rest of London put together, and this walk picks out just a few of its many highlights. Start by exploring the wonderful 12th-century **1 St Bartholomew-the-Great** (p146), whose atmospheric interior has been used frequently as a film set. Head through the Tudor gatehouse and turn right towards the colourful Victorian arches of **2 Smithfield Market** (p149). Head northeast along Long Lane and take a right at Aldersgate St. Follow the roundabout to the right and nip up the stairs (or take the lift) to the **3 Museum of London** (p151). After exploring the museum's excellent free galleries turn left onto the highwalk and pause to examine the ruins of the **4 Roman city walls** and behind them the distinctive towers of the **5 Barbican** (p150). Descend from the highwalk and cross over to Wood St to find the **6 tower of St Alban** (1698),

all that's left of a Wren-designed church destroyed in WWII bombing. Turn left into Love Lane and right into Aldermanbury – the impressive 15th-century **7 Guildhall** (p147) is on your left, behind a modern extension. Crossing its courtyard – note the black outline of the Roman amphitheatre – continue east onto Gresham St, taking a right into Prince's St and emerging onto the busy Bank intersection lined with neoclassical temples to commerce. Behind the Duke of Wellington statue is a metal pyramid detailing the many significant buildings here. From the **8 Royal Exchange** (p150), follow Cornhill and take a right down Gracechurch St. Turn left into wonderful **9 Leadenhall Market** (p148), roughly where the Roman forum once stood. As you leave the market's far end, **10 Lloyd's of London** (p152) displays its innards for all to see. Once you turn left onto Lime St, **11 30 St Mary Axe** (p152), or 'the Gherkin', looms before you. Built nearly 900 years after St Bartholomew-the-Great, it's a tangible testimony to the city's ability to constantly reinvent itself.

SKY POD
BAR

Map p450 (⌂0333 772 0020; www.skygarden.london; L35, 20 Fenchurch St, EC3; ⏰7am-1am; ⊖Monument) You'll need a Sky Garden (p146) booking to access this rooftop bar, and if you'd like a guaranteed table to sit at, you're best to book one at the same time. The views are extraordinary, although it does get cold up here in winter. Note, they don't accept shorts, sportwear, trainers or flip flops after 5pm.

CITY OF LONDON DISTILLERY
BAR

Map p450 (⌂020-7936 3636; www.cityoflondondistillery.com; 22 Bride Lane, EC4; ⏰4-11pm Mon-Sat; ⊖Blackfriars) Hogarth's famous *Gin Lane* print provides a warning before you descend the stairs to one of the few bars in London to distill its own 'mother's ruin' on site. If you'd like to know more about what goes on in the shiny distilling vats, proudly displayed behind glass windows, book a tour or attend a gin-making class.

HACK & HOP
CRAFT BEER

Map p450 (⌂020-7583 8117; www.thehackandhop.com; 35 Whitefriars St, EC4; ⏰11.30am-11pm Mon-Fri, noon-5pm Sat & Sun; 🛜; ⊖Blackfriars) From 5pm weekdays, suited Fleet St workers descend on this specialist beer bar for a craft beer and burger before heading home. There's a good range of craft beers and real ales, many of them from London brewers.

FOLLY
BAR

Map p450 (⌂0845 468 0102; www.thefollybar.com; 41 Gracechurch St, EC3; ⏰7.30am-late Mon-Fri, 10am-late Sat, 10am-6pm Sun; ⊖Monument) Workers in London's concrete jungle flock to this two-level garden-style cafe-bar for a restorative dose of greenery (both real and faux) and picnic-table seating. Come knock-off time there's barely enough space to twirl a cocktail umbrella. There's a full menu on offer too, with a strong emphasis on burgers and steaks, and positively sinful desserts.

MADISON
COCKTAIL BAR

Map p450 (⌂020-3693 5160; www.madisonlondon.net; rooftop, 1 New Change, EC4; ⏰11am-midnight Mon-Wed, to 1am Thu-Sat, to 9pm Sun; ⊖St Paul's) Perched atop One New Change with a drop-dead gorgeous view of St Paul's, Madison offers a large open-air roof terrace with a restaurant on one side and a cocktail bar on the other; we come for the latter. Drinkers must be over 21; no trainers or flip flops admitted, however fashionable. Expect to queue.

SHIP
PUB

Map p450 (⌂020-7702 4422; www.shipec3.co.uk; 3 Hart St, EC3; ⏰11.30am-11pm Mon-Fri; ⊖Tower Hill) This small and very smart 1802 pub with a nautical theme is a short walk from Tower Hill. The Upper Deck dining room looks like a film set and serves better-than-average pub grub.

BLACKFRIAR
PUB

Map p450 (⌂020-7236 5474; www.nicholsonspubs.co.uk; 174 Queen Victoria St, EC4; ⏰10am-11pm Mon-Sat, noon-10.30pm Sun; ⊖Blackfriars) Built in 1875 on the site of a Dominican monastery (hence the name and the corpulent chap above the door), this prominent pub was famously saved from demolition in the 1960s by poet Sir John Betjeman. The unusual monastic-themed friezes date from an art-nouveau makeover in 1905. It serves a good selection of ales, along with speciality sausages and chops.

YE OLDE CHESHIRE CHEESE
PUB

Map p450 (⌂020-7353 6170; Wine Office Court, 145 Fleet St, EC4; ⏰11.30am-11pm Mon-Fri, noon-11pm Sat; ⊖Chancery Lane) Rebuilt in 1667 after the Great Fire, this is one of London's most famous pubs, accessed via a narrow alley off Fleet St. Over its long history, Dr Johnson, Thackeray and Dickens have all supped in its gloriously gloomy surrounds. The vaulted cellars are thought to be remnants of a 13th-century Carmelite monastery.

COUNTING HOUSE
PUB

Map p450 (⌂020-7283 7123; www.the-counting-house.com; 50 Cornhill, EC3; ⏰10am-11pm Mon-Fri; 🛜; ⊖Bank) With its counters and basement vaults, this award-winning pub certainly looks and feels comfortable in the former headquarters of NatWest Bank (1893), with its domed skylight and elegantly curved central bar. This is a favourite of City boys and girls, who come for the good range of real ales and the speciality pies (from £12).

WINE PANTRY
WINE BAR

Map p450 (⌂020-3751 9410; www.ewsco.co.uk; 8 Devonshire Row, EC2; ⏰11am-8pm Mon, 11am-11pm

Tue-Fri, 2-8pm Sat) Aiming to demonstrate that the phrase 'quality English wine' isn't an oxymoron, this shop sells bottles of homegrown still and sparkling wine to take away or drink by the glass – along with local gin and whisky. It makes for an interesting stop, but the bright lighting effectively kills the atmosphere.

HOOP & GRAPES   PUB
Map p450 (www.nicholsonspubs.co.uk; 47 Aldgate High St, EC3; ⊗10am-11pm Mon-Fri; ⊜Aldgate) For a pub that survived the Great Fire by 50m, the Hoop & Grapes is surprisingly lacking in atmosphere. The current structure probably dates from the 17th century, but it's said that the foundations were built in the 13th and hide a tunnel that once led to the Tower of London.

EL VINO   WINE BAR
Map p450 (☑020-7353 6786; www.elvino.co.uk; 47 Fleet St, EC4; ⊗11.30am-3pm & 5-8pm Mon-Fri; ⊜Blackfriars) A venerable institution that plays host to barristers, solicitors and other legal types from the Royal Courts of Justice across the way, this wood-lined wine bar (one of four in a small chain) has one of the better wine lists in the City. El Vino featured as Pomeroy's in the TV series *Rumpole of the Bailey*.

⭐ ENTERTAINMENT

BARBICAN CENTRE   PERFORMING ARTS
Map p450 (☑020-7638 8891; www.barbican.org. uk; Silk St, EC2; ⊗box office 10am-8pm; ⊜Barbican) Home to the London Symphony Orchestra and the BBC Symphony Orchestra, the Barbican (p150) also hosts scores of other concerts, focusing in particular on jazz, folk, world and soul artists. Dance is also performed here, while the cinema screens recent releases as well as film festivals.

BRIDEWELL THEATRE   THEATRE
Map p450 (☑020-8881 2201; www.sbf.org.uk; Bride Lane, EC4; ⊜Blackfriars) This unique small theatre started in 1994 in an old Victorian swimming pool. It's run by the St Bride Foundation, which was founded in 1891 to promote the then-vibrant printing

culture of nearby Fleet St. The theatre stages evening performances by amateur and professional groups, and the Lunchbox Theatre program offers bite-sized 45-minute renditions of plays during weekday lunch hours.

 ## SHOPPING

Unless you want to buy a suit, business shirt or snazzy tie, the City doesn't hold much shopping appeal. The Royal Exchange has a good selection of high-end brand-name boutiques. Aside from the busy One New Change shopping centre, not much is open on the weekend.

LONDON SILVER VAULTS   ARTS & CRAFTS
Map p450 (☑020-7242 3844; www.silvervaults london.com; 53-63 Chancery Lane, WC2; ⊗9am-5.30pm Mon-Fri, to 1pm Sat; ⊜Chancery Lane) The 30-odd shops that work out of these secure subterranean vaults make up the largest collection of silver under one roof in the world. The different businesses tend to specialise in particular types of silverware – from cutlery sets to picture frames, animal sculptures and lots of jewellery.

ST PAUL'S CATHEDRAL
SHOP   GIFTS & SOUVENIRS
Map p450 (☑020-7246 8363; www.stpaulsshop. org.uk; crypt, St Paul's Cathedral, EC4; ⊗9am-5pm; ⊜St Paul's) The place to come for essentials such as St Paul's snow globes and silk scarves printed with Cathedral artworks, the crypt shop also sells all of the usual Beefeater and doubledecker bus souvenirs.

ONE NEW CHANGE   SHOPPING CENTRE
Map p450 (www.onenewchange.com; 1 New Change, EC4M; ⊗10am-6pm Mon-Wed & Sat, 10am-8pm Thu & Fri, noon-6pm Sun; ⊜St Paul's) Opened in 2010, this glitzy shopping centre has all the usual chain-store suspects (Topshop/Topman, Mango, Next, H&M, Banana Republic, Boots and Oliver Bonas), but the highlight is the public roof terrace with its extraordinary views of the St Paul's dome.

The South Bank

WATERLOO | BANKSIDE & SOUTHWARK | LONDON BRIDGE | BERMONDSEY | ROTHERHITHE

Neighbourhood Top Five

❶ Tate Modern (p160) Finding out what all the fuss is about by exploring this magnificent, and now extended, modern- and contemporary-art collection.

❷ London Eye (p165) Revolving in leisurely fashion above London's panoramic cityscape in this iconic Ferris wheel.

❸ Borough Market (p163) Stimulating your taste buds on a gastronomic tour of discovery at this gourmet market.

❹ Oblix (p172) Sipping a coffee or cocktail in the Shard for riveting views of the city.

❺ Shakespeare's Globe (p162) Getting a Bard's-eye view of Elizabethan theatrics at this authentic recreation of a 17th-century theatre.

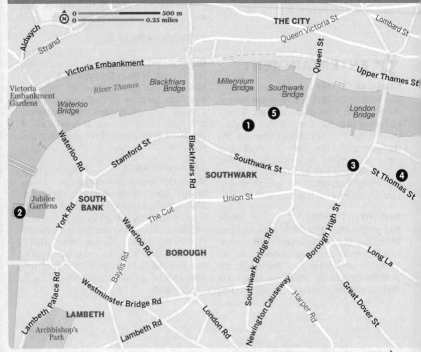

For more detail of this area see Map p452 ➡

Explore the South Bank

The drawcard sights on the South Bank stretch west–east in a manageable riverside melange, so exploring on foot is best. If you're pressed for time, allocate a day to walk from the London Eye to London Bridge, with just a couple of sightseeing stops along the way (the London Eye, say, and the Tate Modern).

If you have even the slightest thespian disposition, you should make time for a play. Shakespeare's Globe (p162) is a once-in-a-lifetime opportunity, and the neighbourhood is home to other world-renowned theatres, too. Plan ahead if you're picky about what performance you'd like to see and where you sit; otherwise, book on the spur of the moment for same-day or standby tickets.

The area around Maltby Street Market (p171) really only comes to life at weekends (Saturdays especially), when the market is in full swing, microbreweries convert into 'tap rooms' and the railway arches open up their wholesale secrets to individual customers for the day.

It pays to plan ahead a night at the South Bank's higher-end bars and restaurants, especially those with views; if your heart is set on eating or drinking at a particular place, book a slot rather than chancing it on a walk-in.

Local Life

➡ **Hang-outs** Cool Londoners love Maltby Street Market (p171) for its gourmet sandwiches, crazy cocktails and rollicking atmosphere.

➡ **Museums** Locals earmark the Friday and Saturday late-night opening (till 10pm) at the Tate Modern (p160) to view the art when crowds have thinned.

➡ **Artisan food and drink** Be it for their next dinner party or just for a treat, Londoners love buying delicious products at Borough Market (p163), trying local gin at Jensen (p173) or enjoying craft beer from the Bermondsey Beer Mile (p173).

Getting There & Away

➡ **Underground** The South Bank is lashed into the tube system by stations at Waterloo, Southwark, London Bridge and Bermondsey, all on the Jubilee Line. The Northern Line runs through London Bridge and Waterloo; the Bakerloo Line runs through Waterloo.

➡ **Walking** Cross to South Bank from the City over Tower Bridge or the Millennium Bridge, or from the West End across Waterloo Bridge. Each offers sublime views of the city.

➡ **Bicycle** Jump on a Santander Bike and wheel it!

➡ **Bus** The Riverside RV1 runs around the South Bank and Bankside, linking all the main sights (running between Covent Garden and Tower Gateway).

Lonely Planet's Top Tip

To collect the main sights, trace the Silver Jubilee Walk and the South Bank section of the Thames Path along the southern riverbank, but do venture further inland for the best eating and drinking.

✖ Best Places to Eat

➡ Arabica Bar & Kitchen (p170)

➡ Padella (p170)

➡ Skylon (p169)

➡ Baltic (p170)

➡ Watch House (p171)

For reviews, see p169.

THE SOUTH BANK

🍺 Best Places to Drink

➡ Little Bird Gin (p173)

➡ Scootercaffe (p171)

➡ Brew By Numbers (p173)

➡ Oblix (p172)

➡ Mayflower (p173)

For reviews, see p171.

◉ Best Theatres

➡ Shakespeare's Globe (p174)

➡ National Theatre (p174)

➡ Unicorn Theatre (p174)

➡ Young Vic (p175)

➡ Old Vic (p175)

For reviews, see p174. ➡

TOP SIGHT
TATE MODERN

The public's love affair with this phenomenally successful modern- and contemporary-art gallery shows no sign of cooling more than 15 years after it opened. In fact, so enraptured are art-goers with the Tate Modern that the Tate decided to expand: its daring 10-storey geometric extension at the back, named Switch House, opened in 2016.

Boiler House

The original gallery lies in what was once Bankside Power Station. Now called Boiler House, it is an imposing sight: a 200m-long building, made of 4.2 million bricks. Its conversion into an art gallery was a masterstroke of design: the 'Tate Modern effect' is clearly as much about the building and its location (cue the ever popular balconies on level 3 with their magnificent views of St Paul's) as it is about the mostly 20th-century art inside.

Turbine Hall

The first thing to greet you as you pour down the ramp off Holland St at the main entrance is the astounding 3300-sq-metre Turbine Hall. Originally housing the power station's humungous electricity generators, this vast space has become the commanding venue for large-scale installation art and temporary exhibitions. Some art critics swipe at its populism, particularly the 'participatory art' (Carsten Höller's funfair-like slides *Test Site;* Doris Salcedo's enormous *Shibboleth* fissure in the floor; and Robert Morris' climbable geometric sculpture), but others insist this makes art more accessible. Note, if you enter instead from the river entrance, you'll end up on the more-muted level 1.

DON'T MISS

- ➡ Turbine Hall
- ➡ Special exhibitions
- ➡ Views of St Paul's Cathedral from Boiler House level 3 balconies
- ➡ The tanks
- ➡ Viewing gallery on level 10 of Switch House

PRACTICALITIES

- ➡ Map p452, D3
- ➡ www.tate.org.uk
- ➡ Bankside, SE1
- ➡ admission free
- ➡ ⏱10am-6pm Sun-Thu, to 10pm Fri & Sat
- ➡ 🛜 ♿
- ➡ ⊖Blackfriars, Southwark, London Bridge

Switch House

The new Tate Modern extension takes its name from the former electrical substation that still occupies the southeast end of the site. To echo its sister building, it is also constructed of brick, although here these are slightly lighter and have been artistically laid out in a lattice to let light in (and out – the building looks stunning after dark).

The interior is rather stark, with raw, unpolished concrete (the original look of the Tanks) vaguely reminiscent of decrepit brutalist buildings, but the exhibition space is fantastic, giving the collection the room it deserves to breathe and shine.

The Tanks

The three huge subterranean tanks once stored fuel for the power station. These unusual circular spaces are now dedicated to showing live art, performance, installation and film, or 'new art' as the Tate calls it.

Viewing Gallery: Level 10

The views from level 10 are, as you would expect, sweeping. The river views are perhaps not quite as iconic as the full frontal St Paul's view that you get from Boiler House, but from here you get to see Boiler House itself, and a lot more in every direction. The views of the Shard as you look to the east are especially good. And best of all, they are free.

Permanent Collection

Tate Modern's permanent collection is arranged by both theme and chronology on levels 2 and 4 of Boiler House and levels 0, 2, 3 and 4 of Switch House. The emphasis in the latter is on art from the 1960s onwards.

More than 60,000 works are on constant rotation, which can be frustrating if you'd like to see one particular piece, but keeps it thrilling for repeat visitors. Helpfully, you can check the excellent website to see whether a specific work is on display – and where.

Special Exhibitions

With the opening of Switch House, the Tate Modern has increased the number of special exhibitions it hosts. You will find the exhibits on levels 3 and 4 of Boiler House and level 2 of Switch House; all are subject to admission charges (adult tickets cost £12.50 to £18.50; children enter free).

Past special exhibitions have included retrospectives on Henri Matisse, Edward Hopper, Frida Kahlo, Roy Lichtenstein, August Strindberg, Nazism and 'Degenerate' Art, and Joan Miró.

TATE-TO-TATE BOAT

For the most scenic of culture trips, take the Tate Boat (www.tate.org.uk/visit/tate-boat; one-way adult/child £8/4) between the Bankside Pier at Tate Modern and the Millbank Pier at its sister museum, Tate Britain (p90).

STARCHITECTS

Swiss architects Herzog & de Meuron scooped the prestigious Pritzker Architecture Prize for their transformation of empty Bankside Power Station, which closed in 1981. Leaving the building's single central 99m-high chimney, adding a two-storey glass box onto the roof and employing the cavernous Turbine Hall as a dramatic entrance space were three strokes of genius. Herzog & de Meuron also designed the new Tate extension, Switch House.

PRES PANAYIOTIS/SHUTTERSTOCK ©

TOP SIGHT
SHAKESPEARE'S GLOBE

Unlike other venues for Shakespearean plays, the Globe was designed to resemble the original as closely as possible, from the materials to the open-air stage and arena, which means exposing the audience to London's fickle skies. Watching a play here is experiencing Shakespeare at its best, and touring the theatre will make you appreciate how unique this venue is.

The current Globe is located just a few hundred metres from its original location on Park St. The original structure was one of the first purpose-built theatres to be established in London – until then, playing companies used inns, college halls or private homes to stage their plays.

Despite the worldwide popularity of Shakespeare over the centuries, the Globe was almost a distant memory when American actor (and, later, film director) Sam Wanamaker came searching for it in 1949. Undeterred by the fact that the theatre's foundations had vanished beneath a row of heritage-listed Georgian houses, Wanamaker set up the Globe Playhouse Trust in 1970 and began fundraising for a memorial theatre. Work started just 200m from the original Globe site in 1987. Wanamaker died four years before the new theatre opened in 1997.

Shakespeare wrote for both outdoor and indoor theatre, and an indoor playhouse had always been part of the Globe's ambitions. In 2014 this was realised with the opening of the **Sam Wanamaker Playhouse**, a candlelit Jacobean theatre.

A visit to the Globe includes an informative tour of the theatre, departing half-hourly, and sometimes also the Playhouse. You'll gain access to the exhibition space beneath the theatre, which has fascinating exhibits about Shakespeare and theatre in the 17th century, including costumes and props, and also includes fun live talks and demonstrations. Or you can of course take in a play (p174): a 'groundling' ticket (standing) costs just £5.

DON'T MISS

➡ Exhibition Hall and tour
➡ Interior of the Globe Theatre
➡ Sam Wanamaker Playhouse

PRACTICALITIES

➡ Map p452, D3
➡ www.shakespeares globe.com
➡ 21 New Globe Walk, SE1
➡ adult/child £16/9
➡ ⏰9am-5pm
➡ 🚻
➡ ⊜Blackfriars, London Bridge

TOP SIGHT
BOROUGH MARKET

Located in this spot in some form or another since the 13th century, 'London's Larder' has enjoyed an astonishing renaissance in the past 15 years. Always overflowing with food lovers, inveterate gastronomes, wide-eyed visitors and Londoners in search of inspiration for their next dinner party, this fantastic market has become firmly established as a sight in its own right.

Foodscapes

The market specialises in high-end fresh products so you'll find the usual assortment of fruit and vegetable stalls, cheesemongers, butchers, fishmongers and bakeries, as well as delis and gourmet stalls selling spices, nuts, preserves and condiments. This gastronomic ensemble makes the most eye-catching and mouth-watering displays, and there are plenty of visitors strolling with cameras at the ready. Prices tend to be high but many traders offer free samples, a great perk for visitors and locals alike.

DON'T MISS

➡ Free samples

➡ Foodscapes (really!)

➡ Enjoying takeaway by the river

PRACTICALITIES

➡ Map p452, E4

➡ www.boroughmarket.org.uk

➡ 8 Southwark St, SE1

➡ ⏰10am-5pm Wed & Thu, 10am-6pm Fri, 8am-5pm Sat

➡ ⊖London Bridge

Foodstalls

Food window-shopping (and sampling) over, you'll be able to grab lunch in one of the myriad takeaway stalls – choose from anything from sizzling gourmet sausages, chorizo sandwiches, falafel wraps and raclette portions (cheese melted over cured meats and potatoes). There's also an almost unreasonable number of cake stalls – walking out without a treat will be a challenge! Many of the lunch stalls cluster in Green Market (the area closest to Southwark Cathedral). Allow £4 to £8 for a takeaway dish.

◉ SIGHTS

◉ Waterloo

ROUPELL ST
STREET

Map p452 (Roupell St, SE1; ⊖Waterloo) Waterloo station isn't exactly scenic, but wander around the backstreets of this transport hub and you'll find some amazing architecture. Roupell St is an astonishingly pretty row of workers' cottages, all dark bricks and coloured doors, dating back to the 1820s. The street is so uniform it looks like a film set.

The same architecture extends to Theed and Whittlesey Streets (which run parallel to Roupell St to the north). The terraced houses were developed for artisan workers by John Palmer Roupell, a gold refiner, between the 1820s and the 1840s. They have survived both WWII damage and the many developments of the area intact.

NATIONAL THEATRE
THEATRE

Map p452 (🖉020-7452 3000; www.national theatre.org.uk; South Bank, SE1; 🚹; ⊖Waterloo) The nation's flagship theatre complex comprises three auditoriums for performances (p174). Likened by Prince Charles to a nuclear power station, the theatre's purpose-designed architecture is considered an icon of the brutalist school. Fantastic **backstage tours** lasting 1¼ hours (adult/child £9.50/8.25) are available. Every tour is different but you're likely to see rehearsals and changes of sets or bump into actors in the corridors. There is at least one tour per day, and often more. Consult the website for exact times and make sure you book.

There are also architecture tours (£12.50), family tours (£9.50) and costume tours (£12.50).

★LONDON DUNGEON
HISTORIC BUILDING

Map p452 (www.thedungeons.com/london; County Hall, Westminster Bridge Rd, SE1; adult/child £30/24; ⊙10am-5pm Mon-Fri, to 6pm Sat & Sun; 🚹; ⊖Waterloo, Westminster) Older kids tend to love the London Dungeon, as the terrifying queues during school holidays and weekends testify. It's all spooky music, ghostly boat rides, macabre hangman's drop-rides, fake blood and actors dressed up as torturers and gory criminals (including Jack the Ripper and Sweeney Todd), with interactive scares galore.

The highlights are the vaudevillian delights of being sentenced by a mad, bewigged judge on trumped-up charges, the utterly disorienting Whitechapel Labyrinth, the Drop Dead Drop Ride (which has you 'plummeting' to your death by hanging from the gallows) and Escape the Great Fire of London, rounded off with a stop in the Tavern.

It takes just over 1½ hours to work your way through the gory dungeon. Buy tickets online to avoid the queues and save a few pounds. Note that children younger than eight may find some parts too scary.

LONDON SEA LIFE AQUARIUM
AQUARIUM

Map p452 (www.visitsealife.com; County Hall, Westminster Bridge Rd, SE1; adult/child £25.50/20.40; ⊙10am-6pm Mon-Fri, 9.30am-7pm Sat & Sun; 🚹; ⊖Waterloo, Westminster) Displays look somewhat dated, but there are some stand-out sights, including the shark tunnel, the ray lagoon, the Gentoo penguin enclosures (penguins jump and dive at mesmerising speed) and Frozen Planet, with its flickering northern lights. Feeds and talks are scheduled throughout the day, so your chances of catching one during your visit are high.

Book online to save up to 30% on the admission price; combined tickets offering good discounts are also available with the London Eye (p165), the London Dungeon (p164) and Madame Tussauds (p106).

COUNTY HALL
HISTORIC BUILDING

Map p452 (Westminster Bridge Rd, SE1; ⊖Westminster or Waterloo) Begun in 1909 but not completed until 1922, this grand building with its curved, colonnaded facade was the home of the London County Council, subsequently the Greater London Council, until 1986. It now houses a number of attractions.

◉ Bankside & Southwark

TATE MODERN
MUSEUM

See p160.

SHAKESPEARE'S GLOBE
HISTORIC BUILDING

See p162.

MILLENNIUM BRIDGE
BRIDGE

Map p452 (⊖St Paul's, Blackfriars) The elegant steel, aluminium and concrete Millennium Bridge staples the south bank of the Thames, in front of Tate Modern, to the north bank, at the steps of Peter's Hill below St Paul's Cathedral. The low-slung frame designed by Sir Norman Foster and

TOP SIGHT
LONDON EYE

It's hard to remember what London looked like before the landmark London Eye (officially the Coca-Cola London Eye) began twirling at the southwestern end of Jubilee Gardens in 2000. Not only has it fundamentally altered the South Bank skyline but, standing 135m tall in a fairly flat city, it is visible from numerous locations.

A ride – or 'flight', as it is called here – in one of the wheel's 32 glass-enclosed eye pods takes a gracefully slow 30 minutes and, weather permitting, you can see 25 miles in every direction from the top. Don't let poor weather put you off, either: the close-up views of Westminster, just across the river, are probably the highlight of the ride. Interactive tablets provide great information (in six languages) about landmarks as they come up in the skyline.

It can feel like you'll spend more time in the queue than you will in the pod, but don't be discouraged: it is worth the wait, and those close-up, vertical shots of the Eye will look terrific.

DID YOU KNOW?

➜ The Eye is the focal point of the capital's New Year's Eve fireworks, for which it is rigged with some 12,000 fireworks.

PRACTICALITIES

➜ Map p452, A4

➜ ☎0871-222 4002

➜ www.londoneye.com

➜ adult/child £23.45/18.95

➜ ⊙11am-6pm Sep-May, 10am-8.30pm Jun-Aug

➜ ⊜Waterloo, Westminster

THE SOUTH BANK SIGHTS

Antony Caro looks spectacular, particularly when lit up at night with fibre optics, and the view of St Paul's from the South Bank has become one of London's iconic images.

GOLDEN HINDE   SHIP
Map p452 (☎020-7403 0123; www.goldenhinde. com; St Mary Overie Dock, Cathedral St, SE1; self-guided tours adult/child £6/4.50, events adult/child £7/5; ⊙10am-5.30pm; ⊛; ⊜London Bridge) Stepping aboard this replica of Sir Francis Drake's famous Tudor ship will inspire genuine admiration for the admiral and his rather short-statured (average height 1.6m) crew, which numbered between 40 and 60. It was in a tiny five-deck galleon just like this that Drake and his crew circumnavigated the globe between 1577 and 1580. Visitors can explore the ship independently or join a guided tour led by a costumed actor – children love these.

CLINK PRISON MUSEUM   MUSEUM
Map p452 (☎020-7403 0900; www.clink.co.uk; 1 Clink St, SE1; adult/child £7.50/5.50; ⊙10am-6pm Mon-Fri, to 7.30pm Sat & Sun; ⊛; ⊜London Bridge) This one-time private jail, known as the Liberty of the Clink, was used to detain debtors, prostitutes, thieves and numerous Protestants and Catholics during the Reformation. The museum relates the story of its most (in)famous inmates and explains at length – with props, storyboards and original objects – the many ways they could be tortured. Not suitable for children under seven years.

ROSE THEATRE   THEATRE
Map p452 (☎020-7261 9565; www.rosetheatre. org.uk; 56 Park St, SE1; ⊜London Bridge) FREE The Rose, for which Christopher Marlowe and Ben Jonson wrote their greatest plays and in which Shakespeare learned his craft, is unique: its original 16th-century foundations were discovered in 1989 beneath an office building and given a protective concrete cover. Administered by the nearby Globe Theatre, the Rose is only open to the public on set open days and for performances; check the website for details.

◉ London Bridge

BOROUGH MARKET   MARKET
See p163.

TOP SIGHT
SOUTHWARK CATHEDRAL

The earliest surviving parts of this relatively small cathedral are the **retrochoir** at the eastern end, which contains four chapels and was part of the 13th-century Priory of St Mary Overie, some ancient arcading by the southwest door, 12th-century wall cores in the north transept, and an arch that dates from the original Norman church. But most of the cathedral is Victorian.

One of the more intriguing sights is a selection of **medieval roof bosses** from the 15th century, close to the baptismal font. Walk up the north aisle of the nave and on the left you'll see the **tomb of John Gower**, the 14th-century poet who was the first to write in English. Cross into the choir to admire the 16th-century **Great Screen** separating the choir from the retrochoir.

In the south aisle of the nave have a look at the green alabaster **monument to William Shakespeare**. Beside the monument is a **plaque to Sam Wanamaker** (1919–93), American playwright and founder of the recreated **Shakespeare's Globe** (p162) theatre. Do hunt down the exceedingly fine **Elizabethan sideboard** in the north transept.

DON'T MISS
➡ Retrochoir
➡ Ancient arcading
➡ Great Screen

PRACTICALITIES
➡ Map p452, E3
➡ 020-7367 6700
➡ www.cathedral.southwark.anglican.org
➡ Montague Cl, SE1
➡ ☺8am-6pm Mon-Fri, 8.30am-6pm Sat & Sun
➡ ⊖London Bridge

SHARD
NOTABLE BUILDING

Map p452 (www.theviewfromtheshard.com; 32 London Bridge St, SE1; adult/child £30.95/24.95; ☺10am-10pm; ⊖London Bridge) Puncturing the skies above London, the dramatic splinter-like form of the Shard has rapidly become an icon of London. The viewing platforms on floors 69 and 72 are open to the public and the views are, as you'd expect from a 244m vantage point, sweeping, but they come at a hefty price – book online at least a day in advance to save £5.

Audio guides in 11 languages are available. To take in the view for less, visit one of the building's restaurants or bars; you'll pay less than half the viewing platform ticket price for breakfast or a cocktail at **Aqua Shard** (Map p452; www.aquashard.co.uk; 31st fl, 31 St Thomas St, SE1; ☺10.30am-1am Sun-Thu, to 2am Fri & Sat; ⊖London Bridge) or Oblix (p172) where the views are still spectacular. If you choose Gŏng (p172) for a drink, be aware there is a £30 minimum spend per person.

HMS BELFAST
SHIP

Map p452 (www.iwm.org.uk/visits/hms-belfast; Queen's Walk, SE1; adult/child £14.50/7.25; ☺10am-5pm; ⊖London Bridge) HMS *Belfast* is a magnet for kids of all ages. This large, light cruiser – launched in 1938 – served in WWII, helping to sink the German battleship *Scharnhorst,* shelling the Normandy coast on D-Day and later participating in the Korean War. Its 6in guns could bombard a target 14 land miles distant. Displays offer a great insight into what life on board was like, in peace times and during military engagements.

OLD OPERATING THEATRE MUSEUM & HERB GARRET
MUSEUM

Map p452 (www.oldoperatingtheatre.com; 9a St Thomas St, SE1; adult/child £6.50/3.50; ☺10.30am-5pm; ⊖London Bridge) This unique museum, 32 steps up a spiral stairway in the tower of **St Thomas Church** (1703), is the unlikely home of Britain's oldest operating theatre. Rediscovered in 1956, the garret was used by the apothecary of St Thomas's Hospital to store medicinal herbs. The museum looks back at the horror of 19th-century medicine – all pre-anaesthetic and pre-antiseptic. You can browse the natural remedies, including snail water for venereal disease, and recoil at the fiendish array of amputation knives and blades. There are

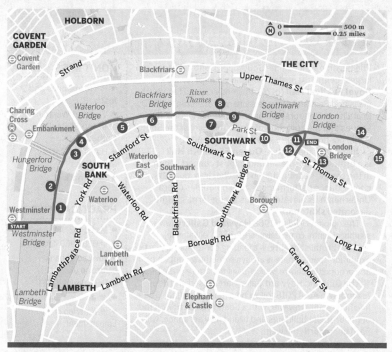

🏃 Neighbourhood Walk
South Bank Stroll

START WESTMINSTER TUBE STATION
END LONDON BRIDGE TUBE STATION
LENGTH 2.8 MILES; 3½ HOURS

From Westminster tube station, cross the river on Westminster Bridge and admire the views of Big Ben. As you reach the South Bank, the first building you'll pass is the sombre ❶**County Hall** (p164), seat of London's government from 1922 until Thatcher dissolved the Greater London Council in 1986.

The ❷**London Eye** (p165) gracefully rotates next to it and the atmosphere on this stretch of the river is always party-like, with ice-cream vans, street performers, dozens of visitors and Londoners on their lunchtime run. Push on east past the ❸**Southbank Centre** (p168) and pause to admire the acrobatics of teenagers in the graffitied skatepark underneath ❹**Queen Elizabeth Hall** (p174).

Carry on strolling along the river, past the boutiques of ❺**Gabriel's Wharf** and the ❻**Oxo Tower**. After 20 to 30 minutes you'll emerge in front of the imposing ❼**Tate Modern** (p160); note the new extension at the back (opened in 2016), which echoes the industrial brick architecture of the original power station. Opposite is the ❽**Millennium Bridge** (p164), Sir Norman Foster's 'blade of light'.

Just 100m past the Tate is the magnificently rebuilt ❾**Shakespeare's Globe** (p162). Walk under Southwark Bridge, which is beautifully lit at night, past the perennially busy ❿**Anchor Bankside pub** (p172), and down the maze of streets leading to ⓫**Southwark Cathedral** (p166).

Spreading around the railway arches is ⓬**Borough Market** (p163), London's premier gourmet produce market. Lording dramatically over this area is the ⓭**Shard** (p166), the EU's tallest building and modern London icon. Pass London Bridge and the intimidating ⓮**HMS Belfast** (p166) for glorious views of Tower Bridge before arriving at ⓯**City Hall** on your right, nicknamed 'the egg'. Finally, retrace your steps to the London Bridge tube station.

TOP SIGHT
SOUTHBANK CENTRE

The flagship venue of the Southbank Centre, Europe's largest centre for performing and visual arts, is the **Royal Festival Hall** (p174). Its gently curved facade of glass and Portland stone is more humane than its 1970s brutalist neighbours. It is one of London's leading music venues and the epicentre of life on this part of the South Bank, hosting cafes, restaurants, shops and bars.

Just north, the austere **Queen Elizabeth Hall** (p174) is a brutalist icon, the second-largest concert venue in the centre, hosting chamber orchestras, quartets, choirs, dance performances and sometimes opera. Underneath its elevated floor is a long-term, graffiti-decorated **skatepark**.

The opinion-dividing 1968 **Hayward Gallery** (www.southbankcentre.co.uk; Belvedere Rd, SE1; ⊖Waterloo), another brutalist beauty, is a leading contemporary-art exhibition space. There is always something happening in and around the centre, which gives the area a great buzz.

The QEH and Hayward Gallery are closed and due to reopen in April 2018 following a major overhaul. The finished result, however, with a floating glass box on top of the brutalist buildings and brand new art space, will have been worth the wait.

DON'T MISS
➡ Performances and festivals
➡ Views of Wesminster and St Paul's Cathedral
➡ Hayward Gallery exhibitions
➡ Skatepark

PRACTICALITIES
➡ Map p452, A4
➡ ☎020-7960 4200
➡ www.southbankcentre.co.uk
➡ Belvedere Rd, SE1
➡ 🛜♿
➡ ⊖Waterloo or Embankment

---

talks on Victorian surgery and medicine preparation on Saturdays and Sundays at 2pm; book ahead.

GIBBON'S RENT   GARDENS
Map p452 (Gibbon's Rent, SE1; ⊖London Bridge) Buried between soaring blocks of flats, this tiny alley has been transformed by locals into a secret garden lined with potted plants. A small wooden wardrobe, thumbing its nose at the gargantuan Shard looming in the distance, acts as a book-swap library. Annoyingly there are no benches to sit and relax. There are two entrances: one on Magdalen St and one on Holyrood St.

LONDON BRIDGE EXPERIENCE
& LONDON TOMBS   MUSEUM
Map p452 (www.thelondonbridgeexperience.com; 2-4 Tooley St, SE1; adult/child £27.95/22.50; ⊗10am-5pm Mon-Fri, 9.30am-6pm Sat & Sun; ⊖London Bridge) Stuffed away in the vaults beneath New London Bridge (dating from 1973), this historical attraction takes you on a whistle-stop tour of London's most famous span. Follow bridge history, from the Romans to Peter de Colechurch's 'Old London Bridge' (1209) lined with shops, to the

American Robert McCulloch, who bought the 1831 version of London Bridge in 1967 for US$2.5 million, transporting it to Arizona and rebuilding it at Lake Havasu City, where it can be seen today.

CROSSBONES GARDEN   GARDENS
Map p452 (www.crossbones.org.uk; cnr Union Street & Redcross Way, SE1; ⊗noon-2pm Mon-Fri; ⊖Borough, London Bridge) This peaceful, if slightly ramshackle garden sits on a site known as Crossbones, an unconsecrated burial ground where those living on the margins of society were buried until 1853. Some 50,000 people were buried here over the centuries, most of them women (who worked as prostitutes) and children. Since the 1990s, volunteers have fought to preserve the site from development and transform it into a garden of remembrance.

◉ Bermondsey

FASHION & TEXTILE MUSEUM   MUSEUM
Map p452 (☎020-7407 8664; www.ftmlondon.org; 83 Bermondsey St, SE1; adult/child £9.90/free; ⊗11am-6pm Tue, Wed, Fri & Sat, to 8pm Thu,

to 5pm Sun; ⊖London Bridge) This brainchild of designer Zandra Rhodes has no permanent collection, just quarterly temporary exhibitions, which have included retrospectives on Swedish fashion, the evolution of underwear and 20th-century art in textiles.

WHITE CUBE BERMONDSEY — GALLERY

Map p452 (www.whitecube.com; 144-152 Bermondsey St, SE1; ⊙10am-6pm Tue-Sat, noon-6pm Sun; ⊖London Bridge) FREE The newest and largest of the White Cube galleries, this spot impresses with its large exhibition spaces, which lend themselves to monumental pieces or expansive installations using several mediums. White Cube is the brainchild of Jay Jopling, dealer to the stars of the Brit Art movement. He made his reputation in the 1990s by exhibiting then-unknown artists such as Damien Hirst and Antony Gormley.

✘ EATING

With the presence of Borough Market, Maltby Street Market and numerous food and drink businesses, London Bridge and Bermondsey attract the cream of eating options on the South Bank. The area around the Southbank Centre is full of chains. Head 'inland' towards Waterloo and Southwark to discover authentic gastronomic gems.

✘ Waterloo

MASTERS SUPER FISH — FISH & CHIPS $

Map p452 (✆020-7928 6924; www.masterssuperfish.com; 191 Waterloo Rd, SE1; mains £8-12; ⊙5.30-10.30pm Mon, noon-3pm & 5.30-10.30pm Tue-Sat; ⊖Waterloo) This popular place serves excellent fish brought in fresh daily from Billingsgate Market and grilled rather than fried if desired. It's low on charm but gets full marks for flavour and authenticity.

★SKYLON — MODERN EUROPEAN $$

Map p452 (✆020-7654 7800; www.skylon-restaurant.co.uk; 3rd fl, Royal Festival Hall, Southbank Centre, Belvedere Rd, SE1; 3-course menu grill/restaurant £25/30; ⊙grill noon-11pm Mon-Sat, to 10.30pm Sun, restaurant noon-2.30pm & 5.30-10.30pm Mon-Sat & noon-4pm Sun; ⊖Waterloo) This excellent restaurant inside the Royal Festival Hall (p174) is divided into grill and fine-dining sections by a large bar

(p171). The decor is cutting-edge 1950s: muted colours and period chairs (trendy then, trendier now), while floor-to-ceiling windows bathe you in magnificent views of the Thames and the city. The six-course restaurant tasting menu costs £59.

KONDITOR & COOK — BAKERY $

Map p452 (www.konditorandcook.com; 22 Cornwall Rd, SE1; cakes £2-4, hot food £3.85-6.55; ⊙7.30am-7pm Mon-Fri, 8.30am-6pm Sat, 11am-5pm Sun; ⊖Waterloo) This elegant cake shop and bakery produces wonderful cakes – lavender and orange, lemon and almond – massive raspberry meringues, cookies, and loaves of warm bread with olives, nuts and spices. It also serves hot takeaway food such as quiche or risotto, popular with local office workers. Daily menu posted on the website.

CASSE-CROÛTE — FRENCH $$

Map p452 (✆020-7407 2140; www.cassecroute.co.uk; 109 Bermondsey St, SE1; mains £18.50; ⊙noon-10pm Mon-Sat, to 4pm Sun; ⊖London Bridge) You'll have to keep reminding yourself that you are in London and not in France, so typical is the interior of a French brasserie or bistro. The fare, too, is quintessentially French, from *lapin à la moutarde* (rabbit in mustard sauce) to *île flottante* (a soft-set meringue in vanilla custard) and there's an all-French wine list. All-day service, however, is definitely a London touch!

CUT — BRITISH $$

Map p452 (www.thecutbar.com; Young Vic, The Cut, SE1; mains £12-17; ⊙9am-11pm Mon-Fri, from 10am Sat; ⊖Waterloo) This laid-back, all-day brasserie at the front of the Young Vic (p175) theatre serves well-executed bistro fare – risottos, burgers, pasta, grilled cuts of meat and fish – as well as pastries and hot drinks throughout the day. The £10 lunch menu for a main and a drink (weekdays except Wednesday) is a snip.

OXO TOWER BRASSERIE — MODERN EUROPEAN $$$

Map p452 (✆020-7803 3888; www.harveynichols.com/restaurant/the-oxo-tower/brasserie; OXO Tower Wharf, SE1; mains £17-27, 3-course menu £32; ⊙noon-11pm Mon-Sat, to 10pm Sun; ⊖Waterloo) The iconic Oxo Tower's conversion, with this restaurant on the 8th floor, helped spur much of the local dining renaissance. In the stunning glassed-in terrace you have a front-row seat for the best view in London, and you'll pay handsomely for it.

Fish dishes usually comprise half the menu, and vegetarians are well catered for too.

✖ Bankside & Southwark

★ BALTIC
EASTERN EUROPEAN **$$**

Map p452 (☎020-79281111; www.balticrestaurant. co.uk; 74 Blackfriars Rd, SE1; mains £10.50-19, 2-course lunch menu £17.50; ☺noon-3pm & 5.30-11.15pm Tue-Sun, 5.30-11.15pm Mon; ✐; ⊜Southwark) In a bright and airy, high-ceilinged dining room with glass roof and wooden beams, Baltic is travel on a plate: dill and beetroot, dumplings and blini, pickle and smoke, rich stews and braised meat. From Polish to Georgian, the flavours are authentic and the dishes beautifully presented. The wine and vodka lists are equally diverse.

★ ANCHOR & HOPE
GASTROPUB **$$**

Map p452 (www.anchorandhopepub.co.uk; 36 The Cut, SE1; mains £12-20; ☺noon-2.30pm Tue-Sat, 6-10.30pm Mon-Sat, 12.30-3pm Sun; ⊜Southwark) A stalwart of the South Bank food scene, the Anchor & Hope is a quintessential gastropub: elegant but not formal, and utterly delicious (European fare with a British twist). The menu changes daily but think salt marsh lamb shoulder cooked for seven hours; wild rabbit with anchovies, almonds and rocket; and panna cotta with rhubarb compote.

UNION STREET CAFE
ITALIAN **$$$**

Map p452 (☎020-7592 7977; www.gordonramsay .com/union-street-cafe; 47-51 Great Suffolk St, SE1; mains £20-27, 1-/2-course lunch menu £12/24; ☺noon-midnight Mon-Sat, to 6pm Sun; ✐⛭; ⊜Southwark) There's not a scrap of snootiness about this canteen-style Gordon Ramsay bistro. The dining room is industrial-chic and staff are lovely. On the plate it's a yummy mix of classic antipasti, pasta, meats and more unusual Italian dishes. On Sundays £15 will get you free-flowing prosecco to accompany your lunch.

✖ London Bridge

★ PADELLA
ITALIAN **$**

Map p452 (www.padella.co; 6 Southwark St, SE1; dishes £5-11; ☺noon-4pm & 5-10pm Mon-Sat, noon-5pm Sun; ✐; ⊜London Bridge) Yet another fantastic addition to the foodie enclave of Borough Market (p163), Padella is a small, energetic bistro specialising in handmade pasta dishes, inspired by the owners' extensive culinary adventures in Italy. The portions are small, which means that, joy of joys, you can (and should!) have more than one dish. Outstanding. The downside is the perennial queue (no reservations). In the evenings the restaurant uses a virtual queue system, where they take your number and text you when your table is ready.

MAGDALEN
MODERN BRITISH **$$**

Map p452 (☎020-7403 1342; www.magdalen restaurant.co.uk; 152 Tooley St, SE1; mains £16.50-26, 2-/3-course lunch Mon-Fri £16.50/19.50; ☺noon-2.30pm Mon-Fri & 6-9.30pm Mon-Sat; ⊜London Bridge) You can't go wrong with this formal dining room, where the welcome is warm and the service excellent. The Modern British fare adds its own appetising spin to familiar dishes (grilled calves' kidneys, creamed onion and sage, roast cod with chickpeas, grilled courgettes and pickled lemon). The desserts and English cheese selection are another delight.

TAPAS BRINDISA
TAPAS **$$**

Map p452 (☎020-7357 8880; www.brindisatapas kitchens.com; 18-20 Southwark St, SE1; tapas £6-20; ☺10am-11.30pm Mon-Fri, 9am-11.30pm Sat, 10am-10.30pm Sun; ⊜London Bridge) This tapas restaurant is appropriately located on the corner of Borough Market (p163), London's foodie paradise. It doesn't take reservations, and come evening it's not unusual to see people queuing out into the street for a table, but it's worth the wait. It also has a deli around the corner and other branches across the city.

EL PASTÓR
MEXICAN **$$**

Map p452 (www.tacoselpastor.co.uk; 6-7a Stoney St, SE1; dishes £2.50-8.50; ☺noon-3pm & 6-11pm Mon-Sat; ⊜London Bridge) The cavernous entrance on Stoney St reveals a Mexican eatery rocking the industrial-chic look. El Pastór specialises in tacos and quesadillas, which are made fresh daily. Fillings are delicious but the portions are tiny – one taco or quesadilla is devoured in just two mouthfuls (especially when smothered in one of the house salsas), so double up on everything.

★ ARABICA BAR & KITCHEN
MIDDLE EASTERN **$$$**

Map p452 (☎020-3011 5151; www.arabicabarand kitchen.com; 3 Rochester Walk, Borough Market, SE1; dishes £6-14; ⊘11am-11pm Mon-Fri, 8.30am-11.30pm Sat, 11am-9pm Sun; ⚲; ⊜London Bridge) Pan–Middle Eastern cuisine is a well-rehearsed classic these days, but Arabica Bar & Kitchen has managed to bring something fresh to its table: the decor is contemporary and bright, the food delicate and light, and there's an emphasis on sharing (two to three small dishes per person). The downside of this tapas approach is that the bill adds up quickly.

✘ Bermondsey

★ WATCH HOUSE   CAFE $
Map p452 (www.watchhousecoffee.com; 193 Bermondsey St, SE1; mains from £4.95; ⊘7am-6pm Mon-Fri, 8am-6pm Sat, 9am-5pm Sun; ⚲; ⊜Borough, London Bridge) 🖉 Saying that the Watch House nails the sandwich wouldn't really do justice to this tip-top cafe: the sandwiches really are delicious, and use artisan breads from a local baker. But there is also great coffee, and treats for the sweet-toothed. The small but lovely setting is a renovated 19th-century watch-house from where guards looked out for grave robbers in the next-door cemetery.

MALTBY STREET MARKET   MARKET $
Map p452 (www.maltby.st; Maltby St, SE1; dishes £5-10; ⊘9am-4pm Sat, 11am-4pm Sun; ⊜Bermondsey) Started as an alternative to the juggernaut that is Borough Market (p163), Maltby Street Market is becoming a victim of its own success, with brick and mortar shops and restaurants replacing the old workshops, and throngs of visitors. That said, it boasts some original – and all top-notch – food stalls selling smoked salmon from east London, African burgers, seafood and lots of pastries.

ST JOHN BAKERY   BAKERY $
Map p452 (www.stjohngroup.uk.com; 72 Druid St, SE1; pastries/bread from £1.50/3; ⊘9am-4pm Sat & Sun; ⚲; ⊜London Bridge) One of the many secrets hiding under the railway arches of Druid St, St John Bakery opens its iron shutter to visitors at the weekend (it's a wholesale bakery during the week). The main draw for visitors is likely to be the now legendary doughnuts, although we'll wholeheartedly recommend any of the cakes or breads.

M MANZE   BRITISH $
Map p452 (www.manze.co.uk; 87 Tower Bridge Rd, SE1; mains from £2.95; ⊘11am-2pm Mon, 10.30am-2pm Tue-Thu, 10am-2.30pm Fri & Sat; ⊜Borough) Dating from 1902, M Manze started off as an ice-cream seller before moving on to selling its legendary staples: minced-beef pies. It's a classic operation, from the ageing tilework to the traditional workers' menu: pie and mash, pie and liquor (parsley-based sauce) eels jellied or stewed. Vegetarian available. Eat in or take away.

🍷 DRINKING & NIGHTLIFE

The South Bank is a strange combination of good, down-to-earth boozers, which just happen to have been here for hundreds of years, and modern bars – some of them very fancy indeed – patronised by a trendy, well-heeled set.

🍸 Waterloo

★ KING'S ARMS   PUB
Map p452 (☏020-7207 0784; www.thekingsarmslondon.co.uk; 25 Roupell St, SE1; ⊘11am-11pm Mon-Fri, noon-11pm Sat, noon-10.30pm Sun; ⊜Waterloo) Relaxed and charming, this neighbourhood boozer at the corner of a terraced Waterloo backstreet was a funeral parlour in a previous life. The large traditional bar area, complete with open fire in winter, serves up a good selection of ales and bitters. It gets packed with after-work crowds between 6pm and 8pm.

★ SCOOTERCAFFE   BAR
Map p452 (132 Lower Marsh, SE1; ⊘8.30am-11pm Mon-Fri, 10am-midnight Sat, to 11pm Sun; 📶; ⊜Waterloo) A well-established fixture on the up-and-coming Lower Marsh road, this funky cafe-bar and former scooter repair shop with a Piatti scooter in the window serves killer hot chocolates, coffee and decadent cocktails. Unusually, you're allowed to bring in takeaway food. The tiny patio at the back is perfect for soaking up the sun.

SKYLON   BAR
Map p452 (www.skylon-restaurant.co.uk; Royal Festival Hall, Southbank Centre, Belvedere Rd, SE1; ⊘noon-1am Mon-Sat, to 10.30pm Sun; 📶; ⊜Waterloo) Ravishing 1950s decor and show-stopping views make Skylon a memorable

choice for a drink or meal (p169). You'll have to come early to bag one of the tables at the front with plunging views of the river. Drinks-wise, just ask: from superb seasonal cocktails to infusions and a staggering choice of wine and whiskys.

FOUR CORNERS CAFE
CAFE

Map p452 (www.four-corners-cafe.com; 12 Lower Marsh, SE1; ⏰7.30am-6.30pm Mon-Fri, 9am-5pm Sat; 🛜; 🚇Waterloo) With its excellent coffee (from Ozone Roasters) and unusually large selection of teas, Four Corners Cafe attracts a loyal following. Occasional visitors will feel at home with the travel theme: from the map-lined coffee counter to the old guide-book collection. The place has a buzz. You can even trade your old guidebooks (if they don't have it already) for free coffee.

🍸 Bankside & Southwark

DANDELYAN
COCKTAIL BAR

Map p452 (www.mondrianlondon.com; Mondrian London, 20 Upper Ground, SE1; ⏰4pm-1am Mon-Wed, noon-2am Thu-Sat, to 12.30am Sun; 🛜; 🚇Southwark) Riverside Dandelyan isn't your average hotel lobby bar: it's a destination in its own right. The cocktails – featuring unexpected ingredients such as Douglas fir, chalk bitters and dandelion capillaire – are as original as the Alice in Wonderland–like decor of the green marble bar, green walls and curtains, and extravagant pink banquettes.

RUMPUS ROOM
COCKTAIL BAR

Map p452 (www.mondrianlondon.com; Mondrian London, 20 Upper Ground, SE1; ⏰5pm-1am Tue & Wed, to 2am Thu-Sat; 🛜; 🚇Southwark) Located on the 12th floor of the Mondrian Hotel, this is something of a show-stopper, with knock-out views of the city and a roof terrace to boot. The emphasis is on fabulous cocktails. Dress to impress and book if possible. There's live music on Wednesdays.

ANCHOR BANKSIDE
PUB

Map p452 (34 Park St, SE1; ⏰11am-11pm Sun-Wed, to midnight Thu-Sat; 🚇London Bridge) A mainstay recommendation – but with good reason – this riverside boozer dates back to the 17th century. Trips to the terrace are rewarded with superb views across the Thames but brace for a constant deluge of drinkers. Eighteenth-century dictionary writer Samuel Johnson, whose brewer

friend owned the joint, drank here, as did diarist Samuel Pepys before that.

🍸 London Bridge

★ OBLIX
BAR

Map p452 (www.oblixrestaurant.com; 32nd fl, Shard, 31 St Thomas St, SE1; ⏰noon-11pm; 🚇London Bridge) On the 32nd floor of the Shard (p166), Oblix offers mesmerising vistas of London. You can come for anything from a coffee (£3.50) to a cocktail (from £10) and enjoy virtually the same views as the official viewing galleries of the Shard (but at a reduced cost and with the added bonus of a drink). Live music every night from 7pm.

The downside is Oblix's popularity: it can be hard to get in, especially at meal-times when many of the tables are reserved for diners. Note that reasonably smart attire is expected, so no trainers/sneakers or flip flops. Children welcome before 6pm.

GŌNG
BAR

Map p452 (☎020-7234 8208; www.gong-shangri-la.com; Level 52, Shangri-La Hotel, Shard, 31 St Thomas St; ⏰noon-1am Mon-Sat, to midnight Sun; 🛜; 🚇London Bridge) Cool Gōng on the 52nd floor of the Shard, in the Shangri-La (p350) hotel, is London's highest bar. Naturally sunset's the optimum time, and it's all about cocktails, Champagne and wine. There's a £30 minimum spend per person (easy to achieve) and tables are allocated for 90 minutes. You're encouraged to book but walk-ins are allowed. No children.

RAKE
PUB

Map p452 (☎020-7407 0557; www.utobeer.co.uk; 14 Winchester Walk, SE1; ⏰noon-11pm Mon-Fri, 11am-11pm Sat, noon-10pm Sun; 🚇London Bridge) With a fantastic line of beers to slake any thirst, the Rake offers more than 130 labels – many of them international craft brews – at any one time. There are 10 taps, and the selection of craft beers, real ales, lagers and ciders (with one-third-pint measures) changes constantly. It's a teensy place yet always busy; the bamboo-decorated decking outside is especially popular.

GEORGE INN
PUB

Map p452 (NT; ☎020-7407 2056; www.national trust.org.uk/george-inn; 77 Borough High St, SE1; ⏰11am-11pm; 🚇London Bridge) Owned and leased by the National Trust, this magnificent old boozer is London's last

THE SOUTH BANK DRINKING & NIGHTLIFE

surviving galleried coaching inn, dating from 1677 (after a fire destroyed it the year before) and mentioned in Dickens' *Little Dorrit*. It is on the site of the Tabard Inn, where the pilgrims in Chaucer's *The Canterbury Tales* gathered before setting out on the road.

★COFFEE HOUSE   COFFEE

Map p452 (The Gentlemen Baristas; www.the gentlemenbaristas.com; 63 Union St, SE1; coffee £1.50-2.90; ⊘7am-6pm Mon-Fri, 8.30am-5pm Sat, 10am-4pm Sun; 🛜; ⊕London Bridge, Borough) This addition to the Bankside coffee scene is a godsend, and for barista-worshipping coffee lovers it's the place to come. There may be a slight whiff of pretension about the mac-wielding media types who choose to hang out here, but it's still a top spot with enough space to linger peacefully over a flat white.

🍷 Bermondsey

★BREW BY NUMBERS   MICROBREWERY

Map p452 (www.brewbynumbers.com; 79 Enid St, SE1; ⊘6-10pm Fri, 11am-8pm Sat; ⊕Bermondsey) This microbrewery's raison d'être is experimentation. Everything from its 'scientific' branding (the numbers refer to the type of beer – porter, pale ale etc – and recipe) to its enthusiasm for exploring new beer styles and refashioning old ones (*saison* for instance, an old Belgian beer drunk by farm workers) is about broadening the definition of beer.

★LITTLE BIRD GIN   COCKTAIL BAR

Map p452 (www.littlebirdgin.com; Maltby St, SE1; ⊘10am-4pm Sat, from 11am Sun; ⊕London Bridge) This South London–based distillery opens a pop-up bar in a workshop at Maltby Street Market (p171) to ply merry punters with devilishly good cocktails (£5 to £7), served in jam jars or apothecary's glass bottles.

ANSPACH & HOBDAY   MICROBREWERY

Map p452 (www.anspachandhobday.com; 118 Druid St, SE1; ⊘5-9pm Fri, 10.30am-5.30pm Sat, 12.30-5pm Sun; ⊕London Bridge) It's all about porter at this microbrewery, although lighter ales are also brewed. Beer aficionados will love trying brews from the experimental range; beers come in large 750ml bottles and are rotated regularly. There's a nice outdoor seating area.

40 MALTBY STREET   WINE BAR

Map p452 (www.40maltbystreet.com; 40 Maltby St, SE1; ⊘5.30-10pm Wed & Thu, 12.30-2.30pm & 5.30-10pm Fri, 11am-10pm Sat; ⊕London Bridge) 🍴 This tunnel-like wine-bar-cum-kitchen sits under the railway arches that support trains as they travel in and out of London Bridge. It is first and foremost a wine importer focusing on organic vintages, but its hospitality venture has become incredibly popular. The wine recommendations are obviously top-notch and the food – simple, gourmet bistro fare – is spot on.

DOODLE BAR   BAR

Map p452 (60 Druid St, SE1; ⊘6-11pm Wed, noon-11pm Thu, to midnight Fri & Sat, noon-6pm Sun; 🛜; ⊕Bermondsey) Awaken the artist within and pop down to this funtastic Bermondsey bar within a railway arch. A former pop-up in Battersea before migrating to SE1, there are blackboards to be doodled up, so call up your muse, your inner Banksy, MC Escher or Matt Groening – and get chalking. There's ping pong too.

JENSEN   DISTILLERY

Map p452 (www.jensengin.com; 55 Stanworth St, SE1; ⊘10am-4pm Sat, from 11am Sun; ⊕London Bridge) A micro gin distillery, Jensen Gin produces two main kinds: Bermondsey Dry, a variation of the famous London Dry gin; and Old Tom, a more intense, opaque gin that is unsweetened. The distillery throws open its doors at weekends for tastings, sales (750ml bottles cost £20 to £25) and cocktails (£5.95).

GARRISON PUBLIC HOUSE   GASTROPUB $$

Map p452 (www.thegarrison.co.uk; 99-101 Bermondsey St, SE1; mains £13-22; ⊘8-11.30am, noon-3pm & 6-10pm; 🖉; ⊕London Bridge) The Garrison's traditional green-tiled exterior and rather distressed beach-shack interior are both appealing, but it's the food – poached hake, harissa-laced chicken and delicious cooked breakfasts – that lures punters to this evergreen Bermondsey gastropub.

🍷 Rotherhithe

★MAYFLOWER   PUB

Map p462 (www.mayflowerpub.co.uk; 117 Rotherhithe St, SE16; ⊘11am-11pm Mon-Sat, noon-10.30pm Sun; ⊕Rotherhithe) This 16th-century pub is named after the vessel that took the pilgrims to America in 1620. The ship set sail from Rotherhithe, and Captain Christopher Jones supposedly charted its course here while supping schooners. The pub oozes character and history, from the candles to the wood-panelling and dark interior. There's seating on a small back terrace overlooking the Thames.

⭐ ENTERTAINMENT

The South Bank of London is home to some heavy hitters when it comes to London's theatre scene. Music and performing arts are big at the Southbank Centre. Last-minute tickets are often available, so if you haven't booked, don't forget about spontaneity!

⭐SHAKESPEARE'S GLOBE THEATRE

Map p452 (☑020-7401 9919; www.shakespeares globe.com; 21 New Globe Walk, SE1; seats £20-45, standing £5; ⊖Blackfriars or London Bridge) If you love Shakespeare and the theatre, the Globe (p162) will knock your theatrical socks off. This authentic Shakespearean theatre is a wooden 'O' without a roof over the central stage area, and although there are covered wooden bench seats in tiers around the stage, many people (there's room for 700) do as 17th-century 'groundlings' did, and stand in front of the stage.

Because the building is quite open to the elements, you may have to wrap up. Groundlings note: umbrellas are not allowed, but cheap raincoats are on sale. Unexpected aircraft noise is unavoidable too.

The theatre season runs from late April to mid-October and includes works by Shakespeare and his contemporaries such as Christopher Marlowe.

If you don't like the idea of standing in the rain or sitting in the cold, opt for an indoor candlelit play in the **Sam Wanamaker Playhouse**, a Jacobean theatre similar to the one Shakespeare would have used in winter. The programming also includes opera.

⭐NATIONAL THEATRE THEATRE

Map p452 (Royal National Theatre; ☑020-7452 3000; www.nationaltheatre.org.uk; South Bank, SE1; ⊖Waterloo) England's flagship theatre showcases a mix of classic and contemporary plays performed by excellent casts in three theatres (Olivier, Lyttelton and Dorfman). Artistic director Rufus Norris, who started in April 2015, made headlines in 2016 for announcing plans to stage a Brexit-based drama.

Travelex tickets, costing just £15 and which you can book in advance, are available for certain performances; same-day tickets, which you must buy in person at the box office, cost £15 to £18; Friday Rush tickets cost £20, and are released online every Friday at 1pm for performances the following week. Under-18s pay half price.

⭐UNICORN THEATRE THEATRE

Map p452(☑020-76450560;www.unicorntheatre. com; 147 Tooley St, SE1; ⊖London Bridge) It seems only natural that one of the first theatres dedicated to young audiences would make its home in a neighbourhood of heavy-hitting theatres. Its rationale is that the best theatre for children should be judged against the same standards as the best theatre for adults. The productions are therefore excellent, wide-ranging and perfectly tailored to their target audience.

ROYAL FESTIVAL HALL CONCERT VENUE

Map p452 (☑020-7960 4200; www.southbank centre.co.uk; Southbank Centre, Belvedere Rd, SE1; 🛜; ⊖Waterloo) Royal Festival Hall's amphitheatre seats 2500 and is one of the best places for catching world- and classical-music artists. The sound is fantastic, the programming impeccable and there are frequent free gigs in the wonderfully expansive foyer.

QUEEN ELIZABETH HALL CONCERT VENUE

Map p452 (QEH; www.southbankcentre.co.uk; Southbank Centre, Belvedere Rd, SE1; ⊖Waterloo) This concert hall hosts music and dance performances on a smaller scale to the nearby Royal Festival Hall, both part of the Southbank Centre. The Hall re-opens in April 2018 after its 21st-century facelift.

SOUTHBANK CENTRE CONCERT VENUE

Map p452 (☑0844 875 0073; www.southbank centre.co.uk; Belvedere Rd, SE1; ⊖Waterloo) The Southbank Centre comprises several venues – Royal Festival Hall, Queen Elizabeth Hall and Purcell Room – hosting a wide range of performing arts. As well as regular programming, it organises fantastic festivals, including **London Wonderground** (circus and cabaret), **Udderbelly** (a festival of comedy in all its guises) and **Meltdown** (a music event curated by the best and most eclectic names in music).

RAMBERT DANCE COMPANY   DANCE

Map p452 (☑020-8630 0600; www.rambert.
org.uk; 99 Upper Ground, SE1) The innovative
Rambert Dance Company is the UK's foremost contemporary dance troupe, performing at venues across London, the UK and
abroad.

BFI SOUTHBANK   CINEMA

Map p452 (☑020-7928 3232; www.bfi.org.uk;
Belvedere Rd, SE1; tickets £8-12; ⊙10am-11pm;
⊖Waterloo) Tucked almost out of sight under
the arches of Waterloo Bridge, the British
Film Institute (BFI) contains four cinemas
that screen thousands of films each year
(many art house); a gallery devoted to the
moving image; and a mediatheque, where
you watch film and TV highlights from the
BFI National Archive.

OLD VIC   THEATRE

Map p452 (☑0844 871 7628; www.oldvictheatre.
com; The Cut, SE1; ⊖Waterloo) American actor Kevin Spacey took the theatrical helm
of this London theatre in 2003, giving it a
new lease of life. He was succeeded in April
2015 by Matthew Warchus (who directed
Matilda the Musical and the film *Pride*),
whose aim is to bring an eclectic programming to the theatre: expect new writing, as
well as dynamic revivals of old works and
musicals.

YOUNG VIC   THEATRE

Map p452 (☑020-7922 2922; www.youngvic.org;
66 The Cut, SE1; ⊖Southwark or Waterloo) This
ground-breaking theatre is as much about
showcasing and discovering new talent as
it is about people discovering theatre. The
Young Vic features actors, directors and
plays from across the world, many tackling
contemporary political and cultural issues,
such as the death penalty, racism or corruption, and often blending dance and music
with acting.

BFI IMAX CINEMA   CINEMA

Map p452 (www.odeon.co.uk/cinemas/bfi_imax;
1 Charlie Chaplin Walk, SE1; adult/child from
£16/12; ⊡; ⊖Waterloo) The IMAX Cinema
of the British Film Institute (BFI) (p175) is
the biggest screen in the UK. It shows 2D
and 3D documentaries about travel, space
and wildlife, which last anywhere from 40
minutes to 1½ hours, as well as recently released blockbusters.

🛍 SHOPPING

**The South Bank isn't a big shopping
destination; the scene here is more about
serendipitous finds in independent
designer boutiques or vintage markets
than purposeful souvenir hunting.**

UTOBEER   FOOD & DRINKS

Map p452 (www.utobeer.co.uk; Borough Market,
Unit 24, Middle Row, SE1; ⊙11am-5.30pm Mon-Fri,
9am-5pm Sat; ⊖London Bridge) This beer shop
inside Borough Market (p163) stocks around
700 international bottled beers, with a large
selection of both American and European
brews to take away. Its sister pub, The Rake,
(p172) is just outside the market.

LOVELY & BRITISH   GIFTS & SOUVENIRS

Map p452 (☑020-7378 6570; www.facebook.
com/LovelyandBritish; 132a Bermondsey St, SE1;
⊙10am-6pm; ⊖London Bridge) As the name
suggests, this gorgeous Bermondsey boutique prides itself on stocking prints, jewellery and homewares (crockery especially)
from British designers. It's an eclectic mix
of wares, with very reasonable prices,
which make lovely presents or souvenirs.

SOUTHBANK CENTRE SHOP   HOMEWARES

Map p452 (www.southbankcentre.co.uk; Festival Tce, SE1; ⊙10am-9pm Mon-Fri, to 8pm Sat,
noon-8pm Sun; ⊖Waterloo) This is the place
to come for quirky London books, '50s-in-
spired homewares, original prints and creative gifts for children. The shop is rather
eclectic but you're sure to find unique gifts
or souvenirs to take home.

NATIONAL THEATRE GIFT SHOP   BOOKS

Map p452 (☑020-74523456; www.nationaltheatre.
org.uk; South Bank, SE1; ⊙9.30am-10.45pm Mon-
Sat; ⊖Waterloo) You'll find an extensive selection of books covering literature, history, art
and more, as well as National Theatre merchandise and unusual gifts. Jewellery and
children's gifts are lined up next to fold-out
craft-beer maps and skull-shaped erasers.

SOUTH BANK BOOK MARKET   MARKET

Map p452 (Riverside Walk, SE1; ⊙11am-7pm,
shorter hours winter; ⊖Waterloo) The South
Bank Book Market sells prints and secondhand books daily under the arches of
Waterloo Bridge. You'll find anything here,
from fiction to children's books, and comics
to classics.

Kensington & Hyde Park

KNIGHTSBRIDGE & SOUTH KENSINGTON | HYDE PARK & KENSINGTON GARDENS | CHELSEA & BELGRAVIA | VICTORIA & PIMLICO

Neighbourhood Top Five

❶ Victoria & Albert Museum (p178) Thumbing through an encyclopaedic A–Z of decorative and design works from across the globe while admiring the astonishing architecture and making hordes of unexpected discoveries.

❷ Natural History Museum (p182) Becoming hypnotised by the awe-inspiring stonework and inexhaustible collection of this world-leading museum, while putting aside time to delve into its bucolic Wildlife Garden.

❸ Hyde Park (p184) Enjoying a picnic in London's green lung and exploring its many sights and gorgeous scenery.

❹ Science Museum (p186) Nurturing a wide-eyed fascination for the complexities of the world and the cosmos in this electrifying museum.

❺ Harrods (p199) Big-time shopping – or just window-shopping!

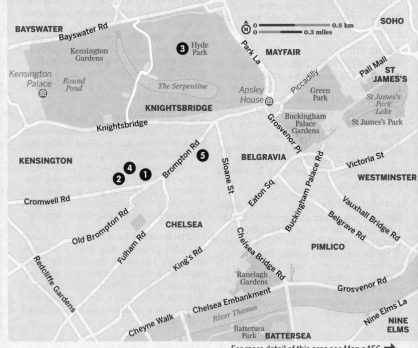

For more detail of this area see Map p456 ➡

Explore Kensington & Hyde Park

You can navigate a serious learning curve or at least catch up on all you forgot since high school at South Kensington's magnificent museums of the arts and sciences. You'll need several days – and considerable calorific reserves – to do them all justice. Museums open at 10am, so you don't have to set your alarm too early, but being near the front of the queue when the doors open means useful elbow room.

Shoppers will make an eager beeline for Knightsbridge, Harrods and Harvey Nichols, but there are also tranquil shopping escapes – such as John Sandoe Books and Peter Harrington – to sidestep the jostling crowds.

For a sight-packed day visit Hyde Park and conjoined Kensington Gardens – crucial for seeing why Londoners love their green spaces. Begin by exploring the opulence of Apsley House before walking across the park, via the Serpentine, to the Albert Memorial, Royal Albert Hall and Kensington Palace.

Outstanding restaurants will be with you every step of the way: Kensington, Knightsbridge and Chelsea take their dining particularly seriously, so some of your fondest memories could well be gastronomic, whether you're grazing, snacking or plain feasting.

Local Life

➜ **Hang-outs** Rub shoulders with discerning drinkers at the Anglesea Arms (p198) or Queen's Arms (p198) or snap your fingers with local jazz hounds at the swinging 606 Club (p198) and Pheasantry (p199).

➜ **Museums** Late-night Fridays at the Victoria & Albert (p178) mean fewer crowds (especially children) and locals can get a look-in.

➜ **Parks** When the sun's out, Londoners dust off their shades, get outdoors to expanses of green like Hyde Park (p184) and lie on the grass reading chunky novels.

Getting There & Away

➜ **Tube** Kensington and Hyde Park are well connected to the rest of London via South Kensington, Sloane Sq, Victoria, Knightsbridge and Hyde Park Corner stations. The main lines are Circle, District, Piccadilly and Victoria.

➜ **Bus** Handy routes include 74 from South Kensington to Knightsbridge and Hyde Park Corner; 52 from Victoria to High St Kensington; 360 from South Kensington to Sloane Sq and Pimlico; and 11 from Fulham Broadway to the King's Rd, Sloane Sq and Victoria.

➜ **Bicycle** Santander Cycles (p415) are very handy for pedal-powering your way into, out of and around the neighbourhood.

Lonely Planet's Top Tip

Catch the Queen's Life Guard (Household Cavalry) departing for Horse Guards Parade at 10.28am (9.28am Sundays) from Hyde Park Barracks for the daily Changing of the Guard, performing a ritual that dates to 1660. They troop via Hyde Park Corner, Constitution Hill and the Mall. It's not as busy as the Changing of the Guard at Buckingham Palace and you can get closer to the action.

✕ Best Places to Eat

➜ Tom's Kitchen (p196)
➜ Five Fields (p197)
➜ Dinner by Heston Blumenthal (p192)
➜ Launceston Place (p196)
➜ Pimlico Fresh (p197)

For reviews, see p192.➜

🍷 Best Places to Drink

➜ Tomtom Coffee House (p198)
➜ Phene (p198)
➜ Queen's Arms (p198)
➜ Buddha Bar (p198)
➜ Anglesea Arms (p198)

For reviews, see p197.➜

⊙ Best Shopping

➜ Harrods (p199)
➜ Conran Shop (p200)
➜ John Sandoe Books (p199)
➜ Peter Harrington (p200)
➜ Pickett (p200)

For reviews, see p199.➜

KENSINGTON & HYDE PARK

TOP SIGHT
VICTORIA & ALBERT MUSEUM

The Museum of Manufactures, as the V&A was known when it opened in 1852, was part of Prince Albert's legacy to the nation in the aftermath of the successful Great Exhibition of 1851. Its original aims – which still hold today – were the 'improvement of public taste in design' and 'applications of fine art to objects of utility'. It's done a fine job so far.

Collection

Through 146 galleries, the museum houses the world's greatest collection of decorative arts, from ancient Chinese ceramics to modernist architectural drawings, Korean bronze and Japanese swords, cartoons by Raphael, gowns from the Elizabethan era, ancient jewellery, a Sony Walkman – and much, much more.

Entrance

Entering under the stunning blue-and-yellow blown-glass **chandelier** by Dale Chihuly, you can grab a museum map (£1 donation requested) at the information desk. (If the 'Grand Entrance' on Cromwell Rd is too busy, there's another around the corner on Exhibition Rd, or you can enter from the tunnel in the basement, if arriving by tube.) A new entrance on Exhibition Rd was unveiled in 2017.

Level 1

The street level is mostly devoted to art and design from India, China, Japan, Korea and Southeast Asia, as well as European art. One of the museum's highlights is the **Cast Courts** in rooms 46a and 46b, containing staggering plaster casts collected in the Victorian era, such as Michelangelo's *David*, acquired in 1858.

DON'T MISS

➡ Jewellery Gallery
➡ Raphael cartoons
➡ Cast Courts
➡ Ardabil Carpet
➡ TT Tsui (China) Gallery

PRACTICALITIES

➡ Map p456, C4
➡ 020-7942 2000
➡ www.vam.ac.uk
➡ Cromwell Rd, SW7
➡ admission free
➡ ⏰10am-5.40pm Sat-Thu, to 10pm Fri
➡ South Kensington

The **TT Tsui (China) Gallery** (rooms 44 and 47e) displays lovely pieces, including a beautifully lithe wooden statue of Guanyin (a Mahayana bodhisattva) seated in a regal *lalitasana* pose from AD 1200; also check out a leaf from the 'Twenty Views of the Yuanmingyuan Summer Palace' (1781–86), revealing the Haiyantang and the 12 animal heads of the fountain (now ruins) in Beijing. Within the subdued lighting of the **Japan Gallery** (room 45) stands a fearsome suit of armour in the Domaru style. More than 400 objects are within the **Islamic Middle East Gallery** (room 42), including ceramics, textiles, carpets, glass and woodwork from the 8th century up to the years before WWI. The exhibition's highlight is the gorgeous mid-16th-century **Ardabil Carpet**.

For fresh air, the landscaped **John Madejski Garden** is a lovely shaded inner courtyard. Cross it to reach the original **Refreshment Rooms** (Morris, Gamble and Poynter Rooms), dating from the 1860s and redesigned by McInnes Usher McKnight Architects (MUMA), who also renovated the **Medieval and Renaissance galleries** (1350–1600) to the right of the Grand Entrance.

Level 2 & 4

The **British Galleries**, featuring every aspect of British design from 1500 to 1900, are divided between levels 2 (1500–1760) and 4 (1760–1900). Level 4 also boasts the **Architecture Gallery** (rooms 127 to 128a), which vividly describes architectural styles via models and videos, and the spectacular, brightly illuminated **Contemporary Glass Gallery** (room 129).

Level 3

The **Jewellery Gallery** (rooms 91 to 93) is outstanding; the mezzanine level – accessed via the glass-and-perspex spiral staircase – glitters with jewel-encrusted swords, watches and gold boxes. The **Photographs Gallery** (room 100) is one of the nation's best, with access to over 500,000 images collected since the mid-19th century. **Design Since 1945** (room 76) celebrates design classics from a 1985 Sony credit-card radio to a 1992 Nike 'Air Max' shoe, Peter Ghyczy's Garden Egg Chair from 1968 and the now ubiquitous selfie stick.

Level 6

Among the pieces in the **Ceramics Gallery** (rooms 136 to 146) – the world's largest – are standout items from the Middle East and Asia. The **Dr Susan Weber Gallery** (rooms 133 to 135) celebrates furniture design over the past six centuries.

Victoria & Albert Museum

HALF-DAY HIGHLIGHTS TOUR

The art- and design-packed V&A is vast: we have devised an easy-to-follow tour of the museum highlights to help cover some signature pieces while also allowing you to appreciate some of the grandeur of the museum architecture.

Enter the V&A by the Grand Entrance off Cromwell Rd and immediately turn left to explore the Islamic Middle East Gallery and to

discover the sumptuous silk-and-wool **❶ Ardabil Carpet**. Among the pieces from South Asia in the adjacent gallery is the terrifying automated **❷ Tipu's Tiger**. Continue to the outstanding **❸ Fashion Gallery** with its displays of clothing styles through the ages. The magnificent gallery opposite houses the **❹ Raphael Cartoons**, large paintings by Raphael used to weave tapestries for the Vatican. Take the stairs to level 2 and the Britain 1500–1760 Gallery; turn left in the

Raphael Cartoons
These seven drawings by Raphael, depicting the acts of St Peter and St Paul, were the full-scale preparatory works for seven tapestries that were woven for the Sistine Chapel in the Vatican.

Fashion Gallery
With clothing from the 18th century to the present day, this circular and chronologically arranged gallery showcases evening wear, undergarments and iconic fashion milestones, such as 1960s dresses designed by Mary Quant.

The Great Bed of Ware
Created during the reign of Queen Elizabeth I, its headboard and bedposts are etched with ancient graffiti; the 16th-century oak Great Bed of Ware is famously name-dropped in Shakespeare's *Twelfth Night*.

LEVEL 1

Stairs to Level 2

Main Entrance

❹ ❸ ❷ ❶

Gift Shop

Tsui China Collection

Japan Gallery

Cast Courts

John Madejski Garden

LEVEL 2

Britain 1500–1760 Gallery

❺ Stairs from Level 1

❻ Stairs to Level 3

The Ardabil Carpet
One of the world's most beautiful carpets, the Ardabil was completed in 1540, one of a pair commissioned by Shah Tahmasp, ruler of Iran. The piece is most astonishing for the artistry of the detailing and the subtlety of design.

Tipu's Tiger
This disquieting 18th-century wood-and-metal mechanical automaton depicts a European being savaged by a tiger. When a handle is turned, an organ hidden within the feline mimics the cries of the dying man, whose arm also rises.

GREG BALFOUR EVANS / ALAMY STOCK PHOTO ©

gallery to find the **5** **Great Bed of Ware**, beyond which rests the exquisitely crafted artistry of **6** **Henry VIII's Writing Box**. Head up the stairs into the Metalware Gallery on level 3 for the **7** **Hereford Screen**. Continue through the Ironwork and Sculpture Galleries and through the Leighton Corridor to the glittering **8** **Jewellery Gallery**. Exit through the Stained Glass gallery, at the end of which you'll find stairs back down to level 1.

TOP TIPS

➡ Museum attendants are always at hand along the route for information.

➡ Photography is allowed in most galleries, except the Jewellery Gallery, the Raphael Cartoons and in exhibitions.

➡ Avoid daytime crowds: visit the V&A in the evening, till 10pm on Fridays.

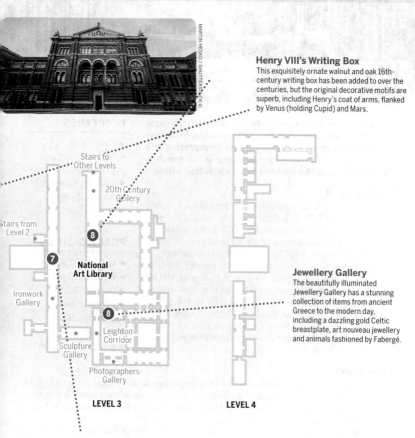

MARTIN HESKO / SHUTTERSTOCK ©

Henry VIII's Writing Box
This exquisitely ornate walnut and oak 16th-century writing box has been added to over the centuries, but the original decorative motifs are superb, including Henry's coat of arms, flanked by Venus (holding Cupid) and Mars.

Stairs to Other Levels

20th Century Gallery

Stairs from Level 2

8

7

National Art Library

Ironwork Gallery

8

Leighton Corridor

Sculpture Gallery

Photographers Gallery

LEVEL 3

LEVEL 4

Jewellery Gallery
The beautifully illuminated Jewellery Gallery has a stunning collection of items from ancient Greece to the modern day, including a dazzling gold Celtic breastplate, art nouveau jewellery and animals fashioned by Fabergé.

The Hereford Screen
Designed by Sir George Gilbert Scott, this awe-inspiring choir screen is a labour of love, originally fashioned for Hereford Cathedral. It's an almighty conception of wood, iron, copper, brass and hardstone, and there were few parts of the V&A that could support its great mass.

TOP SIGHT
NATURAL HISTORY MUSEUM

A sublime house of worship to science, this colossal building is infused with the irrepressible Victorian spirit of collecting, cataloguing and interpreting the natural world. The museum building is as much a reason to visit as the world-famous collection within.

Hintze Hall

This grand central hall resembles a cathedral nave – quite fitting, as it was built in a time when the natural sciences were challenging the biblical tenets of Christian orthodoxy. Naturalist and first superintendent of the museum Richard Owen celebrated the building as a 'cathedral to nature'.

After 81 years in the Mammals Hall, in 2017 the blue whale skeleton was relocated to Hintze Hall, with the famous cast of a **diplodocus skeleton** (nicknamed Dippy) making way for the colossal mammal. The transfer itself was a mammoth and painstaking engineering project, disassembling and preparing the 4.5-tonne bones for reconstruction in a dramatic diving posture that will greet visitors to the museum.

Blue Zone

Undoubtedly the museum's star attraction, the **Dinosaurs Gallery** takes you on an impressive overhead walkway, past a dromaeosaurus (a small and agile meat eater) before reaching a roaring animatronic T-rex and then winding its way through skeletons, fossils, casts and fascinating displays about how dinosaurs lived and died.

Another highlight of this zone is the **Mammals & Blue Whale Gallery**, with its life-size blue whale model and extensive displays on cetaceans. Lest we forget we are part of the animal kingdom, the museum has also dedicated a gallery to **Human Biology**, where you'll be able to understand more about what makes us tick (senses, hormones, our brain and so on).

Green Zone

While children love the Blue Zone, adults may prefer the Green Zone, especially the **Treasures in Cadogan Gallery**, on the 1st floor, which houses the museum's most prized possessions, each with a unique history. Exhibits include a chunk of moon rock, an Emperor Penguin egg collected by Captain Scott's expedition and a first edition of Charles Darwin's *On the Origin of Species*.

Equally rare and exceptional are the gems and rocks in the **Vault**, including a Martian meteorite and the largest emerald ever found. marvel at the trunk section of a 1300-year-old **giant sequoia tree** on the 2nd floor: its size is mind-boggling.

Red Zone

This zone explores the ever-changing nature of our planet and the forces shaping it. The earthquake simulator (in the **Volcanoes and Earthquakes Gallery**), which recreates the 1995 Kobe earthquake in a grocery store is a favourite, as is the **From the Beginning Gallery**, which retraces Earth's history.

In **Earth's Treasury**, you can find out more about our planet's mineral riches and how they are being used in our everyday lives – from jewellery to construction and electronics.

Access to most of the galleries in the Red Zone is via **Earth Hall** and a very tall escalator that disappears into a huge metal sculpture of the Earth. The most intact **stegosaurus fossil skeleton** ever found is displayed at the base.

Orange Zone

The **Darwin Centre** is the beating heart of the museum: this is where the museum's millions of specimens are kept and where its scientists work. The top two floors of the amazing 'cocoon' building are dedicated to explaining the kind of research the museum does – windows allow you to see the researchers at work.

If you'd like to find out more, pop into the **Attenborough studio** (named after famous naturalist and broadcaster David Attenborough) for one of the daily talks with the museum's scientists. The studio also shows films throughout the day.

Exhibitions

The museum hosts regular exhibitions (admission fees apply), some of them on a recurrent basis. **Wildlife Photographer of the Year** (adult £10.50-13.50, child £6.50-8, family £27-36.90; ⊘Oct-Sep), with its show-stopping images, is now in its 50th year, and **Sensational Butterflies** (www.nhm.ac.uk; Natural History Museum, Cromwell Rd, SW7; £5.85, family £19.80; ⊘Apr-Sep; ⊜South Kensington), a tunnel tent on the East Lawn that swarms with what must originally have been called 'flutter-bys', has become a firm summer favourite.

ICE SKATING AT THE MUSEUM

From Halloween to January, a section by the East Lawn of the museum is transformed into a glittering and highly popular ice rink, complete with a hot-drinks stall. Our advice: book your slot well ahead, browse the museum and skate later.

OUTDOOR TRANSFORMATION

The museum is transforming its outdoor spaces, tripling the Wildlife Garden in size, creating a piazza in the eastern grounds and adding a geological and palaeontological timeline walk.

MUSEUM SHOP

As well as the obligatory dinosaur figurines and animal soft toys, the museum's shop has a huge and brilliant collection of children's books about nature, animals and, of course, dinosaurs. On the adult side, beautiful jewellery and lovely stationery are treats to look out for.

KENSINGTON & HYDE PARK NATURAL HISTORY MUSEUM

TOP SIGHT
HYDE PARK

One of London's largest royal parks spreads itself over 142 hectares of neat gardens, wild expanses of overgrown grass and glorious trees. As well as being a fantastic green space in the middle of London, it is home to a handful of fascinating sights and hosts **Winter Wonderland (p201) from November to January.**

The eastern half of the park is covered with expansive lawns, which become one vast picnic-and-frolic area on sunny days. The western half is more untamed, with plenty of trees and areas of wild grass.

If you're after somewhere more colourful (and some shade), head to the **Rose Garden**, a beautifully landscaped garden with flowers year-round. It's an ideal spot in which to sit and contemplate for a while.

A little further west, you'll find the **Holocaust Memorial Garden**, a simple stone marker in a grove of trees.

Speakers' Corner

Frequented by Karl Marx, Vladimir Lenin, George Orwell and William Morris, **Speakers' Corner** in the northeastern corner of Hyde Park is traditionally the spot for oratorical flourishes and soapbox ranting. If you've got something to get off your chest, do so on Sunday, although you'll mainly have fringe dwellers, religious fanatics and hecklers for company. It's the only place in Britain where demonstrators can assemble without police permission, a concession granted in 1872 after serious riots 17 years before when 150,000 people gathered to demonstrate against the Sunday Trading Bill before Parliament, only to be unexpectedly ambushed by police concealed within Marble Arch.

Some historians also link Speakers' Corner with the nearby Tyburn gallows, where condemned criminals might speak to the crowd before being hanged.

DON'T MISS

→ The Serpentine Galleries

→ Speakers' Corner

→ Diana, Princess of Wales Memorial Fountain

PRACTICALITIES

→ Map p456, D2

→ www.royalparks.org. uk/parks/hyde-park

→ ⊙5am-midnight

→ ⊖Marble Arch, Hyde Park Corner, Queensway

Diana, Princess of Wales Memorial Fountain

This memorial fountain is dedicated to the late Princess of Wales. Envisaged by the designer Kathryn Gustafson as a 'moat without a castle' and draped 'like a necklace' around the southwestern edge of Hyde Park near the Serpentine Bridge, the circular double stream is composed of 545 pieces of Cornish granite, its waters drawn from a chalk aquifer more than 100m below ground. Unusually, visitors are actively encouraged to splash about, to the delight of children.

The SolarShuttle (p201) ferries passengers from the Serpentine Boathouse to the fountain on weekends from March to September (every day from mid-July to late August).

The Serpentine

Hyde Park is separated from Kensington Gardens by the L-shaped Serpentine, a small lake once fed by waters from the River Westbourne. You can have a swim too – between May and September – at the Serpentine Lido (p201), where a swimming area within the lake is ring-fenced. There is also a paddling pool for children.

If you'd rather stay dry, rent a paddle boat from the Serpentine Boathouse (p201).

The Serpentine Galleries

Constituting some of the most important contemporary-art spaces in town, these two galleries are a major draw. South of the Serpentine lake is the original **Serpentine Gallery** (📞020-7402 6075; www.serpentinegalleries.org; Kensington Gardens, W2; ⊙10am-6pm Tue-Sun; 📶; FREE), in which Damien Hirst, Andreas Gursky, Louise Bourgeois, Gabriel Orozco, Tomoko Takahashi and Jeff Koons have all exhibited. The setting is the 1930s former tea pavilion in Kensington Gardens.

In 2013 the gallery opened the **Serpentine Sackler Gallery** within **the Magazine**, a former gunpowder depot, across the Serpentine Bridge in Hyde Park. Built in 1805, it was augmented with a daring, undulating extension designed by Pritzker Prize–winning architect Zaha Hadid.

The galleries run a full program of exhibitions, readings, talks and open-air cinema screenings. A leading architect who has never previously built in the UK is annually commissioned to build a new 'Summer Pavilion' nearby, open from June to October.

HISTORY

Henry VIII expropriated the park from the church in 1536, after which it emerged as a hunting ground for kings and aristocrats; later it became a popular venue for duels, executions and horse racing. In the early 17th century it was the first royal park to open to the public. It was also the famous venue of the Great Exhibition in 1851, and during WWII, it became a vast potato bed. These days, it's an occasional concert and music-festival venue and in winter the site of Winter Wonderland.

ROYAL GUN SALUTES

Royal Gun Salutes are fired in Hyde Park on 10 June for the Duke of Edinburgh's birthday and on 14 November for the Prince of Wales's birthday. The salutes are fired at midday and include 41 rounds (21 is standard, but being a royal park, Hyde Park gets a bonus 20 rounds).

DECK CHAIRS

Found the perfect spot? Hire a **deck chair** (one/four hours £1.60/4.60, all day £8). They are available throughout the park from March to October, weather permitting.

SCIENCE MUSEUM

With seven floors of interactive and educational exhibits, this scientifically spellbinding museum will mesmerise adults and children alike.

The most popular galleries are on the ground floor (Level Zero), starting with **Exploring Space**, which features genuine rockets and satellites and a full-size replica of 'Eagle', the lander that took Neil Armstrong and Buzz Aldrin to the moon in 1969.

Next is the **Making the Modern World Gallery**, a visual feast of locomotives, planes, cars, engines and other revolutionary inventions (penicillin, cameras and other innovations).

The fantastic **Information Age Gallery** on Level 2 showcases how information and communication technologies have transformed our lives since the 19th century. Standout displays include wireless transmissions sent by a sinking *Titanic,* the first BBC radio broadcast and a Soviet BESM 1965 super computer. The **Atmosphere Gallery** explains the science of the world's climate over billions of years and tackles the issue of current climate change.

The 3rd-floor (Level 3) **Flight Gallery** (free tours 1pm most days) is a favourite place for children, with its gliders, hot-air balloons and aircraft, including the Gipsy Moth, that Amy Johnson flew to Australia in 1930. Also check out the designs for an early aerial steam carriage – a futile attempt to harness steam power for flight. This floor also features a **Red Arrows 3D flight-simulation theatre** (adult/children £6/5) and a **Fly 360 degree flight-simulator capsules** (£12 per capsule). Also on the 3rd floor, interactive **Wonderlab** (£6) explores scientific phenomena in a fun and educational way, with daily shows.

If you've kids under the age of five, pop down to the basement (Level –1) and the Garden, where there's a fun-filled play zone, including a water-play area, besieged by tots in orange waterproof smocks.

DON'T MISS

➡ Exploring Space Gallery
➡ Information Age Gallery
➡ Making the Modern World Gallery
➡ Flight Gallery
➡ Flight simulators

PRACTICALITIES

➡ Map p456, C4
➡ www.sciencemuseum.org.uk
➡ Exhibition Rd, SW7
➡ admission free
➡ ⊙10am-6pm
➡ 🛜
➡ ⊖South Kensington

⊙ SIGHTS

⊙ Knightsbridge & South Kensington

NATURAL HISTORY MUSEUM　　　MUSEUM
See p182.

VICTORIA & ALBERT MUSEUM　　　MUSEUM
See p178.

SCIENCE MUSEUM　　　MUSEUM
See p186.

BROMPTON ORATORY　　　CHURCH
Map p456 (✆020-7808 0900; www.brompton
oratory.co.uk; 215 Brompton Rd, SW7; ⊙7am-
8pm; ⊜South Kensington) The Church of the
Immaculate Heart of Mary, also known
as the London Oratory and the Oratory of
St Philip Neri, is a Roman Catholic church
second in size in London only to the in-
complete Westminster Cathedral. Built in
Italian baroque style in 1884, the interior
is swathed in marble and statuary; much
of the decorative work predates the church
and was imported from Italian churches.
The church was employed by the KGB during the Cold War as a dead-letter box.

There is a busy schedule of services (five
in English and Latin on weekdays, four on
Saturday and throughout the day on Sunday), including a Solemn Mass in Latin on
Sundays (11am).

**ROYAL COLLEGE OF
MUSIC MUSEUM**　　　MUSEUM
Map p456 (✆020-7591 4842; www.rcm.ac.uk/
museum; Prince Consort Rd, SW7; ⊜South Kensington) FREE This illustrious museum is
closed for rebuilding and redevelopment
until 2019. Till then, a part of the museum
collection can be explored digitally online
via the website.

⊙ Hyde Park & Kensington Gardens

HYDE PARK　　　PARK
See p184.

ROYAL ALBERT HALL　　　HISTORIC BUILDING
Map p456 (✆0845 401 5034, box office 020-
7589 8212; www.royalalberthall.com; Kensington
Gore, SW7; tour adult/child £12.75/5.75; ⊜South

Kensington) Built in 1871 thanks in part to
the proceeds of the 1851 Great Exhibition
organised by Prince Albert (Queen Victoria's husband), this huge, domed, red-
brick amphitheatre, adorned with a frieze
of Minton tiles, is Britain's most famous
concert venue and home to the BBC's Promenade Concerts (the Proms) every summer.
To find out about the hall's intriguing history and royal connections, and to gaze out
from the Gallery, book an informative one-
hour front-of-house **grand tour** (Map p456;
✆020-7589 8212; adult/child £13/6; ⊙hourly
9.30am-4.30pm).

The hall was never intended as a concert
venue but as a 'Hall of Arts and Sciences', so
it spent the first 133 years of its existence
tormenting everyone with shocking acoustics. The 85 huge mushroom-like fibreglass
acoustic reflectors first dangled from the
ceiling in 1969, and a further massive refurbishment was completed in 2004. There's
a whole range of other tours, from a grand
tour to a secret-history tour, an afternoon-
tea tour, an architectural tour, behind-the-
scenes tour and tours with dining provided.

★**ALBERT MEMORIAL**　　　MONUMENT
Map p456 (✆tours 020-8969 0104; Kensington
Gardens; tours adult/concession £9/8; ⊙tours
2pm & 3pm 1st Sun of month Mar-Dec; ⊜Knights-
bridge, Gloucester Rd) This splendid Victorian
confection on the southern edge of Kensington Gardens is as ostentatious as its subject. Purportedly humble, Queen Victoria's
German husband Albert (1819–61) explic-
itly insisted he did not want a monument.
Ignoring the good prince's wishes, the Lord
Mayor instructed George Gilbert Scott to
build the 53m-high, gaudy Gothic memorial
– the 4.25m-tall gilded statue of the prince,
surrounded by 187 figures representing the
continents (Asia, Europe, Africa and America), the arts, industry and science, went up
in 1876.

An eye-opening blend of mosaic, gold
leaf, marble and Victorian bombast, the
renovated monument is topped with a cru-
cifix. The statue was painted black for 80
years, originally – some say – to disguise
it from WWI Zeppelins (nonetheless, the
memorial was selected by German bombers
during WWII as a landmark). To step beyond the railings for a close-up of the staggering 64m-long *Frieze of Parnassus* along
the base – carved in situ and described by
Scott as 'perhaps one of the most laborious

TOP SIGHT
KENSINGTON PALACE

Built in 1605, Kensington palace became the favourite royal residence under William and Mary of Orange in 1689, and remained so until George III became king and relocated to Buckingham Palace. Today, it remains a royal residence, with the likes of the Duke and Duchess of Cambridge (Prince William and his wife Kate) and Prince Harry living here.

A large part of the palace is open to the public, however, including the King's and Queen's State Apartments. The **King's State Apartments** are the most lavish, starting with the **Grand Staircase**, a dizzying feast of trompe l'oeil. The beautiful **Cupola Room**, once the venue of choice for music and dance, is arranged with gilded statues and a gorgeous painted ceiling. The **Drawing Room** lies beyond.

Visitors can also access **Victoria's apartments** where Queen Victoria (1819–1901) was born and lived until she became Queen. An informative narrative about her life is told through personal effects and extracts from her journals.

The **sunken garden** in the garden to the palace is ablaze with flowers in spring and summer.

DON'T MISS

➡ Cupola Room
➡ Grand Staircase
➡ Victoria's apartments
➡ Sunken garden

PRACTICALITIES

➡ Map p456, A3
➡ www.hrp.org.uk/kensingtonpalace
➡ Kensington Gardens, W8
➡ adult/child £19/free;
➡ ◷10am-6pm Mar-Oct, to 4pm Nov-Feb
➡ ⊖High St Kensington

works of sculpture ever undertaken' – join one of the 45-minute tours.

KENSINGTON GARDENS — PARK
Map p456 (✆0300 061 2000; www.royalparks.org.uk/parks/kensington-gardens; ◷6am-dusk; ⊖Queensway or Lancaster Gate) A gorgeous collection of manicured lawns, tree-shaded avenues and basins immediately west of Hyde Park, the picturesque 107-hectare expanse of Kensington Gardens is technically part of Kensington Palace, located in the far west of the gardens.The large **Round Pond** is enjoyable to amble around and also worth a look are the lovely fountains in the **Italian Gardens** (Map p456; ⊖Lancaster Gate), believed to be a gift from Albert to Queen Victoria; they are now the venue of a handy new cafe.

The **Diana, Princess of Wales Memorial Playground** (Map p456; ⊖Queensway), in the northwest corner of the gardens, has some pretty ambitious attractions for children. Next to the playground stands the delightful **Elfin Oak** (Map p456), a 900-year-old tree stump carved with elves, gnomes, witches and small creatures. George Frampton's

celebrated **Peter Pan statue** (Map p456; ⊖Lancaster Gate) is close to the lake, while the astonishing Albert Memorial (p187) is in the south of Kensington Gardens, facing the Royal Albert Hall (p187).

WELLINGTON ARCH — MUSEUM
Map p456 (www.english-heritage.org.uk/visit/places/wellington-arch; Hyde Park Corner, W1; adult/child £4.70/2.80, with Apsley House £10.50/6.30; ◷10am-6pm Apr-Sep, to 4pm Nov-Mar; ⊖Hyde Park Corner) Dominating the green space throttled by the Hyde Park Corner roundabout, this imposing neoclassical 1826 arch originally faced the Hyde Park Screen, but was shunted here in 1882 for road widening. Once a police station, it is now a gallery with temporary exhibitions and a permanent display about the history of the arch. The open-air balconies (accessible by lift) afford unforgettable views of Hyde Park, Buckingham Palace and the Mall.

Originally crowned by a disproportionately large equestrian statue of the Duke of Wellington (which now stands in Aldershot in Hampshire), it was replaced by the current four-horse *Peace Descending on the*

Quadriga of War, Europe's largest bronze sculpture, in 1912.

SERPENTINE LAKE
LAKE

Map p456 (☑020-7262 1330; ⊜Knightsbridge, South Kensington) Hyde Park is separated from Kensington Gardens by the squiggly Serpentine lake, created when the Westbourne River was dammed in the 1730s. At Christmas, it's the site of a brass-balls swimming race, and in summer people like to rent pedalos (adult/child per hour £12/5). A solar ferry called the SolarShuttle (p201) goes at a river-snail's pace from the boathouse to the Lido Café. In operation yearround (operators assure us), we presume it must depend on the weather.

⊙ Chelsea & Belgravia

★MICHELIN HOUSE
HISTORIC BUILDING

Map p456 (81 Fulham Rd, SW3; ⊜South Kensington) Built for Michelin between 1905 and 1911 by François Espinasse, and completely restored in 1985, the building blurs the stylish line between art nouveau and art deco. The iconic roly-poly Michelin Man (Bibendum)

appears in the exquisite modern stained glass (the originals were removed at the outbreak of WWII and stored in the Michelin factory in Stoke-on-Trent, but subsequently vanished), while the lobby is decorated with tiles showing early-20th-century cars.

★NATIONAL ARMY MUSEUM
MUSEUM

Map p456 (☑020-7730 0717; www.nam.ac.uk; Royal Hospital Rd, SW3; ⊘10am-5.30pm, to 8pm 1st Wed of the month; ⊜Sloane Sq) **FREE** This inventively redesigned museum vibrantly relates the history of the British Army, from the perspective of its servicemen and servicewomen. The museum reopened with a big bang in 2017, with five brand-new state-of-the-art galleries, including the **Soldier Gallery**, the **Army Gallery**, the **Society Gallery** (exploring society's relationship with the army), the **Battle Gallery** (the army at war) and the **Insight Gallery** (on the impact of the British Army through the world). Free talks, workshops and tours are also hosted: see the website for details.

On the Ground Floor Lower Level, **Play Base** (£4.50) offers a fun and immersive experience for under 9s (including an assault course and the chance to clamber aboard a

TOP SIGHT
APSLEY HOUSE

This stunning house, containing exhibits about the Duke of Wellington, who defeated Napoleon Bonaparte at Waterloo, was once the first building to appear when entering London from the west and was therefore known as 'No 1 London'. Still one of London's finest, Apsley House was designed by Robert Adam for Baron Apsley in the late 18th century, but later sold to the first Duke of Wellington, who lived here until he died in 1852.

In 1947 the house was given to the nation; 10 of its rooms are open to the public. Wellington memorabilia, including his **death mask**, fills the basement gallery, while there's an astonishing **collection of china and silver,** including a dazzling **Egyptian service**, a divorce gift from Napoleon to Josephine, which she declined.

The stairwell is dominated by Antonio Canova's staggering 3.4m-high **statue** of a fig-leafed Napoleon with titanic shoulders, adjudged by the subject as 'too athletic'. The 1st-floor **Waterloo Gallery** contains paintings by Velázquez, Rubens, Van Dyck, Bruegel, Murillo and Goya. A highlight is the elaborate Portuguese silver service, presented to Wellington in honour of his triumph over 'Le Petit Caporal'. Check the website for details of evening openings, when you can explore the house after dark.

DON'T MISS

➡ Egyptian service
➡ Canova's statue of Napoleon
➡ Waterloo Gallery paintings

PRACTICALITIES

➡ Map p456, F3
➡ ☑020-7499 5676 www.english-heritage.org.uk/visit/places/apsley-house
➡ 149 Piccadilly, W1
➡ adult/child £9.30/5.60, with Wellington Arch £11.20/6.70
➡ ⊘11am-5pm Wed-Sun Apr-Oct, 10am-4pm Sat & Sun Nov-Mar
➡ ⊜Hyde Park Corner)

command liaison vehicle), with six one-hour sessions from 9.40am to 4.20pm. There's a cafe (10am to 5pm) too, for museum-weary legs, caffeine requirements and snacks.

SAATCHI GALLERY   GALLERY
Map p456 (www.saatchigallery.com; Duke of York's HQ, King's Rd, SW3; ⊕10am-6pm; ⊖Sloane Sq) **FREE** This enticing gallery hosts temporary exhibitions of experimental and thought-provoking work across a variety of media. The white and sanded bare-floorboard galleries are magnificently presented; at the time of writing, Richard Wilson's mesmerising *20:50* – one of the main draws to the museum – had unfortunately been taken off display, so check ahead. A cool shop chips in on the 1st floor.

Check the website for dates when the galleries may be shut for ticketed exhibitions.

KING'S ROAD   STREET
Map p456 (⊖Sloane Sq) At the counter-cultural forefront of London fashion during the technicolour '60s and anarchic '70s (Ian Fleming's fictional spy James Bond had a flat in a square off the road), the King's Rd today is more a stamping ground for the leisure-class shopping set. The last green-haired Mohawk punks – once tourist sights in themselves – shuffled off sometime in the 1990s. Today it's all Bang & Olufsen, Kurt Geiger and a sprinkling of specialist shops; even pet canines are slim and snappily dressed.

In the 17th century, Charles II fashioned a love nest here for himself and his mistress Nell Gwyn, an orange-seller turned actress at the Drury Lane Theatre. Heading back to Hampton Court Palace at eventide, Charles would employ a farmer's track that inevitably came to be known as the King's Rd.

CHELSEA PHYSIC GARDEN   GARDENS
Map p456 (☏020-7352 5646; www.chelsea physicgarden.co.uk; 66 Royal Hospital Rd, SW3; adult/child £10.50/6.95; ⊕11am-5pm Mon, to 6pm Tue-Fri & Sun Apr-Oct, 9.30am-4pm Mon-Fri Nov-Mar; ⊖Sloane Sq) You may bump into a wandering duck or two as you enter this walled pocket of botanical enchantment, established by the Apothecaries' Society in 1673 for students working on medicinal plants and healing. One of Europe's oldest of its kind, the small grounds are a compendium of botany, from carnivorous pitcher plants to rich yellow flag irises, a cork oak from Portugal, the largest outdoor fruiting olive tree in the British Isles, rare trees and shrubs.

The site, not far from the river, ensures a slightly warmer microclimate to protect nonnative plants. The fascinating pharmaceutical garden grows plants used in contemporary Western medicine; the Garden of World Medicine has a selection of plants used by indigenous peoples in Australia, China, India, New Zealand and North America. There's also a heady perfume and aromatherapy garden plus a fine cafe near the shop; enter from Swan Walk. Pick up an audio guide or join a free tour (held three or more times daily); a host of courses and lectures detail plant remedies.

ROYAL HOSPITAL CHELSEA   MUSEUM
Map p456 (www.chelsea-pensioners.co.uk; Royal Hospital Rd, SW3; ⊕grounds 10am-4.30pm Mon-Sat, Great Hall shuts daily noon-2pm, museum 10am-4pm Mon-Fri; ⊖Sloane Sq) **FREE** Designed by Christopher Wren, this superb structure was built in 1692 to provide shelter for ex-servicemen. Since the reign of Charles II, it has housed hundreds of war veterans, known as Chelsea Pensioners. They're fondly regarded as national treasures, and cut striking figures in the dark-blue greatcoats (in winter) or scarlet frock coats (in summer) that they wear on ceremonial occasions.

The **museum** contains a huge collection of war medals bequeathed by former residents and plenty of information about the institution's history and its residents. Visitors can also peek at the hospital's Great Hall refectory, Octagon Porch, chapel and courtyards. Chelsea Pensioner–led tours are also available (adult/child £12/7).

Former Prime Minister Margaret Thatcher is buried here, in the old **cemetery**. The extensive grounds are home to the Chelsea Flower Show, the annual jamboree of the gardening world, held in May.

CARLYLE'S HOUSE   HISTORIC BUILDING
Map p456 (☏020-7352 7087; www.nationaltrust. org.uk/carlyles-house; 24 Cheyne Row, SW3; adult/child £6.50/3.25; ⊕11am-5pm Wed-Sun Mar-Oct; ⊖Sloane Sq) From 1834 until his death in 1881, the eminent Victorian essayist and historian Thomas Carlyle dwelt in this three-storey terrace house, bought by his parents when it was surrounded by open fields in what was then a deeply unfashionable part of town. The lovely Queen Ann house – built in 1708 – is magnificently

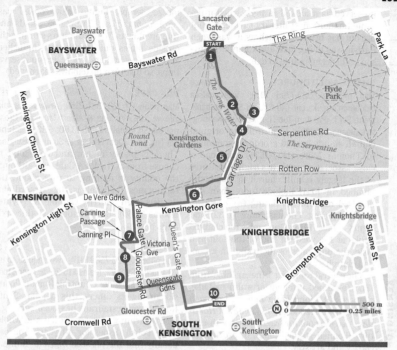

Neighbourhood Walk
Gardens & Mews

START LANCASTER GATE TUBE STATION
END NATURAL HISTORY MUSEUM
LENGTH 2.2 MILES; 1½ HOURS

Begin outside Lancaster Gate tube station and head to the park. Bear left at the **1 Italian Gardens** (p188) – thought to be a gift from Prince Albert to Queen Victoria – and follow the path along Long Water until you reach **2 The Arch**, an imposing statue by Henry Moore that affords fantastic views of Kensington Palace, the Tudors' favourite palace and current residence of Princes William and Harry. As you reach the road, glance left at the **3 Serpentine Sackler Gallery** (p185), a former gun depot with a modern extension designed by prize-winning architect Zaha Hadid.

Cross the **4 bridge** over the Serpentine and take in the views. Turn right into Kensington Gardens, walk past the **5 Serpentine Gallery** (p185), a famous contemporary-art gallery, and make your way south to the **6 Albert Memorial** (p187), a Victorian Gothic confection commemorating the Prince Consort. Carry on west through the park and exit at Palace Gate. Walk down and turn right onto Canning Place. Take a moment to admire the gorgeous **7 Canning Mews** to your right and also take a long look up De Vere Gardens and its lengthy line of grand houses. Turn left onto Canning Passage and then left again onto Victoria Grove. The boutiques and wisteria-clad houses on this little square could be straight out of a Cotswold village. Bear right along **8 Launceston Place** and walk on past ivy-covered walls and exquisite houses: some of the most coveted real estate in London. Take a small detour down **9 Kynance Mews** on the right (there is a public right of way until about halfway down the mews) to see the storybook cottages.

Take a left at Cornwall Gardens; cross to Queen's Gate Gardens, then turn right at Queen's Gate (all these streets are lined with white stuccoed buildings typical of the area): the **10 Natural History Museum** is just ahead of you. The main entrance is a little further along on Cromwell Rd.

preserved as it looked in 1895, when it became London's first literary shrine. It's not big but has been left much as it was when Carlyle was living here and Chopin, Tennyson and Dickens came to call.

CHELSEA OLD CHURCH   CHURCH

Map p456 (☎020-7795 1019; www.chelsea oldchurch.org.uk; cnr Old Church St & Embankment, SW3; ⏰2-4pm Tue-Thu; ⊖South Kensington, Sloane Sq) This beautiful and original church stands behind a bronze monument to Thomas More (1477–1535), who had a close association with it. Original features of the largely rebuilt church (it was badly bombed in 1941) include more than one hundred monuments dating from 1433 to 1957, including Thomas More (1532) and Henry James (1916). Don't miss the chained books at the western end of the southern aisle, the only ones of their kind in a London church.

The central tome is a 'Vinegar Bible' from 1717 (so-named after an erratum in Luke, chapter 20), alongside a *Book of Common Prayer* from 1723 and a 1683 copy of *Homilies*. Also look out for fragments of 17th-century Flemish stained glass, of exceptional clarity and artistry.

✖ EATING

Quality and cashola being such easy bedfellows, you'll find some of London's finest establishments in the smart hotels and ritzy mews of Chelsea, Belgravia and Knightsbridge, but choice exists in all budget ranges. Chic and cosmopolitan South Kensington has always been reliable for pan-European options.

✖ Knightsbridge & South Kensington

COMPTOIR LIBANAIS   LEBANESE $

Map p456 (☎020-7225 5006; www.comptoir libanais.com; 1-5 Exhibition Rd, SW7; mains from £8.50; ⏰8.30am-midnight Mon-Sat, to 10.30pm Sun; 🛜; ⊖South Kensington) If your battery's flat hoovering up South Kensington's museums, this colourful, good-looking and brisk restaurant just round the corner from the tube station is a moreish stop for Lebanese

mezze, wraps, tagine (slow-cooked casseroles), *mana'esh* (flatbreads), salads and fine breakfasts. When the sun's shining, the outside tables quickly fill with munchers and people-watchers. There are no reservations, so just turn up (elbows sharpened).

V&A CAFE   CAFE $

Map p456 (☎020-7581 2159; www.vam.ac.uk/info/va-cafe; Victoria & Albert Museum, Cromwell Rd, SW7; mains £7.45-13.50; ⏰10am-5.15pm Sat-Thu, to 9.30pm Fri; 🛜; ⊖South Kensington) There is plenty of hot and cold food to choose from at the V&A Café, and although the quality is nothing to rave about, the setting most definitely is: the extraordinarily decorated Morris, Gamble & Poynter Rooms (1860) show Victorian Gothic style at its best.

DAQUISE   POLISH $$

Map p456 (☎020-7589 6117; www.daquise.co.uk; 20 Thurloe St, SW7; mains £15-20; ⏰noon-11pm; ⊖South Kensington) Counting Roman Polanski among its diners, this popular South Kensington restaurant has been serving a heart-warming range of vodkas and wholesome Polish dishes for 60 years. You can usually find the oft-seen *bigos* (a 'hunter's stew' of cabbage and pork), *pierogi* (dumplings) and an abundance of soups on the reasonably priced and regularly varying menu. The express lunch is excellent value at £10.

L'ETO   CAFE $$

Map p456 (www.letocaffe.co.uk; 243 Brompton Rd, SW3; mains £11.50-19.95; ⏰9am-10pm Sun-Wed, to 11pm Thu-Sat; 🛜📷; ⊖South Kensington, Knightsbridge) With its all-day service, this upmarket cafe has found an excellent niche between the museum district of South Kensington and the shopping vortex of Knightsbridge. The salad bar and eye-popping sweets counter are great, although the à la carte menu is good too, if a little over-priced.

★DINNER BY HESTON BLUMENTHAL   MODERN BRITISH $$$

Map p456 (☎020-7201 3833; www.dinnerby heston.com; Mandarin Oriental Hyde Park, 66 Knightsbridge, SW1; 3-course set lunch £45, mains £28-44; ⏰noon-2pm & 6-10.15pm Mon-Fri, noon-2.30pm & 6-10.30pm Sat & Sun; 🛜; ⊖Knightsbridge) Sumptuously presented Dinner is a gastronomic tour de force, taking diners on a journey through British culinary history (with inventive modern inflections). Dishes carry historical dates to convey context, while the restaurant interior is a design triumph, from the glass-walled kitchen and its overhead clock mechanism to the large windows looking onto the park. Book ahead.

Also on hand is a 16th-century Tudor-style private room that seats 12 guests, who dine at an extravagant Sapele and Rosewood oval table. Set lunches are available Monday to Friday.

BAR BOULUD   INTERNATIONAL $$$
Map p456 (www.barboulud.com/london; Mandarin Oriental Hyde Park, 66 Knightsbridge, SW1; mains £15-34, 2-/3-course lunch menu £18/21; ⊙noon-11pm; 🛜⏳; ❺Knightsbridge) Combining French gastronomy with American influences must have raised a few chef's eyebrows in Daniel Boulud's native France, but diners vote with their forks, whether they choose the *saumon au beurre blanc* or the 'Yankee' burger.

The drinks list is just as trans-Atlantic with a spectacular cellar (the wine list is 27 pages long) and equally great cocktails (the white cosmopolitan, with vodka, elderflower liqueur and white cranberry is to die for). The set lunch is available daily between noon and 6.30pm.

ZUMA   JAPANESE $$$
Map p456 (🕿020-7584 1010; www.zuma restaurant.com; 5 Raphael St, SW7; mains £15-75; ⊙noon-3pm Mon-Fri, to 3.30pm Sat & Sun, 6-11pm Mon-Sat, to 10.30pm Sun; 🛜; ❺Knightsbridge) Zuma oozes style – a modern-day take on the traditional Japanese *izakaya* ('a place to stay and drink sake'), where drinking and eating harmonise. The *robata* (chargrilled) dishes are the stars of the show; wash them down with one of 40 types of sake on offer. Booking is advised, although there are walk-in spaces at the *robata* and sushi counters.

RIB ROOM   BRITISH $$$
Map p456 (🕿020-7858 7250; www.theribroom. co.uk; Jumeirah Carlton Tower, Cadogan Place, SW1; mains from £24, 2-/3-course set lunch £28/32; ⊙7-11am Mon-Sat, 8-11am Sun, 12.30-2.45pm Tue-Fri, to 3.30pm Sun, 6.30-10pm Tue, to 10.30pm Wed-Sat; 🛜; ❺Knightsbridge) Head chef Ian Rudge's faultless preparation is the cornerstone of the much-lauded carnivorous menu at the Rib Room, satiating

Knightsbridge diners with steaks, cutlets, roast rib of beef and oysters with aplomb since the swinging '60s. Prices may steady your hand, but the food is superlative (and well-priced set meals come with a glass of Champagne). Service is outstanding. The three-course set lunch on Sunday is £55.

🍴 Hyde Park & Kensington Gardens

MAGAZINE   INTERNATIONAL $$
Map p456 (🕿020-7298 7552; www.magazine-restaurant.co.uk; Serpentine Sackler Gallery, West Carriage Dr, W2; mains £13-24, 2-/3-course lunch menu £17.50/21.50; ⊙9am-6pm Tue-Sat; 🛜; ❺Lancaster Gate, Knightsbridge) Located in the elegant extension of the Serpentine Sackler Gallery (p185), Magazine is no ordinary museum cafe. The food is as contemporary and elegant as the building, and artworks from current exhibitions add yet another dimension. The afternoon tea (£25, with one cocktail) is particularly original: out with cucumber sandwiches, in with gin-cured sea trout, goat's curd and coconut granita.

Magazine opens for dinner on Fridays and Saturdays from April to September, with the added bonus of live music.

ORANGERY   CAFE $$
Map p456 (🕿020-3166 6113; www.orangery kensingtonpalace.co.uk; Kensington Palace, Kensington Gardens, W8; mains £12.50-16.50, afternoon tea £27.50; ⊙10am-5pm; ⏳; ❺Queensway, High St Kensington) The Orangery, housed in an 18th-century conservatory on the grounds of Kensington Palace (p188), is lovely for a late breakfast or lunch, but the standout experience here is English afternoon tea. Book ahead to bag a table on the beautiful terrace.

OGNISKO   POLISH $$
Map p456 (🕿020-7589 0101; www.ognisko restaurant.co.uk; 55 Prince's Gate, Exhibition Rd, SW7; mains £7-20, 2-/3-course set lunch £18.50/22; ⊙noon-3pm & 5.30-11.15pm, to 10.30pm Sun; 🛜; ❺South Kensington) Ognisko has been a stalwart of the Polish community in London since 1940 (it's part of the Polish Hearth Club). The grand dining room is stunning, bathed in light from tall windows and adorned with modern art and chandeliers, and the food couldn't be more authentic: try the delicious *pierogi*

Parks & Gardens

Glance at a colour map of town and be struck by how much is olive green. London has some of the world's most superb urban parkland, most of it well-tended,accessible and a delight in any season.

Hyde Park

Perhaps London's most famous and easily accessed expanse of urban greenery, Hyde Park is astonishing for the variety of its landscapes and trees. The lovely Serpentine separates it from that other grand London park, Kensington Gardens.

Greenwich Park

Delightfully hilly, elegantly landscaped and bisected by the Meridian Line, Greenwich Park offers sweeping perspectives from its highest point. London's oldest enclosed royal park, it is home to herds of deer and some of Greenwich's top highlights.

Victoria Park

Named after its eponymous royal benefactor, Victoria Park is one of East London's most pleasant and popular parks, enjoying an expensive regeneration several years back. In summer it becomes a venue for live music and festivals.

Richmond Park

An epic expanse of greenery down southwest, royal Richmond Park is home to herds of deer, sublime views and a fantastic collection of trees, ponds,woodland and grass. Shake off the urban fumes and immerse yourself in its wild expanses.

Kew Gardens

To fall for Kew Gardens, all you need is an eye for fine architecture, a fondness for exploration and a sense of natural curiosity. Children will adore the treetop walkway and the fantastic play zones.

Hyde Park (p184) **2.** Palm House, Kew Gardens (p314)
Bucks, Richmond Park (p316)

❶ FINE BUT AFFORDABLE DINING

Chelsea and Kensington have some of the finest – and most expensive – restaurants in London. One way of enjoying them without breaking the bank is to go for the set lunch menus, which offer great value (two to three courses for less than £30).

(dumplings stuffed with cheese and potatoes) or the blinis.

LAUNCESTON PLACE
MODERN BRITISH $$$

Map p456 (☑020-7937 6912; www.launceston place-restaurant.co.uk; 1a Launceston Pl, W8; 2-/3-course set lunch £25/30, 3-course dinner £30-60; ⊙noon-2.30pm Wed-Sat, to 3.30pm Sun, 6-10pm Tue-Sat, 6.30-9pm Sun; ☏; ⊖Gloucester Rd, High St Kensington) This exceptionally handsome, superchic Michelin-starred restaurant is hidden away almost anonymously on a picture-postcard Kensington street of Edwardian houses. Prepared by London chef Ben Murphy, dishes occupy the acme of gastronomic pleasures and are accompanied by an award-winning wine list. The adventurous will aim for the six-course tasting menu (£75; vegetarian version available) or the 'reduced' five-course version (£49).

The pre-theatre dinner (£30) is available in the early evening.

MIN JIANG
CHINESE $$$

Map p456 (☑020-7361 1988; www.minjiang. co.uk; Royal Garden Hotel, 10th fl, 2-24 Kensington High St, W8; mains £12-68, lunch set menu £40-55, dinner set menu £70-88; ⊙noon-3pm & 6-10.30pm; ☑; ⊖High St Kensington) Min Jiang serves up seafood, excellent wood-fired Peking duck (*běijīng kǎoyā;* half/ whole £33/60), *dim sum* (from £4.80) and sumptuously regal views over Kensington Palace and Gardens. The menu is diverse, with a sporadic accent on spice (the Min Jiang is a river in Sichuan).

✖ Chelsea & Belgravia

★ TOM'S KITCHEN
MODERN EUROPEAN $$

Map p456 (☑020-7349 0202; www.tomskitchen. co.uk/chelsea; 27 Cale St, SW3; mains £16-30, 2-/3-course lunch menu £16.50/19.50; ⊙8am-2.30pm & 6-10.30pm Mon-Fri, 9.30am-3.30pm & 6-10.30pm Sat, to 9.30pm Sun; ☏☑; ⊖South Kensington) 🖊 Recipe for success: mix one part relaxed and smiling staff, and one part light and airy decor to two parts divine food and voilà: you have Tom's Kitchen. Classics such as grilled steaks, burgers, slow-cooked pork belly and chicken schnitzel are cooked to perfection, while seasonal choices such as the homemade ricotta or pan-fried scallops are sublime.

The restaurant goes to great lengths to support British farmers, growers and fishers. You can read about their suppliers online, or in little cards in the restaurant.

DAYLESFORD ORGANIC
DELI $$

Map p456 (☑020-7881 8060; www.daylesford organic.com; 44b Pimlico Rd, SW1; mains £8-17; ⊙8am-8pm Mon-Sat, 10am-4pm Sun; ☏☑; ⊖Sloane Sq) A chomping ground for the Chelsea and Pimlico set, with a deli counter, a farmhouse shop and a modernist cafe serving delicious breakfasts, light lunches and afternoon teas.

PAINTED HERON
INDIAN $$

Map p456 (☑020-7351 5232; www.thepainted heron.com; 112 Cheyne Walk, SW10; mains £13.50-20, 2-course lunch menu £15.94; ⊙11.30am-3.30pm & 6-11pm; ☑; ⊖Sloane Sq) The rather formal setting – starched white tablecloths, cubby holes and leather banquettes – is softened by intimate lighting in the evenings and affable service on all occasions. As for the food, it's a delight, from classics such as biryani and tikka masala to Modern Indian innovations such as venison curry with red wine and chocolate samosas for dessert.

LOTS ROAD PUB & DINING ROOM
GASTROPUB $$

(☑020-73526645; www.lotsroadpub.com; 114 Lots Rd, SW10; mains £12-20; ⊙noon-11pm Mon-Sat, to 10.30pm Sun; ⊖Fulham Broadway) Light floods through the windows into the high-ceilinged, wood-lined, curved dining area and onto the black-and-chrome bar, where choice wines are sold by the glass. Service is tip-top and the regularly changing menu may read as standard fare – beef, salmon, lamb – but it's all delicious.

Sunday roasts are deservedly popular, and don't miss the sticky toffee pudding.

★FIVE FIELDS   MODERN BRITISH $$$

Map p456 (☏020-78381082; www.fivefieldsrestaurant.com; 8-9 Blacklands Tce, SW3; 3-course set meal £65, tasting menu £85; ⊘6.30-10pm Tue-Sat; ☎; ⊖Sloane Sq) The inventive British prix fixe cuisine, consummate service and enticingly light and inviting decor are hard to resist at this triumphant Chelsea restaurant – now with a Michelin star – but you'll need to plan early and book way up front. It's only open five nights a week.

★GORDON RAMSAY   FRENCH $$$

Map p456 (☏020-7352 4441; www.gordonramsayrestaurants.com/restaurant-gordon-ramsay; 68 Royal Hospital Rd, SW3; 3-course lunch/dinner £65/110; ⊘noon-2.30pm & 6.30-11pm Mon-Fri; ☎; ⊖Sloane Sq) One of Britain's finest restaurants and London's longest-running with three Michelin stars, this is hallowed turf for those who worship at the altar of the stove. It's true that it's a treat right from the taster to the truffles, but you won't get much time to savour it all. Bookings are made in specific sittings and you dare not linger; book as late as you can to avoid that rushed feeling. The blowout Menu Prestige (£145) is seven courses of perfection.

★RABBIT   MODERN BRITISH $$

Map p456 (☏020-3750 0172; www.rabbit-restaurant.com; 172 King's Rd, SW3; mains £6-24, set lunch £13.50; ⊘noon-midnight Tue-Sat, 6-11pm Mon, noon-6pm Sun; ☏; ⊖Sloane Sq) Three brothers grew up on a farm. One became a farmer, another a butcher, while the third worked in hospitality. So they pooled their skills and came up with Rabbit, a breath of fresh air in upmarket Chelsea. The restaurant rocks the agri-chic (yes) look and the creative, seasonal modern British cuisine is fabulous.

The drinks list is just as good, with a great selection of wines from the family vineyard in Sussex, and local beers and ciders.

MEDLAR   MODERN EUROPEAN $$$

Map p456 (☏020-7349 1900; www.medlarrestaurant.co.uk; 438 King's Rd, SW10; set lunch £25-35, 2-/3-course dinner £41/49; ⊘noon-3pm & 6.30-10.30pm Mon-Fri, 6-10.30pm Sat, 6-9.30pm Sun; ☎; ⊖Fulham Broadway, Sloane Sq) With its uncontrived yet crisply modern and cool green-on-grey design, Medlar is a King's Rd sensation. With no à la carte menu and scant pretentiousness, the prix fixe modern European cuisine is delightfully assured: the menu changes with the season but tries hard to promote British ingredients as well as underrated meats such as pigeon and guinea fowl, all beautifully presented.

HUNAN   CHINESE $$$

Map p456 (☏020-7730 5712; www.hunanlondon.com; 51 Pimlico Rd, SW1; lunch/dinner from £42.80/66.80; ⊘noon-2pm & 6.30-11pm Mon-Sat; ☏; ⊖Sloane Sq) In business for over three decades, this understated Chinese restaurant imaginatively exercises a no-menu policy, so just present your preferences and let the *dachu* (chef) get cracking. A meal will comprise 12 to 18 small, tapas-style dishes – many with a pronounced Taiwan accent (despite the name) – to encourage a spectrum of flavour and colour. Vegetarian options available.

✖ Victoria & Pimlico

★PIMLICO FRESH   CAFE $

Map p456 (☏020-7932 0030; 86 Wilton Rd, SW1; mains from £4.50; ⊘7.30am-7.30pm Mon-Fri, 9am-6pm Sat & Sun; ⊖Victoria) This friendly two-room cafe will see you right whether you need breakfast (French toast, bowls of porridge laced with honey or maple syrup), lunch (homemade quiches and soups, 'things' on toast) or just a good old latte and cake.

KAZAN   TURKISH $$

Map p456 (☏020-7233 7100; www.kazanrestaurant.com; 93-94 Wilton Rd; mains £6.50-25, set menu from £27.50; ⊘noon-3pm & 5.30-10pm, to 10.30pm Fri; ⊖Victoria) Aromatic Kazan gets repeated thumbs up for its set Turkish meze, shish kebabs and *kulbasti* (rosemary-rubbed grilled fillet of lamb). Flavours are rich and faultless, service is attentive and the Ottoman ambience alluring, but not over the top. Seafood and vegetarian options available. Booking ahead is recommended.

🍷 DRINKING & NIGHTLIFE

Kensington, Chelsea and Belgravia do not have London's oldest and most time-seasoned watering holes, but several very charming, characterful and distinctive pubs provide a congenial environment for a pint.

★ANGLESEA ARMS   PUB

Map p456 (📞020-73737960; www.angleseaarms. com; 15 Selwood Tce, SW7; ⏱11am-11pm Mon-Sat, noon-10.30pm Sun; ⓢSouth Kensington) Seasoned with age and decades of ale-quaffing patrons (including Charles Dickens, who lived on the same road, and DH Lawrence), this old-school pub boasts considerable character and a strong showing of brews, while the terrace out front swarms with punters in warmer months. Arch-criminal Bruce Reynolds masterminded the Great Train Robbery over drinks here.

★TOMTOM COFFEE HOUSE   CAFE

Map p456 (📞020-7730 1771; www.tomtom.co.uk; 114 Ebury St, SW1; ⏱8am-5pm Mon-Fri, 9am-6pm Sat & Sun; 🛜; ⓢVictoria) Tomtom has built its reputation on its amazing coffee: not only are the drinks fabulously presented (forget ferns and hearts in your latte, here it's peacocks fanning their tails), but the selection is dizzying; from the usual espresso-based suspects to filter, and a full choice of beans. You can even spice things up with a bonus tot of cognac or whisky (£3).

The cafe also serves lovely food throughout the day, from breakfast and toasties on sourdough bread to homemade pies (mains £5 to £10).

PHENE   BAR

Map p456 (www.thephene.com; 9 Phene St, SW3; ⏱noon-11pm Mon-Fri, 10am-11pm Sat, to 10pm Sun; 🛜; ⓢSloane Sq) This beautiful bar/pub in the heart of Chelsea is a hit – from the red banquette in the stylish dining room to the elegant terrace for summer evenings, and from the excellent selection of beers brewed by the capital's many small breweries to the original G&Ts (lots of different gins and flavoured tonics).

QUEEN'S ARMS   PUB

Map p456 (www.thequeensarmskensington. co.uk; 30 Queen's Gate Mews, SW7; ⏱noon-11pm Mon-Sat, to 10.30pm Sun; ⓢGloucester Rd) Just around the corner from the Royal Albert Hall is this blue-grey-painted godsend. Located in an adorable cobbled mews setting off bustling Queen's Gate, it beckons with a cosy interior and a right royal selection of ales – including selections from small, local cask brewers – and ciders on tap. In warm weather, drinkers stand outside in the mews (only permitted on one side).

The fine pub menu is good for dinner, with burger-and-a-beer offers on Mondays for a tenner.

BUDDHA BAR   BAR

Map p456 (📞020-3667 5222; www.buddhabar london.com; 145 Knightsbridge, SW1; cocktails from £15; ⏱5pm-midnight Mon-Fri, noon-midnight Sat, to 11.30pm Sun; 🛜; ⓢKnightsbridge) When you've shopped your legs off in Knightsbridge, this serenely seductive zone welcomes you into a world of Chinese bird-cage lanterns, subdued lighting, tucked-away corners and booths, perfect for sipping on a Singapore Sling and chilling out. The restaurant downstairs continues the Oriental theme, serving pan-Asian specialities.

DRAYTON ARMS   PUB

Map p456 (📞020-7835 2301; www.thedrayton armssw5.co.uk; 153 Old Brompton Rd, SW5; ⏱noon-11pm Mon, to 11.30pm Tue & Wed, to midnight Thu & Fri, 10am-midnight Sat, to 11.30pm Sun; ⓢGloucester Rd) This vast, comely Victorian corner boozer is delightful inside and out, with some bijou art-nouveau features (sinuous tendrils and curlicues above the windows and the doors), contemporary art on the walls, a fabulous coffered ceiling and a heated beer garden. The crowd is both hip and down-to-earth; great beer and wine selection. The pub has a studio theatre too, with nightly productions at 8pm.

☆ ENTERTAINMENT

This isn't the neighbourhood for cutting-edge clubs, but if jazz floats your boat, a couple of standout venues should top your London list.

★606 CLUB   BLUES, JAZZ

(📞020-7352 5953; www.606club.co.uk; 90 Lots Rd, SW10; ⏱7-11.15pm Sun-Thu, 8pm-12.30am Fri & Sat; 🚇Imperial Wharf) Named after its old address on the King's Rd that cast a spell over jazz lovers London-wide back in the '80s, this fantastic, tucked-away basement jazz club and restaurant gives centre stage to contemporary British-based jazz musicians nightly. The club can only serve alcohol to nonmembers who are dining, and it is highly advisable to book to get a table.

There is no entry charge, but a 'music charge' (£10 Sunday to Thursday and £14 Friday and Saturday) will be added to your food/drink bill at the end of the evening; it's open for occasional Sunday lunches.

★ROYAL ALBERT HALL CONCERT VENUE

Map p456 (☑0845 401 5034; www.royalalbert hall.com; Kensington Gore, SW7; ⊜South Kensington) This splendid Victorian concert hall hosts classical music, rock and other performances, but is famously the venue for the BBC-sponsored Proms. Booking is possible, but from mid-July to mid-September Proms punters queue for £5 standing (or 'promenading') tickets that go on sale one hour before curtain-up. Otherwise the box office and prepaid-ticket collection counter are through door 12 (south side of the hall).

A variety of tours of the Albert Hall are also available.

★PHEASANTRY LIVE MUSIC

Map p456 (☑020-7351 5031; www.pizzaexpress. com/kings-road; 152-154 King's Rd, SW3; from £12; ◷11.30am-11pm; ⊜Sloane Sq, South Kensington) Currently run by Pizza Express, the Pheasantry on King's Rd ranges over three floors, with a lovely garden at the front for alfresco dining, but the crowd-puller is the live cabaret and jazz in the basement. A grade II–listed 19th-century building, the Pheasantry has been a ballet academy, a boho bar and a nightclub (where Lou Reed once sang).

Shows are generally at 8pm or 8.30pm; book online.

CADOGAN HALL CONCERT VENUE

Map p456 (☑020-7730 4500; www.cadoganhall. com; 5 Sloane Tce, SW1; tickets £10-40; ⊜Sloane Sq) Home of the Royal Philharmonic Orchestra, 950-seat Cadogan Hall is a major venue for classical music, opera and choral music, with occasional dance, rock, jazz and family concerts.

ROYAL COURT THEATRE THEATRE

Map p456 (☑020-7565 5000; www.royal courttheatre.com; Sloane Sq, SW1; tickets £12-38; ⊜Sloane Sq) Equally renowned for staging innovative new plays and old classics, the Royal Court is among London's most progressive theatres and has continued to foster major writing talent across the UK. There are two auditoriums: the main Jerwood Theatre Downstairs, and the much smaller studio Jerwood Theatre Upstairs. Tickets for Monday performances are £12.

A limited number of restricted-view standing places go on sale one hour before each Jerwood Theatre Downstairs performance for just 10p each. Contact the theatre to check on availability.

CINÉ LUMIÈRE CINEMA

Map p456 (☑020-7871 3515; www.institut-francais.org.uk; 17 Queensberry Pl, SW7; ⊜South Kensington) Attached to South Kensington's French Institute, Ciné Lumière's large 300-seat art-deco *salle* (cinema) screens absorbing international seasons (including the London Spanish Film Festival; www. londonspanishfilmfestival.com) and classic and recently released French cinema and international films, subtitled in English.

🛍 SHOPPING

Frequented by models, celebrities, and Russian oligarchs, and awash with new money (much from abroad), this well-heeled part of town is all about high fashion, glam shops, groomed shoppers and iconic top-end department stores. Even the charity shops along the chic King's Rd resemble fashion boutiques.

★JOHN SANDOE BOOKS BOOKS

Map p456 (☑020-7589 9473; www.johnsandoe. com; 10 Blacklands Tce, SW3; ◷9.30am-6.30pm Mon-Sat, 11am-5pm Sun; ⊜Sloane Sq) The perfect antidote to impersonal book superstores, this atmospheric three-storey bookshop in 18th-century premises is a treasure trove of literary gems and hidden surprises. It's been in business for six decades and loyal customers swear by it, while knowledgeable booksellers spill forth with well-read pointers and helpful advice.

HARRODS DEPARTMENT STORE

Map p456 (☑020-7730 1234; www.harrods.com; 87-135 Brompton Rd, SW1; ◷10am-9pm Mon-Sat, 11.30am-6pm Sun; ⊜Knightsbridge) Garish and stylish in equal measures, perennially crowded Harrods is an obligatory stop for visitors, from the cash-strapped to the big spenders. The stock is astonishing, as are many of the price tags. High on kitsch, the 'Egyptian Elevator' resembles something out of an Indiana Jones epic, while the memorial fountain to Dodi and Di (lower ground floor) merely adds surrealism.

Many visitors don't make it past the ground floor where designer bags, the myriad scents from the perfume hall and the mouth-watering counters of the food hall provide plenty of entertainment. The latter actually makes for an excellent, and surprisingly affordable, option for a picnic in nearby Hyde Park. From 11.30am to midday on Sunday, it's browsing time only.

PETER HARRINGTON   BOOKS

Map p456 (☑020-7591 0220; www.peter harrington.co.uk; 100 Fulham Rd, W3; ⏱10am-6pm Mon-Sat; ⊜South Kensington) Over three floors, Peter Harrington has a huge collection of first editions (in generally fine quality), signed modern art prints (Andy Warhol, Pablo Picasso, Bridget Riley, Elisabeth Frink, MC Escher, Damien Hirst among others) and more. Pick up a signed first edition, first printing of F Scott Fitzgerald's *The Great Gatsby* (£250,000) or a more affordable first edition of Dr Seuss's *Daisy-Head Mayzie* (£150).

PICKETT   GIFTS & SOUVENIRS

Map p456 (☑020-7823 5638; www.pickett.co.uk; cnr Sloane St & Sloane Tce, SW1; ⏱9.30am-6.30pm Mon-Tue & Thu-Fri, 10am-7pm Wed, to 6pm Sat; ⊜Sloane Sq) 🌱 Walking into Picketts as an adult is a bit like walking into a sweet shop as a child: the exquisite leather goods are all so colourful and beautiful that you don't really know where to start. Choice items include the perfectly finished handbags, the exquisite roll-up backgammon sets and the men's grooming sets. All leather goods are made in Britain.

There are actually two shops next door to each other: one for men, one for women. Women's clutch bags start at around £345; men's bags range between £245 and over £1000. Everything bought here is delightfully gift-wrapped too.

HARVEY NICHOLS   DEPARTMENT STORE

Map p456 (www.harveynichols.com; 109-125 Knightsbridge, SW1; ⏱10am-8pm Mon-Sat, 11.30am-6pm Sun; ⊜Knightsbridge) At London's temple of high fashion, you'll find Chloé and Balenciaga bags, the city's best denim range, a massive make-up hall with exclusive lines and great jewellery. The food

hall and in-house restaurant, **Fifth Floor**, are, you guessed it, on the 5th floor. From 11.30am to midday, it's browsing time only.

JO LOVES   COSMETICS

Map p456 (☑020-7730 8611; www.joloves.com; 42 Elizabeth St, SW1; ⏱10am-6pm Mon-Wed, Fri & Sat, to 7pm Thu, noon-5pm Sun; ⊜Victoria) Famed British scent-maker Jo Malone opened Jo Loves in 2013 on a street where she once had a Saturday job as a young florist, featuring the entrepreneur's signature candles, fragrances and bath products in a range of delicate scents – Arabian amber, white rose and lemon leaves, oud and mango. All products come exquisitely wrapped in red boxes with black bows.

CONRAN SHOP   DESIGN

Map p456 (☑020-7589 7401; www.conran shop.co.uk; Michelin House, 81 Fulham Rd, SW3; ⏱10am-6pm Mon, Tue & Fri, to 7pm Wed & Thu, to 6.30pm Sat, noon-6pm Sun; ⊜South Kensington) The original design store (going strong since 1987), the Conran Shop is a treasure trove of beautiful things – from radios to sunglasses, kitchenware to children's toys and books, bathroom accessories to greeting cards. Browsing bliss. Spare some time to peruse the magnificent art nouveau/deco Michelin House the shop belongs to.

LIMELIGHT MOVIE ART   VINTAGE

Map p456 (☑020-7751 5584; www.limelightmovie art.com; 313 King's Rd, SW3; ⏱11.30am-6pm Mon-Sat; ⊜Sloane Sq, South Kensington) This spiffing poster shop is a necessary stop for collectors of vintage celluloid memorabilia, nostalgic browsers or film buffs. Prints are all original and prices start at around £70 for the smaller formats (such as lobby cards) but can go into four figures for larger, rarer posters.

PENHALIGON'S   FASHION & ACCESSORIES

Map p456 (☑020-7823 9733; www.penhaligons. com; 132 King's Rd, SW3; ⏱9.30am-6.30pm Mon-Sat, to 7pm Wed, 11.30am-6.30pm Sun; ⊜Sloane Sq) Stepping through the door of this cute branch of the famous perfumery, sitting cosily on the corner of Bywater St, is like walking into a floral spray of hyacinths, roses and peonies. The beautifully presented bottled perfumes make exquisite gifts.

RIPPON CHEESE   FOOD

Map p456 (☑020-7931 0628; www.rippon cheeselondon.com; 26 Upper Tachbrook St, SW1;

⊘8am-4.30pm Mon-Fri, 8.30am-5pm Sat; ⊖Victoria, Pimlico) A potently inviting pong greets you as you near this cheesemonger with its 500 varieties of mostly English and French cheeses. Ask the knowledgeable staff for recommendations (and taste as you go!) and stock up for a picnic in a London park.

PETER JONES DEPARTMENT STORE
Map p456 (⊘020-7730 3434; www.peterjones. co.uk; Sloane Sq, SW1; ⊘9.30am-7pm Mon-Tue & Thu-Sat, to 8pm Wed, noon-6pm Sun; ⊖Sloane Sq) An upmarket department store, Peter Jones's fortes are china, furnishings and gifts, though it stocks accessories and cosmetics too.

BRITISH RED CROSS VINTAGE
Map p456 (⊘020-7376 7300; 69-71 Old Church St, SW3; ⊘10am-6pm Mon-Sat; ⊖Sloane Sq) The motto 'One man's rubbish is another man's treasure' couldn't be truer in this part of London, where the 'rubbish' is made up of designer gowns, cashmere jumpers and perhaps a first edition or two. Obviously the price tags are a little higher than in your run-of-the-mill charity shop (£40 rather than £5 for a jumper or jacket), but it's still a bargain for the quality and browsing is half the fun.

T2 FOOD & DRINKS
Map p456 (⊘020-7584 5280; www.t2tea.com; 96 King's Rd, SW3; ⊘10am-7pm Mon-Sat, noon-6pm Sun; ⊖Sloane Sq) This Australian brand is the tea lovers' answer to the coffee craze of the last few years. There are dozens of blends from around the world to choose from, which all come packaged in funky bright-orange cardboard boxes. The original teaware is another draw.

🏃 SPORTS & ACTIVITIES

WINTER WONDERLAND AMUSEMENT PARK
Map p456 (www.hydeparkwinterwonderland. com; Hyde Park; ⊖Hyde Park Corner) From November to January, this six-week attraction in Hyde Park is full of winter festivities, shows, ice-skating, circus acts and more.

PURE GYM GYM
Map p456 (⊘0845 676 6500; www.puregym. com; The South Kensington Estate, 63-81 Pelham St, SW7; ⊖South Kensington) Pure Gym has over 40 gyms around the city.

HYDE PARK TENNIS & SPORTS CENTRE TENNIS
Map p456 (⊘020-7262 3474; www.willtowin. co.uk/hyde-park-centreinfo; South Carriage Dr, Hyde Park; tennis per hr adult £11-14, child £7-10; ⊘8am-6pm; ⊖Knightsbridge) Has six outdoor hard tennis courts, a bowling green (£8 per person per hour), a nine-hole putting course (£6) and an outdoor gym, as well as a cafe. Peak hours (after 5pm) are priciest for tennis.

SERPENTINE SOLARSHUTTLE BOAT BOATING
Map p456 (⊘020-7262 1989; www.solarshuttle. co.uk; adult/child £5/3) Ferries passengers from the Serpentine Boathouse to the Diana, Princess of Wales Memorial Fountain (p185) at weekends from March to September (every day from mid-July to late August).

SERPENTINE BOATHOUSE BOATING
Map p456 (⊘020-7262 1330; adult/child per 30min £10/4, per 1hr £12/5; ⊖Hyde Park Corner or Knightsbridge) Rent a paddle boat from the Serpentine Boathouse.

SERPENTINE LIDO SWIMMING
Map p456 (⊘020-7706 3422; Hyde Park, W2; adult/child £4.80/1.80; ⊘10am-6pm daily Jun-Aug, to 6pm Sat & Sun May; ⊖Hyde Park Corner, Knightsbridge) Perhaps the ultimate London pool is inside the Serpentine lake. This fabulous lido is open May to August. Sun loungers are available for £3.50 for the whole day.

Clerkenwell, Shoreditch & Spitalfields

CLERKENWELL | FINSBURY & ST LUKE'S | SPITALFIELDS | SHOREDITCH & HOXTON | FINSBURY & ST LUKE'S

Neighbourhood Top Five

1 Shoreditch nightlife (p218) Donning your craziest outfit, grooming your beard and heading to Shoreditch for cocktails and carousing in clubs such as Cargo.

2 Super Market Sunday (p221) Crawling the markets with the multicultural masses on a sunny Sunday

along Brick Lane and Spitalfields.

3 Geffrye Museum (p206) Stepping back through the living rooms of time at this wonderfully evocative domestic-interiors museum.

4 Vintage shopping in Spitalfields (p220) Finding that unique vinyl, 1960s dress or art-deco poster

in one of Spitalfields' vintage shops, including Blitz London.

5 Brick Lane (p207) Strolling through this unique neighbourhood, which bears witness to London's long migration history.

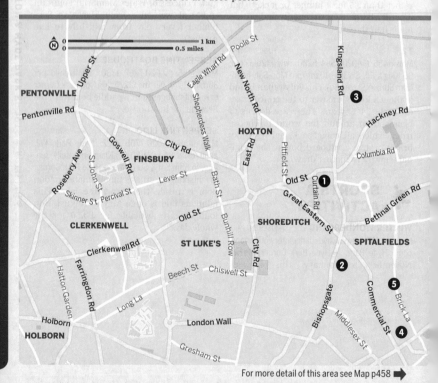

For more detail of this area see Map p458 ➡

Explore Clerkenwell, Shoreditch & Spitalfields

Swing by during the day to explore the area's boutiques, vintage shops, markets and cafes. But make sure you come back after dark for a meal at one of the many excellent eateries, followed by an evening flitting between kooky cocktail bars and subterranean nightspots.

Shoreditch can get pretty wild on Friday and Saturday nights, and many places stay open until dawn. Spitalfields is great fun too, although slightly more subdued. Clerkenwell by comparison is positively sedate.

Sunday is a great day to join the crowds shrugging off their hangovers with a stroll through Spitalfields' many markets, but note that Clerkenwell is eerily quiet.

Local Life

→ **Nights out with a difference** Mingle with London's hiperati at DreamBagsJaguarShoes (p217); learn to life draw or play ping pong at the Book Club (p217); or take a swing class at the Queen of Hoxton (p216), followed by alfresco drinks on the rooftop.

→ **Coffee crawl** The area has so many excellent cafes that a mild caffeine tremor is de rigueur. Sink a silky flat white or a shotgun espresso at Prufrock Coffee (p210), Shoreditch Grind (p211), Ozone Coffee Roasters (p212) or Allpress Espresso (p217).

→ **The pho mile** Spend some time working out which is your favourite Vietnamese restaurant on the Kingsland Rd/Old St strip (p211).

Getting There & Away

→ **Underground** Farringdon and Barbican stations on the Circle, Hammersmith & City and Metropolitan Lines are stopping-off points for Clerkenwell. These lines and Central Line also head through Liverpool St, the closest tube stop to Spitalfields. Old St, on the Bank branch of the Northern Line, is the best stop for the western edge of Hoxton and Shoreditch.

→ **Overground** Shoreditch High St and Hoxton are the closest stations to Spitalfields and the eastern parts of Shoreditch and Hoxton.

→ **Bus** Clerkenwell and Old St are connected with Oxford St by the 55 and with Waterloo by the 243. The 38 runs up Rosebery Ave and edges past Exmouth Market on its way from Victoria to Islington. The 8 and 242 zip through the city and up Shoreditch High St.

Lonely Planet's Top Tip

Fancy a late one? **333 Mother** (p216), **XOYO** (p216), **Cargo** (p218) and the **Horse & Groom** (p218) all stay open until at least 3am on weekends. **Brick Lane Beigel Bake** (p213) will serve you munchies throughout the night, and for breakfast with a pint, the **Fox & Anchor** (p215) throws back its doors at 7am (8.30am on weekends).

CLERKENWELL, SHOREDITCH & SPITALFIELDS

✗ Best Places to Eat

→ Clove Club (p213)
→ Hawksmoor (p214)
→ Polpo (p208)
→ Foxlow (p210)
→ Gate (p210)

For reviews, see p208.➡

🍷 Best Places to Drink

→ Worship St Whistling Shop (p216)
→ Ye Olde Mitre (p215)
→ Zetter Townhouse Cocktail Lounge (p215)
→ Cocktail Trading Co (p218)
→ Fox & Anchor (p215)
→ Queen of Hoxton (p216)

For reviews, see p214.➡

🔒 Best Places to Shop

→ Sunday UpMarket (p219)
→ Old Spitalfields Market (p220)
→ Collectif (p219)
→ Rough Trade East (p219)
→ Magma (p220)

For reviews, see p219.➡

◉ SIGHTS

Clerkenwell, Shoreditch and Spitalfields make up in atmosphere and history for what they lack in 'big ticket sights'. Here you'll come across some of London's oldest buildings, and poignant reminders of the capital's long history of migration. Far from simply being a historical repository, however, the area is the heart of London's creative industry, and it very much feels like it is actively shaping the next chapter in London's history.

◉ Clerkenwell

ST JOHN'S GATE   HISTORIC BUILDING

Map p458 (www.museumstjohn.org.uk; St John's Lane, EC1M; ◉10am-5pm daily Jul-Sep, Mon-Sat Oct-Jun; ◉Farringdon) **FREE** This remarkable Tudor gate dates from 1504. During the 12th century, the Knights Hospitaller (a Christian and military order with a focus on providing care to the sick) established a priory here. Inside is a small museum that covers the history of the order (including rare examples of the knights' armour), as well as its 19th-century revival in Britain as the secular Order of St John and the foundation of St John Ambulance.

The gate was erected as a grand entrance to the priory and survived despite most of the buildings being destroyed when Henry VIII dissolved monasteries throughout England between 1536 and 1540. It enjoyed a varied afterlife, not least as a Latin-speaking coffee house, which was run without much success by William Hogarth's father during Queen Anne's reign. Restored in the 19th century, it also housed the Old Jerusalem Tavern, where writers and artists, including Charles Dickens, met.

Try to time your visit to catch one of the comprehensive 80-minute **guided tours** (11am and 2.30pm Tuesdays, Fridays and Saturdays) of the gate and the priory church (p204). You'll also be shown upstairs to the sumptuous 1902 chapter hall and council chamber, which are still used by the order to this day. Suggested tour donation £5.

ST JOHN'S PRIORY CHURCH   CHURCH

Map p458 (www.museumstjohn.org.uk; St John's Sq, EC1M; ◉guided tour only; ◉Farringdon) The Priory Church is one of London's oldest churches. This whole area was originally part of the medieval St John's Priory and is now associated with the revived Order of St John. The walled garden, planted with

---

◉ TOP SIGHT
DENNIS SEVERS' HOUSE

This quirky hotchpotch of a cluttered house (built c 1724) is named after the late American eccentric who restored and turned it into what he called a 'still-life drama'. Severs was an artist who lived in the house (in a similar way to the original inhabitants) until his death in 1999.

Visitors today find they've entered the home of a family of Huguenot silk weavers, who were common to the Spitalfields area in the 18th century. However, while you see the Georgian interiors, with meals and drinks half-abandoned and rumpled sheets, and while you smell cooking and hear creaking floorboards, your 'hosts' always remain tantalisingly just out of reach.

From the cellar to the bedrooms, the interiors demonstrate both the original function and design of the rooms as well as the highs and lows of the area's history. The family's fortunes fade as you progress upstairs, ending in a state of near-destitution on the upper level.

The 'plot' isn't exactly obvious, but no matter, the house is wonderfully evocative and makes for a unique experience.

DON'T MISS

➜ Silent Night tours
➜ The house cat
➜ Hogarth tableau

PRACTICALITIES

➜ Map p458, G6
➜ ☎020-7247 4013
➜ www.dennissevers house.co.uk
➜ 18 Folgate St, E1
➜ day/night £10/15
➜ ◉noon-2pm & 5-9pm Mon, 5-9pm Wed & Fri, noon-4pm Sun
➜ ◉Liverpool St

medicinal herbs and flowers, was built as a memorial to St John's workers who died during the world wars. Sadly the church can only be visited on a guided tour, along with St John's Gate (p204).

If the somewhat boxy church doesn't seem like it ever belonged to a medieval priory, that's because it didn't. The real treasure lies beneath, where the nave of the original church has been preserved as a darkened crypt. Built in the 1380s in the Norman Romanesque style, it's one of the oldest buildings in London. Inside there's a alabaster effigy of a Castilian knight (1575) and a battered monument portraying the last prior, Sir William Weston, as a decaying body in a shroud (a memento mori designed to remind viewers of their own mortality).

The nave once abutted a large circular chancel that was demolished following the dissolution of the priory. Outside, the outline of the original church has been traced onto the square.

CHARTERHOUSE   HISTORIC BUILDING
Map p458 (☑020-7253 9503; www.thecharter house.org; Charterhouse Sq, EC1M; ⊙11am-5pm Tue-Sun; ⊜Barbican) FREE From a monastery, to a Tudor mansion, to the charitable foundation that's operated here since 1611, Charterhouse has played a discreet but important part in London's story. Visitors have free access to the small museum, the chapel and the main court, but must join a one-hour tour to see more (£10 and well worth it). These run three times daily and take in the most historic rooms and courts, and the cloister.

Although Charterhouse was founded in 1371 as a Carthusian monastery (the name derives from Chartreuse in France, where the order is based), the site's history began in 1348 when what is now Charterhouse Sq was used as a plague burial ground during the great epidemic of the Black Death. Some of the bodies were recently excavated during the Crossrail works (a new underground train line) and one skeleton is exhibited in the museum.

In 1537 the monastery was dissolved and the property transferred to King Henry VIII. The prior and 15 of the monks were executed. They were the first of England's Catholic martyrs of the Reformation and three of them were subsequently canonised.

The king sold the property in 1545 to Sir Edward North, who converted it into his London mansion, knocking down the

original church and much of the cloister in the process. In 1611 it was purchased by Thomas Sutton, known at the time as the 'richest commoner in England'. In his will, Sutton directed that it should become a school for boys and an almshouse for 'destitute gentlemen'. Around 40 pensioners (known as 'brothers') still live here today; women were admitted for the first time in 2017. Charterhouse School moved to Surrey in 1872 and is still going strong.

ST ETHELDREDA'S   CHURCH
Map p458 (☑020-7405 1061; www.stetheldreda. com; 14 Ely Pl, EC1; ⊙8am-5pm Mon-Sat, to 12.30pm Sun; ⊜Chancery Lane) FREE More than just a gorgeous oasis of peace, this stunner of a church is also the oldest Roman Catholic church in the UK, dating from the reign of Edward I. The town chapel of the Bishops of Ely dates from the mid-13th century to 1570 and is named after 7th-century East Anglian princess and Fenland saint Etheldreda. The church was saved during the Great Fire of London by an abrupt change in the wind.

The church was also hit in WWII by a Luftwaffe bomb that came through the roof during the Blitz and put paid to its surviving stained glass; the beautiful great east window was replaced in 1952.

MARX MEMORIAL LIBRARY   LIBRARY
Mapp458(☑020-72531485;www.marx-memorial-library.org; 37a Clerkenwell Green, EC1R; tours £5; ⊙tours 1pm Tue & Thu; ⊜Farringdon) Built in 1738 to house a Welsh charity school, this unassuming building is an interesting reminder of Clerkenwell's radical history. From here in 1902 and 1903, during his European exile, Lenin edited 17 editions of the Russian-language Bolshevik newspaper

Iskra (Spark). In 1933, 50 years after the death of Karl Marx and around the time of the Nazi book burnings, it was decided that the building would be converted into a library to honour the founder of communism.

Copies of *Iskra* have been preserved in the library, along with other socialist literature, Spanish Civil War banners and relics from various industrial disputes. Tours visit the room where Lenin worked and the building's 15th-century cellar.

If you think it's odd that Clerkenwell should have a memorial to Marx, you might be surprised to learn that from 1942 to 1951 a bust of Lenin stood in Holford Sq in neighbouring Finsbury, gazing towards his former residence. After being repeatedly vandalised it was moved to Islington Town Hall, where it remained on display until 1996, when it was consigned to a museum.

◉ Finsbury & St Luke's

BUNHILL FIELDS CEMETERY
Map p458 (Bunhill Row, EC1; ◷8am-dusk; ⊖Old St) This cemetery just outside the city walls has been a burial ground for more than 1000 years. 'Bunhill' probably derives from the area's macabre historical name – 'Bone Hill'. Famous burials include literary giants Daniel Defoe, John Bunyan and William Blake. It's a lovely place for a stroll, and a rare green space in this built-up area.

WESLEY'S CHAPEL CHURCH
Map p458 (www.wesleyschapel.org.uk; 49 City Rd, EC1Y; ◷10am-4pm Mon-Sat; ⊖Old St) Built in 1778, this warm and welcoming church was the place of work and worship for John Wesley, the founder of the Methodist Church. You can learn more about him in the **Museum of Methodism** downstairs, and visit his house (at the front) and his grave (behind the church).

◉ Spitalfields

Crowded around its famous market and grand parish church, Spitalfields has long been one of the capital's most multicultural areas. Waves of Huguenot (French Protestant), Jewish, Irish and, more recently, Indian and Bangladeshi immigrants have made Spitalfields home.

A walk along Brick Lane is the best way to experience the sights, sounds and smells

---

TOP SIGHT
GEFFRYE MUSEUM

If you like nosing around other people's homes, you'll love this museum devoted to middle-class domestic interiors.

Built in 1714 as a home for poor pensioners, these beautiful ivy-clad almshouses have been converted into a series of living rooms, dating from 1630 to the Victorian era. An extension completed in 1998 contains several 20th-century rooms (a flat from the 1930s, a 1960s suburban lounge and an all-too-familiar 1990s loft-style apartment) as well as a gallery for temporary exhibits, a shop and a cafe.

The rear **garden** is also organised by era, mirroring the museum's exploration of domesticity through the centuries. There's also a very impressive walled **herb garden**, featuring 170 different plants. The lawns at the front are a popular spot for lazing about.

One of the almshouses has been completely restored to show the living conditions of the original pensioners in the 18th and 19th centuries. It's the absolute attention to detail that impresses, right down to the vintage newspaper left open on the breakfast table. The setting is so fragile, however, that **tours** (adult/child £4/free) are only held a few times a month; check the website for up-to-date tour dates.

DON'T MISS
→ Period rooms
→ Period and herb gardens (April to October)
→ Almshouse interior

PRACTICALITIES
→ Map p458, G2
→ www.geffrye-museum.org.uk
→ 136 Kingsland Rd, E2
→ admission free
→ ◷10am-5pm Tue-Sun
→ ⊖Hoxton

of Bangladeshi London, but to get a sense of what Georgian Spitalfields was like, branch off to Princelet, Fournier, Elder and Wilkes streets. Having fled persecution in France, the Huguenots set up shop here from the late 17th century, practising their trade of silk weaving. The attics of these grand town houses were once filled with clattering looms and the area became famous for the quality of its silk, even providing the material for Queen Victoria's coronation gown.

CHRIST CHURCH SPITALFIELDS CHURCH

Map p458 (☑020-7377 2440; www.ccspitalfields. org; Commercial St, E1; ☺10am-4pm Mon-Fri, 1-4pm Sun; ☻Liverpool St) This imposing English baroque structure, with a tall spire sitting on a portico of four great Tuscan columns, was designed by Nicholas Hawksmoor and completed in 1729. The heaviness of the exterior gives way to a brilliantly white and lofty interior, with Corinthian columns and large brass chandeliers.

BRICK LANE STREET

Map p458 (☻Shoreditch High St, Liverpool St) Full of noise, colour and life, Brick Lane is a vibrant mix of history and modernity, and a palimpsest of cultures. Today it is the centrepiece of a thriving Bengali community in an area nicknamed Banglatown. The southern part of the lane is one long procession of curry and balti houses intermingled with fabric shops and Indian supermarkets.

Sadly the once-high standard of cooking in the curry houses is a distant memory, so you're probably better off trying subcontinental cuisine in Whitechapel.

Just past Hanbury St is the converted Old Truman Brewery (p207), a series of buildings on both sides of the lane that was once London's largest brewery. The Director's House on the left harks back to 1740; the old Vat House across the road with its hexagonal bell tower is early 19th century; and the Engineer's House next to that dates from 1830. The brewery stopped producing beer in 1989, and in the 1990s it became home to a host of independent music businesses, small shops and hip clubs and bars. North of here Brick Lane is a very different place, stuffed with eclectic clothing stores, excellent bagel bakeries, and plenty of cafes and bars.

OLD TRUMAN BREWERY HISTORIC BUILDING

Map p458 (www.trumanbrewery.com; 91 Brick Lane, E1; ☻Shoreditch High St) Founded here in the 17th century, Truman's Black Eagle Brewery was, by the 1850s, the largest brewery in the world. Spread over a series of brick buildings and yards straddling both sides of Brick Lane, the complex is now completely given over to edgy markets, pop-up fashion stores, vintage clothes shops, indie record hunters, cafes, bars and live-music venues. Beer may not be brewed here any more, but it certainly is consumed.

After decades of decline, Truman's Brewery finally shut up shop in 1989 – temporarily as it turned out, with the brand subsequently resurrected in 2010 in new premises in Hackney Wick. In the 1990s the abandoned brewery premises found new purpose as a deadly cool hub for boozy Britpoppers and while it may not have quite the same cachet today, it's still plenty popular.

Several of the buildings are heritage listed, including the Director's House at 91 Brick Lane (built in the 1740s); the old Vat House directly opposite, with its hexagonal bell tower (c 1800); and the Engineer's House right next to it, dating from the 1830s.

19 PRINCELET ST MUSEUM

Map p458 (☑020-7247 5352; www.19princelet street.org.uk; 19 Princelet St, E1; ☺infrequent; ☻Liverpool St) FREE This 1719 Huguenot town house originally housed a prosperous family of weavers, before becoming home to waves of immigrants, including Polish, Irish and Jewish families, the last of which built a synagogue in the back garden in 1869. In keeping with the house's multicultural past, it's now home to a museum of immigration and diversity. The house urgently needs repair and so opens infrequently; check the website. Donations welcome.

BRICK LANE GREAT MOSQUE MOSQUE

Map p458 (Brick Lane Jamme Masjid; www.bricklane jammemasjid.co.uk; 59 Brick Lane, E1; ☻Liverpool St) No building symbolises the different waves of immigration to Spitalfields quite as well as this one. Built in 1743 as the New French Church for the Huguenots, it was a Methodist chapel from 1819 until it was transformed into the Great Synagogue for Jewish refugees from Russia and central Europe in 1898. In 1976 it changed faiths yet again, becoming the Great Mosque. Look for the sundial, high up on the Fournier St frontage.

☉ Shoreditch & Hoxton

Hoxditch? Shoho? Often (confusingly) used interchangeably by Londoners, Hoxton and Shoreditch signify the area stretching north and east from the roundabout at Old St tube station. The name Shoreditch relates to a settlement that grew up immediately north of the old city, around the junction of two important Roman thoroughfares: Kingsland Rd and Old St. Shoreditch was the name of the parish, within which was the village of Hoxton. These days Hoxton is generally known as the area to the north of Old St, up to Kingsland Rd, with Shoreditch being the roads to the south, stretching to the east as far as Brick Lane. But switch them around, or get them confused, and no one will bat an eyelid.

✕ EATING

In addition to a wealth of fantastic cafes and restaurants, this area has popular food markets with stalls devoted to a wide variety of cuisines. Check out Exmouth Market and Whitecross St Market for weekday lunches, and Brick Lane (p207) and the surrounding streets on Sundays. Hoxton's Kingsland Rd and Old St are well known for their reasonably priced Vietnamese eateries.

✕ Clerkenwell

★ POLPO
ITALIAN $

Map p458 (☎020-7250 0034; www.polpo.co.uk; 3 Cowcross St, EC1M; dishes £4-12; ⊙11.30am-11pm Mon-Sat, to 4pm Sun; ⊖Farringdon) Occupying a sunny spot on semi-pedestrianised Cowcross St, this sweet little place serves rustic Venetian-style meatballs, *pizzette*, grilled meat and fish dishes. Portions are larger than your average tapas but a tad smaller than a regular main – the perfect excuse to sample more than one of the exquisite dishes. Exceptional value for money.

PANZO
PIZZA $

Map p458 (www.panzopizza.com; 50 Exmouth Market, EC1R; pizza £8.50; ⊙noon-10.30pm Mon-Sat; ☑; ⊖Farringdon) Never has pizza looked more mouth-watering than at Panzo's: oblong-shaped, loaded with toppings and enjoyed in a dining room bathed in the

🏃 Neighbourhood Walk
East End Then & Now

START LIVERPOOL ST STATION
END OLD ST STATION
LENGTH 1.8 MILES; 1½ HOURS

This route leads straight through the heart of historic, multicultural Spitalfields and on to hipper-than-thou Shoreditch. You'll find it at its liveliest on a Sunday, when the various markets are effervescing – but be prepared for a much slower stroll. During the rest of the week, there are still plenty of diverting shops and bars to break your stride.

Leaving the tube station, cross busy Bishopsgate, turn left and then right when you come to ❶ **Middlesex St**. This used to be known as Petticoat Lane, after the lacy women's undergarments that were sold here, but that proved too saucy for the authorities and the name was changed in 1830 – to Middlesex!. The East End locals weren't nearly so prudish and the ragtag Sunday market that's been based here for more than 400 years is still known by its former name.

Veer left into Widegate St and continue into narrow ❷ **Artillery Passage**, one of Spitalfields' most atmospheric lanes, lined with historic shopfronts and drinking dens. From here, a left then a right will bring you onto Gun St and, at its far end, ❸ **Old Spitalfields Market** (p220).

Enter the market and turn right into the covered lane lined with fancy gift shops and eateries – a far cry from the fruit-and-veggie stands that the market was famous for until 1991 when 'New Spitalfields' opened in Leyton. Continue on through the artisan craft and fashion stalls of the market proper and then step out onto Commercial St. Just over the road is the ❹ **Ten Bells** (p219) pub – famous as one of Jack the Ripper's possible pick-up joints – and the hulking presence of ❺ **Christ Church** (p207). Running between the two, Fournier St is one of Spitalfields' most intact Georgian streetscapes. As you wander along, note the oddball, Harry Potterish numbering (11½ Fournier St) and keep an eye out for famous artsy residents Tracey Emin and

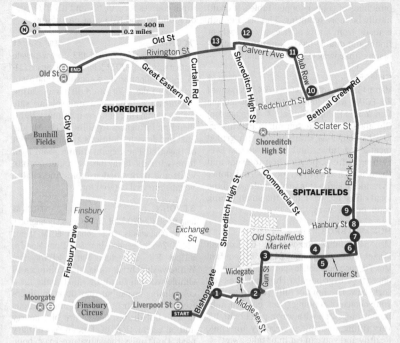

Gilbert & George. The last building on the left of Fournier St is **6 Brick Lane Great Mosque** (p207). Turn left onto buzzing and colourful **7 Brick Lane** (p207). Today this narrow but famous thoroughfare is the centrepiece of a thriving Bengali community in an area nicknamed Banglatown. Expect to be cajoled by eager touts as you pass the long procession of curry houses. For the most part the standard is pretty average, despite extravagant claims to the contrary. Stop at the corner of **8 Hanbury St** to admire the graffiti and then continue on to **9 Old Truman Brewery** (p207). North of here Brick Lane is a very different place, stuffed with eclectic clothing shops, old-time Jewish bagel bakeries and a surfeit of cafes and bars. Further up, at the traffic lights cross Bethnal Green Rd, turn left and then veer right onto Redchurch St, where there are more interesting independent shops to peruse. As you turn right into Club Row, keep an eye out for an elaborate black-and-red piece of street sculpture called **10 Portal**, dedicated to the artist CityZenKane's late son. Leafy Club Row terminates in **11 Arnold Circus**, a circular intersection topped with a wooded mound and a

bandstand. Until 1891 this was the heart of London's worst slum, the Old Nichol rookery. Nearly 6000 people lost their homes when the slum was cleared, most having no choice but to rent similarly impoverished rooms further east. The rubble from the 730 demolished houses lies under the bandstand. Take the third road on the left (Calvert Ave) and walk past **12 St Leonard's Church** (built in the Palladian style in around 1740) to Shoreditch High St. Turn left and cross over to Rivington St.

Just past the railway bridge, look out for a wrought-iron gate on the right leading into **13 Cargo** (p218). Just inside the gate, protected under perspex, there's a piece by famous graffiti artist Banksy picturing a security guard holding a poodle on a leash. Banksy's just one of many accomplished street artists to have left their mark on Shoreditch's streets – you'll spot plenty more as you continue along Rivington St. At the end of Rivington, turn right onto Great Eastern St and then veer left onto traffic-clogged Old St. Believed to have had its origins as a Roman road, it remains a major route. Soon the distinctive arcs straddling the Old St tube station will come into view.

pink hues of copper-topped tables. It could hardly be more tempting. The pizza dough is made from a mix of rice, soy and wheat flours and double-baked – unusual, but delicious. Takeaway (£6.50) available too.

CHIFAFA
TURKISH $

Map p458 (www.chifafa.com; 45-47 Clerkenwell Rd, EC1M; wraps from £5.40; ⊙11.30am-9pm Mon-Wed, to 11.30pm Thu-Sat; ⊘; ⊖Farringdon) Chifafa serves what you might call luxury kebabs: delicious wraps filled with grilled meats, vegetables and tasty sauces. Everything is fresh, prepared on the spot and there isn't a deep-fryer or inverted doner pyramid in sight. It is very popular with the local office crowd. Eat in the small dining room or take away.

HUMMUS BROS
CAFE $

Map p458 (https://hbros.co.uk; 62 Exmouth Market, EC1R; mains from £4.65; ⊙11am-5pm Mon-Fri, noon-5pm Sat, to 4pm Sun; ⊛⊘; ⊖Farringdon) ⊘ Ever-popular Hummus Bros can sort you with a bowl of filling hummus with your choice of topping (beef, chicken, tabbouleh etc) eaten with warm pita bread. It's very filling, enticing at virtually any time, healthy and you can eat in or take away.

PRUFROCK COFFEE
CAFE $

Map p458 (www.prufrockcoffee.com; 23-25 Leather Lane, EC1N; mains £4-7; ⊙8am-6pm Mon-Fri, 10am-5pm Sat & Sun; ⊛⊘; ⊖Farringdon) Not content with being one of the kings of London's coffee-bean scene (it offers barista training and workshops in 'latte art'), Prufrock also dishes up delicious breakfasts, lunches and cuppa-friendly pastries and snacks. Judging by the number of laptops, plenty of customers treat it as their office.

★ FOXLOW
STEAK $$

Map p458 (www.foxlow.co.uk; 69-73 St John St, EC1; mains £12-24; ⊙noon-3pm & 5.30-10.30pm Mon-Sat, 10am-3.30pm Sun; ⊛⊘⊙; ⊖Farringdon) ⊘ This lovely brasserie builds on the extensive experience of its founders (of Hawksmoor fame), who always put the quality of their ingredients centre stage. You can therefore expect succulent dry-aged steaks from Ginger Pig beef, slow-cooked ribs, fried chicken and terrific Sunday roasts. The atmosphere is cosy, inviting and relaxed, and staff are chummy. Vegetarians and vegans are well catered for.

There are good-value set meals at lunchtime and early evening on weekdays (two/three courses for £15/18), and it's BYO beer on Mondays and BYO wine on Tuesdays.

★ GATE
VEGETARIAN $$

Map p458 (⊘020-7278 5483; www.thegate restaurants.com; 370 St John St, EC1V; mains £11-15; ⊙noon-10pm; ⊘⊙; ⊖Angel) The Gate can probably take a lot of credit for elevating vegetarian cuisine from uninspiring side dishes to starring in its own culinary right. Blending influences from India, the Middle East and Jewish traditions, the food is a riot of flavours. The elegant dining room is in tune with its Islington surrounds: white walls and dark wooden tables and chairs. Vegans are well catered for.

ST JOHN
BRITISH $$

Map p458 (⊘020-7251 0848; www.stjohngroup. uk.com/spitalfields; 26 St John St, EC1M; mains £14.80-24.90; ⊙noon-3pm & 6-11pm Mon-Fri, 6-11pm Sat, 12.30-4pm Sun; ⊖Farringdon) Whitewashed brick walls, high ceilings and simple wooden furniture don't make for a cosy dining space but they do keep diners free to concentrate on St John's famous nose-to-tail dishes. Serves are big, hearty and a celebration of England's culinary past. Don't miss the signature roast bone marrow and parsley salad (£8.90).

MORITO
TAPAS $$

Map p458 (⊘020-7278 7007; www.morito.co.uk; 32 Exmouth Market, EC1R; dishes £6.50-9.50; ⊙noon-4pm & 5-11pm Mon-Sat, noon-4pm Sun; ⊛; ⊖Farringdon) This diminutive eatery is a wonderfully authentic take on a Spanish tapas bar and has excellent eats. Seats are at the bar, along the window, or on one of the small tables inside or out. It's relaxed, convivial and often completely crammed; reservations are taken for lunch, but dinner is first come, first served, with couples generally going to the bar.

COMPTOIR GASCON
FRENCH, DELI $$

Map p458 (⊘020-7608 0851; www.comptoir gascon.com; 63 Charterhouse St, EC1M; mains £10-22.50; ⊙noon-2.30pm & 5.30-9.30pm Tue-Sat; ⊛; ⊖Farringdon) The menu is divided into 'best of duck' and 'charcoal grill' sections at this oddly angular bistro-deli specialising in the food and wine of southwest France. It may not sound very French, but we find it hard to go past the juicy duck burger (£9.50) – *sans* foie gras, naturally.

ST JOHN BREAD & WINE
BRITISH $$

Map p458 (☑020-7251 0848; www.stjohngroup.uk.com; 94-96 Commercial St, E1; mains £14.70-18; ⊗8am-4pm & 6-11pm; ⊖Shoreditch High St) Offers nose-to-tail traditional British fare (potted pork, devilled kidneys, meaty pies) in a simple, clean and bright space. It also has an excellent selection of British cheeses and puddings.

CARAVAN
INTERNATIONAL $$

Map p458 (☑020-7833 8115; www.caravanrestaurants.co.uk; 11-13 Exmouth Market, EC1R; mains £17.50-20, brunch £7.50-12; ⊗8am-10.30pm Mon-Fri, 10am-10.30pm Sat, to 4pm Sun; �🛜; ⊖Farringdon) Perfect for a sunny day when its sides are opened onto bustling Exmouth Market, this place is a relaxed affair, offering all-day dining and drinking. The menu has a huge variety of dishes, drawing on flavours from all over the world. The coffee, roasted in the basement, is fantastic.

MODERN PANTRY
FUSION $$

Map p458 (☑020-7553 9210; www.themodernpantry.co.uk; 47-48 St John's Sq, EC1V; mains £13.50-21, breakfast £3.50-9.50; ⊗8am-10pm Mon-Fri, 9am-10.30pm Sat, 10am-10pm Sun; 🛜; ⊖Farringdon) This three-floor Georgian town house in the heart of Clerkenwell has a cracking all-day menu that is almost as pleasurable to read as it is to eat from. Ingredients are sublimely combined into unusual dishes such as miso-marinated onglet steak or Aleppo chilli- and garlic-marinated pork chop. The breakfasts are great too, though portions can be on the small side.

EAGLE
GASTROPUB $$

Map p458 (☑020-7837 1353; www.theeaglefarringdon.co.uk; 159 Farringdon Rd, EC1R; mains £9-17; ⊗noon-3pm & 6.30-10.30pm Mon-Sat, 12.30-4pm Sun; ⊖Farringdon) London's first gastropub may have seen its original owners move on, but it's still a great place for a bite and a pint, especially at lunchtimes when it's relatively quiet. The menu fuses British and Mediterranean elements, and the atmosphere is lively. Watch the chefs work their magic right behind the bar, above which is chalked the menu.

MORO
SPANISH, MOROCCAN $$

Map p458 (☑020-7833 8336; www.moro.co.uk; 34-36 Exmouth Market, EC1R; mains £16.50-24; ⊗noon-2.30pm & 6-10.30pm Mon-Sat, 12.30-2.45pm Sun; ⊖Farringdon) The Moorish cuisine on offer at this Exmouth Market institution

straddles the Straits of Gibraltar, with influences from Spain, Portugal and North Africa – and a bit of Britain added to the mix. If the tables are full, you can often perch at the bar for some tapas, wine and dessert.

✗ Finsbury & St Luke's

LOOK MUM NO HANDS!
CAFE $

Map p458 (☑020-7253 1025; www.lookmumnohands.com; 49 Old St, EC1V; dishes £4.25-11.50; ⊗7.30am-10pm Mon-Fri, from 8.30am Sat, from 9am Sun; 🛜✗; ⊖Barbican) Cyclists and noncyclists alike adore this cafe-workshop, set in a light-filled space looking out onto Old St. Toasties and burgers are the savoury staples; cakes and startlingly impressive coffee complete the offering. There are a few outdoor tables, and staff can loan you a lock if you need to park your wheels.

SHOREDITCH GRIND
CAFE $

Map p458 (www.grind.co.uk; 213 Old St, EC1V; items £2.50-9; ⊗7am-11pm Mon-Thu, to 1am Fri & Sat, 9am-7pm Sun; 🛜; ⊖Old St) Housed in a striking little round building, this hip cafe serves top coffee, cooked breakfasts (until a decadent 3pm) and then rustic pizzas and cocktails after dusk. Sit at a window and watch the hipsters go by.

FIFTEEN
MODERN EUROPEAN $$$

Map p458 (☑020-3375 1515; www.fifteen.net; 15 Westland Pl, N1; mains £22-24, 2-/3-course lunch £19/24, Sun £15-19; ⊗noon-3pm & 6-10.30pm; 🛜; ⊖Old St) It would be easy to dismiss Jamie Oliver's nonprofit restaurant as a gimmick if it weren't so good. It's here the chef pioneered his apprenticeship program that has young chefs from disadvantaged backgrounds train with experienced professionals. The scheme has since extended to other restaurants and Fifteen has sealed its reputation for Modern European fare full of pizzazz. The bar's forte is gin and gin-based cocktails.

✗ Hoxton

SÔNG QUÊ
VIETNAMESE $

Map p458 (www.songque.co.uk; 134 Kingsland Rd, E2; mains £7.20-9.50; ⊗noon-3pm & 5.30-11pm Mon-Fri, noon-11pm Sat, to 10.30pm Sun; ⊖Hoxton) With the kind of demand for seats that most London restaurants can only dream of, this no-frills, hospital-green Vietnamese joint has been feeding the denizens of London for almost 15 years and often has a queue of people waiting. Service can be abrupt but the food is spot on, with two dozen types of fantastic *pho* (noodle soup) to choose from.

KÊU!
VIETNAMESE $

Map p458 (www.vietnamesekitchen.co.uk; 332 Old St, EC1V; items £6.50-8.45; ⊙9am-9pm Mon-Sat; ⊜Old St) This deli-cafe assembles lip-smacking *banh mi* (filled baguettes with fillings such as spicy roast duck or crispy pork belly) to eat in or take away, as well as salads and rice dishes.

VIET GRILL
VIETNAMESE $$

Map p458 (✆020-7739 6686; www.vietnamese kitchen.co.uk; 58 Kingsland Rd, E2; mains £11-14; ✐; ⊜Hoxton) One of the more upmarket options along Kingsland Road, Viet Grill is a low-lit, modern restaurant set over two floors with a buzzy atmosphere and colonial decor. It offers a good selection of Vietnamese curries and meat and fish dishes along with the more traditional *pho* (noodle soup) and *bun* (vermicelli).

CÂY TRE
VIETNAMESE $$

Map p458 (✆020-7729 8662; www.caytre.co.uk; 301 Old St, EC1V; mains £11-15; ⊙noon-11pm Mon-Thu, to 11.30pm Fri & Sat, to 10.30pm Sun; ⊜Old St) Cây Tre serves up all the fresh and fragrant classics to a mix of Vietnamese diners and Hoxton scenesters in a simple but nicely decorated and tightly packed space. It's worth stopping in for the *pho* (noodle soup) – the broth takes 18 hours to make.

✕ Shoreditch

OZONE COFFEE ROASTERS
CAFE $

Map p458 (www.ozonecoffee.co.uk; 11 Leonard St, EC2A; mains £8.50-13.50; ⊙7.30am-9pm Mon-Fri, 9am-5pm Sat & Sun; ☎; ⊜Old St) During the day this Kiwi-run cafe is full of artsy types hunched over their computers and new-media mavens appropriating booth seats for impromptu meetings. Coffee is Ozone's raison d'être (each preparation – latte, espresso, filter, press etc – is allocated a specific blend or coffee bean); but you could instead opt for a New Zealand wine to accompany your risotto or fish of the day.

LEILA'S SHOP
CAFE $

Map p458 (17 Calvert Ave, E2; dishes £5-10; ⊙10am-6pm Wed-Sun; ⊜Shoreditch High St) Tucked away on up-and-coming Calvert Ave, this independent grocery shop doubles as a cafe.

PRINCESS OF SHOREDITCH
MODERN BRITISH $$

Map p458 (✆020-7729 9270; www.theprincess ofshoreditch.com; 76 Paul St, EC2A; mains £13-17; ⊙noon-3pm & 6.30-10pm; ☎; ⊜Old St) The handsome pub downstairs is a buzzy place for a drink, but swirl up the tight spiral staircase and an entirely different Princess presents itself. Polished stemware glistens on wooden Edwardian tables, while the waitstaff buzz around delivering plates of inventive contemporary fare crafted from top-notch British ingredients.

ANDINA
PERUVIAN $$

Map p458 (✆020-7920 6499; www.andinalondon. com; 1 Redchurch St, E2; dishes £6.50-14.50; ⊙8am-11pm Mon-Fri, 10am-11pm Sat & Sun; ☎; ⊜Shoreditch High St) Cheerful Andina sits on the corner of trendy Redchurch St and serves high-quality Peruvian street food. The lively restaurant, set over two floors, is a great place to try creamy *ají de gallina* (chicken casserole), piquant ceviche and succulent grilled meat skewers. Unsurprisingly, it knocks out a mean pisco sour.

ALBION
BRITISH $$

Map p458 (✆020-7729 1051; www.albioncaff. co.uk; 2-4 Boundary St, E2; mains £8-19; ⊙8am-11pm Sun-Thu, to 1am Fri & Sat; ☎⚡; ⊜Shoreditch High St) Those pining for dear Old Blighty's cuisine, *sans* grease and stodge, should earmark a visit to this self-consciously retro 'caff' for top-quality bangers and mash, game-meat pies, Welsh rarebit, devilled kidneys, full English breakfasts and, of course, fish and chips.

EYRE BROTHERS
SPANISH, PORTUGUESE $$$

Map p458 (✆020-7613 5346; www.eyrebrothers. co.uk; 70 Leonard St, EC2A; mains £12-25; ⊙noon-3pm & 6.30-10.45pm Mon-Fri, 7-11pm Sat; ☎; ⊜Old St) The cuisine at this elegant Shoreditch restaurant is Iberian with a touch of African flair, courtesy of the eponymous brothers' upbringing in Mozambique, and it's every bit as exciting as it sounds. The rare acorn-fed Ibérico pork, in particular, is top-notch. It's all accompanied by an extensive list of Portuguese and Spanish wines.

SHOREDITCH COOL

The Shoreditch phenomenon began in the late 1990s, when creative types who had been chased out of the West End by prohibitive rents began taking over warehouses in what was then an urban wasteland, abandoned after the collapse of the fabrics industry. Within a few years the area was seriously cool, boasting oddball bars, clubs, galleries and restaurants that catered to the new media/creative/freelance squad.

Despite the general expectation that the Shoreditch scene would collapse under the weight of its own beards, the regenerated area is still flourishing, with new developments bringing life to some of London's poorest corners, spilling over into nearby Hackney and Bethnal Green.

CLOVE CLUB
GASTRONOMY $$$

Map p458 (☑020-7729 6496; www.theclove club.com; 380 Old St, EC1V; 5-course menu £75; ⊘noon-2pm Tue-Sat, 6-9.30pm Mon-Sat; ☑; ☻Old St) From humble origins as a supper club in a Dalston flat, the Clove Club has transformed into this incredibly impressive Michelin-starred restaurant in Shoreditch Town Hall. Hold onto your hats as you're taken on a culinary canter through multiple courses of intricately arranged, well-thought-out, flavoursome food – including numerous unbidden *amuse-bouches* (complimentary appetisers) and palate cleansers. Unusually, a vegetarian menu is available.

CEREAL KILLER CAFE
CAFE $

Map p458 (☑020-3601 9100; www.cerealkiller cafe.co.uk; 139 Brick Lane, E1; medium cereal £4.30; ⊘8am-8pm; ◧Shoreditch High Street) The first cereal-themed cafe in the country perfectly symbolises the hipster spirit – and gentrification, some might say – of its Shoreditch location. There are 120 cereals on offer and a selection of obscenely calorific but epically delicious hot chocolates.

HKK
CHINESE $$$

Map p458 (☑020-3535 1888; www.hkklondon. com; 88 Worship St, EC2A; mains £12-28, 3-course lunch £38, tasting menu £94; ⊘noon-2.30pm & 6-10pm Mon-Sat; ☑; ☻Liverpool St) If the surrounds are a tad corporate, HKK compensates with the high theatre of chefs slicing and dicing in the centre of the dining room. Duck is a speciality, along with exquisitely constructed dumplings and plenty of other Cantonese delights. Note that the full tasting menu is the only option for dinner.

✖ Spitalfields

BOILER HOUSE
MARKET $

Map p458 (www.boilerhouse-foodhall.co.uk; Old Truman Brewery, 152 Brick Lane, E1; dishes £3-8; ⊘11am-6pm Sat, 10am-5pm Sun; ☑; ☻Liverpool St) More than 30 food stalls selling anything from Argentinian to Vietnamese pitch up in the brewery's impressive old boiler room at the weekend. There is also a bar, and you can sit at the communal tables to tuck in. Come spring and summer, there are dozens more tables in the backyard.

NUDE ESPRESSO
CAFE $

Map p458 (www.nudeespresso.com; 26 Hanbury St, E1; dishes £4.50-12; ⊘7am-6pm Mon-Fri, 9.30am-5pm Sat & Sun; ☻Liverpool St) A simply styled, cosy cafe serving top-notch coffee (roasted across the street). Along with the standard blend, it has rotating single origin coffees and filter as well as espresso-based brews. The sweet treats are delicious, as are the cooked breakfasts, brunch items and light lunches.

BRICK LANE BEIGEL BAKERY
BAKERY $

Map p458 (159 Brick Lane, E2; bagels £1-4.10; ⊘24hr; ☻Shoreditch High St) This relic of the Jewish East End still makes a brisk trade serving dirt-cheap homemade bagels (filled with salmon, cream cheese and/or salt beef) to hungry shoppers and late-night boozers. The queues on Sundays are epic.

GUNPOWDER
INDIAN $$

Map p458 (www.gunpowderlondon.com; 11 White's Row, E1; ⊘noon-3pm & 5.30-10.30 Mon-Sat; ☑; ☻Liverpool St) As you walk into this tiny Indian place, it's the smell that hits you: a delicious blend of spices and incense. The punchy food, inspired by family recipes and home cooking, lives up to this expectation: plates are small and designed for sharing, and the flavours of each dish are divine.

GALVIN HOP   GASTROPUB $$

Map p458 (020-7299 0404; www.galvin restaurants.com; 35 Spital Sq, E1; mains £14.50-19.50; 11.30am-2pm & 6-10.30pm Mon-Sat, 11.30am-9.30pm Sun; ; Liverpool St) It may be the little sister of glamorous Galvin La Chapelle (p214) next door, but this 'pub de-luxe', as it styles itself, is all about giving traditional pub fare a well-executed turn: think premium hot dogs and burgers, fish pie and venison casserole. Go 'bottomless' for brunch for just £10, with your choice of Bloody Mary, prosecco or pilsner.

SOM SAA   THAI $$

Map p458 (www.somsaa.com; 43a Commercial St, E1; dishes £7-16.50; noon-2.30pm Tue-Sat, 5-11pm Mon-Sat; ; Liverpool St) This ever-popular Thai restaurant has come a long way from its early days as a pop-up shop. The menu is relatively short, with a selection of curries, grilled dishes, salads and stir-fries, but the food is authentic and deli-cious. Portions are designed to be shared, although the staff's recommendation of two dishes per person is rather generous. Unusually for a Thai restaurant, there is an extensive drinks list featuring superb cock-tails and a great choice of wines and beers.

POPPIE'S   FISH & CHIPS $$

Map p458 (www.poppiesfishandchips.co.uk; 6-8 Hanbury St, E1; mains £12.20-15.90; 11am-11pm; Liverpool St) This glorious re-creation of a 1950s East End chippy comes complete with waitstaff in pinnies and hairnets, and Blitz memorabilia. As well as the usual fishy suspects, it does those old-time London sta-ples – jellied eels and mushy peas – plus kid-pleasing, sweet-tooth desserts (sticky toffee pudding or apple pie with ice cream), and there's a wine list. Takeaway is a lot cheaper.

ROSA'S   THAI $$

Map p458 (020-7247 1093; www.rosaslondon. com; 12 Hanbury St, E1; mains £8-13; noon-10.30pm; ; Liverpool St) Simply kitted out with low benches and stools, red-fronted Ro-sa's serves tasty Thai food and surprisingly good coffee (courtesy of Monmouth roast-ers). Go for its signature pumpkin curry, one of the zingy salads or a delicious chargrill.

GALVIN LA CHAPELLE   FRENCH $$$

Map p458 (020-7299 0400; www.galvin restaurants.com; 35 Spital Sq, E1; mains £28.50-39, 2-/3-course lunch or early dinner £29/34.50; noon-2.30pm & 6-10.30pm Mon-Sat, noon-3pm & 6-9.30pm Sun; ; Liverpool St) For lash-ings of la-di-da with an extra serve of ooh la la, you can't beat the incredibly grand surrounds of this soaring Victorian hall, inhabited by bow-tied and waistcoated waitstaff and very well-heeled guests. The Michelin-starred menu rises to the chal-lenge, delivering traditional French cuisine with lots of contemporary embellishments. Early diners can take advantage of a good-value set menu.

WRIGHT BROTHERS   SEAFOOD $$$

Map p458 (020-7324 7730; www.thewright brothers.co.uk; 8a Lamb St, E1; mains £22.50-65; noon-10.30pm Mon-Sat, to 9pm Sun; Liver-pool St) For the Wright Brothers, the oyster is their world: they operate the Duchy of Cornwall oyster farm on Prince Charles' es-tate. This chic dining bar serves up freshly shucked shellfish, delicately constructed fish dishes and exquisite cocktails, all on the edge of Spitalfields market.

★HAWKSMOOR   STEAK $$$

Map p458 (020-7426 4850; www.thehawks moor.com; 157 Commercial St, E1; mains £20-50; noon-2.30pm & 5-10.30pm Mon-Sat, noon-9pm Sun; ; Liverpool St) You could easily miss discreetly signed Hawksmoor, but con-firmed carnivores will find it worth seeking out. The dark wood, bare bricks and velvet curtains make for a handsome setting in which to gorge yourself on the best of British beef. The Sunday roasts (£20) are legendary.

🍷 DRINKING & NIGHTLIFE

Shoreditch is the torchbearer of London's nightlife: there are dozens of bars, clubs and pubs, open virtually every night of the week (and until the small hours at weekends) and it can get pretty rowdy. Clerkenwell is more sedate, featuring lovely historic pubs and fine cocktail bars. Spitalfields sits somewhere in between the two extremes and tends to be defined by its City clientele on week nights and market-goers on Saturday and Sunday.

🍸 Clerkenwell

★ZETTER TOWNHOUSE
COCKTAIL LOUNGE   COCKTAIL BAR
Map p458 (✆020-7324 4545; www.thezetter townhouse.com; 49-50 St John's Sq, EC1V; ⊘7.30am-12.45am; 🛜; ⊖Farringdon) Tucked away behind an unassuming door on St John's Sq, this ground-floor bar is decorated with plush armchairs, stuffed animal heads and a legion of lamps. The cocktail list takes its theme from the area's distilling history – recipes of yesteryear plus homemade tinctures and cordials are used to create interesting and unusual tipples. House cocktails are all £10.50.

FABRIC   CLUB
Map p458 (www.fabriclondon.com; 77a Charterhouse Street, EC1M; £5-25; ⊘11pm-7am Fri-Sun; ⊖Farringdon, Barbican) London's leading club, Fabric's three separate dance floors in a huge converted cold store opposite Smithfield meat market draws impressive queues (buy tickets online). FabricLive (on selected Fridays) rumbles with drum 'n' bass and dubstep, while Fabric (usually on Saturdays but also on selected Fridays) is the club's signature live DJ night. Sunday's WetYourSelf! delivers house, techno and electronica.

Following a temporary closure in 2016 due to drug-related deaths, the club operates a strict door policy (you must be over 19 and have a formal ID) and a zero-tolerance policy towards drug use.

★FOX & ANCHOR   PUB
Map p458 (www.foxandanchor.com; 115 Charterhouse St, EC1M; ⊘7am-11pm Mon-Fri, 8.30am-11pm Sat & Sun; 🛜; ⊖Barbican) Behind the Fox & Anchor's wonderful art-nouveau facade is a stunning traditional Victorian pub that has retained its three beautiful snugs at the back of the bar. Fully celebrating its proximity to Smithfield Market, the food is gloriously meaty. Only the most voracious of carnivores should opt for the City Boy Breakfast (£19.50).

JERUSALEM TAVERN   PUB
Map p458 (www.stpetersbrewery.co.uk; 55 Britton St, EC1M; ⊘11am-11pm Mon-Fri; 🛜; ⊖Farringdon) Pick a wood-panelled cubicle at this tiny and highly atmospheric pub housed in a building dating from 1720 and select from the fantastic beverages brewed by St Peter's Brewery in Suffolk. Be warned: it's hugely popular and often very crowded.

★YE OLDE MITRE   PUB
Map p458 (www.yeoldemitreholborn.co.uk; 1 Ely Ct, EC1N; ⊘11am-11pm Mon-Fri; 🛜; ⊖Farringdon) A delightfully cosy historic pub with an extensive beer selection, tucked away in a backstreet off Hatton Garden, Ye Olde Mitre was built in 1546 for the servants of Ely Palace. There's no music, so rooms echo only with amiable chit-chat. Queen Elizabeth I danced around the cherry tree by the bar, they say.

CAFÉ KICK   BAR
Map p458 (✆020-7837 8077; www.cafekick. co.uk; 43 Exmouth Market, EC1R; ⊘11am-11pm Mon-Thu, to midnight Fri & Sat, noon-10.30pm Sun; ⊖Farringdon, Angel) A bare-boards bar with a Continental European feel, where the action centres on a handful of foosball tables. The bar is big on any and all kind of sport, which you can watch on one of the many screens.

BOUNCE   BAR
Map p458 (www.bouncepingpong.com/farringdon; 121 Holborn, EC1N; ⊘4pm-midnight Mon-Thu, to 1am Fri & Sat, to 11pm Sun; ⊖Chancery Lane) This 1950s-themed basement cocktail bar in Holborn is the self-declared home of ping pong, reputedly located in the exact spot the sport was invented. At one end there are 17 table tennis tables – including one from the 2012 London Olympics – and at the other an Italian restaurant. An hour's table hire costs £21 (off-peak) or £29.50 (peak).

VINOTECA   WINE BAR
Map p458 (www.vinoteca.co.uk; 7 St John St, EC1M; ⊘noon-11pm Mon-Sat; 🛜; ⊖Farringdon) Simple yet elegant oak decor, an astonishingly comprehensive wine list and amiable service make this a popular choice with suited City workers and local creatives. All wines are also available by the bottle at the on-site shop, and the food is good too.

THREE KINGS   PUB
Map p458 (7 Clerkenwell Close, EC1R; ⊘noon-11pm Mon-Fri, 5.30-11pm Sat; ⊖Farringdon) This down-to-earth and welcoming backstreet pub attracts a friendly bunch of relaxed locals for its quirky decor, great music and good times.

🍷 Hoxton

GLORY
GAY & LESBIAN

Map p458 (📞020-7684 0794; www.theglory.
co; 281 Kingsland Rd E2; ⊙5pm-midnight Mon-
Thu, to 2am Fri & Sat, 1-11pm Sun; 🚇Haggerston)
A charming cast has taken over this cosy
corner pub, transforming it into one of Lon-
don's most legendary queer cabaret venues.
Order a Twink in Pink or a Schlong Island
Iced Tea from the cocktail list and brace
yourself for whatever wackiness is on offer.
All genders welcome.

HAPPINESS FORGETS
COCKTAIL BAR

Map p458 (www.happinessforgets.com; 8-9 Hoxton Sq, N1; ⊙5-11pm; 🚇; ⊖Old St) This low-lit,
basement bar with good-value cocktails is
relaxed and intimate, overseen by dapper-
looking staff in white shirts and colourful
suspenders. Look for the signs for Ruby cafe
and take the stairs heading down. It's worth
reserving, and you won't want to leave.

WHITE LYAN
BAR

Map p458 (www.whitelyan.com; 153-155 Hoxton
St, N1; ⊙5pm-late Wed-Sun; ⊖Hoxton) All the
tipples are hand-crafted in-house at cool
White Lyan. Zero ice, sugar, fruit or citrus, and no brands, so what you get are
premixed and prechilled drinks from the
fridge every time, including house gin,
whisky, bourbon, vodka, rum, cordials and
infusions. The menu is cutting-edge, but
prices are fairly standard: £10 to £11 for
cocktails and £3 for shots.

BRIDGE
BAR

Map p458 (15 Kingsland Rd, E2; ⊙noon-2.30am;
⊖Hoxton) It doesn't look like much from the
outside, but shuffle into this eastern Mediterranean–style cafe-bar and you'll find an
Aladdin's cave. Upstairs is particularly over
the top. Hold court with a strong drink (coffee or spirits) and a slice of baklava.

RED LION
PUB

Map p458 (41 Hoxton St, N1; ⊙noon-11pm; 🚇;
⊖Old St) Just far enough from Hoxton Sq to
avoid being overrun by weekend blow-ins,
the Red Lion has a local-pub vibe – but giv-
en this is Hoxton, the locals are anything
but typical. It's spread over four floors, but
the roof terrace is the major draw.

333 MOTHER
BAR, CLUB

Map p458 (www.333mother.com; 333 Old St,
EC1V; ⊙noon-2.30am Sun-Thu, to 3am Fri & Sat;
⊖Old St) Hoxton's true old-timer, Mother
just keeps going, despite its hipness halo
slipping slightly. It's quite a relaxed affair
on weekdays, when sipping drinks on the
roof terrace is really very pleasant. Things
heat up on Fridays and Saturdays: DJs start
playing about 8pm downstairs and the
Mother Bar on the 1st floor opens for full-
on revelling from about 10pm.

MACBETH
PUB

Map p458 (www.themacbeth.co.uk; 70 Hoxton St,
N1; ⊙5pm-1am Mon-Thu, to 3am Fri & Sat, to 2am
Sun; 🚇; ⊖Hoxton) This enormous old boozer
on a still-to-be-gentrified stretch, just a
short walk north of Hoxton Sq, is an established stop in the ever-changing Hoxton
scene. It provides a great platform for up-
and-coming music talent and also hosts fun
nights such as artist karaoke (Amy Winehouse, Lady Gaga etc) and themed events.
Admission is usually £5 to £8.

🍷 Shoreditch

★QUEEN OF HOXTON
BAR

Map p458 (www.queenofhoxton.com; 1 Curtain
Rd, EC2A; ⊙4pm-midnight Mon-Wed, to 2am
Thu-Sat; 🚇; ⊖Liverpool St) This industrial-
chic bar has a games room, basement and
varied music nights (including oddballs
such as dance lessons and ukulele jamming
sessions), but the real drawcard is the vast
rooftop bar, decked out with flowers, fairy
lights and even a wigwam. It has fantastic
views across the city.

★WORSHIP ST
WHISTLING SHOP
COCKTAIL BAR

Map p458 (📞020-7247 0015; www.whistlingshop.
com; 63 Worship St, EC2A; ⊙5pm-midnight Mon
& Tue, to 1am Wed & Thu, to 2am Fri & Sat; ⊖Old
St) While the name is Victorian slang for a
place selling illicit booze, this subterranean
drinking den's master mixologists explore
the experimental limits of cocktail chemistry and aromatic science, as well as concocting the classics. Many ingredients are
made with rotary evaporators in the on-site
lab. Also runs cocktail masterclasses.

XOYO

CLUB

Map p458 (www.xoyo.co.uk; 32-37 Cowper St, EC2A; ⊖9pm-4am Fri & Sat, hours vary Sun-Thu; ⊜Old St) This fantastic Shoreditch warehouse club throws together a pulsing and popular mix of gigs, club nights and art events. Always buzzing, it has a varied line-up of indie bands, hip hop, electro, dubstep and much in between, and attracts a mix of clubbers, from skinny-jeaned hipsters to more mature hedonists (but no suits).

SHOREDITCH SKY TERRACE

ROOFTOP BAR

Map p458 (🖉020-3310 5555; www.shoreditch. courthouse-hotel.com; 335-337 Old St, EC1; ⊖4pm-midnight May-Oct; 🕾; ⊜Old St) Set atop the Grade II–listed Courthouse Hotel in the centre of Shoreditch, this rooftop bar has fantastic views of London's skyline. During the week it's a great spot for a date – the atmosphere is lively but tables are spaced far enough apart to ensure privacy. Come the weekend it's more of a party venue, as DJs take the stage.

FIGHT CLUB

BAR

Map p458 (🖉020-3019 3093; www.flightclub darts.com; 2a Worship St, EC2; ⊖noon-midnight Mon-Thu, to 1am Fri & Sat, to 10.30pm Sun; ⊜Moorgate) It's not entirely clear why this darts bar has called itself Fight Club, but in any case we're here to break the first rule and talk about it. The game evokes images of musty pubs and beer-soaked carpets, but this place is super-slick with gleaming decor. Special cameras track the darts in flight, meaning your score pops up automatically on a screen.

KICK

BAR

Map p458 (www.cafekick.co.uk; 127 Shoreditch High St, E1; ⊖noon-11pm Sun-Thu, to 1am Fri & Sat; 🕾; ⊜Shoreditch High St) With its lively vibe, Kick is a fab place to watch big football games. The flag-adorned ground floor features four foosball tables; downstairs has leather sofas and simple tables and chairs; and there are spots on the pavement too. Generous happy hour daily from 4pm to 7pm.

ALLPRESS ESPRESSO

CAFE

Map p458 (www.allpressespresso.com; 58 Redchurch St, E2; ⊖7.30am-5pm Mon-Fri, from 9am Sat & Sun; ⊜Shoreditch High St) Part of the great Antipodean takeover of London cafes, this distant outpost of a New Zealand brand serves perfectly crafted coffee from its neat-as-a-pin roastery. It's a super place

for breakfast: we recommend the mixed plate with salmon (£10.50).

OLD STREET RECORDS

BAR

Map p458 (🖉020-3006 5911; www.oldstreet records.com; 350-354 Old St, EC1; ⊖5pm-midnight Mon-Wed, to 2am Thu-Sat; ⊜Old St) This spacious music bar in the heart of Shoreditch has become an institution in the area. It has live performances six nights a week, ranging across jazz, soul, funk and rock. Housemade pizzas are top-notch, and happy hour runs from 5pm to 8pm.

OLD BLUE LAST

PUB

Map p458 (www.theoldbluelast.com; 38 Great Eastern St, EC2A; ⊖noon-midnight Sun-Thu, to 1am Fri & Sat; 🕾; ⊜Old St) Frequently crammed with a hip teenage-and-up crowd, this scuffed corner pub's edgy credentials are courtesy of *Vice* magazine, the bad-boy rag that owns the place. It hosts some of the best Shoreditch parties and lots of live music.

CALLOOH CALLAY

COCKTAIL BAR

Map p458 (🖉020-7739 4781; www.calloohcallay bar.com; 65 Rivington St, EC2A; ⊖6pm-1am Mon-Sat; ⊜Old St) Given it's inspired by *Jabberwocky*, Lewis Carroll's nonsense poem, this bar's eccentric decor is to be expected. The cocktails are top-notch.

BOOK CLUB

BAR

Map p458 (🖉020-7684 8618; www.wearetbc. com; 100-106 Leonard St, EC2A; ⊖8am-midnight Mon-Wed, to 2am Thu & Fri, 10am-2am Sat, to midnight Sun; 🕾; ⊜Old St) A creative vibe animates this fantastic one-time Victorian warehouse. Book Club hosts DJs and oddball events (life drawing, workshops, twerking lessons and the Crap Film Club) to complement the drinking and enthusiastic ping pong and pool playing. Food is served throughout the day and there's a scruffy basement bar below.

DREAMBAGSJAGUARSHOES

BAR

Map p458 (www.jaguarshoes.com; 32-36 Kingsland Rd, E2; ⊖noon-1am; 🕾; ⊜Hoxton) The bar is named after the pre-existing signs on the two shops whose space it now occupies, a nonchalance that's typical example of we-couldn't-care-less Shoreditch chic. The street-level interior is filled with Formica-topped tables and hung with art. Downstairs there's a larger space where DJs hit the decks at weekends.

BREWDOG
BAR

Map p458 (www.brewdog.com; 51-55 Bethnal Green Rd, E1; ⊙noon-midnight Sun-Thu, to 1am Fri & Sat; 🛜; ⊜Shoreditch High St) BrewDog is an ale aficionado's paradise, with 18 different brews on tap, hundreds by the bottle and, to soak it all up, some excellent burgers (including interesting variations such as brisket and soy). Its own crowd-funded eco-brewery is located Scotland, near Aberdeen, and it stocks other microbrewery beers too.

★CARGO
BAR, CLUB

Map p458 (www.cargo-london.com; 83 Rivington St, EC2A; ⊙noon-1am Sun-Thu, to 3am Fri & Sat; ⊜Shoreditch High St) Cargo is one of London's most eclectic clubs. Under its brick railway arches you'll find a dance floor, a bar and an outside terrace adorned with two original Banksy images. The music policy (hip hop, pop, R&B and club classics) is varied, with plenty of up-and-coming bands also in the line-up. Food is available throughout the day.

HORSE & GROOM
PUB

Map p458 (www.thehorseandgroom.net; 28 Curtain Rd, EC2A; ⊙11.30am-11pm Mon-Wed, to 2am Thu, to 4am Fri, 6pm-4am Sat; ⊜Shoreditch High St) Nicknamed the 'disco pub', this relaxed venue has two intimate spaces with hedonistic nights of house, funk, soul and, of course, disco. The site's had a long history in entertainment – under the women's toilets, archaeologists have found the remains of the theatre where Shakespeare premiered *Romeo and Juliet* and *Henry V*.

CATCH
CLUB

Map p458 (www.thecatchbar.com; 22 Kingsland Rd, E2; ⊙6pm-midnight Mon-Wed, to 2am Thu-Sat, 7pm-1am Sun; ⊜Old St or Shoreditch High St) Catch's interior is eye-catching indeed with its colourful decor. Upstairs you'll hear anything from '90s to funk and hip hop, and a great selection of new and established bands. Downstairs you get a big house-party vibe with DJs who mix up pretty much anything from chart hits to electro and techno.

AQUARIUM
CLUB

Map p458 (www.clubaquarium.co.uk; 256-264 Old St, EC1; ⊙hours vary; ⊜Old St) The real attraction at this big and brash club is the swimming pool and Jacuzzi (towels provided) and the often very-late opening hours (selected nights until 9am). DJs play mainly house and techno to a mainstream,

dressed-up crowd. Trainers (sneakers) are not welcome here.

🍸 Spitalfields

★COCKTAIL TRADING CO
COCKTAIL BAR

Map p458 (www.thecocktailtradingco.co.uk; 68 Bethnal Green Rd, E1; ⊙5pm-midnight Mon-Fri, 2pm-midnight Sat, 2-10.30pm Sun; ⊜Shoreditch High St) In an area famous for its edgy, don't-give-a-damn attitude, this exquisite cocktail bar stands out for its classiness and cocktail confidence. The drinks are truly unrivalled, from the flavours to the presentation – bottles presented in envelopes, ice cubes as big as a Rubik's cube and so on. The decor is reminiscent of a colonial-era gentlemen's club, just warmer and more welcoming.

HAWKSMOOR
COCKTAIL BAR

Map p458 (📞020-7247 7392; www.thehawksmoor.com; 157b Commercial St, E1; ⊙5.30-11pm Mon-Thu, to 1am Fri, noon-1am Sat; 🛜; ⊜Liverpool St) Black leather, bevelled mirror tiles and a copper wall gleam with candlelight in this darkly glamorous basement bar below a popular steak restaurant. The adventurous cocktail list is matched with a good selection of beer, cider and wine, and tempting takes on classic American bar food (burgers, hot dogs and wings).

MAYOR OF SCAREDY CAT TOWN
BAR

Map p458 (www.themayorofscaredycattown.com; 12-16 Artillery Lane, E1; ⊙5pm-midnight Mon-Thu, 3pm-midnight Fri, noon-midnight Sat, to noon-10.30pm Sun; ⊜Liverpool St) This wood and brick secret basement bar is a refreshingly tongue-in-cheek alternative to a downstairs cocktail-bar scene that can take itself too seriously. Enter through the Smeg fridge door in the wall of the Breakfast Club cafe. Give the password (ask to see the Mayor of Scaredy Cat Town) and staff will let you in. Cocktails £9 to £10.

GOLDEN HEART
PUB

Map p458 (110 Commercial St, E1; ⊙11am-midnight Sun-Wed, to 2am Thu-Sat; ⊜Shoreditch High St) It's a distinctly bohemian crowd that mixes in the cosy, traditional interior of this brilliant Spitalfields pub, famous as the watering hole for the cream of London's art crowd. The highlight of a visit a chat with Sandra, the landlord-celebrity who talks to all comers and keeps things fun.

TEN BELLS
PUB

Map p458 (www.tenbells.com; 84 Commercial St, E1; ⏰noon-midnight Sun-Wed, to 1am Thu-Sat; 📶; ⊖Shoreditch High St) This landmark Victorian pub with large windows and beautiful tiles is perfectly positioned for a pint after exploring Spitalfields Market. The most famous of London's Jack the Ripper pubs, it was patronised by his last victim before her grisly end, and possibly by the serial killer himself. Gin menu, pork scratchings and pie of the day offered.

93 FEET EAST
BAR, CLUB

Map p458 (www.93feeteast.co.uk; 150 Brick Lane, E1; ⏰5-11pm Thu, to 1am Fri & Sat, 3-10.30pm Sun; ⊖Liverpool St) Part of the Old Truman Brewery (p207) complex, this venue has a courtyard, three big rooms and an outdoor terrace that gets crowded with a cool East End crowd on sunny afternoons. There are DJs and plenty of live music on offer.

☆ ENTERTAINMENT

★ELECTRIC CINEMA
CINEMA

Map p458 (📞020-3350 3490; www.electric cinema.co.uk; 64-66 Redchurch St, E2; tickets £11-19; ⊖Shoreditch High St) Run by Shoreditch House, an uber-fashionable private member's club, this is cinema-going that will impress a date, with space for an intimate 48 on the comfy armchairs. There's a full bar and restaurant in the complex, and you can take your purchases in with you. Tickets go like crazy, so book ahead.

SADLER'S WELLS
DANCE

Map p458 (📞020-7863 8000; www.sadlerswells. com; Rosebery Ave, EC1R; ⊖Angel) A glittering modern venue that was, in fact, first established in 1683, Sadler's Wells is the most eclectic modern-dance and ballet venue in town, with experimental dance shows of all genres and from all corners of the globe. The Lilian Baylis Studio stages smaller productions.

RICH MIX
LIVE MUSIC

Map p458 (📞020-7613 7498; www.richmix.org. uk; 35-47 Bethnal Green Rd, E1; ⊖Old St) Founded in 2006 in a converted garment factory, this modern cultural centre contains a three-screen cinema, a bar and a theatre. Movies shown are pretty mainstream, but the programming for performing arts is

hugely eclectic, with anything from spoken word to live music and comedy gracing the stage.

CAFÉ 1001
LIVE MUSIC

Map p458 (📞020-7247 6166; www.cafe1001. co.uk; 91 Brick Lane, E1; ⏰6am-midnight; 📶; ⊖Liverpool St) A popular and huge cafe with grills and cakes, lounge seating during the day and a mix of events across two stages in the evenings (DJs, live music, open mic nights, spoken word etc). It gets packed at weekends.

🔒 SHOPPING

This is a top area for discovering cool boutiques and market stalls that showcase up-and-coming designers, not to mention endless vintage stores. There are tonnes of shops on and around Brick Lane, especially in burgeoning Cheshire St, Hanbury St and the Old Truman Brewery. Clerkenwell is mostly known for its jewellery and the work of its artisan craftspeople.

★SUNDAY UPMARKET
MARKET

Map p458 (www.sundayupmarket.co.uk; Old Truman Brewery, 91 Brick Lane, E1; ⏰11am-6pm Sat, 10am-5pm Sun; ⊖Shoreditch High St) The Sunday Upmarket (which in fact opens Saturdays and Sundays) sprawls within the beautiful red-brick buildings of the Old Truman Brewery. You'll find young designers in the Backyard Market (p220), a drool-inducing array of food stalls in the Boiler House (p213), antiques and bric-a-brac in the Tea Rooms (p220) and a huge range of vintage clothes (p220) in the basement across the street.

★COLLECTIF
FASHION & ACCESSORIES

Map p458 (www.collectif.co.uk; 58 Commercial St, E1; ⏰10am-6pm; ⊖Liverpool St) If you love the feminine silhouette of the 1940s and the pin-up look of the 1950s, you will swoon over Collectif's vintage-inspired dresses, shirts, coats and accessories.

★ROUGH TRADE EAST
MUSIC

Map p458 (www.roughtrade.com; Old Truman Brewery, 91 Brick Lane, E1; ⏰9am-9pm Mon-Thu, to 8pm Fri, 10am-8pm Sat, 11am-7pm Sun; ⊖Shoreditch High St) It's no longer directly associated with the legendary record label (home to The Smiths, The Libertines and The Strokes, among many others), but this huge record shop is still the best for music of an indie, soul, electronica and alternative persuasion. In addition to an impressive selection of CDs and vinyl, it also dispenses coffee and stages promotional gigs.

★OLD SPITALFIELDS MARKET   MARKET

Map p458 (www.oldspitalfieldsmarket.com; Commercial St, E1; ◷10am-5pm Mon-Fri & Sun, 11am-5pm Sat; ◉Liverpool St) Traders have been hawking their wares here since 1638 and it's still one of London's best markets. Today's covered market was built in the late 19th century, with the more modern development added in 2006. Sundays are the biggest and best days, but Thursdays are good for antiques and Fridays for independent fashion. There are plenty of food stalls too.

★MAGMA   BOOKS, GIFTS

Map p458 (www.magmabooks.com; 117-119 Clerkenwell Rd, EC1R; ◷10am-7pm Mon-Sat; ◉Chancery Lane) This much-loved shop sells coffee-table books, magazines and almost anything on the design cutting edge. It has some lovely children's books and activity sets too. Great for present shopping.

VINTAGE (UP)MARKET   VINTAGE

Map p458 (www.vintage-market.co.uk; Old Truman Brewery, F Block, 85 Brick Lane, E1; ◷11am-6pm Thu-Sat, 10am-5pm Sun; ◉Liverpool St) This basement market has a fabulous selection of vintage fashion, posters and vinyls, and even the odd piece of furniture. Although it is part of the Sunday Upmarket (p219), it is open from Thursday to Sunday.

BLITZ LONDON   VINTAGE

Map p458 (www.blitzlondon.co.uk; 55-59 Hanbury St, E1; ◷11am-7pm; ◉Liverpool St) One of the capital's best secondhand clothes stores, with more than 20,000 hand-selected items of men's and women's clothing, shoes and accessories spanning four decades since the 1960s. You'll find anything from mainstream brands such as Nike to designer labels such as Burberry.

BACKYARD MARKET   MARKET

Map p458 (www.backyardmarket.co.uk; 146 Brick Lane, E1; ◷11am-6pm Sat, 10am-5pm Sun; ◉Shoreditch High St) Just off Brick Lane, the Backyard Market fills a large brick warehouse (part of the Old Truman Brewery complex) with stalls selling designer clothes, ceramics, jewellery, unique prints and funky furniture titbits.

E.C.ONE   JEWELLERY

Map p458 (☑020-7713 6185; www.econe.co.uk; 41 Exmouth Market, EC1R; ◷10am-6pm Mon-Sat; ◉Farringdon) Husband-and-wife team Jos and Alison Skeates sell gorgeous contemporary collections by British and international jewellery designers. Watch the jewellers at work at the rear of the shop.

TATTY DEVINE   JEWELLERY

Map p458 (☑020-7739 9191; www.tattydevine.com; 236 Brick Lane, E2; ◷10am-6.30pm Mon-Fri, 11am-6pm Sat, 10am-5pm Sun; ◉Shoreditch High St) Harriet Vine and Rosie Wolfenden make hip and witty perspex jewellery that's become the favourite of many young Londoners. Their original designs feature all manner of flora- and fauna-inspired necklaces, as well as creations sporting moustaches, dinosaurs and bunting. Name necklaces (made to order; from £27.50) are also a treat.

TEA ROOMS   ANTIQUES

Map p458 (www.bricklane-tearooms.co.uk; Old Truman Brewery, 91 Brick Lane, E1; ◷11am-6pm Sat, 10am-5pm Sun; ◉Liverpool St) Whether you're after a vintage suitcase, some mismatched crockery for that shabby-chic feel, antique furniture or unique souvenirs, this warren of stalls should see you right.

HOUSE OF HACKNEY   HOMEWARES

Map p458 (www.houseofhackney.com; 131 Shoreditch High St, E1; ◷10am-7pm Mon-Sat, 11am-5pm Sun; ◉Shoreditch High St) Selling everything from furniture to china and clothing, all in the zaniest of prints, this store is well worth a look. If you ever wanted to have your coffee mug match the jungle print on your wallpaper and lampshade, it's the store for you.

BOXPARK   SHOPPING CENTRE

Map p458 (www.boxpark.co.uk; 2-10 Bethnal Green Rd, E1; ◷11am-7pm Mon-Sat, noon-6pm Sun; ◉; ◉Shoreditch High St) A great place to find both up-and-coming and established brands, Boxpark is a quirky shopping mall created from shipping containers. The series of tiny container shops (pop-up or permanent) sells a wide variety of items: fashion, design, gifts, art and wine. Head to the upper level for restaurants, bars and a terrace.

MR START
CLOTHING

Map p458 (http://mr-start.com; 40 Rivington St, EC2A; ⊙10.30am-6.30pm Mon-Wed & Fri, to 7pm Thu, 11am-6pm Sat, noon-5pm Sun; ⊖Old St) This supremely elegant and cool menswear boutique is brought to you by fashion designer Philip Start. It offers casualwear as well as tailoring, all made with gorgeous textiles – think cashmere, merino, silk and the finest cottons.

PRESENT
CLOTHING

Map p458 (www.present-london.com; 140 Shoreditch High St, E1; ⊙10.30am-7pm Mon-Fri, 11am-6.30pm Sat, to 5pm Sun; ⊖Shoreditch High St) Everything for the hip and financially endowed gentleman, including designer gear, shoes and chutney.

BRICK LANE MARKET
MARKET

Map p458 (www.visitbricklane.org; Brick Lane, E1; ⊙9am-5pm Sun; ⊖Shoreditch High St) Spilling out into its surrounding streets, this irrepressibly vibrant market fills a vast area with household goods, bric-a-brac, secondhand clothes, cheap fashion and ethnic food.

HATTON GARDEN
JEWELLERY

Map p458 (www.hatton-garden.net; EC1N; ⊖Farringdon) If you're in the market for classic settings or unmounted stones, stroll along Hatton Garden jewellery quarter – it's chock-a-block with gold, diamond and jewellery shops, especially at its southern end.

Over the quiet Easter weekend of 2015, in a heist worthy of a Hollywood film, thieves using a stolen industrial-sized diamond-tipped drill cut through a 50cm reinforced-concrete wall to break into the basement vault of a safe-deposit company here. They escaped with an estimated £60 million of loot.

CRAFT CENTRAL
ARTS & CRAFTS

Map p458 (www.craftcentral.org.uk; 33-35 St John's Sq, EC1M; ⊖Farringdon) Headquarters for a not-for-profit organisation supporting local craftspeople and designers, Craft Central has a small shop showcasing work from a different artisan every week. The real trick is to time your visit with one of the biannual Made In Clerkenwell open days (admission £3), when more than 100 designers open up their workshops and sell their wares.

SUPER MARKET SUNDAY

Head to the East End on a Sunday and it can feel as though you can't move for markets. Starting at Columbia Road Flower Market (p226) in East London and working your way south via Brick Lane and its Sunday UpMarket (p219) to Old Spitalfields Market (p220) makes for a colourful consumerist crawl.

LABOUR & WAIT
HOMEWARES

Map p458 (www.labourandwait.co.uk; 85 Redchurch St, E2; ⊙11am-6pm Tue-Sun; ⊖Shoreditch High St) Dedicated to simple and functional, yet scrumptiously stylish, traditional British and European homewares, Labour & Wait specialises in items by independent manufacturers who make their products the old-fashioned way. Browse shaving soaps, enamel coffee pots, luxurious lambswool blankets, elegant ostrich-feather dusters and even kitchen sinks.

ABSOLUTE VINTAGE
VINTAGE

Map p458 (☏020-7247 3883; www.absolute vintage.co.uk; 15 Hanbury St, E1; ⊙11am-7pm; ⊖Liverpool St) As well as the secondhand clothes for men and women, check out the mammoth vintage shoe collection here. There are colours and sizes for all, with footwear ranging from designer to something out of your grandparents' storage.

🏃 SPORTS & ACTIVITIES

JUNKYARD GOLF
MINIGOLF

Map p458 (www.junkyardgolfclub.co.uk; 91 Brick Lane, E1; per person £9.50; ⊙4-11pm Mon-Thu, from noon Fri-Sun; ⊖Shoreditch High St) Based in the Old Truman Brewery (p207) – a graffiti-covered warehouse – Junkyard Golf has four minigolf courses, each with nine holes, and all themed around, well, junk. The four bars ensure you won't go thirsty, and streetfood traders are on hand with cheese toasties, hot dogs and nachos. Children under 18 allowed Sunday to Wednesday till 7pm only.

East London & Docklands

WAPPING | WHITECHAPEL | BETHNAL GREEN | DALSTON | HACKNEY | BOW & MILE END | LIMEHOUSE | ISLE OF DOGS | ROYAL VICTORIA DOCKS | LOWER LEA VALLEY | DE BEAUVOIR TOWN | ENTERTAINMENT | SHOPPING | SPORTS & ACTIVITIES

Neighbourhood Top Five

❶ Columbia Road Flower Market (p226) Stopping to smell the roses amid the bedlam and barrow-boy banter of London's most fragrant market.

❷ Queen Elizabeth Olympic Park (p232) Reliving Games memories among extensive parklands dotted wtih interesting architec-ture, sports centres and even an urban beach.

❸ Broadway Market (p242) Strolling along the Regent's Canal, feasting from a market stall, perusing the stores and then staking a place at one of the pubs.

❹ Museum of London Docklands (p229) Discovering the city's maritime past amidst the ultramodern tower blocks of the Isle of Dogs.

❺ Whitechapel Gallery (p225) Musing over edgy exhibitions at a gallery with a reputation for championing fresh new talent.

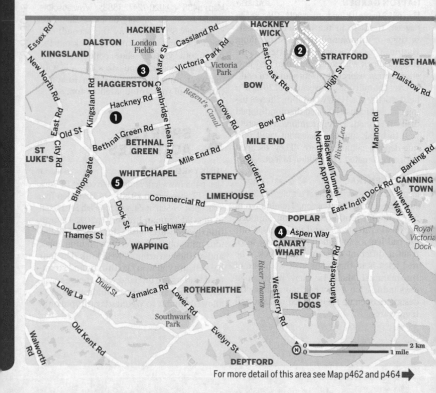

For more detail of this area see Map p462 and p464 ➡

Explore East London & Docklands

East London doesn't really have what you might call blockbuster sights, and the main attractions are quite spread out. It includes the heart of the old East End (Whitechapel, Bethnal Green, Stepney, Mile End, Bow) and most of London's historic Docklands (Wapping, Limehouse, the Isle of Dogs, Royal Victoria Docks), along with gritty but hip Hackney and Dalston to the north, and Stratford further east.

Your best bet is to head to a sight that interests you and then spend some time exploring the surrounding neighbourhood before popping back on public transport to visit the next place. Time your visit to Bethnal Green for a Sunday so that you can experience the flower market before heading to the Museum of Childhood. Save strolling around the cluster of sights at Queen Elizabeth Olympic Park for a sunny day.

Local Life

➡ **Picnics** On sunny Saturdays, East Londoners of all stripes grab goodies from Broadway Market (p242) and head to London Fields (p227) for a picnic and a dip in the Lido.

➡ **Gallery** With free admission and no permanent collection, there's always something new to check out at Whitechapel Gallery (p225).

➡ **Old-style caffs** The spirit of the pre-war East End survives in ungentrified eateries such as E Pellicci (p233) and F Cooke (p236).

Getting There & Away

➡ **Underground** Three lines cut straight through the East End: the Central Line (stopping at Bethnal Green, Mile End and Stratford) and the conjoined District and Hammersmith & City Lines (Whitechapel, Mile End).

➡ **Overground** Trains play a bigger part in the network here than they do in other parts of London, with three main lines and stops in Wapping, Whitechapel, Bethnal Green, London Fields, Dalston, Hackney, Hackney Wick and Stratford.

➡ **DLR** Starting at Tower Gateway or Bank, the DLR provides a scenic link to Limehouse and the Isle of Dogs, as well as joining the dots with Stratford.

➡ **Bus** The 277 bus (Highbury Corner to the Isle of Dogs) is handy for Victoria Park.

Lonely Planet's Top Tip

The most relaxed way to explore East London is along the water. Cyclists and pedestrians can drop to Regent's Canal at the bottom of Broadway Market and follow the waterway to Limehouse. Branching east at Victoria Park, the Hertford Union Canal delivers you to Hackney Wick and Olympic Park. From Limehouse Basin you can also pick up the Thames Path and follow it to St Katharine Docks.

✗ Best Places to Eat

➡ Corner Room (p234)
➡ Berber & Q (p235)
➡ Towpath (p235)
➡ Yuu Kitchen (p233)
➡ Typing Room (p234)

For reviews, see p233.➡

🍷 Best Places to Drink

➡ Netil360 (p240)
➡ High Water (p238)
➡ Satan's Whiskers (p238)
➡ Cat & Mutton (p239)
➡ Dove Freehouse (p239)

For reviews, see p237.➡

◉ Best Places for Local History

➡ Museum of London Docklands (p229)
➡ Sutton House (p227)
➡ Ragged School Museum (p229)
➡ Hackney Museum (p227)
➡ House Mill (p232)

WORTH A DETOUR

CABLE STREET

Cutting a line between Wapping and Whitechapel, Cable St takes its name from the use of the length of the thoroughfare to twist hemp rope into ships' cables (similarly named, the shorter and narrower Twine Ct runs south from here). It's most famous for the Battle of Cable St (1936), in which the British fascist Oswald Mosley planned to march a bunch of his blackshirts into the area, supposedly as a celebration of the fourth anniversary of the British Union of Fascists. Although pockets of fascist supporters existed in the East End, the march was successfully repelled by local people – over 100,000 Jews, communists, dockers, trade unionists and other ordinary East Enders turned out in solidarity against them. At No 236 you'll find the old St George's Town Hall, its west wall completely covered in a large, vibrant **mural** commemorating the riots.

The church just behind this building is **St George-in-the-East**, erected by Nicholas Hawksmoor in 1729 and badly damaged in the Blitz. All that now remains is the tower and exterior walls, enclosing a smaller modern core.

⊙ SIGHTS

⊙ Wapping

Once notorious for slave traders, drunk sailors and prostitutes, the towering early-19th-century warehouses of Wapping (pronounced 'whopping') still give an atmospheric picture of the area's previous existence.

Although there's nothing to actually mark it, down on the riverside below Wapping New Stairs (near the marine police station) was Execution Dock, where convicted pirates were hanged and their bodies chained in a gibbet at low tide, to be left until three tides had washed over their heads. Among the more famous people who died this way was Captain William Kidd, hanged here in 1701, and whose grisly tale you can read about in the nearby Captain Kidd (p237) pub.

ST KATHARINE DOCKS   HARBOUR
Map p462 (☑020-7264 5287; www.skdocks.
co.uk; 50 St Katharine's Way, E1; ⊖Tower Hill)
Sitting in the shadow of Tower Bridge, this once-booming part of London's Docklands was built in 1828 by engineer-extraordinaire Thomas Telford. To make way for it, 1250 'insanitary' houses were razed and 11,300 people made homeless. The dock was badly bombed during WWII and was finally abandoned altogether in 1968. Its current incarnation, as a marina for luxury yachts, surrounded by cafes, restaurants and twee shops, dates from the 1980s.

It's the perfect starting point for a stroll along the Thames Path to Wapping and Limehouse.

ST GEORGE-IN-THE-EAST   CHURCH
Map p462 (☑020-7481 1345; www.stgeorge
intheeast.org; 16 Cannon St Rd, E1; ⓢShadwell
DLR) This church was erected by Nicholas Hawksmoor in 1729 and badly damaged in the Blitz. All that now remains is a shell enclosing a smaller modern core.

CABLE STREET MURAL   PUBLIC ART
Map p462 (236 Cable St, E1; ⓢDLR Shadwell)
Painted on the side of the former St George's Town Hall (now a library), this large mural commemorates the riots that took place here in October 1936 when the British fascist Oswald Mosley led a bunch of his blackshirt thugs into the area to intimidate the local Jewish population. They were repelled by local people – Jews and non-Jews alike.

⊙ Whitechapel

WHITECHAPEL ROAD   STREET
Map p462 (E1; ⊖Whitechapel) The East End's main thoroughfare hums with a constant cacophony of Asian, African, European and Middle Eastern languages, its busy shops and market stalls selling everything from Indian snacks to Nigerian fabrics and Turkish jewellery, as the area's multitudinous ethnic groupings rub up against each other more or less comfortably. It's a chaotic and poor place, but it's full of life.

Within a few minutes' walk of Whitechapel tube station you'll pass the enormous East London Mosque (p226). Behind it, on Fieldgate St, is oversized Tower House (p225) – once a hostel and then a dosshouse, but now a redeveloped apartment block. Past residents include Joseph Stalin and authors Jack London and George Orwell. The latter described it in detail in *Down and Out in Paris and London* (1933).

Whitechurch Rd morphs into Mile End Rd at the intersection with Cambridge Heath Rd, but just before it does you'll find the Blind Beggar (p225). William Booth, the founder of the Salvation Army, preached his first streetside sermon outside this pub in 1865; there's a statue (p225) to his memory near the beginning of Mile End Rd. The pub is also famous as the place where notorious gangster Ronnie Kray shot and killed George Cornell in 1966 during a turf war over control of the East End's organised crime. He was jailed for life and died in 1995.

It's worth strolling 150m along Mile End Rd to take a look at the Trinity Green Almshouses (p225). Built for injured or retired sailors in 1695, the two rows of almshouses run at right angles away from the street, facing a lawn and a central chapel with a clock tower.

TRINITY GREEN ALMSHOUSES
HISTORIC BUILDING

Map p462 (Mile End Rd, E1; ⊖Whitechapel) These poorhouses were built for injured or retired sailors in 1695. The two rows of almshouses run at right angles away from the street, facing a village-type green and a chapel with a clock tower.

BLIND BEGGAR
HISTORIC BUILDING

Map p462 (337 Whitechapel Rd, E1; ⊖Whitechapel) William Booth, the founder of the Salvation Army, preached his first streetside sermon outside this pub in 1865. It's also famous as the place where notorious gangster Ronnie Kray shot and killed George Cornell in 1966 during a turf war over control of the East End's organised crime. Kray was jailed for life and died in 1995.

WILLIAM BOOTH STATUE
MONUMENT

Map p462 (Mile End Rd; ⊖Whitechapel) A statue of the Salvation Army founder, erected near the place where he gave his first streetside sermon.

EAST LONDON & DOCKLANDS SIGHTS

TOP SIGHT
WHITECHAPEL GALLERY

A firm favourite of art students and the avant-garde cognoscenti, this ground-breaking gallery doesn't have a permanent collection but instead is devoted to hosting edgy exhibitions of contemporary art (only some of which are ticketed). It first opened the doors of its main art-nouveau building in 1901 and in 2009 it extended into the library next door, doubling its exhibition space to 10 galleries.

Founded by Victorian philanthropist Canon Samuel Barnett to bring art to the East End, the gallery made its name staging exhibitions by both established and emerging artists, including the first UK shows by Pablo Picasso (whose *Guernica* was exhibited here in 1939), Jackson Pollock, Mark Rothko, Frida Kahlo and Nan Goldin. British artists David Hockney and Gilbert & George also debuted here.

The gallery's ambitiously themed shows change every couple of months and there's often live music, poetry readings, talks and films on Thursday evenings. It also co-sponsors several awards, including the Max Mara Art Prize for UK-based female artists and the Jarman Awards for artists working with moving images.

DON'T MISS

➜ Rachel Whiteread's frieze of gilded leaves on the art-nouveau facade
➜ Bookshop

PRACTICALITIES

➜ Map p462, B5
➜ ☎020-7522 7888
➜ www.whitechapelgallery.org
➜ 77-82 Whitechapel High St, E1
➜ admission free
➜ ⊙11am-6pm Tue, Wed & Fri-Sun, to 9pm Thu
➜ ⌖
➜ ⊖Aldgate East

TOWER HOUSE
NOTABLE BUILDING

Map p462 (81 Fieldgate St, E1; ⊝Whitechapel) This enormous building, now redeveloped as an apartment block, was once a hostel and then a dosshouse. Past residents include Joseph Stalin and authors Jack London and George Orwell. The latter describes it in detail in his *Down and Out in Paris and London* (1933).

EAST LONDON MOSQUE
MOSQUE

Map p462 (☎020-7650 3000; www.eastlondon mosque.org.uk; 46-92 Whitechapel Rd, E1; ☺10am-10pm; ⊝Whitechapel) This large mosque is capped with a dome and one large and two smaller minarets, each topped with a crescent moon. The exterior is relatively unadorned except for some accents in blue tile. Unless you're coming to pray, visits should be pre-arranged.

⊙ Bethnal Green

★COLUMBIA ROAD FLOWER MARKET
MARKET

Map p462 (www.columbiaroad.info; Columbia Rd, E2; ☺8am-3pm Sun; ⊝Hoxton) A wonderful explosion of colour and life, this weekly market sells a beautiful array of flowers, pot plants, bulbs, seeds and everything you might need for the garden. It's a lot of fun and the best place to hear proper Cockney barrow-boy banter ('We got flowers cheap enough for ya muvver-in-law's grave' etc). It gets really packed, so go as early as you can, or later on when the vendors sell off the cut flowers cheaply.

V&A MUSEUM OF CHILDHOOD
MUSEUM

Map p462 (☎020-8983 5200; www.museum ofchildhood.org.uk; Cambridge Heath Rd, E2; ☺10am-5.45pm; ♿; ⊝Bethnal Green) FREE Housed in a purpose-built Victorian-era building, this branch of the Victoria & Albert Museum (p178) is aimed at both kids (with play areas, interactive exhibits and dressing-up boxes) and nostalgic grown-ups who come to admire the antique toys. From teddies, doll's houses and dolls to Meccano, Lego and computer games, it's a wonderful toy-cupboard trip down memory lane.

HACKNEY CITY FARM
FARM

Map p462 (www.hackneycityfarm.co.uk; 1a Goldsmiths Row, E2; ☺10am-4.30pm Tue-Sun; ⊝Hoxton) FREE If there's a less bucolic landscape than Hackney Rd, we can't imagine it. All the more reason to bring a slice of the country to kids who have only ever known eggs to have come from a supermarket. There are plenty of animals to pat and, after ap-

---

A HERO RISES IN THE EAST

Daniel Mendoza (1764–1836), the father of 'scientific boxing' who billed himself as 'Mendoza the Jew', was the first bare-knuckle boxer to employ strategy and speed in the ring. Mendoza was born in Aldgate and left school at age 13, taking odd jobs as a porter, being taunted as an outsider and getting into scrapes. He was eventually discovered by 'gentleman boxer' Richard Humphreys, 20 years his senior, who took him under his wing and started him training. Mendoza developed a style of fighting in direct opposition to the norm of the day, where two fighters would stand face to face and slug it out until one collapsed.

Mendoza began a highly successful career in the ring, but eventually fell out with his mentor. His most infamous fight came during a grudge match in 1788 with Humphreys. Just as Mendoza was about to administer the coup de grâce, Humphreys' second grabbed Mendoza's arm, a moment caught in a contemporary print called *Foul Play* on display in the National Portrait Gallery. Mendoza went on to fight Humphreys fairly two more times, emerging the victor and moral superior.

Mendoza was the first sportsman in Britain to achieve cult status – a veritable David Beckham of 18th-century London. He made (and lost) a fortune, wrote his memoirs and a how-to book called *The Art of Boxing*, mixed with the high and mighty (including royalty) and sold branded trinkets and images of himself. Most importantly he advanced the cause of Jews in a country that had only allowed them back the century before. People learned for the first time that a Jew could and would fight back – and win.

227

propriate hand washing, a cafe serving homemade gelato.

◉ Dalston

RIDLEY ROAD MARKET   MARKET
Map p462 (www.hackney.gov.uk/ridley-road-market; Ridley Rd, E8; ⊙9.30am-5pm Mon-Sat; ⊜Dalston Kingsland) Massively popular with the ethnically diverse community it serves, this market is best for its exotic fruit and vegetables, whole fish and colourful fabrics. You'll also find the usual assortment of plastic tat, cheap clothing and joss sticks.

DALSTON EASTERN CURVE GARDENS   GARDENS
Map p462 (www.dalstongarden.org; 13 Dalston Lane, E8; ⊙11am-7pm Sun-Thu, to 10pm Fri & Sat; ⊜Dalston Junction) FREE This garden is typical of the kind of grassroots regeneration happening around Dalston: a project led by the community, for the community – and a roaring success. There's a simple cafe and regular workshops and events, from gardening sessions to acoustic music. It's a nice place to rest your legs or to meet friendly locals.

The site used to be a derelict railway line and old sleepers have been used to make a boardwalk and raised beds for the veggie patch. Sadly a question mark hangs over the garden's future as there are plans to redevelop the neighbouring shopping centre.

◉ Hackney

SUTTON HOUSE   HISTORIC BUILDING
Map p462 (NT; ☑020-8986 2264; www.nationaltrust.org.uk/sutton-house; 2-4 Homerton High St, E9; adult/child £5.40/2.75; ⊙noon-5pm Wed-Sun, daily Aug, closed Jan; ⊜Hackney Central) It would be quite possible to walk straight past this relatively inconspicuous brick house without noticing its great age. Originally known as Bryk Place, it was built in 1535 by Sir Ralph Sadleir, a prominent courtier of Henry VIII, when Hackney was still a village. Highlights include the Linenfold Parlour, where the Tudor oak panelling on the walls has been carved to resemble draped cloth; the panelled Great Chamber; the Victorian study; and the Georgian parlour.

Abandoned and taken over by squatters in the 1980s, Sutton House could have been lost to history. Enter the National Trust, which has set about conserving and pre-

serving it – including some of the squatters' artwork upstairs. The house is also used by community groups for language classes and music therapy.

VIKTOR WYND MUSEUM OF CURIOSITIES, FINE ART & NATURAL HISTORY   MUSEUM
Map p462 (www.thelasttuesdaysociety.org; 11 Mare St, E8; £5; ⊙noon-11pm Wed-Sun; ⊜Bethnal Green) Museum? Art project? Cocktail bar? This is not a venue that's easily classifiable. Inspired by Victorian-era cabinets of curiosities (wunderkabinnet), Wynd's wilfully eccentric collection includes stuffed birds, pickled genitals, two-headed lambs, shrunken heads, a key to the Garden of Eden, dodo bones, celebrity excrement and a gilded hippo skull which belonged to Pablo Escobar. A self-confessed 'incoherent vision of the world displayed through wonder', make of it what you will. Or stop by for a cocktail at the bar upstairs.

A subjective and thought-provoking collection, it's an admirable and frequently illuminating attempt to convey the wonder and horrors of the natural world. There are also exhibitions, lectures and taxidermy workshops. You must be over 21 to enter.

ST AUGUSTINE'S TOWER   CHURCH
Map p462 (☑020-8986 0029; www.hhbt.org.uk; Mare St, E8; ⊜Hackney Central) Set at the edge of the beautiful St John's Churchyard Gardens, this 13th-century tower is the oldest building in Hackney and the only remains of a church that was demolished in 1798. The tower's 135 steps can be climbed on occasional open days; see the website for details.

HACKNEY MUSEUM   MUSEUM
Map p462 (☑020-8356 3500; www.hackney.gov.uk/museum; 1 Reading Lane, E8; ⊙9.30am-5.30pm Tue, Wed, Fri & Sat, to 8pm Thu; ⊜Hackney Central) FREE Devoted to items relating to Hackneyites past and present, this interesting little museum is as diverse as the ethnically mixed community it serves. Most exhibits are everyday things used by everyday people, but more unusual items include a 1000-year-old Saxon log boat and a coin from the 'Hackney hoard'. This was one of 160 gold coins discovered in 2007 after being hidden by a Jewish family who moved to Hackney to escape the Nazis, only to die in the Blitz.

EAST LONDON & DOCKLANDS SIGHTS

LONDON FIELDS PARK

Map p462 (Richmond Rd, E8; ⊜London Fields) A strip of green in an increasingly hip part of Hackney, London Fields is where locals hang out after a meander up Broadway Market (p242). The park also has two children's play areas, a decent pub and the London Fields Lido (p243).

◉ Bow & Mile End

VICTORIA PARK PARK

Map p462 (www.towerhamlets.gov.uk/victoria park; Grove Rd, E3; ⊙7am-dusk; ⊜Hackney Wick) The 'Regent's Park of the East End', this 86-hectare leafy expanse of ornamental lakes, monuments, tennis courts, flower beds and lawns was opened in 1845. It was the first public park in the East End, given the go-ahead after a local MP presented Queen Victoria with a petition of 30,000 signatures. It quickly gained a reputation as the 'People's Park' when many rallies were held here. Large public events still occur, including the annual Lovebox and Field Day music festivals.

During WWII the park was largely closed to the public and was used as a base for antiaircraft guns and as an internment camp for Italian and then German prisoners of war.

MILE END PARK PARK

Map p462 (www.towerhamlets.gov.uk/mileend park; ⊜Mile End) The 36-hectare Mile End Park is a long, narrow series of interconnected green spaces wedged between Burdett and Grove Rds and Regent's Canal. Landscaped to great effect during the millennium year, it incorporates a go-kart track, a skate park, an ecology area, a climbing wall and a sports stadium. The centrepiece, though, is architect Piers Gough's plant-covered Green Bridge linking the northern and southern sections of the park over busy Mile End Rd.

TOWER HAMLETS
CEMETERY PARK CEMETERY

Map p462 (www.fothcp.org; Southern Grove, E3; ⊜Mile End) Opened in 1841 this 13-hectare cemetery was the last of the 'Magnificent Seven': suburban cemeteries (including Highgate and Abney Park) created by an act of Parliament in response to London's rapid population growth. Some 270,000 souls were laid to rest here until the cemetery was closed to burials in 1966 and

---

CANARY WHARF DEVELOPMENT

You'd probably never guess it while gazing up at the skyscrapers that dominate Canary Wharf, but from the 16th century until the mid-20th century, this area was the centre of the world's greatest port, making it the hub of the British Empire and its enormous global trade. At the docks here, cargo was landed from around the world, bringing jobs to a tight-knit working-class community. Even up to the start of WWII this community still thrived, but that all changed when the docks were badly firebombed during the Blitz.

After the war the docks were in no condition to cope with the postwar technological and political changes as the British Empire evaporated. At the same time enormous new bulk carriers and container ships demanded deep-water ports and new loading and unloading techniques. From the mid-1960s, dock closures followed one another as fast as they had opened, and the number of dock workers dropped from as many as 50,000 in 1960 to about 3000 by 1980.

The financial district that exists at Canary Wharf today was begun by the London Docklands Development Corporation, a body established by the Thatcher government in the freewheeling 1980s to take pressure for office space off the City. This rather artificial enclave had a shaky start. The low-rise toytown buildings had trouble attracting tenants, the Docklands Light Railway – the main transport link – had teething troubles, and the landmark One Canary Wharf tower had to be rescued from bankruptcy twice. Now, however, the place swarms during the working week with dark-suited office workers en route to their desks in the sky.

---

turned into a park and local nature reserve

TOP SIGHT
MUSEUM OF LONDON DOCKLANDS

Housed in an 1802 warehouse, this museum combines artefacts and multimedia displays to chart the city's history through its river and docks. The best strategy is to begin on the 3rd floor in the introductory **No. 1 Warehouse** section and work your way down through the ages. The **Trade Expansion** gallery includes a reconstructed late-18th-century Legal Quay and an iron gibbet once used to display the bodies of executed pirates. The most illuminating and disturbing gallery is **London, Sugar & Slavery**, which examines the city's role in the transatlantic slave trade.

Highlights of the second floor include **Sailortown**, a re-creation of the cobbled streets, bars and lodging houses of a mid-19th-century dockside community. There are also fascinating displays about the docks during the world wars and their controversial transformation into London's second financial district during the 1980s.

There's lots for kids to enjoy, including the hands-on **Mudlarks** gallery, where children can explore the Thames' history, tip the clipper, try on old-fashioned diving helmets and construct a simple model of Canary Wharf.

The museum stages special exhibitions every few months, for which there is usually a charge.

DON'T MISS
➡ Sailortown
➡ London, Sugar & Slavery
➡ Docklands at War
➡ New Port New City

PRACTICALITIES
➡ Map p464, A1
➡ ☏020-7001 9844
➡ www.museumof london.org.uk/ docklands
➡ West India Quay, E14
➡ admission free
➡ ⏲10am-6pm
➡ 🛜
➡ ❒DLR West India Quay

---

in 2001. Today it's an eerily beautiful site, its crumbling Victorian monuments draped in ever-encroaching greenery.

RAGGED SCHOOL MUSEUM MUSEUM
Map p462 (☏020-8980 6405; www.ragged schoolmuseum.org.uk; 46-50 Copperfield Rd, E3; ⏲10am-5pm Wed & Thu, 2-5pm 1st Sun of month; ❒Mile End) FREE Both adults and children are inevitably charmed by this combination of mock Victorian schoolroom (with hard wooden benches and desks, slates, chalk, inkwells and abacuses), re-created East End kitchen and social-history museum. The school closed in 1908, but you can experience what it would have been like during its Sunday openings, when you can take part in a lesson. As a pupil you'll be taught reading, writing and 'rithmetic by a strict school ma'am in full Victorian regalia.

The museum celebrates the legacy of Dr Thomas Barnardo, who founded this school for destitute East End children in 1877. 'Ragged' refers to the pupils' usually torn, dirty and dishevelled clothes. Sunday lessons take place at 2.15pm and 3.30pm (donations requested).

◉ Limehouse

There isn't much to Limehouse, although it became the centre of London's Chinese community – its first Chinatown – after 300 sailors settled here in 1890. It gets a mention in Oscar Wilde's *The Picture of Dorian Gray* (1891), when the protagonist passes by this way in search of opium.

ST ANNE'S LIMEHOUSE CHURCH
Map p462 (☏020-7987 1502; www.stanneslime house.org; Commercial Rd, E14; ⏲services only; ❒DLR Westferry) Nicholas Hawksmoor's earliest church (built 1714–27) still boasts the highest church clock in the city. In fact, the 60m-high tower was until recently a 'Trinity House mark' for navigation on the Thames, which is why it often flies the Royal Navy's white ensign.

◎ Isle of Dogs

This odd protuberance on a loop in the Thames, made an island by various dock basins and canals, is completely dominated by the cluster of tower blocks at Canary Wharf. Londoners are divided on their opinion of this area – despite its perceived soullessness, its radical redevelopment is certainly impressive.

The centrepiece is Cesar Pelli's One Canada Square (p230) building. It's surrounded by more recent towers housing a wealth of financial giants.

Etymologists are still out to lunch over the origin of the island's name. Some believe it relates to the royal kennels, which were located here during the reign of Henry VIII. Others maintain it's a corruption of the Flemish word *dijk* (dyke), recalling the Flemish engineers who shored up the area's muddy banks.

MUDCHUTE   FARM
Map p464 (☑020-7515 5901; www.mudchute.org; Pier St, E14; ☻9am-5pm; ⓕ; ⛟DLR Mudchute) ✎**FREE** Entering Mudchute Park from East Ferry Rd through the canopy of trees, you're greeted by the surprising sight of cows and sheep roaming in 13 grassy hectares of parkland. There are also pigs, goats, horses, llamas, alpacas, donkeys, ducks, turkeys, chickens...junior city slickers love this place! Looking back to the skyscrapers of Canary Wharf gives you a clear sense of the contrasts of this part of London. There's also a good cafe and a farm shop.

ONE CANADA SQUARE   NOTABLE BUILDING
Map p464 (1 Canada Sq, E14; ☻Canary Wharf) Cesar Pelli's pyramid-capped 235m-high skyscraper was built in 1991, and was the UK's tallest building when it opened in 1991 – a title it held until 2010 when the Shard knocked it off its perch.

◎ Royal Victoria Docks

THE CRYSTAL   MUSEUM
Map p462 (www.thecrystal.org; 1 Siemens Brothers Way, E16; adult/child £8/free; ☻10am-5pm Tue-Sat; ⛟DLR Royal Victoria) ✎ Although at times it does come over like an expensive advertisement for technology firm Siemens – whose groundbreaking sustainable building it inhabits – the Crystal's highly interactive displays on urban sustainability and the pressures facing the modern city are thoroughly engaging. There's also a cafe, with views over Royal Victoria Dock. You can tie it in with a cable-car (p230) journey across the river to North Greenwich.

EMIRATES AIR LINE   CABLE CAR
Map p462 (www.emiratesairline.co.uk; 27 Western Gateway, E16; one-way adult/child £4.50/2.30, with Oyster Card £3.40/1.70; ☻7am-10pm Mon-Fri, 9am-10pm Sat & Sun; ☻North Greenwich) Capable of ferrying 2400 people per hour across the Thames in either direction, this cable car makes quick work of the journey from the Greenwich Peninsula to the Royal Docks. Although it's mostly patronised by tourists for the views over the river – and the views are ace – it's also listed on the London Underground map as part of the transport network, meaning you can pay with your Oyster Card and nab a discount while you're at it.

BILLINGSGATE FISH MARKET   MARKET
Map p462 (☑020-7987 1118; www.billingsgatefishmarket.org; Trafalgar Way, E14; ☻4-8am Tue-Sat; ⛟DLR Blackwall) This wholesale fish market is open to the public, but you'll have to be up at the crack of dawn to see it in action. Formally established in 1699 in the City between London Bridge and the Tower, the market moved to Poplar in 1982 and currently sells 25,000 tonnes of seafood annually.

◎ Lower Lea Valley

From the mills of Cistercian monks in the 1st century to the Stratford railway hub of the 1880s (from which goods from the Thames were transported all over Britain), the tidal Lower Lea Valley had long been the source of what Londoners required to fuel their industries. However, before building work on the Queen Elizabeth Olympic Park began in 2008, this vast area of East London had become derelict, polluted and largely ignored.

Creating world-class sporting facilities for the 2012 Olympic Games was at the forefront of this area's redevelopment, but this was well balanced with the aim of regenerating the area for generations to come. More than 30 new bridges were built to criss-cross the River Lea. Waterways in and around the park were upgraded, with waste

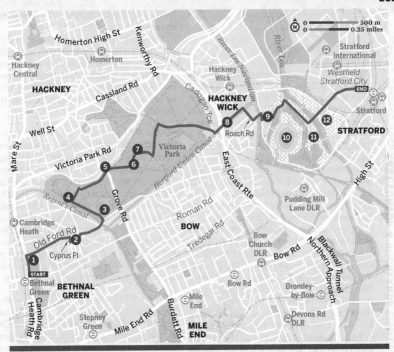

Neighbourhood Walk
East End Eras

START BETHNAL GREEN STATION
END STRATFORD STATION
LENGTH 3.6 MILES, 2½ HOURS

This route offers an insight into the old and new of East London. Exit the tube station towards the ❶ **Museum of Childhood** (p226). Just past the museum, turn right into Old Ford Rd, then continue to Cyprus Pl and turn right. The surrounding area was heavily bombed during WWII and the many tower blocks were subsequently erected on the bomb sites. As you turn left into beautifully preserved ❷ **Cyprus St** you'll get a taste of what Victorian Bethnal Green would have looked like. At the end of the street turn left then right, back onto Old Ford Rd. Just over Regent's Canal lies ❸ **Victoria Park** (p228). Take the path on the left along the lake until you reach the ❹ **Dogs of Alciabiades** howling on plinths. Turn right here and then right again at the next gate. When you reach the ornate wrought-iron gates, cross the road and enter the eastern section of the park near the ❺ **Royal Inn**

(p240). Veer right for a look at the neo-Gothic ❻ **Burdett-Coutts Memorial** (1862), a former public fountain that was a gift of Angela Burdett-Coutts, once the richest woman in England and a prominent philanthropist. From here, ramble on past ❼ **East Lake** to the park's eastern tip and exit via St Mark's Gate. Cross Cadogan Tce and join the much-graffitied ❽ **canal path**. This area is Hackney Wick, home to a warren of warehouses and a community of artists. Cross the canal at the metal footbridge with the big hoop, continue onto Roach Rd and then turn left to cross the bridge and enter ❾ **Queen Elizabeth Olympic Park** (p232). Keeping the main ❿ **stadium** on your right, cross the River Lea and walk through the playground towards the tangled tentacles of the ⓫ **ArcelorMittal Orbit** (p232). Turn left, cross the bridge and examine the elegant curves of the ⓬ **London Aquatics Centre** (p243). From here you can either head straight on to Stratford Station or continue following the river north to explore the park's wetlands and the Lee Valley VeloPark.

cleared and contaminated soil cleaned on a massive scale.

★QUEEN ELIZABETH
OLYMPIC PARK   PARK
Map p462 (www.queenelizabetholympicpark.
co.uk; E20; ⊖Stratford) The glittering centre-piece of London's 2012 Olympic Games, this vast 227-hectare expanse includes the main Olympic venues as well as playgrounds, walking and cycling trails, gardens, and a diverse mix of wetland, woodland, meadow and other wildlife habitats as an environmentally fertile legacy for the future. The main focal point is London Stadium (p232), with a Games capacity of 80,000, scaled back to 54,000 seats for its new role as the home ground for West Ham United FC.

Other signature buildings include the London Aquatics Centre (p243), Lee Valley VeloPark (p243), ArcelorMittal Orbit (p232) and the Copper Box Arena (p241), a 6000-seat indoor venue for sports and concerts. Then there's the BeachEast (p232), an artificial sandy beach on the River Lea, and **Here East**, a vast 'digital campus' covering an area equivalent to 16 football fields.

For a different perspective on the park, or if you're feeling lazy, take a tour through its waterways with Lee & Stort Boats (p243).

ARCELORMITTAL ORBIT   TOWER
Map p462 (📞0333 800 8099; www.arcelormittal orbit.com; 3 Thornton St, E20; adult/child £12/6, with slide £17/11; ⊙11am-5pm; ⊖Stratford) Love it or loathe it, Turner Prize–winner Anish Kapoor's 115m-high, twisted-steel sculpture towers strikingly over the southern end of Queen Elizabeth Olympic Park. In essence it's an artwork, but at the 80m mark it also offers an impressive panorama from its mirrored viewing platform, which is accessed by a lift from the base of the sculpture (the tallest in the UK). A dramatic tunnel slide running down the tower is the world's highest and longest, coiling 178m down to ground level.

Descend 4m (via a caged external staircase) from the platform for more vistas, interpretative screens and an outside section. From here, you can opt to skip down 455 steps to the ground (accompanied by soundscapes of London) or hop back in the lift. Alternatively, weave your way down on the superb tunnel slide (worth the extra £5), which takes 40 seconds to get you back

down. For further thrills, take a **free-fall abseil** off the tower (£85, book ahead).

The tower has had its share of critics, with the *Daily Mail* likening it to a collision between two cranes. London's former mayor Boris Johnson famously described it as a giant hubble-bubble pipe (we think he means a shisha water pipe) and so the 'hubble-bubble tower' it is.

HOUSE MILL   HISTORIC BUILDING
Map p462 (📞020-8980 4626; www.housemill.
org.uk; Three Mill Lane, E3; adult/child £3/free; ⊙11am-4pm Sun May-Oct, 1st Sun only Mar, Apr & Dec; ⊖Bromley-by-Bow) One of two remaining mills from a trio that once stood on this small island in the River Lea, House Mill (1776) operated as a sluice tidal mill, grinding grain for a nearby distillery until 1941. Tours, which run according to demand and last about 45 minutes, take visitors to all four floors of the mill and offer a fascinating look at traditional East End industry.

LONDON STADIUM   STADIUM
Map p462 (📞020-8522 6157; www.london stadium.com; Queen Elizabeth Olympic Park, E20; tours adult/child £19/11; ⊙tours 10am-4.15pm; 🚈DLR Pudding Mill Lane) Still known to most Londoners as the Olympic Stadium, this large sports ground is the main focal point of Queen Elizabeth Olympic Park (p232). It had a Games capacity of 80,000, which has been scaled back to 54,000 seats for its new role as the home ground for West Ham United FC. It's also used for athletics and other large sporting events and concerts. When nothing's on, self-guided multimedia tours are available (check the website before heading out).

BEACHEAST   BEACH
Map p462 (www.beacheast.co.uk; Stratford Waterfront, E20; adult/child £2/1; ⊙10am-10pm late Jul–early Sep; ⊖Stratford) One thousand tons of sand dumped onto Queen Elizabeth Olympic Park gets you the largest city beach in the UK, so sharpen up your sandcastle-making skills and then sink a chilled *cuba libra* at the bar to toast your efforts. With funfair rides (£2 to £4), a vast kids' paddling pool, events and beach sports, it only opens for the hottest weeks – and longest days – of summer.

EATING

East London's multiculturalism has ensured that its ethnic cuisine stretches far and wide, with some fantastic low-key eateries serving authentic and value-for-money fare. But the area's gentrification has introduced a slew of gastropubs and some more upmarket restaurants, too. Excellent coffee shops have sprouted up all over the East End, though you can still – if you must – find plenty of greasy-spoon caffs, or a traditional pie with mash and liquor (parsley sauce). Places to head if you want to sniff out your own favourites include Columbia Rd, Broadway Market and the streets just to the north of Victoria Park.

Whitechapel

TAYYABS PUNJABI $

Map p462 (☑020-7247 9543; www.tayyabs.co.uk; 83-89 Fieldgate St, E1; mains £5.60-16; ☺noon-11.30pm; ☑; ☻Whitechapel) This buzzing (OK, crowded) Punjabi restaurant is in another league to its Brick Lane equivalents. *Seekh* kebabs (tandoor-cooked mince skewers), masala fish and other starters served on sizzling hot plates are delicious, as are accompaniments such as dhal, naan and raita. On the downside, it can be noisy, service can be haphazard and queues often snake out the door.

★YUU KITCHEN ASIAN $$

Map p462 (☑020-7377 0411; www.yuukitchen. com; 29 Commercial St, E1; dishes £4.50-8.50; ☺5.30pm-late Mon & Tue, noon-2.30pm & 5.30pm-late Wed-Fri, noon-4pm & 5.30pm-late Sat & Sun; ☑; ☻Aldgate East) Manga images pout on the walls and birdcages dangle from the ceiling at this fun, relaxed eatery. Dishes are either bite-sized or designed to be shared, and while the focus is mainly Asian, some dishes from further along the Pacific Rim pop up too. Hence Hawaiian *poke* (raw fish) sits alongside Vietnamese rolls and showstopping *bao* (Taiwanese steamed buns).

CAFÉ SPICE NAMASTÉ INDIAN $$

Map p462 (☑020-7488 9242; www.cafespice. co.uk; 16 Prescot St, E1; mains £7-25; ☺noon-3pm & 6.15-10.30pm Mon-Fri, 6.30-10.30pm Sat; ☑; ☻Tower Hill) TV chef Cyrus Todiwala

has taken an old magistrates court just a 10-minute walk from Tower Hill, decorated it in carnival colours and filled it with fragrant aromas. The Parsi and Goan menu is famous for its superlative *dhansaak* (lamb stew with rice and lentils), but the tandoori and vegetarian dishes are just as good.

Wapping

SMITH'S SEAFOOD $$$

Map p462 (☑020-7488 3456; www.smithsrestaurants.com; 22 Wapping High St, E1; mains £17-39, 2-/3-course lunch £22/27, dinner £25/30; ☺noon-4pm & 6-10.30pm Mon-Sat, noon-5.30pm Sun; ☻Tower Hill) Thames views through floor-to-ceiling windows distract admirably from a slightly dated ambience, as do the wonderful dishes that progress from the kitchen. The menu is enormous and while seafood dominates, there are some meat and vegetarian dishes as well. Mains are served with a choice of chips, salad, mushy peas or seasonal vegetables. Save room for the steamed pudding.

Bethnal Green

E PELLICCI CAFE $

Map p462 (☑020-7739 4873; www.epellicci. com; 332 Bethnal Green Rd, E2; dishes £1.60-9; ☺7am-4pm Mon-Sat; ☻Bethnal Green) Opened in 1900, this diminutive Anglo-Italian caff captures the distilled essence of the old East End. Portions are generous and although the food's nothing special (fry-ups, pasta, sandwiches), the warm welcome and the banter from the gregarious staff and rag-tag collection of local characters crammed around tightly packed tables make it well worth a visit.

GALLERY CAFE VEGETARIAN $

Map p462 (☑020-8980 2092; www.stmargarets house.org.uk; 21 Old Ford Rd, E2; mains £6-9; ☺8am-8pm; ☻☑; ☻Bethnal Green) Set in the basement of a lovely Georgian building, this pretty cafe serves simple but delicious vegan and vegetarian fare to relaxed locals. Sadly the service can be just as relaxed. There's a cute courtyard at the front for sunny days. Check the website for sporadic evening events such as live music, comedy and film nights.

COCKNEY RHYMING SLANG

Traditionally cockneys were people born within earshot of the Bow Bells – the church bells of **St Mary-le-Bow** (p147) on Cheapside. Since few people actually live in the City these days, this definition has broadened to take in those living further east. The term cockney is often used to describe anyone speaking what is also called estuarine English (in which 't' and 'h' are routinely dropped and glottal stops – what the two 't's sound like in 'bottle' – abound).

True cockney speech also uses something called rhyming slang, which may have developed among London's costermongers (street traders) and criminals as a code to avoid police attention. This code replaced common nouns and verbs with rhyming phrases. So 'going up the apples and pears' meant going up the stairs, the 'trouble and strife' was the wife, 'telling porky pies' was telling lies and 'would you Adam and Eve it?' was 'would you believe it?' Over time the second of the two words tended to be dropped so the rhyme vanished.

Few, if any, people still use pure cockney but a good many still understand it. You're more likely to come across it in residual phrases such as 'telling porkies' (lying), 'use your loaf' ('loaf of bread' for head), 'ooh, me plates' ('plates of meat' for feet) or 'me old china' ('china plate' for mate).

★ **CORNER ROOM** MODERN BRITISH **$$**
Map p462 (☑020-7871 0460; www.townhallhotel. com/cornerroom; Patriot Sq, E2; mains £13-14, 2-/3-course lunch £19/23; ⊙7.30-10am, noon-3pm & 6-9.45pm; ☻Bethnal Green) Someone put this baby in the corner, but we're certainly not complaining. Tucked away on the 1st floor of the Town Hall Hotel, this relaxed restaurant serves expertly crafted dishes with complex yet delicate flavours, highlighting the best of British seasonal produce.

BISTROTHEQUE MODERN BRITISH **$$**
Map p462 (☑020-8983 7900; www.bistro theque.com; 23-27 Wadeson St, E2; mains £17-24, 3-course early dinner £25; ⊙6-10.30pm Mon-Fri, 11am-4pm & 6-10.30pm Sat & Sun; ☻Bethnal Green) Aside from being too cool to have a sign, this warehouse conversion ticks all the boxes of a contemporary upmarket London bistro (the name made more sense when there was a club-like cabaret space downstairs). The food and service are uniformly excellent.

PARADISE GARAGE BRITISH **$$**
Map p462 (☑020-7613 1502; www.paradise254. com; 254 Paradise Row, E2; mains £19-20, brunch £9-12; ⊙6-10pm Tue-Fri, 11am-3pm & 6-10pm Sat, 11am-3pm Sun; ☻Bethnal Green) White tiles and dangling bare lightbulbs have transformed this old railway arch into a sharp-looking restaurant, with a menu to match. The kitchen puts an interesting spin on best-of-British produce such as Cornbury Park fallow deer and Welsh lamb. Dishes are beautifully presented and the service is excellent. In summer, tables are set up out the front.

BRAWN EUROPEAN **$$**
Map p462 (☑020-7729 5692; www.brawn.co; 49 Columbia Rd, E2; mains £15-19; ⊙noon-3pm Tue-Sat, 6-10.30pm Mon-Sat, noon-4pm Sun; ☻Hoxton) There's a French feel to this relaxed corner bistro, yet the menu wanders into Italian and Spanish territory as well, and even tackles that British institution, the Sunday lunch (three courses £28). Dishes are seasonally driven and delicious, and there's an interesting selection of European wine on offer.

LAXEIRO TAPAS **$$**
Map p462 (☑020-7729 1147; www.laxeiro.co.uk; 93 Columbia Rd, E2; tapas £4.50-13; ⊙11-3pm & 7-11pm Tue-Fri, 9am-4.30pm Sat & Sun; ☻Hoxton) Regulars return to this homely yet stylish restaurant for the friendly service and authentic tapas – the barbecued lamb is a sure-fire winner. The handful of more ambitious dishes includes large serves of paella to be shared. In summer there are tables outside on the picturesque street.

★ **TYPING ROOM** MODERN BRITISH **$$$**
Map p462 (☑020-7871 0461; www.typingroom. com; Town Hall Hotel, Cambridge Heath Rd, E2; 5-course meal £65; ⊙6-10pm Tue & Wed, noon-2.30pm & 6-10.30pm Thu-Sat; ☻Bethnal Green) The chefs at the Typing Room couldn't get away with Ramsay-esque outbursts as their kitchen is positioned, theatre-like, at the

entrance of the elegant but informal dining room. Just as well, as it might distract from the painstakingly prepared and exquisitely plated dishes they turn out. Service is faultless, and there's an interesting wine list to boot.

✖ Bow & Mile End

EMPRESS   MODERN BRITISH $$
Map p462 (☑020-8533 5123; www.empresse9.co.uk; 130 Lauriston Rd, E9; mains £15-19; ⊙6-10.15pm Mon, noon-3.30pm & 6-10.15pm Tue-Sat, 10am-9.30pm Sun; ▣277) This upmarket pub conversion belts out delicious modern British cuisine in very pleasant surroundings. On Mondays there's a £10 main-plus-drink deal and on weekends it serves an excellent brunch.

✖ De Beauvoir Town

★TOWPATH   CAFE $
Map p462 (☑020-7254 7606; rear 42-44 De Beauvoir Cres, N1; mains £7-9.50; ⊙9am-5pm Tue-Sun; ⊜Haggerston) Occupying four small units on the Regent's Canal towpath, this simple cafe is a super place to sit in the sun and watch the ducks and narrowboats glide by. The coffee and food are excellent too, with delicious cookies and brownies on the counter and cooked dishes chalked up on the blackboard daily.

★BERBER & Q   NORTH AFRICAN $$
Map p462 (☑020-7923 0829; www.berberandq.com; 338 Acton Mews, E8; mains £12-17; ⊙6-11pm Tue-Fri, 11am-3pm & 6-11pm Sat & Sun; ⊜Haggerston) A mouth-watering barbecue smell greets you as you enter under the railway arches to this very cool Berber-style grill house. Smoked aubergine mezze comes loaded with garlic, sumac and juicy bursts of pomegranate, and is served with charred pita. Lamb shawarma (kebab) is meltingly tender, while piquant treats include harissa hot wings, *merguez* (beef sausage), green chermoula chicken thighs and spiced beef kofte.

DUKE'S BREW & QUE   AMERICAN $$
Map p462 (☑020-3006 0795; www.dukesbrewandque.com; 33 Downham Rd, N1; mains £12-21; ⊙6-10.30pm Mon-Fri, noon-4pm & 5.30-10.30pm Sat & Sun; ⊜Haggerston) The house speciality at this attractive 18th-century pub is ribs

– pork or beef – smoked over hickory and lovingly barbecued until the meat falls off the bone. Washed down with a beer from the nearby Beavertown Brewery, it is lip-smackin' food par excellence. The weekend brunch is similarly delicious with pancakes and whopper omelettes filled with barbecue cuts.

✖ Dalston

CHICK 'N' SOURS   CHICKEN $
Map p462 (☑020-3620 8728; www.chicknsours.co.uk; 390 Kingsland Rd, E8; mains £8-12; ⊙6-10pm Tue-Fri, noon-3.30pm & 6-10pm Sat & Sun; ⊜Haggerston) It's a simple scenario but a goodie: fried free-range chicken and sours served in a hip little place with crazy tiling, patterned lino and a big red neon sign. Serves are substantial and come with a variety of sauces and on-trend extras such as pickled watermelon. Crispy Schezuan aubergine is a zingy way to start, washed down with a gin sour.

L'ATELIER   CAFE $
Map p462 (☑020-7254 3238; www.facebook.com/LatelierDalston; 31 Stoke Newington Rd, N16; mains £4-9; ⊙8am-6pm; ▦◪; ⊜Dalston Kingsland) L'Atelier sports the kitsch/vintage decor that is standard in N16 – mismatched furniture, retro posters, fresh flowers at every table – with French music and the smell of espresso coffee for added ambience. It's a lovely spot to grab an all-day breakfast, salad or open sandwich and a cup of something.

MANGAL OCAKBASI   TURKISH $$
Map p462 (☑020-7275 8981; www.mangal1.com; 10 Arcola St, E8; mains £8-14; ⊙noon-midnight; ▦◪; ⊜Dalston Kingsland) Mangal is the quintessential Turkish *ocakbasi* (open-hooded charcoal grill, the mother of all barbecues): brightly lit, smoky and serving superb mezze, grilled vegetables, lamb chops, quail and a lip-smacking assortment of kebabs. Serves are massive. BYO alcohol. This is the original Mangal but some argue that Mangal 2, just around the corner on Stoke Newington Rd, has more atmosphere.

A LITTLE OF WHAT YOU FANCY   MODERN BRITISH $$
Map p462 (☑020-7275 0060; www.alittleofwhatyoufancy.info; 464 Kingsland Rd, E8; mains £16-17; ⊙6.30-10pm Thu-Fri, 11am-10pm Sat & Sun;

Dalston Junction) Tables are adorned with flowers and candles at this cosy little bistro, setting a suitably romantic scene. Indian and Italian influences combine with the best of British on the menu, but nothing is too tricksy and the serves are substantial.

ROTORINO
ITALIAN $$

Map p462 (020-7249 9081; www.rotorino. com; 434 Kingsland Rd, E8; mains £15-16; 6-11pm Mon-Sat, noon-9pm Sun; Dalston Junction) Decked out with blue tiles, 1950s lino and exposed brick, Rotorino's chic interior comes as a welcome surprise, especially after stepping off such a shabby section of Kingsland Rd. The menu is divided into 'antipasti', 'pasta', 'wood grill' and 'stove'.

✕ Hackney

CLIMPSON & SONS
CAFE $

Map p462 (www.climpsonandsons.com; 67 Broadway Market, E8; dishes £4-6; 7.30am-5pm Mon-Fri, 9am-5pm Sat & Sun; London Fields) Small and sparsely furnished, this deservedly popular cafe has assumed the name of the butcher that once stood here. The coffee is superb – it roasts its own just around the corner – and it also does a fine line in breakfasts, sandwiches, salads and pastries.

F COOKE
BRITISH $

Map p462 (020-7254 6458; 9 Broadway Market, E8; mains £2.70-4; 10am-7pm Mon-Sat; London Fields) If you want a glimpse of pre-gentrification Broadway Market, head to F Cooke pie-and-mash shop. This family business has been going strong since 1900, and the shop has its original signage and tiles, along with plenty of family photographs around the walls and sawdust on the floor. It still serves warm jellied eels, too!

RANDY'S WING BAR
AMERICAN $

Map p462 (020-8555 5971; www.randyswingbar.co.uk; 28 East Bay Lane, E20; mains £7.50-9; 6-11pm Mon & Tue, noon-11.30pm Wed-Sat, noon-6pm Sun; Hackney Wick) What began life as a street-food cart has developed into a fully fledged restaurant, and happily the flavours have been unaffected by the presence of a roof. Unsurprisingly, chicken wings are the signature dish, with six varieties on offer, from Indian and Korean to good ole American. There are also three similarly multicultural burgers.

GREEN PAPAYA
VIETNAMESE, CHINESE $

Map p462 (020-89855486; www.green-papaya.com; 191 Mare St, E8; mains £7-12; noon-3pm & 5-11pm Tue-Fri, 1-10.30pm Sat & Sun; London Fields) This neighbourhood restaurant differentiates itself from the great mass of East London Vietnamese joints by incorporating hand-pulled noodle and lamb dishes from Xi'an in central China. The Vietnamese side of the menu is particularly strong on seafood dishes.

LITTLE GEORGIA
GEORGIAN $

Map p462 (020-7739 8154; www.facebook.com/littlegeorgiahackney; 87 Goldsmith's Row, E2; brunch dishes £5-9, dinner £10-13; 10am-11pm Tue-Sun; Hoxton) A charming slice of the Caucasus in East London, this cosy eatery is an good introduction to the cuisine of Georgia. During the day it serves cooked breakfasts and a delicious range of salads and sandwiches.

ELLORY
MODERN BRITISH $$

Map p462 (020-3095 9455; www.ellorylondon.com; 1 Westgate St, E8; mains £16; 6pm-midnight Mon-Fri, noon-3pm & 6pm-1am Sat, noon-4pm & 6-9.30pm Sun; London Fields) Scratchy vinyl plays in an industrial-chic space with exposed ducting and lights that look like naval mines: so far, so hipster. But Elllory is far from ordinary, adding quirky touches to deceptively simple dishes such as roast chicken and steamed broccoli. Service is charming and competent, and there's free sparkling water on tap and a good-value set lunch on Sundays.

LEGS
MODERN BRITISH $$

Map p462 (020-34418765; www.legsrestaurant.com; 120 Morning Lane, E9; dishes £8-13; 6-11pm Wed-Fri, 10am-11pm Sat, 10am-5pm Sun; Hackney Central) It doesn't look like much, but this small, cafe-style place has developed a reputation for creating inventive dishes out of the freshest seasonal produce. Weekend brunches are legendary, while in the evening they offer a range of small- to medium-sized dishes fit for sharing, and an interesting wine list to wash it all down with.

FORMANS
BRITISH $$

Map p462 (020-8525 2365; www.formans.co.uk; Stour Rd, E3; mains £15-20, brunch £6-10; 7-11pm Thu & Fri, 10am-2pm & 7-11pm Sat, noon-3pm Sun; Hackney Wick) Curing fish since 1905, riverside Formans boasts prime views over the Olympic stadium and an edgy free gallery overlooking its smokery. The menu includes a delectable choice of smoked salmon (including its signature 'London cure'), plenty of other seafood, a few nonfishy things and delicious sponge puddings. There's a great selection of British wines and spirits too.

LARDO   ITALIAN $$

Map p462 (☑020-8985 2683; www.lardo.co.uk; 197-201 Richmond Rd, E8; mains £9-17; ⊘11am-10.30pm; ⊖Hackney Central) A simple, one-room affair that celebrates *lardo* – the cured back fat of rare-breed pigs scented with aromatic herbs. You'll find it on excellent pizzas and among the antipasti. A couple of pasta and main dishes round out the menu.

✖ Isle of Dogs

THE GUN   BRITISH $$

Map p464 (☑020-7515 5222; www.thegundocklands.com; 27 Coldharbour, E14; mains £16-29; ⊘11.30am-midnight; 🛜; ⊖Canary Wharf) Set at the end of a residential street that somehow survived the Blitz, this early 18th-century riverside pub has been seriously dolled up, but still manages to ooze history. It's claimed that Lord Nelson had secret assignations with Lady Emma Hamilton here (hence the names on the toilet doors). The menu's excellent, focusing on British meats, especially game.

PLATEAU   FRENCH $$$

Map p464 (☑020-7715 7100; www.plateau-restaurant.co.uk; L4 Canada Place, E14; mains £24-32; ⊘11.30am-10.30pm Mon-Sat; 🍴; ⊖Canary Wharf) Occupying a squat glass box right in the centre of the Canary Wharf business district, Plateau's Eero Saarinen tulip chairs fill up with tower-block escapees at lunchtime, making the most of the excellent set-lunch menu (two/three courses £25/28) and park views. Options include tasty soups and perfectly cooked fish dishes.

🍷 DRINKING & NIGHTLIFE

The locus of London cool continues in its relentless march east, from Soho in the 1960s to Shoreditch in the 1990s, **and now Dalston, Hackney and Hackney Wick. Dalston has the liveliest strip, but there are also great venues scattered around warehouses in the vicinity of Hackney's Mare St and along the canals in Hackney Wick. Head to Broadway Market, Columbia Rd or Whitechapel for rejuvenated historic pubs.**

🍷 Wapping

PROSPECT OF WHITBY   PUB

Map p462 (☑020-7481 1095; www.taylor-walker.co.uk; 57 Wapping Wall, E1; ⊘noon-11pm; 🛜; ⊖Wapping) Once known as the Devil's Tavern due to its unsavoury clientele, the Prospect first opened its doors in 1520, although the only part of the original pub remaining is the flagstone floor. Famous patrons have included Charles Dickens and Samuel Pepys. There's a smallish terrace overlooking the Thames, a restaurant upstairs, open fires in winter and a pewter-topped bar.

TOWN OF RAMSGATE   PUB

Map p462 (☑020-7481 8000; www.townoframsgate.pub; 62 Wapping High St, E1; ⊘noon-midnight Mon-Sat, to 11pm Sun; 🛜; ⊖Wapping) This ancient pub was built in 1545 on the site of an older watering hole, the Hostel, which served ale during the Wars of the Roses. Its historic ambience is complemented by river views and healthy servings of food from its carvery.

CAPTAIN KIDD   PUB

Map p462 (☑020-7480 5759; 108 Wapping High St, E1; ⊘noon-11pm; 🛜; ⊖Wapping) With its large windows, fine beer garden and displays recalling the hanging nearby of the eponymous pirate in 1701, this is a favourite riverside pub. Although it inhabits a 17th-century building, the pub itself only dates from the 1980s. It stocks a good range of Samuel Smith craft beer from Yorkshire.

🍷 Whitechapel

INDO   PUB

Map p462 (☑020-7247 4926; 133 Whitechapel Rd, E1; ⊘noon-1am Sun-Thu, to 3am Fri & Sat; 🛜; ⊖Whitechapel) Bang opposite the East London Mosque (p226), this tiny pub has battered old tables, pews and a couple of knackered Chesterfields under the only window. Friendly staff work the beautifully tat-cluttered bar and serve stone-baked pizzas to craft-beer drinkers with the munchies. There's art for sale on the walls, DJs on weekend nights and interesting bands on an irregular schedule.

CULPEPER
PUB

Map p462 (☎020-7247 5371; www.theculpeper. com; 40 Commercial St, E1; ⊙11am-midnight Sun-Thu, to 2am Fri & Sat; ⊜Aldgate East) Stripped back to bare bricks and smartened up with potted plants and industrial light fixtures, this corner pub serves an interesting selection of wine, beer and cocktails to a fashionable young crowd. The highlight is the rooftop greenhouse and terrace bar (summer only).

ARCHERS
PUB

Map p462 (☎020-7650 7869; www.thearchers pub.com; 42 Osborn St, E1; ⊙4pm-midnight Mon-Fri, noon-1am Sat, noon-11pm Sun; ⊜Aldgate East) Zhooshed up precisely enough but not too much, this great old corner pub remains a cosy spot for a pint. Jar-like light fixtures cast shadows on the pistachio panelling, while charming staff chat and flirt with the clientele over the polished wooden bar.

Bethnal Green

★SATAN'S WHISKERS
COCKTAIL BAR

Map p462 (☎020-7739 8362; www.facebook. com/satanswhiskers; 343 Cambridge Heath Rd, E2; ⊙5pm-midnight; ⊜Bethnal Green) Unassuming and indeed unappealing till you get inside, this little cocktail bar exorcises first impressions with welcoming staff, an ever-changing drinks menu, crazy taxidermy and good music, making it a memorable stop on a Bethnal Green crawl.

CARPENTER'S ARMS
PUB

Map p462 (☎020-7739 6342; www.carpenters armsfreehouse.com; 73 Cheshire St, E2; ⊙4-11.30pm Mon-Wed, noon-11.30pm Thu-Sun; 🛜; ⊜Shoreditch High St) Once owned by infamous gangsters the Kray brothers (who bought it for their old ma to run), this chic yet cosy pub has been beautifully restored and its many wooden surfaces positively gleam. A back room and small yard provide a little more space for the convivial drinkers. There's a huge range of draught and bottled beers and ciders.

ROYAL OAK
PUB

Map p462 (☎020-7729 2220; www.royaloak london.com; 73 Columbia Rd, E2; ⊙4-11pm Mon-Fri, noon-midnight Sat, 11am-10.30pm Sun; ⊜Hoxton) This lovely wood-panelled pub really hits its stride on Sundays when London's famous flower market (p226) is just outside the door. There's a handsome central bar with a better-than-average wine list, plus a little garden at the back.

SAGER + WILDE
WINE BAR

Map p462 (☎020-8127 7330; www.sagerand wilde.com; 193 Hackney Rd, E2; ⊙5pm-midnight Mon-Fri, 2pm-midnight Sat & Sun; 🛜; ⊜Hoxton) A handsome addition to the East End drinking scene, this quietly stylish wine bar offers a modish bar-bites menu, an eye-catching glass-brick bar counter and excellent wines by the bottle and glass. There are a few outdoor tables for street-side supping.

LAST TUESDAY SOCIETY
CLUB

Map p462 (☎020-7998 3617; www.thelast tuesdaysociety.org; Viktor Wynd Museum of Curiosities, Fine Art & Natural History, 11 Mare St, E8; ⊜Bethnal Green) Runs fantastic masked balls on various occasions (St Valentine's Day, summer party, Halloween etc). Advance booking required.

BETHNAL GREEN WORKING MEN'S CLUB
CLUB

Map p462 (☎020-7739 7170; www.workersplay time.net; 42-44 Pollard Row, E2; ⊙pub 6pm-late Wed-Sat, club hours vary; ⊜Bethnal Green) As it says on the tin, this is a true working men's club. Except that this one has opened its doors and let in all kinds of off-the-wall club nights, including trashy burlesque, gay and lesbian shindigs, retro nights, beach parties and bake-offs. Expect sticky carpets, a shimmery stage set and a space akin to a school-hall disco.

Dalston

★HIGH WATER
COCKTAIL BAR

Map p462 (☎020-7241 1984; www.highwater london.com; 23 Stoke Newington Rd, N16; ⊙5pm-12.30am; 🚆Dalston Kingsland) Table service is offered but if you're the kind that likes to indulge in random conversations with complete strangers, we'd suggest you grab a seat at the bar. And that way you can interrogate the charming staff about what corners of their largely self-devised cocktail list will best cater to your taste, then watch them concoct it.

DALSTON SUPERSTORE GAY & LESBIAN
Map p462 (⌖020-7254 2273; www.dalstonsuper store.com; 117 Kingsland High St, E8; ⊗11.45am-late; ⊜Dalston Kingsland) Bar, club or diner? Gay, lesbian or straight? Dalston Superstore is hard to pigeonhole, which we suspect is the point. This two-level industrial space is open all day but really comes into its own after dark when there are club nights in the basement.

SHACKLEWELL ARMS PUB
Map p462 (⌖020-7249 0810; www.shackle wellarms.com; 71 Shacklewell Lane, E8; ⊗5pm-midnight Mon-Thu, 5pm-3am Fri, noon-3am Sat, noon-midnight Sun; ⊜Dalston Kingsland) Dalston's premier indie-rock pub is as sticky-floored and grungy as you'd hope it would be. There's a popular pool table and a garden bar, but the main attraction is the band room, which stages live music most nights. They've a long-standing association with the **Field Day** (www.fielddayfestivals.com; Victoria Park, E3; ⊗Jun; ⊜Hackney Wick) music festival, hosting a stage in Victoria Park and the afterparty.

RUBY'S COCKTAIL BAR
Map p462 (www.rubysdalston.com; 76 Stoke Newington Rd, N16; ⊗6.30pm-midnight Tue-Thu, to 2am Fri & Sat; ⊜Dalston Kingsland) Tucked away in a basement, this artfully dishevelled, candlelit cocktail bar delivers a speakeasy vibe, although you're more likely to hear hair metal being played than honky-tonk piano. On Fridays and Saturdays they open a much larger lounge next door and let loose some feel-good disco tunes. Plus there are £5 cocktail specials on (when else but) Ruby Tuesdays.

FARR'S SCHOOL OF DANCING BAR
Map p462 (⌖020-7923 4553; www.farrs schoolofdancing.com; 17-19 Dalston Lane, E8; ⊗4pm-midnight Mon-Fri, noon-1am Sat, noon-11pm Sun; ☎; ⊜Dalston Junction) There was actually a dance school here in the 1930s, but rest assured, nobody's going to expect you to tackle a tango in this big, knowingly grungy boozer nowadays. You could, however, conceivably bust a move to '80s tunes as the evening progresses. Expect a big central bar, mismatched tables topped with candles and flowers, and a relaxed, good-time crowd.

NEST CLUB
Map p462 (www.ilovethenest.com; 36 Stoke New-ington Rd, N16; ⊗10pm-4am Thu-Sat; ⊜Dalston Kingsland) The occasional big-name DJ joins the up-and-comers at this low-ceilinged Dalston dance club.

DALSTON ROOF PARK ROOFTOP BAR
Map p462 (⌖020-7275 0825; www.bootstrap company.co.uk; Print House, 18 Ashwin St, E8; ⊗9am-3pm Mon, 9am-3pm & 5-11pm Tue-Fri, 3pm-midnight Sat, 3-10pm Sun May-Sep; ⊜Dalston Junction) It's spaces like Dalston Roof Park that make you regret the fact that London isn't sunny year-round. Be-cause when you sit in the colourful chairs on the bright-green AstroTurf looking over the Dalston skyline with a drink in your hand, it really is something. Purchase a £12 annual membership and head on up.

De Beauvoir Town

DRAUGHTS CAFE, BAR
Map p462 (www.draughtslondon.com; 337 Acton Mews, E8; entry £5; ⊗10am-11pm; ☒Haggerston) London's first board-game themed cafe/bar – it has over 600 to choose from – offers a delightfully geeky way to while away an af-ternoon. Food, wine and ale are served all day, and there is even a 'game guru' on hand to explain rules and advise which games are best suited to your group's wants.

Hackney

★**CAT & MUTTON** PUB
Map p462 (⌖020-7249 6555; www.catand mutton.com; 76 Broadway Market, E8; ⊗noon-midnight Sun-Fri, 10am-1am Sat; ⊜London Fields) At this fabulous Georgian pub, Hackney hipsters sup pints under the watchful eyes of hunting trophies, black-and-white pho-tos of old-time boxers and a large portrait of Karl Marx. If it's crammed downstairs, as it often is, head up the spiral staircase to the comfy couches. DJs spin funk, disco and soul on the weekends.

★**DOVE FREEHOUSE** PUB
Map p462 (⌖020-7275 7617; www.dovepubs. com; 24-28 Broadway Market, E8; ⊗noon-11pm; ☎; ⊜London Fields) Alluring at any time, the

Dove has a rambling series of rooms and a wide range of Belgian Trappist, wheat and fruit-flavoured beers. Drinkers spill on to the street in warmer weather, or hunker down in the low-lit back room with board games when it's chilly.

★NETIL360 ROOFTOP BAR

Map p462 (www.netil360.com; 1 Westgate St, E8; ☉10am-10pm Wed-Fri, noon-11pm Sat & Sun Apr-Nov; ☎; ⊜London Fields) Perched atop Netil House, this uber-hip rooftop cafe-bar offers incredible views over London, with brass telescopes enabling you to get better acquainted with workers in the Gherkin. In between drinks you can knock out a game of croquet on the AstroTurf, or perhaps book a hot tub for you and your mates to stew in.

MARTELLO HALL BAR

Map p462 (☑020-3889 6173; www.martellohall. com; 137 Mare St, E8; ☉8am-midnight Sun-Wed, to 3am Thu-Sat; ☎; ⊜London Fields) If Dr Jekyll was a louche Hackney hipster, this is where he'd hang out – sipping on gin made by Nicola, the bar's own shiny copper still. A steampunky belt-driven fan whirs overhead, while liqueur bottles glitter like secret elixirs in the candlelight. At the rear, an open kitchen turns out *torta fritta* (fried dumplings), pizza and £15 weekend 'bottomless brunches'.

HOWLING HOPS MICROBREWERY

Map p462 (☑020-3583 8262; www.howlinghops. co.uk; 9a Queen's Yard, White Post Lane, E9; ☉noon-11pm; ☎; ⊜Hackney Wick) You won't find cans, bottles or barrels in this pleasantly grungy brewery bar; just 10 gleaming tanks containing ales and lagers straight from the source. They share the old Victorian warehouse with the wonderful-smelling Billy Smokes Barbecue and there's also a counter serving excellent coffee.

CRATE BREWERY MICROBREWERY

Map p462 (☑020-8533 3331; www.cratebrewery. com; 7 Queen's Yard, White Post Lane, E9; ☉noon-11pm; ☎; ⊜Hackney Wick) No wonder hipsters swarm to Hackney Wick: these Victorian warehouses make ideal craft breweries. Inside, pizza and various cask beers and ciders are dispensed under light fixtures fashioned from old bed springs. On Sunday days, the canalside tables fill up quickly.

PEOPLE'S PARK TAVERN PUB

Map p462 (☑020-8533 0040; www.peoplespark tavern.pub; 360 Victoria Park Rd, E9; ☉noon-midnight Sun-Thu, 1pm-2am Fri & Sat; ☎; ⊜Homerton) If you're wandering through Victoria Park and fancy either a refreshing beverage or a game of minigolf, here's where to head. There's a fabulous beer garden, right on the park, and it also has an in-house microbrewery. Comedy, live music and DJs are all part of a busy weekly entertainment roster.

ROYAL INN ON THE PARK PUB

Map p462 (☑020-8985 3321; www.royalinnon thepark.com; 111 Lauriston Rd, E9; ☉noon-11pm; ☎; ☒277) On the northern border of Victoria Park, this excellent establishment – once a poster pub for Transport for London – has 10 real ales and Belgian and Czech beers on tap, outside seating to the front and a large courtyard at the back.

NO 90 BAR

Map p462 (☑020-8986 0090; www.number 90bar.co.uk; 90 Wallis Rd, E9; ☉noon-11.30pm Wed-Sun; ⊜Hackney Wick) Occupying a cavernous brick warehouse right on the canal, No 90 serves craft beer, wine and cocktails to local artists and Sunday sippers. DJs play most nights and there's occasional live music, and hipster bingo on the last Wednesday of the month.

KING EDWARD VII PUB

(☑020-8534 2313; www.facebook.com/KingEddiesE15; 47 Broadway, E15; ☉11am-midnight; ⊜Stratford) Built in the 19th century, this lovely old boozer has a series of handsome rooms set around a central bar. The front bar and saloon are the most convivial, and there's a little courtyard at the back. Thursday is open-mic night.

🍺 Limehouse

GRAPES PUB

Map p462 (☑020-7987 4396; www.thegrapes. co.uk; 76 Narrow St, E14; ☉noon-11pm; ☒DLR Limehouse) One of Limehouse's renowned historic pubs, the Grapes dates from 1583 and has insinuated its way into the writing of Pepys, Dickens, Wilde, Arthur Conan Doyle and Peter Ackroyd. It really is tiny, especially the riverside terrace, which can only really comfortably fit about a half-dozen close friends, but its cosy wood-lined interior exudes plenty of old-world charm.

AN EAST LONDON PLAYLIST

➤ *'Mile End'* – Pulp (1995)

➤ *'Dagenham Dave'* – Morrissey (1995)

➤ *'Dalston'* – Razorlight (2004)

➤ *'Ill Manors'* – Plan B (2012)

➤ *'River Lea'* – Adele (2015)

OLD SHIP
GAY

Map p462 (☑020-7791 1301; www.oldship.net; 17 Barnes St, E14; ⊘noon-midnight; ⓓDLR Limehouse) In every respect this is your typical little East End corner pub...except, that is, for the drag-queen cabaret shows on Sundays and Saucy Sophie's quiz on Wednesdays.

WHITE SWAN
GAY

Map p462 (☑020-7780 9870; www.bjswhiteswan. com; 556 Commercial Rd, E14; ⊘8pm-2am Tue-Thu, 8pm-5am Fri & Sat, 5pm-2am Sun; ⓓDLR Limehouse) The White Swan is a fun East End kind of place, with a large dance floor, a basement club and a more relaxed pub area. Club classics and cheesy pop predominate, and there are regular drag shows and singalongs around the piano.

☆ ENTERTAINMENT

WILTON'S
THEATRE

Map p462 (☑020-7702 2789; www.wiltons.org. uk; 1 Graces Alley, E1; tour £6; ⊘tours 6pm most Mondays, bar 5-11pm Mon-Sat; ⊖Tower Hill) A gloriously atmospheric example of a Victorian music hall, Wilton's hosts a variety of shows, from comedy and classical music to theatre and opera. One-hour guided tours offer an insight into its fascinating history. The **Mahogany Bar** is a great way to get a taste of the place if you're not attending a performance.

WHISTLE PUNKS
AXE THROWING

Map p462 (www.whistlepunks.com; 22-36 Raven Row, E1; 90min £22-29; ⊘6pm-9.30pm Wed-Fri, noon-7.30pm Sat; ⊖Whitechapel) If you want to bury the hatchet with hipsters, head to Whistle Punks, where you can try axe-throwing. It's basically darts on steroids, and once you've been shown how to minimise the chances of mortally wounding your companions, you'll take part in a tournament. Sensibly, there is no bar.

VORTEX JAZZ CLUB
JAZZ

Map p462 (☑020-7254 4097; www.vortex jazz.co.uk; 11 Gillet Sq, N16; ⊘8pm-midnight; ⓡDalston Kingsland) With a fantastically varied menu of jazz, the Vortex hosts an outstanding line-up of musicians, singers and songwriters from the UK, the USA, Europe, Africa and beyond. It's a small venue so make sure you book if there's an act you particularly fancy.

HACKNEY EMPIRE
THEATRE

Map p462 (☑020-8985 2424; www.hackney empire.co.uk; 291 Mare St, E8; ⊖Hackney Central) One of London's most beautiful theatres, this renovated Edwardian music hall (1901) offers an extremely diverse range of performances – from hard-edged political theatre to musicals, opera and comedy. It's one of the very best places to catch a pantomime at Christmas.

GENESIS
CINEMA

Map p462 (☑020-7780 2000; www.genesis cinema.co.uk; 93-95 Mile End Rd, E1; ⊖Stepney Green) Snuggle up under a blanket on a couch to watch a flick at this wonderful little five-screen cinema.

COPPER BOX ARENA
CONCERT VENUE

Map p462 (☑020-8221 4900; http://copperbox arena.org.uk; Copper St, E20; badminton 1hr £11, gym day pass £10; ⊘7am-10pm; ⊖Hackney Wick) The handball arena during the 2012 Olympic Games, this 7000-seat indoor venue is now used for for badminton, other sports and concerts.

CAFE OTO
LIVE MUSIC

Map p462 (www.cafeoto.co.uk; 18-22 Ashwin St, E8; ⊘9.30am-late; 🛜; ⊖Dalston Junction) Dedicating itself to promoting experimental and alternative musicians, this is Dalston's premier venue for hipsters to stroke their beards while listening to electronic bleeps, Japanese psychedelica or avant folk. Set in a converted print warehouse, it's one of London's most idiosyncratic live-music venues. When there are no gigs on, it's open as a cafe-bar.

DALSTON JAZZ BAR
JAZZ

Map p462 (☑020-7254 9728; www.dalstonjazz bartheclub.co.uk; 4 Bradbury St, N16; ⊘11pm-3am Thu-Sat; ⊖Dalston Kingsland) Hidden just off the chaos of Kingsland High St, Dalston Jazz Bar also operates as a neighbourhood cocktail bar and eatery. The jazz part of the equation only kicks in late at night, late in the week, with live musicians and 'jazz DJs' from Thursday to Saturday.

ARCOLA THEATRE
THEATRE

Map p462 (☑020-7503 1646; www.arcolatheatre. com; 24 Ashwin St, E8; ⊖Dalston Junction) Dalston's a fair schlep from the West End, but drama buffs still flock to this innovative theatre for its adventurous and eclectic productions. A unique annual feature is **Grimeborn**, an opera festival focusing on lesser known or new works – it's Dalston's answer to East Sussex's world-famous Glyndebourne opera festival, taking place around the same time (August).

RIO CINEMA
CINEMA

Map p462 (☑020-7241 9410; www.riocinema.org. uk; 107 Kingsland High St, E8; ⊠Dalston Kingsland) The Rio is Dalston's neighbourhood art-house, classic and new-release cinema, and a venue for non-mainstream festivals such as the East End Film Festival, the London Turkish Film Festival and the Fringe! Queer Film & Arts Fest. It also holds regular Q&A sessions with film directors.

🔒 SHOPPING

There are some wonderfully quirky little stores lining Columbia Rd and Broadway Market, although some only open on the weekends. If you're after something a little more mainstream, the vast Westfield Stratford City can't fail to satisfy. There's also a shopping mall beneath the Canary Wharf skyscrapers, with similar shops, bars and restaurants. Bargain hunters in the know stake out the outlet stores along Hackney's Morning Lane and Chatham Place.

★ BROADWAY MARKET
MARKET

Map p462 (www.broadwaymarket.co.uk; Broadway Market, E8; ⊘9am-5pm Sat; ☐394) There's been a market down this pretty street since the late 19th century. The focus these days is artisan food, arty knickknacks, books, records and vintage clothing. Stock up on edible treats then head to London Fields (p227) for a picnic.

GLITTERATI
VINTAGE

Map p462 (☑020-7739 7739; 148 Columbia Rd, E2; ⊘10.30am-5pm Sat & Sun; ⊖Hoxton) If you're the kind of person who likes to wear 1930s couture and costume jewellery while reading original Penguin books and sipping gin poured from a crystal decanter, this is precisely the place for you.

HACKNEY WALK
FASHION & ACCESSORIES

Map p462 (www.hackneywalk.com; 163 Morning Lane, E9; ⊘10am-6pm; ⊖Hackney Central) Tucked between Morning Lane and the train tracks, this new development has created a discount fashion precinct out of an area already known for its Burberry and Pringle of Scotland outlet stores. Newcomers include big brands such as Zadig & Voltaire, Gieves & Hawkes and Nike, with end-of-run stock at up to 70% off regular prices.

PRINGLE OF SCOTLAND OUTLET STORE
CLOTHING

Map p462 (☑020-8533 1158; www.pringle scotland.com; 90 Morning Lane; ⊘10am-6.30pm Mon-Sat, 11am-5pm Sun; ⊖Hackney Central) There are proper bargains to be had at this excellent outlet store that stocks seconds and end-of-line items from the Pringle range. Expect high-quality merino, cashmere and lambswool knitwear for both men and women.

BEYOND RETRO
VINTAGE

Map p462 (☑020-7923 2277; www.beyondretro. com; 92-100 Stoke Newington Rd, N16; ⊘10am-7pm Mon-Sat, 11.30am-6pm Sun; ⊖Dalston Kingsland) A riot of colour, furbelow, frill, feathers and flares, this vast store has every imaginable type of vintage clothing for sale, from hats to shoes. There's another branch in **Bethnal Green** (Map p462; ☑020-7613 3636; www.beyondretro.com; 110-112 Cheshire St, E2; ⊘10am-7pm Mon-Sat, 11.30am-6pm Sun; ⊖Shoreditch High St).

TRAID
CLOTHING

Map p462 (☑020-7923 1396; www.traid.org.uk; 106-108 Kingsland High St, E8; ⊘11am-7pm Mon-Sat, to 5pm Sun; ⊖Dalston Kingsland) Banish every preconception you have about charity shops, for Traid is nothing like the ones you've seen before: big and bright, with not a whiff of mothball. The offerings aren't necessarily vintage but rather quality, contemporary secondhand clothes for a fraction of the usual prices. It also sells its own creations made from offcuts.

BURBERRY OUTLET STORE
CLOTHING

Map p462 (www.burberry.com; 29-31 Chatham Pl, E9; ⊘10am-7pm; ⊖Hackney Central) This outlet shop has excess international stock from the reborn-as-trendy Brit brand's current and last-season collections. Prices are around 30% lower than those in the main shopping centres – but still properly pricey.

WESTFIELD STRATFORD CITY   MALL
(http://uk.westfield.com; Westfield Ave, E20; ⊙10am-9pm Mon-Fri, 9am-9pm Sat, noon-6pm Sun; 🕾; ⊖Stratford) Right by Queen Elizabeth Olympic Park, this is Britain's third-largest mall – a behemoth containing more than 250 shops, 70 places to eat and drink, a 17-screen cinema, a bowling alley, a 24-hour casino and a Premier Inn hotel.

🏃 SPORTS & ACTIVITIES

LONDON AQUATICS CENTRE   SWIMMING
(📞020-8536   3150;   www.londonaquatics centre.org; Carpenters Rd, E20; adult/child from £4.95/2.50; ⊙6am-10.30pm; ⊖Stratford) The sweeping lines and wave-like movement of Zaha Hadid's award-winning Aquatics Centre make it the architectural highlight of Queen Elizabeth Olympic Park (p232). Bathed in natural light, the 50m competition pool beneath the huge undulating roof (which sits on just three supports) is an extraordinary place to swim. There's also a second 50m pool, a diving area, a gym, a creche and a cafe.

LEE VALLEY VELOPARK   CYCLING
Map p462 (📞0300 0030 613; www.visitleevalley.org.uk/velopark; Abercrombie Rd, E20; 1hr taster £40, pay & ride from £4, bike & helmet hire adult/child from £12/8; ⊙9am-10pm; 🕾; ⊖DLR Stratford International) The beautifully designed, cutting-edge Queen Elizabeth Olympic Park (p232) velodrome is open to the public – either to wander through and watch the pros tear around the steep-sloped circuit, or to have a go yourself. Both the velodrome and the attached BMX park offer taster sessions. Mountain bikers and road cyclists can attack the tracks on a pay-and-ride basis.

ALFRED LE ROY   CRUISE
Map p462 (www.alfredleroy.com; Queen's Yard, White Post Lane, E9; from £13; ⊙Sat & Sun; ⊖Hackney Wick) When it's not moored as a floating bar outside Crate Brewery, this narrowboat heads out on booze cruises through Queen Elizabeth Olympic Park. On Saturdays it heads upriver to Springfield Park at noon, and downriver to Limehouse Basin at 3.30pm. Two-hour Sunday cruises (various times) offer a £25 all-you-can-drink prosecco, Bloody Mary and mimosa add-on. Book online.

LONDON FIELDS LIDO   SWIMMING
Map p462 (📞020-7254 9038; www.better.org. uk/leisure/london-fields-lido; London Fields West Side, E8; adult/child £4.80/2.85; ⊙6.30am-9pm; ⊖London Fields) Built in the 1930s but abandoned by the '80s, this heated 50m Olympic-size outdoor pool reopened in 2006 and once again gets packed with swimmers and sunbathers during summer.

LEE & STORT BOATS   CRUISE
Map p462 (📞0845 116 2012; www.leeandstort boats.co.uk; Stratford waterfront pontoon, E20; adult/child £9/4; ⊙daily Apr-Sep, Sat & Sun Mar & Oct; ⊖Stratford) Lee & Stort offers 45-minute tours on the waterways through Queen Elizabeth Olympic Park (p232). Check the display boards in the park for departure times, which are usually on the hour from midday onwards.

EAST LONDON & DOCKLANDS SPORTS & ACTIVITIES

Hampstead & North London

KING'S CROSS & EUSTON | REGENT'S PARK | PRIMROSE HILL | CAMDEN TOWN | HAMPSTEAD | HIGHGATE | HIGHBURY | ISLINGTON | KENTISH TOWN | BARNSBURY | STOKE NEWINGTON

Neighbourhood Top Five

① **Hampstead Heath** (p254) Enjoying the sweeping views of London from Parliament Hill; getting a culture fix at beautiful Kenwood; and slumping in a couch at the Garden Gate pub to recover.

② **Camden Market** (p253) Soaking up the sights, sounds, smells and frantic energy of the legendary market.

③ **British Library** (p246) Discovering the treasures of the nation's library and marvelling at the sheer volume of knowledge stored within its walls.

④ **Wellcome Collection** (p250) Enjoying a thought-provoking afternoon exploring questions of life, death and art at this intriguing gallery.

⑤ King's Cross (p249) Marvelling at the metamorphosis of the area from industrial wasteland to supercool new neighbourhood.

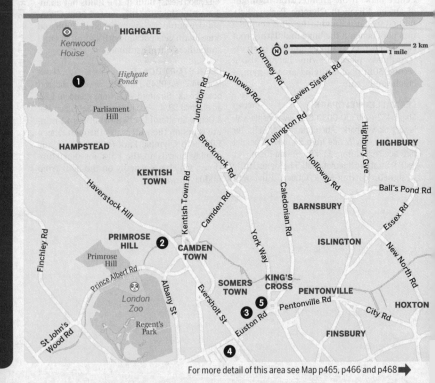

For more detail of this area see Map p465, p466 and p468 ➡

Explore Hampstead & North London

North London is a big place – you could spend a week exploring its parks, checking out the sights, lounging in gastropubs and sampling the nightlife. So if you're short on time, you'll have to pick and choose carefully.

Hampstead Heath (p254) and Camden Market (p253) should be on top of your list. Camden Town has an intoxicating energy, while Hampstead Heath offers glorious walks, city views, wonderful art and an insight into how North Londoners spend their weekends. Note, however, that there are steep inclines in this part of London, so sightseeing can be quite tiring. Because these are residential areas, they tend to be quiet during the week and busy at weekends.

King's Cross, on the other hand, with its central location and numerous offices, is busier on weekdays. It's a great place to hang out – be it for an alfresco lunch, an ice cream or a drink. There are also a couple of museums to explore, and on weekends you can visit the exquisite St Pancras building (p249).

Consider walking along Regent's Canal (p252) to link places such as King's Cross, Camden, and Regent's Park (p252) – it's a route that's both practical and delightful.

Local Life

➡ **Live music** North London is well known for being the home of indie rock. Music fans flock to numerous bars and theatres around Camden Town and Kentish Town to hear bands aiming for the big time.

➡ **Sunday pub lunches** Hampstead is a particularly good place to experience this institution of English life, although there are plenty of suitable venues all over North London.

➡ **Swimming** Hampstead Heath ponds (p270) are open year-round, and a small group of hard-core aficionados swim every day, rain or shine.

Getting There & Away

➡ **Underground** North London is served by the Northern, Piccadilly, Victoria, Jubilee and Bakerloo Lines. Additionally the Circle, Hammersmith & City and Metropolitan Lines call into King's Cross St Pancras, Euston Sq and Baker St.

➡ **Overground** The Overground crosses North London from east to west, with useful stops at Highbury & Islington, Caledonian Rd & Barnsbury, Camden Rd and Hampstead Heath.

➡ **Bus** There is a good network of buses in North London connecting various neighbourhoods to each other and the centre of the city. Buses are particularly useful for getting to the zoo (route 274) and the northern part of Hampstead Heath (210).

Lonely Planet's Top Tip

If the sun's shining, drop any plans you might have made and head straight to a park. North London has some of the capital's biggest and best green spaces. Pack a picnic and then do as Londoners do: head to the pub afterwards!

Best Places to Eat

➡ Trullo (p263)
➡ Roti King (p258)
➡ Ruby Violet (p258)
➡ Ottolenghi (p263)
➡ Hook Camden Town (p261)

For reviews, see p258.➡

Best Places to Drink

➡ Holly Bush (p266)
➡ Drink, Shop & Do (p264)
➡ Edinboro Castle (p265)
➡ Bar Pepito (p264)
➡ Euston Tap (p264)

For reviews, see p264.➡

Best Places for Live Music

➡ Proud Camden (p265)
➡ Dublin Castle (p269)
➡ O2 Forum (p269)
➡ KOKO (p267)
➡ Jazz Cafe (p267)

For reviews, see p267.➡

HAMPSTEAD & NORTH LONDON

TOP SIGHT
BRITISH LIBRARY

Consisting of low-slung red-brick terraces and fronted by a large plaza featuring an oversized statue of Sir Isaac Newton, Colin St John Wilson's British Library building is a love-it-or-hate-it affair (Prince Charles once famously likened it to a secret-police academy). Completed in 1998, it's home to some of the greatest treasures of the written word.

The Collection
The British Library is the nation's principal copyright library, which means that it automatically receives a copy of everything published in Britain and Ireland. Among its more than 150 million items are historic manuscripts, books, maps, journals, newspapers and sound recordings.

King's Library
At the centre of the building is the wonderful King's Library, the 85,000-volume collection of King George III, displayed in a beautiful six-storey, 17m-high **glass-walled tower**.

The collection is considered to be one of the most significant of the Enlightenment period. After being bequeathed to the nation by George IV in 1823, it was kept at the British Museum, in the specially built King's Library Gallery. After a bomb fell on the collection during WWII, it was moved to the Bodleian Library in Oxford and finally moved back to London in 1998 when the new British Library opened.

DON'T MISS
➡ Sir John Ritblat Gallery
➡ King's Library
➡ Temporary exhibitions

PRACTICALITIES
➡ Map p466, A6
➡ www.bl.uk
➡ 96 Euston Rd, NW1
➡ admission free
➡ ⊘galleries 9.30am-6pm Mon & Fri, to 8pm Tue-Thu, to 5pm Sat, 11am-5pm Sun
➡ 📶
➡ ⊖King's Cross St Pancras

Sir John Ritblat Gallery

Housing the Treasures of the British Library, the library's most precious and high-profile documents, this darkened gallery is the highlight of any visit. The collection spans almost three millennia and contains manuscripts, religious texts, maps, music scores, autographs, diaries and more.

Rare texts from all the main religions include the **Codex Sinaiticus**, the first complete text of the New Testament, written in Greek in the 4th century; a **Gutenberg Bible** (1455), the first Western book printed using movable type; and the spectacularly illustrated **Jain sacred texts**.

It holds historical documents, including one of four remaining copies of the **Magna Carta** (1215), the charter credited with setting out the basis of human rights in English law. Not so important, but extremely poignant, is **Captain Scott's final diary**, including an account of fellow explorer Lawrence Oates' death.

Literature is also well represented, with **Shakespeare's First Folio** (1623) and manuscripts by some of Britain's best-known authors, such as Lewis Carroll, Jane Austen, George Eliot and Thomas Hardy. Music fans will love **The Beatles' handwritten lyrics** (including *A Hard Day's Night* scribbled on the back of one of Julian Lennon's birthday cards), and original scores by Bach, Handel, Mozart and Beethoven.

Exhibitions

The library runs regular high-profile exhibitions in the PACCAR gallery, all connected to its records; admission charges vary. Smaller free exhibitions take place around the library, and focus on particular authors, genres or themes (science fiction, the census, crime fiction etc).

The Philatelic Exhibition

Based on various collections amassed in the 19th century, the Philatelic Exhibition now consists of more than 80,000 items, including stamps from almost every country. The sliding racks are designed to reduce the stamps' exposure to light.

BOOKS BY THE NUMBERS

What you can see of the library is just the tip of the iceberg. Under your feet, on five basement levels, run 625km of shelving (growing by 12km every year).

READER PASS

To access the reading rooms and the bulk of the library collection, you'll need to apply for a Reader Pass. Anyone can apply but passes are only issued if you can demonstrate a need to see specific items in the collection – usually for an academic or specific research purpose. Passes are issued for a period of one month to three years.

TOP SIGHT
ZSL LONDON ZOO

Established in 1828, these zoological gardens are among the oldest in the world – they're actually from where the word 'zoo' originated. The emphasis nowadays is firmly placed on conservation, education and breeding, with fewer species and more spacious conditions. The zoo is involved in conservation efforts in more than 50 countries.

The zoo's latest development is **Land of the Lions**, a new enclosure that seeks to re-create the environment of Gir National Park in India (complete with signs in Hindi, rickshaws and colourful props) where the last Asiatic lions live in the wild. There are four lions in the enclosure, as well as Hanuman langur monkeys and Ruppell's griffon vultures.

Tiger Territory is a little slice of Indonesian forest and the home of the zoo's two endangered Sumatran tigers and their two cubs (born in June 2016). The enclosure allows the animals to climb and bathe as well as to wander around freely.

With its underwater viewing area, **Penguin Beach** is another popular attraction. It's a key element of the zoo's breeding program of Humboldt, macaroni and rockhopper penguins.

Rainforest Life – a slice of the humid South American rainforest complete with sloths, monkeys and birds – is one of several immersive exhibits where the animals wander freely among visitors. Others include the **In with the Lemurs** enclosure, where the very curious and playful ring-tailed lemurs will come within touching distance, and **Butterfly Paradise**, where myriad butterflies and moths flutter from flower to flower.

You'll also find plenty to see indoors, should you come on a rainy or cold day, and the excellent play area will allow children to let rip their inner lion/chimp without frightening the real animals!

DON'T MISS

- ➡ Tiger Territory
- ➡ Land of the Lions
- ➡ Penguin Beach
- ➡ Gorilla Kingdom
- ➡ Rainforest Life

PRACTICALITIES

- ➡ Map p468, B4
- ➡ www.zsl.org/zsl-london-zoo
- ➡ Outer Circle, Regent's Park, NW1
- ➡ adult/child £29.75/22
- ➡ ⏰10am-6pm Apr-Sep, to 5.30pm Mar & Oct, to 4pm Nov-Feb
- ➡ 🚼
- ➡ 🚌274

⊙ SIGHTS

North London is a collection of small neighbourhoods, originally ancient villages that were slowly drawn into London as the metropolis expanded. It's a very green area, home to some of the most wonderful park spaces in the city. Sights are pretty scattered in the northern half of the area, where you'll need some leg power to explore hilly Hampstead and around. King's Cross, however, is a lot more compact. A walk along Regent's Canal will link Regent's Park, Camden and King's Cross.

⊙ King's Cross & Euston

King's Cross used to be something of a blind spot on London's map, somewhere you only ever went through rather than to. The surrounding streets were the capital's red-light district, and when the British Library first opened here in 1998, drug addicts could regularly be found in the toilets. In fact, it was the area's reputation that poured cold water on plans to renovate the hotel at St Pancras station in the 1980s and 1990s.

Fast forward a couple of decades and King's Cross's transformation isn't far removed from the metamorphosis of Stratford following the 2012 Olympic Games. Not only do friends now gather and chat on the plaza in front of King's Cross station, but families also stroll through the former railyards behind the station, along broad avenues lined with trees. This one-time industrial wasteland has become home to hip new eateries, glitzy corporate headquarters and lots of green spaces.

BRITISH LIBRARY LIBRARY
See p246.

ST PANCRAS STATION & HOTEL HISTORIC BUILDING
Map p466 (✆020-8241 6921; www.stpancras london.com; Euston Rd, NW1; ⊖King's Cross St Pancras) Looking at the jaw-dropping Gothic splendour of St Pancras, it's hard to believe that the 1873 Midland Grand Hotel languished empty for years and even faced demolition in the 1960s. Now home to a five-star hotel, 67 luxury apartments and the Eurostar terminal, the entire complex has been returned to its former glory. Tours (£20; 10.30am, noon, 2pm &

3.30pm weekends) take you on a fascinating journey through the building's history, from its inception as the southern terminus for the Midlands Railway line.

Designed by George Gilbert Scott (who also built the Albert Memorial in Hyde Park), the Midland Grand Hotel was the most luxurious hotel in London when it first opened. All of the materials (including the stone, iron and 60 million red bricks) were brought down from the Midlands as a showcase for the kind of products the railway link could provide. The whole thing cost an astounding £438,000 – somewhere between £500 and £600 million in today's money.

You can get an idea of the original over-the-top decor in the **Gilbert Scott Bar**, which was originally the hotel's reception. The neighbouring dining room (now a fine-dining restaurant run by acclaimed chef Marcus Wareing) showcases the more restrained style of a 1901 refurbishment. The building was incredibly modern for its time, with England's first hydraulic lift, London's first revolving door and a thick layer of concrete between the floors to act as a firebreak. Ironically this contributed to its undoing, as it made it extremely difficult to adapt the rooms to new trends such as private bathrooms and electricity (the lighting was gas).

The hotel closed in 1935 and was used for railway offices and finally abandoned in 1988. It was only when plans to use St Pancras as the Eurostar terminal came up in the 1990s that local authorities decided to renovate the building and open a hotel. The Eurostar first arrived at **St Pancras International** in 2007 and **St Pancras Renaissance London Hotel** opened its doors in 2011.

Tours take you up the glorious grand staircase and along the exquisitely decorated corridors into one of the 37 remaining original Victorian rooms. They then head into the station proper, where sky-blue iron girders arc over what was, at the time, the largest unsupported space ever built. A modern addition to the concourse is **Meeting Place**, a giant statue of two lovers embracing, by sculptor Paul Day – be sure to examine the wonderful railway-themed frieze winding around its base. Also worth a look is the fabulously ornate **Booking Office Bar & Restaurant** (Map p466; info@ luxuryvacationsuk.com; ⊙6.30am–midnight Sun-Wed, to 1am Fri & Sat;), housed in the station's original ticket office.

GRANARY SQUARE   SQUARE

Map p466 (www.kingscross.co.uk; Stable St, N1; ⊖King's Cross St Pancras) Positioned by a sharp bend in the Regent's Canal north of King's Cross Station, Granary Sq is at the heart of a major redevelopment of a 27-hectare expanse once full of abandoned freight warehouses. Its most striking feature is a fountain made of 1080 individually lit water jets, which pulse and dance in sequence. On hot spring and summer days, it becomes a busy urban beach.

The vast brick 1851 warehouse fronting the square is now home to some excellent eateries and the main campus of the Central St Martins University of the Arts, including its **Platform Theatre** (www.platform-theatre.com). Also worth noting is the wavy glass frontage of the nearby **Kings Place** building. Completed in 2008, it's home to a concert hall, restaurants, commercial galleries and the offices of the *Guardian* and *Observer* newspapers. The excellent gallery House of Illustration (p251) is at No 2.

LONDON CANAL MUSEUM   MUSEUM

Map p466 (📞020-7713 0836; www.canalmuseum.org.uk; 12-13 New Wharf Rd, N1; adult/child £5/2.50; ⊙10am-4.30pm Tue-Sun & bank holidays; ⊖King's Cross St Pancras) This little museum traces the history of the Regent's Canal and explores what life was like for families living and working on Britain's impressively long and historic canal system. The exhibits in the stables upstairs are dedicated to the history of canal transport in Britain, including recent developments such as the clean-up of the Lea River for the 2012 Olympic Games. The museum is housed in a warehouse dating from 1858, where ice was once stored in two deep wells.

The ice trade was huge in Victorian London, with 35,000 tonnes imported from Norway in 1899 alone, arriving in the city at Regent's Canal Dock before being transported along the canal. You can access the wharf at the back of the museum where narrow boats are moored.

CAMLEY STREET
NATURAL PARK   NATURE RESERVE

Map p466 (www.wildlondon.org.uk; 12 Camley St, N1; ⊙10am-4pm Nov-Mar, to 5pm Apr-Oct; ⊖King's Cross St Pancras) A tiny nature reserve sounds like an unlikely find in such an urban part of London, yet Camley Street truly is wild, cramming three different habitats (woodland, grassland and wetland) for birds,

---

TOP SIGHT
WELLCOME COLLECTION

The Wellcome Collection styles itself as a 'free destination for the incurably curious', a pretty accurate tag for an institution that seeks to explore the links between medicine, science, life and art. It's a serious topic, but the genius of the museum is that it presents it in an accessible way. The building is light and modern, with varied and interactive displays ranging from interviews with researchers, doctors and patients, to art depicting medicine and models of human organs.

The heart of the permanent collection is Sir Henry Wellcome's eccentric array of objects from around the world. Wellcome (1853–1936), a pharmacist, entrepreneur and collector, was fascinated by medicine and amassed from different civilisations more than one million objects associated with life, birth, death and sickness.

In the **Medicine Now** gallery, interactive displays and provocative artworks are designed to make you ponder humanity and the human body.

The museum also runs outstanding (and free) temporary exhibitions on topics exploring the frontiers of modern medicine, its place in society and its history.

DON'T MISS

➜ Temporary exhibitions

➜ Medicine Now permanent exhibition

➜ Medicine Man, featuring objects from Henry Wellcome's personal collection

PRACTICALITIES

➜ Map p468, F6

➜ www.wellcomecollection.org

➜ 183 Euston Rd, NW1

➜ admission free

➜ ⊙10am-6pm Tue, Wed & Fri-Sun, to 10pm Thu

➜ ⊖Euston Sq, Euston

WALKING ALONG REGENT'S CANAL

The canals that were once a trade lifeline for the capital have now become a favourite escape for Londoners, providing a quiet walk away from traffic and crowds. For visitors, an added advantage of **Regent's Canal** (p252) towpath is that it provides an easy (and delightful) shortcut across North London.

You can, for instance, walk from Little Venice to Camden in less than an hour; on the way, you'll pass Regent's Park, London Zoo, Primrose Hill, beautiful villas designed by architect John Nash as well as redevelopments of old industrial buildings into trendy blocks of flats. Allow 15 to 20 minutes between Camden and Regent's Park, and 25 to 30 minutes between Regent's Park and Little Venice. There are plenty of exits on the way and signposts all along.

If you decide to continue on, it's worth stopping at the **London Canal Museum** (p250) in King's Cross to learn more about the canal's history. Shortly afterwards you'll hit the 878m-long Islington Tunnel and have to take to the roads for a spell. After joining the path again near Colebrooke Row, you can follow the water all the way to the Thames at Limehouse Basin, or divert on to the Hertford Union Canal at Victoria Park and head to **Queen Elizabeth Olympic Park** (p252).

butterflies, amphibians and plant life into its tiny space. There is an informative visitor centre and well-maintained paths to explore.

★GASHOLDER PARK   PARK

Map p466 (⊖King's Cross St Pancras) Part of the impressive redevelopment of the King's Cross area, this urban green space right by Regent's Canal is a masterpiece of regeneration. The cast iron structure used to be the frame of Gasholder No 8, the largest gas storage cylinder in the area (which was originally located across the canal). Carefully renovated, and with the addition of a central lawn, beautiful benches and a mirrored canopy, it has metamorphosed into a gorgeous pocket park.

KING'S CROSS STATION   HISTORIC BUILDING

Map p466 (www.kingscross.co.uk/kings-cross-station; Euston Rd; ⊖King's Cross St Pancras) With its clean lines and the simple arches of its twin train sheds, you might be forgiven for thinking that King's Cross is a more modern building than its show-off neighbour St Pancras, but in fact it opened its doors more than a decade earlier. Built in 1852 in the classic muddy-yellow London stock brick, it stands apart from the prevailing Victorian sensibility of more is more.

In 2012 a major refurbishment was completed, with the opening of a new departures terminal under an exceedingly beautiful, curving, canopy-like roof formed from a lattice-like web of steel. Shabby extensions have been removed from the front of the building, showcasing the facade and

opening up an expansive plaza crowned with a **Henry Moore sculpture**.

Of course, for many people – especially of the more junior persuasion – King's Cross Station means just one thing: the departure point for Hogwarts School of Witchcraft and Wizardry. You'll need to be embarking on an actual train journey to visit the platforms, so the kind people at Network Rail have moved the magical portal leading to **platform 9¾** to a more convenient location in the new departures terminal. A sign has been permanently erected, along with a trolley half disappearing into the wall and carrying a trunk and an owl cage. You can have your picture taken by wizards from the Harry Potter Shop (p270) next door.

HOUSE OF ILLUSTRATION   GALLERY

Map p466 (www.houseofillustration.org.uk; 2 Granary Sq, N1C; adult/child £7.50/4; ⊙10am-6pm Tue-Sun; ⊖King's Cross St Pancras) This charity-run gallery founded by the legendary Sir Quentin Blake (famed as the illustrator of Roald Dahl's books) opened in 2014 and is the UK's sole public gallery purely dedicated to illustration. It stages ever-changing exhibitions – everything from cartoons and book illustrations to advertisements and scientific drawings.

⊙ Regent's Park

ZSL LONDON ZOO   ZOO

See p248.

★**REGENT'S CANAL**   CANAL

Map p468 To escape the crowded streets and enjoy a picturesque, waterside side stretch of North London, take to the canals that once played such a vital role in the transport of goods across the capital. The towpath of the Regent's Canal also makes an excellent shortcut across North London, either on foot or by bike. In full, the ribbon of water runs 9 miles from Little Venice (where it connects with the Grand Union Canal) to the Thames at Limehouse.

You can make do with walking from Little Venice to Camden Town in less than an hour, passing Regent's Park (p252) and London Zoo (p248), as well as beautiful villas designed by architect John Nash and redevelopments of old industrial buildings. Allow 25 to 30 minutes between Little Venice and Regent's Park, and 15 to 20 minutes between Regent's Park and Camden Town. There are plenty of well-signed exits along the way.

If you decide to continue on, it's worth stopping at the London Canal Museum (p250) in King's Cross to learn more about the canal's history. Shortly afterwards you'll hit the 878m-long Islington Tunnel and have to take to the roads for a spell. After joining the path again near Colebrooke Row, you can follow the water all the way to the Thames at Limehouse Basin, or divert on to the Hertford Union Canal at Victoria Park (p228) and head to Queen Elizabeth Olympic Park (p232).

REGENT'S PARK   PARK

Map p468 (www.royalparks.org.uk; ☉5am–dusk; ⊖Regent's Park, Baker St) The most elaborate and formal of London's many parks, Regent's Park is one of the capital's loveliest green spaces. Among its many attractions are London Zoo (p248), Regent's Canal (p252), an ornamental lake and sports pitches where locals meet to play football, rugby and volleyball. **Queen Mary's Gardens**, towards the south of the park, are particularly pretty, especially in June when the roses are in bloom. Performances take place here in an open-air theatre (p268) during summer.

The Prince Regent, the future George IV, commissioned star architect John Nash (the man behind Buckingham Palace, Marble Arch and Brighton's Royal Pavilion) to design the park in what was once a royal hunting ground. The original design included a royal palace and houses for the

aristocracy. Although only a fraction of the grand scheme ever came to fruition, you can get some idea of what Nash might have achieved by the look of the buildings along the Outer Circle.

ABBEY ROAD STUDIOS   HISTORIC BUILDING

(www.abbeyroad.com; 3 Abbey Rd, NW8; ⊖St John's Wood) Beatles aficionados can't possibly visit London without making a pilgrimage to this famous recording studio in St John's Wood. The studios themselves are off-limits, so you'll have to content yourself with examining the decades of fan graffiti on the fence outside. Stop-start local traffic is long accustomed to groups of tourists lining up on the zebra crossing to re-enact the cover of the fab four's 1969 masterpiece *Abbey Road*. In 2010 the crossing was rewarded with Grade II heritage status.

For a strangely engrossing real-time view of the crossing, hit the 'live' tab for the webcam on the studio's website; you can even find your own crossing shot by punching in your time. To reach Abbey Road Studios, take the tube to St John's Wood, cross the road, follow Grove End Rd to its end and turn right. Don't do what some disappointed fans do and head to Abbey Rd Station in West Ham – it's no relation of the true site and miles off course. There are at least 10 Abbey Rds in London, adding to confusion.

LORD'S   STADIUM

(☎020-7616 8500; www.lords.org; St John's Wood Rd, NW8; tours adult/child £20/12; ☉4-6 tours daily; ☎; ⊖St John's Wood) The 'home of cricket' is a must for any devotee of this particularly English game. Book early for the Test matches here, but cricket buffs should also take the absorbing and anecdote-filled 100-minute tour of the ground and facilities (online booking required). Tours take in the famous Long Room, where members watch the games surrounded by portraits of cricket's great and good, and a museum featuring evocative memorabilia that will appeal to fans old and new.

The famous little urn containing the Ashes, the prize of the most fiercely contested competition in cricket, resides here permanently. There are no tours on major match days; tour hours vary through the year, so see the website for details.

LONDON CENTRAL MOSQUE   MOSQUE

Map p468 (www.iccuk.org; 146 Park Rd, NW8; ⊖St John's Wood) Completed in 1977 this striking large white mosque is topped with a glistening golden dome and a minaret, and can hold more than 5000 worshippers. Provided you take your shoes off and dress modestly (females must cover their hair), you're welcome to go inside but, as is the way with mosques, the interior is intentionally simple.

⊙ Primrose Hill

Wedged between well-heeled Regent's Park and grungy Camden, the little neighbourhood of Primrose Hill is high on the property wish list of many Londoners – but utterly unaffordable for most. With its independent boutiques, good restaurants and appealing pubs, it has a rare village feel.

PRIMROSE HILL   PARK
Map p468 (⊖Chalk Farm) On summer weekends, Primrose Hill park is absolutely packed with locals enjoying a picnic and the extraordinary views over the city skyline. Come weekdays, however, and there are mostly just dog walkers and nannies. It's a lovely place to enjoy a quiet stroll or an alfresco sandwich.

⊙ Camden Town

JEWISH MUSEUM LONDON   MUSEUM
Map p468 (www.jewishmuseum.org.uk; 129-131 Albert St, NW1; adult/child £7.50/3.50; ⊙10am-5pm Sat-Thu, to 2pm Fri; ⊖Camden Town) This interesting little museum has permanent displays pertaining to the Jewish faith, the history of Jewish people in Britain and the Holocaust. One of its more important artefacts is a *mikveh* (sunken ritual bath), which was uncovered from Milk St in the City of London in 2001. It dates from the mid-12th century, shortly before the Jews were expelled from England for nearly four centuries.

⊙ Hampstead

The most well-heeled and leafy part of North London, Hampstead has long been associated with intellectuals and artists, although these days it's mainly bankers and foreign oligarchs who can afford to buy property here.

TOP SIGHT
CAMDEN MARKET

Although – or perhaps because – it stopped being cutting-edge several thousand cheap leather jackets ago, Camden Market attracts millions of visitors each year and is one of London's most popular attractions. What started out as a collection of attractive craft stalls beside Camden Lock on the Regent's Canal now extends most of the way from Camden Town tube station to Chalk Farm tube station.

There are three main market areas – **Buck Street Market**, **Camden Lock Market** and **Stables Market** (p269) – although they seem to blend together with the crowds snaking along and the 'normal' shops lining the streets. You'll find a bit of everything: clothes (of variable quality) in profusion, bags, jewellery, arts and crafts, candles, incense and myriad decorative titbits.

The area across the road from the Lock Market is being developed as a high-end retail outfit complete with boutique hotel. The development will be complete in 2018 and many fear that it might affect Camden's rollicking atmosphere.

There are dozens of food stalls at the Lock Market, courtesy of food collective KERB (p261). You can eat at the big communal tables or by the canal.

DON'T MISS

➡ Stables Market
➡ Camden Lock Market
➡ Lunch at the food stalls

PRACTICALITIES

➡ Map p468, D2
➡ www.camdenmarket.com
➡ Camden High St, NW1
➡ ⊙10am-6pm
➡ ⊖Camden Town, Chalk Farm

ℹ WILLOW ROAD & FENTON HOUSE TICKETS

Visitors interested in seeing both No 2 Willow Road (p254) and Fenton House (p254) should consider a combined ticket (£11) to save a few pounds. The two sights are only about 15 minutes' walk from each other across leafy Hampstead.

FENTON HOUSE   HISTORIC BUILDING

Map p465 (NT; ☎020-7435 3471; www.national trust.org.uk/fenton-house; Hampstead Grove, NW3; adult/child £7.70/3.80; ☺11am-5pm Wed-Sun Mar-Oct; ☻Hampstead) One of the oldest houses in Hampstead, this late-17th-century merchant's residence has a charming walled garden with roses and an orchard, and fine collections of porcelain and keyboard instruments, including a 1612 harpsichord once played by Handel. The interior is very evocative thanks to original Georgian furniture and period art such as 17th-century needlework pictures.

NO 2 WILLOW ROAD   NOTABLE BUILDING

Map p465 (NT; ☎020-7435 6166; www.national trust.org.uk/2-willow-road; 2 Willow Rd, NW3; adult/child £6.50/3.25; ☺11am-5pm Wed-Sun Mar-Oct; ☻Hampstead Heath) Fans of modern architecture will want to swing past this property, the central house in a block of three designed by the 'structural rationalist' Ernö Goldfinger in 1939. Many think it looks like the sort of mundane 1950s architecture you see everywhere. It may do now, but 2 Willow Rd was a forerunner in this style.

The interior has cleverly designed storage space, amazing light (rooms that couldn't have a side window have a skylight) and a collection of artworks by Henry Moore, Max Ernst and Bridget Riley. It's accessible to all, thanks to hugely knowledgeable staff. Entry is by guided tour only (11am, noon, 1pm & 2pm) until 3pm, after which unguided visits are allowed.

KEATS HOUSE   HISTORIC BUILDING

Map p465 (www.cityoflondon.gov.uk/keats; 10 Keats Grove, NW3; adult/child £6.50/free; ☺11am-5pm Wed-Sun; ☻Hampstead Heath) This elegant Regency house was home to the golden boy of the Romantic poets, John Keats, from

◉ TOP SIGHT
HAMPSTEAD HEATH

Sprawling Hampstead Heath, with its rolling woodlands and meadows, feels a million miles away – despite being approximately four – from the City of London. It covers 320 hectares, most of it woods, hills and meadows, and is home to about 180 bird species, 23 species of butterflies, grass snakes, bats and a rich array of flora.

It's a wonderful place for a ramble, especially to the top of **Parliament Hill**, which offers expansive views across the city and is one of the most popular places in London to fly a kite. Alternatively head up the hill to Kenwood, with its grand 18th-century house and landscaped gardens, or lose yourself in the West Heath. Signage is limited, but getting a little lost is part of the experience.

If walking is too pedestrian for you, the bathing ponds are another major attraction. There are separate ones for men and women and a slightly less secluded mixed pond (p270).

Once you've had your fill of fresh air and/or culture, do as Londoners do and head to one of the wonderful pubs nearby for a restorative pint.

DON'T MISS

➡ Views from Parliament Hill

➡ Strolling in the woodlands

➡ Kenwood

PRACTICALITIES

➡ Map p465, B3

➡ www.cityoflondon. gov.uk

➡ ☻Hampstead Heath, Gospel Oak

TOP SIGHT
KENWOOD HOUSE

This magnificent neoclassical mansion stands at the northern end of Hampstead Heath in a glorious sweep of landscaped gardens that lead down to a picturesque lake.

The 17th-century house, which was remodelled by Robert Adam in the 1760s, was extensively refurbished in 2013, with rooms repainted in their original colours. The **Great Library**, with its powder-pink and sky-blue vaulted ceiling and vignette paintings, is magnificent.

The house was rescued from developers in the 1920s by Lord Iveagh Guinness, a member of the famous brewing family, who donated it and its wonderful collection of art to the nation. The **Iveagh Bequest**, as it is known, contains paintings by Rembrandt (one of his many self-portraits), Constable, Gainsborough, Reynolds, Hals, Vermeer and Van Dyck and is one of the finest small collections in Britain. Head up the great stairs for the Suffolk Collection, consisting of Jacobean portraits by William Larkin and a set of royal Stuart portraits.

The gardens are another highlight, and you'll find sculptures by Henry Moore and Barbara Hepworth on the lawn. The old servants' wing now houses a sit-down cafe and a snack bar with an ice-cream counter.

DON'T MISS

➜ Rembrandt self-portrait
➜ The Great Library
➜ Strolling in the landscaped gardens

PRACTICALITIES

➜ Map p465, B2
➜ EH
➜ www.english-heritage.org.uk;
➜ Hampstead Lane, NW3
➜ ⊘10am-5pm
➜ 🚼
➜ 🚌210
➜ FREE

1818 to 1820. It was here that Keats met his fiancée Fanny Brawne, literally the girl next door. And it was here that he wrote many of his most celebrated poems. The house is sparsely but evocatively furnished and the museum does a great job of recounting Keats' short and intense life.

There is a 10-minute biographical film shown downstairs and listening stations upstairs where you can listen to some of Keats' poems and excerpts from letters written by both him and Fanny Brawne.

FREUD MUSEUM   MUSEUM
(www.freud.org.uk; 20 Maresfield Gardens, NW3; adult/child £8/free; ⊘noon-5pm Wed-Sun; ⊖Finchley Rd) After fleeing Nazi-occupied Vienna in 1938, Sigmund Freud lived the last year of his life here. The fascinating Freud Museum maintains his study and library much as he left it, with his couch, books and collection of small Egyptian figures and other antiquities, all of which he'd managed to bring with him from Austria. One room upstairs is dedicated to his daughter, Anna, who was also an eminent psychoanalyst and lived in the house until her death in 1982.

You'll find information on psychoanalysis, excerpts of dream analyses scattered around the house, and plenty of information about the large Freud family.

⊙ Highgate

HIGHGATE WOOD   PARK
Map p465 (www.cityoflondon.gov.uk; Archway Rd, N10; ⊘7.30am-sunset; ⊖Highgate) 🌳 With more than 28 hectares of ancient woodland, this park is a wonderful spot for a walk any time of the year. It's also teeming with life: 70 different bird species have been recorded here, along with seven types of bat, 12 types of butterfly and 80 kinds of spider. There's a huge clearing in the centre for sports, and it also has a popular playground and a cafe.

⊙ Highbury

ARSENAL EMIRATES STADIUM   STADIUM
Map p466 (📞020-7619 5000; www.arsenal.com/tours; Hornsey Rd, N5; tours self-guided adult/child £20/10, guided £40; ⊘10am-6pm Mon-Sat, to 4pm Sun; ⊖Holloway Rd) When Arsenal's

TOP SIGHT
HIGHGATE CEMETERY

A Gothic wonderland of shrouded urns, obelisks, broken columns, sleeping angels, Egyptian-style tombs and overgrown graves, Highgate is a Victorian Valhalla spread over 20 wonderfully wild and atmospheric hectares. On the eastern side you can pay your respect to the graves of Karl Marx and Mary Ann Evans (better known as novelist George Eliot). The real highlight, however, is the overgrown **West Cemetery**, where a maze of winding paths leads to the Circle of Lebanon – rings of tombs flanking a circular path and topped with a majestic cedar of Lebanon.

Admission to the West Cemetery is by **guided tour** (adult/child £12/6; ⏲1.45pm Mon-Fri, every 30min 11am-3pm Sat & Sun Nov-Feb, to 4pm Mar-Oct;) only; bookings are essential for weekday tours. Tours of the **East Cemetery** (adult/child £8/4) take place at 2pm on Saturdays.

The most well-known recent interment was that of singer George Michael, who died on Christmas Day 2016 and was buried alongside his mother in March 2017. Also of note is Russian dissident Alexander Litvinenko, who died under sinister circumstances in 2006 when the radioactive isotope Polonium 210 somehow made it into his tea in a Mayfair hotel.

DON'T MISS

➡ Karl Marx's grave
➡ Tour of the West Cemetery
➡ Circle of Lebanon

PRACTICALITIES

➡ Map p465, D2
➡ www.highgatecemetery.org
➡ Swain's Lane, N6East Cemetery
➡ adult/child £4/free
➡ ⏲10am-5pm Mon-Fri, 11am-5pm Sat & Sun
➡ Ⓔ Archway

---

new stadium opened in 2006, fans claimed it would never be the same again. It's true that the 64,000-seat stadium lacks some of the bonhomie of the old Highbury ground, but it's still a sell-out at every game. Match tickets are tricky to come by, even if you have a first-born to sacrifice, so if you're a fan, consider taking a stadium tour instead.

Self-guided audio tours (available in nine languages) are very entertaining, or you could shell out for a guided tour with a former Arsenal player. Both options take you everywhere, from the back entrance used by the players to the entertainment suites where corporate bigwigs watch the game. You'll get to walk to the pitch through 'the tunnel', sit on the team's pitch-side benches and even check out the changing rooms (which are complete with spa and physio suite on Arsenal's side).

Tours include entry to a museum that focuses on the history of the club and its fans, and is therefore likely to only interest the most ardent Arsenal supporters. Visits finish in the stadium's enormous shop, where Arsenal merchandise of every guise is available.

⊙ Islington

Gathered around attractive Upper St, Islington is generally portrayed in the press as a hotbed of champagne socialism, due in part to its association with New Labour in the 1990s (the Blairs famously lived here, along with other key figures). The area's gentrification is reflected in design stores, excellent eateries and a thriving theatre scene, but there are still enough raucous pubs and live-music venues to add some edge.

Less than 200 years ago, Islington was still a quiet village surrounded by farmland, set on the banks of the pleasantly languid New River (most of which is now below street level). Two medieval roads out of London met at what is now Islington High St: one led directly from the City and the other from the Smithfield meat market. Subsequently, Islington became an important rest stop, both for visitors to the City and for livestock. Inns sprung up in the area from the 10th century, the most famous of which was the Angel, which became particularly fashionable in the 18th century when it doubled as a theatre, starting a theatrical tradition that continues in Islington to this day.

Before 1855, Upper St was a veritable livestock highway, with an annual traffic flow that included 50,000 cattle and half a million sheep. By the end of that century, Islington had completely lost its rural feel under the weight of a soaring population. During WWII, 78,000 homes were damaged in the borough and 958 Islingtonians died in air raids.

CRYSTAL MAZE LIVE CHALLENGE

Map p466 (☑08448 718 805; www.the-crystal-maze.com; 10-14 White Lion St, N1; £52.50; ⊖Angel) It's back! The '90s game show of the same name – a British television cult classic – has been reincarnated for the public. The result is hugely impressive and all but identical to the real thing, right down to the animated hosts and challenging games and puzzles, which teams must conquer to gather crystals, which give added time in the dome finale. Book (a long way) in advance.

ST MARY'S CHURCH CHURCH

Map p466 (www.stmaryislington.org; Upper St, N1; ⊖Highbury & Islington or Angel) Although there has been a church on this site since the 12th century, the oldest part of the present-day St Mary's is the tower, with its distinctive spire, dating from 1754. The rest of this elegant Georgian church was rebuilt after being destroyed during the Blitz. The surrounding churchyard is now a leafy little park.

ESTORICK COLLECTION OF
MODERN ITALIAN ART GALLERY

Map p466 (www.estorickcollection.com; 39a Canonbury Sq, N1; adult/child £6.50/free; ⊙11am-6pm Wed-Sat, noon-5pm Sun; ⊖Highbury & Islington) Housed in a listed Georgian building, the Estorick is the only gallery in Britain devoted to Italian art, and one of the leading collections of futurist painting in the world. The collection of paintings, drawings, etchings and sculpture was amassed by American writer and art dealer Eric Estorick and his wife, Salome. The permanent collection includes works by greats such as Giacomo Balla, Umberto Boccioni, Gino Severini, Amedeo Modigliani and Carlo Carrà.

Well-conceived and fascinating special exhibitions have included many 20th-century art movements and lesser-known artists from Italy and beyond. There's also a garden cafe, a small shop and an extensive library.

WORTH A DETOUR

WILLIAM MORRIS GALLERY

Fans of Victoriana and the Arts & Crafts movement should make time for this sensational little **gallery** (☑020-8496 4390; www.wmgallery.org.uk; Lloyd Park, Forest Rd, E17; ⊙10am-5pm Wed-Sun; ⊖Walthamstow Central) FREE. Located in Walthamstow in northeast London, it is the former family home of designer William Morris (1834–96), founder of iconic interior design company Morris & Co, famous far and wide for his patterned wallpaper.

The beautiful Georgian mansion re-opened in August 2012 after two years of extensive renovations and the exhibition inside is truly world class. The gallery gives pride of place to Morris's wide-ranging artistic endeavours, with a fantastic workshop explaining his production processes, and a wonderfully evocative recreation of his shop. But it depicts a much more complete portrait of the artist by also covering his writing (for which he was more famous than he was for his designs in his lifetime) and activism. Morris was appalled by the consequences of industrialisation on manufacturing processes and quality, on people's living conditions and on the environment, and he became a socialist in the 1880s, campaigning tirelessly against capitalism.

The strength of the gallery is its beauty and interactive quality, which children will love. Kids will also love the lovely park at the back, complete with play area. The 1st floor hosts temporary exhibitions. The gallery's **shop** sells beautiful, Morris-inspired design objects and the **Tea Room** in the glasshouse is the perfect place for a break or a light lunch.

To get here from Walthamstow Central tube station, turn right and then first left into Hoe St. Continue on this road for 600m and then turn left into Gaywood Rd. The gallery is across the road, at the end of the street.

ALEXANDRA PARK & PALACE

Built in 1873 as North London's answer to Crystal Palace, **Alexandra Palace** (www.alexandrapalace.com; Alexandra Palace Way, N22; Alexandra Palace) suffered the ignoble fate of burning to the ground only 16 days after opening. Encouraged by attendance figures, investors decided to rebuild and it reopened just two years later. During WWI, it housed German prisoners of war and in 1936 it was the scene of the world's first TV transmission – a variety show called *Here's Looking at You*. The palace burned down again in 1980 but was rebuilt for the third time and opened in 1988.

Today 'Ally Pally' (as it is affectionately known) is a multipurpose conference and exhibition centre, with additional facilities including an indoor ice-skating rink, a panoramic bar, and a popular playground and boating lake. It hosts occasional club nights and concerts, too.

The park in which it stands sprawls over some 196 hectares. Locals come to enjoy the sweeping views of London and a farmers market on Sundays. The fireworks held here on Bonfire Night are some of the most spectacular in town, lighting up the city skyline.

CANONBURY SQUARE   SQUARE

Map p466 (Canonbury Rd, N1; 8am-dusk; Highbury & Islington) A short walk from bustling Upper St, this pretty, park-like square was once home to authors Evelyn Waugh and George Orwell. The latter moved here with his family after his flat in St John's Wood was destroyed during the Blitz. His house at number 27b is marked by a blue plaque, while Waugh's residence at number 17 is unmarked. It's worth pausing in the park to soak up the atmosphere and peruse the dedications on the benches.

Just around the corner, on Canonbury Pl, is privately owned **Canonbury Tower**, a relic of the area's original manor house. Dating from 1509, the house was known to have hosted famous figures such as Sir Francis Bacon and Queen Elizabeth I.

EATING

North London is full of eating gems, including historic pubs, smart cafes, market stalls and ethnically diverse restaurants. It's particularly good for vegetarians, with some excellent exclusively vegetarian and vegan establishments and plenty of others offering a good meat-free selection.

King's Cross & Euston

RUBY VIOLET   ICE CREAM $

Map p466 (www.rubyviolet.co.uk; Midlands Goods Shed, 3 Wharf Rd, N1C; 1/2 scoops £3/5.50; 10am-7pm Sun-Thu, to 10pm Fri & Sat; King's Cross St Pancras) This parlour is taking ice cream to the next level: flavours are wonderfully original (masala chai, Belgian chocolate, raspberry and sweet potato) and toppings and hot sauces are housemade. Plus, there's Pudding Club on Friday and Saturday nights, when you can sink your spoon into mini baked Alaskas or hot chocolate fondant and ice cream.

Ruby Violet makes a point of using the finest ingredients, be they organic, free-range or grown by small producers.

ROTI KING   MALAYSIAN $

Map p468 (40 Doric Way, NW1; mains £5-7; noon-3pm & 5-10.30pm Mon-Fri, noon-10.30pm Sat; Euston) The neon sign pointing you in the direction of this pocket-sized basement restaurant doesn't look too promising. Step inside the white-tiled eatery, however, and you know you're in safe hands. It's all about roti canai, a flaky flatbread typical of Malaysia, served with fragrant bowls of curry or stuffed with tasty fillings. A genuine budget option that isn't a sandwich or a salad – hurrah.

DIWANA BHEL POORI HOUSE   INDIAN $

Map p468 (020-7387 5556; www.diwanabph.com; 121-123 Drummond St, NW1; mains £5.10-8.95; noon-11.30pm Mon-Sat, to 10.30pm Sun; Euston) One of the best Indian vegetarian restaurants in London, Diwana specialises in Bombay-style *bhel poori* (a tangy, soft and crunchy 'party mix' dish) and *dosas* (filled crispy pancakes made from rice flour). Solo diners should consider a *thali* (a complete meal consisting of lots of small dishes).

The all-you-can-eat lunchtime buffet (£7) is legendary, and there are daily specials.

REAL FOOD MARKET
MARKET **$**

Map p466 (www.realfoodfestival.co.uk; King's Cross Sq, N1; dishes £4-8; ☺noon-7pm Wed-Fri; ✐; ⊖King's Cross St Pancras) This lovely market brings together two dozen gourmet food stalls three times a week. You can get anything from lovely cheeses, cured meats, smoked haddock and artisan bread to take-away dishes such as wraps, curries and delicious cakes.

WAITROSE KING'S CROSS
SUPERMARKET **$**

Map p466 (www.waitrose.com; Midland Goods Shed, 1 Wharf Rd, N1C; ☺8am-10pm Mon-Sat, noon-6pm Sun; ⊖King's Cross St Pancras) The branch of this gourmet supermarket isn't your typical supermarket experience: not only does it have an excellent takeaway section with lovely salads and deli-type fare, but it also has a bakery, a juice bar, a coffee bar and a wine bar. Perfect for a decadent picnic by the canal.

KING'S LIBRARY CAFÉ
MODERN BRITISH **$**

Map p466 (1st fl, British Library, 96 Euston Rd, N1; mains £5-10; ☺9.30am-5pm Mon-Fri, to 4pm Sat; ☎; ⊖King's Cross St Pancras) A cafeteria offering a range of hot and cold mains – pick from the well-assorted salad bar, or the pie, pasta or curry of the day. The seating area has great views of the towering King's Library.

ADDIS
AFRICAN **$**

Map p466 (☎020-7278 0679; www.addisrestaurant.co.uk; 40-42 Caledonian Rd, N1; mains £9-12; ☺noon-2.30pm & 6-10.30pm; ✐; ⊖King's Cross St Pancras) Cheery Addis serves pungent Ethiopian dishes such as *ayeb be gomen* (cottage cheese with spinach and spices) and *fuul musalah* (crushed fava beans topped with feta cheese, falafel and sautéed in ghee), which are eaten on a platter-sized piece of soft but slightly elastic injera bread. The restaurant is normally full of African diners, which we take as a good sign.

FOODILIC
CAFE **$**

Map p466 (www.foodilic.com; 260 Pentonville Rd, N1; mains £4-8; ☺8am-7pm Mon-Fri, from 9am Sat; ✐; ▣King's Cross St Pancras) An enticing display of salads, quiches and *feuilletés* (savoury pastries) covers the counter, presenting plenty of difficult choices – but at these prices you can afford to pile your plate high. Seating is limited to half-a-dozen mushroom-shaped chunky wooden tables at the rear. The food is half price for the last hour.

GRAIN STORE
INTERNATIONAL **$$**

Map p466 (☎020-7324 4466; www.grainstore.com; 1-3 Stable St, N1C; mains £13-20.50; ☺10am-11.30pm Mon-Sat, 10.30am-3.30pm Sun; ✐; ⊖King's Cross St Pancras) Fresh seasonal vegetables take top billing at Bruno Loubet's bright and breezy Granary Sq restaurant. Meat does appear but it lurks coyly beneath leaves, or adds crunch to mashes. The creative menu gainfully plunders from numerous cuisines to produce dishes that are simultaneously healthy and delicious.

CARAVAN
INTERNATIONAL **$$**

Map p466 (☎020-7101 7661; www.caravanrestaurants.co.uk; 1 Granary Sq, N1C; mains £7-19.50; ☺8am-10.30pm Mon-Fri, 10am-10.30pm Sat, 10am-4pm Sun; ☎✐; ⊖King's Cross St Pancras) Housed in the lofty Granary Building, Caravan is a vast industrial-chic destination for tasty fusion bites from around the world. You can opt for several small plates to share tapas style, or stick to main-sized plates. The outdoor seating area on Granary Sq is especially popular on warm days.

KARPO
EUROPEAN **$$**

Map p466 (☎020-3096 9900; www.karpo.co.uk; 23-27 Euston Rd, NW1; mains £11-19, breakfast £7-10; ☺7am-10pm Mon-Sat, 8am-9pm Sun; ⊖King's Cross St Pancras) There is something utterly refreshing about Karpo, with its bright, modern space, 'living wall', gracious service and delicious, seasonal brasserie-style menu served round the clock. It all looks effortless. Breakfasts include the usual eggy suspects, as well as smoothies and pancakes.

✖ Primrose Hill

MANNA
VEGETARIAN **$$**

Map p468 (☎020-7722 8028; www.mannav.com; 4 Erskine Rd, NW3; mains £12-14; ☺noon-3pm & 6.30-10pm Tue-Sat, noon-7.30pm Sun; ✐; ⊖Chalk Farm) Tucked away on a side street, this upmarket little place does a brisk trade in inventive vegetarian and vegan cooking. The menu features mouth-watering, beautifully presented dishes incorporating elements of Californian, Mexican and Asian cuisine with nods to the raw-food trend. The cheesecake of the day is always a hit. The two-course lunch menu is a steal for £11.

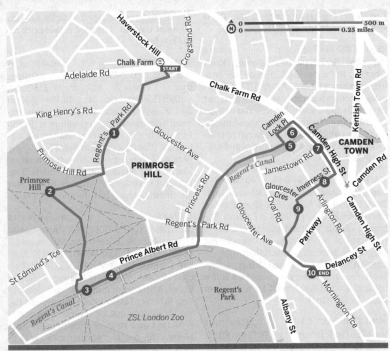

Neighbourhood Walk
A Northern Point of View

START CHALK FARM TUBE STATION
END EDINBORO CASTLE
LENGTH 4KM; TWO HOURS

This walk takes in North London's most interesting locales, including celebrity-infested Primrose Hill and chaotic Camden Town, home to loud guitar bands and the last of London's cartoon punks. When you come out of Chalk Farm station, cross the road and walk up Regent's Park Rd. Turn left on the railway bridge and continue up the southern, boutique-lined stretch of **1 Regent's Park Rd.** This is one of London's most affluent neighbourhoods, home to many darlings of the women's mags, so keep your eyes open for famous faces.

When you reach **2 Primrose Hill** (p253), walk to the top of the park where you'll find a classic view of central London's skyline. On sunny days the park is full of revellers sunbathing, enjoying a picnic or a kick-about. Walk down the hill through the park, bearing right towards Primrose Hill

Lodge. Cross the road and join the towpath along **3 Regent's Canal,** turning left. You'll walk past the large aviary at **4 London Zoo** (p248), quaint narrow boats, superb mansions and converted industrial buildings. At **5 Camden Lock,** turn left and head into the **6 Camden Lock Market** (p269). With its original fashion, ethnic art and dozens of food stalls, it's a fun, buzzing place, particularly at weekends. Exit onto **7 Camden High St,** taking note of the giant Doc Martin boots, angels and dragons projecting from the upper levels of the shops. Turn right onto **8 Inverness St,** which hosts its own little market and is lined with bars. At **9 Gloucester Cres** turn left and walk past the glorious Georgian townhouses. At the end of the road, turn left then cross Parkway onto Delancey St and make a beeline for the **10 Edinboro Castle** (p265), where this walk ends with a well-deserved drink! Warning: if it's a balmy spring or summer day, you may be there a while. And when you're ready to go home, Camden Town tube station is just a five-minute walk away.

✗ Camden Town

★ HOOK CAMDEN TOWN
FISH & CHIPS $

Map p468 (www.hookrestaurants.com; 65 Parkway, NW1; mains £8-12; ⏰noon-3pm & 5-10pm Mon-Thu, noon-10.30pm Fri & Sat, to 9pm Sun; 👶; ⊖Camden Town) 🏊 In addition to working entirely with sustainable small fisheries and local suppliers, Hook makes all its sauces on site and wraps its fish in recycled materials, supplying diners with extraordinarily fine-tasting morsels. Totally fresh, the fish arrives in panko breadcrumbs or tempura batter, with seaweed salted chips. Craft beers and fine wines are also on hand.

Sauces go beyond the usual suspects, and range from ketchup and tartare to garlic truffle, chipotle, hot mango and lime, chimichurri and piri-piri. There's also a great kids' menu, free-range chicken and tacos. All that and the setting has all the breezy simplicity of the seaside.

★ CHIN CHIN LABS
ICE CREAM $

Map p468 (www.chinchinlabs.com; 49-50 Camden Lock Pl, NW1; ice cream £4-5; ⏰noon-7pm Sun-Thu, to 10pm Fri & Sat; ⊖Camden Town) This is food chemistry at its absolute best. Chefs prepare the ice-cream mixture and freeze it on the spot by adding liquid nitrogen. Flavours change regularly and match the seasons (spiced hot cross bun, passionfruit and coconut, for instance). Sauces and toppings are equally creative. Try the ice-cream sandwich if you can: ice cream wedged inside gorgeous brownies or cookies.

It's directly opposite the giant Gilgamesh statue inside Camden Lock Market.

KERB CAMDEN MARKET
MARKET $

Map p468 (www.kerbfood.com; Camden Lock Market; mains £6-8; ⏰noon-5pm; 👶; ⊖Camden Town) From Argentinian to Vietnamese, the KERB food market collective is like an A – Z of world cuisines. Each stall looks more mouth-watering than the next, and there should be enough choice to keep even the fussiest of eaters happy. Eat on the big communal tables or find a spot somewhere along the canal.

MARKET
MODERN BRITISH $$

Map p468 (📞020-7267 9700; www.marketrestaurant.co.uk; 43 Parkway, NW1; 2-course lunch menu £11.50, mains £15-20; ⏰noon-2.30pm & 6-10.30pm Mon-Sat, 11am-3pm Sun; ⊖Camden Town) This fabulous restaurant is an ode to

---

NORTH LONDON'S BEST VEGETARIAN RESTAURANTS

North London is the place to be for creative, filling and absolutely delicious vegetarian cuisine to suit all tastes. Here are some of the best. Note: unlike the others, Addis is not, strictly speaking, vegetarian but Ethiopian cuisine has a rich vegetarian tradition, which is well represented in the restaurant's menu.

Addis (p259)

Manna (p259)

Woodlands (p262)

Rasa (p264)

---

great, simple British food, with a measure of French sophistication thrown in. The light and airy space (bare brick walls, steel tables and basic wooden chairs) reflects this stripped-back approach.

NAMAASTE KITCHEN
INDIAN $$

Map p468 (📞020-7485 5977; www.namaastekitchen.co.uk; 64 Parkway, NW1; mains £10.50-19; ⏰noon-3pm & 5.30-11pm Mon-Fri, noon-11pm Sat & Sun; 👶; ⊖Camden Town) Although everything's of a high standard, if there's one thing you should try at Namaaste, it's the kebab platter: the meat and fish coming off the kitchen grill are beautifully tender and incredibly flavoursome. The bread basket is another hit, with specialities such as spiced *missi roti* making a nice change from the usual naan.

YORK & ALBANY
MODERN BRITISH $$

Map p468 (📞020-7388 3344; www.gordonramsay restaurants.com/york-and-albany; 127-129 Parkway, NW1; mains £11.50-25, 2-/3-course lunch £20/24; ⏰7am-3pm & 6-11pm Mon-Sat, 7am-9pm Sun; 👶; ⊖Camden Town) Part of chef Gordon Ramsay's culinary empire, this lively hotel brasserie serves British classics in its light-filled dining room. It also churns out great wood-fired pizzas and offers some sort of meal/drink deal most weeknights.

✗ Kentish Town

DIRTY BURGER
BURGERS $

Map p465 (📞020-3310 2010; www.eatdirty burger.com; 79 Highgate Rd, NW5; burgers £6-7; ⏰noon-midnight Mon-Thu, to 1am Fri, 9am-1am

Sat, to 11pm Sun; ⊖Kentish Town) Apart from eggs with sausages or bacon until 11am at weekends, this chic shack serves nothing but burgers (including a vegetarian version), fries and milkshakes. And *what* burgers: thick, juicy and wonderfully messy, with mustard, gherkin and cheese. The shack is located in the backyard behind Pizza East restaurant. There isn't much dining space, so take away to Hampstead Heath instead.

✗ Hampstead

GINGER & WHITE   CAFE $

Map p465 (www.gingerandwhite.com; 4a-5a Perrins Ct, NW3; mains £4.50-8.50; ⊘7.30am-5.30pm Mon-Fri, 8.30am-5.30pm Sat & Sun; 🛜🖉🚼; ⊖Hampstead) This lovely cafe on a quiet alleyway is a long-standing Hampstead favourite for its excellent coffee, simple but delicious food and light, airy set-up. Depending on the time of day, you'll find yummy mummies, young professionals using the window seats as office space and devoted locals on a first-name basis with staff.

WOODLANDS   INDIAN $

Map p465 (☑020-7794 3080; www.woodlandsrestaurant.co.uk; 102 Heath St, NW3; dishes £5-8, thali £19; ⊘noon-2.45pm Fri-Sun, 6-10.45pm Tue-Sun; 🖉; ⊖Hampstead) Don't expect cutting-edge decor or faultless service, but this South Indian restaurant is a great bet for an affordable vegetarian meal in Hampstead. It caters superbly to vegan, gluten-free and dairy-free diners too.

WELLS TAVERN   GASTROPUB $$

Map p465 (☑020-7794 3785; www.thewellshampstead.co.uk; 30 Well Walk, NW3; mains £12-25; ⊘noon-11pm; 🛜; ⊖Hampstead) This popular gastropub has a surprisingly modern interior, given its traditional exterior. The menu is proper posh English pub grub – Cumberland sausages, mash and onion gravy, and full roasts with all the trimmings. At weekends you'll need to fight to get a table if you haven't booked ahead. The outdoor tables are prime spots for contemplation.

STAG   GASTROPUB $$

Map p465 (☑020-7722 2646; www.thestagnw3.com; 67 Fleet Rd, NW3; mains £9-17.50; ⊘noon-11pm; ⊖Hampstead Heath) Although the Stag is a fantastic pub for craft beer, it's known in North London for its outstanding food

– the Sunday roast and beef-and-ale pie in particular. The summer barbecue in the garden is another delight. The only drawback is that service can be slow.

GAUCHO   ARGENTINE $$$

Map p465 (☑020-7431 8222; www.gauchorestaurants.co.uk; 64 Heath St, NW3; mains £16.50-60, 2-/3-course lunch £24.50/27.50; ⊘11.30am-11pm Sun-Wed, to midnight Thu-Sat; ⊖Hampstead) Carnivores rejoice; this is one of the finest places in London for a steak. There are several branches of this Argentinian grill across the capital, but this one has the advantage of being less busy than its counterparts and it serves a special *asado* (barbecue) menu, complete with alfresco seating, when the weather permits.

✗ Barnsbury

IBERIA   GEORGIAN $$

Map p466 (☑020-7700 7750; www.iberiarestaurant.co.uk; 294-296 Caledonian Rd, N1; mains £8.90-17; ⊘5-11pm Tue-Fri, 1-11pm Sat, 1-9pm Sun; ⊖Caledonian Rd & Barnsbury) On an insalubrious strip of affordable ethnic eateries, Iberia stands out for its pleasant surrounds, friendly service and excellent traditional Georgian fare. If you're not familiar with the cuisine, expect a meaty morph of Russian and Middle Eastern flavours.

✗ Islington

LE MERCURY   FRENCH $

Map p466 (☑020-7354 4088; www.lemercury.co.uk; 140a Upper St, N1; mains £10.95; ⊘noon-1am Mon-Sat, to 11pm Sun; ⊖Highbury & Islington, Angel) An excellent and wildly popular budget French eatery, Le Mercury seems to have everything you could need in its winning formula: romantic atmosphere with candlelit, petite tables and plants everywhere, combined with superb French food at unbeatable prices. Londoners have long known about this place, so reservations are advised.

CHILANGO   MEXICAN $

Map p466 (www.chilango.co.uk; 27 Upper St, N1; burritos & tacos £6-7; ⊘11.30am-10pm; 🖉; ⊖Angel) The good value and tastiness of Chilango's Mexican fare is no secret among Islingtonians on a budget. Burritos come bursting to the seams with your choice of

STOKE NEWINGTON

East of Holloway and north of Dalston, **Stoke Newington** is a step too far off the beaten track for most visitors to London, which is a shame, as there are a few excellent reasons to seek it out. Set on the old Roman road heading north from the City of London, Stokey (as the locals call it) was a small village on the edge of the woods where travellers might stop to water their horses right up until Tudor times. Despite being gobbled up by London in the intervening centuries, it still retains traces of a village feel.

Enchanting **Abney Park Cemetery** (www.abneypark.org; Stoke Newington Church St, N16; ⊘8am-dusk; ☐73) was bought and developed by a private firm in 1840 as a burial ground and arboretum catering for central London's overflow. It was a dissenters (ie non–Church of England) cemetery and many of the most influential Presbyterians, Quakers and Baptists are buried here, including the Salvation Army founder, William Booth. The derelict chapel at its centre could be right out of a horror film, and the atmosphere of the whole place is rather spooky.

After being neglected for several decades, during which time it turned into a delightfully overgrown ruin and developed a reputation as a gay cruising ground, its care was taken over by a charitable trust in 1991. It's now a managed wilderness, providing an important urban habitat for birds, butterflies and bugs – if you're very lucky you might spot tawny owls or sparrowhawks.

meat (chicken, prawns, pork or beef), beans, salad, rice and sauces. Vegetarians are well catered for too. Eat in the bright, colourful interior or take it away.

⭐ DUKE OF CAMBRIDGE GASTROPUB **$$**

Map p466 (☑020-7359 3066; www.dukeorganic. co.uk; 30 St Peter's St, N1; mains £13.50-22; ⊘noon-11pm Mon-Sat, to 10.30pm Sun; ☑☻; ☻Angel) ⌖ The UK's first certified organic pub is a great place to avoid the crowds, as it's tucked some way down a side street in Islington where casual passers-by rarely tread. It has a fantastic selection of beers and ales on tap, a great (biodynamic) wine list and an interesting organic menu with a Mediterranean bent.

⭐ OTTOLENGHI BAKERY, MEDITERRANEAN **$$**

Map p466 (☑020-7288 1454; www.ottolenghi. co.uk; 287 Upper St, N1; breakfast £5.50-10.50, mains lunch/dinner from £12.90/11; ⊘8am-10.30pm Mon-Sat, 9am-7pm Sun; ☑; ☻Highbury & Islington) Mountains of meringues tempt you through the door of this deli-restaurant, where a sumptuous array of baked goods and fresh salads greets you. Meals are as light and bright as the brilliantly white interior design, with a strong influence from the eastern Mediterranean.

⭐ TRULLO ITALIAN **$$**

Map p466 (☑020-7226 2733; www.trullorestaurant.com; 300-302 St Paul's Rd, N1; mains £13-21; ⊘12.30-2.45pm & 6-10.15pm Mon-Sat, 12.30-3pm Sun; ☻Highbury & Islington) Trullo's daily homemade pasta is delicious, but the main attraction here is the charcoal grill, which churns out the likes of succulent Italian-style pork chops, steaks and fish. The extensive and all-Italian wine list is another hit. Service is excellent, although dinner time can get packed; reservations are essential.

YIPIN CHINA CHINESE **$$**

Map p466 (☑020-7354 3388; www.yipinchina. co.uk; 72 Liverpool Rd, N1; mains £8-22; ⊘noon-11pm; ☑; ☻Angel) The kind of Chinese restaurant that's usually full of Chinese people (ie the good kind of restaurant), Yipin specialises in the spicy, fragrant, colourful cuisine of Hunan, and there are plenty of fiery Sichuanese and familiar Cantonese dishes to choose from, too. The lengthy picture menu makes the choosing (slightly) easier.

SMOKEHOUSE BARBECUE **$$**

Map p466 (☑020-7354 1144; www.smokehou-seislington.co.uk; 63-69 Canonbury Rd, N1; mains £14-18.50; ⊘5-11pm Mon-Fri, noon-midnight Sat, to 10.30pm Sun; ☜; ☻Highbury & Islington) In this lovely, light-filled pub, elegantly turned out in dark wood and whitewashed walls, you'll find a meaty menu of international dishes, all imbued – as the name suggests – with a smoky flavour (everything is grilled, roasted or smoked on the premises). Ingredients are carefully sourced and skilfully combined, and there is a particularly extensive beer list. The little leafy garden is a boon in warmer months.

KIPFERL
AUSTRIAN $$

Map p466 (www.kipferl.co.uk; 20 Camden Passage, N1; mains £7.50-17.50; ⊙noon-10pm Mon, 9am-10pm Tue-Sat, 10am-8pm Sun; ⊜Angel) Part cafe, part restaurant and totally Austrian, Kipferl serves classic comfort food such as Wiener schnitzel, *Käsespatzle* (egg noodles with cheese) and spinach dumplings. Otherwise just sidle in and choose a coffee from the 'colour palette' menu that's typical of Viennese cafes, and pick from the mouth-watering selection of cakes (Sacher torte, *Apfelstrudel* etc).

✕ Stoke Newington

RASA
INDIAN $

(☏020-7249 0344; www.rasarestaurants.com; 55 Stoke Newington Church St, N16; mains £4.50-6.75; ⊙6-10.45pm Mon-Fri, noon-3pm & 6-11pm Sat & Sun; ✎; ☏73) The flagship of the Rasa chain, this South Indian vegetarian eatery is Stoke Newington's best-known restaurant. Friendly service, a calm atmosphere, reasonable prices and outstanding food from the Indian state of Kerala are its distinctive features. The multicourse Keralan Feast (£17) is for the ravenous only.

GOOD EGG
MIDDLE EASTERN $$

(http://thegoodeggn16.com; 93 Stoke Newington Church St, N16; dishes £6.50-17.50; ⊙9am-4pm Mon, to 11pm Tue-Fri, 10am-11pm Sat & Sun; ✎👶; ☏73) Working the culinary trend of the moment – Levantine food meets modern European cuisine – the Good Egg, with its long opening hours, is many things to many people: a family-friendy cafe, a trendy restaurant and the best place in Stoke Newington for brunch. The trick is that it consistently delivers. Expect queues.

🍷 DRINKING & 🍸 NIGHTLIFE

Camden Town is one of North London's favoured drinking areas, with more bars and pubs pumping out music than you could ever manage to crawl between. The hills of Hampstead are a real treat for old-time-pub aficionados, while

Islington is known for its theatre pubs and tucked-away wine and cocktail bars. As for King's Cross, there are new places opening all the time, many in converted Victorian buildings.

🍷 King's Cross & Euston

★ BAR PEPITO
WINE BAR

Map p466 (www.barpepito.co.uk; 3 Varnishers Yard, The Regent's Quarter, N1; ⊙5pm-midnight Mon-Sat; ⊜King's Cross St Pancras) This intimate Andalusian bodega specialises in sherry and tapas. Novices fear not: the staff are on hand to advise. They're experts at food pairings (top-notch ham and cheese selections). To go the whole hog, try a tasting flight of selected sherries with snacks to match.

★ DRINK, SHOP & DO
BAR

Map p466 (☏020-7278 4335; www.drinkshopdo.co.uk; 9 Caledonian Rd, N1; ⊙7.30am-midnight Mon-Thu, 7.30am-2am Fri, 10.30am-2am Sat, to 6pm Sun; 🔊; ⊜King's Cross St Pancras) This kooky little outlet will not be pigeonholed. As its name suggests, it is many things to many people: a bar, a cafe, an activities centre, a disco even. But the idea is that there will always be drinking (be it tea or gin), music and things to do – anything from dancing to building Lego robots.

★ EUSTON TAP
BAR

Map p468 (☏020-3137 8837; www.eustontap.com; 190 Euston Rd, NW1; ⊙noon-11pm; ⊜Euston) This specialist drinking spot inhabits a monumental stone structure on the approach to Euston Station. Craft beer devotees can choose between eight cask ales, 20 keg beers and 150 brews by the bottle. Grab a seat on the pavement, take the tight spiral staircase upstairs or buy a bottle to take away. It's part of a twinset with the **Northern Tap** across the street, which specialises in craft beer from northern England (Euston Station being the gateway to the north).

CAMINO
BAR

Map p466 (www.camino.uk.com; 3 Varnishers Yard, The Regent's Quarter, N1; ⊙noon-midnight Sun-Thu, to 1am Fri & Sat; 🔊; ⊜King's Cross St Pancras) Festive Camino is popular with London's Spanish community and therefore feels quite authentic. Drinks, too, are representative of what you'd find in Spain: cava, Estrella on tap and a long all-Spanish wine list. It's a brilliant place to watch football –

international games in particular – and DJs hit the turntables on weekends. In summer the courtyard gets absolutely crammed.

ORIGIN COFFEE ROASTERS CAFE

Map p466 (96 Euston Rd, NW1; ⊘7.30am-6pm Mon-Fri, 9am-4pm Sat, 10am-4pm Sun) This beautiful little cafe scores highly on design but even more on its coffee. One of just a handful of outlets from specialist coffee roaster Origin, whose raison d'être is provenance and processing, it offers regularly changing feature coffees and a selection of espresso-based concoctions and filter options.

BIG CHILL HOUSE BAR

Map p466 (www.wearebigchill.com; 257-259 Pentonville Rd, N1; ⊘11am-midnight Sun-Wed, to 1am Thu, to 3am Fri & Sat; 🛜; ⊜King's Cross St Pancras) Come the weekend, the only remotely chilled-out space in this large, buzzy bar is its first-rate and generously proportioned rooftop terrace. It's run by the people behind the Big Chill record label, so it can be counted on for a varied roster of live music and DJs. The sound system is fantastic and entry is free most nights.

EGG LDN CLUB

Map p466 (www.egglondon.co.uk; 200 York Way, N7; ⊘11pm-6am Tue, to 7am Fri, to 9am Sat; ⊜Caledonian Rd, King's Cross St Pancras) Egg has a superb layout with two vast exposed-concrete rooms, a wooden loft space, a garden and a roof terrace. It specialises in house and techno and attracts some heavyweight DJs, particularly on Saturday nights. At weekends it runs a free shuttle bus from 11pm onwards, leaving from outside 68 York Way, outside King's Cross Station.

BRITISH LIBRARY COFFEE SHOP CAFE

Map p466 (Upper ground fl, British Library, 96 Euston Rd, NW1; ⊘9.30am-7.30pm Mon-Thu, to 5.30pm Fri, to 4.30pm Sat & Sun; 🛜) The coffee comes courtesy of Nude Espresso, a delicious micro-roaster in the East End. There are plenty of sweet and savoury snacks to enjoy along with your drinks, too.

🍷 Primrose Hill

QUEEN'S PUB

Map p468 (www.thequeensprimrosehill.co.uk; 49 Regent's Park Rd, NW1; ⊘11am-11pm; 🛜; ⊜Chalk Farm) Perhaps because this is Primrose Hill, the Queen's is a bit more cafe-like than your average pub. Still, it's a good one, with a creditable wine and beer selection and, more importantly, plenty of people-watching to do while sipping your pint – Jude Law has been known to come here for a tipple.

🍷 Camden Town

★PROUD CAMDEN BAR

Map p468 (www.proudcamden.com; Stables Market, Chalk Farm Rd, NW1; ⊘11am-1.30am Mon-Sat, to midnight Sun; ⊜Chalk Farm) Proud occupies a former horse hospital within Stables Market, with private booths in the old stalls, fantastic artworks on the walls (the main bar acts as a gallery during the day) and a kooky garden terrace complete with a hot tub. It's also one of Camden's best music venues, with live bands and DJs most nights (entry free to £15).

★EDINBORO CASTLE PUB

Map p468 (www.edinborocastlepub.co.uk; 57 Mornington Tce, NW1; ⊘11am-11pm; 🛜; ⊜Camden Town) Large and relaxed Edinboro offers a refined atmosphere, gorgeous furniture perfect for slumping into, a fine bar and a full menu. The highlight, however, is the huge beer garden, complete with warm-weather barbecues and decorated with coloured lights on long summer evenings. Patio heaters come out in winter.

LOCK TAVERN PUB

Map p468 (www.lock-tavern.com; 35 Chalk Farm Rd, NW1; ⊘noon-midnight Mon-Thu, to 1am Fri & Sat, to 11pm Sun; ⊜Chalk Farm) A Camden institution, the black-clad Lock Tavern rocks: it's cosy inside, and there's a rear beer garden and a great roof terrace from where you can watch the market throngs. Beer is plentiful here and it proffers a prolific roll call of guest bands and well-known DJs at weekends to rev things up. Dancing is encouraged. Entry is always free.

HER UPSTAIRS GAY & LESBIAN

Map p468 (www.herupstairs.co.uk; 18 Kentish Town Rd, NW1; ⊘5pm-1am Sun-Thu, to 3am Fri & Sat; ⊜Camden Town) A mainly young, alternative, multigendered crowd follows the light of the pink chandeliers up to this drag-driven bar. Grab a drink under the mismatched tasselled lampshades and enjoy whatever oddball entertainment is on offer.

BLUES KITCHEN
PUB

Mapp468(020-73875277;www.theblueskitchen. com; 111-113 Camden High St, NW1; noon-midnight Mon-Thu, to 3am Fri & Sat, 10am-1am Sun; Camden Town) The Blues Kitchen's recipe for success is simple: select brilliant blues bands, host them in a fabulous bar, make it (mostly) free and offer some excellent food and drink. Which means that the crowds keep on comin'. There's live music every night – anything from folk to rock 'n' roll – and blues jams from 8.30pm on Sundays.

BREWDOG CAMDEN
BAR

Map p468 (www.brewdog.com; 113 Bayham St, NW1; noon-11.30pm Mon-Thu, to midnight Fri & Sat, to 10.30pm Sun; ; Camden Town) The hair of this particular dog is craft beer, with around 20 different brews on tap. BrewDog's own brewery is up in Scotland, but more than half of the bar's stock is comprised of guest beers sourced from boutique breweries the world over. Mop it all up with a burger or a hot dog.

Kentish Town

BULL & GATE
PUB

Map p465 (www.bullandgatenw5.co.uk; 389 Kentish Town Rd, NW5; 11am-11pm Sun-Thu, to midnight Fri & Sat; ; Kentish Town) Once one of the best places to see unsigned but promising talent, the legendary Bull & Gate's old-school music venue has metamorphosed into an elegant gastropub-cum–piano bar. The upstairs bar has been lavishly decorated in the spirit of an old gentleman's club – expect cocktails and live jazz on Fridays and Saturdays.

Hampstead

★HOLLY BUSH
PUB

Map p465 (www.hollybushhampstead.co.uk; 22 Holly Mount, NW3; noon-11pm Mon-Sat, to 10.30pm Sun; ; Hampstead) This beautiful Grade II–listed Georgian pub opens to an antique interior, with open fires in winter. It has a knack for making you stay longer than you planned. Set above Heath St, in a secluded hilltop location, it's reached via the Holly Bush Steps.

SPANIARD'S INN
PUB

Map p465 (www.thespaniardshampstead.co.uk; Spaniards Rd, NW3; noon-11pm; ; 210) Dating from 1585, this historic tavern has more character than a West End musical. It was highwayman Dick Turpin's hangout between robbery escapades, but it's also served as a watering hole for more savoury characters such as author Charles Dickens and Romantic poets Shelley, Keats and Byron. It even gets a mention in *Dracula*. There's a big, blissful garden that gets crammed at weekends.

GARDEN GATE
PUB

Map p465 (www.thegardengatehampstead.co.uk; 14 South End Rd, NW3; noon-11pm Sun-Fri, 10am-11.30pm Sat; ; Hampstead Heath) At the bottom of the heath hides this gem of a pub, a 19th-century cottage with a gorgeous beer garden. The interior is wonderfully cosy, with dark-wood tables, upholstered chairs and an assortment of distressed sofas. It serves Pimms and lemonade in summer and mulled wine in winter, both ideal after a long walk. The food's good too.

Highgate

★FLASK
PUB

Map p465 (www.theflaskhighgate.com; 77 Highgate West Hill, N6; noon-11pm; ; Highgate) Charming nooks and crannies, an old circular bar and an enticing beer garden make this 1663 pub the perfect place for a pint en route between Hampstead Heath and Highgate Cemetery. In winter huddle down in the cosy interior and enjoy the Sunday roast and open fires. It's like a village pub in the city.

BOOGALOO
BAR

Map p465 (020-8340 2928; www.theboogaloo. co.uk; 312 Archway Rd, N6; 5pm-midnight Mon-Wed, to 1am Thu, 4pm-2am Fri, 12.30pm-2am Sat, to midnight Sun; ; Highgate) 'London's Number 1 Jukebox' is how Boogaloo flaunts itself: its celebrity-musician-selected jukebox playlists feature the favourite 10 songs of the likes of Nick Cave, Sinead O'Connor and Kate Moss, to name but a few. There's plenty to boogie to (and dance classes to perfect your moves), as well as live music, pub quizzes and comedy nights.

If you're into music in a big way, you won't regret the trek to come here.

🍷 Islington

BULL
PUB

Map p466 (www.thebullislington.co.uk; 100 Upper St, N1; ⊗noon-midnight; 📶; ⊖Angel) One of Islington's liveliest pubs (with DJs on weekend nights and sports events on TV), the Bull serves a large range of draught lager, real ales, fruit beers, ciders and wheat beer, plus a good selection of wine. The mezzanine is generally a little quieter than downstairs, although on weekend nights you'll often struggle to find a seat.

69 COLEBROOKE ROW
COCKTAIL BAR

Map p466 (www.69colebrookerow.com; 69 Colebrooke Row, N1; ⊗5pm-midnight Sun-Thu, to 2am Fri & Sat; ⊖Angel) Also known as 'the bar with no name', this tiny establishment may be nothing much to look at, but it has a stellar reputation for its cocktails (£10.50). The seasonal drinks menu is steeped in ambitious flavours and blends, with classic drinks for more conservative palates. Hard to find a seat at the best of times, so make sure you book ahead.

ELK IN THE WOODS
BAR

Map p466 (📞020-7226 3535; www.the-elk-in-the-woods.co.uk; 37-39 Camden Passage, N1; ⊗9am-11pm; ⊖Angel) A wonderful take on a stylish countryside hunters pub, this comfy Islington bar-cafe is equally notable for its good, simple food. With its large, rough oak-wood tables, old mirrors, stuffed deer head and friendly staff, this is a spot to savour. Come early in the evenings, as tables are sought-after and it's not the kind of bar you stand in.

CASTLE
PUB

Map p466 (www.thecastleislington.co.uk; 54 Pentonville Rd, N1; ⊗11am-11pm; 📶; ⊖Angel) A gorgeous, boutique pub with a winning formula of snazzy decor (wooden floors, designer wallpaper, soft furnishings and large maps on the walls), good gastropub food, a rotating selection of craft beers and, to top it all off, a wonderful roof terrace.

CRAFT BEER CO
CRAFT BEER

Map p466 (www.thecraftbeerco.com; 55 White Lion St, N1; ⊗4-11pm Mon-Thu, noon-1am Fri & Sat, to 10.30pm Sun; ⊖Angel) Riding the wave of the craft beer craze, this lovely pub is pushing the envelope by offering its drinkers a daily beer menu with dozens of brews from around the world, whether from kegs, casks, bottles or cans. Naturally, it has a burger menu to turn a couple of pints into a night.

🍷 Stoke Newington

AULD SHILLELAGH
PUB

(www.theauldshillelagh.co.uk; 105 Stoke Newington Church St, N16; ⊗11am-midnight; 🚌73) We're going out on a limb and calling this London's best Irish pub. The staff are sharp, the Guinness is good and the live entertainment is frequent and varied (from trad bands to rappers, sometimes even both at once). It's a great spot to watch the rugby or football and there's a beer garden out the back.

☆ ENTERTAINMENT

North London is the home of indie rock, and many a famous band started out playing in the area's grungy bars. You can be sure to find live music of some kind every night of the week. A number of venues are multipurpose, with gigs in the first part of the evening (generally around 7pm or 8pm), followed by club nights beginning around midnight.

★JAZZ CAFE
LIVE MUSIC

Map p468 (📞020-7485 6834; www.thejazzcafelondon.com; 5 Parkway, NW1; ⊖Camden Town) The name would have you think jazz is the main staple, but it's only a small slice of what's on offer. The intimate club-like space also serves up funk, hip hop, R&B, soul and rare groove, with big-name acts regularly dropping in. Saturday club night is soul night, with two live sets from the house band.

★KOKO
LIVE MUSIC

Map p468 (www.koko.uk.com; 1a Camden High St, NW1; ⊖Mornington Cres) Once the legendary Camden Palace, where Charlie Chaplin, the Goons and the Sex Pistols performed, and where Prince played surprise gigs, KOKO is maintaining its reputation as one of London's better gig venues. The theatre has a dance floor and decadent balconies, and attracts an indie crowd. There are live bands most nights and hugely popular club nights on Saturdays.

A NORTH LONDON PLAYLIST

➡ *'Driving In My Car'* – Madness (1982), NW5 (2009)

➡ *'London'* – The Smiths (1987)

➡ *'King's Cross'* – Pet Shop Boys (1987)

➡ *'For Tomorrow (Visit To Primrose Hill Extended)'* – Blur (1993)

➡ *'Come Back to Camden'* – Morrissey (2004)

➡ *'Pentonville'* – Babyshambles (2005)

★ SCALA   LIVE MUSIC

Map p466 (☏020-7833 2022; www.scala.co.uk; 275 Pentonville Rd, N1; ⊖King's Cross St Pancras) Opened in 1920 as a salubrious golden-age cinema, Scala slipped into porn-movie hell in the 1970s only to be reborn as a club and live-music venue in the noughties. It's one of the best places in London to catch an intimate gig and is a great dance space too, hosting a diverse range of club nights.

★ CECIL SHARP HOUSE   TRADITIONAL MUSIC

Map p468 (www.cecilsharphouse.org; 2 Regent's Park Rd, NW1; ⊖Camden Town) If you've ever fancied clog stamping, hanky waving or bell jingling, this is the place for you. Home to the English Folk Dance and Song Society, this institute keeps all manner of wacky folk traditions alive, with performances and classes held in its gorgeous mural-covered Kennedy Hall. The dance classes are oodles of fun; no experience necessary.

ANGEL COMEDY   COMEDY

Map p466 (www.angelcomedy.co.uk; 2 Camden Passage, N1; ⊘shows 8pm; ⊖Angel) There's free comedy every night at this great little club upstairs at the Camden Head. Monday is improv night, and on other evenings you might get anything from a new act to a famous name road-testing new material; check the website for listings. Donations are gratefully received.

ELECTRIC BALLROOM   LIVE MUSIC

Map p468# (☏020-7485 9006; www.electricballroom.co.uk; 184 Camden High St, NW1; ⊖Camden Town) One of Camden's historic venues, the Electric Ballroom has been entertaining North Londoners since 1938. Many great bands and musicians have played here, from Blur to Paul McCartney, The Clash and U2. There are constantly changing club

nights on Fridays, while on Saturdays it hosts Propaganda, a crowd-pleaser featuring dance anthems from the '70s, '80s and '90s, as well as current hits.

KING'S HEAD THEATRE   THEATRE

Map p466 (www.kingsheadtheatre.com; 115 Upper St, N1; ⊖Angel) This stalwart pub theatre hosts new plays and musicals, along with revivals of classics. Classical music and opera are part of the mix, too.

LORD'S   SPECTATOR SPORT

(☏020-7432 1000; www.lords.org; St John's Wood Rd, NW8; ☏; ⊖St John's Wood) For cricket devotees a trip to Lord's is often as much a pilgrimage as anything else. As well as being home to Marylebone Cricket Club, the ground hosts Test matches, one-day internationals and domestic cricket finals. International matches are usually booked months in advance, but tickets for county cricket fixtures are reasonably easy to come by.

REGENT'S PARK OPEN AIR THEATRE   THEATRE

Map p468 (☏0844 826 4242; www.openairtheatre. org; Queen Mary's Gardens, Regent's Park, NW1; ⊘May-Sep; ♿; ⊖Baker St) A popular and very atmospheric summertime fixture in London, this 1250-seat outdoor auditorium plays host to four productions a year: famous plays (Shakespeare often features), new works, musicals and usually one production aimed at families.

ROUNDHOUSE   CONCERT VENUE

Map p468 (www.roundhouse.org.uk; Chalk Farm Rd, NW1; ⊖Chalk Farm) Built as a railway repair shed in 1847, this unusual Grade II–listed round building became an arts centre in the 1960s and hosted legendary bands before falling into near-dereliction in 1983. Its 21st-century resurrection as a creative hub has been a great success and it now hosts everything from big-name concerts to dance, circus, stand-up comedy, poetry slams and improvisation.

UNION CHAPEL   CONCERT VENUE

Map p466 (www.unionchapel.org.uk; 19 Compton Tce, N1; ⊖Highbury & Islington) One of London's most atmospheric and individual music venues, the Union Chapel is an old church that still holds services as well as concerts – mainly acoustic – and the monthly **Live at the Chapel** comedy club. It also runs **Daylight Music**: free gigs that regularly take place on Saturdays from noon to 2pm.

DUBLIN CASTLE
LIVE MUSIC

Map p468 (www.thedublincastle.com; 94 Parkway, NW1; ⊘1pm-2am; ⊖Camden Town) Live punk or alternative bands play most nights in this comfortably grungy pub's back room (cover charges are usually between £4.50 and £7). DJs take over after the bands on Friday, Saturday and Sunday nights.

HAMPSTEAD THEATRE
THEATRE

(☑020-7722 9301; www.hampsteadtheatre.com; Eton Ave, NW3; ⊖Swiss Cottage) The Hampstead is famed for staging new writing and taking on emerging directors. It was an early champion of Harold Pinter, which shows it knows a good thing when it sees one.

O2 FORUM
CONCERT VENUE

Map p465 (www.academymusicgroup.com; 9-17 Highgate Rd, NW5; tickets from £18.50; ⊖Kentish Town) You can find your way to the O2 Forum – once the famous Town & Country Club – by the ticket touts that line the way from Kentish Town tube station. This art-deco former cinema (built 1934) is spacious yet intimate enough for bands and comedians starting to break through (or big names a little past their prime).

ALMEIDA
THEATRE

Map p466 (☑020-7359 4404; www.almeida.co.uk; Almeida St, N1; £10-38; ⊖Highbury & Islington) Housed in a Grade II–listed Victorian building, this plush 325-seat theatre can be relied on for imaginative programming. Its emphasis is on new, up-and-coming talent.

 # SHOPPING

Shopping in Camden Town is all about market stalls, Doc Martin boots and secondhand clothes. Islington is great for antiques, quality vintage clothes and design objects.

★STABLES MARKET
MARKET

Map p468 (www.camdenmarket.com; Chalk Farm Rd, NW1; ⊘10am-6pm; ⊖Chalk Farm) Connected to the Lock Market, the Stables is the best part of the Camden Market complex, with antiques, Asian artefacts, rugs, retro furniture and clothing. As the name suggests, it used to be an old stables complex,

complete with horse hospital, where up to 800 horses (who worked hauling barges on Regent's Canal) were housed.

★ANNIE'S VINTAGE COSTUME & TEXTILES
VINTAGE

Map p466 (www.anniesvintageclothing.co.uk; 12 Camden Passage, N1; ⊘11am-6pm; ⊖Angel) One of London's most enchanting vintage shops, this high-end boutique has costumes to make you look like Greta Garbo. Famous designers come here for inspiration, so you might also get to do some celebrity spotting.

★CAMDEN LOCK MARKET
MARKET

Map p468 (www.camdenmarket.com; 54-56 Camden Lock Pl, NW1; ⊘10am-6pm; ⊖Camden Town) Right next to the canal lock, this is the original Camden Market, with diverse food stalls, ceramics, furniture, oriental rugs, musical instruments and clothes.

★CAMDEN PASSAGE MARKET
ANTIQUES

Map p468 (www.camdenpassageislington.co.uk; Camden Passage, N1; ⊘8am-6pm Wed & Sat; ⊖Angel) Not to be confused with Camden Market, Camden Passage is a pretty cobbled lane in Islington lined with antique stores, vintage-clothing boutiques and cafes. Scattered along the lane are four separate market areas devoted to antique curios and whatnots. The main market days are Wednesday and Saturday (although the shops are open all week). Stallholders know their stuff, so bargains are rare.

MARY'S LIVING & GIVING SHOP
CLOTHING

Map p466 (138 Upper St; ⊘10am-6pm Mon-Sat, noon-4pm Sun) This is not your average charity shop: the boutique is done up beautifully and the quality of the clothes on offer is top-notch. Allow £60 to £80 for designer dresses and jackets; £7 to £10 for high-street brand tops. There is a small selection of children's clothes too.

FORTNUM & MASON
FOOD & DRINKS

Map p466 (www.fortnumandmason.com; Unit 1a, St Pancras International Station, Pancras Rd, N1; ⊘7am-8pm Mon-Sat, 8am-8pm Sun; ⊖King's Cross St Pancras) This small branch of the renowned department store, its first in more than 300 years, offers a good array of its signature teas (loose leaf or teabags) and coffees, which are great for last-minute presents and souvenirs if you're boarding a Eurostar. It also runs a cafe.

EXCLUSIVO
FASHION & ACCESSORIES

Map p465 (2 Flask Walk, NW3; ⊗10.30am-6pm; ⊖Hampstead) If you've ever dreamed of owning a pair of Manolo Blahniks or a Pucci dress, but have always baulked at the price, Exclusivo might just be your chance. This tiny shop specialises in top-quality secondhand designer garments and accessories, and while prices remain high (£100 to £500 for a dress, for instance), they are a fraction of the original price tag.

SAMPLER
WINE

Map p466 (☎020-7226 9500; www.thesampler. co.uk; 266 Upper St, N1; ⊗11.30am-9pm Mon-Sat, to 7pm Sun; ⊖Highbury & Islington) One of London's leading wine shops, this brilliant place allows you to sample up to 80 different wines before buying. Just load up a smart card and use it to sample from the machines – from as little as 30p for a sample and up to £20 for a good vintage. Wines are organised by grape variety. Staff are friendly and knowledgeable.

GILL WING
GIFTS & SOUVENIRS

Map p466 (www.gillwing.co.uk; 194-195 Upper St, N1; ⊗9am-6pm, from 10am Sun; ⊖Highbury & Islington) Inhabiting multiple stores on Upper St, Gill Wing sells shoes (at number 192), kitchenware (at 190) and jewellery (at 182), but our favourite is its flagship gift shop. It's basically impossible to walk past without doing a double take at the colourful window full of glasses, cards, children's toys and other eclectic titbits.

HARRY POTTER SHOP AT PLATFORM 9¾
GIFTS & SOUVENIRS

Map p466 (www.harrypotterplatform934.com; King's Cross Station, N1; ⊗8am-10pm Mon-Sat, 9am-9pm Sun; ⊖King's Cross St Pancras) With Pottermania refusing to die down and Diagon Alley impossible to find, when your junior witches and wizards are seeking a wand of their own, take the family directly to King's Cross Station. This little wood-panelled store also stocks jumpers sporting the colours of Hogwarts' four houses (Gryffindor having pride of place) and assorted merchandise, including, of course, the books.

HOUSMANS
BOOKS

Map p466 (www.housmans.com; 5 Caledonian Rd, N1; ⊗10am-6.30pm Mon-Sat, noon-6pm Sun; ⊖King's Cross St Pancras) If you're searching for hard-to-find tomes on a progressive, radical, pacifist, feminist, socialist or communist theme, this long-standing, not-for-profit bookshop is your best bet.

🏃 SPORTS & ACTIVITIES

★ HAMPSTEAD HEATH PONDS
SWIMMING

Map p465 (www.cityoflondon.gov.uk; Hampstead Heath, NW5; adult/child £2/1; ⊖Hampstead Heath) Set in the midst of the gorgeous heath, Hampstead's three bathing ponds (men's, women's and mixed) offer a cooling dip in murky brown water. Despite what you might think from its appearance, the water is tested daily and meets stringent quality guidelines.

The men's and women's ponds are open year-round and are supervised by a lifeguard. Opening times vary with the seasons, e.g. from 7am or 8am until 3.30pm in winter and 8.30pm at the height of summer. The men's pond is particularly popular with gay men and the surrounding lawns are a prime sunbathing and posing spot whenever the sun's out. There's also a nude sunbathing area within the changing-room enclosure. The mixed pond closes in winter. It's the least secluded of the three and can sometimes get crowded in summer.

Notting Hill & West London

HIGH ST KENSINGTON | NOTTING HILL & WESTBOURNE GROVE | EARL'S COURT & WEST BROMPTON | MAIDA VALE | SHEPHERD'S BUSH | HAMMERSMITH | KENSINGTON HIGH ST | HAMMERSMITH & CHISWICK | ENTERTAINMENT

Neighbourhood Top Five

1 **Portobello Road Market** (p274) Spending a Saturday afternoon browsing eclectic stalls selling street food, antiques and fashion, among other things, and putting your feet up in a local cafe or pub.

2 **Design Museum** (p273) Getting your camera out at this fabulous museum dedicated to the importance of design in everyday life.

3 **Boat Trip** (p275) Boarding a boat for the leisurely trip between Little Venice and Camden, along Regent's Canal.

4 **Windsor Castle** (p280) Raising a pint in the garden or snug interior of this classic tavern on Campden Hill Road.

5 **Electric Cinema** (p283) Cosying up in a front-row double bed with a glass of vino at one of the UK's oldest cinemas.

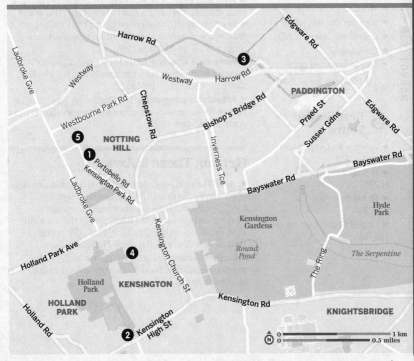

For more detail of this area see Map p470 and p472 ➡

Lonely Planet's Top Tip

To make the best of your time at Portobello Road Market, do a one-way circuit (p276) between Notting Hill Gate and Ladbroke Rd tube stations. The flow tends to go from Notting Hill to Ladbroke Grove, but either way works fine.

✕ Best Places to Eat

➡ Potli (p279)

➡ Ledbury (p279)

➡ River Cafe (p280)

➡ Gate (p280)

➡ Snaps + Rye (p278)

For reviews, see p277.➡

🍷 Best Places to Drink

➡ Troubadour (p281)

➡ Windsor Castle (p280)

➡ Scarsdale Tavern (p281)

➡ Dove (p282)

➡ Earl of Lonsdale (p280)

For reviews, see p280.➡

⊙ Best Guided Tours

➡ London Waterbus Company (p285)

➡ Brompton Cemetery (p275)

➡ 18 Stafford Terrace (p273)

➡ Kensal Green Cemetery (p275)

Explore Notting Hill & West London

Most people come to West London for three reasons: for Portobello Road Market, for outstanding dining, or because they're sleeping in one of the area's choice accommodation options.

West London is sight-light, but you should allow half a day for the the Design Museum and Portobello Road Market and another half day to walk along the Grand Union Canal towards Little Venice, maybe with a pint at one of the waterside pubs en route.

Some excellent restaurant and entertainment options will save those staying in the area from legging it into the West End (although it's close enough to do so if you want). For eating, Notting Hill has a great concentration of good names, but cast your net further and land superb pickings in Hammersmith and Shepherd's Bush.

For nightlife, Notting Hill and Shepherd's Bush are the most vibrant, while Kensington is home to one of the capital's most interesting roof-top clubs. Other areas will be pretty quiet once the pubs have rung the 11pm bell.

Local Life

➡ **Fruit and vegetable markets** Although also popular with tourists, Portobello Road Market (p274) is where many Notting Hill residents shop for their daily fruit and veg. Another good fruit and veg market is Shepherd's Bush Market (p285).

➡ **Waterside strolling** Little Venice (p275) is very popular at the weekend when families go for a walk along the canal's tow paths.

➡ **Affordable pampering** The Porchester Spa (p286) is run by Westminster Council and is cheaper than typical commercial spas.

Getting There & Away

➡ **Tube** The west–east Central Line stops at Queensway (Bayswater), Notting Hill Gate and Shepherd's Bush. For Paddington, Westbourne Grove and the western end of Shepherd's Bush, there's the painfully slow Hammersmith & City Line. Earl's Court and Hammersmith are on the zippy Piccadilly Line.

➡ **Bicycle** Santander Cycles (p415) are useful to get from one neighbourhood to another, with docking stations across West London.

 SIGHTS

A large and fairly spread out neighbourhood – well linked by public transport – West London has several interesting house museums as well as the new Design Museum, recently relocated (and massively expanded) from its former position by the Thames. Portobello Road Market is the main draw to Notting Hill for most visitors.

⊙ High St Kensington

HOLLAND PARK   PARK

Map p472 (Ilchester Pl; ⊙7.30am-dusk; ⊖High St Kensington, Holland Park) This handsome park divides into dense woodland in the north, spacious and inviting lawns by Holland House, sports fields for the beautiful game and other exertions in the south, and some lovely gardens, including the restful Kyoto Garden. The park's many splendid peacocks are a gorgeous sight and an adventure playground keeps kids occupied. Holland House – largely bombed to smithereens by the Luftwaffe in 1940 – is the venue of Opera Holland Park (p283) in summer.

LEIGHTON HOUSE   HOUSE

Map p472 (⌨Mon-Fri 020-7602 3316, Sat & Sun 020-7471 9160; www.leightonhouse.co.uk; 12 Holland Park Rd, W14; adult/child under 12yr £12/free; ⊙10am-5.30pm Wed-Mon; ⊖High St Kensington) Sitting on a quiet street just west of Holland Park and designed in 1866 by George Aitchison, Leighton House was home to the eponymous Frederic, Lord Leighton (1830–96), a painter belonging to the Aesthetic movement. The ground floor is served up in an Orientalist style, its exquisite **Arab Hall** added in 1879 and densely covered with blue and green tiles from Rhodes, Cairo, Damascus, and Iznik in Turkey.

18 STAFFORD TERRACE   HOUSE

Map p472 (⌨Mon-Fri 020-7602 3316, Sat & Sun 020-7938 1295; www.rbkc.gov.uk/subsites/museums/18staffordterrace1.aspx; 18 Stafford Tce, W8; adult/child £7/5, tours £10/8; ⊙guided tours 11am, self-guided tours 2-5.30pm Wed, Sat & Sun mid-Sep–mid-Jun; ⊖High St Kensington) Formerly known as Linley Sambourne House, 18 Stafford Terrace, tucked away behind Kensington High St, was the home of *Punch* cartoonist and amateur photographer Linley Sambourne and his wife Marion from 1875 to 1914. What you see is

NOTTING HILL & WEST LONDON SIGHTS

⊙ TOP SIGHT
DESIGN MUSEUM

Relocated in 2016 from its former Thames location to a stunning new £83m home by Holland Park, this slick museum is dedicated to popularising the importance and influence of design in everyday life. With a revolving program of special exhibitions, the museum is a crucial pit stop for anyone with an eye for modern and contemporary aesthetics.

Splendidly housed in the refitted former Commonwealth Institute (which opened in 1962), the lavish interior – all smooth Douglas fir and marble – is itself a design triumph.

Most exhibitions are ticketed (from £10), as are talks in the auditorium (from £5), but the extensive 2nd-floor **Designer Maker User** gallery is free. Exploring the iconography of design classics, the gallery contains almost 1000 objects that trace the history of modern design, from 1980s Apple computers to water bottles, typewriters, floppy discs and a huge advert for the timeless VW Beetle.

You can also encounter the museum's **Designers in Residence** on the 2nd floor when the room is open (otherwise you can see them working through the glass). Also note the original stained glass in the shop on the ground floor, where you can also find a cafe (a restaurant, **Parabola**, is on the 2nd floor).

DON'T MISS

➡ Designer Maker User gallery

➡ Designers in Residence

➡ The stained glass in the shop

➡ The museum's architecture

PRACTICALITIES

➡ Map p472, E2

➡ ⌨020-7940 8790

➡ www.designmuseum.org

➡ 224-238 Kensington High St, W8

➡ admission free

➡ ⊙10am-6pm, to 8pm 1st Fri of the month

➡ 🛜

➡ ⊖High St Kensington

TOP SIGHT
PORTOBELLO ROAD MARKET

Buzzing Portobello Road Market is an iconic London attraction with an eclectic mix of street food, fruit and veg, antiques, curios, collectibles, vibrant fashion and trinkets. The shops along Portobello Rd open daily and the fruit and veg stalls (from Elgin Cres to Talbot Rd) only close on Sunday. The busiest day by far is Saturday, when antique dealers set up shop (from Chepstow Villas to Elgin Cres), but it's all elbows. This is also when the fashion market (beneath Westway, from Portobello Rd to Ladbroke Rd) is in full swing – although you can also browse for fashion on Friday and Sunday.

Among the vintage and 'firsthand' fashion stalls of Westway, you'll also find accessories, shoes, jewellery and CDs. More upmarket, Portobello Green Arcade (p284) is home to some cutting-edge clothing and jewellery designers and niche outlets. Across the way, Acklam Village Market (p278) is a popular weekend streetfood market with snacks from across the globe.

Continue on Portobello Rd towards trendy Golborne Rd (famous for vintage furniture, vintage-clothes shops and cool cafes) and you'll hit the 'new goods' section, with kitchenware, bric-a-brac and more fruit and veg stalls – as well as secondhand goods, despite this being the 'new goods' market.

DON'T MISS

➡ Fashion market
➡ Designers at Portobello Green Arcade
➡ Fruit and veg stalls
➡ Antiques market

PRACTICALITIES

➡ Map p470, B4
➡ www.portobello market.org
➡ Portobello Rd, W10
➡ ⊙8am-6.30pm Mon-Wed, Fri & Sat, to 1pm Thu
➡ ⊜Notting Hill Gate, Ladbroke Grove

---

pretty much the typical home of a comfortable middle-class Victorian family, with dark wood, Turkish carpets and sumptuous stained glass throughout. You can visit some nine rooms by 75-minute guided morning tours (costumed on Saturdays) or by self-guided visits in the afternoons.

Twilight tours (£12) are an atmospheric time to visit, held on the third Wednesday of the month at 7pm, but advance booking is crucial.

ST MARY ABBOTS   CHURCH
Map p472 (☑020-7937 5136; www.smaw8.org; Kensington Church St; ⊜High St Kensington) Designed by Sir George Gilbert Scott and sporting the tallest spire in London, lovely St Mary Abbots – right on the corner of Kensington Church St and Kensington High St – is a haven of peace and calm. The church, with its huge and inviting interior, is currently undergoing ambitious restoration. St Mary Abbots was seriously damaged by the Luftwaffe in 1944.

⊙ Notting Hill & Westbourne Grove

MUSEUM OF BRANDS, PACKAGING & ADVERTISING   MUSEUM
Map p470 (☑020-7243 9611; www.museumof brands.com; 111-117 Lancaster Rd, W11; adult/ child £9/5; ⊙10am-6pm Tue-Sat, 11am-5pm Sun; ⊜Ladbroke Grove) This recently relocated shrine to nostalgia is the brainchild of consumer historian Robert Opie, who has amassed advertising memorabilia and packaging since the age of 16. There are early Monopoly sets, the first appearances of Mickey Mouse and Disney, a primitive version of Cluedo, Teazie-Weazie powder shampoo, radios, TVs, and ephemera celebrating cultural/consumer icons the Fab Four, Mork and Mindy, Star Wars, Star Trek, Buzz Lightyear, Pokemon et al. An annual adult ticket is £20.

NOTTING HILL CARNIVAL

Every year, for three days that include the last weekend of August, Notting Hill echoes to the beats of calypso, ska, reggae and soca sounds of Notting Hill Carnival. Launched in 1964 by the local Afro-Caribbean community, which was keen to celebrate its culture and traditions, it has grown to become Europe's largest street festival (over two million visitors in total) and a highlight of the annual calendar in London.

The carnival includes events showcasing the five main 'arts': the 'mas' (derived from masquerade), which is the main costume parade; pan (steel bands); calypso music; static sound systems (anything goes, from reggae, dub and funk to drum 'n' bass); and the mobile sound systems. The 'mas' is generally held on the Monday and is the culmination of the carnival's celebrations. Processions finish around 9pm, although parties in bars, restaurants and seemingly every house in the neighbourhood go on late into the night.

Another undisputed highlight of the carnival is the food: there are dozens of Caribbean food stands and celebrity chefs such as Levi Roots often make an appearance.

⦿ Earl's Court & West Brompton

BROMPTON CEMETERY   CEMETERY
Map p472 (☏020-7352 1201; www.royalparks.org.uk/parks/brompton-cemetery; Old Brompton Rd, SW5; tour £6; ☺7am-dusk; ⊜West Brompton, Fulham Broadway) The United Kingdom's sole cemetery owned by the Crown, this atmospheric 19th-century, 16-hectare boneyard's most famous denizen may be suffragette Emmeline Pankhurst, but it's also fascinating as the possible inspiration for many of Beatrix Potter's characters. A local resident in her youth, Potter may have noted some of the names on headstones: there's a Mr Nutkin, Mr McGregor, Jeremiah Fisher, Tommy Brock – even a Peter Rabbet! The chapel and colonnades at one end are modelled on St Peter's in Rome.

Two-hour **tours** depart at 2pm every Sunday from May to August (and two Sundays a month in September, October, November, March and April) from the chapel itself. At the time of writing, visits to the catacombs were to become a more regular option, due to their popularity (see www.brompton-cemetery.org.uk for details). The catacombs can also be visited during the annual summer open day.

CHELSEA FOOTBALL CLUB   STADIUM
Map p472 (☏0871 984 1955; www.chelseafc.com; Stamford Bridge, Fulham Rd, SW6; tours adult/child £21/15; ☺museum 9.30am-5pm, tours 10am-3pm; ⊜Fulham Broadway) Chelsea (aka the Blues) is one of London's wealthiest football clubs, and Stamford Bridge is

hallowed turf for fans after a souvenir kit or a tour of the stadium. Book online for cheaper tickets.

⦿ Maida Vale

LITTLE VENICE   CANAL
Map p470 (⊜Warwick Avenue) It was Lord Byron who dreamed up this evocative phrase to describe the junction between Regent's Canal (p251) and the **Grand Union Canal**, a confluence overseen by beautiful mansions and navigated by colourful narrow boats. The canals go back to the early 19th century when the government was trying to develop new transport links across the country.

GRAND UNION CANAL   CANAL
Map p470 (⊜Warwick Ave) Dating from the early 19th century, the Grand Union Canal actually finishes up in Birmingham (you can journey much of its length by bicycle): horse-drawn barges were ideal for carrying coal and other bulk commodities such as grain or ice (the latter was imported from Norway by ship to Limehouse and then conveyed along the canal). Little Venice is an important mooring point for narrow boats (many of them permanent homes), which keeps the boating spirit bubbling away.

⦿ Shepherd's Bush

KENSAL GREEN CEMETERY   CEMETERY
(☏020-8969 0152; www.kensalgreencemetery.com; Harrow Rd, W10; tours £7; ☺9am-5pm Mon-Sat, 10am-5pm Sun, to 6pm Sun in summer; ⊜Kensal Green) For many years the most

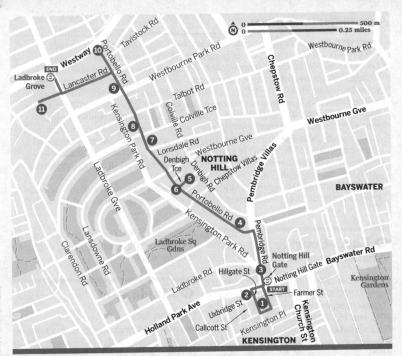

Neighbourhood Walk
Notting Hill

START NOTTING HILL GATE STATION
END LADBROKE GROVE STATION
LENGTH 1.5 MILES; TWO HOURS

A small and manageable neighbourhood, Notting Hill is best visited for Portobello Road Market (heaving on Saturdays). From Notting Hill Gate tube station, leave the south exit and turn left down Farmer St into **1 Hillgate Village**, with its picture-postcard painted houses. Callcott St is particularly photogenic. Loop back around and leave Hillgate St by the iconic **2 Coronet cinema** featured in *Notting Hill* (it's no longer a cinema). Turn right and cross at the lights to the junction with Pembridge Rd; the tollgate – the 'gate' of Notting Hill Gate – once stood here. Along Pembridge Rd, at the junction with Kensington Park Rd, was once the main entrance to the huge 19th-century **3 Hippodrome**. The Hippodrome vanished in the 1840s, although its layout survives in the road contours to the west. Bend into Portobello Rd and note the blue plaque high

at **4 No 22**, commemorating George Orwell, who lived here. Keep walking along Portobello Rd and pop into charming **5 Denbigh Terrace**, with its pastel-coloured houses. Note the steeple of sand-coloured **6 St Peter's Church** to the west on the far side of Portobello Rd. Continue along Portobello Rd and note the **7 shop** named 'Notting Hill' at No 142 on your right: the bookshop of William Thacker (Hugh Grant) in the eponymous film. Further along, stop outside the historic **8 Electric Cinema** (p283); observe the tiling by the pavement and pop in to take view the classic interior. Down further, cross Westbourne Park Rd. The blue front door at **9 280 Westbourne Park Rd**, William Thacker's flat in the film *Notting Hill*, still attracts devotees. At **10 Portobello Green Arcade** (p284), stop to browse a clutch of invigorating designer clothes shops and quirky boutiques. Backtrack a bit down Portobello Rd and turn west into Lancaster Rd to visit the excellent **11 Museum of Brands, Packaging & Advertising** (p274). Ladbroke Grove tube station is a short walk north.

fashionable necropolis in England (you wouldn't be seen dead anywhere else), Kensal Green Cemetery accepted its first occupants in 1833, and the Gothic boneyard is the final resting place of many illustrious names, including Charles Babbage, Isambard Kingdom Brunel, Wilkie Collins, Anthony Trollope, William Makepeace Thackeray, Baden Powell and the almost comically named Dr Albert Isaiah Coffin.

Supposedly based on the Cimetière du Père-Lachaise in Paris, the cemetery is distinguished by its Greek Revival architecture, arched entrances and the outrageously ornate tombs that bear testimony to 19th-century delusions of grandeur. Two-hour **tours** of the cemetery are offered on Sundays at 2pm (from March to October; first and third Sundays per month other times) by the Friends of Kensal Green Cemetery (www.kensalgreen.co.uk). Some of these tours also visit the catacombs beneath the Anglican Chapel (although at the time of writing, they were still closed for the restoration of the chapel). The cemetery is laid out alongside the Grand Union Canal (p275), which makes for splendid walks alongside the water, especially if the sun obliges.

⊙ Hammersmith

FULHAM PALACE   HISTORIC BUILDING

(www.fulhampalace.org; Bishop's Ave, SW6; ⊙palace 12.30-4.30pm Mon-Thu, noon-5pm Sun summer, earlier hours in winter, gardens dawn-dusk daily; ⊖Putney Bridge) FREE Within glorious stumbling distance of the Thames, this summer home of the bishops of London from 704 to 1975 is a lovely blend of architectural styles immersed in beautiful gardens. Until 1924, when it was filled with rubble, the longest moat in England enclosed the palace. The oldest surviving chunk is the little red-brick Tudor gateway, while the main building dates from the mid-17th century and was remodelled in the 19th century. Ongoing restoration work is due to complete in 2019 – it's open throughout.

The lovely courtyard draws watercolourists on sunny days and the genteel **Drawing Room Café** (mains £5-12; ⊙9.30am-5pm Apr-Oct, to 4pm Nov-Mar) at the rear, looking out onto the gorgeous lawn, is a superlative spot for some carrot cake and a coffee. There's also a pretty and recently restored **walled garden** (10.15am to 4.15pm summer, to 3.45pm winter) and, detached from the main house, a Tudor Revival **chapel** designed by William Butterfield in 1866.

There are two permanent displays inside the palace relating the history of the building and its inhabitants. **Guided tours** (£6, children free, 1½ hours, four to five tours per month) usually take in the **Great Hall**, the **Victorian chapel**, **Bishop Sherlock's Room** and the **Dining Room**. There are also **garden walks** (£6, 1¼ hours); check the website for dates and times. The lawn is also a venue for **Luna Cinema**, the popular summer outdoor-cinema club that shows films at famous spots around town and the UK; summer jazz evenings are also staged.

The surrounding land, once totalling almost 15 hectares but now reduced to just over five, forms **Bishop's Park**, a beautiful park with a lovely promenade along the river and the usual assortment of playgrounds, fountains and cafe. Tours (£6) also take in the park.

WILLIAM MORRIS SOCIETY   MUSEUM

Map p472 (☑020-8741 3735; www.williammorris society.org; 26 Upper Mall, W6; ⊙2-5pm Thu & Sat; ⊖Ravenscourt Park) FREE Tucked away in the coach house and basement of Kelmscott House (William Morris' former home), this small riverside museum stages temporary exhibitions on all things William Morris. It has a downstairs shop (with a fireplace designed by Morris) and a still-working printing press (demonstrations given on Saturdays).

✕ EATING

West London has some excellent dining choices, generally – though not exclusively – at the more affordable end of the budget spectrum. You'll find everything from international street food (Acklam Village Market), pie and mash, fish and chips, and Japanese fast food to Danish treats, smart Greek and top-end gourmet cuisine.

✕ Notting Hill & Westbourne Grove

HONEST BURGERS
BURGERS $

Map p470 (☑020-7229 4978; www.honest burgers.co.uk; 189 Portobello Rd, W11; mains from £8.50; ⊙11.30am-11pm Mon-Sat, to 10pm Sun, brunch 9.30am-1pm Sat & Sun; ☎; ⊜Ladbroke Grove) When the burger munchies strike, this Portobello branch of the winning, no-nonsense Brixton chain can sit you down for a helping of its juicy trademark dish, with a serving of its irresistible rosemary salted chips. Brunch at weekends is also a popular fixture for granola, bacon sandwiches or bubble and squeak.

ARANCINA
ITALIAN $

Map p470 (☑020-7221 7776; www.arancina. co.uk; 19 Pembridge Rd, W11; mains £3-23.50; ⊙8am-11pm Mon-Sat, 9am-11pm Sun; ⊜Notting Hill Gate) Arancina always has a scrum of people round it thanks to the whiff of freshly baked pizza, Sicilian snacks and the cut-out orange Fiat Cinquecento (500; the original '60s version) in the window. Try the *arancine* (fried balls of rice with fillings; £3), the creamy desserts known as *cannolo siciliano* (£3.50) or a slice of perfect pizza.

There's another branch not far away at 19 Westbourne Grove.

LOWRY & BAKER
CAFE $

Map p470 (☑020-8960 8534; 339 Portobello Rd, W10; mains from £6; ⊙8am-4pm Mon-Sat, from 10am Sun; ☎; ⊜Labroke Grove, Westbourne Park) All wobbly seats, duffed-up tables, and mismatched cups, saucers and cutlery, this appealing cafe has a shabby jumble-sale charm, fine Monmouth coffee and tasty platters. It's a great spot for breakfast (homemade granola, toasted brioche etc), brunch (such as avocado on toast with poached eggs) or just to put your feet up after schlepping around Portobello Market.

TAQUERÍA
MEXICAN $

Map p470 (☑020-7229 4734; www.taqueria. co.uk; 139-143 Westbourne Grove; tacos £7.20-10.50; ⊙noon-11pm Mon-Thu, to 11.30pm Fri & Sat, to 10.30pm Sun; ☎; ⊜Notting Hill Gate) ✿ You won't find fresher or more limp (they're not supposed to be crispy!) tacos anywhere in London because these ones are made on the premises. Starting life as a stall on

Portobello Rd and recently refurbished, it's a small casual place with a great vibe, committed to environmental mores: the eggs, chicken and pork are free-range, the meat British, the fish MSC-certified and the milk and cream organic.

ACKLAM VILLAGE MARKET
MARKET $

Map p470 (www.acklamvillage.com; 4-8 Acklam Rd, W10; ⊙11am-7pm Sat & Sun; ⊜Ladbroke Grove) Stuffed under the Westway, this lively and aromatic street-eats market at the north end of Portobello Rd serves snacks from all over the globe: take your pick from Palestinian, African, Peruvian, Chinese, Mexican, Greek, Moroccan, Polish, Portuguese or plain old British. A bar is on hand for alcoholic lubrication, with craft beers and live sounds.

COCKNEY'S PIE AND MASH
PIES $

Map p470 (☑020-8960 9409; 314 Portobello Rd, W10; ⊙11.30am-5.30pm Tue-Thu, to 7pm Fri, to 5.30pm Sat) For fine helpings of London's staples: pie and mash, jellied eels, liquor (parsley sauce).

SNAPS + RYE
DANISH $$

Map p470 (☑020-8964 3004; 93 Golborne Rd, W10; 4-course dinner £37, mains from £10; ⊙8am-6pm Tue-Wed, to 11pm Thu, Fri & Sat, 10am-5pm Sun; ☎; ⊜Ladbroke Rd, Westbourne Park) ✿ This neat Danish restaurant along Golborne Rd has made Nordic waves in this corner of London. Trendily frugal and achingly cool, the clean sparseness is complemented by a delicious menu: Nordic yoghurt granola, full Danish breakfast, fish kedgeree or house-cured herring salad, all finished with meringues kys (a kind of Eton mess, the menu intones) and lubricated with a Danish craft beer. Skål!

★MAZI
GREEK $$

Map p470 (☑020-7229 3794; www.mazi.co.uk; 12-14 Hillgate St, W8; mains £9-24; ⊙noon-3pm Tue-Sun, 6.30-10.30pm Mon-Sat & 6.30-10pm Sun; ☎; ⊜Notting Hill Gate) Where long-standing Costa's Grill did business for decades, Mazi has shaken up the Greek tradition along pretty Hillgate St, concocting a lively menu of modern and innovative platters (many of sharing size) in a bright and neat setting, with a small back garden (for summer months) and an all-Greek wine list. It's both small and popular, so reservations are important.

★GEALES
SEAFOOD $$

Map p470 (☑020-7727 7528; www.geales.com; 2 Farmer St, W8; 2-course express lunch £9.95, mains £9-37.50; ☺noon-3pm & 6-10.30pm Tue-Fri, noon-10.30pm Sat, noon-4pm Sun; 🛜; ⊖Notting Hill Gate) Frying since 1939 – a bad year for the European restaurant trade – Geales has endured with its quiet location on the corner of Farmer St. The succulent fish in crispy batter is a fine catch, but the fish pie is also worth angling for. Look out for the good-value (two-course, one coffee) express lunch, available from Tuesday to Friday.

★LEDBURY
FRENCH $$$

Map p470 (☑020-7792 9090; www.theledbury. com; 127 Ledbury Rd, W11; 4-course set lunch £70, 4-course dinner £115; ☺noon-2pm Wed-Sun & 6.30-9.45pm daily; 🛜; ⊖Westbourne Park or Notting Hill Gate) With two Michelin stars and swooningly elegant, Brett Graham's artful French restaurant attracts well-heeled diners in jeans with designer jackets. Dishes such as hand-dived scallops, Chinese water deer, smoked bone marrow, quince and red leaves or Herdwick lamb with salt-baked turnips, celery cream and wild garlic are triumphs. London gastronomes have the Ledbury on speed-dial, so reservations well in advance are crucial.

✖ Kensington High St

WASABI
JAPANESE $

Map p472 (www.wasabi.uk.com; Kensington Arcade, Kensington High St, W8; mains £5-8; ☺10am-10pm Mon-Sat, 11am-9pm Sun; 🛜; ⊖High St Kensington) This bright sit-down and takeaway branch of the superb Japanese sushi and bento chain, has fantastic rice sets, noodles, rolls and salads, all good value and perfect for a fast lunch. Branches all over central London.

✖ Shepherd's Bush

★POTLI
INDIAN $

Map p472 (☑020-8741 4328; www.potli.co.uk; 319-321 King St, W6; weekday 1-/2-course set lunch £7.95/10.95, mains £7.50-15; ☺noon-2.30pm Mon-Sat, 6-10.15pm Mon-Thu, 5.30-10.30pm Fri & Sat, noon-10pm Sun; 🛜; ⊖Stamford Brook, Ravenscourt Park) With its scattered pieces from Mumbai's Thieves Market, Indian-market-kitchen/bazaar cuisine, homemade pickles and spice mixes, plus an accent on genuine flavour, tantalising Potli deftly captures the aromas of its culinary home. Downstairs there's an open kitchen and service is friendly, but it's the alluring menu – where flavours are teased into a rich and authentic Indian culinary experience – that's the real crowd-pleaser.

KERBISHER & MALT
FISH & CHIPS $

Map p472 (www.kerbisher.co.uk; 164 Shepherd's Bush Rd, W6; mains £6-7; ☺noon-10pm Tue-Sat, to 9.30pm Sun & Mon; 🛜; ⊖Hammersmith) 🍴 Peacock-blue-fronted Kerbisher & Malt serves up sustainably sourced, delectable, battered or grilled coley, haddock, pollock, cod and plaice that has made waves. Served in a box to go, the value coley and chips (£6), chip butties (£2.50) or tasty double-fried chips (£2.30) are good news, while white-tile walls and chunky wooden tables casts this as a no-nonsense but handsome chippie.

MR FALAFEL
MIDDLE EASTERN $

Map p472 (☑07440 557681; www.mrfalafel. co.uk; Units T4–T5, Shepherd's Bush Market, W12; falafels from £4.25; ☺11am to 6pm Mon-Sat; ☑; ⊖Shepherd's Bush Market) This popular cafe is the place for Palestinian falafel wraps, done to a turn.

PATIO
POLISH $$

Map p472 (☑020-8743 5194; www.patiolondon. com; 5 Goldhawk Rd, W12; mains £8.50-14.90, 2-/3-course set meal £15.50/16.95; ☺noon-3pm & 6-11pm Mon-Fri, 5-11.30pm Sat & Sun; 🍴; ⊖Shepherd's Bush, Goldhawk Rd) Cluttered with curios and antiques, this cosy restaurant serves terrific and authentic home-style Polish food, presided over by a kindly matriarch who knows and sees all.

PRINCESS VICTORIA
GASTROPUB $$

Map p472 (☑020-8749 5886; www.princess victoria.co.uk; 217 Uxbridge Rd, W12; mains £11.50-22.50; ☺11.30am-11pm Mon-Thu, to midnight Fri & Sat, to 10.30pm Sun; 🛜; 🚍207, 607, ⊖Shepherd's Bush Market) Grandly restored, the roomy interior of this imposing former Victorian gin palace soaks up pretty much any hubbub thrown at it, with ample elbow space and a setting of gorgeous skylights and period details. The menu is a gastronomic triumph, wine-lovers are well supplied and the walled herb garden at the rear is a choice setting for one of the gin-infused cocktails.

✗ Hammersmith & Chiswick

★GATE
VEGETARIAN $$

Map p472 (020-8748 6932; http://thegate restaurants.com/hammersmith.php; 51 Queen Caroline St, W6; mains £13-16; ⊘noon-2.30pm Mon-Fri, noon-3pm Sat & Sun, 6-10.30pm daily; 🛜🍴; ⊖Hammersmith) One of London's best vegetarian restaurants, this good-looking eatery could do with better *feng shui* (behind the Hammersmith Apollo, off Hammersmith flyover), but the inventive menu (asparagus tart, wild mushroom risotto cake, aubergine schnitzel), great weekend brunches, welcoming staff and relaxed atmosphere make the trek here worthwhile. Bookings crucial.

RIVER CAFE
ITALIAN $$$

Map p472 (020-7386 4200; www.rivercafe. co.uk; Rainville Rd, Thames Wharf, W6; mains from £18; ⊘12.30-2.30pm & 7-9pm Mon-Sat, noon-3pm Sun; 🛜; ⊖Hammersmith) The Thames-side name that spawned the world-famous eponymous cookery books offers simple, precise cooking that showcases seasonal ingredients sourced with fanatical expertise; the menus change daily. Booking is essential, as it's Michelin-starred and a favourite of cashed-up local gastronomes.

🍷 DRINKING & NIGHTLIFE

West London has everything from historic riverside boozers to smart Kensington classic pubs, microbrewery bars stuffed with choice, tucked-away boozers, roof-top garden clubs and pubs perched by the canal. It's worth coming here for a pub crawl alone.

🍸 Notting Hill & Westbourne Grove

WINDSOR CASTLE
PUB

Map p472 (www.thewindsorcastlekensington. co.uk; 114 Campden Hill Rd, W11; ⊘noon-11pm Mon-Sat, to 10.30pm Sun; 🛜; ⊖Notting Hill Gate) A classic tavern on the brow of Campden Hill Rd, this place has history, nooks and charm on tap. It's worth the search for its historic compartmentalised interior, roaring fire (in winter), delightful beer garden (in summer) and affable regulars (all seasons). According to legend, the bones of Thomas Paine (author of *Rights of Man*) are in the cellar.

EARL OF LONSDALE
PUB

Map p470 (277-281 Portobello Rd, W11; ⊘noon-11pm Mon-Fri, 10am-11pm Sat, noon-10.30pm Sun; ⊖Notting Hill Gate, Ladbroke Grove) A perfect bolthole for those traipsing Portobello Rd and named after the *bon vivant* founder of the AA (Automobile Association, *not* Alcoholics Anonymous), the Earl is peaceful during the day, with both old biddies and young hipsters inhabiting the reintroduced snugs. There are Samuel Smith's ales, a fantastic backroom with sofas, banquettes, open fires, a magnificent beer garden and cheery staff.

NOTTING HILL ARTS CLUB
CLUB

Map p470 (www.nottinghillartsclub.com; 21 Notting Hill Gate, W11; ⊘6pm-late Mon-Fri, 4pm-late Sat & Sun; 🛜; ⊖Notting Hill Gate) London simply wouldn't be what it is without places like NHAC. Cultivating the underground music scene, this small basement club attracts a musically curious and experimental crowd. Dress code: no suits and ties.

UNION TAVERN
PUB

Map p470 (020-7286 1886; www.union-tavern. co.uk; 45 Woodfield Rd, W9; ⊘noon-11pm Mon-Thu, to midnight Fri & Sat, to 10.30pm Sun; 🛜; ⊖Westbourne Park) With just the right mix of shiny gastropub, rough-and-ready local appeal, good Grand Union Canal location (with waterside terrace) and a really strong selection of craft beers, this pub is a super choice for a pint or two on your way to or from Portobello Road Market.

PORTOBELLO STAR
COCKTAIL BAR

Map p470 (020-3588 7800; www.portobello starbar.co.uk; 171 Portobello Rd, W11; cocktails from £6; ⊘11am-11.30pm Sun-Thu, to 12.30am Fri & Sat; 🛜; ⊖Ladbroke Grove) Gin and alluring cocktailsare on the menu at this former pub, refreshed into a nifty, narrow cocktail bar. The Portobello Star also runs Ginstitute (p286) is up the road.

♥ Kensington High St

★ROOF GARDENS   CLUB
Map p472 (www.roofgardens.virgin.com;   99
Kensington High St, W8; club £20, gardens free;
☺club 10pm-2am Fri & Sat, gardens 9am-5pm on
selected dates; 🕿; ⊖High St Kensington) Atop
the former Derry and Toms building is this
enchanting venue – a nightclub with 0.6
hectares of gardens and resident flamingos.
The wow factor requires £20 entry (you
must register on the guest list via the website before going) and drinks are £10 a pop.
Open only to over-21s, the dress code is 'no
effort, no entry' (leave the onesie at home).

There are three different gardens (dating from 1938): the stunningly beautiful
Spanish gardens inspired by the Alhambra
in Granada; the Tudor gardens, all nooks,
crannies and fragrant flowers; and the
Woodlands gardens, home to fully grown
oak trees and four flamingos.

When the club is not in full swing, the
gardens can be visited year-round by the
public, free of charge (although they are often hired out for private parties, so phone
ahead to check). Events through the year
range from barbecues on balmy summer
evenings to live music throughout the winter. Enter from Derry St.

SCARSDALE TAVERN   PUB
Map p472 (☎020-7937 1811; www.scarsdaletav-
ern.co.uk; 23a Edwardes Sq, W8; ☺noon-11pm
Mon-Sat, to 10.30pm Sun; 🕿; ⊖High St Kensington) This Fuller's pub quietly located along
Edwardes Sq is a lovely place for a pint of
ale or some very satisfying food. There's a
constant bevy of garrulous drinkers out the
front in warmer weather, who never want
to go home.

♥ Maida Vale

WARRINGTON   PUB
Map p470 (☎020-7286 8282; www.faucetinn.
com/warrington; 93 Warrington Cres, W9;
☺8am-11pm Mon-Thu, to midnight Fri & Sat,
to 10.30pm Sun; 🕿; ⊖Warwick Ave or Maida
Vale) Built in 1857, this former high-end
brothel is an ornate, art-nouveau feast
of a pub, with mosaic floors, pillared
portico and heaps of style. The huge saloon bar, dominated by a marble-topped
hemispherical counter with a carved
mahogany base and a vast stained-glass

window by Tiffany, is a fabulous place to
sample a range of four real ales.

WATERWAY   BAR
Map p470 (☎020-7266 3557; www.thewaterway.
co.uk; 54 Formosa St, W9; ☺10.30am-11pm Mon-
Fri, 10am-11pm Sat, to 10.30pm Sun; 🕿; ⊖War-
wick Ave) Don't come here for the selection
of beer or ales or the expensive nosh; this
place, hard by the Grand Union Canal in
Little Venice, is all about location, and it's
hard to imagine a better place to while
away a weekend afternoon. Children are
welcome until 9.30pm.

♥ Earl's Court & West Brompton

★TROUBADOUR   BAR
Map p472 (☎020-7341 6333; www.troubadour.
co.uk; 263-267 Old Brompton Rd, SW5; ☺cafe
8.30am-12.30am, club 8pm-12.30am or 2am; 🕿;
⊖Earl's Court) On a comparable spiritual
plane to Paris' Shakespeare and Company
Bookshop, this eccentric, time-warped
and convivial boho bar-cafe has been ser-
enading drinkers since 1954. (Deep breath)
Adele, Paolo Nutini, Ed Sheeran, Joni
Mitchell and (deeper breath) Jimi Hendrix
and Bob Dylan have performed here, and
there's still live music (folk, blues) and a
large, pleasant garden open in summer.

ATLAS   PUB
Map p472 (☎020-7385 9129; www.theatlaspub.
co.uk; 16 Seagrave Rd, SW6; ☺5-11pm Mon,
noon-3pm & 5-11pm Tue-Thu, noon-11pm Fri &
Sat, to 10.30pm Sun; 🕿; ⊖West Brompton) A
garrulous hubbub frequently spilling from
its ivy-clad and port-coloured facade, this
Victorian-era pub tempts locals, visitors,
foodies and drinkers alike with a delicious
wood-panelled interior, a winning Mediterranean menu, a lovely side courtyard and a
fine range of beers and wines.

♥ Shepherd's Bush

PARADISE BY WAY OF
KENSAL GREEN   BAR
(☎020-8969 0098; www.theparadise.co.uk; 19
Kilburn Lane, W10; ☺4pm-midnight Mon-Wed, to
1am Thu, to 2am Fri, noon-2am Sat, to 11.30pm
Sun; 🕿; ⊖Kensal Green) With its statues,
religious paintings, gaunt oil portraits,

NOTTING HILL & WEST LONDON DRINKING & NIGHTLIFE

panelling and dense drapes, the wildly eclectic, eccentric, boho and gothic Kensal Green bar-club is an excellent choice for offbeat charm and downright panache. The British menu is superb, and club nights Speakerboxxx (hip hop and R&B) on Fridays and Get it Good (disco, house and hip hop) on Saturdays are massive.

BREW DOG
BAR

Map p472 (✆020-8749 8094; www.brewdog.com; 15-19 Goldhawk Rd, W12; ⊘noon-midnight Mon-Sat, to 10.30pm Sun; 🛜; ⊜Shepherd's Bush or Goldhawk Rd) Craft beer – from its brewery in Scotland as well as guest beers from far and wide – is the name of the game at specialists Brew Dog, with over 40 on tap, including the heady punch of Coffee and Cigarettes (12.1%) or the decidedly milder and amusingly named Nanny State (0.5%); alternatively aim down the middle and sink a Dead Pony Club (3.8%).

LIBRARY BAR
BAR

Map p472 (www.bushtheatre.co.uk; 7 Uxbridge Rd; ⊘10am-11pm Mon-Sat; 🛜; ⊜Shepherd's Bush Market) Tread the bare wood floorboards of this roomy bar/cafe in this erstwhile library, and grab a paperback play or two from the dense collection stuffed onto shelves. A new garden terrace has been added recently, bringing a further alfresco dimension. It's a great place to grab a brekkie, sink a cocktail or draught beer, or hang out for some pre-theatre snacking.

📍 Hammersmith

DOVE
PUB

Map p472 (✆020-8748 9474; www.dovehammersmith.co.uk; 19 Upper Mall, W6; ⊘11am-11pm Mon-Sat, noon-10.30pm Sun; 🛜; ⊜Hammersmith, Ravenscourt Park) Severely inundated by the epic floodwaters of 1928, this gem of a 17th-century Fuller's pub revels in historic charm and superb Thames views. Scottish poet James Thompson was reputedly inspired to write the lyrics of 'Rule Britannia' here in the 18th century. It was Graham Greene's local, Hemingway and Dylan Thomas drank here too, and William Morris lived nearby.

To your right as you walk in is what was once listed as the world's smallest bar. If the sun comes out, fight for a spot on the lovely terrace (forget it on Boat Race day). In winter, warm your toes by the open fire.

OLD SHIP W6
PUB

Map p472 (✆020-8748 2593; www.oldshipw6.co.uk; 25 Upper Mall, W6; ⊘11am-11pm Mon-Thu, to midnight Fri, 9am-midnight Sat, to 11pm Sun; 🛜; ⊜Ravenscourt Park, Stamford Brook) Decorated with sculls, oars and nautical prints, the Old Ship and its shiny, buttoned leather sofas would hardly merit a diversion but for its terrific waterside perch, which guarantees superb al fresco Thames views from the balcony upstairs or the ground-floor terrace. Dating from 1722, the pub is wall-to-wall with spectators during the annual Oxford and Cambridge Boat Race.

☆ ENTERTAINMENT

Theatre, live music, opera, comedy, classic deco cinemas screening art-house and independent films: they're all covered in West London.

★ BUSH THEATRE
THEATRE

Map p472 (✆020-8743 5050; www.bushtheatre.co.uk; 7 Uxbridge Rd, W12; ⊘10am-11pm Mon-Sat; ⊜Shepherd's Bush) This rehoused and reinvigorated West London theatre is renowned for encouraging new talent and independent, new playwriting. Its success since 1972 is down to strong writing from the likes of Jonathan Harvey, Conor McPherson, Stephen Poliakoff and Mark Ravenhill. It also has an excellent cafe and bar. The theatre hosts the three-day **Shubbak Festival**, London's largest biennial festival of contemporary Arab culture.

The **Shepherd's Bush Comedy Festival** is also held here in summer.

PUPPET THEATRE BARGE
PUPPET THEATRE

Map p470 (✆020-7249 6876; www.puppetbarge.com; 35 Blomfield Rd, W9; adult/child £12/8.50; ⊍Warwick Avenue) This utterly charming marionette (aka puppet) theatre can be found in a converted barge moored in Little Venice – an area as pretty as it sounds. The theatre has been there for almost 40 years and holds regular performances during weekends and school holidays.

GATE PICTUREHOUSE
CINEMA

Map p470 (✆0871 902 5731; www.picturehouses.co.uk; 87 Notting Hill Gate, W11; tickets £7-13.50; ⊜Notting Hill Gate) Opened in 1911, the Gate's single screen has one of London's most charming art-deco cinema interiors, with

INDIE CINEMAS

If you love cinema, you're in for a treat with West London's quirky picture houses, including the Electric Cinema (p283) and the Gate Picturehouse (p282). Features include sofas (beds, even), alcoholic drinks (not simply permitted, but encouraged), Q&A events with directors, and much more – this is how cinema should be! Tickets are slightly more expensive than run-of-the-mill movie houses.

director Q&As and a wealth of cinema clubs, including the E4 Slackers Club (students) and Silver Screen (over-60s). Cheapest tickets on Mondays. Sink a drink in the foyer bar before or after your film (a mix of art-house and mainstream).

ELECTRIC CINEMA
CINEMA

Map p470 (☑020-7908 9696; www.electric cinema.co.uk; 191 Portobello Rd, W11; tickets £8-22.50; ⊖Ladbroke Grove) Having notched up its centenary in 2011, the Electric is one of the UK's oldest cinemas, updated. Avail yourself of the luxurious leather armchairs, sofas, footstools and tables for food and drink in the auditorium, or select one of the six front-row double beds! Tickets are cheapest on Mondays.

EVENTIM APOLLO
LIVE PERFORMANCE

Map p472 (☑0844 249 4300; www.eventim apollo.com; 45 Queen Caroline St, W6; £10-65; 🐾; ⊖Hammersmith) Hosting such musical titans as Sting, Kate Bush and Paul Weller as well as comedians, celebrity scientists such as Professor Brian Cox and travelling roadshows, this 3655-seat 1930s venue (formerly known as the Hammersmith Apollo) is one of London's leading performance and live-music venues.

OPERA HOLLAND PARK
OPERA

Map p472 (☑0300 999 1000; www.operaholland park.com; Holland Park, W8; tickets £18-77; ⊖High St Kensington, Holland Park) Sit under the 1000-seat canopy, temporarily erected every summer for a nine-week season in the middle of Holland Park (p273), for a mix of crowd pleasers and rare (even obscure) works. Five operas are generally performed each year.

O2 SHEPHERD'S
BUSH EMPIRE
CONCERT VENUE

Map p472 (☑020-8354 3300; www.academy musicgroup.com/o2shepherdsbushempire; Shepherd's Bush Green, W12; tickets £15-40; 🐾; ⊖Shepherd's Bush) This famous midsized venue (standing capacity is 2000) attracts all manner of top acts (Muse, La Roux) and back-catalogue giants (Dead Kennedys, the Jesus and Mary Chain). The floor doesn't slope, so if you're not so tall, the view from up the back in the stalls may not be good (it's worth paying for the balcony, or arrive early and get up front).

RIVERSIDE STUDIOS
PERFORMING ARTS

Map p472 (☑020-8237 1000; www.riverside studios.co.uk; Crisp Rd, W6; ⊖Hammersmith) Shut at the time of writing while undergoing redevelopment, but due to reopen in 2018, the Riverside hosts an eclectic mix of performing arts, from circus to theatre and comedy, and also doubles as an art-house cinema. There are a popular restaurant and bar on hand, with terrace views of the Thames and Hammersmith Bridge.

LYRIC HAMMERSMITH
THEATRE

Map p472 (☑020-8741 6850; www.lyric.co.uk; King St, Lyric Sq, W6; tickets £15-40; ⊖Hammersmith) Recently refurbished and extended with a new wing, the Lyric turns classics on their head, staging a stimulating choice of productions from the highbrow to more accessible theatre.

KNOCK2BAG
COMEDY

Map p472 (☑07870-212189; Bar FM, 184 Hopgood St, W12; ⊖Shepherd's Bush Market) Big comedy names and more fringe acts, with a sister outfit in Shoreditch.

 SHOPPING

Save most of your shopping energy for the bonanza of independent shops around Portobello Rd and its famous market. Kensington Church St is excellent for antiques, as well as independent niche retailers for collectibles and gifts and top-grade charity shops. For vast mall shopping with everything under one roof, head to Westfield.

PORTOBELLO ROAD MARKET
CLOTHING, ANTIQUES

See p274.

CHINESE TEA COMPANY
TEA

Map p470 (☑020-8960 0096; www.the-chinese-tea-company.com; 14 Portobello Green Arcade, 281 Portobello Rd, W10; ☺11am-6pm Mon-Sat; ☻Ladbroke Grove) Owner Juyan proffers pointers in the world of Chinese tea at this bijou specialist shop in Portobello Green Arcade. Whatever your choice of Chinese tea (chá) – Pu'er, Tie Guanyin, Jasmine, Mogan Shan red tea or Lion's Peak Long Jing – you'll find it here, as well private tea tastings (£25 to £30).

ADAM
CLOTHING

Map p470 (☑020-8960 6944; www.adamoflondon.com; 11 Portobello Green Arcade, 281 Portobello Rd, W11; ☺10am-5.30pm Tue-Sat, noon-5pm Sun; ☻Ladbroke Grove) Short of a Crombie to go with your mohair suit (with 1.5in lapels and 6in vent) and button-down shirt? Adam has all your mod needs and provides a fascinating look into the well-dressed and trim niche of classic mod clothing in the big smoke. Look for the Quadrophenia still in the window.

YASTIK
HOMEWARES

Map p472 (☑020-3538 7981; www.yastikbyrifatozbek.com; 8 Holland St, W8; from £280; ☺10am-6pm Tue-Sat; ☻High St Kensington) The lovely patterns and colours of the cushions in rows at petite Yastik (Turkish for 'pillow') employ hand woven ikats and suzani embroidery, based on and inspired by designs from across Central Asia. They may not be cheap, but they're gorgeous and make ideal gifts.

ROYAL TRINITY HOSPICE
CLOTHING

Map p472 (☑020-7361 1530; www.royaltrinityhospice.london/kensington; 31-33 Kensington Church St, W8; ☺10am-6pm Mon-Sat, 11am-5pm Sun; ☻High St Kensington) For designer labels and top-end items in female clothing, shoes and bags, it's well worth a browse through this well-supplied charity shop on Kensington Church St. Stock turnover is pretty high, so fresh items are always coming in, and the sister shop alongside has menswear and further odds and ends.

JAPANESE GALLERY
ART

Map p472 (日本美術; ☑020-7229 2934; www.japanesegallery.co.uk; 66d Kensington Church St, W8; ☺10am-6pm; ☻High St Kensington, Notting Hill Gate) Offers a large range of original, fine and historic Ukiyo-e ('pictures of the floating world') woodblock Japanese prints. Prices range from under £100 to much more for museum-quality examples. The shop also sells a range of beautiful Japanese cards for occasions. Staff are very helpful and can help you choose.

FOUND AND VISION
VINTAGE

Map p470 (☑020-3620 5755; www.foundandvision.com; 104 Golborne Rd, W10; ☺10am-6pm; ☻Ladbroke Grove) A glorious selection makes this funky Golborne Rd stop – its name a play on Bowie's synth-led classic from 1977 album Low – a paradise for hunters of vintage clothing, with an abundance of killer 1970s lounge suits, Adolfo knit dresses, Vivienne Westwood blouses, Missoni sweaters, Versace tops and much more.

LUTYENS & RUBINSTEIN
BOOKS

Map p470 (☑020-7229 1010; www.lutyensrubinstein.co.uk; 21 Kensington Park Rd, W11; ☺10am-6pm Mon, to 6.30pm Tue-Fri, to 6pm Sat, 11am-5pm Sun; ☻Ladbroke Grove) Lutyens & Rubinstein is a tremendous, compact (ground floor and basement) and terribly discerning bookshop. It's a squeeze, but the small size pays dividends. Established by a company of literary agents, the focus is on 'excellence in writing', as determined by customers and readers, so every book comes recommended. Don't expect huge piles of best-sellers or stuffed dump-bins.

NOTTING HILL BOOKSHOP
BOOKS

Map p470 (☑020-7229 5260; www.thenottinghillbookshop.co.uk; 13 Blenheim Cres; ☺9am-7pm Mon-Sat, 10am-6pm Sun; ☻Ladbroke Grove) This fine, rather small, general bookshop – the inspiration behind the bookshop in Hugh Grant and Julia Roberts' monster rom-com Notting Hill – still sees a regular stream of pilgrims (of all ages) who pose outside for snaps. An understandable and very browseable accent on travel books endures, but fiction provides equilibrium and there's a strong children's section at the rear.

PORTOBELLO GREEN ARCADE
CLOTHING

Map p470 (www.portobellodesigners.com; 281 Portobello Rd, W10; ☻Ladbroke Grove) Portobello Green Arcade is home to some cutting-edge clothing and jewellery designers as well as small, independent niche shops such as Adam and Chinese Tea Company.

CERAMICA BLUE
HOMEWARES

Map p470 (☑020-7727 0288; www.ceramicablue. co.uk; 10 Blenheim Cres, W11; ☺10am-6.30pm Mon-Sat, noon-5pm Sun; ☺Ladbroke Grove) A lovely spot for colourful, eclectic and handsome crockery, imported from more than a dozen countries. There are Japanese eggshell-glaze teacups, serving plates with tribal South African designs, candelabra from Italy, gorgeous tablecloths from Provence, hand-decorated glass from Turkey, hand-painted terracotta from Spain, coloured glass plates from Germany, fun tea-towels and much more.

WESTFIELD
MALL

Map p472 (☑020-3371 2300; http://uk.westfield. com/london; Ariel Way, W12; ☺10am-10pm Mon-Sat, noon-6pm Sun; ☺Wood Lane) With a humongous cousin in Stratford (and one tipped for Croydon for 2020–21), this gigantic recession-busting shopping mecca was London's first mall. As well as the 380-odd shops that reside here (all franchises), Westfield has a raft of eateries (again, chains only), bars, a cinema and regular events, from fashion shows to book signings.

ROUGH TRADE WEST
MUSIC

Map p470 (☑020-7229 8541; www.roughtrade. com; 130 Talbot Rd, W11; ☺10am-6.30pm Mon-Sat, 11am-5pm Sun; ☺Ladbroke Grove) With its underground, alternative and vintage rarities, this home of the eponymous punk-music label remains a haven for vinyl junkies.

RETRO WOMAN
VINTAGE

Map p470 (☑020-7565 5572; www.mgeshops. com; 20 Pembridge Rd, W11; ☺10am-8pm; ☺Notting Hill Gate) More secondhand than vintage, but very popular, Retro Woman has racks upon racks of hand-me-down fashion and big-name designer goodies, including an astonishing selection of shoes (of Imelda Marcos proportions) and self-confessed 'nylon monstrosities' from the '70s. There's another branch a bit further along Pembridge Rd, at No 32.

SHEPHERD'S BUSH MARKET
MARKET

Map p472 (www.myshepherdsbushmarket.com; ☺9am-6pm Mon-Sat; ☺Shepherd's Bush, Goldhawk Rd) Running since 1914, this fruit-and-veg market stretches underneath the Hammersmith & City and Circle Lines between Goldhawk Rd and Shepherd's Bush tube stations. Popular with local African and Afro-Caribbean communities, it's stockpiled with mangoes, passionfruit, okra, plantains, sweet potatoes and other exotic fare.

HONEST JON'S
MUSIC

Map p470 (☑020-8969 9822; www.honestjons. com; 278 Portobello Rd, W10; ☺10am-6pm Mon-Sat, 11am-5pm Sun; ☺Ladbroke Grove) Flogging old-school reggae, jazz, funk, soul, dance and blues vinyl to Notting Hill's musical purists since 1974, with a large volume of CDs. Check the extensive listings, including the rarest of the rare, on the website.

RELLIK
VINTAGE

Map p470 (☑020-8962 0089; www.relliklondon. co.uk; 8 Golborne Rd; ☺10am-6pm Tue-Sat; ☺Westbourne Park) Incongruously located opposite one of London's most notorious tower blocks – the godawful-yet-heritage-listed concrete Trellick Tower – Rellik is a fashionista favourite retro store. It stocks vintage numbers from the 1920s to the 1980s, and rummaging among the frippery, it's not unusual to find an Yves Saint-Laurent coat, a Chloe suit or an Ossie Clark dress.

BISCUITEERS
FOOD

Map p470 (☑020-7727 8096; www.biscuiteers. com/biscuiteers-shop-icing-notting-hill; 194 Kensington Park Rd, W11; ☺10am-6pm Mon-Sat, 11am-5pm Sun; Ⓤ Notting Hill Gate) Achieving an almost surreal level of quaintness, Biscuiteers is a Notting Hill cafe specialising in hand-iced treats, ranging from biscuits to cupcakes to chocolates. You can try your own hand at the art of icing decoration by joining one of the on-site classes.

🏃 SPORTS & ACTIVITIES

★ LONDON WATERBUS COMPANY
CRUISE

Map p470 (☑020-7482 2550; www.londonwater bus.co.uk; 32 Camden Lock Pl, NW1; adult/child one-way £9/7.50, return £14/12; ☺hourly 10am-5pm Apr-Sep, weekends only & less frequent departures other months; ☺Warwick Ave, Camden Town) This enclosed barge runs enjoyable 50-minute trips on Regent's Canal between Little Venice and Camden Lock, passing by Regent's Park and stopping at London Zoo. There are fewer departures outside high season – check the website for schedules.

One-way tickets (adult/child £25/18), including entry to London Zoo, allowing passengers to disembark within the zoo grounds are available. Buy tickets aboard the narrowboats.

GINSTITUTE
COOKING

Map p470 (☑020-3034 2234; www.theginstitute. com; 186 Portobello Rd, W11; adult £110; ☺noon-11.30pm Mon-Sat, to 11pm Sun; Ⓤ Notting Hill Gate) Ginstitute offers a thoroughly interactive gin experience. You'll learn about the history of the beverage in Britain – which is as fascinating as it is depressing – and how it's made. Includes a cocktail reception, a gin lecture, a 70cl bottle of Portobello Road No 171 gin, a 70cl bottle of your personally devised gin blend.

QUEENS ICE & BOWL
SKATING

Map p470 (☑020-7229 0172; www.queens iceandbowl.co.uk; 17 Queensway; adult/child £12.50/11.50, skate hire £3; ☺10am-6.45pm & 8-10.45pm daily, children's classes 4.45-5.30pm Tue & Thu; Ⓔ Queensway) London may have a generous crop of winter outdoor ice rinks, but Queen's Ice Rink in Queensway is open all year. A great hit with novices and ice-skaters of all ages, the rink has been sending generations of youngsters and adults, arms whirling, around its ice for decades. There's a fun ten-pin bowling alley (10am to 11pm, £8.95/7.50 per adult/child per game) right alongside.

PORCHESTER SPA
SPA

Map p470 (☑020-7313 3858; www.porchester spatreatments.co.uk; Porchester Centre, Queensway, W2; £28.55; ☺10am-10pm; Ⓔ Bayswater, Royal Oak) Housed in a gorgeous, art-deco building, the Porchester is a no-frills spa run by Westminster Council. With a 30m swimming pool, a large Finnish-log sauna, two steam rooms, three Turkish hot rooms and a massive plunge pool, there are plenty of affordable treatments on offer including massages and male and female pampering/ grooming sessions.

It's women only on Tuesdays, Thursdays and Fridays all day and between 10am and 2pm on Sundays; men only on Mondays, Wednesdays and Saturdays. Couples are welcome from 4pm to 10pm on Sundays.

Greenwich & South London

GREENWICH | LAMBETH, KENNINGTON, ELEPHANT AND CASTLE & VAUXHALL | CLAPHAM & WANDSWORTH |
BRIXTON | BATTERSEA | DULWICH & FOREST HILL

Neighbourhood Top Five

❶ Royal Observatory
(p289) Standing astride two
hemispheres and exploring
the cosmos then savouring
the epic views over London
from Greenwich Park.

❷ Brixton Village (p296)
Hanging out in this fun and
ever-funky area.

❸ Horniman Museum
(p296) Exploring the eclectic wonders of the museum,
before enjoying a picnic in
its beautiful gardens.

❹ Deptford (p302) Discovering the dichotomy of
this district, with its Georgian architecture, state-
of-the-art Laban Theatre

dance academy and worka-
day market.

❺ Imperial War Museum
(p294) Browsing a tremen-
dous and riveting collection
on war, conflict, weaponry
and military action in a former psychiatric hospital.

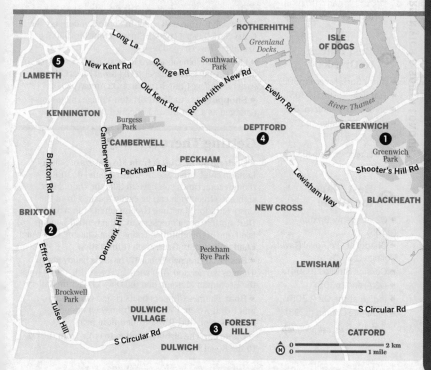

For more detail of this area see Map p474, p476 and p477 ➡

Lonely Planet's Top Tip

A fun way to reach Docklands from Greenwich (or vice versa) is via the foot tunnel under the Thames. From the Island Gardens park on the Isle of Dogs, enjoy the splendid view of Greenwich that Venetian artist Canaletto portrayed in his *Greenwich Hospital from the North Bank of the Thames* (1752), now in the National Maritime Museum's art collection.

◉ Best Places to Eat

➜ Koi Ramen Bar (p298)

➜ May the Fifteenth (p300)

➜ Trinity (p301)

➜ Mamalan (p299)

➜ Chez Bruce (p301)

For reviews, see p298.

◉ Best Places to Drink

➜ Cutty Sark Tavern (p303)

➜ Trafalgar Tavern (p303)

➜ Shrub and Shutter (p303)

➜ Greenwich Union (p303)

➜ Lost & Co (p303)

For reviews, see p303.

◉ Best Places for Music

➜ O2 Academy Brixton (p305)

➜ Chapel at Old Royal Naval College (p292)

➜ Corsica Studios (p304)

➜ O2 Arena (p305)

➜ Indigo at the O2 (p305)

➜ St Alfege Church (p293)

For reviews, see p305. ➡

Explore Greenwich & South London

Until recently Londoners talked as if the Thames was the huge barrier between north and south that it was in the Middle Ages. But with more attractions, better transport links and increased pedestrian areas, the allure to go south has become irresistible. Quaint Greenwich (*gren-itch*) is packed with grand architecture, while gorgeous parks and standout museums bring growing fleets of visitors. With the Royal Observatory and the renovated Queen's House, Greenwich should be one of the highlights of any visit to London – allow a day, particularly if you want to head down the river to the Thames Barrier.

Find time for an afternoon or a night out in edgy and artistic Brixton. Battersea and Wandsworth are home to lovely parks and a visit is ideally rounded off with a beer in a fantastic local pub. Lambeth boasts both the medieval London residence of the Archbishop of Canterbury and the incomparable Imperial War Museum. Dulwich and Forest Hill are home to excellent galleries and museums, while Bexleyheath and Eltham will reward day trippers with unusual architectural gems.

Local Life

➜ **Hang-outs** Spending a Saturday or Sunday afternoon in the pub is time well spent in South London; try the Cutty Sark Tavern (p303), Shrub & Shutter (p303) or Trafalgar Tavern (p303).

➜ **Live music** Join music fans in Brixton at Dogstar (p305) and in Greenwich at Chapel at Old Royal Naval College (p292), St Alfege Church (p293) or O2 Arena (p305).

➜ **Shopping** Art-inclined Brixton Village (p296) has emerged as a vibrant and eclectic hub of local life.

Getting There & Away

➜ **Underground, DLR & train** Most areas of South London can be reached by Underground or DLR, though sometimes you have to take the train. Most sights in Greenwich can be easily reached from the Cutty Sark for Maritime Greenwich (its full name) DLR station, but a quicker way from central London is on one of the mainline trains from Charing Cross or London Bridge to Greenwich train station.

➜ **Bus** From Greenwich, bus 177 or 180 is handy for the Thames Barrier and Woolwich. In Forest Hill, the P4 links the Horniman Museum and the Dulwich Picture Gallery.

➜ **Boat** Thames Clippers boats run to Greenwich and Royal Arsenal Woolwich from the London Eye, Embankment and Tower Millennium piers.

➜ **Cable car** The airborne option to cross from the O2 to the Royal Docks.

GARY PERKIN/SHUTTERSTOCK ©

◉ TOP SIGHT
ROYAL OBSERVATORY & GREENWICH PARK

The Royal Observatory is where the study of the sea, the stars and time converge. The prime meridian charts its line through the grounds of the observatory, chosen quite arbitrarily in 1884, to divide the globe into the eastern and western hemispheres. The observatory sits atop a hill within leafy and regal Greenwich Park, London's oldest royal park.

Royal Observatory

Unlike most other attractions in Greenwich, the Royal Observatory contains free-access areas (such as Weller Astronomy Galleries) and ones you pay for (Meridian Line, Flamsteed House and Camera Obscura).

Flamsteed House & Meridian Courtyard

Charles II ordered construction of the Christopher Wren–designed **Flamsteed House**, the original observatory building, on the foundations of Greenwich Castle in 1675 after closing the observatory at the Tower of London. Today it contains the magnificent **Octagon Room** and the rather simple apartment where the Astronomer Royal, John Flamsteed, and his family lived. Here you'll also find the brilliant **Time Galleries**, explaining how the longitude problem – how to accurately determine a ship's east–west location – was solved through astronomical means and the invention of the marine chronometer.

In the **Meridian Courtyard**, where the globe is decisively sliced into east and west, visitors can delightfully straddle both hemispheres, with one foot on either side of the meridian line. Every day the red **Time Ball** at the top of the Royal Observatory drops at 1pm, as it has done ever since 1833.

DON'T MISS

→ Meridian Courtyard
→ Flamsteed House
→ Camera Obscura
→ Views of London from the statue of General Wolfe
→ Astronomy Centre
→ Greenwich Park

PRACTICALITIES

→ Map p477, D3
→ www.rmg.co.uk
→ Greenwich Park, Blackheath Ave, SE10
→ adult/child £9.50/5, with Cutty Sark £18.50/8.50
→ ⊙10am-5pm Sep-Jun, to 6pm Jul & Aug
→ ℝDLR Cutty Sark, DLR Greenwich, Greenwich

PRIME TARGET

On 15 February 1894, the Royal Observatory was the unexpected target of a bomb plot. The bomber – a 26-year-old French anarchist called Martial Bourdin – managed to blow his left hand off in the bungled attack and died from his wounds soon afterwards. The choice of the Royal Observatory as a target was never understood, but it was undamaged. The bombing later found literary recognition in Joseph Conrad's novel *The Secret Agent* and the anarchist appears in the TS Eliot poem *Animula* under the name Boudin.

GROUND ZERO

The Greenwich meridian was selected as the global prime meridian at the International Meridian Conference in Washington DC in 1884. Greenwich became the world's ground zero for longitude and standard for time calculations, replacing the multiple meridians that had existed till then. Greenwich was assisted in its bid by the earlier US adoption of Greenwich Mean Time for its own national time zones. In any case, the majority of world trade already used sea charts that identified Greenwich as the prime meridian.

There's also a telescope on a platform with amazing views over London, and a map of what you can see.

Astronomy Centre & Peter Harrison Planetarium

The southern half of the observatory contains the highly informative (and free) **Weller Astronomy Galleries**, where you can touch the oldest object you will ever encounter: part of the Gibeon meteorite, a mere 4.5 billion years old! Other engaging exhibits include an orrery (mechanical model of the solar system, minus the as-yet-undiscovered Uranus and Neptune) from 1780, astronomical documentaries, a first edition of Newton's *Principia Mathematica* and the opportunity to view the Milky Way in multiple wavelengths. This is also the venue of the annual Insight Astronomy Photographer of the Year exhibition, with its astonishing images. To take stargazing further, pick up a Skyhawk telescope from the shop.

The state-of-the-art **Peter Harrison Planetarium** – London's only planetarium – can cast entire heavens onto the inside of its roof. It runs at least five informative shows a day. Booking advised.

Camera Obscura

Situated in a small brick summerhouse next to the Meridian Courtyard, this astonishing room projects a live image of Queen's House – and the people moving in front of it and the boats on the Thames behind – onto a table. Enter through two layers of thick curtains – to keep the light out; make sure you close them behind you to keep the room as dark as possible.

Greenwich Park

This is one of London's loveliest expanses of green (p292), with a rose garden, picturesque walks, Anglo-Saxon tumuli and astonishing views from the crown of the hill near near the **Statue of General Wolfe** towards Canary Wharf – the financial district across the Thames. Covering 74 hectares, it's the oldest enclosed royal park and is partly the work of André Le Nôtre, the landscape architect who designed the palace gardens of Versailles.

The park contains a lovely teahouse near the Royal Observatory, a cafe behind the National Maritime Museum, a deer park, tennis courts in the southwest and a boating lake at the **Queen's House** (p293) end. There's also **Ranger's House** (p293) and the park is full of chestnut trees - head there in October and pick the nuts from the ground.

TOP SIGHT
OLD ROYAL NAVAL COLLEGE

Home to the University of Greenwich and Trinity College of Music, the Old Royal Naval College is one of London's most gracious and historic sites. There are two main sections open to the public, as well as huge grounds. When all is said and done, it's worth taking the Greenwich Foot Tunnel to view the spectacle from the far side of the Thames.

When Christopher Wren was commissioned by King William III and Queen Mary II to construct a naval hospital here in 1692, he conceived it in two separate halves to protect the river views from the Queen's House, Inigo Jones' Renaissance masterpiece to the south. Designed as a dining hall (p292) for retired sailors, this is one of Europe's greatest banquet halls, containing the largest painting in Europe, the baroque painted ceiling by artist Sir James Thornhill.

Off the Upper Hall is the **Nelson Room**, originally designed by Nicholas Hakwsmoor. In January 1806, the brandy-soaked (for embalming purposes of course) body of the great naval hero lay in state here before his funeral at St Paul's Cathedral.

The beautiful **Painted Hall** is shut till 2019 for an ambitious conservation effort, however visitors can still visit the Painted Hall through Painted Hall Ceiling Tours, climbing an observation deck to take a closer look at the paintings. Tours are £10 and last 45 minutes; tickets can be booked online on the Old Royal Naval College website.

With its mix of ancient Greek and naval motifs, the beautiful **chapel** (p292) in the Queen Mary Building is decorated in an elaborate rococo style with lots of trompe l'œil details. The chapel is famed for its excellent acoustics and regularly hosts concerts; check the Old Royal Naval College's website for details. Note the astonishing neoclassical ceiling, decorated in a tantalising and triumphant blend of cream and light blue. Regular services are also held throughout the week.

DON'T MISS

→ Painted Hall
→ Concerts in the chapel
→ Artefacts from Henry VIII's Palace of Placentia

PRACTICALITIES

→ Map p477, C2
→ www.ornc.org
→ 2 Cutty Sark Gardens, SE10
→ admission free
→ ⊙10am-5pm, grounds 8am-11pm
→ ℝ DLR Cutty Sark

⊙ SIGHTS

⊙ Greenwich

ROYAL OBSERVATORY
HISTORIC BUILDING
See p289.

OLD ROYAL NAVAL COLLEGE
HISTORIC BUILDING
See p291.

★ GREENWICH PARK
PARK
Map p477 (☎030-0 061 2380; www.royalparks. org.uk; King George St, SE10; ☉6am-around sunset; ⊠DLR Cutty Sark, ⊠Greenwich, Maze Hill) This is one of London's loveliest expanses of green, with a rose garden, picturesque walks, Anglo-Saxon tumuli and astonishing views from the crown of the hill near the Royal Observatory (p289) towards Canary Wharf – the financial district across the Thames. Covering 74 hectares, it's the oldest enclosed royal park and is partly the work of André Le Nôtre, the landscape architect who designed the palace gardens of Versailles.

PAINTED HALL
HISTORIC BUILDING
Map p477 (☎020-8269 4799; www.ornc.org; Old Royal Naval College, SE10; ⊠DLR Cutty Sark) FREE Designed as a dining hall for retired sailors, this is one of Europe's greatest banquet halls, containing the largest painting in Europe, the Baroque painted ceiling by artist Sir James Thornhill. An illusory architectural composition frames King William III and Queen Mary II, original patrons of the Painted Hall and the Old Royal Naval College, enthroned amidst symbols of their triumph and Britain's naval power. Beneath William's feet grovels the defeated French king, Louis XIV, furled flag in hand. The hall is shut till 2019 for an ambitious conservation effort.

CHAPEL AT OLD ROYAL NAVAL COLLEGE
CHURCH
Map p477 (www.ornc.org; SE10; ☉10am-5pm Mon-Sun; ⊠DLR Cutty Sark) With its mix of ancient Greek and naval motifs, the neoclassical Chapel of St Peter and St Paul in the Queen Mary Building at Old Royal Naval College (p291) is decorated in an elaborate rococo style with lots of trompe l'oeil details. The eastern end of the chapel is dominated by the *Preservation of St Paul after Shipwreck at Malta* painting by the 18th-century American artist Benjamin West.

⊙ TOP SIGHT
NATIONAL MARITIME MUSEUM

Narrating the long and eventful history of seafaring Britain, this museum's highlights include *Miss Britain III* (the first boat to top 100mph on open water), the 19m-long golden state barge built in 1732 for Frederick, Prince of Wales, the huge **ship's propeller** and the colourful figureheads installed on the ground floor. Families will also love the **ship simulator** and the **children's gallery**.

Voyagers: Britons and the Sea houses JMW Turner's largest work, the huge 1824 oil painting *The Battle of Trafalgar* is hung in its namesake gallery on the ground floor.

On the 1st floor, **Traders: the East India Company and Asia** looks at Britain's 19th-century maritime trade with the East, while **The Atlantic: Slavery, Trade, Empire** explores the triangular trade between Europe, Africa and America from the 1600s to the 1850s.

On the 2nd floor, the superb **Nelson, Navy, Nation** gallery focuses on the Royal Navy during the conflict-ridden 17th century.

Opening in 2018, a new **Exploration Wing** will contain four galleries: Pacific Exploration, Polar Worlds, Tudor and Stuart Seafarers and Sea Things, devoted to the theme of exploration and human endeavour.

DON'T MISS
➡ JMW Turner's *The Battle of Trafalgar*
➡ Frederick's golden state barge
➡ *Miss Britain III*
➡ Ship simulator

PRACTICALITIES
➡ Map p477, C2
➡ www.rmg.co.uk/ national-maritime-museum
➡ Romney Rd, SE10
➡ admission free
➡ ☉10am-5pm
➡ ⊠DLR Cutty Sark

TOP SIGHT
CUTTY SARK

The last of the great clipper ships to sail between China and England in the 19th century and one of Greenwich's great photo-ops, the fully restored *Cutty Sark* endured massive fire damage a decade ago during a £25 million restoration. Launched in 1869 in Scotland, it made eight voyages to China in the 1870s, sailing out with a mixed cargo and coming back with a bounty of tea.

The exhibition in the ship's hold tells its story as a tea clipper at the end of the 19th century (and then a carrier of wool and mixed cargo). As you make your way up, there are films, interactive maps and plenty of illustrations and props to get an idea of what life on board was like.

On the top deck, you can visit the crew's cramped living quarters and the officers' plush cabins. Visits end in the basement gallery located underneath the hull, which rests on a glass 'sea' design by architect Nicola Grimshow and appears to be floating. There's also an intriguing collection of **figureheads** below deck, one of the largest of its kind in the world. Another fire took hold in 2014, but fire crews were quick to respond and extinguish the blaze.

DON'T MISS

➡ Hull views from the basement gallery

➡ Interactive displays on the voyages of the *Cutty Sark*

➡ Top-deck living quarters

➡ Figureheads collection

PRACTICALITIES

➡ Map p477, B2

➡ ✆020-8312 6608

➡ www.rmg.co.uk/cuttysark

➡ King William Walk, SE10

➡ adult/child £13.50/7

➡ ⊙10am-5pm Sep-Jun, to 6pm Jul & Aug

➡ ℞DLR Cutty Sark

QUEEN'S HOUSE   HISTORIC BUILDING
Map p477 (www.rmg.co.uk/queens-house; Romney Rd, SE10; ⊙10am-5pm; ℞DLR Cutty Sark) **FREE** The first Palladian building by architect Inigo Jones after he returned from Italy is as enticing for its form as for its art collection. The house was begun in 1616 for Anne of Denmark, wife of James I, but was not completed until 1638, when it became the home of Charles I and his queen, Henrietta Maria. The beautiful helix-shaped (and reportedly haunted) **Tulip Stairs** form England's first set of centrally unsupported stairs: they constitute a peerless photo op for upward shots.

The **Great Hall** is a lovely cube shape with an elaborately tiled floor, laid in 1635 and best viewed from the gallery. Turner Prize-winning artist Richard Wright recently worked on a fine and intricate design for the ceiling in gold leaf. Don't miss the immaculately restored painted ceiling in the **Queen's Presence Chamber** on the 1st floor. An ambitious restoration of the house was unveiled in 2017, with 22 rooms in Queen's House devoted to art over a 400-year period, marking the building's 400th anniversary.

RANGER'S HOUSE   MUSEUM
Map p477 (Wernher Collection; EH; ✆020-8294 2548; www.english-heritage.org.uk; Greenwich Park, Chesterfield Walk, SE10; adult/child £7.60/4.60; ⊙guided tours at 11.30am & 2pm Sun-Wed late Mar-Sep; ℞Greenwich, DLR Cutty Sark) This elegant Georgian villa, built in 1723, once housed the ranger of Greenwich Park (p292) and now contains a collection of 700 works of fine and applied art (medieval and Renaissance paintings, porcelain, silverware, tapestries) amassed by Julius Wernher (1850–1912), a German-born railway engineer's son who struck it rich in the diamond fields of South Africa in the 19th century. The Spanish Renaissance jewellery collection is the best in Europe. Book in advance. Note that the **rose garden** fronting the Ranger's House makes a visit in June even more special.

ST ALFEGE CHURCH   CHURCH
Map p477 (www.st-alfege.org; Greenwich Church St, SE10; ⊙11am-4pm Mon-Fri, 10am-4pm Sat, noon-4pm Sun; ℞Greenwich, DLR Cutty Sark) Designed by Nicholas Hawksmoor to replace a 13th-century church and consecrated in 1718, lovely St Alfege features a

restored mural by James Thornhill (whose work can also be found in the Painted Hall (p292) at the nearby Royal Naval College (p291) and at St Paul's Cathedral (p153)), a largely wood-panelled interior, and an intriguing keyboard from the Tudor period with middle keyboard octaves. Henry VIII was also baptised at the church. Free concerts take place at 1.05pm on Thursdays and most Saturdays.

GREENWICH FOOT TUNNEL   TUNNEL
Map p477 (Cutty Sark Gardens, SE10; ⊘24hr; ⓇDLR Cutty Sark) Reached via glass-topped domes (with lifts and steps) on either side of the river, this white-tiled Victorian-era 370m-long pedestrian tunnel provides an atmospheric back route from Greenwich to the Isle of Dogs; it's also an excellent diversion on foot to get a photo-op of Greenwich from the far side of the river. At an average walking pace, the journey is only around 10 minutes, but can be done faster – especially if you can't handle the feeling of the river just 50ft overhead!

FAN MUSEUM   MUSEUM
Map p477 (☑020-83051441; www.thefanmuseum. org.uk; 12 Crooms Hill, SE10; adult/child £4/3; ⊘11am-5pm Tue-Sat, noon-5pm Sun; ⓇGreen-

wich, ⊜Cutty Sark) For fan fans, this lovely museum, entirely devoted to the things you flap to cool down, has a wonderful collection of over 5000 fans, including ivory, tortoiseshell, peacock-feather and folded-fabric examples, alongside kitsch battery-powered versions and huge ornamental Welsh fans. The setting, an 18th-century Georgian town house, also has an Orangery (p304), with lovely trompe l'œil murals, a fan-shaped garden and afternoon tea (£8) four days a week (Tues, Fri, Sat and Sun).

O2   NOTABLE BUILDING
Map p461 (www.theo2.co.uk; Peninsula Sq, SE10; ⊜North Greenwich) The 380m-wide circular O2 cost £750 million to build at the end of the last century. Once much derided as the definitive white elephant, it finally found its calling as a multipurpose venue hosting big-ticket concerts, sporting events and blockbuster exhibitions. There are dozens of bars and restaurants inside and you can actually scale the outside with an outfit called Up at the O2 (p307). It's located on the Greenwich Peninsula, just 10 minutes by bus from Greenwich itself and on the Jubilee line.

TOP SIGHT
IMPERIAL WAR MUSEUM

Fronted by a pair of intimidating 15in naval guns, this riveting museum is housed in what was the third home of the Bethlehem Royal Hospital, also known as Bedlam. Although its focus is on military action involving British or Commonwealth troops during the 20th century, it rolls out the carpet to war in the wider sense.

The highlight is the state-of-the-art **First World War Galleries** opened in 2014 on the lower level (here floor zero) to mark the 100th anniversary of the start of the conflict. It takes a hard look at those who experienced the war both on the front line and at home. In the forecourt and the atrium above are **Witnesses to War** – everything from a Battle of Britain Spitfire and a towering German V-2 rocket to a Reuters Land Rover damaged by rocket attack in Gaza and a section of the World Trade Center in New York.

One of the most challenging sections is the extensive **Holocaust Exhibition** (not recommended for under 14s) on the 3rd floor. **Curiosities of War** is a jumble sale of fascinating items such as a makeshift bar used by the Dam Busters crew in 1943, taken from the museum's collection.

DON'T MISS
➡ First World War Galleries
➡ Holocaust Exhibition
➡ Battle of Britain Spitfire
➡ Curiosities of War

PRACTICALITIES
➡ Map p476, C2
➡ www.iwm.org.uk
➡ Lambeth Rd, SE1
➡ admission free
➡ ⊘10am-6pm
➡ ⊜Lambeth North

THAMES BARRIER

This sci-fi-looking barrier is designed to protect London from flooding and, with rising sea levels and surge tides, vulnerable London is likely to become increasingly dependent on the barricade. Completed three decades ago, the barrier consists of 10 movable gates anchored to nine concrete piers, each as tall as a five-storey building. Each of the 10 steel gates is 20m high and weighs 3300 tonnes. The silver roofs on the piers house the operating machinery that rotates the gates against excess water. Tested monthly, they make a glitteringly surreal sight, straddling the river in the lee of a giant warehouse.

The Thames is a tidal river, with its tide rising and falling twice a day – a difference in levels of up to 8m – and once a fortnight there's also a stronger 'spring' tide. The danger comes when the spring tide coincides with an unexpected surge, which pushes massive amounts of extra water upriver. The barrier has been built to prevent that water pouring over the riverbanks and flooding nearby houses. Environmentalists are already talking about a bigger, wider damming mechanism further towards the mouth of the river on the North Sea before the current barrier comes to the expected end of its design life in about 2035.

The barrier looks best when raised, and the only guaranteed time this happens are when the mechanisms are checked once a month. For exact dates and times, check with the **Thames Barrier Information Centre** (📞020-8305 4188; www.gov.uk/the-thames-barrier).

If you're coming from central London, take a train to Charlton from Charing Cross or London Bridge. Walk east along Woolwich Rd to Eastmoor St, which leads northward to the centre. If you're coming from Greenwich, you can pick up bus 177 or 180 along Romney Rd and get off at the Thames Barrier stop. The closest tube station is North Greenwich, from where you can pick up bus 472 or 161. **Thames River Service** (Map p477; 📞020-7930 4097; www.thamesriverservices.co.uk; adult/child one-way £12.50/6.25, return £16.50/8.25) boats also travel to and from the barrier, although they don't dock here.

BEACONSFIELD GALLERY

GALLERY

Map p476 (📞020-7582 6465; www.beaconsfield.ltd.uk/about; 22 Newport St, SE11; ⏱11am-5pm Wed-Sun; 🚇Vauxhall) **FREE** Housed in an old Victorian school, this contemporary art gallery hosts a steady stream of exhibitions, talks and events. The on-site cafe serves ethically sourced, homemade vegetarian and vegan dishes, and organic coffee from its vintage Italian espresso machine.

☉ Lambeth, Kennington, Elephant and Castle & Vauxhall

GARDEN MUSEUM

MUSEUM

Map p476 (📞020-7401 8865; www.gardenmuseum.org.uk; St Mary-at-Lambeth, Lambeth Palace Rd, SE1; adult/child under 6 £10/free; ⏱10.30am-5pm Sun-Fri, to 4pm Sat, closed 1st Mon of month; 🚇Lambeth North) Housed in the disused church of St Mary-at-Lambeth, this peaceful, green-fingered museum takes a close look at the 17th-century, father-and-son Tradescant team, widely travelled gardeners to Charles I and Charles II. Its trump card, though, is charming **knot garden**, a replica of a 17th-century formal garden, with topiary hedges clipped into an intricate, twirling design. The museum reopened after major renovations in May 2017.

FLORENCE NIGHTINGALE MUSEUM

MUSEUM

Map p476 (📞020-7188 4400; www.florence-nightingale.co.uk; St Thomas' Hospital, 2 Lambeth Palace Rd, SE1; adult/child £7.50/3.80; ⏱10am-5pm; 🚇Westminster, Waterloo) This small but almost perfect museum looks at the life and legacy of Florence Nightingale (1820–1910), considered the founder of modern nursing. Her story is told through memorabilia and documents – don't miss her (now stuffed) pet owl Athena and the lantern she famously carried while visiting the wards at night. Most illuminating are her letters and, highlight of the collection, a recording of her voice made in 1890, by which time she'd become one of the world's first A-list celebrities.

LAMBETH PALACE   HISTORIC BUILDING

Map p476 (www.archbishopofcanterbury.org/pages/the-garden.html; Lambeth Palace Rd, SE1; ⊖Lambeth North) A gorgeous red- and fired-brick Tudor gatehouse, dating from 1495 and located beside the church of St Mary-at-Lambeth, leads to Lambeth Palace, the official London residence of the Archbishop of Canterbury. Although the palace is not open to the public, the gardens (£5) occasionally are; check the website for dates and times.

◉ Clapham & Wandsworth

CLAPHAM   AREA

Map p474 (⊖Clapham Common) Famed for its huge common, a verdant venue for many outdoor summer events and sports, affluent Clapham (Clopeham in the Domesday Book) is a popular and distinctly middle-class neighbourhood in South London. The main thoroughfare, Clapham High St, starts at the common's northeastern edge and is lined with bars, restaurants and shops.

WANDSWORTH COMMON   PARK

Map p474 (☒Wandsworth Common, Clapham Junction) Wilder and more overgrown than the nearby common in Clapham, Wandsworth Common is full of couples pushing prams when the sun's out. On the western side is a pleasant collection of streets known as the **toast rack**, because of their alignment: Baskerville, Dorlcote, Henderson, Nicosia, Patten and Routh Rds (all lined with Georgian houses). A blue plaque at 3 Routh Rd announces the home of former prime minister David Lloyd George.

A fenced off wooden tower without sails is all that survives of **Wandsworth Common Windmill** (Windmill Rd, SW18; ☒Clapham Junction), a small 19th-century smock mill on Windmill Road.

◉ Brixton

BRIXTON VILLAGE   MARKET

Map p474 (www.brixtonmarket.net/brixton-village; Atlantic Rd, SW9; ⊘8am-11.30pm Tue-Sun, to 6pm Mon; ⊖Brixton) This revitalised covered market has enjoyed an eye-catching renaissance in the past half-dozen years, prompted by an initiative to offer a period

---

TOP SIGHT
HORNIMAN MUSEUM

Comprising the collection of wealthy tea merchant Frederick John Horniman, this museum is a treasure trove of discoveries, from a huge stuffed walrus and slowly undulating moon jellyfish to a nasty 17th-century torture chair from Spain and a knockout musical-instruments exhibition.

On the ground and 1st floors is the **Natural History Gallery**, with animal skeletons, pickled specimens and dusty cupboards. When the 19th-century Apostle Clock from Germany strikes 4pm, the saints troop out past Jesus and only Judas turns away from him. Children adore the **Hands On Base Gallery**, where you can touch, wear and play around with thousands of objects.

On the lower ground floor you'll find the **African Worlds Gallery** and the **Music Gallery**. The latter displays thousands of instruments, from Native American rattles and early English keyboards to Indonesian *gamelan* and Ghanaian drums. There are touch screens so you can hear what they sound like.

The **aquarium** in the basement is small but state of the art and the 6.5 hectares of hillside **gardens** (complete with views of London as far as Wembley) are magnificent.

DON'T MISS
- ➡ Hands On Base Gallery
- ➡ Aquarium
- ➡ Music Gallery
- ➡ Apostle Clock
- ➡ Gardens

PRACTICALITIES
- ➡ ☑020-8699 1872
- ➡ www.horniman.ac.uk
- ➡ 100 London Rd, Forest Hill, SE23
- ➡ museum & gardens free, exhibitions ticketed
- ➡ ⊘museum 10.30am-5.30pm, gardens 7.15am-sunset Mon-Sat, 8am-sunset Sun
- ➡ ☒Forest Hill

DANSON HOUSE

Palladian villa **Danson House** (☏020-8303 7777; Danson Park, Bexleyheath, Kent DA6; adult/child £8/free; ⊕10am-4pm Sun; ☒Bexleyheath)was built by John Boyd, an East India Company director, in 1766. Saved from demolition in 1995, the house was painstakingly renovated based on mid-19th-century watercolours by Sarah Johnston. The house now serves as the official Register Office for the London Borough of Bexley and is only open on Sunday. The English-style garden and surrounding park are a delight and the tearoom (open daily 9am to 5pm) in the one-time breakfast room serves wholesome food. It's a 20-minute walk southwest from the Bexleyheath train station.

Highlights include the dining room's reliefs and 17 wall paintings celebrating love and romance; the chinoiserie salon; the library, with a fair few 'decorative' books; the music room, with its functioning organ; the dizzying spiral staircase; and the original Victorian kitchens.

of free rent to outfits setting up in the dilapidated 1930s Granville Arcade. Cafes and restaurants have swarmed in along with a host of inventively inclined shops, which happily cohabit with butchers, greengrocers and bazaars.

BRIXTON WINDMILL   NOTABLE BUILDING

Map p474 (☏020-7926 6056; www.brixtonwindmill.org; Blenheim Gardens, SW2; ⊕Apr-Oct; ☒45 or 59, ☺Brixton, then) Quite a sight (and terrific photo-op) and built for John Ashby in 1816, this is the closest windmill to central London still in existence. Later powered by gas and milling as recently as 1934, it's been refitted with sails and machinery and is open to the public for free guided tours from April to October, usually on the second weekend of every month. Check the website for dates and times.

BLACK CULTURAL ARCHIVES   CULTURAL CENTRE

Map p474 (☏020-3757 8500; www.bcaheritage. org.uk; 1 Windrush Sq, SW2; ⊕10am-6pm Tue-Sat; ☒Brixton, ☺Brixton) **FREE** Housed in a heritage centre in the heart of Brixton, the Black Cultural Archives puts on seminal photographic exhibitions, many in association with the V&A, and organises workshops, lectures and performances. There's also a reading room and reference library (10am to 4pm Wednesday to Friday). It's open to 7pm on the second Thursday of the month.

⊙ Battersea

BATTERSEA PARK   PARK

Map p474 (☏020-8871 7530; www.batterseapark. org; ⊕8am-dusk; ☒Battersea Park) Sprinkled with sculptures by Henry Moore and Barbara Hepworth, these 50 hectares of gorgeous greenery stretch between Albert and Chelsea bridges. To the north is the Peace Pagoda (p298). There are lakes and plenty of sporting facilities – rent bicycles and other pedal conveyances from London Recumbents (p307).

There's also an art space called the **Pump House Gallery** (☏020-8871 7572; www. pumphousegallery.org.uk; ⊕11am-4pm Wed-Sun) **FREE** and a **Children's Zoo** (☏020-7924 5826; www.batterseaparkzoo.co.uk; adult/child £8.95/6.95; ⊕10am-5.30pm Apr-Oct, to 4.30pm Nov-Mar).

BATTERSEA POWER STATION   HISTORIC BUILDING

Map p474 (www.batterseapowerstation.co.uk; 188 Kirtling St, SW8; ☒Battersea Park) Its four smokestacks famously celebrated on Pink Floyd's *Animals* album cover, Battersea Power Station is one of South London's best-known monuments. Built by Giles Gilbert Scott (who also designed the power station that's now the Tate Modern, and the iconic red telephone box) in 1933, the station was snuffed out in 1983 only to enter an existential limbo for more than three decades. It's now being redeveloped as a mixed residential and commercial space.

Luck turned for the mighty brick building in 2011 when a £8 billion master plan to redevelop the site, right on the Thames, was approved. Plans include thousands of new homes, retail and corporate space and two new tube stations on the extended Northern line at Battersea Park and Nine Elms, where the new US Embassy will relocate after leaving Grosvenor Sq in Mayfair. Shops, restaurants and cafes in the first phase, Circus West Village, opened in 2017. The chimneys – which have been dismantled and are being reconstructed, reinforced with steel and repainted – will be finished by 2020, as will the embassy, the first new homes and the new tube stations. The total redevelopment isn't expected to be finished until 2024. Watch this space.

PEACE PAGODA SHRINE
Map p474 (Battersea Park; ⃝Battersea Park) Erected in 1985 by a group of Japanese Buddhists to commemorate Hiroshima Day (6 August), the pagoda in Battersea Park (p297) displays the Buddha in the four stages of his life.

⊙ Dulwich & Forest Hill

DULWICH PICTURE GALLERY GALLERY
(⃝020-8693 5254; www.dulwichpicturegallery. org.uk; Gallery Rd, SE21; adult/child £7/free; ⊘10am-5pm Tue-Sun; ⃝; ⃝West Dulwich) The world's first public art gallery, the small Dulwich Picture Gallery was designed by the idiosyncratic architect Sir John Soane

between 1811 and 1814 to house nearby Dulwich College's collection of paintings by Raphael, Rembrandt, Rubens, Reynolds, Lorrain, Gainsborough, Poussin, Canaletto, Van Dyck and many more. Unusually, the collector Noel Desenfans and painter Sir Peter Francis Bourgeois chose to have their mausoleums, lit by a moody *lumière mystérieuse* (mysterious light) created with tinted glass, placed among the pictures.

DULWICH PARK PARK
(College Rd, SE21; ⊘8am-dusk; ⃝West Dulwich, North Dulwich) With its hectares of green space and much-loved bicycle hire putting fleets of novel, low-slung bikes under the feet of enthusiastic kids, Dulwich Park is one of London's most handsome and enjoyable parks. Bikes can be hired from London Recumbents (p307), near the Old College Gate in the west of the park. The park **playground** is great for toddlers.

✗ EATING

★**KOI RAMEN BAR** NOODLES $
Map p474 (⃝07796 463 972; www.koiramenbar. co.uk; Pop Brixton, 49 Brixton Station Rd, SW9; from £4.50; ⊘11.30am-10.30pm Mon-Thu, to 11.30pm Fri & Sat, to 10.30pm Sun; ⃝Brixton, ⃝Brixton) Blink-and-you'll-miss-it Koi has a secret weapon to alert passers-by: the ever-enticing aroma of noodles and a chirpy band of staff. There's a thin – negligible is a better word – counter for your *tonkotsu* ramen (£6) before you snap your chopsticks

RED HOUSE

From the outside, **Red House** (NT; ⃝020-8304 9878; www.nationaltrust.org.uk/red-house; 13 Red House Lane, Bexleyheath, Kent DA6; adult/child £7.70/3.80; ⊘11am-5pm Wed-Sun mid-Feb–Oct, 11am-5pm Fri-Sun Nov-late Dec; ⃝Bexleyheath) is reminiscent of a gingerbread house wrought in stone. It was built in 1859 by Victorian designer William Morris – of Morris wallpaper fame. The nine rooms open to the public, including two bedrooms only recently accessible after being shut up for more than a century, bear all the elements of the Arts and Crafts movement to which Morris adhered – Gothic art here, some religious symbolism there, an art nouveau–like sunburst over there.

Furniture by Morris and the house's designer, Philip Webb, are on display, as are stained glass, paintings and murals (some only recently revealed under the wallpaper) by Edward Burne-Jones. Recent conservation work revealed a previously unknown pre-Raphaelite wall painting. The one-time kitchen has been converted into a lovely cafe. Entry before 1.30pm is by guided tour only; tours leave half-hourly from 11am.

The surrounding gardens were designed by Morris 'to clothe' the house. Don't miss the well with a conical roof, inspired by a traditional oast house used for drying hops. It's a 15-minute walk south from the Bexleyheath station.

ELTHAM PALACE

Rayon heir Stephen Courtauld (of Courtauld Gallery fame) and his wife Virginia (Ginie) built this art-deco mansion (EH; www.english-heritage.org.uk; Court Yard, Eltham, SE9; adult/child £14.40/8.60; ⊙10am-6pm Sun-Fri Apr-Sep, to 5pm Sun-Fri Oct, to 4pm Sun Nov-Feb, 10am-4pm Sun-Fri Mar; ℝEltham, Mottingham) next to a 15th-century medieval hall between 1933 and 1937. From the impressive entrance hall with its dome, African black-bean-panelled walls and huge circular carpet with geometric shapes, to the black-marble dining room with silver-foil ceiling and heavy black doors decorated with lacquered animal figures, it appears the couple had taste as well as money.

A £1.7 million refurbishment has opened up areas previously closed to the public. These include the decorated map room off Ginie's boudoir, where the couple plotted their extensive travels, and the basement, converted to a deluxe air-raid shelter during the Blitz. The couple also, rather fashionably for the times, had a pet lemur – the heated cage, complete with tropical murals and a bamboo ladder leading to the ground floor for the spoiled (and vicious) 'Mah-jongg' is also on view.

A royal palace was built on this site in 1305 and was, for a time, the boyhood home of Henry VIII, before the Tudors decamped to Greenwich. Little of that palace remains, apart from the restored Great Medieval Hall incorporated into the mansion. Its hammerbeam roof is generally rated the third best in the country, behind those at Westminster Hall and Hampton Court Palace. The 8 hectares of gardens include a rockery and moat with working bridge.

Visitors view the mansion's 20 rooms on a self-paced tour with an entertaining handheld multimedia guide.

Eltham Palace is equidistant – about a 20-minute walk – from Eltham and Mottingham stations (trains from London Bridge).

and plunge in. The ramen are delicious, including the miso tofu vegetarian version, served with a light, tasty broth.

★MAMALAN   CHINESE $

Map p474 (www.mamalan.co.uk; Unit 18, Brixton Village, SW9; dishes £4-9; ⊙noon-4pm Mon, to 10.30pm Tue-Sun; ⊕Brixton) For authentic, handmade Beijing street food – dumplings, noodles, salads and snacks – this cute-as-a-button eatery in Brixton Village is the business. We can't get enough of its beef noodle soup and pork and Chinese leaf dumplings! There's another branch on **The Pavement** (Map p474; www.mamalan.co.uk; 8 The Pavement, SW4; dishes £4-9; ⊙noon-3.30pm & 6-10pm Mon-Fri, noon-10pm Sat & Sun; ⊕Clapham Common).

★FRANCO MANCA   PIZZA $

Map p474 (www.francomanca.co.uk; 4 Market Row, SW9; pizzas £4.50-6.95; ⊙noon-5pm Mon, noon-11pm Tue-Fri, 11.30am-11pm Sat, 11.30am-10.30pm Sun; ⊕Brixton) The Brixton branch of Franco Manca remains a perennial local favourite and draws pizza enthusiasts from far and wide. The restaurant only uses its own sourdough, fired up in a wood-burning brick oven. There are no reservations, so

beat the queues by arriving early, avoiding lunch hours and Saturday.

POP BRIXTON   MARKET $

Map p474 (49 Brixton Station Rd; ⊙9am-11pm Sun-Wed, to midnight Thu-Sat; ⊕Brixton) There's a scrummy eclectic range of small kitchens serving international street food in Pop Brixton, making it ideal snacking territory. Koi Ramen Bar (p298) is an excellent choice for *tonkotsu* noodles, while for Cantonese fare, head to Duck Duck Goose (p300).

PAUL RHODES BAKERY   BAKERY $

Map p477 (37 King William Walk, SE10; tarts from £1.80; ⊙7am-6pm; ℝDLR Cutty Sark) This handy corner bakery is a tip-top spot for a snack, baked goodies and a coffee. There's delights such as courgette, kale, hummus and tomato or chicken, bacon and avocado baguettes, marvellous lemon and citrus tarts, gorgeous chocolate tarts and vanilla cheesecake, served up by smiling staff. It's also open early.

KERBISHER & MALT   FISH & CHIPS $

Map p474 (☎020-3417 4350; www.kerbisher.co.uk; 50 Abbeville Rd, SW4; mains from £6;

☺4.30-10pm Tue-Thu, noon-2.30pm & 4.30-10pm Fri, noon-10pm Sat, to 9pm Sun; ⊝Clapham Common, Clapham South) 🖉 In London, Kerbisher & Malt have done for fish and chips what Franco Manca did for pizza, hitting the ground running with some fantastic, fresh and well-priced food. Expect double-fried chips, homemade sauces, sustainably sourced fish, their own brew beer and a limited, but very affordable, menu.

GODDARDS AT GREENWICH   BRITISH $

Map p477 (☏020-8305 9612; www.goddards atgreenwich.co.uk; 22 King William Walk, SE10; dishes £3.30-7.30; ☺10am-7pm Sun-Thu, to 8pm Fri & Sat; ⏒DLR Cutty Sark) If you're keen to try that archetypal English dish, pie and mash (minced beef, steak and kidney or even chicken in pastry with mashed potatoes), do so at this Greenwich institution, which always attracts a motley crowd. Jellied eels, mushy peas and 'liquor' (a green sauce made from parsley and vinegar) are optional extras.

GREENWICH MARKET   MARKET $

Map p477 (www.greenwichmarketlondon.com/food-and-drink; College Approach, SE10; ☺9am-5.30pm; 🅿🖉; ⏒DLR Cutty Sark) Perfect for snacking your way through a world atlas of food while browsing the other market stalls. Come here for delicious food to take away, from Spanish tapas and Thai curries to sushi, Ethiopian vegetarian, French crêpes, dim sum, Mexican burritos and lots more.

★MAY THE FIFTEENTH   MODERN EUROPEAN $$

Map p474 (☏020-8772 1110; www.maythe15th.com; 47 Abbeville Rd, SW4; mains £15-18; ☺6-11pm Tue, noon-11pm Wed-Fri, 9.30am-11pm Sat, to 9.30pm Sun; 🔊; ⊝Clapham Common, Clapham South) Formerly the Abbeville Kitchen, this has a local feel with its little terrace and cosy dining room yet its appeal is universal. The menu changes daily, but expect a blend of modern British and European cuisine, with dishes such as suet-crusted beef-and-onion pie and Cornish pollock, violet artichokes, chickpeas, Gordal olives and anchovies. Seasonal produce is emphasised. You'll always find a large piece of meat to share between two or three such as slow-cooked lamb or rib of Dexter beef. On Saturdays from 10am to 3pm, it's brunch all the way.

★BUENOS AIRES CAFE   ARGENTINE $$

(☏020-8315 5333; www.buenosairescafe.co.uk; 17 Royal Pde, SE3; mains £9-31; ☺noon-2.30pm & 6-10.30pm Mon-Fri, noon-4pm & 6-10.30pm Sat & Sun; 🔊; ⏒Blackheath) As you would expect from an Argentinian eatery, the beef is superb but what seals it is the gorgeous decor (all wood furniture and oversized posters), the excellent wine list, stellar service and wonderful homemade pasta and pizza (55% of today's population in Argentina is of Italian origin, hence this delightful culinary heritage). Views of the heath all get the thumbs up too. Bookings essential.

There's another branch in Greenwich.

★RIVINGTON GRILL   BRITISH $$

Map p477 (☏020-8293 9270; www.rivington greenwich.co.uk; 178 Greenwich High Rd, SE10; mains £11.25-18.25; ☺noon-11pm Mon-Fri, from 10am Sat & Sun; ⏒Greenwich) This younger sister of the trendy bar and grill in Hoxton is every bit as stylish, with seating on two levels overlooking a lovely long bar. The seasonally adjusted menu is totally British, with chicken pie, lamb chops, suckling pig and luxury pies rubbing shoulders with grilled sardines, fish and chips and apple-and-rhubarb crumble. Warm and friendly welcome. The full English breakfast (£12.25) at weekends is awesome.

DUCK DUCK GOOSE   CHINESE $$

Map p474 (www.duckduckgooselondon.com; Pop Brixton, 49 Station Rd, SW9; mains £4-30; ☺noon-3.30pm & 6.30-10pm Tue-Thu & Sun, to 11pm Fri & Sat; ⏒Brixton, ⊝Brixton) Make no bones about it, this Cantonese canteen is no-frills but it's what you'd find shoved down a steamy side street off Mong Kok, Kowloon-way. So are the flavours: load up on char siu (roast pork), roast duck, roast goose or steamed bream with ginger and spring onion and sink a Tsingtao (totally wrong side of China, but it's still China's best beer).

BUENOS AIRES CAFE   CAFE $$

Map p477 (☏020-8858 9172; www.buenosaires cafe.co.uk/greenwich-restaurant; 15 Nelson Rd, SE10; 2-3-course lunch £11.95/14.95, mains £6.95-28.95; 🔊🖵; ⏒DLR Cutty Sark) Take a seat in the sunlight-filled orangery at the rear of this traditionally styled Argentine cafe for a very relaxing coffee at the heart of Greenwich, or choose the courtyard garden. The front is all-wood – conservative, but pleasant too – with the walls covered in Maradona stills. Dishes are superb steaks, pasta and pizza. Ask about tango evenings.There's another branch in Blackheath (p300).

PHARMACY 2
BRITISH $$

Map p476 (☑020-3141 9333; www.pharmacy restaurant.com; Newport Street Gallery, Newport St, SE11; £12.50-26.50; ☺10am-midnight Tue-Sat, to 6pm Sun; 🛜🚲; ☻Vauxhall) Located within Damien Hirst's Newport Street Gallery, this restaurant is most notable for its amazing pill-inspired decor. The original Pharmacy in Notting Hill was madly popular in its late '90s heyday, and while the sequel hasn't quite achieved those giddy heights, there's an enjoyable, slightly surreal buzz. The menu has some decent seafood – look out for the soft-shell crab burger.

A vegetarian and kids menu makes the restaurant surprisingly inclusive too.

CHAPTERS
BRASSERIE $$

(☑020-8333 2666; www.chaptersrestaurants. com; 43-45 Montpelier Vale, SE3; mains £8.50-14.95, 2/3-course lunch £12.95/14.95, dinner £14.95/17.95; ☺8am-11pm Mon-Sat, to 9pm Sun; 🛜🚲🖶; 🚇Blackheath) This excellent restaurant in Blackheath Village is a sophisticated brasserie offering, you guessed it, all day dining. It achieves a high standard in its cuisine, service and atmosphere, whether you're here for the beer-battered haddock, slow-roast pork belly or one of Chapters' ace breakfasts. Set lunches are available Monday to Friday, and set dinners from Monday to Thursday. Food and service are consistently high quality and you can come for anything from coffee and cake to dinner.

BRUNSWICK HOUSE
MODERN BRITISH $$

Map p476 (☑020-7720 2926; 30 Wandsworth Rd, SW8; mains £14.20-18.40, 2-3-course lunch menu £18/21; ☺noon-3pm & 6-10.30pm Mon-Sat, noon-3pm Sun; 🛜; ☻Vauxhall) This boutique cafe, housed in a lone Georgian house marooned between high-rises and a roundabout and sharing space with an architectural salvage company, serves modern British fare that's as simple and elegantly executed as the oversized posters on the walls, the assorted lanterns and the vintage furniture. The weekday lunch menu is also available from 6pm to 7pm.

OLD BREWERY
MODERN BRITISH $$

Map p477 (☑020-3437 2222; www.oldbrewery greenwich.com; Pepys Bldg, Old Royal Naval College, SE10; mains £11-25; ☺10am-10pm Mon-Sat, to 10.30pm Sun; 🛜🖶; 🚇DLR Cutty Sark) Acquired by Young's in 2016 and entirely refurbished, this excellent and handsome choice within the grounds of the Old Royal Naval College (p291) is both a ravishing restaurant and a pub, with a heady range of craft beers and cocktails. There's outside seating for sunny days.

DRAGON CASTLE
CHINESE $$

Map p476 (☑020-7277 3388; www.dragoncastle london.com; 100 Walworth Rd, SE17; mains £8.80-27; ☺noon-11pm; 🛜🚲; ☻Elephant & Castle) It's hard to imagine that one of the best non-chain Chinese restaurants in London is hidden here in deepest, darkest Kennington. The duck, pork and seafood (deep-fried crispy oysters, crab with black bean) are renowned, but come for the dim sum (noon to 4.30pm), especially at lively weekend lunchtime. Good-value set menus are available for four or more diners.

★ TRINITY
BRITISH $$$

Map p474 (☑020-7622 1199; www.trinityrestaurant.co.uk; 4 The Polygon, SW4; 2-3-course lunch menu £35/39, mains £17-35; ☺12.30-2.30pm & 6.30-10pm Mon-Sat, 12.30-3pm Sun; 🛜; ☻Clapham Common) Named after the nearby church and holder of a Michelin star, Adam Byatt's good-looking Clapham Old Town restaurant is a light and delectable spot near the common. Service, attentive and unobtrusive, delivers a strong wine list and a mouth-watering menu displaying considerable culinary artistry. It's a formal, classic address that sees many returnees and stages guest chef evenings. Reservations recommended.

★ CHEZ BRUCE
FRENCH $$$

(☑020-8672 0114; www.chezbruce.co.uk; 2 Bellevue Rd, SW17; 3-course menu lunch £35-39.50, 3-course dinner £55; ☺noon-2.30pm Mon-Fri, to 3pm Sat & Sun, 6.30-10pm Mon-Thu, to 10.30pm Fri & Sat, to 9.30pm Sun; 🛜; 🚇Wandsworth Common) Though Michelin-starred and in business for over two decades, Chez Bruce still insists on a winning local feel that accommodates all comers. The rustic exterior, beside leafy Wandsworth Common, belies a crisp modern interior. The wine list is an all-star cast, and the food sublime. Bookings essential.

HONEST BURGERS
BURGERS

Map p474 (☑020-3693 9690; www.honest burgers.co.uk; 75 Venn St, SW4; mains £8.50-12.75; ☺11.30am-11pm Mon-Thu, to midnight Fri, 9.30am-midnight Sat, 9.30am-10pm Sun; 🛜🖶; ☻Clapham Common) You can carry on east to Brixton for the original **branch** (Map p474;

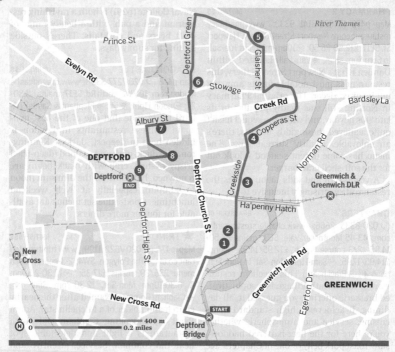

🏃 Neighbourhood Walk
Deptford

START DEPTFORD BRIDGE DLR & STATION
END DEPTFORD RAILWAY STATION
LENGTH 1.5 MILES; THREE HOURS

This walk explores edgy Deptford, just west of Greenwich, once an important and wealthy dockyard and ship-building centre, and now a district in transition, with galleries and art centres squeezing in between pie and mash shops, and pubs turning into bars. From the station walk up Deptford Church St and turn right into **1 Creekside**, a street that's lined with galleries and artist studios with regularly changing art exhibitions, including **2 Art Hub Gallery** and **3 Cockpit Arts**. A short distance north is the plastic-clad **4 Laban Theatre** (p306), home to the largest contemporary dance school in Europe. The turf-covered mounds in front conceal debris cleared from the site. Follow Copperas St to the creek then head north to join Glaisher St. Just beyond the new footbridge is a **5 statue of Peter the Great** recalling the Russian tsar's four-month stay in 1698, when he came to Deptford to learn more about new

developments in shipbuilding. The original party dude, Peter stayed with diarist John Evelyn and his drunken parties badly damaged the writer's house. Walk south along Deptford Green to the late-17th-century **6 St Nicholas Church**, which contains a memorial to playwright Christopher Marlowe, murdered in a Deptford tavern brawl at the age of 29 in 1593 and may be buried here. The skull and crossbones over the lychgate entrance may have inspired the Jolly Roger pirate flag. Running off Deptford Green, delightful **7 Albury St** is lined with Georgian buildings that once housed Deptford's naval officers. Notice the exquisite wood carvings decorating many of the doorways. To the south is the baroque **8 St Paul's Church**, built in 1730. In the churchyard in front is the grave of Mydiddee, a native Tahitian who returned with Captain Bligh on the HMS *Providence* and died here almost immediately in 1793. Walk over to Deptford High St and, if the day is right, land in the centre of **9 Deptford Market**, a colourful market held three days a week. Deptford railway station is just north.

Unit 12, Brixton Village, SW9; ⏰11.30am-4pm Mon, to 10.30pm Tue-Sat, to 10pm Sun; 🛜; ⬤Brixton), or stop off on this side-street outpost for terrific burgers, the best of a few burger bars in this part of Clapham. Specials add some spice and zest to an otherwise very dependable, but short, menu. It's a hip, friendly and welcoming branch and the weekend brunch is fantastic; kids menu too.

Monday to Thursday deal: burger and chips plus a voucher for a ticket to the Clapham Picture House (p305) for £16.

DRINKING & NIGHTLIFE

★SHRUB AND SHUTTER BAR

Map p474 (☑020-7326 0643; www.theshruband shutter.com; 336 Coldharbour Lane, SW9; cocktails from £8; ⏰5pm-late Tue-Sat; 🛜; ⬤Brixton) Many punters – some who travel a long way – are here to write home about the winning modern British menu, but are instead instantly waylaid by the sublimely innovative and fantastically good-looking cocktails at buzzing Brixton bar-restaurant Shrub and Shutter, served up by cheery staff who rarely put a foot wrong.

★DRAFT HOUSE PUB

Map p474 (☑020-7097 5140; www.drafthouse. co.uk; 94 Northcote Rd, SW11; ⏰4-11pm Mon-Wed, to midnight Thu, 3pm-midnight Fri, 11am-midnight Sat, 11am-10.30pm Sun; 🛜; ⬤Clapham Junction, Wandsworth Common) Taking beer seriously, standout Draft House – where middle-class cash and high expectations effortlessly dovetail – is no slouch. There's 18 ales, stouts and lagers on tap, over 50 varieties of bottled beers and a seasonally adjusted menu (served through the day) with excellent brunches, standout burgers, moreish beer food and sticky deserts. Outside seating.

★CUTTY SARK TAVERN PUB

Map p477 (☑020-8858 3146; www.cutty sarkse10.co.uk; 4-6 Ballast Quay, SE10; ⏰11.30am-11pm Mon-Sat, noon-10.30pm Sun; 🛜; ⬤DLR Cutty Sark) Housed in a delightful bow-windowed, wood-beamed Georgian building directly on the Thames, the Cutty Sark is one of the few independent pubs left in Greenwich. Half a dozen cask-conditioned ales on tap line the bar, there's an inviting riverside seating area opposite and

an upstairs dining room looking out on to glorious views. It's a 10-minute walk from the DLR station.

★GREENWICH UNION PUB

Map p477 (☑020-8692 6258; www.greenwich union.com; 56 Royal Hill, SE10; ⏰noon-11pm Mon-Fri, 10am-11pm Sat, 10am-10.30pm Sun; 🛜; ⬤DLR Greenwich) The award-winning Union plies six or seven Meantime microbrewery beers, including raspberry and wheat varieties, and a strong list of ales, plus bottled international brews. It's a handsome place, with duffed-up leather armchairs and a welcoming long, narrow aspect leading to a conservatory and beer garden at the rear.

★LOST & CO BAR

Map p474 (☑020-7622 2112; www.lostangel.co.uk; 339 Battersea Park Rd, SW11; ⏰noon-midnight Sun-Wed, to 1am Thu, to 2am Fri & Sat; 🛜; ⬤Wandsworth Rd, Battersea Park, Queenstown Rd) This fantastic cocktail bar-cum-restaurant fills with a fun and hedonistic crowd while the garden at the back is the venue for many a summer drinking session. DJs take over on weekends, with roasts and live acoustic music on Sunday afternoons.

★TRAFALGAR TAVERN PUB

Map p477 (☑020-8858 2909; www.trafalgar tavern.co.uk; 6 Park Row, SE10; ⏰noon-11pm Mon-Thu, noon-midnight Fri, 10am-midnight Sat, 10am-11pm Sun; ⬤DLR Cutty Sark) This elegant tavern with big windows overlooking the Thames is steeped in history. Dickens apparently knocked back a few here – and used it as the setting for the wedding breakfast scene in *Our Mutual Friend* – and prime ministers Gladstone and Disraeli used to dine on the pub's celebrated whitebait.

THE BEAR PUB

(☑07903 088009; 296a Camberwell New Rd, SE5; ⏰5-11.30pm Mon-Wed, 4pm-midnight Thu, to 1am Fri, noon-1am Sat, to 11.30pm Sun; 🛜; ⬤Denmark Hill, ⬤Oval) Ale-hounds and craft-beer aficionados will find the journey to Camberwell a trip well rewarded by this quality boozer where it's never hard to find a seat, there's an enticing 20 beers and ciders on tap and the crowd is cool and relaxed. The gastro pub food wins praise too: what more do you need?

BALHAM BOWLS CLUB PUB

(☑020-8673 4700; www.balhambowlsclub.com; 7-9 Ramsden Rd, SW12; ⏰4-11pm Mon-Wed, to

GREENWICH & SOUTH LONDON DRINKING & NIGHTLIFE

midnight Thu, to 1am Fri, noon-1am Sat, noon-11pm Sun; 🛱; ⊜Balham) This former lawn bowling clubhouse no longer has its green, but it's lost none of its retro allure. 'BBC' is now one of the best pubs in South London. The vintage furnishings and decor, and eclectic jumble of spacious wood-panelled rooms create an atmosphere of old-world charm.

FRANK'S
BAR

(www.frankscafe.org.uk; 10th fl, 95a Rye Lane, SE15; ⊙5-11pm Tue-Fri, 11am-11pm Sat & Sun Jun-Sep; 🛱; ⊜Peckham Rye) The superlative views of the city from this alfresco bar, set on the 10th floor of a multistorey car park, have punters queuing round the block on sunny days. The bare concrete space has a simple wooden bar, benches and a big red canopy, as well as a cracking little cocktail list, craft beer on tap, snacks and sharing platters. Some may find the long-drop toilets a nasal challenge.

CORSICA STUDIOS
CLUB

Map p476 (☑020-7703 4760; www.corsicastudios.com; 4/5 Elephant Rd, SE17; free-£17.50; ⊙hours vary; 🛱; ⊜Elephant & Castle) It's places like Corsica Studios that have given the once-rough Elephant & Castle area an edge. This not-for-profit, underground club is a well-known venue for electronic music. It's a small, intimate space with excellent sound and a mix of gigs and club nights till 3am weekdays and 6am weekends.

MARKET HOUSE
PUB

Map p474 (☑020-7095 9443; www.market-house.co.uk; 443 Coldharbour Lane, SW9; ⊙3-11pm Mon-Thu, to 3am Fri, 1pm-4am Sat, 1-11pm Sun; 🛱; ⊜Brixton) The designer-wallpapered, vintage-furnished, cocktail-serving, pop-up catering, Victorian-era Market House is something of a departure for an area traditionally associated with grotty pubs – and it's a roaring success at that. The late (and free) opening hours on the weekend music nights are especially popular with locals.

MASON'S ARMS
PUB

Map p474 (☑020-7622 2007; www.masons-arms-battersea.co.uk; 169 Battersea Park Rd, SW8; ⊙noon-11pm; 🛱; 🚆Battersea Park) This lovely boozer is a favourite of Battersea residents for its winning combination of relaxed atmosphere, beer garden on sunny days (and open fire for winter blues) and terrific British dishes (mains £10.50 to £21).

EAGLE
GAY

Map p476 (☑020-7793 0903; www.eaglelondon.com; 349 Kennington Lane, Vauxhall, SE11; ⊙8pm-late Tue-Thu, 9pm-4am Fri & Sat, 8pm-3am Sun; 🛱; ⊜Vauxhall) This fantastic place is a haven of alternative queer goings-on in muscle-bound Vauxhall. Open six nights a week with a different feel each night with Men Inc (£5) every Friday and the legendary Horse Meat Disco (from £6) on Sunday.

RVT
GAY

Map p476 (Royal Vauxhall Tavern; ☑020-7820 1222; www.rvt.org.uk; 372 Kennington Lane, SE11; entry £4-8; ⊙7pm-midnight Mon-Thu, 9pm-3am Fri, 9pm-2am Sat, 3pm-midnight Sun; ⊜Vauxhall) Rough around the edges to say the least, the Royal Vauxhall Tavern is the perfect antidote to the gleaming new wave of uppity gay venues now crowding Vauxhall's gay village. Saturday's Duckie, tagged 'London's Authentic Honky Tonk', is the club's signature queer performance night, while Sunday Social is cabaret and dance till midnight and on Monday it's the fun Big Bingo Show!

ORANGERY
CAFE

Map p477 (☑020-8305 1441; www.thefanmuseum.org.uk; full tea £8; ⊙1.45-3.45pm Tue & Sun,12.30-4.30pm Fri & Sat; 🚆Greenwich, ⊜Cutty Sark) Round out your trip to the Fan Museum (p294) with a trip to this muralled orangery, with a fan-shaped garden and afternoon tea four days a week.

EFFRA HALL TAVERN
PUB

Map p474 (www.theeffra.com; 38a Kellett Rd, SW2; ⊙4-11pm Mon-Wed, to midnight Thu-Fri, noon-midnight Sat, noon-11pm Sun; ⊜Brixton) This rather rundown old boozer brings you closer to the heart of the Brixton Afro-Caribbean vibe than any other pub in the area, thanks to the spicy Jamaican menu and regular live jazz. The patio out back is fringed with palm trees, while the interior is all shabby Victorian splendour. For bites, expect jerk chicken, Caribbean curry, Red Stripe beer-battered cod and plantain slices.

FIRE LONDON
GAY

Map p476 (☑020-3242 0040; www.firelondon.net; 39 Parry St, SW8; £5-15; ⊙11pm-10am Thu-Sat; ⊜Vauxhall) Regularly hosting the best gay club nights in London, Fire is an expansive, smart space under Vauxhall's railway arches, with a pronounced lean towards house and techno. Its outdoor garden is a rare thing on the clubbing scene – good to watch the sunrise! The club attracts a lot of straight clubbers too.

HOIST
GAY

Map p476 (www.thehoist.co.uk; Arches 47b&c, South Lambeth Rd, SW8; ☺9pm-1am Wed, 8pm-midnight Thu, 10pm-3am Fri, 10pm-4am Sat, 10pm-1am Sun; ☻Vauxhall) One of Europe's most famous fetish clubs, the Hoist is a one-stop shop for guys into leather and uniforms. The dress code is very strict – everyone has to wear boots and rubber, leather, uniform or nothing (as in starkers). Check out the array of fetish nights on the website.

DOGSTAR
BAR

Map p474 (☎020-7733 7515; http://dogstar brixton.com; 389 Coldharbour Lane, SW9; ☺4-11pm Tue & Wed, to 2am Thu, to 4am Fri & Sat, noon-10pm Sun; ☻Brixton) Downstairs, this long-running local institution has a cavernous DJ and live-music bar, mobbed by a young South London crowd. The main bar is as casual as you'd expect from a converted pub – comfortable sofas, big wooden tables – so dressing to kill is not obligatory. Dogstar Comedy on Thursday.

TWO BREWERS
GAY

Map p474 (☎020-7819 9539; www.the2brewers. com; 114 Clapham High St, SW4; after 10pm £3-8; ☺5pm-2am Sun-Thu, to 4am Fri & Sat; ☎; ☻Clapham Common) Clapham exudes an inner-suburban feel, the High St in particular, but the long-standing Two Brewers endures as one of the best London gay bars outside the gay villages of Soho, Shoreditch and Vauxhall. Here there's a friendly, laid-back, local crowd who come for a quiet drink during the week and some madcap cabaret and dancing at weekends.

Admission after 10pm is £3 on Monday, Tuesday, Wednesday and Thursday, £7 on Friday, £8 on Saturday and £4 on Sunday.

☆ ENTERTAINMENT

★O2 ACADEMY BRIXTON
LIVE MUSIC

Map p474 (www.o2academybrixton.co.uk; 211 Stockwell Rd, SW9; ☺most nights doors open 7pm; ☻Brixton) It's hard to have a bad night at the Brixton Academy, even if you leave with your soles sticky with beer, as this cavernous former-5000-capacity art-deco theatre always thrums with bonhomie. There's a properly raked floor for good views,

as well as plenty of bars and an excellent mixed bill of established and emerging talent. Most shows are 14-plus.

British electronic band Leftfield were once banned from the venue after their volume levels caused the ceiling to crumble. No selfie sticks or GoPros.

O2 ARENA
LIVE MUSIC

Map p462 (www.theo2.co.uk; Peninsula Sq, SE10; ☎; ☻North Greenwich) One of the city's major concert venues, hosting all the biggies – the Rolling Stones, Paul Simon and Sting, One Direction, Ed Sheeran and many others – inside the 20,000-capacity arena. It's also a popular venue for sporting events and you can even climb the roof for ranging views with Up at the O2 (p307).

CLAPHAM PICTURE HOUSE
CINEMA

Map p474 (☎0871 902 5727; www.picture houses.com; 76 Venn St, SW4; adult/child from £10.50/6.50; ☻Clapham Common) This excellent cinema is a mainstay of Clapham, with an inspiring list of independent and art-house films, as well as mainstream Hollywood fare. The popular bar is another reason to stop by for a pre-movie aperitif. Honest Burgers (p301) across the way does a £16 burger-with-cinema-ticket offer, so you can get dinner, drinks and a film sorted within shuffling distance.

Adult tickets are £7 all day Tuesday.

BRIXTON RITZY PICTUREHOUSE
CINEMA

Map p474 (☎0871 902 5739; www.picturehouses. com; Coldharbour Lane, SW2; adult/child from £10.50/6.50; ☒Brixton, ☻Brixton) Originally opening in 1911, this classic cinema is a cornerstone of Brixton cultural life, attracting both film-goers and drinkers (to its bars and fine cafe). Upstairs at the Ritzy brings you free live music (jazz, blues, reggae and more) as well as comedy and other acts. Films on Mondays are £7.

INDIGO AT THE O2
LIVE MUSIC

Map p462 (☎020-8463 2000; www.theo2. co.uk/events/venue/indigo-at-the-o2; Peninsula Square, SE10; ☎; ☻North Greenwich) The Indigo at the O2 may be smaller than the O2, but seats 2750, making it one of London's larger venues.

OVAL
SPECTATOR SPORT

Map p476 (☎0844 375 1845; www.kiaoval.com; Kennington, SE11; international match £35-450, county £15-45, tour adult/child £20/10; ☻Oval)

Home to the Surrey County Cricket Club, the Oval is south London's cricketing home. As well as Surrey matches, it also regularly hosts international test matches. Getting tickets for county games is relatively straightforward, but it's much harder for international fixtures. The season runs from April to September; ground tours are available all year around – but need to be booked in advance (see the website).

LABAN THEATRE DANCE

Map p477 (☏020-8463 0100; www.trinitylaban. ac.uk; Creekside, SE8; tickets £6-15; ⓡDLR Greenwich) Home of the Trinity Laban Conservatoire of Music and Dance, the Laban Theatre is the largest and best-equipped contemporary dance school in Europe and presents student dance performances, graduation shows and regular shows by the resident troupe, Transitions Dance Company. Its stunning £23 million home was conceived by Herzog & de Meuron, designers of the Tate Modern.

MINISTRY OF SOUND CLUB

Map p476 (☏020-7740 8600; www.ministry ofsound.com; 103 Gaunt St, SE1; entry £10-22; ◔10pm-6.30am Fri, 11am-7am Sat; ☎; ⊖Elephant & Castle) This legendary club-cum-enormous-global-brand (four bars, three dance floors) lost some 'edge' in the early noughties but, after pumping in top DJs, firmly rejoined the top club ranks. Friday is the Gallery trance night, while Saturday sessions offer the crème de la crème of house, electro and techno DJs.

UP THE CREEK COMEDY

Map p477 (www.up-the-creek.com; 302 Creek Rd, SE10; tickets £5-15; ◔7-11pm Thu & Sun, to 2am Fri & Sat; ⓡDLR Cutty Sark) Bizarrely enough, the hecklers can be funnier than the acts at this great club. Mischief, rowdiness and excellent comedy are the norm, with the Blackout open-mic night on Thursdays (www. the-blackout.co.uk; £5) and Sunday specials (www.sundayspecial.co.uk; £7). There's an after-party disco on Fridays and Saturdays.

BATTERSEA ARTS CENTRE THEATRE

Map p474 (☏020-7223 2223; www.bac.org.uk; Lavender Hill, SW11; ⎙77 or 345, ⓡClapham Junction) This arts centre suffered severe fire damage in 2015, but continues to operate a busy schedule of innovative performances and activities while the Grand Hall is rebuilt.

 # SHOPPING

POP BRIXTON MARKET

Map p474 (www.popbrixton.org; 49 Brixton Station Rd, SW9; ◔9am-11pm Sun-Wed, to midnight Thu-Sat; ⊖Brixton) One of the latest in the growing number of venues that have clocked on to using old shipping containers for hosting pop-up bars, restaurants and shops, Pop Brixton is a brilliant community initiative with a buzzing atmosphere, particularly on weekends, and holds regular events and classes (some free), including t'ai chi, capoeira, yoga and wood engraving.

It plans to operate until August 2018, but hopefully will continue beyond that if the lease can be extended.

BRIXTON VILLAGE MARKET

Map p474 (www.brixtonmarket.net/brixton-village; Atlantic Rd; ◔8am-11.30pm Tue-Sun, to 6pm Mon; ⊖Brixton) A revitalised and very hip transformation of Granville Arcade near Brixton Market, with a host of inventively inclined shops and fantastic restaurants and cafes.

ARTICLE CLOTHING

Map p474 (Atlantic Rd, SW9; ◔11am-7pm Tue-Sat, to 5pm Sun; ⊖Brixton) Snappy Article (there's a branch up in Hoxton) is a cool addition to Brixton, with a sharp line of up-to-the-minute men's togs and shoes. Very trim and neat indeed.

BATTERSEA FLOWER STATION HOMEWARES

Map p474 (☏020-7978 4253; www.battersea flowerstation.co.uk; 16 Winders Rd, SW11; ◔9am-5pm Mon-Fri, from 9.30am Sat, from 11am Sun; ⓡClapham Junction) With its punning name you might think this charming garden centre, squeezed into a sliver of land alongside some railway tracks, would be happy to rest on its florals. But there's more: it doubles as a florist, and even on busy weekends the friendly staff will treat you like you're the only customer.

TOOTING MARKET MARKET

(☏020-8672 4760; www.tootingmarket.com; 21-23 Tooting High St, SW17; ◔8am-6pm Mon-Thu, to 10.30pm Fri & Sat, 9am-5pm Sun; ⊖Tooting Broadway) A stalwart of the South London shopping scene, Tooting Market has been operating since 1930 (but may be facing demolition due to Crossrail 2, a proposed rail link). There is an excellent variety of stalls, selling everything from vintage clothing (look for Amber Skye's Wardrobe) to African sculptures (look for Maat Foundation). The atmosphere is at its boisterous best at weekends.

GREENWICH MARKET
MARKET

Map p477 (www.greenwichmarketlondon.com; College Approach, SE10; ⊗9.30am-5pm; 🚇DLR Cutty Sark) One of the smallest of London's ubiquitous markets, but Greenwich Market holds its own in quality. On Tuesdays, Wednesdays, Fridays and weekends, stallholders tend to be small, independent artists, offering original prints, wholesome beauty products, funky jewellery and accessories, cool fashion pieces and so on. On Tuesdays, Thursdays and Fridays, you'll find vintage, antiques and collectables. Loads of street food too.

VILLAGE BOOKS
BOOKS

(☎020-8693 2808; www.village-books.co.uk; 1d Calton Ave, Dulwich Village, SE21; ⊗9am-5.30pm Mon-Sat, 11am-5pm Sun; 🚇North Dulwich) Village Books is so small you could swing the proverbial dead cat and dislodge books from all four walls. But tininess is this shop's forte, with a wealth of knowledge and experience from staff, including the ever-resourceful owner, Hazel Broadfoot. There is an extensive and excellent children's book section.

BRIXTON MARKET
MARKET

Map p474 (www.brixtonmarket.net; Electric Ave & Granville Arcade; ⊗8am-6pm Mon, Tue & Thu-Sat, to 3pm Wed; 🚇Brixton) A heady, cosmopolitan blend of silks, wigs, knock-off fashion, halal butchers and the occasional Christian preacher assembles on Electric Ave. Tilapia fish, pig's trotters, yams, mangoes, okra, plantains and Jamaican *bullah* (gingerbread) cakes are just some of the exotic products on sale.

CASBAH RECORDS
MUSIC

Map p477 (☎020-8858 1964; www.casbah records.co.uk; 320-322 Creek Rd, SE10; ⊗11.30am-6pm Mon, 10.30am-6pm Tue-Fri, 10.30am-6pm Sat & Sun; 🚇DLR Cutty Sark) This funky meeting ground of classic, vintage and rare vinyl (Bowie, Rolling Stones, soul, rock, blues, jazz, indie etc) – as well as CDs, DVDs and memorabilia – originally traded at Greenwich Market before upgrading to this highly browsable shop.

JOY
FASHION & ACCESSORIES

Map p474 (☎020-7924 9654; www.joythestore. com; 518 Brixton Rd, SW11; ⊗10am-7pm Mon-Sat, 10.30am-6pm Sun; 🚇Brixton) This funky shop does a great line in retro floral frocks and blouses, hip T-shirts, polo shirts and an imaginative range of inventive gift ideas and quirky accessories.

20 STOREY
GIFTS & SOUVENIRS

Map p474 (☎07939-956712; 2a Market Row, SW9; ⊗10am-6.30pm Mon-Sat, from 11am Sun; 🚇Brixton) A shop with a sense of humour, 20 Storey is your essential stop for funky mugs, great cards, gadgets, gimmicky gifts, posters and original books.

🏃 SPORTS & ACTIVITIES

GO APE BATTERSEA
OUTDOORS

Map p474 (☎0845 519 1672; www.goape.co.uk/ days-out/battersea; Battersea Park, SW11; adult/ child £35/27; ⊗9am-4pm Wed-Sun; 🚇Battersea Park) This popular treetop adventure franchise has finally strung up shop in central London, and the location couldn't be better. As you clamber across precarious bridges, whoosh down zip lines (the longest is 50m!) and scale cargo nets, you'll be rewarded with views of Battersea Park and the city skyline. Perfect for families, and for a date with a difference.

LONDON RECUMBENTS
CYCLING

(☎020-8299 6636; www.londonrecumbents. co.uk; Ranger's Yard, Dulwich Park; per hr £10-20; ⊗10am-5pm, closes earlier Dec-Feb; 🚇West Dulwich, North Dulwich) Rents fun recumbent bicycles and other pedal conveyances for adults and kids. Last hires are an hour before closing.

UP AT THE O2
ADVENTURE SPORTS

Map p462 (www.theo2.co.uk/upattheo2; The O2, Greenwich Peninsula, SE10; from £28; ⊗hours vary; 🚇North Greenwich) London isn't exactly your thrill-seeking destination, but this ascent of the O2 (p294) is not for the faint-hearted. Equipped with climbing suit and harness, you'll scale the famous entertainment venue to reach a viewing platform perched 52m above the Thames with sweeping views of Canary Wharf, the river, Greenwich and beyond. Hours vary depending on the season (sunset and twilight climbs also available).

Richmond, Kew & Hampton Court

RICHMOND & KEW | PUTNEY & BARNES | CHISWICK | TWICKENHAM | WIMBLEDON | HAMPTON COURT

Neighbourhood Top Five

1 Listening out for poltergeists along the galleries and vaults of majestic **Hampton Court Palace** (p310) before getting lost in the maze.

2 Plunging into the luxuriant green expanses, wooded thickets and tropical foliage of **Kew Gardens** (p314).

3 Turning your back on urban London to discover a pristine pocket of wilderness at the **London Wetland Centre** (p318).

4 Sinking a pint of beer at the historic riverside **White Cross pub** (p322) while trying to avoid being cut off by the high tide.

5 Exploring London's wild side, roaming at will around **Richmond Park** (p316).

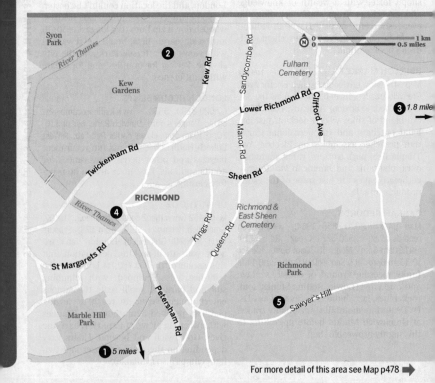

For more detail of this area see Map p478 ➡

Explore Richmond, Kew & Hampton Court

Richmond, Kew and Hampton Court is the London you barely knew existed and you'll need a few days getting to fathom the charms of this adorable neighbourhood. The shiny city is a galaxy away: this is where the green and pleasant land of England commences. Start early in the morning with Kew Gardens, but you may find yourself there the entire day, getting magnificently lost. If you escape, head south to laze by the river in grand Richmond, Instagramming some of London's most delightful river views. Richmond Park and Wimbledon Common offer rambling opportunities galore. Several excellent hotels allow you to overnight here, if you wish, so your explorations can continue to Hampton Court Palace, the UK's most magnificent chunk of Tudor architecture; ghost hunters will want to check out this famously haunted palace to really get into the 'spirit' of things. Night-times are pretty low-key in the neighbourhood, but you've a bevy of waterside pubs to treat you to a more languorous perspective of the city as it melds with pastoral England. You might not find yourself coming here exclusively to shop, but bring your wallet as there's no shortage of fine dining to fill your tummy.

Local Life

➜ **Hang-outs** Get into the riverside pub-lunch mood joining locals quaffing beer at the City Barge (p322) or White Cross (p322).

➜ **Greenery** Londoners from all over town bolt down to Richmond Park (p316) and Kew Gardens (p314) for weekend great escapes.

➜ **River views** Join locals jogging by the river, walking their dogs or catching some sunshine north and south of Richmond Bridge (p317).

Getting There & Away

➜ **Train & Underground** Both Kew Gardens and Richmond are on the District Line and London Overground; Richmond train station can be reached from Clapham Junction. Trains run to Hampton Court station from Waterloo. East Putney, Putney Bridge, Fulham Broadway and Chiswick Park are on the District Line.

➜ **Boat** Services run several times daily from Westminster Pier to Kew and on to Hampton Court Palace (boats sometimes stop at Richmond).

Lonely Planet's Top Tip

A manageable section of the fantastic Thames Path (p319) is the 4 miles between Putney Bridge and Barnes Footbridge. Taking around 90 minutes, most of the walk is very rural and at times you will only be accompanied by birdsong and the gentle swish of the river. From the footbridge, Chiswick train station is about 0.75 miles to the northwest. For more details, see the River Thames Alliance's Visit Thames site (www.visitthames.co.uk).

✕ Best Places to Eat

➜ Glasshouse (p321)

➜ Gelateria Danieli (p321)

➜ Chez Lindsay (p321)

➜ Orange Pekoe (p321)

➜ Petersham Nurseries Cafe (p322)

For reviews, see p321.➜

♟ Best Places to Drink

➜ White Cross (p322)

➜ City Barge (p322)

➜ White Hart (p323)

➜ Crooked Billet (p323)

➜ Tap on the Line (p322)

For reviews, see p322.➜

◉ Best Guided Tours

➜ Kew Explorer (p324)

➜ Hampton Court Palace (p310)

➜ Strawberry Hill (p319)

➜ Ham House (p316)

⊙ TOP SIGHT
HAMPTON COURT PALACE

London's most spectacular Tudor palace, this 16th-century icon concocts an imposing sense of history, from the huge kitchens and grand living quarters to the spectacular gardens, complete with a 300-year-old maze.

History of the Palace

Hampton Court Palace was built by Cardinal Thomas Wolsey in 1515, but was coaxed from him by Henry VIII just before Wolsey (as chancellor) fell from favour. It was already one of the most sophisticated palaces in Europe when, in the 17th century, Sir Christopher Wren was commissioned to build an extension. The result is a beautiful blend of Tudor and 'restrained baroque' architecture. The palace was opened to the public by Queen Victoria in 1838.

Entering the Palace

Passing through the magnificent main gate, you arrive first in the **Base Court** and beyond that **Clock Court**, named after its 16th-century astronomical clock. The panelled rooms and arched doorways in the **Young Henry VIII's Story** upstairs from Base Court provide a rewarding introduction: note the Tudor graffiti on the fireplace. Off Base Court to the right as you enter, and acquired by Charles I in 1629, Andrea Magenta's nine-painting series *The Triumphs of Caesar* portray Julius Caesar returning to Rome in a triumphant procession.

DON'T MISS

- ➡ Great Hall
- ➡ Chapel Royal
- ➡ William III & Mary II's Apartments
- ➡ Gardens and maze
- ➡ Cumberland Art Gallery
- ➡ Henry VIII's crown

PRACTICALITIES

- ➡ Map p478
- ➡ www.hrp.org.uk/hamptoncourtpalace
- ➡ adult/child/family £23/11.50/57
- ➡ ⊙10am-6pm Apr-Oct, to 4.30pm Nov-Mar
- ➡ 🚢Hampton Court Palace, 🚉Hampton Court

Henry VIII's State Apartments

The stairs inside Anne Boleyn's Gateway lead up to Henry VIII's Apartments, including the stunning **Great Hall**. The **Horn Room**, hung with impressive antlers, leads to the **Great Watching Chamber** where guards controlled access to the king. Henry VIII's dazzling gemstone-encrusted **crown** has been re-created – the original was melted down by Oliver Cromwell – and sits in the **Royal Pew** (open 10am to 4pm Monday to Saturday and 12.30pm to 1.30pm Sunday), which overlooks the beautiful **Chapel Royal** (still a place of worship after 450 years).

Tudor Kitchens & Great Wine Cellar

Also dating from Henry's day are the delightful Tudor kitchens, used to prepare meals for a royal household of 1200 people. Don't miss the Great Wine Cellar, which handled the 300 barrels each of ale and wine consumed here annually in the mid-16th century.

William III's & Mary II's Apartments

A tour of William III's Apartments, completed by Wren in 1702, takes you up the grand **King's Staircase**. Highlights include the **King's Presence Chamber**, dominated by a throne backed with scarlet hangings. During a devastating fire in 1986 which gutted an entire wing of the palace, staff were ready to cut the huge portrait of William III from its frame with knives, if necessary. The sumptuous **King's Great Bedchamber**, with a bed topped with ostrich plumes, and the **King's Closet** (where His Majesty's toilet has a velvet seat) should not be missed. Restored and recently reopened, the unique **Chocolate Kitchens** were built for William and Mary in about 1689. William's wife Mary II had her own apartments, accessible via the fabulous **Queen's Staircase** (decorated by William Kent).

Georgian Private Apartments

The Georgian Rooms were used by George II and Queen Caroline on the court's last visit to the palace in 1737. Do not miss the fabulous Tudor **Wolsey Closet** with its early 16th-century ceiling and painted panels, commissioned by Henry VIII.

Gardens & Maze

Beyond the palace are the stunning gardens; keep an eye out for the **Real Tennis Court**, dating from the 1620s. Originally created for William and Mary, the **Kitchen Garden** is a magnificent re-creation.

No one should leave Hampton Court without losing themselves in the 800m-long **maze** (adult/child/family £4.20/2.60/12.30; ☺10am-5.15pm Apr-Oct, to 3.45pm Nov-Mar; 🚌 Hampton Court Palace, 🚆 Hampton Court), also accessible to those not entering the palace.

TO THE PALACE BY BOAT

Between April and September, the palace can be reached by boat on the 22-mile route along the Thames from Westminster Pier in central London (via Kew and Richmond), but can take up to four hours (depending on the tide). Boats (single adult/child £17/8.50) are run by Westminster Passenger Services Association.

HAUNTED HAMPTON COURT

With a history this old and eventful, a para-normal dimension is surely mandatory. Arrested for adultery and detained in the palace in 1542, Henry's fifth wife, Catherine Howard, was dragged screaming down a gallery by her guards after an escape bid. Her ghost is said to do a repeat performance, uttering 'unearthly shrieks' in the Haunted Gallery leading to the Royal Pew (she must be a tireless ghost as she also haunts the Tower of London).

Hampton Court Palace

A DAY AT THE PALACE

With so much to explore in the palace and seemingly infinite gardens, it can be tricky knowing where to begin. It helps to understand how the palace has grown over the centuries and how successive royal occupants embellished Hampton Court to suit their purposes and to reflect the style of the time.

As soon as he had his royal hands upon the palace from Cardinal Thomas Wolsey,

Henry VIII began expanding the ❶ **Tudor architecture**, adding the ❷ **Great Hall**, the exquisite ❸ **Chapel Royal**, the opulent Great Watching Chamber and the gigantic ❹ **Tudor kitchens**. By 1540 it had become one of the grandest and most sophisticated palaces in Europe. James I kept things ticking over, while Charles I added a new tennis court and did some serious art-collecting, including pieces that can be seen in the ❺ **Cumberland Art Gallery**.

VISITBRITAIN / GETTY IMAGES ©

❼ The Maze

Around 150m north of the main bulding

Created from hornbeam and yew and planted in around 1700, the maze covers a third of an acre within the famous palace gardens. A must-see conclusion to Hampton Court, the maze takes the average visitor about 20 minutes to reach the centre.

Tudor Kitchens

These vast kitchens were the engine room of the palace, and had a staff of 200 people. Six spit-rack-equipped fireplaces ensured roast meat was always on the menu (to the tune of 8200 sheep and 1240 oxen per year).

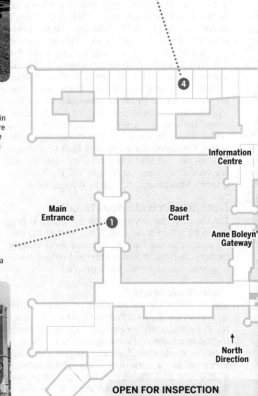

Tudor Architecture

Dating to 1515, the palace serves as one of the finest examples of Tudor architecture in the nation. Cardinal Thomas Wolsey was responsible for transforming what was originally a grand medieval manor house into a stunning Tudor palace.

KIEVVICTOR / SHUTTERSTOCK ©

Information Centre

Main Entrance

Base Court

Anne Boleyn Gateway

↑ **North Direction**

OPEN FOR INSPECTION

The palace was opened to the public by Queen Victoria in 1838.

After the Civil War, puritanical Oliver Cromwell warmed to his own regal proclivities, spending weekends in the comfort of the former Queen's bedroom and selling off Charles I's art collection. In the late 17th century, William and Mary employed Sir Christopher Wren for baroque extensions, chiefly the William III Apartments, reached by the **6 King's Staircase**. William III also commissioned the world-famous **7 maze**.

TOP TIPS

➡ Ask one of the red-tunic-garbed warders for anecdotes and information.

➡ Tag along with a themed tour led by costumed historians or do a dusk till dawn sleepover at the palace.

➡ Grab one of the audio tours from the Information Centre.

The Great Hall
This grand dining hall is the defining room of the palace, displaying what is considered England's finest hammer-beam roof, 16th-century Flemish tapestries that depict the story of Abraham, and some exquisite stained-glass windows.

Chapel Royal
The blue-and-gold vaulted ceiling was originally intended for Christ Church, Oxford, but was installed here instead; the 18th-century oak reredos was carved by Grinling Gibbons. Books on display include a 1611 1st edition of the King James Bible, printed by Robert Barker.

Chapel Court Garden

❷

❸

Clock Court

❺

Fountain Court

❻

The King's Staircase
One of five rooms at the palace painted by Antonio Verrio and a suitably bombastic prelude to the King's Apartments, the overblown King's Staircase adulates William III by elevating him above a cohort of Roman emperors.

GORDON BELL / SHUTTERSTOCK ©

Cumberland Art Gallery
The former Cumberland Suite, designed by William Kent, has been restored to accommodate a choice selection of some of the finest works from the Royal Collection.

TOP SIGHT
KEW GARDENS

A staggering 24% of London is a green patchwork of domestic gardens, sprouting some 2.5 million trees. Throw in London's abundant parkland, and you have one of the greenest cities on the planet. The 132-hectare gardens at Kew are the finest product of the British botanical imagination and really should not be missed. No worries if you don't know your quiver tree from your alang-alang: a visit to Kew is a journey of discovery for all.

Botanical Collection
As well as being a public garden, Kew is a pre-eminent research centre, maintaining its reputation as the most exhaustive botanical collection in the world.

Palm House
Assuming you come by tube and enter via Victoria Gate, you'll come almost immediately to the enormous and elaborate 700-glass-paned Palm House, a domed hothouse of metal and curved sheets of glass dating from 1848, enveloping a splendid display of exotic tropical greenery; an aerial walkway offers a parrot's-eye view of the lush vegetation. The huge Jurassic cycad (*Encephalartos altensteinii*) here is the world's oldest pot plant. Just northwest of the Palm House stands the tiny and irresistibly steamy **Waterlily House** sheltering the gigantic *Victoria cruziana* waterlily, whose vast pads can support the weight of a small adult.

Princess of Wales Conservatory
The angular Princess of Wales Conservatory houses plants in 10 different climatic zones – everything from a desert to a mangrove swamp. Look out for stone plants, which resemble

DON'T MISS
➡ Palm House
➡ Temperate House
➡ Treetop Walkway
➡ Kew Palace
➡ Chinese Pagoda

PRACTICALITIES
➡ Map p478, C2
➡ www.kew.org
➡ Kew Rd, TW9
➡ adult/child £14/2.50
➡ ⏱10am-6.30pm Apr-Aug, closes earlier Sep-Mar
➡ 🚢Kew Pier, 🚇Kew Bridge, ⊝Kew Gardens

pebbles (to deter grazing animals), carnivorous plants, gigantic waterlilies, cacti and a collection of tropical orchids.

Arboretum

Covering two thirds of the gardens, the **arboretum** refers to the more than 14,000 trees at Kew, which are often gathered together according to genera. You can find everything from eucalyptus trees to giant redwoods and Japanese pagoda trees.

Kew Palace

Built in 1631 and the smallest of the royal palaces, adorable red-brick Kew Palace, in the northwest of the gardens, is a former royal residence once known as Dutch House. It was the favourite home of George III and his family; his wife, Queen Charlotte, died here in 1818 (you can see the very chair in which she expired). Don't miss the recently restored **Royal Kitchens** next door.

Chinese Pagoda

Clad in scaffolding at the time of writing, Kew's 49.5m-tall eight-sided pagoda (1762), designed by William Chambers (who designed Somerset House), is one of the Kew Gardens' architectural icons. During WWII the pagoda withstood the blast from a stick of Luftwaffe bombs exploding nearby, and was also secretly employed by the Ministry of Defence to test bomb trajectories (which involved cutting holes in each floor). Current restorations – due to be completed in 2018 – will return its former full colours, along with the 80 dragons that once decorated the pagoda.

Other Highlights

Several long vistas (**Cedar Vista**, **Syon Vista** and **Pagoda Vista**) are channelled by trees from vantage points within Kew Gardens. The idyllic, thatched **Queen Charlotte's Cottage** in the southwest of the gardens was popular with 'mad' George III and his wife; the beautiful carpets of bluebells around here are a draw in spring. Opened in 2016, the 320m-long **Great Broad Walk Borders** is the longest double herbaceous border in the UK. The **Marianne North Gallery** displays the botanical paintings of Marianne North, an indomitable traveller who roamed the continents from 1871 to 1885, painting plants along the way.

VISITING THE GARDENS

Spring is a spectacular season to visit, but any time of the year is fine. Most visitors arrive by tube or train, but from April to October, boats run by the Westminster Passenger Services Association, sail from Westminster Pier to Kew Pier. Kids can explore the fun-filled Treehouse Towers (an outdoor play area) and Climbers and Creepers (an interactive botanical zone). Popular summer concerts bring music to Kew (visit the website for more info). Luna Cinema (www.thelunacinema.com) stages outdoor films at Kew Gardens in the warmer months.

BOTANICAL BOBBIES

Kew Gardens is also home to its very own police force – the Kew Constabulary – one of the world's smallest police forces!

KEW EXPLORER

If you want a good overview of the gardens, jump aboard the Kew Explorer (p324), which allows you to hop on and off at stops along the way.

⊙ SIGHTS

Leafy Richmond, Kew & Hampton Court have some of London's most eye-catching sights. Visiting them affords the chance to get river-side and enjoy delightful visions of pastoral London. Hampton Court Palace, Kew Gardens, the London Wetland Centre, the sights of Richmond and charms of Wimbledon rank among London's best offerings for visitors, botanists, historians, architecture enthusiasts, river fans, tennis buffs, those in flight from the pollution of central London or hikers in search of vast, green expanses.

⊙ Richmond & Kew

KEW GARDENS
GARDENS

See p314.

RICHMOND PARK
PARK

Map p478 (☑0300 061 2200; www.royalparks.org.uk/parks/richmond-park; ⊙7am-dusk; ⊟Richmond) At almost 1000 hectares (the largest urban parkland in Europe), this park offers everything from formal gardens and ancient oaks to unsurpassed views of central London 12 miles away. It's easy to flee the several roads slicing up the rambling wilderness, making the park perfect for a quiet walk or a picnic with the kids, even in summer when Richmond's riverside heaves. Coming from Richmond, it's easiest to enter via Richmond Gate or from Petersham Rd.

Herds of more than 600 red and fallow deer basking under the trees are part of its magic, but they can be less than docile in rutting season (September and October) and when the does bear young (May to July), so keep your distance (over 50m) during these times. Birdwatchers will love the diverse habitats, from neat gardens to woodland and assorted ponds. Floral fans should visit **Isabella Plantation**, a stunning 16-hectare woodland garden created after WWII, in April and May when the rhododendrons, azaleas and camellias bloom.

Set in a beautiful 13-hectare garden and affording great views of the city from the back terrace, **Pembroke Lodge** (Map p478; www.pembroke-lodge.co.uk; ⊙9am-5.30pm Apr-Oct, to just before dusk Nov-Mar) was the childhood home of Bertrand Russell. The Georgian tea rooms can garnish your visit with warm scones and clotted cream from 9am to 5.30pm.

The pastoral vista from **Richmond Hill** (Map p478) has inspired painters and poets for centuries and still beguiles. It's the only view (which includes St Paul's Cathedral 10 miles away) in the country to be protected by an act of Parliament.

HAM HOUSE
HISTORIC BUILDING

Map p478 (☑020-8940 1950; www.nationaltrust.org.uk/ham-house-and-garden; Ham, TW10; whole property adult/child/family £10.80/5.40/27, garden adult/child/family £4/2/10.20; ⊙house noon-4pm Sat-Thu late Mar–mid-Nov, by tour only Jan-Mar; gardens 11am-4pm Sat-Thu Jan–mid-Feb & Nov–mid-Dec, 11am-5pm Sat-Thu mid-Feb–Oct; ⊟371, ⊟Richmond, ⊟Richmond) Known as 'Hampton Court in miniature', much haunted redbrick Ham House was built in 1610 and became home to the first Earl of Dysart, unluckily employed as 'whipping boy' to Charles I. Inside it's grandly furnished; the Great Staircase is a fine example of Stuart woodworking. Look out for ceiling paintings by Antonio Verrio, a miniature of Elizabeth I by Nicholas Hilliard and works by Constable and Reynolds. The grounds slope delightfully down to the Thames and lovely 17th-century formal gardens await exploration.

The garden ticket also allows you access to the below stairs rooms. For spooky thrills, nocturnal after-hours ghost tours (£22) delve into Ham House's paranormal dimensions. A cafe (10am to 5pm) is open for light refreshments. Just opposite the Thames and accessible by small ferry is Marble Hill Park and its splendid mansion (p318).

RICHMOND GREEN
PARK

Map p478 (⊟Richmond, ⊟Richmond) A short walk west of the Quadrant (the road at the tube exit) is Richmond Green with its mansions and delightful pubs. In the Middle Ages, jousting tournaments were held here and today it's an absolute picture on a sunny day. Cross the green diagonally for the attractive remains of **Richmond Palace** (Map p478) – the main entrance and red-brick gatehouse – built in 1501. On the northeast side of the green, facing Richmond Theatre (p323), is Little Green (a smaller green).

THAMES AT RICHMOND

The stretch of the river from Twickenham Bridge to Petersham and Ham is one of the prettiest in London. The action is mostly around five-span Richmond Bridge (p317), built in 1777. Just before it, along one of the loveliest parts of the Thames, is tiny Corporation Island, colonised by flocks of feral parakeets. The gorgeous walk to Petersham can be crowded in nice weather; it's best to cut across pastoral Petersham Meadows (p317) and continue to Richmond Park for peace and quiet. There are several companies near Richmond Bridge, including Richmond Bridge Boathouses (p324), that offer skiff hire.

Alternatively walk north from Twickenham Bridge, alongside the Old Deer Park, past the two obelisks and climb onto **Richmond Lock** (Map p478; Richmond, St Margarets, Richmond) and footbridge, dating from 1894.

RICHMOND BRIDGE BRIDGE

Map p478 (Richmond, Richmond) This five-span bridge, built in 1777, is London's oldest surviving crossing and was only widened for traffic in 1937. According to the *Richmond Bridge Act* of 1772, vandalism of the bridge was punished with 'transportation to one of His Majesty's Colonies in America for the space of seven years'.

PETERSHAM MEADOWS PARK

Map p478 (Richmond, Richmond) Once part of the Ham House estate, pastoral Petersham Meadows – where cows still graze - is a perfectly bucolic slice of rural England, especially if you don't have time to visit the English countryside proper.

ORANGERY HISTORIC BUILDING

(Kew Gardens, TW9) Designed by Sir William Chambers, this elegant grade I listed plant house in Kew Gardens is home to a restaurant and cafe.

⊙ Putney & Barnes

PUTNEY & BARNES AREA

(Barnes, Putney) Called *Putelei* in the Domesday Book of 1086, Putney is most famous as the starting point of the annual **Oxford and Cambridge Boat Race** (www.theboatrace.org; late Mar/early Apr). Barnes is less well known and more 'villagey' in feel. The best way to approach Putney is to follow the signs from Putney Bridge tube station for the footbridge (which runs parallel to the rail track), admiring the gorgeous riverside houses, with their gardens fronting the Thames, and thereby avoiding the tatty High St until the last minute.

⊙ Chiswick

CHISWICK HOUSE HISTORIC BUILDING

(020-8995 0508; www.chgt.org.uk; Burlington Lane, Chiswick Park, W4; adult/child £6.70/4, gardens free; gardens 7am-dusk, house 10am-6pm Sun-Wed Apr-Sep, to 5pm Oct; Chiswick, Turnham Green) Designed by the third Earl of Burlington (1694–1753) – fired up with passion for all things Roman after his grand tour of Italy – this stunner of a neo-Palladian pavillion with an octagonal dome and colonnaded portico is a delight. The almost overpoweringly grand interior includes the coffered dome of the Upper Tribunal – left ungilded, the walls below are decorated with eight enormous paintings.

Admire the stunningly painted ceiling (by William Kent) of the **Blue Velvet Room** and look out for carvings of the pagan vegetative deity, the Green Man, in the marble fireplaces of the **Green Velvet Room**.

Lord Burlington also planned the house's original gardens, now **Chiswick Park**, a huge 26-hectare expanse surrounding the house, but they have been much altered since his time and were fully restored in 2010. Children will love them – look out for the stone sphinxes near the Cedar of Lebanon trees (another sphinx made of lead can be found in the Lower Tribuna).

Home to a splendid 19th-century conservatory and a gateway designed by Inigo Jones, Chiswick House also has an excellent cafe. Download an audio tour from the website.

The house is about a mile southwest of the Turnham Green tube station and 750m northeast of Chiswick train station.

HOGARTH'S HOUSE
HISTORIC BUILDING

(📞020-8994 6757; www.hounslow.info/arts/hogarthshouse; Hogarth Lane, W4; ⊙noon-5pm Tue-Sun; ⊖Turnham Green) **FREE** Home between 1749 and 1764 to artist and social commentator William Hogarth, this small house displays his caricatures and engravings, with such works as the haunting *Gin Lane* (and the less well-known, more affirmative *Beer Street*), *Marriage-à-la-mode* and copies of *A Rake's Progress* and *The Four Stages of Cruelty*.

The low ceiling of the narrow staircase is a head-bumping reminder that the Sergeant Painter to the King was under 5ft tall at full stretch. The house was bombed by the Luftwaffe in 1940, but the artist's mulberry tree survived and still flourishes in the garden (which would be a quiet retreat were it not for the roaring dual carriageway beyond the wall), accompanied by daffodils in spring. Prints and postcards are available from the downstairs shop. At the time of writing, the garden was being restored.

RUSSIAN ORTHODOX CHURCH
CHURCH

(Cathedral of the Dormition of the Mother of God and the Royal Martyrs; www.russianchurchlondon.org/en; 57 Harvard Rd, W4; ⍟Gunnersbury) The star-speckled blue dome of this Russian Orthodox church, soaring above a quiet, residential street in Chiswick, is a slightly surreal reminder of the richness of London's cultural tapestry. The Cathedral of the Dormition of the Mother of God and the Royal Martyrs, to give it its full name, opened in 1999 and has regular services, including one with English translations on Sundays.

⊙ Twickenham

MARBLE HILL HOUSE
HISTORIC BUILDING

Map p478 (📞020-8892 5115; www.english-heritage.org.uk/daysout/properties/marble-hill-house; Richmond Rd, TW1; adult/child/family £7/4.20/18.20; ⊙park 7am-dusk, tours 10.30am & noon Sat, 10.30am, noon, 2.15pm & 3.30pm Sun Apr-Oct; 🅿; ⍟St Margaret's, Richmond, ⊖Richmond) An 18th-century Palladian peach conceived as an idyllic escape from the hurly-burly of city life, this majestic love nest was originally built for George II's mistress Henrietta Howard and later occupied by Mrs Fitzherbert, the secret wife of George IV. The Georgian interior contains some astonishing flourishes, including the hand-painted Chinese wallpaper in the dining parlour

---

⊙ TOP SIGHT
LONDON WETLAND CENTRE

One of Europe's largest inland wetland projects, this 42-hectare centre was transformed from four Victorian reservoirs in 2000 and attracts some 140 species of bird, as well as frogs, butterflies, dragonflies and lizards, plus a thriving colony of watervoles.

From the visitor centre and glass-fronted observatory, meandering paths and boardwalks lead visitors around the grounds, penetrating the reedbed, marsh, fen and watery habitats. The many residents and transients here include black swans, ducks, Bewick's swans, geese, red-crested pochards, sand martins, coots and the rarer bitterns, herons and kingfishers. Don't miss the **Peacock Tower**, a three-storey hide – and magnet for serious birders – on the main lake's eastern edge; other hides are sprinkled around the reserve, including the **Headley Discovery Hide** in the west. A short walk north of the entrance, the wetland's family of sleek-coated **otters** are fed daily at 11am and 2pm (Monday to Friday). Free daily **tours**, which are led by knowledgeable and enthusiastic staff members, are highly recommended. They depart at 11.30am and 2.30pm. Binoculars can be hired from the shop. Check the website for details of events and courses, such as wildlife photography.

DON'T MISS

➡ Peacock Tower
➡ Headley Discovery Hide
➡ Otter feeding
➡ Daily tours

PRACTICALITIES

➡ 📞020-8409 4400
➡ www.wwt.org.uk
➡ Queen Elizabeth's Walk, SW13
➡ adult/child/family £12.75/7/35.55
➡ ⊙9.30am-5.30pm Apr-Oct, to 4.30pm Nov-Mar
➡ ⍟Barnes, ⊖Hammersmith

THAMES PATH

The entire **Thames Path National Trail** is a 184-mile walk stretching from the river's source at Thames Head, near Kemble in the Cotswolds, to the Thames Barrier. It's truly magnificent, particularly in its upper reaches, but tackling the entire course is for the truly ambitious and will need a couple of weeks. Most visitors walk sections of it, such as the 16-mile chunk from Battersea to the barrier, which takes about 6½ hours. There is also a short, but lovely riverside walk from Putney to Barnes (4 miles), or the gorgeous stretch of river from Twickenham Bridge to Petersham and Ham (1.5 miles).

and some delectable furniture. Entrance is only possible on one of the 90-minute guided tours, but you are free to visit the 26-hectare park.

The poet Alexander Pope had a hand in designing the park (containing an ice house and a grotto), which stretches leisurely down to the Thames. In 2017 archaeologists were beginning work on restoring the gardens that Henrietta Howard created in a project expected to last two years.

To get here from St Margaret's station, turn right along St Margaret's Rd, then take the right fork along Crown Rd and turn left along Richmond Rd. Turn right along Beaufort Rd and walk across Marble Hill Park to the house. It is also easily accessible by pedestrian ferry from Ham House. It's a 25-minute walk from Richmond station.

STRAWBERRY HILL   HISTORIC BUILDING

(☑020-8744 1241; www.strawberryhillhouse.org. uk; 268 Waldegrave Rd, TW1; adult/child £12.50/ free; ⊙house 11am-5pm Mon-Wed & Sun, garden 10am-5.30pm daily; ᴙStrawberry Hill, ◉Richmond Station) With its snow-white walls and Gothic turrets, this fantastical and totally restored 18th-century creation in Twickenham is the work of art historian, author and politician Horace Walpole. Studded with elaborate stained glass, the building reaches its astonishing apogee in the gallery, with its magnificent papier-mâché ceiling. For the full magic, join a twilight tour (£20). Last admission to the house is 4pm.

For homemade cakes, quiche and afternoon tea (from £5), pop into the **Cloister Coffee House** (open 10am to 6pm Saturday to Wednesday) and don't overlook exploring the garden. The house is a five- to 10-minute walk from Strawberry Hill train station; otherwise take bus R68 from Richmond tube station.

WORLD RUGBY MUSEUM   MUSEUM

(☑020-8892 8877; www.englandrugby.com; adult/child £8/6; ⊙10am-5pm Tue-Sat, 11am-5pm Sun; ᴙTwickenham, ◉Hounslow East) Shut for redevelopment at the time of writing (to reopen in early 2018), this museum at **Twickenham Stadium** (☑020-8892 8877; www.englandrugby.com/twickenham/; Rugby Rd, Twickenham, TW1; tours adult/child/family £20/12/50; ᴙTwickenham, ◉Hounslow East) showcases old matches in the video theatre and boasts a collection of 10,000 items of rugby memorabilia. Guided tours of the stadium take place at various times every day (except Mondays and match days) and include entry to the museum; see the website for details on times and for news on the relaunch. From Hounslow East tube station take bus 281.

◉ Wimbledon

WIMBLEDON COMMON   PARK

(☑020-8788 7655; www.wpcc.org.uk; ᴙWimbledon, ᴙWimbledon, ◉Wimbledon) Surging on into Putney Heath, Wimbledon Common blankets a staggering 460 hectares of southwest London. An astonishing expanse of open, wild and wooded space for walking (the best mode of exploration), nature trailing and picnicking, the common has its own Wimbledon Windmill (p320), dating from 1817. On the southern side of the common, the misnamed **Caesar's Camp** is what's left of a roughly circular earthen fort built in the 5th century BC. Take bus 93 from Wimbledon tube, train or tram station.

WIMBLEDON LAWN TENNIS MUSEUM   MUSEUM

(☑020-8946 6131; www.wimbledon.com/museum; Gate 4, Church Rd, SW19; adult/child £13/8, museum & tour £25/15; ⊙10am-5.30pm, last admission 5pm; ⓇWimbledon, ⓇWimbledon, ⊝Wimbledon, ⊝Southfields) This ace museum details the history of tennis – from its French precursor *jeu de paume* (which employed the open hand) to the supersonic serves of today's champions. It's a state-of-the-art presentation, with plenty of video clips and a projection of John McEnroe in the dressing room at Wimbledon, but the highlight is the chance to see Centre Court from the **360-degree viewing box**. During the championships in June/July, only those with tickets to the tournament can access the museum.

Riveting facts and figures abound: tennis clothes worn by female tennis players in 1881 weighed up to a gruelling 4.9kg! Compare this with Maria Sharapova's skimpy 2004 Ladies Singles outfit, also on display. The museum houses a cafe and a shop selling all manner of tennis memorabilia. Audio guides are available. Regular 90-minute tours of Wimbledon that take in Centre Court, No 1 Court and other areas of the All England Club also include access to the museum (best to book ahead, online or over the telephone). From Southfields tube station take bus 493, or it's a 15-minute walk; alternatively, take the tube, train or tram to Wimbledon and then take bus 493.

BUDDHAPADIPA TEMPLE   TEMPLE

(☎020-8946 1357; www.watbuddhapadipa.org; 14 Calonne Rd, SW19; ⊙9.30am-5.30pm Mon-Fri, 9am-6pm Sat & Sun; ⓇWimbledon, ⓇWimbledon, ⊝Wimbledon) **FREE** Surrounded by trees in over 1.5 hectares of tranquil Wimbledon land, this delightful Thai Buddhist temple actively welcomes everyone. Accompanying its reflective Buddhist repose, a community feel permeates the temple grounds, with visitors invited in for coffee and a chat. The *wat* (temple) boasts a *bot* (consecrated chapel) decorated with traditional scenes by two leading Thai artists (take your shoes off before entering). Take bus 93 from Wimbledon tube, train or tram station.

WIMBLEDON WINDMILL   NOTABLE BUILDING

(www.wimbledonwindmill.org.uk; Windmill Rd, SW19; adult/child £2/1; ⊙2-5pm Sat, 11am-5pm Sun late Mar-Oct; ℗; ⊝Wimbledon) One of London's few surviving windmills, Wimbledon Windmill is a fine smock mill (ie octagonal-shaped with sloping weatherboarded sides) dating from 1817. The windmill, which ceased operating in 1864, contains a museum with working models on the history of windmills and milling. The adjacent Windmill Tearooms can supply tea, caffeine and sustenance.

WORTH A DETOUR

SYON HOUSE

Just across the Thames from Kew Gardens and today owned by the Duke of Northumberland, **Syon House** (Syon Park; Map p478; ☎020-8560 0882; www.syonpark.co.uk; Brentford, TW7; adult/child £12.50/5.50, gardens only £7.50/4; ⊙house 11am-5pm Wed, Thu & Sun mid-Mar–Oct, gardens & conservatory 10.30am-5pm daily mid-Mar–Oct; ⓇGunnersbury, ⊝Gunnersbury) was once a medieval abbey named after Mt Zion. In 1542 Henry VIII dissolved the order of Bridgettine nuns who peacefully lived here and rebuilt it into a residence. In 1547, they say, God exacted his revenge on the king: when his lead coffin spent the night in Syon en route to Windsor for burial his bloated body exploded, bursting the coffin open and leaving the estate's dogs to lick up the mess.

The house from where Lady Jane Grey ascended the throne for her nine-day reign in 1553 was remodelled in the neoclassical style by Robert Adam in the 18th century and has plenty of Adam furniture and oak panelling. The interior was designed on gender-specific lines, with pastel pinks and purples for the ladies' gallery, and mock Roman sculptures for the men's dining room. Guests at the house have included the great Mohawk chieftain Thayendanegea (Joseph Brant) and Gunpowder Plot conspirator Thomas Percy.

The estate's 16-hectare gardens, with a lake and a magnificent domed Great Conservatory (1826) – the latter inspiring Joseph Paxton to design the Crystal Palace – were landscaped by Capability Brown. Syon Park is filled with attractions for children, including an adventure playground and an aquatic park. Children get free access during school holidays and bank holidays.

Hampton Court

HAMPTON COURT PALACE   PALACE
See p310.

✗ EATING

This neighbourhood excels in a variety of restaurants, cafes and pubs, from Michelin-starred meals to riverside gastropub lunches, gelaterias, tearooms for afternoon tea, or that classic English platter: fish and chips. Picturesque Richmond in particular is popular and diverse as a dining destination.

★ORANGE PEKOE   CAFE $
(020-8876 6070; www.orangepekoeteas. com; 3 White Hart Lane, SW13; cream tea £8.95; 7.30am-5pm Mon-Fri, 9am-5pm Sat & Sun; Barnes Bridge) This delightful Barnes tea shop is a consummate haven for lovers of the tea leaf. Surround yourself with all types of tea and present all your tricky leaf-related questions to the on-site tea sommelier. There's fine coffee, too, plus tasty breakfasts and cakes, ravishing all-day cream teas (scones with clotted cream, strawberry jam and a pot of tea) and the guilty pleasure of full-on traditional afternoon teas, presented in thoroughly English fashion. Reservations recommended.

★GELATERIA DANIELI   GELATO $
Map p478 (020-8439 9807; www.gelateria danieli.com; 16 Brewers Lane, TW9; ice cream from £2.25; 10am-6pm Mon-Sat, 11am-6pm Sun, open later in summer; Richmond, Richmond) Stuffed away down delightful narrow, pinched and flagstone-paved Brewer's Lane off Richmond Green, this tiny gelateria is a joy, and often busy. The handmade ice cream arrives in some two dozen lip-smacking flavours, from Christmas pudding through pistachio, walnut and tiramisu to pinenut and chocolate, scooped into small tubs or chocolate and hazelnut cones. There are milkshakes (£3.75) and coffee too.

RICHMOND HILL BAKERY   BAKERY $
Map p478 (54 Friars Stile Rd; pastries from £1.50; 8am-6pm; Richmond, Richmond) This canine-friendly and homely bakery and cafe occupies a popular and welcoming niche along the marvellously named Friars Stile Rd, supplying Richmond Park ramblers with fine coffee, teas, strawberry tarts, quiches, croissants and cakes. Sun-catchers can aim for one of the tables out the front, or sit behind one of the bay windows. Order your coffee from the front till and collect from the rear.

PIER 1   FISH & CHIPS $
Map p478 (020-8332 2778; www.pier1fishand chipshop.co.uk; 11-13 Petersham Rd, TW10; mains from £8.95; 11.30am-11pm Mon-Sat, to 10.30pm Sun; Richmond, Richmond) The ambience at this fish and chip restaurant is a stylish cut above the rest and the fish – fried or grilled – is delightfully succulent. The fish, served with chips, tartare sauce and a small dish of mushy peas, comes in at £12.95 and is prodigiously sized. The menu also nets a haul of non-fish dishes, from sirloins to roast chicken and vegetable lasagne.

The kids menu gets the nippers a small main, with chips, drink and ice cream for £7.45.

★GLASSHOUSE   MODERN EUROPEAN $$
Map p478 (020-8940 6777; www.glasshouse restaurant.co.uk; 14 Station Pde, TW9; 2-/3-course lunch Mon-Fri £30/35, 2-3-course dinner £45/55; noon-2.30pm & 6.30-10.30pm Mon-Sat, 12.30-3pm & 7-10pm Sun; Kew Gardens, Kew Gardens) A day at Kew Gardens finds a perfect conclusion at this Michelin-starred gastronomic highlight. The glass-fronted exterior envelops a delicately lit, low-key interior, where the focus remains on divinely cooked food. Diners are rewarded with a consistently accomplished menu from chef Berwyn Davies that combines English mainstays with modern European innovation.

The splendid four-course tasting lunch menu is £45 (Monday to Friday); the five-course tasting dinner menu is £70 (Sunday to Thursday).

★CHEZ LINDSAY   FRENCH $$
Map p478 (020-8948 7473; www.chez-lindsay. co.uk; 11 Hill Rise, TW10; mains £12.50-25, 2/3-course set lunch £12.75/15.75; noon-11pm Mon-Sat, to 10pm Sun; Richmond, Richmond) This appetising slice of Brittany at the bottom of Richmond Hill serves wholesome Breton cuisine with a side serving of comfortable ambience and river views. There's an accent on seafood, and house specialities include adorable galettes (buckwheat pancakes, from £3.95) with countless tasty fillings (or plain), washed down

with a variety of hearty (and very dry) Breton ciders. The set lunch is available from Monday to Friday.

MA GOA
INDIAN $$

(☑020-8780 1767; www.ma-goa.com; 242-244 Upper Richmond Rd, SW15; mains £3.95-16.50; ⊙6-10pm Mon, 6.30-10.30pm Tue-Thu, to 11pm Fri & Sat; 🖱🚲; 🚇Putney, 🚌Putney Bridge) This much-loved family-run restaurant specialises in the subtle cuisine of Portugal's former colony of Goa on India's west coast. Winning dishes include the fantastic *chini raan nihari* (pot roasted lamb shank with spices) and the stir-fried Goa chorizo, while the fish dishes are excellent. Vegetarian options are also available.

PETERSHAM NURSERIES CAFE
MODERN EUROPEAN $$$

Map p478 (☑020-8940 5230; www.petersham nurseries.com; Church Lane, off Petersham Rd, TW10; mains £16.50-36; ⊙cafe noon-3pm Tue-Sun, teahouse 9am-5pm Mon-Sat, 11am-5pm Sun) 🍴 In a greenhouse at the back of the fabulously located Petersham Nurseries is this award-winning cafe straight out of the pages of *The Secret Garden*. The confidently executed cuisine includes organic ingredients harvested from the nursery gardens and produce adhering to Slow Food principles. Seasonal plates range from fillets of John Dory with vermentino and asparagus and Cornish native lobster salad. Booking in advance is essential.

There's also a **teahouse** for coffee, tea and cakes through the day and an Italian lunch menu. Because of local residents, and council concerns about traffic increasing with the cafe's popularity, patrons are asked to walk here via the picturesque river towpath, or to use public transport.

🍷 DRINKING & NIGHTLIFE

Richmond may not be on everyone's alcohol radar, but it should be: some of the capital's best, most charming and historic riverside pubs can be found on either side of the Thames. Some of them are lapped by waters at high river tide, or even cut off!

★ CITY BARGE
PUB

(www.metropolitanpubcompany.com/our-pubs/the-city-barge; 27 Strand on the Green, W4; ⊙noon-11pm Mon-Thu, noon-midnight Fri, 10am-midnight Sat, 10am-10.30pm Sun; 🖱; 🚌Gunnersbury) In a line of small riverside cottages facing wooded Oliver's Island (where Cromwell is alleged to have taken refuge), this excellent pub looks straight onto the muddy Thames. Once known as the Navigators Arms, there has been a pub here since the Middle Ages, although the Luftwaffe gave it a dramatic facelift (as has an attractive refurb).

The pub itself claims a lineage dating from the 14th century, which would make it one of London's most ancient pubs. There are three open fires, drinkers spill outside in clement weather and a fine gastropub menu has taken hold. A scene from the Beatles' film *Help!* was shot here, celebrated in framed photo stills. The hefty steel door clangs shut during high tides, which inundate the towpath.

★ WHITE CROSS
PUB

Map p478 (☑020-8940 6844; www.thewhite crossrichmond.com; Water Lane, TW9; ⊙10am-11pm Mon-Sat, to 10.30pm Sun; 🖱; 🚌Richmond) The riverside location and fine food and ales make this bay-windowed pub on the site of a former friary a winner. There are entrances for low and high tides, but when the river is at its highest, Cholmondeley Walk running along the Thames floods and the pub is out of bounds to those not willing to wade. Wellies are provided.

Very occasionally boats have to pick up stranded boozers: a chalkboard lists high-tide times and depths (you can also check the website). Originally called the Waterman's Arms, the pub dates from 1748 and was rebuilt in 1838. Quirky detail: there's a tiny working fireplace *under* the window on your right as you enter.

TAP ON THE LINE
PUB

Map p478 (☑020-8332 1162; www.taponthe line.co.uk; Station Approach, TW9; 🖱; 🚌Kew Gardens) Right by the platform at Kew Gardens tube station (the only London tube station platform with its very own pub), this lovingly restored old tiled Victorian yellow-brick boozer makes for a glorious conclusion to a summer's rambling around Kew. With outside seating in the courtyard at the front, it's also a fine haven for a pub lunch. There's live music on Sundays from 7pm.

WHITE SWAN — PUB

Map p478 (☑020-8744 2951; www.whiteswan twickenham.co.uk; Riverside, TW1; ☺11am-11pm Mon-Sat, to 10.30pm Sun & Mon; ☎; ☒Twickenham) This traditional pub in Twickenham overlooks a quiet stretch of the Thames from what must be one of the most English-looking streets in London. It boasts a fantastic riverside location, a great selection of beer, a loyal crowd of locals and roaring fires in winter. Check the website tide chart to dine outside on the paved garden with Thames water lapping at your table.

CROOKED BILLET — PUB

(☑020-8946 4942; www.thecrookedbillet wimbledon.com; 14-15 Crooked Billet, SW19; ☺11am-11pm Sun-Thu, to midnight Fri & Sat; ☎; ☒Wimbledon) This historic Young's boozer south of Cannizaro Park, just off Wimbledon Common, is brim-full of character, with flagstone floors, open fires and a cosy village-pub personality. Drinkers collapse on the green opposite in summer, while home-cooked food, award-winning ale and seasonal drinks welcome weary ramblers and Wimbledon wayfarers. The Hand in Hand pub next door is another snug option, packed at weekends.

WHITE HART — PUB

(☑020-8876 5177; www.whitehartbarnes.co.uk; the Terrace, SW13; ☺11am-11pm Mon-Thu, 11am-midnight Fri & Sat, noon-9pm Sun; ☎; ☒Barnes Bridge) This riverside Young's pub in Barnes was formerly a Masonic lodge. It's huge, traditional and welcoming downstairs, but the temptation in warmer months is to head to the balcony for Thames views, or to plonk yourself down at one of the riverside tables. When Boat Race (p317) day arrives, the pub is deluged with beer-toting spectators.

☆ ENTERTAINMENT

RICHMOND THEATRE — THEATRE

Map p478 (☑0844 871 7651; www.atgtickets. com/venues/richmond-theatre/; Little Green, TW9; ☒Richmond, ☒Richmond) A magnificent old Victorian building facing Little Green (next to Richmond Green), Richmond Theatre opened in 1899. Designed by architect Frank Matcham, the theatre

ⓘ WIMBLEDON TICKETS

For a few weeks each June and July, the sporting world's attention is fixed on the quiet southern suburb of Wimbledon, as it has been since 1877. Most show-court tickets for the **Wimbledon Championships** (☑020-8944 1066; www.wimbledon.com; Church Rd, SW19; grounds admission £8-25, tickets £41-190) are allocated through public ballot, applications for which usually begin in early August of the preceding year and close at the end of December. Entry into the ballot does not mean entrants will get a ticket. A quantity of show court, outer court, ground tickets and late-entry tickets are also available if you queue on the day of play, but if you want a show-court ticket it is recommended you arrive early the day before and camp in the queue. See www.wimbledon. com for details.

stages a variety of popular plays, operas, ballets, musicals, live music performances and comedy.

🔒 SHOPPING

This is sightseeing rather than shopping territory, but Richmond has a good selection of retail choices for window-shoppers, browsers and shopaholics. Richmond High St is full of chains, but there are some independent stores around. In an enclave of cobbled streets you'll find jewellery shops tucked away down Brewers Lane en route to, or away from, Richmond Green.

TEDDINGTON CHEESE — CHEESE

Map p478 (☑020-8977 6868; www.teddington cheese.co.uk; 74 Hill Rise, TW10; ☺10am-6pm Wed-Sat, 11am-6pm Sun; ☒Richmond, ☒Richmond) As you come down – or head up – Richmond Hill, stop by this cheesemongers that packs a veritable smorgasbord of cheesy delights into a small space. Over 130 different English and international varieties contribute to the aroma and the helpful owner can point you in the right direction, whether it's Garrotxa from

Catalonia, Vacherin Frigbourgeois from Switzerland or Capria from Worcester.

THE OPEN BOOK
BOOKS

Map p478 (📞020-8940 1802; 10 King St, TW9; ⏱9.30am-6pm Mon-Sat, 11am-6pm; 🚆Richmond, ⊖Richmond) Helena Richardson's charming bookshop – fighting off a leviathan Waterstones around the corner – is a mainstay of Richmond reading life. With a terrific range compressed into a small space, this is excellent, unhurried browsing territory and full of surprises; but if you're after something specific, Helena knows her stock inside out.

SPORTS & ACTIVITIES

KEW EXPLORER
BUS

Map p478 (📞020-8332 5648; www.kew.org/kew-gardens/whats-on/kew-explorer-land-train; adult/child £5/2) For a good overview of the gardens, jump aboard this train that allows you to hop on and off at stops along the way, on a 40-minute itinerary. There are seven stops in all along a route that runs in a long loop from the main Victoria Gate, returning to its departure point. The Explorer is also available for private hire.

RICHMOND BRIDGE BOAT HIRE
BOATING

Map p478 (📞020-8948 8270; www.richmond boathire.co.uk; Richmond Bridge; adult/child £8/4; 🚆Richmond, ⊖Richmond) Rents out a variety of rowing boats, including big 12-seaters, for journeys along the Thames. Day rates are £16 for an adult and £6 for a child.

Day Trips from London

Windsor Castle p326

The bastion of British royalty, Windsor Castle overlooks the affluent town of Windsor, picturesquely located along the River Thames.

Oxford p329

The world's oldest university town, Oxford boasts more than three dozen prestigious (and eye-catching) colleges, but also some world-class museums.

Cambridge p334

Awash in exquisite architecture, steeped in history and tradition and renowned for its quirky rituals, Cambridge is the quintessential English university town.

Bath p338

A cultural trendsetter and fashionable haunt for three centuries, Bath has so many architectural gems the entire city has been named a World Heritage Site.

Stonehenge p340

This compelling ring of monolithic stones has been attracting a steady stream of pilgrims, poets and philosophers for the last 5000 years and is still a mystical, ethereal place – a haunting echo from Britain's forgotten past.

TOP SIGHT
WINDSOR CASTLE

The world's largest and oldest continuously occupied fortress, this redoubtable mass of battlements and towers dominates the Berkshire town of Windsor, 25 miles west of London. British monarchs have holed up at Windsor Castle for more than 900 years and it's the Queen's favourite of her several official residences.

History

An earth-and-timber fortress was erected here around 1080 by William the Conqueror, and was rebuilt in stone by his great-grandson, Henry II, in 1170. Edward III added a Gothic palace, while Charles II gave the State Apartments a baroque makeover, creating an 'English Versailles'. George IV swept in with his team of artisans, largely creating today's palace within the castle. As a result of all this rebuilding, the 951-room castle displays a lively range of architectural styles, from half-timbered fired brick to Gothic stonework.

State Apartments

The castle area, covering more than 10 hectares, is divided into three wards. In the Upper Ward, the State Apartments reverberate with style and history. The crossed swords, suits of armour and banners of the **Grand Staircase** set the tone for the two dozen or so rooms open to the public.

The **Grand Vestibule**, presided over by a marble statue of Queen Victoria, displays gifts and spoils from the British Empire, including a life-sized tiger's head of gold with crystal teeth from the throne of Tipu, sultan of Mysore. Here you'll also encounter the musket ball that killed Lord

DON'T MISS

- ➡ Grand Vestibule
- ➡ St George's Hall
- ➡ St George's Chapel
- ➡ Queen Mary's Dolls' House
- ➡ Changing of the Guard

PRACTICALITIES

- ➡ ☎0303 123 7304
- ➡ www.royalcollection. org.uk
- ➡ Castle Hill
- ➡ adult/child £20.50/12
- ➡ ⏰9.30am-5.30pm Mar-Oct, 9.45am-4.15pm Nov-Feb
- ➡ ♿
- ➡ 🚌702 from London Victoria, 🚉London Waterloo to Windsor & Eton Riverside, 🚉London Paddington to Windsor & Eton Central via Slough

Nelson. The **Waterloo Chamber**, commemorating the battle of that name, is filled with portraits of the great and the good by Sir Thomas Lawrence.

From here you move to the **King's Rooms** and **Queen's Rooms**. These 10 chambers are lessons in how the other half lives; they're filled with opulent furniture, tapestries, frescoed ceilings, carved wall panels, and paintings by Hans Holbein, Bruegel, Rembrandt, Peter Paul Rubens, Van Dyck and Gainsborough.

The **Queen's Guard Chamber**, bristling with pistols and swords, gives way to the fabulous **St George's Hall**, the venue of state banquets. On the ceiling the shields of the Knights of the Garter (originally from George IV's time here) were re-created after a devastating fire in 1992. The blank shields record 'degraded' knights who were expelled from the order for various reasons. Next door is the **Lantern Lobby**, a former chapel, where the fire began. End your tour in the **Garter Throne Room**.

Queen Mary's Dolls' House

This astonishing creation off the North Terrace of the Upper Ward is not a toy but a work of artful miniaturisation, designed by Sir Edwin Lutyens for Queen Mary and completed in 1924. At 1:12 scale, an exquisite attention to detail holds sway – it has running water, flushing toilets, electric lights, tiny Crown Jewels, a silver service, vintage wine in the cellar and a fleet of six cars in the garage.

St George's Chapel

Moving westward through the Middle Ward and past the distinctive **Round Tower**, rebuilt in stone from the original Norman keep in 1170, you enter the Lower Ward. This royal chapel, begun by Edward IV in 1475 but not completed until 1528, has a superb nave fashioned in the uniquely English style of Perpendicular Gothic, with gorgeous fan vaulting and massive 'gridiron' stained-glass windows. Serving as a **royal mausoleum**, the chapel contains the tombs of 10 monarchs, including Henry VI, Edward IV, Henry VIII, Charles I, George VI and the late Queen Mother. Note the magnificent Quire, hung with Knights of the Garter banners above the beautifully carved 15th-century wooden stalls. Time your visit well and you can attend **choral evensong** at 5.15pm daily throughout most of the year. The chapel is closed Sundays.

Albert Memorial Chapel

Originally built by Henry III in 1240 and dedicated to Edward the Confessor, this small and highly decorated chapel abutting St George's Chapel was the

ROYAL RESIDENCE

Windsor is used for state occasions and is one of the Queen's principal residences; if she's at home, the Royal Standard, not the Union Flag, flies from the Round Tower.

THE GREAT FIRE

A disastrous fire in 1992 nearly wiped out the State Apartments. Luckily the damage, though severe, was limited and a £37-million, five-year restoration returned the rooms to their former glory.

LOCAL EATS

A La Russe (☎01753-833009; www.alarusse.co.uk; 6 High St, Windsor; mains £12-22, 2-/3-course lunch menu £11/14.50; ⊙noon-2.30pm & 6-9.30pm Mon-Sat) serves tip-top French cuisine a mere hop-and-skip from the castle.

The **Two Brewers** (☎01753-855426; www.twobrewerswindsor.co.uk; 34 Park St, Windsor; mains £12.50-26; ⊙11.30am-11pm Mon-Thu, to 11.30pm Fri & Sat, noon-10.30pm Sun) is a great place to wind down, be it by the flower-decked exterior or the roaring fire in winter.

place of worship for the Order of the Garter until St George's Chapel snatched away that honour. After the death of Prince Albert at Windsor Castle in 1861, Queen Victoria ordered the chapel's elaborate redecoration as a tribute to her husband. A major feature of the restoration is the magnificent vaulted roof – the gold mosaic pieces were crafted in Venice.

Windsor Great Park

South of the castle, **Windsor Great Park** (☏01753-860222; www.windsorgreatpark. co.uk; Windsor; ☉dawn-dusk) ᴳᴿᴱᴱ ranges over a staggering area of 7.7 sq miles. The **Long Walk** is a roughly 3-mile jaunt along a tree-lined path from King George IV Gate to the Copper Horse statue (of George III) on Snow Hill, the park's highest point. The **Savill Garden** (☏01753-860222; www.windsorgreatpark.co.uk; Wick Lane, Englefield Green; adult/child £10.50/free; ☉10am-6pm Mar-Oct, to 4.30pm Nov-Feb; 🅿) is particularly lovely, and located just over 4 miles south of Windsor Castle. By car, take the A308 out of town and follow the brown signs.

Changing of the Guard

A must for any visitor, the changing of the guard is a fabulous spectacle of pomp and ceremony that takes place in the Lower Ward or, when the Queen is in official residence, the Quadrangle in the Upper Ward. It usually happens at 11am on Mondays, Wednesdays, Fridays and Saturdays, weather permitting.

ETON COLLEGE

The largest and most famous public (meaning private and fee-paying) **boys' school** (☏01753-370100; www.etoncollege.com; High St, Eton; adult/child £10/free; ☉tours Fri 2pm & 4pm May-Aug) in England is arguably the most enduring symbol of England's class system. High-profile alumni include 19 British prime ministers, countless princes, kings and maharajas, famous explorers, authors, actors and economists – among them Princes William and Harry, George Orwell, Ian Fleming, John Maynard Keynes, Bear Grylls and Eddie Redmayne.

Eton was founded by Henry VI in 1440 with a view towards educating 70 highly qualified boys awarded a scholarship from a fund endowed by the king. Every year since then, 70 King's Scholars have been chosen, based on the results of a highly competitive exam; these pupils are housed in separate quarters from the 1300 or so other students. All pupils are boarders and must wear formal tailcoats, waistcoats and white collars to lessons (top hats went out in 1948).

Guided tours take in various buildings including the chapel and the Museum of Eton Life. Online booking is recommended.

Oxford

Explore

One of the world's most famous university cities, Oxford is a beautiful, privileged place. It is steeped in history and studded with august buildings, yet maintains the feel of a young city, thanks to its large student population. The elegant honey-toned buildings of the university's colleges, scattered throughout the city, wrap around tranquil courtyards along narrow cobbled lanes, and, inside their grounds, a studious calm reigns. The city's famed spires twirl into the sky above.

Oxford is a wonderful place to wander: the oldest colleges date back to the 13th century, and little has changed inside the hallowed walls since. But along with the rich history, tradition and energetic academic life, there is a busy, lively world beyond the college walls, and the city's nonuniversity majority far outnumber the academic elite. Just as in Cambridge, the existence of 'town' beside 'gown' makes Oxford more than simply a bookish place of learning.

The Best...

→ **Sight** Christ Church (p329)
→ **Place to Eat** Vaults & Garden (p333)
→ **Place to Drink** Turf Tavern (p334)

Getting There & Away

→ **Bus** Oxford's **bus station** (Gloucester Green) is in the centre, near the corner of Worcester and George Sts. The main bus companies are **Oxford Bus Company** (☑01865-785400; www.oxfordbus.co.uk), **Stagecoach** (☑01865-772250; www.stagecoachbus.com) and **Swanbrook** (☑01452-712386; www.swanbrook.co.uk).

Destinations:
Burford (route 853; £3.80, 45 minutes)
Cambridge (X5; £13.50, 3¾ hours)
Cheltenham (route 853; £8, 1½ hours)
Chipping Norton (S3; £4.70, one hour)
London Victoria (Oxford Tube/X90; £15, 1¾ hours)
Woodstock (S3; £3.70, 30 minutes)
National Express (☑0871-7818181; www.nationalexpress.com) coach destinations:
Bath (£8.20, two hours)
Birmingham (£13.50, 2½ hours)

Bristol (£10, three hours)
London Victoria (£16, two hours)
Oxford Bus Company runs 'The Airline' service to/from Heathrow (£23, 1½ hours) and Gatwick (£28, 2-2½ hours) airports.

→ **Train** Oxford's main train station (Botley Rd) is conveniently placed on the western side of the city centre. Destinations include the following:

Birmingham (£18, 1¼ hours)
London Paddington (£25, 1¼ hours)
Manchester (£50, three hours)
Moreton-in-Marsh (£9.90, 35 minutes)
Newcastle (£111, 4½ hours)
Winchester (£17, 1¼ hours)

Oxford Parkway station (Banbury Rd), 4 miles north of the centre, has trains to London Marylebone (£25, one hour). It's convenient if you're staying in Summertown and has bus links to central Oxford.

Need to Know

→ **Area Code** ☑01865
→ **Population** 159,994
→ **Tourist Information** Covers the whole of Oxfordshire, stocks printed Oxford walking guides and books official walking tours.

◉ SIGHTS

★**CHRIST CHURCH**   COLLEGE
(☑01865-276492; www.chch.ox.ac.uk; St Aldate's; adult/child £9/8; ◷10am-5pm Mon-Sat, 2-5pm Sun) The largest of all of Oxford's colleges, with 650 students, and the one with the grandest quad, Christ Church is also most popular with visitors. Its magnificent buildings, illustrious history and latter-day fame as a location for the *Harry Potter* films bring tourists in droves. The college was founded in 1524 by Cardinal Thomas Wolsey, who suppressed the 9th-century monastery existing on the site to acquire the funds for his lavish building project.

Over the years, numerous luminaries have been educated at Christ Church, including Albert Einstein, philosopher John Locke, poet WH Auden, Charles Dodgson (Lewis Carroll; who immortalised the then-dean's daughter in his *Alice in Wonderland* tales), and no fewer than 13 British prime ministers. The main entrance is below the imposing 17th-century **Tom Tower**, the upper part of which was designed by

Oxford

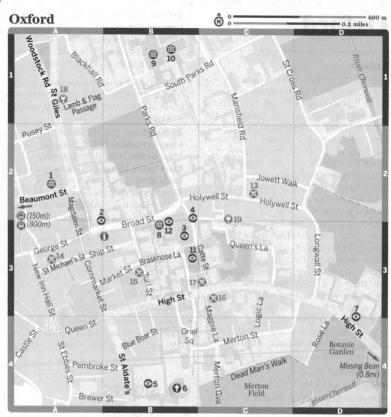

Oxford

◉ Sights

1	Ashmolean Museum	A2
2	Balliol College	A3
3	Bodleian Library	B3
4	Bridge of Sighs	B2
5	Christ Church	B4
6	Christ Church Cathedral	B4
7	Magdalen College	D3
8	Museum of the History of Science	B3
9	Oxford University Museum of Natural History	B1
10	Pitt Rivers Museum	B1
11	Radcliffe Camera	B3
12	Sheldonian Theatre	B3

⊗ Eating

13	Edamamé	C2
14	Handle Bar Cafe & Kitchen	A3
15	Missing Bean	B3
16	Quod	C3
17	Vaults & Garden	C3

◉ Drinking & Nightlife

18	Lamb & Flag	A1
19	Turf Tavern	C2

former student Sir Christopher Wren. Great Tom, the 6-tonne tower bell, still chimes 101 times each evening at 9.05pm (Oxford is five minutes west of Greenwich) to sound the curfew imposed on the original 100 students, plus one added in 1663.

Visitors must head further south down St Aldate's to the visitors' entrance (where there may be queues). From here, you go up to the **Great Hall**, the college's spectacular dining room, with its hammer-beam roof and imposing portraits of past scholars. It was replicated in film studios as the Hogwarts dining hall for the *Harry Potter* films. The hall often closes between noon and 2pm.

Coming down the grand fan-vaulted staircase (where Professor McGonagall welcomed Harry in *Harry Potter and the Philosopher's Stone*), you'll enter **Tom Quad**, Oxford's largest and arguably most impressive quadrangle, with a statue of Mercury in its pond.

From the quad, you access 12th-century **Christ Church Cathedral** (☑01865-276150; www.chch.ox.ac.uk/cathedral; St Aldate's; ☺10am-4.15pm Mon-Sat, 2-4.15pm Sun) [FREE]. It was originally the abbey church and then the college chapel, but was declared a cathedral by Henry VIII when he broke from the Catholic Church, suppressed more monasteries and convents, and gave the college its current name in 1546. It was formerly known as Cardinal's College.

Inside, brawny Norman columns are topped by elegant vaulting, and beautiful stained-glass windows illuminate the walls. Keep an eye out for the 13th-century reliquary of St Frideswide, Oxford's patron saint, whose Anglo-Saxon shrine was a focus of pilgrimage prior to the college being built. Other notable features include the stained-glass depiction of the murder of Thomas Becket, dating from 1320, above the side altar on the right. As this is a working Anglican cathedral, there's no charge to visit it for private prayer or to attend a service – talk to the porters at the main gate. Evensong is held at 6pm most days.

Finally, you'll pass through the 15th-century **cloister**, a relic of the ancient Priory of St Frideswide.

To the south of the college is **Christ Church Meadow**, a leafy expanse bordered by the Rivers Cherwell and Isis, ideal for leisurely walking.

★**BODLEIAN LIBRARY**   LIBRARY
(☑01865-277162; www.bodleian.ox.ac.uk/ bodley; Catte St; tours £6-14; ☺9am-5pm Mon-Sat, 11am-5pm Sun) Oxford's Bodleian Library is one of the oldest public libraries in the world and quite possibly the most impressive one you'll ever see. Visitors are welcome to wander around the central quad and the foyer exhibition space. For £1 you can visit the Divinity School, but the rest of the complex is only accessible on guided tours. Check timings online or at the infor-

mation desk. Advance tickets are available for extended tours only; others must be purchased on the day.

The Bodleian has its roots in a 15th-century collection of books, and its present state is largely due to the efforts of Sir Thomas Bodley, a 16th-century fellow of Merton College. He founded the library in 1602 and, in 1610, came to the agreement with the Stationers' Company of London that it would receive a copy of every single book published in the UK – an agreement that still stands today. The library started off with 20 books; it currently holds more than 12 million items, contains 117 miles of shelving and has seating space for up to 2500 readers. A staggering 5000 books and articles arrive every Wednesday, all of which need to be catalogued and stored.

The oldest part of the library surrounds the Jacobean Gothic **Old Schools Quadrangle**, which dates from the early 17th century and sports some of Oxford's odder architectural gems. On the eastern side of the quad is the **Tower of Five Orders**, an ornate building depicting the five classical orders of architecture. On the western side is the exquisite **Divinity School**, the university's first teaching room. Completed in 1488, it is renowned as a masterpiece of 15th-century English Gothic architecture and has a superb fan-vaulted ceiling sporting the initials of its many benefactors. It featured as the Hogwarts hospital wing in the *Harry Potter* films.

Half-hour mini tours (£6) include the Divinity School and the medieval **Duke Humfrey's library**, where no fewer than five kings, 40 Nobel Prize winners, 26 British prime ministers, and writers such as Oscar Wilde, CS Lewis and JRR Tolkien studied amid rows filled with grand ancient tomes chained to the shelves. It also featured in the *Harry Potter* films as the Hogwarts library. Those wishing to read here (books may not be borrowed) to this day must swear Bodley's Oath, which involves vowing not to bring fire or flames into the library.

Hour-long standard tours (£8) also visit the 17th-century oak-panelled **Convocation House**, where parliament was held during the Civil War, and the **Chancellor's Court**, in which Oscar Wilde and Romantic poet Percy Bysshe Shelley were tried (for debt and promoting atheism, respectively). Extended 1½-hour tours (£14; 9.15am Wednesday and Saturday) include the Radcliffe Camera (p332), the Upper Reading Room and the underground Gladstone Link. Alternatively, pick up a 40-minute audio guide (£2.50).

Some of the library's collections are now housed in the newly renovated **Weston Library** (Broad St), which opened to visitors in 2015.

★**PITT RIVERS MUSEUM**   MUSEUM
(☏01865-270927; www.prm.ox.ac.uk; South Parks Rd; ⊙noon-4.30pm Mon, 10am-4.30pm Tue-Sun) FREE Hidden away through a door at the back of the **Oxford University Museum of Natural History** (☏01865-272950; www.oum.ox.ac.uk; Parks Rd; ⊙10am-5pm; 🛜♿) FREE, this wonderfully creepy anthropological museum houses a treasure trove of half a million objects from around the world – more than enough to satisfy any armchair adventurer. One of the reasons it's so brilliant is the fact there are no computers, interactive displays or shiny modern gimmicks. Dim lighting lends an air of mystery to the glass cases stuffed with prized booty of Victorian explorers.

Objects are mostly divided into themes, rather than cultures, with subjects such as 'Smoking', 'Weapons', 'Body Art' or 'Treatment of Dead Enemies' (a particularly gruesome ensemble). Among the feathered cloaks, silver toe rings, teeth necklaces, Indonesian carvings, blowpipes, shields, magic charms, Noh masks, totem poles, musical instruments, global textiles and shrunken heads, you may spot ceremonial headgear from Uganda worn during circumcision ceremonies, ancient dental implements and a suspended East African boat.

★**ASHMOLEAN MUSEUM**   MUSEUM
(☏01865-278000; www.ashmolean.org; Beaumont St; ⊙10am-5pm Tue-Sun) FREE Britain's oldest public museum, second in repute only to London's British Museum, was established in 1683 when Elias Ashmole presented Oxford University with a collection of curiosities amassed by the well-travelled John Tradescant, gardener to Charles I. Today the museum's four floors feature interactive displays, a giant atrium, glass walls with views into galleries on different levels and a beautifully sited rooftop restaurant. Collections span the world in bright, spacious galleries in one of Britain's best examples of neoclassical architecture.

Historical treasures include Egyptian mummies, Islamic art, Indian textiles, ancient documents, rare porcelain, tapestries, silverware, priceless musical instruments, extensive displays of European art and, famously, the Anglo-Saxon Alfred Jewel.

MAGDALEN COLLEGE   COLLEGE
(☏01865-276000; www.magd.ox.ac.uk; High St; adult/child £6/5; ⊙1pm-dusk Oct-Jun, 10am-7pm Jul & Aug, noon-7pm Sep) Set amid 40 hectares of private lawns, woodlands, river walks and deer park, Magdalen (*mawd*-lin), founded in 1458, is one of the wealthiest and most beautiful of Oxford's colleges. It has a reputation as an artistic college. Some of its notable students have included writers Julian Barnes, Alan Hollinghurst, CS Lewis, John Betjeman, Seamus Heaney and Oscar Wilde, not to mention Edward VIII, TE Lawrence 'of Arabia', Dudley Moore and Cardinal Thomas Wolsey.

Beyond the elegant Victorian gateway, you'll find the medieval chapel and its glorious 15th-century tower. From here move on to the remarkable, restored 15th-century **cloisters**, some of Oxford's finest, with strange animals perched on the buttresses. The fantastic gargoyles and grotesques along the frontage here are thought to have inspired CS Lewis' stone statues in *The Chronicles of Narnia*. Behind the cloisters, lovely **Addison's Walk** leads through the grounds and along the banks of the River Cherwell for just under a mile. In the mid-1870s you might have encountered Oscar Wilde taking his pet lobster for a stroll.

The college also has a fine choir that sings *Hymnus Eucharisticus* at 6am on May Day (1 May) from the top of the 44m bell tower.

RADCLIFFE CAMERA   LIBRARY
(www.bodleian.ox.ac.uk; Radcliffe Sq) The sandy-gold Radcliffe Camera is the quintessential Oxford landmark and undoubtedly one of the city's most photographed buildings. This beautiful, light-filled circular, columned library and reading room that focuses on the humanities was built between 1737 and 1749 in grand Palladian style, and has Britain's third-largest dome. The only way to see the interior is to join an extended 1½-hour tour (£14) of the Bodleian Library (p331).

BALLIOL COLLEGE
COLLEGE

(☏01865-277777; www.balliol.ox.ac.uk; Broad St; adult/child £2/1; ☺10am-dusk) Established in 1263, Balliol College is thought to be the oldest college in Oxford. The huge Gothic wooden doors between the inner and outer quadrangles bear scorch marks from when three Protestant clerics were burned at the stake here in the mid-16th century. Notable alumni include politician Boris Johnson and three former British prime ministers.

MUSEUM OF THE
HISTORY OF SCIENCE
MUSEUM

(☏01865-277280; www.mhs.ox.ac.uk; Broad St; ☺noon-5pm Tue-Sun) **FREE** Science, art, celebrity and nostalgia come together at this fascinating museum, where exhibits include everything from an extensive selection of astrolabes and an equation-covered blackboard used by Einstein in 1931, to the world's finest collection of historical scientific instruments. It's all housed in a lovely 17th-century building.

SHELDONIAN THEATRE
THEATRE

(☏01865-277299; www.admin.ox.ac.uk/sheldonian; Broad St; adult/child £3.50/2.50; ☺10am-4.30pm Mon-Sat Feb-Oct, to 3pm Nov-Jan) Begun in 1663, this monumental building was the first major work of Sir Christopher Wren, then a professor of astronomy. Inspired by the classical Theatre of Marcellus in Rome, it has a rectangular front end, a semicircular back, and railings decorated with classical busts. The ceiling in the main hall is blanketed by a fine 17th-century painting of the triumph of truth over ignorance; the ceiling's remarkable length was made possible by ingenious braces made of shorter timbers.

The Sheldonian is now used for college ceremonies and public concerts, but you can climb to the cupola for good views of the surrounding buildings. Guided tours (adult/child £8/6) are provided on certain days throughout the year. Contact the theatre for details.

BRIDGE OF SIGHS
BRIDGE

(Hertford Bridge; New College Lane) As you stroll along New College Lane, look up at the steeped Bridge of Sighs linking the two halves of Hertford College. Completed in 1914, it's sometimes erroneously referred to as a copy of the famous bridge in Venice, but it bears a much closer resemblance to that city's Rialto Bridge.

✖ EATING & DRINKING

★ **VAULTS & GARDEN**
CAFE $

(☏01865-279112; www.thevaultsandgarden.com; University Church of St Mary the Virgin, Radcliffe Sq; mains £7-10; ☺8.30am-6pm; 📶🍴) Hidden in the vaulted 14th-century Old Congregation House of the University Church, this buzzy local favourite serves a wholesome seasonal selection of soups, salads, pastas, curries, sandwiches and cakes, including plenty of vegetarian and gluten-free options. It's one of Oxford's most beautiful lunch venues, with additional tables in a pretty garden overlooking Radcliffe Sq. Arrive early to grab a seat.

★ **EDAMAMÉ**
JAPANESE $

(☏01865-246916; www.edamame.co.uk; 15 Holywell St; mains £6-9.50; ☺11.30am-2.30pm Wed, 11.30am-2.30pm & 5-8.30pm Thu-Sat, noon-3.30pm Sun; 🍴) The queue out the door speaks volumes about this tiny, deliciously authentic place. All light wood, dainty trays and friendly bustle, this is Oxford's top spot for gracefully simple, flavour-packed Japanese cuisine. Dishes include fragrant chicken miso ramen, tofu stir-fry and, on Thursday nights, sushi. No bookings; arrive early and be prepared to wait. Cash only at lunch.

HANDLE BAR CAFE & KITCHEN
CAFE $

(Bike Zone, 28-32 St Michael's Street; dishes £5-7; ☺8am-10pm Mon-Sat, 10am-7pm Sun; 📶🍴) Hot on Oxford's simmering coffee-culture scene, this bubbly bike-themed cafe gets packed with students, professionals and a few lucky tourists. They're here for luscious, health-focused bites, such as spiced avocado-and-feta toast, kale-wrapped halloumi and fresh-fruit smoothie 'pots', plus tasty cakes, teas and coffees. A raised penny-farthing serves as centrepiece and bikes dangle from the ceiling.

MISSING BEAN
CAFE $

(☏01865-794886; www.themissingbean.co.uk; 14 Turl St; dishes £2-6; ☺8am-6pm Mon-Fri, 9am-6.30pm Sat, 10am-5.30pm Sun; 📶) Inspired by Australia's independent cafe scene, the Missing Bean serves up Oxford's finest coffee, fuelled by its East Oxford roastery – which has its own **branch** (☏01865-794886; www.themissingbean.co.uk; 1 Newtec Pl, Magdalen Rd; ☺7am-2pm Wed-Fri, 10am-2pm Sat). There are loose-leaf teas and smoothies for those less caffeine inclined. Fresh muffins, flapjacks, cakes and ciabattas with all kind of fillings make this a brilliant lunchtime stop.

QUOD
MODERN BRITISH **$$**

(☑01865-202505; www.quod.co.uk; Old Bank Hotel, 91-94 High St; mains £11-20; ⊙7am-11pm; 🛜🖉📶) Popular for its smart, contemporary decor, lively atmosphere and supercentral location, Quod dishes up modern brasserie-style food to the Oxford masses. The two-course weekday set lunch (£12.95) is good value. If you're caught between meals, go for varied international offerings on the all-day menu or, from 3pm to 5.30pm, afternoon tea (£8 to £26).

LAMB & FLAG
PUB

(cnr St Giles & Lamb & Flag Passage; ⊙noon-11pm Mon-Sat, to 10.30pm Sun) Born as a 17th-century tavern, this relaxed wood-walled hideaway is still a good bet for a sturdy pint or glass of wine. It's said that Thomas Hardy wrote part of his novel *Jude the Obscure* within its walls, while authors CS Lewis and JRR Tolkien were once regulars. Pint purchases help fund PhD scholarships at St John's College (which manages the pub).

TURF TAVERN
PUB

(☑01865-243235; www.turftavern-oxford.co.uk; 4-5 Bath Pl; ⊙11am-11pm; 🛜) Squeezed down a narrow alleyway, this tiny medieval pub (dating from at least 1381) is one of Oxford's best loved. It's where US president Bill Clinton famously 'did not inhale'; other patrons have included Oscar Wilde, Stephen Hawking and Margaret Thatcher. Home to 11 real ales, it's always crammed with students, professionals and the odd tourist. Plenty of outdoor seating.

Cambridge

Explore

Abounding with exquisite architecture, exuding history and tradition and renowned for its quirky rituals, Cambridge is a university town extraordinaire. The tightly packed core of ancient colleges, the picturesque riverside 'Backs' (college gardens) and the leafy green meadows surrounding the city give it a more tranquil appeal than its historic rival Oxford.

Like 'the Other Place', as Oxford is known locally, the buildings here seem unchanged for centuries, and it's possible to wander the college buildings and experience them as countless prime ministers, poets, writers and scientists have done. Sheer academic achievement seems to permeate the very walls: cyclists loaded down with books negotiate cobbled passageways, students relax on manicured lawns and great minds debate life-changing research in historic pubs. First-time punters zigzag erratically across the river and those long past their student days wonder what it would have been like to study in such splendid surroundings.

The Best...

➡**Sight** King's College Chapel (p335)
➡**Place to Eat** Midsummer House (p337)
➡**Place to Drink** Eagle (p337)

Getting There & Away

Public transport links to Cambridge are excellent, with frequent connections to London and the rest of the east of England.
➡**Bus** Buses run by **National Express** (☑0871 781 8181; www.nationalexpress.com; Parkside) leave from Parkside. Direct services:

Gatwick £37, 3¾ hours, nine daily
Heathrow £25, 2¾ hours, hourly
London Victoria £5, 2½ hours, two-hourly
Oxford £12, 3½ hours, every 30 minutes
Stansted £10, 45 minutes, two-hourly
➡**Train** The train station is 1.5 miles southeast of the centre. Direct services:

Birmingham New Street £55, three hours, hourly
Ely £5, 15 minutes, three per hour
King's Lynn £10, 50 minutes, hourly
London King's Cross £23, one hour, two to four per hour
Stansted Airport £10, 35 minutes, hourly

Need to Know

➡**Area Code** ☑01223
➡**Population** 123,900
➡**Tourist Information** As well as running escorted tours, the tourist office also has information about self-guided walks.

Cambridge

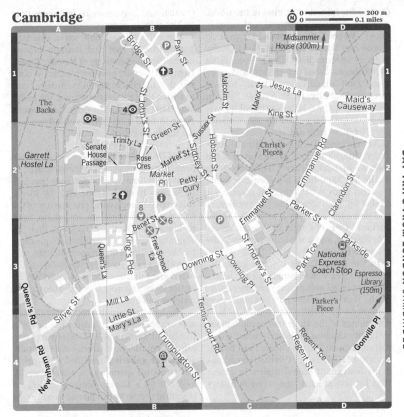

Cambridge

◉ Sights

⊗ Eating

◉ Drinking & Nightlife

◉ SIGHTS

★ KING'S COLLEGE CHAPEL   CHURCH
(☎ 01223-331212; www.kings.cam.ac.uk; King's Pde; adult/child £9/free; ⊙ 9.30am-3.30pm Mon-Sat & 1.15-2.30pm Sun term time, 9.30am-4.30pm daily university holidays) In a city crammed with showstopping buildings, this is a scene-stealer. Grandiose 16th-century King's College Chapel is one of England's most extraordinary examples of Gothic architecture. Its inspirational, intricate 80m-long fan-vaulted ceiling is the world's largest and soars upwards before exploding into a series of stone fireworks. This hugely atmospheric space is a fitting stage for the chapel's world-famous choir; hear it sing during the free and magnificent **evensong** during term time (5.30pm Monday to Saturday, 10.30am and 3.30pm Sunday).

★ TRINITY COLLEGE   COLLEGE
(www.trin.cam.ac.uk; Trinity St; adult/child £3/1; ⊙ 10am-3.30pm Nov-Mar, to 5pm Jul-Oct) The largest of Cambridge's colleges, Trinity offers an extraordinary Tudor gateway, an air of supreme elegance and a sweeping Great

Court – the largest of its kind in the world. It also boasts the renowned and suitably musty **Wren Library** (www.trin.cam.ac.uk; ⊙noon-2pm Mon-Fri year-round, plus 10.30am-12.30pm Sat term time) FREE, containing 55,000 books dated before 1820 and more than 2500 manuscripts. Works include those by Shakespeare, St Jerome, Newton and Swift – and AA Milne's original *Winnie the Pooh;* both Milne and his son, Christopher Robin, were graduates.

As you enter Trinity through the part-gilded gate, have a look at the **statue** of the college's founder, Henry VIII, that adorns it. His left hand holds a golden orb, while his right grips not the original sceptre but a table leg, put there by student pranksters and never replaced. It's a wonderful introduction to one of Cambridge's most venerable colleges, and a reminder of who really rules the roost.

In the **Great Court** beyond, scholastic humour gives way to wonderment, thanks to its imposing architecture and sheer size. To the right of the entrance is a small tree, planted in the 1950s and reputed to be a descendant of the apple tree made famous by Trinity alumnus Sir Isaac Newton. Other alumni include Francis Bacon, Lord Byron, Tennyson, HRH Prince Charles (legend has it his bodyguard scored higher in exams than he did), at least nine prime ministers

(British and international) and more than 30 Nobel Prize winners.

The college's vast **hall** has a dramatic hammer-beam roof and lantern; beyond lie the dignified cloisters of **Nevile's Court**. Henry VIII would have been proud to note, too, that his college would eventually come to throw the best party in town, the lavish **May Ball** (⊙early Jun) in early June, though you will need a fat purse, and a friend on the inside, to get an invitation.

★FITZWILLIAM MUSEUM   MUSEUM
(www.fitzmuseum.cam.ac.uk; Trumpington St; by donation; ⊙10am-5pm Tue-Sat, noon-5pm Sun) FREE Fondly dubbed 'the Fitz' by locals, this colossal neoclassical pile was one of the first public art museums in Britain, built to house the fabulous treasures that the seventh Viscount Fitzwilliam bequeathed to his old university. Expect Roman and Egyptian grave goods, artworks by many of the great masters and some quirkier collections: banknotes, literary autographs, watches and armour.

The building's unabashedly over-the-top appearance sets out to mirror its contents; this ostentatious jumble of styles mixes mosaic with marble, and Greek with Egyptian. The **lower galleries** are filled with priceless treasures spanning the ancient world; look out for a Roman funerary couch, an inscribed copper votive plaque from Yemen

---

FANCY A PUNT?

Gliding a self-propelled punt along the Backs is a blissful experience – once you've got the hang of it. It can also be a manic challenge to begin. If you wimp out, you can always opt for a relaxing chauffeured punt.

Punt hire costs around £20 to £28 per hour; 45-minute chauffeured trips of the Backs cost about £15 to £19 per person. One-way trips to Grantchester (1½ hours) start at around £18 per person.

Punting looks pretty straightforward but, believe us, really – it's not. So here are some tips to stop you zigzagging wildly across the river, losing your pole and falling in.
➡ Standing at the back end of the punt, lift the pole out of the water at the side of the punt.
➡ Let the pole slide through your hands to touch the bottom of the river.
➡ Tilt the pole forward (that is, in the direction of travel of the punt) and push down to propel the punt forward.
➡ Twist the pole to free the end from the mud at the bottom of the river, and let it float up and trail behind the punt. You can then use it as a rudder to steer.
➡ If you haven't fallen in yet, raise the pole out of the water and into the vertical position to begin the cycle again.
➡ Hold on to the pole, particularly when passing under Clare Bridge, as students sometimes snatch them for a giggle.

(c AD 100–200), a figurine of Egyptian cat goddess Bastet, splendid Egyptian sarcophagi and mummified animals, plus dazzling illuminated manuscripts. The **upper galleries** showcase works by Leonardo da Vinci, Titian, Rubens, the Impressionists, Gainsborough, Constable, Rembrandt and Picasso; standout works include the tender *Pietà* by Giovanni del Ponte and Salvator Rosa's dark and intensely personal *L'Umana Fragilita*.

The Fitz has a tragic footnote: although begun by George Basevi in 1837, he didn't live to see its completion. While working on Ely Cathedral he stepped back to admire his handiwork, slipped and fell to his death.

One-hour guided tours (£6) of the museum are held at 2.30pm Saturdays.

ROUND CHURCH   CHURCH
(www.christianheritage.org.uk; Bridge St; £2.50; ⊙10am-5pm Tue-Sat, 1.30-4pm Sun) Cambridge's intensely atmospheric Round Church is one of only four such structures in England. It was built by the mysterious Knights Templar in 1130 and shelters an unusual circular nave ringed by chunky Norman pillars. The carved stone faces crowning the pillars bring the 12th century vividly to life.

The church's position on Bridge St reminds you of its original role; that of a chapel for pilgrims crossing the river.

✖ EATING & DRINKING

ESPRESSO LIBRARY   CAFE $
(www.espressolibrary.co.uk; 210 East Rd; mains £6.90-9.50; ⊙7am-6pm Mon-Sat, from 8am Sun; 🎧🍴) A chilled soundtrack and customers with laptops at almost every table signal that this industrial-chic cafe is a student favourite. That'll be partly down to the wholesome food – think frittata with sweet potatoes and spinach, and juicy portobello mushrooms in brioche buns – and partly down to some cracking coffee.

SMOKEWORKS   BARBECUE $$
(www.smokeworks.co.uk; 2 Free School Lane; mains £10-19; ⊙11.45am-10.30pm Mon-Thu, to 11pm Fri & Sat, to 9.30pm Sun; 🎧) This dark, industrial-themed dining spot draws discerning carnivores and local hipsters with its melt-in-your-mouth ribs, wings and wonderfully smoky pulled pork. The service is friendly and prompt, and the salted caramel milkshakes come in a glass the size of your head.

PINT SHOP   MODERN BRITISH $$
(🖉01223-352293; www.pintshop.co.uk; 10 Peas Hill; mains £12.50-25.50; ⊙noon-10pm Mon-Fri, 11am-10.30pm Sat, 11am-10pm Sun) Popular Pint Shop's vision is to embrace eating and drinking equally. To this end, it's both a busy bar specialising in craft beer (10 on keg and six on draft) and a stylish dining room serving classy versions of traditional grub (dry-aged steaks, gin-cured sea trout, charcoal-grilled plaice). All in all, hard to resist.

★MIDSUMMER HOUSE   MODERN BRITISH $$$
(🖉01223-369299; www.midsummerhouse.co.uk; Midsummer Common; 5/8 courses £56.50/120; ⊙noon-1.30pm Wed-Sat, 7-8.30pm Tue-Thu, 6.30-9.30pm Fri & Sat; 🖉) At the region's top table, chef Daniel Clifford's double-Michelin-starred creations are distinguished by depth of flavour and immense technical skill. Sample transformations of coal-baked celeriac, Cornish crab, and roast pigeon with wild garlic, before a sweet pear, blueberry and white chocolate delight.

Wine flights start at £45. Unusually, there are vegetarian versions of both set menus.

★EAGLE   PUB
(www.eagle-cambridge.co.uk; Benet St; ⊙8am-11pm Mon-Sat, to 10.30pm Sun; 🎧🍴) Cambridge's most famous pub has loosened the tongues and pickled the grey cells of many an illustrious academic; among them Nobel Prize–winning scientists Crick and Watson, who discussed their research into DNA here (note the blue plaque by the door). Fifteenth-century, wood-panelled and rambling, the Eagle's cosy rooms include one with WWII airmen's signatures on the ceiling.

The food, served all day, is good too.

Bath

Explore

Britain is littered with beautiful cities, but precious few compare to Bath. Home to some of the nation's grandest Georgian architecture – not to mention one of the world's best-preserved Roman bathhouses – this slinky, sophisticated, snooty city, founded on top of natural hot springs, has been a tourist draw for nigh on 2000 years.

Bath's heyday really began during the 18th century, when local entrepreneur Ralph Allen and his team of father-and-son architects, John Wood the Elder and Younger, turned this sleepy backwater into the toast of Georgian society, and constructed fabulous landmarks such as the Circus and Royal Crescent.

The Best...

➡**Sight** Roman Baths (p338)
➡**Place to Eat** Circus (p340)
➡**Place to Drink** Star Inn (p341)

Getting There & Away

➡**Bus** Bath's **bus and coach station** (Dorchester St) is near the train station.

National Express coaches run direct to London (£33, 3½ hours, eight to 10 daily). Two-hourly services also run to London Heathrow (£27, three hours). Services to many other destinations change at Bristol.

Local buses:

Bristol bus 38/39/X39; £5.50, 50 minutes, four per hour Monday to Saturday, half-hourly on Sunday

Wells bus 173; £5.50, one hour 15 minutes, two per hour Monday to Saturday, hourly Sunday)

➡**Train** Bath Spa station is at the south end of Manvers St. Many services connect through Bristol, including those to the southwest and north of England.

Direct services:

Bristol £7.30, 15 minutes, three per hour
Cardiff Central £20, one hour, hourly
London Paddington £38, 1½ hours, half-hourly
Salisbury £18, one hour, hourly

Need to Know

➡**Area Code** ☑01225
➡**Population** 88,900
➡**Tourist Information** Bath Tourist Office Calls are charged at the premium rate of 50p per minute.

⊙ SIGHTS

★ROMAN BATHS
HISTORIC BUILDING

(☑01225-477785; www.romanbaths.co.uk; Abbey Churchyard; adult/child £15.50/9.80; ☺9.30am-6pm Sep-Jun, 9am-10pm Jul & Aug) In typically ostentatious style, the Romans constructed a complex of bathhouses above Bath's three natural hot springs, which emerge at a steady 46°C (115°F). Situated alongside a temple dedicated to the healing goddess Sulis-Minerva, the baths now form one of the best-preserved ancient Roman spas in the world, and are encircled by 18th- and 19th-century buildings. Bath's premier attraction can get very busy. To dodge the worst of the crowds, avoid weekends, and July and August.

★ROYAL CRESCENT
ARCHITECTURE

Bath is famous for its glorious Georgian architecture, and it doesn't get any grander than this semicircular terrace of majestic town houses overlooking the green sweep of Royal Victoria Park. Designed by John Wood the Younger (1728–82) and built between 1767 and 1775, the houses appear perfectly symmetrical from the outside, but the owners were allowed to tweak the interiors, so no two houses are quite the same. **No 1 Royal Crescent** (☑01225-428126; www.no1royalcrescent.org.uk; adult/child/family £10/4/22; ☺noon-5.30pm Mon, 10.30am-5.30pm Tue-Sun Feb-early Dec) offers you an intriguing insight into life inside.

A walk east along Brock St from the Royal Crescent leads to **The Circus**, a ring of 33 houses divided into three semicircular terraces. Plaques on the houses commemorate famous residents such as Thomas Gainsborough, Clive of India and David Livingstone. The terrace was designed by John Wood the Elder, but he died in 1754, and the terrace was completed by his son in 1768.

To the south along Gravel Walk is the **Georgian Garden** (off Royal Ave; ☺9am-5pm) FREE, restored to resemble a typical 18th-century town-house garden.

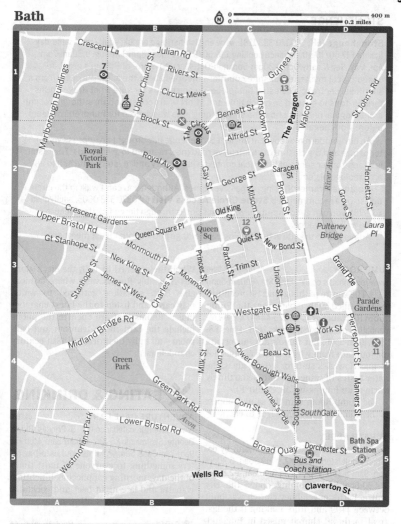

DAY TRIPS FROM LONDON BATH

Bath

◉ Sights
1 Bath Abbey	D3
2 Bath Assembly Rooms	C2
3 Georgian Garden	B2
4 No 1 Royal Crescent	B1
5 Pump Room	C4
6 Roman Baths	D4
7 Royal Crescent	A1
8 The Circus	B2

⊗ Eating
9 Adventure Cafe Bar	C2

10 Circus	B2
Pump Room Restaurant	(see 5)
11 Sotto Sotto	D4

⊖ Drinking & Nightlife
12 Salamander	C3
13 Star Inn	C1

⊕ Sports & Activities
Bath Abbey Tower Tours	(see 1)

STONEHENGE

Stonehenge (EH; ☑0370 333 1181; www.english-heritage.org.uk; adult/child same-day tickets £17.50/10.50, advance booking £16.50/9.90; ⊙9am-8pm Jun-Aug, 9.30am-7pm Apr, May, Sep & early Oct, 9.30am-5pm mid-Oct–Mar; ℗) is one of Britain's great archaeological mysteries: despite countless theories about the site's purpose, from a sacrificial centre to a celestial timepiece, no one knows for sure what drove prehistoric Britons to expend so much time and effort on its construction, although recent archeological findings show the surrounding area was sacred for hundreds of years before work began.

An ultramodern makeover at ancient Stonehenge has brought an impressive visitor centre and the closure of an intrusive road (now restored to grassland). The result is a far stronger sense of historical context, with dignity and mystery returned to an archaeological gem.

A pathway frames the ring of massive stones. Although you can't walk in the circle, unless on a recommended **Stone Circle Access Visit** (☑0370 333 0605; adult/child £32/19), you can get close-up views. Admission is through timed tickets – secure a place well in advance.

Admission to the site is free for English Heritage and National Trust members.

PUMP ROOM   HISTORIC BUILDING

(www.romanbaths.co.uk; Stall St; ⊙10am-5pm) FREE The centre of this grand 19th-century room is filled with tables from the **Pump Room Restaurant** (☑01225-444477; www.romanbaths.co.uk; Stall St; snacks £6-8, dishes £8-12; ⊙10am-5pm), but there's also an ornate spa fountain from which Bath's famous hot springs flow. Ask staff for a (free) glass; the water tastes of minerals and is startlingly warm at an impressive 38°C (100°F).

The Pump Room is in the same complex as the Roman Baths, but is free to enter.

★**BATH ABBEY**   CHURCH

(www.bathabbey.org; Abbey Churchyard; by donation adult/student £4/2; ⊙9.30am-5.30pm Mon, 9am-5.30pm Tue-Fri, to 6pm Sat, 1-2.30pm & 4.30-6pm Sun) Looming above the city centre, Bath's huge abbey church was built between 1499 and 1616, making it the last great medieval church raised in England. Its most striking feature is the west facade, where angels climb up and down stone ladders, commemorating a dream of the founder, Bishop Oliver King.

Tower tours (adult/child £6/3; ⊙11am-4pm Mon-Sat Nov-Mar, 10am-5pm Apr-Aug, 10am-4pm Sep & Oct) leave on the hour from Monday to Friday, and every half-hour on Saturdays.

BATH ASSEMBLY ROOMS   HISTORIC BUILDING

(NT; www.nationaltrust.org.uk; 19 Bennett St; ⊙10.30am-6pm Mar-Oct, to 5pm Nov-Feb) FREE When they opened in 1771, the city's glorious Assembly Rooms were where fashionable Bath socialites gathered to waltz, play cards and listen to the latest chamber music. Rooms that are open to the public include the card room, tearoom and ballroom – all lit by their original 18th-century chandeliers.

✖ EATING & DRINKING

ADVENTURE CAFE BAR   CAFE $

(www.adventurecafebar.co.uk; 5 Princes Bldgs, George St; mains £5-10; ⊙8am-3am Mon-Fri, 9am-3am Sat & Sun; ☑) This cool cafe-bar offers something to everyone at most times of the day: morning cappuccino, lunchtime ciabatta and late-night beer and cocktails. There's great outdoor seating at the back.

★**CIRCUS**   MODERN BRITISH $$

(☑01225-466020; www.thecircusrestaurant.co.uk; 34 Brock St; mains lunch £10-15, dinner £17-21; ⊙10am-midnight Mon-Sat) Chef Ali Golden has turned this bistro into one of Bath's destination addresses. Her taste is for British dishes with a Continental twist, à la the late British food writer Elizabeth David: rabbit, Wiltshire lamb and West Country fish are all infused with herby flavours and rich sauces. It occupies an elegant town house near the Circus. Reservations recommended.

SOTTO SOTTO   ITALIAN $$

(☏01225-330236; www.sottosotto.co.uk; 10
North Pde; mains £10-24.50; ⊘noon-2pm &
5-10pm; ✐) The setting – an artfully lit
vaulted brick chamber – is superb, and the
food matches it for style. Authentic Italian
dishes are likely to include Parma-ham-
wrapped sea bass sautéed in white wine,
and a spicy seafood and Tuscan bean pasta.
Top tip: don't forgo the garlicky sautéed
spinach side.

★STAR INN   PUB

(www.abbeyales.co.uk; 23 The Vineyards, off the
Paragon; ⊘noon-2.30pm & 5.30-11pm Mon-Fri,
noon-midnight Sat, to 10.30pm Sun) Few pubs
are registered relics, but the Star is that,
and it still has many of its 19th-century bar
fittings. It's the brewery tap for Bath-based
Abbey Ales; some ales are served in traditional jugs, and you can even ask for a pinch
of snuff in the 'smaller bar'.

SALAMANDER   PUB

(☏01225-428889; www.bathales.com; 3 John
St; ⊘11am-midnight Mon-Thu, to 1am Fri & Sat,
to 11pm Sun; ☎) Owned by Bath Ales, local
favourite 'the Sally' serves house beers such
as amber Gem and the stronger Wild Hare
Pale Ale. Food is served upstairs in the dining room.

Sleeping

Hanging your hat (or anything else) in London can be painfully expensive, and you'll almost always need to book well in advance. Decent hostels are easy to find but aren't as cheap as you might hope. Hotels range from no-frills chains through to the world's most ritzy establishments, such as the Ritz itself. B&Bs are often better value and more atmospheric than hotels.

Hotels

London has a grand roll call of stately hotels and many are experiences in their own right. Standards at the top end are high, but so are the prices. Quirkiness and individuality can be found in abundance, alongside dyed-in-the-wool traditionalism. While a rung or two down in overall quality and charm, mid-range chain hotels generally offer good locations and dependable comfort. A new trend is for smart hotels with tiny but well-designed rooms and larger communal spaces for spreading out in; prices often start extremely reasonably for these but rise sharply for last-minute bookings. Demand can often outstrip supply – especially on the bottom step of the market – so book ahead, particularly during holiday periods and in summer.

B&Bs

Bed and breakfasts generally come in at a tier below hotels, often promising boutique-style charm and a more personal level of service. Handy B&B clusters appear in Paddington, South Kensington, Victoria and Bloomsbury.

Hostels

Generally the cheapest form of accommodation, hostels can be both an affordable and a sociable option. They vary widely in quality, so choose carefully. Those with a reputation as party hostels can be a lot of fun, but don't expect to get much sleep. As well as dorm rooms, many also offer twin and double rooms, sometimes with en-suite bathrooms. These private rooms are often better than what you'd get for an equivalent price in a budget hotel.

Apartments

If you're in London for a week or more, a short-term or serviced apartment may make sense. They usually come with cooking and laundry facilities, and rates at the bottom end are comparable to a B&B. At the top end are luxurious pads you may never want to leave.

Rates & Booking

Deluxe hotel rooms cost from around £350 per double, but there's good variety at the top end, so you should find a room from about £200 offering superior comfort without the prestige. Some boutique hotels also occupy this bracket. There's a noticeable dip in quality below this price, with notable exceptions. Under £100 and you're at the more serviceable, budget end of the market. Look out for weekend deals that can put a better class of hotel within reach. Rates often slide in winter. Book directly through the hotel website for the best online deals or promotional rates. Hostelling International (HI) members net discounts on YHA accommodation.

Lonely Planet's Top Choices

citizenM Tower of London (p348) Designer digs at reasonable prices with extraordinary views.

Hoxton Hotel (p351) Cool location, nifty looks and very cheap rooms.

South Place (p348) Boutique comfort and cheeky charm.

Hazlitt's (p347) A step back into the Georgian era in the middle of Soho.

40 Winks (p353) Two gorgeously designed rooms in the historic East End.

Best by Budget

£

Qbic (p353) Well-designed little rooms available at a steal if booked early enough.

Clink78 (p354) Heritage hostel in a former magistrates court.

YHA London Oxford Street (p345) Centrally positioned hostel with excellent shared facilities.

££

citizenM Tower of London (p348) Small but perfectly formed rooms, some with killer views.

Hoxton Hotel (p351) Outstanding value for its location and design.

40 Winks (p353) Whimsically decorated boutique B&B in the East End.

£££

Hazlitt's (p347) Old-world elegance in a terrific location.

South Place (p348) Artsy boutique offering on the edge of the City.

Knightsbridge Hotel (p350) Elegant rooms in a 200-year-old house.

Best Hostels

Clink78 (p354) Excellent facilities in an unusual courthouse setting.

YHA London Oxford Street (p345) The smallest and most personable of London's YHAs.

Safestay Holland Park (p355) A bright addition to the only surviving wing of a Jacobean mansion.

St Christopher's Village (p349) Large, newly renovated party hostel.

Safestay London Elephant & Castle (p358) Funky hostel in a Georgian building.

Best Heritage Hotels

Hazlitt's (p347) Immerse yourself in the 1718 ambience and modern comforts.

Ritz London (p346) There's only one Ritz and it reigns supreme.

Corinthia (p346) Victorian jewel in the crown near the seat of power.

The Goring (p346) Delectable slice of classy, classic England.

Brown's Hotel (p347) London's oldest hotel still remains near the top of the heap.

Best B&Bs

40 Winks (p353) Two eccentrically furnished designer rooms.

Barclay House (p356) Ticks every box – and a few more.

Aster House (p350) Great location with charming hosts.

17 Homestead Rd (p355) Two pristine rooms in a Victorian town house.

37 Trevor Square (p350) Chic and spacious rooms in Knightsbridge.

Reservations

➡ To access the best prices, book rooms as far in advance as possible, especially for weekends and holiday periods.

➡ Prices tend to peak at weekends except for business-orientated hotels in the City, where prices usually drop on Friday, Saturday and Sunday nights.

➡ Most hotels will match prices on booking sites if you book directly, and this may come with extra perks such as free breakfast or a later checkout.

Tax

➡ Value-added tax (VAT; 20%) is added to hotel rooms. Hotels almost always include VAT in their advertised rates.

Checking In & Out

➡ Check-in is usually 2pm, though most places will let you check in earlier if your room is available, or at the very least let you leave your luggage. Check-out is usually between 10am and noon.

Breakfast

➡ Breakfast may be included in the room rate. Often this is a continental breakfast; a cooked breakfast might cost extra.

OOD	FOR	AGAINST
t End	Close to main sights; great transport links; wide range of accommodation in all budgets; good restaurants.	Busy tourist areas; expensive.
The City	Near St Paul's and Tower of London; good transport links; handy central location; quality hotels; some cheaper weekend rates.	Very quiet at weekends; a business district so high prices during the week.
The South Bank	Near Tate Modern, London Eye and Southbank Centre; cheaper than West End; excellent pubs and views.	Many chain hotels; choice limited.
Kensington & Hyde Park	Excellent for South Kensington museums and shopping; great accommodation range; stylish area; good transport.	Quite expensive; drinking and nightlife options limited.
Clerkenwell, Shoreditch & Spitalfields	Hip area with great bars and nightlife; excellent for boutique hotels.	Few top sights.
East London	Markets, multicultural feel; great restaurants and traditional pubs.	Limited sleeping options; some areas less safe at night.
North London	Leafy; vibrant nightlife; pockets of village charm; excellent boutique hotels and hostels; great gastropubs; quiet during the week.	Noncentral and away from main sights.
West London	Good shopping, markets and pubs; excellent boutique hotels; good transport.	Pricey; light on top sights.
Greenwich & South London	Great boutique options; leafy escapes; near top Greenwich sights.	Sights spread out beyond Greenwich; transport limited.
Richmond, Kew & Hampton Court	Smart riverside hotels; semirural pockets; quiet; fantastic riverside pubs.	Sights spread out; a long way from central London.

🛏 The West End

SOHOSTEL
HOSTEL £

Map p440 (📞020-8821 5154; www.sohostel.
co.uk; 91 Dean St, W1; dm/tw £25/55; ⊝@🛜;
⊖Tottenham Court Road) Offering a frankly
unbeatable location in the middle of Soho,
this brightly painted establishment offers
spacious, clean rooms and decent communal areas – including a Hawaiian-themed
roof garden and bar, where you can find
locally brewed beer and homemade pizza.

HOXTON HOLBORN
HOTEL £

Map p438 (📞020-7661 3000; http://thehoxton.
com; 199-206 High Holborn, WC1; r £90-260;
✳@🛜; ⊖Holborn) This branch of the Hoxton hotel chain continues the tradition of
offering stylish yet affordable accommodation in 174 rooms that vary enormously in
size and comfort. At the lowest end is the
aptly named Shoebox (a snip from as low as
£90) through Snug and Cosy to the top-end
Roomy, which has a king-size bed. The central location remains the same for all.The
buzzy lobby has computers for guest use,
maps and newspapers. Hubbard & Bell, a
convivial cafe, bar and grill, is also here.

GEORGE HOTEL
B&B £

Map p444 (📞020-7387 8777; www.georgehotel.
com; 58-60 Cartwright Gardens, WC1; s/tw/tr
from £68/95/150, with bathroom £100/150/175;
@🛜; ⊖Russell Sq) Housed in three crescent
town houses dating to around 1810, the
George is a friendly chap, if a tad old-fashioned. There's no lift or air-conditioning,
but there are fans in each of the 40 rooms.
Lone travellers might consider room 26 or
103 with views of the gardens in front.

YHA LONDON OXFORD STREET
HOSTEL £

Map p440 (📞020-7734 1618; www.yha.org.uk/
hostel/london-oxford-street; 14 Noel St, W1; dm
£18-36, tw £50-85; @🛜; ⊖Oxford Circus) The
most central of London's seven YHA hostels is also one of the most intimate with
just 104 beds. The excellent shared facilities include a fuchsia-coloured kitchen and
bright, funky lounge. Dormitories have
three or four beds, and there are doubles
and twins. The in-house shop sells coffee
and beer. Free wi-fi in common areas. The
hostel offers free daily walking tours at
10.30am and a pub crawl at 7pm.

GENERATOR LONDON
HOSTEL £

Map p444 (📞020-7388 7666; www.generatorhos
tels.com/london; 37 Tavistock Pl, WC1; dm/r from
£15/68; ✳🛜; ⊖Russell Sq) With its industrial
lines and funky decor, the huge Generator
(it has more than 870 beds) is one of central London's grooviest budget spots. The
bar, complete with pool tables, stays open
until 3am and there are frequent themed
parties. Dorm rooms have between four and
12 beds; backing it up are twins and triples.

There is no kitchen, but breakfast is provided and the large canteen serves bargain
dinners from £4.50. Public areas are a delight, especially the large TV lounge, with
comfy theatre-style seating.

FIELDING HOTEL
BOUTIQUE HOTEL ££

Map p438 (📞020-7836 8305; www.thefielding
hotel.co.uk; 4 Broad Ct, Bow St, WC2; s/d/q from
£110/170/190; ✳🛜; ⊖Covent Garden) Hidden
away in a pedestrianised court in the heart
of Covent Garden, this pretty, exceptionally friendly 25-room hotel (named after the
novelist Henry Fielding, who lived nearby)
has been furnished to a very high standard:
bathrooms have lovely walk-in showers, and
rooms are beautifully done up and fully
air-conditioned. The hotel doesn't provide
breakfast but the area is full of cafes.

HOTEL LA PLACE
HOTEL ££

Map p446 (📞020-7486 2323; www.hotellaplace.
com; 17 Nottingham Pl, W1; s/d from £115/180;
✳@🛜🛗; ⊖Baker St) The 18 rooms here
are very much in the traditional mode, but
impeccably cared for and have updated
bathrooms. All double rooms have king-
size beds with orthopaedic mattresses, and
the friendly management has installed a
24-hour wine bar on the ground floor and
an ice machine on the 2nd floor. The two-
level suite and connecting rooms are good
for families.

JESMOND HOTEL
B&B ££

Map p444 (📞020-7636 3199; www.jesmondhotel.
org.uk; 63 Gower St, WC1; s £75-95, d £95-125,
tr £140-165, q £150-185, all incl breakfast; @🛜;
⊖Goodge St) The rooms at this popular,
15-room family-run Georgian-era hotel in
Bloomsbury are basic but clean and cheerful (four are with shared bathroom): there's
a small, pretty garden, and the price tag is
very attractive indeed. There's also laundry
service and good breakfasts for kicking off
your London day. Location is highly central.

HARLINGFORD HOTEL
HOTEL ££

Map p444 (☑020-7387 1551; www.harlingford hotel.com; 61-63 Cartwright Gardens, WC1; s/d/ tr £95/135/160; @🐾🖥; ⊖Russell Sq) With a modern interior with lashings of mauve and royal blue and green-tiled bathrooms, this stylish Georgian 43-room hotel in Bloomsbury is arguably the best on a street where competition is fierce. The welcome is always warm and the price unbeatable, but there's lots of stairs and no lift. Room 10 looks on to the tranquil garden.

THE ACADEMY
BOUTIQUE HOTEL ££

Map p444 (☑020-7631 4115; www.theacademy hotel.co.uk; 21 Gower St, WC1; s/d/ste from £140/170/190; 🖥🐾; ⊖Goodge St) This beautiful, terribly English hotel ranges through five Georgian town houses in Bloomsbury. The 49 lovely rooms are kitted out with fluffy feather duvets, elegant furnishings and the latest in creature comforts. A conservatory overlooks a leafy back garden with a fish pond and there's a cosy breakfast room. No lift.

★ZETTER TOWNHOUSE MARYLEBONE
BOUTIQUE HOTEL £££

Map p446 (☑020-7324 4577; www.thezetter townhouse.com/marylebone; 28-30 Seymour St, W1; d from £210, studio £300-520; @🐾; ⊖Marble Arch) We've always loved the Zetter group of hotels and this new boutique number with two dozen rooms only increases our passion. From Seymour's Parlour, a kind of library/lounge lobby named after a fictional 'wicked' uncle, to the comfy back rooms dressed in black and burgundy on the ground floor and above, it's a blend of fusty style, kitsch and good humour.

Superior rooms have four-poster beds with canopies (did we see a Union Flag?) and coffee machines. Lear's Loft is a suite reached by its own staircase.

★BEAUMONT
HOTEL £££

Map p446 (☑020-7499 1001; www.thebeaumont. com; Brown Hart Gardens, W1; d/studio/ste incl breakfast from £495/720/1575; 🖥🐾; ⊖Bond St) A stylish and very handsome smaller-scale luxury hotel, the 73-room Beaumont is all art-deco opulence. Fronted by an arresting stainless-steel-and-oak cuboid sculpture by Antony Gormley called *Room* (which encompasses part of a £1725 per night suite), the striking white building dates from 1926. Rooms and suites are swish and elegant, with a 1920s modernist aesthetic.

Don't miss the iconic American Bar (p126) off the main lobby. Room prices include local drop-offs in the hotel's vintage Daimler.

★ROSEWOOD LONDON
HOTEL £££

Map p438 (☑020-7781 8888; www.rosewood hotels.com/en/london; 252 High Holborn, WC1; d from £440-750, ste £1100-1400; P🖥@🐾🖥; ⊖Holborn) What was once the grand Pearl Assurance building (dating from 1914) now houses the stunning Rosewood hotel, where an artful marriage of period and modern styles thanks to designer Tony Chi can be found in its 262 rooms and 44 suites. British heritage is carefully woven throughout the bar, restaurant, deli, lobby and even the housekeepers' uniforms.

We love Swedish artist Agnetha Sjögren's dog sculpture in the lobby, the (live) house dog and the little metal animals on the guest-room doors.

★HAYMARKET HOTEL
HOTEL £££

Map p438 (☑020-7470 4000; www.firmdale hotels.com/hotels/london/haymarket-hotel; 1 Suffolk Pl, off Haymarket, SW1; r/ste £335/505; 🖥🐾🖥🐾; ⊖Piccadilly Circus) With the trademark colours and lines of hotelier/designer duo Tim and Kit Kemp, the Haymarket is scrumptious, with hand-painted Gournay wallpaper, signature fuchsia and green designs in the 50 different guest rooms, a sensational 18m pool with mood lighting, an exquisite library lounge with honesty bar, and original artwork throughout.

We love the dog silhouettes on the chairs and bar stools in the Brumus Bar, which takes its name from the owner's late pooch.

★RITZ LONDON
LUXURY HOTEL £££

Map p448 (☑020-7493 8181; www.theritzlondon. com; 150 Piccadilly, W1; r/ste from £380/850; P🖥@🐾; ⊖Green Park) What can you say about a hotel that has lent its name to the English lexicon? This 136-room caravanserai has a spectacular position overlooking Green Park and is supposedly the Royal Family's home away from home (it does have a royal warrant from the Prince of Wales and is very close to the palace). All rooms have Louis XVI–style interiors and antique furniture. Various formal-dress and smart-casual codes (shirt and tie) apply in some of the hotel's outlets. For stunning cocktails in art-deco opulence, take a seat in the Rivoli Bar (p121).

★**DORSET SQUARE HOTEL** HOTEL **£££**

Map p446 (☎020-77237874; www.firmdalehotels.com/hotels/london/dorset-square-hotel; 39-40 Dorset Sq, NW1; s/d from £200/265; ❄️☎️; ⊖Baker St) Two combined Regency town houses form this gorgeous 38-room Firmdale Hotel overlooking leafy Dorset Sq, where Lord's Old Ground was laid in 1787 (which explains the cricket memorabilia in glass cases in the lobby and cricket-ball doorknobs). Bright and breezy guest rooms are snazzily attired with modern, eye-catching fabrics and snappy designs. Wonderful service.

Room 15 on the ground floor has its own little patio giving on to Gloucester Pl. The in-house restaurant, the **Potting Shed** (mains £16.50 to £24.50), is a cut above.

★**COVENT GARDEN HOTEL** BOUTIQUE HOTEL **£££**

Map p438 (☎020-78061000; www.firmdalehotels.com/hotels/london/covent-garden-hotel;10 Monmouth St, WC2; d/ste from £335/550; ❄️☎️; ⊖Covent Garden) This gorgeous and discreet 58-room boutique hotel housed in a former French hospital features antiques, gorgeous, bright fabrics and quirky bric-a-brac to mark its individuality. There's an excellent bar-restaurant off the lobby and two stunning guest lounges with fireplaces (note the beautiful marquetry desk) on the 1st floor, which come into their own in the winter. Rooms on the ground floor (like room 5) are larger and have higher ceilings.

★**LONDON EDITION** HOTEL **£££**

Map p444 (☎020-7781 0000; www.editionhotels.com/london; 10 Berners St, W1; d/ste from £375/900; ❄️☎️; ⊖Tottenham Court Rd) Step into the lobby of the London Edition and you're greeted by a stunning combination of old and new – from the stucco ceiling hangs an Ingo Maurer pendulum, reflecting the ornate surrounds in all directions. The 173 wood-panelled rooms are uncomplicated, with mid-century elements and faux-fur throws.

All the rooms are adorned by photographic portraits of Dutch photographer Hendrik Kerstens' daughter Paula in myriad poses inspired by Holland's Golden Age in the 17th century.

THE GORING HOTEL **£££**

Map p448 (☎020-7396 9000; www.thegoring.com; Beeston Pl, SW1; r/ste from £430/1340; ❄️☎️; ⊖Victoria) Kate Middleton spent her last night as a commoner in the Royal Suite (£8400 per night) before joining the Royal Family, propelling the Goring into an international media glare. Glistening with chandeliers, sumptuous furnishings and overseen by highly professional staff, this family-owned hotel with 61 rooms is a grand, albeit highly relaxed, slice of Englishness, with a delightful garden.

ME LONDON HOTEL **£££**

Map p438 (☎020-7395 3400; www.melia.com/en/hotels/united-kingdom/london/me-london; 336-337 The Strand; d £285-375, ste from £525; 🅿️❄️☎️; ⊖Temple, Covent Garden) The Foster + Partners–designed 157-room ME London at the southwestern curve where the Strand meets Aldwych is all sophisticated and natty cool. All rooms – also designed by Foster + Partners – are super-neat, ultramodern and classy, with dizzy-making floor-to-ceiling windows. The Radio Rooftop Bar (p124) also has some of the best views in town from its alfresco terrace. Terrace rooms on the 8th and 9th floors come with balcony.

CORINTHIA HOTEL **£££**

Map p448 (☎020-7930 8181; www.corinthia.com; Whitehall Place, SW1; d/ste £425/1380; ❄️☎️🏊; ⊖Embankment) With hotels from Malta to St Petersburg, the Corinthia group's crown jewel is this grand Victorian property in Whitehall. It's as smart as can be, but never overbearing and stuffy. A stay here is a delight, with perfect rooms (total: 297), flawless service, tempting afternoon tea and a location that ensconces you at the very heart, but just beyond the bustle of London.

GRAZING GOAT HOTEL **£££**

Map p446 (☎020-7724 7243; www.thegrazinggoat.co.uk; 6 New Quebec St, W1; d £210-250; ☎️; ⊖Marble Arch) On an attractive little street lined with boutiques and cafes, this upmarket pub (ground floor) and dining room (1st floor) has eight tasteful rooms in a contemporary country style with wood-panelled walls painted teal and bird prints throughout. All rooms have king-size beds, vintage-style DAB radios and iPod docks. Superior rooms are larger with bigger beds, bathtubs and fans.

NADLER SOHO BOUTIQUE HOTEL **£££**

Map p440 (☎020-3697 3697; www.nadlerhotels.com/the-nadler-soho.html; 10 Carlisle St, W1; s £180, d £190-320, ste £400; ❄️@☎️; ⊖Tottenham Court Rd) In the heart of Soho, this

78-room boutique hotel is a sleek mix of creams, tans and blacks, with a good range of rooms, all with mini kitchens complete with microwave and fridge. Service is welcoming and smooth; guests are offered discounts at nearby bars and restaurants. Hew Locke's sculpture *Selene* above the entrance represents, appropriately enough, 'sleep'.

SAVOY HOTEL £££

Map p438 (020-7836 4343; www.fairmont.com/savoy; The Strand, WC2; r £485-700, ste from £895; P ❄ 🛜 🏊; ⊖Charing Cross) A night surrounded by the Edwardian and art-deco grandeur of the iconic Savoy is never a casual choice, considering the price, but as one of life's treats you can't go wrong. The £220 million refit has put fizz back into this classic, and it's all here: river views, 265 sumptuous rooms, pre-eminent restaurants and the much-loved American Bar (p126).

HAZLITT'S HISTORIC HOTEL £££

Map p440 (020-7434 1771; www.hazlittshotel.com; 6 Frith St, W1; s/d/ste from £200/230/600; ❄ 🛜; ⊖Tottenham Court Rd) Built in 1718 and comprising four original Georgian houses, this Soho gem was the one-time home of essayist William Hazlitt (1778–1830). The 30 guest rooms have been furnished with original antiques from the appropriate era and boast a profusion of seductive details, including panelled walls, mahogany four-poster beds, antique desks, Oriental carpets, sumptuous fabrics and fireplaces in every room.

CLARIDGE'S LUXURY HOTEL £££

Map p446 (020-7629 8860; www.claridges.co.uk; Brook St, W1; r/ste from £450/780; P ❄ @ 🛜 🐾; ⊖Bond St) Claridge's, with 203 rooms, is one of London's iconic five-star hotels. Celebrated for its sumptuous art-deco features (including 1930s vintage furniture that once graced the staterooms of the decommissioned SS *Normandie*), it has recently added a more modern touch with a series of rooms and suites designed by David Linley, the Queen's nephew.

SOHO HOTEL HOTEL £££

Map p440 (020-7559 3000; www.firmdalehotels.com/hotels/london/the-soho-hotel; 4 Richmond Mews, W1; r/ste from £380/585; P ❄ 🛜; ⊖Oxford Circus) The hip Soho has all the hallmarks of the eclectically chic duo Tim and Kit Kemp writ large over 91 individually fashioned guest rooms, each light-filled with floor-to-ceiling windows. Colours are soft, yet vivacious and creative, and the loving attention to design extends to a stunning black cat sculpture by Fernando Botero at the entrance.

BROWN'S HOTEL HOTEL £££

Map p448 (020-7493 6020; www.roccofortehotels.com/hotels-and-resorts/browns-hotel; 30 Albemarle St, W1; r/ste from £500/2000; ❄ 🛜 🐾; ⊖Green Park) London's oldest hostelry, this landmark hotel was created in 1837 from 11 town houses. Each of the 115 rooms has been individually decorated by designer Olga Polizzi, and many feature antiques and original artworks. The public areas are lovely: the traditional **English Tea Room** is all Edwardian oak panelling and working fireplaces while the **Donovan Bar** has a stunning 19th-century stained-glass window.

WALDORF HILTON HISTORIC HOTEL £££

Map p438 (020-7836 2400; www.hilton.co.uk/waldorf; Aldwych, WC2; r from £310; ❄ 🛜 🏊 🐾; ⊖Temple, Covent Garden) The glorious Edwardian splendour of this renovated old pile dating to 1908 still lives on in the heritage-listed Palm Court. The rooms feature some very contemporary designs, but the hotel is working hard to make the best of its heritage and anecdote-filled history, with its tea dances, historic tours, a pianist in the reception area, and a Louis XVI–style restaurant, Homage. Great swimming pool too.

BOOKING WEBSITES

Visit London (www.visitlondon.com) Huge range of listings from the city's official tourism portal.

London Town (www.londontown.com) Excellent last-minute offers on boutique hotels and B&Bs.

Alastair Sawdays (www.sawdays.co.uk) Hand-picked selection of boltholes in the capital.

Lonely Planet (www.lonelyplanet.com/london) Hundreds of properties.

ONE ALDWYCH
HOTEL **£££**

Map p438 (☑020-7300 1000; www.onealdwych. co.uk; 1 Aldwych, WC2; d £270-500, ste £520-1500; P✻☎✉; ☻Covent Garden) Housed in former art-nouveau-style newspaper offices (1907), One Aldwych is an upbeat hotel with tasteful artworks throughout. The 105 spacious and stylish rooms are replete with raw silk curtains, natural tones, daily fresh flowers and huge bathtubs. The circular suites (like suite 200) have fabulous views of the Strand, the Thames and Waterloo Bridge from two windows.

🛏 The City

LONDON ST PAUL'S YHA
HOSTEL **£**

Map p450 (☑020-7236 4965; www.yha.org.uk/ hostel/london-st-pauls; 36 Carter Lane, EC4; dm/ tw/d from £18/65/89; @☎; ☻St Paul's) Housed in the former boarding school for St Paul's Cathedral choir boys, this 213-bed hostel has notable period features, including Latin script in a band around the exterior. There's no kitchen, no lift and no en-suite rooms, but there is a comfortable lounge and a cafe.

★ CITIZENM TOWER OF LONDON
DESIGN HOTEL **££**

Map p450 (☑020-3519 4830; www.citizenm.com; 40 Trinity Sq, EC3; r from £125; ✻@☎; ☻Tower Hill) Downstairs it looks like a rich hipster's living room, with well-stocked bookshelves, kooky art, Beefeater knick-knacks and lots of work space. Rooms are compact but well-designed, with an iPad to open the curtains, control the TV and adjust the shower lighting. It's worth paying an extra £30 for the extraordinary Tower views, although they're even better from the 7th-floor bar.

APEX LONDON WALL
HOTEL **££**

Map p450 (☑020-7562 3030; www.apexhotels. co.uk; 7-9 Copthall Ave, EC2; r from £152; ✻☎; ☻Bank) Given its position right at the heart of the financial district, it's unsurprising that this upmarket hotel feels a tad corporate. On the upside, the staff are delightful, the rooms are extremely comfortable, there's a small gym, prices drop substantially on the weekends, and you even get to take a rubber ducky home with you.

MOTEL ONE LONDON – TOWER HILL
HOTEL **££**

Map p450 (☑020-7481 6420; www.motel-one. com; 24-26 Minories, EC3; s/d from £98/113;

✻☎; ☻Aldgate) Part of a German chain, this almost budget option is just a short hop from the Tower of London. The 290 rooms are small but fully equipped, with a sleek contemporary design. If you feel a little cramped, there's a large, stylish lounge bar downstairs.

★ SOUTH PLACE
BOUTIQUE HOTEL **£££**

Map p450 (☑020-3503 0000; www.southplace hotel.com; 3 South Pl, EC2; d/ste from £232/740; ✻☎; ☻Moorgate) A hip, design-led boutique hotel, South Place impresses at every turn. From the art-filled lobby and espionage-inspired theme (a Russian spy ring was once located in this area) to the Michelin-starred seafood restaurant and 80 beautifully laid-out rooms – every detail has been carefully considered. There are even cheeky hangover and sex kits alongside the British products in the luxurious minibar.

CHEVAL THREE QUAYS
APARTMENT **£££**

Map p450 (☑020-3725 5333; www.chevalresi dences.com; 40 Lower Thames St, EC3; apt from £369; ✻☎; ☻Tower Hill) Positioned right on the doorstep of the Tower of London, these elegant, spacious, modern apartments have all the comforts of home, including full kitchen and laundry facilities. Those facing south have small balconies, providing the perfect perch for afternoon gin and tonics with extraordinary river views.

ANDAZ LIVERPOOL STREET
HOTEL **£££**

Map p450 (☑020-7961 1234; https://londonliver-poolstreet.andaz.hyatt.com; 40 Liverpool St, EC2; r £295; ✻☎; ☻Liverpool St) Built as the Great Eastern Hotel in 1884, this is the London flagship for Hyatt's Andaz chain. There's no reception, just black-clad staff who check you in on iPads. Splashes of red add zing to the spacious, elegant rooms, and there are three restaurants, two bars, a pub, a health club and a Masonic temple hidden in the basement.

🛏 The South Bank

ST CHRISTOPHER'S VILLAGE
HOSTEL **£**

Map p452 (☑020-7939 9710; www.st-christophers. co.uk; 163 Borough High St, SE1; dm/r incl breakfast from £11.40/50; ☎; ☻London Bridge) This 230-bed party-zone hostel has new bathrooms, fresh paint, pod beds with privacy curtains, reading lights, power sockets (British and European) and USB ports, and refurbished common areas. Its two bars, Belushi's and Dugout, are perennially popular. Dorms have four to 33 beds (following the introduction of triple bunks); breakfast and linen are included.

The hotel was about to embark on a big expansion when we visited, with capacity doubling by 2018. Oasis, the female-only wing of the hostel, is very popular, with dorms of up to 12 beds.

WALRUS
HOSTEL £

Map p452 (☎020-7928 4368; www.thewalrus barandhostel.com; 172 Westminster Bridge Rd, SE1; dm incl breakfast £16-30; ☎; ⊖Waterloo) This little hostel gets top marks for trying so hard (and succeeding!) at creating a welcoming, individual, friendly and cosy hostel in the big smoke. The corridors and stairs are on the shabby side but the dorms (sleeping from four to 22) and bathrooms are spick and span. The downside is the noise from the street and railway, but at this price...

★CITIZENM
BOUTIQUE HOTEL ££

Map p452 (☎020-3519 1680; www.citizenm. com/london-bankside; 20 Lavington St, SE1; r £109-249; ❋@☎; ⊖Southwark) If citizenM had a motto, it would be 'Less fuss, more comfort'. The hotel has done away with things it considers superfluous (room service, reception, heaps of space) and instead has gone all out on mattresses and bedding (heavenly super-king-sized beds), state-of-the-art technology (everything from mood lighting to TV is controlled through a tablet computer) and superb decor.

SHANGRI-LA HOTEL
AT THE SHARD
HOTEL £££

Map p452 (☎020-7234 8000; www.shangri-la. com/london/shangrila; 31 St Thomas St, SE1; d/ ste from £400/750; ❋@☎☎; ⊖London Bridge) Unsurprisingly for a hotel occupying levels 34 to 52 of the Shard, there are breathtaking views everywhere you look in the Shangri-La: be it the floor-to-ceiling windows in the bedrooms, the panoramic bathrooms (you've never had such a good view while having a bath), the Skypool, the bar or the restaurant. The decor is a stylish blend of Chinese-influenced and modern.

The Shard's tapering shape puts the suites on lower floors, and each guest room is slightly different in design. Rooms are the latest cry in comfort and technology, with Nespresso coffee machines, iPod docking

stations, a pillow menu and Washlet toilets (with a mind-boggling array of options).

🛏 Kensington & Hyde Park

MEININGER
HOSTEL £

Map p455 (☎020-3318 1407; www.meininger-hostels.com; Baden Powell House, 65-67 Queen's Gate, SW7; dm £16-50, s/tw from £60/70; ❋@☎; ⊖Gloucester Rd or South Kensington) Housed in the late-1950s Baden Powell House opposite the Natural History Museum, this 48-room German-run 'city hostel and hotel' has spick-and-span rooms – most are dorms of between four and 12 beds, with podlike showers. There is also a handful of private rooms. It has good security and nice communal facilities, including a bar and a big roof terrace, plus a fantastic location.

ASTOR HYDE PARK
HOSTEL £

Map p455 (☎020-7581 0103; www.astorhostels. com; 191 Queen's Gate, SW7; dm/d from £19/60; @☎; ⊖Gloucester Rd or High St Kensington) Wood-panelled walls, bay windows with leaded lights, plus a 19th-century vibe and a posh address just over from the Royal Albert Hall. This hostel has 150 beds in rooms over five floors (no lift), including dorms with five to 12 beds, and a good kitchen and spacious lounge. The hostel only accepts guests between the ages of 18 and 40.

All-you-can-eat breakfast is £1.

CHERRY COURT HOTEL
B&B £

Map p455 (☎020-7828 2840; www.cherry courthotel.co.uk; 23 Hugh St, SW1; s/d/tr/f £65/75/110/135; ❋@☎; ⊖Victoria) The brightly coloured rooms may be pocket-sized, but they're clean and tidy at this five-floor Victorian house hotel (no lift). Rates are very attractive for this part of town. The heartfelt welcome from the (responsive) Patel family is a real bonus, as is the handy breakfast basket (fresh fruit, cereal bar and fruit juice), which you can eat in or take away.

37 TREVOR SQUARE
B&B ££

Map p455 (☎020-7823 8186; www.37trevor square.co.uk; 37 Trevor Sq, SW7; s/d £120/200; ☎; ⊖Knightsbridge) Finding the cosy town house of 37 Trevor Square in the real-estate hot spot of Knightsbridge is a genuine discovery. Rooms are chic, homely and rather spacious, especially the lower-ground double. Serving breakfast in her glorious kitchen overlooking Trevor Sq, Margaret has lived in the area for years and has plenty of tips to offer. There's no lift.

LIME TREE HOTEL   BOUTIQUE HOTEL ££

Map p455 (☑020-7730 8191; www.limetreehotel. co.uk; 135-137 Ebury St, SW1; s incl breakfast £120-160, d & tw £180-210, tr £230; @ ☎; ⊖Victoria) Family-run for over three decades, this beautiful 25-bedroom Georgian town house hotel is all comfort, British designs and understated elegance. Rooms are individually decorated, many with open fireplaces and sash windows, but some are smaller than others, so enquire. There is a lovely back garden for late-afternoon rays (picnics encouraged on summer evenings). Rates include a hearty full-English breakfast. No lift.

★NUMBER SIXTEEN   HOTEL ££

Map p455 (☑020-7589 5232; www.firmdale hotels.com/hotels/london/number-sixteen; 16 Sumner Pl, SW7; s from £192, d £240-396; ❄ @ ☎ ⫯; ⊖South Kensington) With uplifting splashes of colour, choice art and a sophisticated-but-fun design ethos, Number Sixteen is simply ravishing. There are 41 individually designed rooms, a cosy drawing room and a fully stocked library. And wait till you see the idyllic, long back garden set around a fountain, or sit down for breakfast in the light-filled conservatory. Great amenities for families.

KNIGHTSBRIDGE HOTEL   HOTEL £££

Map p455 (☑020-7584 6300; www.firmdale hotels.com/hotels/london/knightsbridge-hotel; 10 Beaufort Gardens, SW3; s/d/ste from £258/270/462; ❄ @ ☎ ⫯; ⊖Knightsbridge) A gorgeous six-floor peach, the 44-room Knightsbridge occupies a 200-year-old house on a quiet, no-through-traffic, tree-lined street. Each room is different, with elegant and beautiful interiors finished in a sumptuous, subtle and modern English style. The hotel goes out of its way to cater to children with board games, London activity books, kiddy cutlery and a kids' menu.

ASTER HOUSE   B&B £££

Map p455 (☑020-7581 5888; www.asterhouse. com; 3 Sumner Pl, SW7; s £180, d £240-375; ❄ @ ☎; ⊖South Kensington) The trump cards of this Victorian town house in South Kensington are its location and the charming welcome of its hosts. The plant-filled Orangerie is an atmospheric place for breakfast, but the standard of the decor is rather underwhelming for the price. Continental buffet breakfast included.

ARTIST RESIDENCE   BOUTIQUE HOTEL £££

Map p455 (☑020-78286684; www.artistresidence london.co.uk; 52 Cambridge St, SW1; r £180-350; ❄ ☎; ⊖Pimlico or Victoria) It's not cheap, but this superbly distinctive boutique Pimlico hotel elevates the concept of shabby chic to new heights: sporadic bare brick and each piece of furniture and decor individually sourced and crafted, from the reclaimed parquet floors and vintage furniture to retro Smeg fridges. All rooms have rainforest showers – for grand free-standing baths, upgrade to the suites.

BEAUFORT HOUSE   APARTMENT £££

Map p455 (☑020-7584 2600; www.beaufort house.co.uk; 45 Beaufort Gardens, SW3; 1-4 bedroom apt £443-1350; ❄ ☎; ⊖Knightsbridge) Run by very helpful, friendly and welcoming staff, these stylish, comfortable and fully equipped serviced apartments in a grand building on a quiet cul-de-sac off Brompton Rd are ideally located for the breathless shopping vortex of Knightsbridge. Free access to a nearby health club; no minimum stay requirement outside high season.

AMPERSAND HOTEL   BOUTIQUE HOTEL £££

Map p455 (☑020-7589 5895; www.ampersand hotel.com; 10 Harrington Rd, SW7; s £170-192, d £216-360; ❄ @ ☎; ⊖South Kensington) It feels light, fresh and bubbly in the Ampersand, where smiling staff wear denims and waistcoats rather than impersonal dark suits. The common rooms are colourful and airy, and the stylish rooms are decorated with wallpaper designs celebrating the nearby arts and sciences of South Kensington's museums.

LEVIN HOTEL   HOTEL £££

Map p455 (☑020-7589 6286; www.thelevinhotel. co.uk; 28 Basil St, SW3; r incl breakfast from £285-345, ste £435; P ❄ @ ☎; ⊖Knightsbridge) The luxury 12-room Levin is a bijou boutique gem. Attention to detail (US, EU, UK and Asian sockets in every room, Nespresso coffee machines, fine Egyptian linen, underfloor heating in bathrooms, iPads on request), exquisite design and highly hospitable service create a delightful stay. The gorgeous continental buffet breakfast is complimentary. The car park is £40 per day.

LANESBOROUGH
HOTEL £££

Map p455 (☏020-7259 5599; www.lanesborough. com; Hyde Park Corner, SW1; r from £490; P ❋ @ �; ⊖Hyde Park Corner) Where visiting divas doze and foreign royalty hang their crowns, this former hospital (St George's) boasts 93 lavishly appointed guest rooms and suites, and exudes a regal opulence. All guests receive personal round-the-clock butlers, and staff are impeccably turned out in bowler hats and morning suits. The hotel opened a brand-new luxury spa in 2017.

GORE
HOTEL £££

Map p455 (☏020-7584 6601; www.gorehotel. com; 190 Queen's Gate, SW7; r from £195; P ❋ �; ⊖Gloucester Rd) With obliging staff in tails, twinkling chandeliers, walls crowded with framed portraits and prints, and enough wood-panelling to put paid to a sizeable chunk of prime woodland, this fantastic 50-room hotel wallows in old England charm. The suites are especially lavish (Judy Garland aficionados can sleep on her bed – shipped over from the US – in her namesake suite). Rolling Stones fans won't feel left out either – they can celebrate the *Beggars Banquet* album launch in the bar where it happened.

BLAKES
HOTEL £££

Map p455 (☏020-7370 6701; www.blakeshotels. com; 33 Roland Gardens, SW7; d from £384; ❋ @ ⓢ; ⊖Gloucester Rd or South Kensington) Five Victorian houses cobbled into one hotel and incomparably designed by Anouska Hempel, Blakes oozes panache. Each of its 45 guest rooms is elegantly decked out in a distinctive, flamboyant style: expect four-poster beds (with and without canopies), rich fabrics, plenty of Asian influences, and antiques set on bleached hardwood floors.

For that extra bit of privacy and comfort, there's an 18th-century mews house, priced accordingly.

🛏 Clerkenwell, Shoreditch & Spitalfields

★HOXTON HOTEL
HOTEL ££

Map p458 (☏020-7550 1000; www.hoxtonhotels. com; 81 Great Eastern St, EC2; r £69-259; ❋ ⓢ; ⊖Old St) In the heart of hip Shoreditch, this sleek hotel takes the low-cost airline approach to selling its rooms – book long enough ahead and you might pay just £69. The 210 renovated rooms are small but stylish, with flat-screen TVs, desks, fridges with complimentary bottled water and milk, and breakfast (orange juice, granola, yoghurt and banana) in a bag delivered to your door.

★CITIZENM
DESIGN HOTEL ££

Map p458 (www.citizenm.com; 6 Holywell Lane, EC2A; r from £119; @ ⓢ; ⊖Shoreditch High St) citizenM's winning combination of awesome interior design and a no-nonsense approach to luxury (yes to king-sized beds and high-tech pod rooms; no to pillow chocolates and room service) is right at home in hipster Shoreditch. Room rates are just right, and the convivial lounge/bar/reception downstairs always seems to be on the right side of busy.

HUB
HOTEL ££

Map p458 (www.hubhotels.co.uk; 86 Brick Lane, E1; r £60-150; ❋ ⓢ; ⊖Liverpool St) Hub is a boon for travellers on a budget: rooms really are small but they have everything you need and are done in a breezy, clever design with a zingy lime-and-white colour scheme that doesn't make them feel oppressive. By trading internal space, you'll be rewarded with a phenomenal location, comfy beds, good wi-fi and even a small desk.

MALMAISON
BUSINESS HOTEL ££

Map p458 (☏020-3750 9402; www.malmaison. com; 18-21 Charterhouse Sq, EC1M; r £109-400; ❋ ⓢ; ⊖Farringdon) Facing a leafy square in Clerkenwell, this chic 97-room hotel in a converted nurses' home has been given a total refit and now revels in understated 1970s chic. The cocktail bar in the reconfigured lobby is a centre of continental cool and the luminous subterranean restaurant is a delight. Prices vary considerably and can be much cheaper at weekends.

★ZETTER TOWNHOUSE
BOUTIQUE HOTEL £££

Map p458 (www.thezettertownhouse.com; 49-50 St John's Sq, EC1V; r/ste from £221/380; ❋ ⓢ; ⊖Farringdon) The 13 rooms in this elegant Georgian town house are uniquely decorated in period style, but with witty touches, such as headboards made from reclaimed fairground carousels, and garish colour schemes. Rooms aren't huge, but what it lacks in size it definitely makes up for in personality and charm. The exquisite cocktail lounge (p215) downstairs (which doubles as a breakfast room) is another reason to stay.

★ FOX & ANCHOR   BOUTIQUE HOTEL £££

Map p458 (☑020-7250 1300; www.foxandanchor. com; 115 Charterhouse St, EC1; r/ste from £169/199; 🛜; ⊖Farringdon or Barbican) A characterful option in a handy location above a glorious pub, this delightful hotel offers just six small but sumptuous rooms, each individually decorated and many with roll-top zinc bathtubs. For the ultimate luxury, choose the Market Suite, which has a king-sized bed and its own private rooftop terrace.

You can have breakfast in the splendid Fox & Anchor pub downstairs, which is legendary for its meat-charged City Boy Breakfast (£19.50). Vegetarians fear not: there are plenty of lovely egg variations, as well as yoghurt and porridge.

★ ROOKERY   HERITAGE HOTEL £££

Map p458 (☑020-7336 0931; www.rookeryhotel. com; 12 Peter's Lane, Cowcross St, EC1; d/ste from £209/419; ❄🛜; ⊖Farringdon) This charming warren of 33 rooms has been built within a row of 18th-century Georgian houses and fitted out with period furniture (including a museum-piece collection of Victorian baths, showers and toilets), original wood panelling shipped over from Ireland and artwork selected personally by the owner. Highlights: the small courtyard garden, and the library with its honesty bar and working fireplace.

ACE HOTEL   HOTEL £££

Map p458 (☑020-7613 9800; www.acehotel.com/ london; 100 Shoreditch High St, E1; r £175-600; ❄🛜❄; ⊖Shoreditch High St) Part of a small, seriously hip US chain, this hotel prides itself on creating a relaxed atmosphere while maintaining exacting standards. From the guitars, turntables and record libraries in the deluxe rooms to the Pot Noodles and Yorkshire tea in the minibar, there's a real sense of fun, although it must be said that the aesthetic is rather masculine.

The hotel's restaurant (Hoi Polloi), cafe (Bulldog Edition) and basement bar (Miranda) are destinations in their own right, and the popular lobby offers a space to sit, with free wi-fi available to all. The hotel also has four complimentary bikes for guests to use.

SHOREDITCH ROOMS   BOUTIQUE HOTEL £££

Map p458 (☑020-7739 5040; www.shoreditch house.com/hotel; Shoreditch House, Ebor St, E2; r £175-325; ❄🛜❄; ⊖Shoreditch High St) Part of a private members' club but with rooms available to all, Shoreditch Rooms is quite upfront about the size of its 26 rooms, categorising them as tiny, small and small-plus. Each room is freshly decorated in a vaguely Cape Cod style, with light-grey wood panelling and sparkly white linen. Small-plus rooms have amazing balconies.

Guests get to use the gorgeous rooftop heated pool and gym. The sumptuous Cowshed products in the guest rooms are made at the group's Babington House estate in Somerset.

ZETTER HOTEL   BOUTIQUE HOTEL £££

Map p458 (☑020-7324 4444; www.thezetter. com; 86-88 Clerkenwell Rd, EC1; d from £210, studio £300-438; ❄🛜🏠; ⊖Farringdon) 🐾 The Zetter Hotel is a temple of cool minimalism with an overlay of colourful kitsch on Clerkenwell's main thoroughfare. Built using sustainable materials on the site of a derelict office, its 59 rooms are relatively spacious for the area. The rooftop studios are the real treat, with terraces commanding superb views. There is a hot-drink station on every floor for guest use.

🛏 East London

WOMBAT'S CITY HOSTEL   HOSTEL £

Map p461 (☑020-7680 7600; www.wombats-hostels.com/london; 7 Dock St, E1; dm/d £25/116; ⊖@🛜🏠; ⓤTower Hill) An ideal base to explore London's East End, this hostel offers light and airy budget accommodation in a historical setting. With its vaulted brick ceiling, the bar has a cosy atmosphere; the terrace, complete with hammocks, is ideal for lazy summer evenings.

LUXURY INN   GUESTHOUSE £

Map p461 (☑020-7683 3056; www.theluxuryinn. com; 156 Tottenham Rd, N1; r from £85; ❄❄; ⊖Dalston Junction) There are only four bedrooms in this modern conversion of a small brick warehouse, situated on a pleasant tree-lined street that's surprisingly close to bustling, grimy Kingsland Rd. There's no reception or owners on site, but there's a spacious communal lounge and kitchen, and Netflix in each of the bright and airy rooms.

QBIC

DESIGN HOTEL £

Map p461 (☏020-3021 3300; www.qbichotels.com; 42 Adler St, E1; r from £54; ❄☎; ⊖Aldgate East) ✎ There's a modern feel to this snappy hotel, with white tiling, neon signs, and vibrant art and textiles. Rooms are sound-insulated, mattresses excellent and rainforest showers powerful. Prices vary widely depending on when you book, and the cheapest are windowless.

AVO

HOTEL £

Map p461 (☏020-3490 5061; www.avohotel.com; 82 Dalston Lane, E8; r from £79; ❄☎; ⊖Dalston Junction) Positioned above a restaurant on traffic-clogged Dalston Lane, this family-run boutique hotel is a surprising find. It has just six rooms, all with mango-wood furnishings, gleaming black-and-grey bathrooms, memory-foam mattresses, iPod docks and Elemis toiletries. Double-glazing keeps things quiet.

★40 WINKS

B&B ££

Map p461 (☏020-7790 0259; www.40winks.org; 109 Mile End Rd, E1; s/d/ste £120/195/295; ☎; ⊖Stepney Green) Short on space but not on style, this 300-year-old town house in Stepney Green oozes quirky charm. There are just two bedrooms (a double and a compact single) which share a bathroom – or you can book both as a spacious suite. Owned by a successful designer, the rooms are uniquely and extravagantly decorated with an expert's eye. Book far ahead.

TOWN HALL HOTEL
& APARTMENTS

HOTEL ££

Map p461 (☏020-7871 0460; www.townhallhotel.com; Patriot Sq, E2; r from £172; ❄☎⊠; ⊖Bethnal Green) Set in a former Edwardian town hall (1910) updated with art-deco features in the 1930s, this 97-room hotel

was the council's headquarters until 1965. The design aesthetic of the hotel combines these eras beautifully, with the addition of cutting-edge contemporary art by London-based artists. Each room has quirks from the original structure, and the apartments are extremely well equipped.

🛏 North London

★CLINK78

HOSTEL £

Map p466 (☏020-7183 9400; www.clinkhostels.com/london/clink78; 78 King's Cross Rd, WC1; dm/r incl breakfast from £16/65; @☎; ⊖King's Cross St Pancras) This fantastic 630-bed hostel is housed in a 19th-century magistrates courthouse where Charles Dickens once worked as a scribe and members of the Clash stood trial in 1978. It features pod beds (including overhead storage space) in four- to 16-bed dormitories. There's a top kitchen with a huge dining area and a busy bar – Clash – in the basement.

Parts of the hostel are heritage listed, including six cells that have been converted into bedrooms and a pair of wood-panelled court rooms used as a cinema and internet room. There are all-female dorms. You'll find an ATM and change machine conveniently placed in the lobby. Linen and breakfast included: toast and spreads, cereal, juice, tea and coffee (7am to 10.30am).

CLINK261

HOSTEL £

Map p466 (☏020-7183 9400; www.clinkhostels.com/london/clink261; 261 Grays Inn Rd, WC1; dm/r incl breakfast from £13/65; @☎; ⊖King's Cross St Pancras) A 170-bed hostel with bright, funky dorms that sleep four to 18; good bathrooms; bunk beds fitted with a privacy panel; and individual lockers for valuables. There's a great self-catering kitchen and a

---

FEW-FRILLS CHAINS

London has various discount hotel chains that offer clean and modern – if somewhat institutional – accommodation for reasonable rates.

Days Hotel (www.daysinn.co.uk) Just two branches in central London.

easyHotel (www.easyhotel.com) Functional, with orange-moulded-plastic rooms, some without windows; seven branches in London.

Express by Holiday Inn (www.hiexpress.co.uk) One of the more upmarket chains on this list, with 18 London branches.

Premier Inn (www.premierinn.com) Excellent local chain with generally high standards; in large numbers.

Travelodge (www.travelodge.co.uk) Serviceable rooms, few public facilities.

STUDENT DIGS

During university holidays (mid-March to late April, late June to September, and mid-December to mid-January), student dorms and halls of residence are open to paying visitors. Choices include **LSE Vacations** (☑020-7955 7676; www.lsevacations.co.uk; s/tw/tr incl breakfast from £45/65/90; ☎), whose eight halls include **Bankside House** (☑020-7955 7676; www.lsevacations.co.uk; 24 Sumner St, SE1; s/tw/tr/q incl breakfast from £68/89/119/133; ☎; ⊖Southwark) and **High Holborn Residence** (Map p438 ☑020-7107 5737; www.lsevacations.co.uk; 178 High Holborn, WC1; s/d from £36/45; ☎; ⊖Holborn). **King's Venues** (☑020-7848 1700; www.kingsvenues.com; s £40-60) handles six residences, including the centrally located **Great Dover St Apartments** (☑020-7407 0068; www.kingsvenues.com; 165 Great Dover St, SE1; ☎; ⊖Borough) and **Stamford St Apartments** (☑020-7848 4664; www.kingsvenues.com; 127 Stamford St, SE1; s incl breakfast £59; ☎; ⊖Waterloo).

---

cosy TV lounge in the basement. Continental breakfast and linen are included.

★ ROSE & CROWN
B&B ££

(☑020-7923 3337; www.roseandcrownn16.co.uk; 199 Stoke Newington Church St, N16; s £96, d £132-180, ste £198; P☎; ⊡73, ⊡Stoke Newington) At the top of a street packed with great pubs, shops and cafes, this grand family-friendly boozer offers six beautifully decorated, contemporary rooms. The deluxe double and suite have sitting areas and free-standing bathtubs as well as original features from the pub's days as a Truman brewery. Guests have access to a lovely roof terrace. The above-average breakfast is served in a cute dining room.

MEGARO
BOUTIQUE HOTEL ££

Map p466 (☑020-7843 2222; www.hotelmegaro.co.uk; Belgrove St, WC1; d from £120, f £195; ❄☎♿; ⊖King's Cross St Pancras) There are many things that commend the Megaro: the 49 indulgently large rooms, lovely decor, in-room creature comforts (espresso machines, fresh milk, rainforest showerheads), attentive service and an excellent bar-restaurant. There is some noise from the street, so if you're a light sleeper, go high or towards the back.

Many rooms, including the very large family ones (202 and 302) that face the train station, have Murphy (or wall) beds to accommodate extra sleepers.

GREAT NORTHERN HOTEL
HISTORIC HOTEL £££

Map p466 (GNH; ☑020-3388 0800; www.gnh london.com; King's Cross Station, Pancras Rd, N1; r from £180; ❄@☎; ⊖King's Cross St Pancras) Built as the world's first railway hotel in 1854, the GNH is now a boutique hotel in a classic style reminiscent of luxury sleeper trains. Exquisite artisanship is in evidence everywhere. And in addition to the two lively bars and a restaurant, there's a 'pantry' on every floor, from which you can help yourself to hot or cold drinks and snacks, including cakes baked daily.

YORK & ALBANY
BOUTIQUE HOTEL £££

Map p468 (☑020-7387 5700; www.gordonram sayrestaurants.com/york-and-albany; 127-129 Parkway, NW1; d incl breakfast £175-255, ste £305; ❄☎♿☎; ⊖Camden Town) Luxurious yet cosy, the York & Albany oozes Georgian charm. Many of the rooms have feature fireplaces, plus antique furniture, beautiful floor-to-ceiling windows, lush bathrooms (with underfloor heating) and Egyptian-cotton bed linen. All nine rooms and suites have Sky TV and coffee machines. We love the four-poster bed and sunken bathroom in room 5.

ST PANCRAS RENAISSANCE LONDON HOTEL
LUXURY HOTEL £££

Map p466 (☑020-7841 3540; www.stpancras renaissance.co.uk; Euston Rd, NW1; d from £230; ❄☎☎☎; ⊖King's Cross St Pancras) Housed in the former Midland Grand Hotel (1873), a red-brick Gothic Victorian marvel designed by Sir George Gilbert Scott, the St Pancras Renaissance counts 245 rooms but only 38 of them are in the original building; the rest are in an extension at the back and are rather bland.

🛏 West London

SAFESTAY HOLLAND PARK
HOSTEL £

Map p472 (☑020-3326 8471; www.safestay.co.uk; Holland Walk, W8; dm £20, r from £60; ☎;

⊖High St Kensington or Holland Park) This fresh place replaced the long-serving YHA hostel running here since 1958. With a bright and bold colour design, the hostel has four- to eight-bunk dorm rooms, twin-bunk and single-bunk rooms, free wi-fi in the lobby and a fabulous location in the Jacobean east wing of Holland House in Holland Park (p273), the only part that survived a Luftwaffe onslaught.

LONDON HOUSE HOTEL   HOTEL £

Map p470 (📞020-7243 1810; www.londonhouse hotels.com; 81 Kensington Gardens Sq, W2; d £80-160; ❈🖤; ⊖Bayswater) This good-value, snappy-looking hotel in a rather grand Regency-style building looks over Kensington Gardens Sq. The 103 rooms may be on the small side, as are the bathrooms, but each is clean and pleasantly furnished, while the setting is peaceful. The best rooms have views onto the leafy square.

17 HOMESTEAD RD   B&B £

Map p472 (📞020-7385 6773; www.fulham bedandbreakfastlondon.co.uk; 17 Homestead Rd, SW6; d & tw £95-110; 🖤; ⊖Fulham Broadway or Parsons Green) With its pristine buff-coloured carpets, this charming and completely spotless two-room B&B is housed in a Victorian terraced property. The ambience is lovingly maintained with lashings of elbow grease (and a no-shoes policy) from the friendly and welcoming owner, Fiona. Breakfasts are simple (muesli, toast, orange juice, tea or coffee). Book ahead.

YHA EARL'S COURT   HOSTEL £

Map p472 (📞0345 371 9114; www.yha.org.uk/ hostel/london-earls-court; 38 Bolton Gardens, SW5; dm £23-32, d & tw from £79, tr from £89, q from £129; 🖤; ⊖Earl's Court) There's some lovely original tiling on the floor as you enter this fine old property on a quiet, leafy street in Earl's Court, although most other period detailing has been overlaid. Most accommodation (186 beds) is in clean, airy dormitories of between four and 10 metal bunk beds. Common areas are spacious; showers and toilets are clean and staff helpful.

GARDEN COURT HOTEL   HOTEL £

Map p470 (📞020-7229 2553; www.garden courthotel.co.uk; 30-31 Kensington Gardens Sq, W2; s £40-99, d £50-129, tr £65-149, q £75-179; @🖤; ⊖Bayswater) Run by the same family since 1954, the very clean Garden Court

is a reliable choice in its price range. The decor is simple, with decorative wallpaper and basic furniture. Prices can dip as low as £36 per night during the slack season. The cheapest singles are quite small and not en suite, but have a private shower room outside the room.

★MAIN HOUSE   HOTEL ££

Map p470 (📞020-7221 9691; www.themainhouse. co.uk; 6 Colville Rd, W11; ste £120-150; 🖤; ⊖Ladbroke Grove, Notting Hill Gate or Westbourne Park) The four adorable suites at this peach of a Victorian midterrace house on Colville Rd make this a superb choice. Bright and spacious rooms are excellent value and come with vast bathrooms and endless tea and coffee. Cream of the crop is the uppermost suite, occupying the entire top floor. There's no sign, but look for the huge letters 'SIX'. Minimum three-night stay.

The well-spoken, amenable and friendly owner, Caroline, is also a font of local knowledge, and if she has popped out, the staff are very helpful too.

★BARCLAY HOUSE   B&B ££

Map p472 (📞077 6742 0943; www.barclayhouse london.com; 21 Barclay Rd, SW6; s from £110, d £135-168; @🖤; ⊖Fulham Broadway) The three dapper, thoroughly modern and comfy bedrooms in this shipshape Victorian house are a dream, from the Philippe Starck shower rooms, walnut furniture, double-glazed sash windows and underfloor heating to the small, thoughtful details (fumble-free coat hangers, drawers packed with sewing kits, plasters and maps). The cordial, music-loving owners – bursting with tips and handy London knowledge – concoct an inclusive, homely atmosphere.

Usually there is a three- to four-night minimum stay. Use of the Seiler grand piano is available by arrangement.

MELROSE GARDENS   B&B ££

Map p472 (📞020-7603 1817; www.staylondon bandb.co.uk; 29 Melrose Gardens, W6; s/tw/d £78/105/120; 🖤; ⊖Goldhawk Rd) Ideal for those seeking peace and a sedate tempo, this charming B&B is run from a typical Victorian family home. Everything is in its right place. It's overseen by cordial hosts Su and Martin, who are quick to dispense handy London info. The only room with its own bathroom is at the very top, while the other two look out over the small garden.

NADLER KENSINGTON
HOTEL ££

Map p472 (☎020-7244 2255; www.thenadler.com; 25 Courtfield Gardens, SW5; s from £99, tw bunk r from £109, d £150-300; ✴@🛜; ⊖Earl's Court) Things – service and design – are snappy and efficient at this sure-footed hotel, and each immaculate room (including the neat bunk-bed rooms) comes with a tiny kitchen (with microwave, minifridge and sink) and a 20in (up to 26in) flat-screen TV. It's well located in a quiet street not too far from Earl's Court tube station for quick journeys to the West End.

SPACE APART HOTEL
HOTEL ££

Map p470 (☎020-7908 1340; www.aparthotel-london.co.uk; 36-37 Kensington Gardens Sq, W2; apt £140-190; ✴@🛜; ⊖Bayswater or Royal Oak) Light, bright, spic-and-span double and triple studio apartments with kitchenette at eye-catching rates. This converted 30-room Georgian building is neatly designed and provides a handy and affordable stay not far from the Notting Hill action. The studios are not big, but for around £20 you can upgrade to a roomier double studio. There's usually a two-night minimum stay.

PORTOBELLO GOLD
INN ££

Map p470 (☎020-7460 4910; www.portobellogold.com; 95-97 Portobello Rd, W11; s/tw/apt incl breakfast from £75/80/170, bunk from £50; 🛜; ⊖Notting Hill Gate) This cheerful guesthouse above a pleasant restaurant and pub (where Bill Clinton once had lunch) has 10 rooms of varying sizes. There are several small doubles (with minuscule shower room) and a couple of twin-bunk rooms. The four-poster suite has antique furnishings, a foldaway four-poster bed and (decorative) open-hearth fireplace, while room/maisonette No 6 boasts a roof terrace with splendid views over Portobello Rd.

TWENTY NEVERN SQUARE
HOTEL ££

Map p472 (☎020-7565 9555; www.20nevernsquare.co.uk; 20 Nevern Sq, SW5; r incl breakfast from £90; 🛜; ⊖Earl's Court) Each room is different at this elegant and stylish four-floor brick hotel overlooking a lovely London square. Cosy, but not especially large, rooms are decorated with Asian-style woodwork, imposing carved-wood beds (some four-poster), venetian blinds and heavy fabrics. Some rooms have bath, others shower. There is a gorgeous conservatory where breakfast is served and a tiny patio.

VANCOUVER STUDIOS
APARTMENT ££

Map p470 (☎020-7243 1270; www.vancouverstudios.co.uk; 30 Prince's Sq, W2; apt £97-350; 🛜; ⊖Bayswater) Everyone will feel at home in this appealing terrace of stylish and affordable apartments, with a restful and charming walled garden. Very well maintained rooms all contain kitchenettes but otherwise differ wildly – ranging from a tiny but well-equipped single to a spacious three-bedroom apartment that sleeps up to six.

EUROPA HOUSE
APARTMENT £££

Map p470 (☎020-7724 5924; www.living-rooms.co.uk/hotel/europa; 79a Randolph Ave, W9; 1-bedroom apt £199-320, 2-bedroom apt £250-485, 3-bedroom apt from £435; ✴🛜👪; ⊖Warwick Ave) In a splendidly leafy area of the city, this set of 14 apartments offers very elegant and classically attired flats, with one- and two-bed apartments and a 153-sq-metre three-bed penthouse apartment on a 14-night minimum stay. Perhaps the best asset is access to the huge, 1.2-hectare enclosed communal garden. Parking is an additional £30 per day.

For families, a kid's concierge is at hand for activities to keep tots entertained.

K + K HOTEL GEORGE
BOUTIQUE HOTEL £££

Map p472 (☎020-7598 8700; www.kkhotels.com; 1-15 Templeton Pl, SW5; s/d from £200/230; P✴🛜; ⊖Earl's Court) From the niftily designed, wide-open foyer to the joyfully huge garden with its glorious lawn, this tidy 154-room boutique hotel just round the corner from Earl's Court tube station has smallish rooms, but they are attractively presented, comfy and come with neat shower. It has a snazzy bar, helpful service throughout, and soft colours. The location is great for zipping into the centre of town.

LA SUITE WEST
BOUTIQUE HOTEL £££

Map p470 (☎020-7313 8484; www.lasuitewest.com; 41-51 Inverness Tce, W2; r £129-279; ✴@🛜; ⊖Bayswater) The black-and-white foyer of the Anouska Hempel–designed La Suite West – bare walls, a minimalist slit of a fireplace, an iPad for guests' use on an otherwise void white-marble reception desk – presages the OCD neatness of rooms hidden down dark corridors. The straight lines, spotless surfaces and sharp angles are accentuated by impeccable bathrooms and softened by comfortable beds and warm service. Downstairs suites have gardens and individual gated entrances.

SLEEPING WEST LONDON

🛏 Greenwich & South London

★ SAFESTAY LONDON ELEPHANT & CASTLE
HOSTEL £

Map p476 (☑020-7703 8000; www.safestay.com; 144-152 Walworth Rd, SE17; dm/d from £28/96; @☎; ⊖Elephant & Castle) Who would have thought that the Labour Party's staid former headquarters would make such a funky hostel? The 18th-century Georgian building has been stunningly renovated: inside, it's all purple and magenta stripes and bright lights, though the 74 rooms are more sober. Most dorms (four to eight beds) are en suite. Enormous bar/lounge with garden.

★ NUMBER 16
B&B ££

Map p477 (☑020-8853 4337; www.st-alfeges. co.uk; 16 St Alfege Passage, SE10; s/d £90/125; ☎; ℝDLR Cutty Sark) One-time sweet shop, this gay-owned B&B has two well-appointed doubles and a single, individually decorated in shades of yellow, blue or green and all with bathroom. The owners do their best to make everyone, gay or straight, feel at home, with chats and cups of tea in the charming basement kitchen. Enter via Roan St.

TOMMYFIELD
HOTEL ££

Map p476 (☑020-7735 1061; www.thetommy field.com; 185 Kennington Lane, SE11; d £119; ✳☎; ⊖Kennington) Above a buzzing gastropub, the trendy Tommyfield offers six stylishly kitted-out rooms with bare-brick, whitewashed walls, all soundproofed and finished to a high standard. Beds are king or superking with white cotton linen, and two of the rooms have bathtubs.

CHURCH STREET HOTEL
BOUTIQUE HOTEL ££

(☑020-7703 5984; www.churchstreethotel.com; 29-33 Camberwell Church St, SE5; s £70-90, d £90-155, tr £160; ✳☎⊞; ℝDenmark Hill) One of London's most individual boutique hotels, this vibrant 27-room establishment is a much-needed shot of tequila into the hotel landscape of London. Run by a half-Spanish, half-English brother duo, the hotel brims with colour, vibrant details and Mexicana (the tiled bathrooms will perk up anyone's day). The smallest rooms share bathrooms. Very off-the-beaten track but transport links are good.

KENNINGTON B&B
B&B ££

Map p476 (☑020-7735 7669; www.kennington bandb.com; 103 Kennington Park Rd, SE11; d £120-150; ☎⊞; ⊖Kennington) With gorgeous bed linen, well-preserved Georgian features and just seven bedrooms and a suite, this lovely B&B in an 18th-century house is tasteful in every regard, from the shining, tiled shower rooms and Georgian shutters to the fireplaces and cast-iron radiators. Not all rooms are en suite, but each has a private shower room. Breakfast is continental; check-out is 11am.

🛏 Richmond, Kew & Hampton Court

PETERSHAM
HOTEL ££

Map p479 (☑020-8940 7471; www.petersham hotel.co.uk; Nightingale Lane, TW10; s/d £130/195, riverview d £260, riverview ste from £450; ☎; ℝRichmond, ⊖Richmond) Neatly perched on the slope down Richmond Hill leading across Petersham Meadows towards the Thames, the impressive four-star Petersham offers stunning Arcadian views at every turn. And its restaurant, with its voluminous windows gazing down to the river, offers some choice panoramas. The 58 rooms are classically styled but those with good river views are dearer. Take bus 65 from Richmond train or tube stations.

★ BINGHAM
BOUTIQUE HOTEL £££

Map p479 (☑020-8940 0902; www.thebingham. co.uk; 61-63 Petersham Rd, TW10; s/d £195/210; ✳☎; ℝRichmond, ⊖Richmond) Just upriver from Richmond Bridge, this lovely riverside Georgian town house is an enticing boutique escape from central London, with 15 very elegant and well-presented rooms – most of them recently restyled. Riverside rooms are naturally pricier, but worth it, as roadside rooms (although deliciously devised and double-glazed) look out over busy Petersham Rd.

Understand London

London Today

London's charmed life has faced challenges in the past but has always overcome them. Even after the plagues, the Great Fire of London and the Blitz bombings, the city carried on. Spiralling property prices and the uncertainty stemming from Brexit are small fry in comparison. In 2017 London was victim to terrorist attacks in locations including London Bridge and Westminster, resulting in an increased police presence. The economy remains buoyant, despite the weak pound, and major investments have been made in public transport.

Best on Film

Passport to Pimlico (1949) Whimsical comedy about a London neighbourhood declaring independence.

Withnail & I (1986) Cult black comedy about two unemployed actors in 1969 Camden.

Bridget Jones's Diary (2001) Eponymous bachelorette seeks and finds love, with London as a gorgeous backdrop.

Skyfall (2012) Sam Mendes' masterful contribution to the James Bond franchise.

Hampstead (2017) An American widow finds unexpected love with a man living wild on Hampstead Heath.

Best in Print

Oliver Twist (Charles Dickens; 1837) Unforgettable characters and a vivid depiction of Victorian London, seen through the eyes of a hapless orphan.

Sour Sweet (Timothy Mo; 1982) Vivid portrayal of a Hong Kong Chinese family moving to London in the 1960s.

London Fields (Martin Amis; 1989) Gripping, dark postmodern study of London lowlife.

London (Edward Rutherfurd; 1997) Sweeping drama that brings London's epic history vividly to life.

White Teeth (Zadie Smith; 2000) Poignant multiethnic romp in postmillennial Willesden.

Going Up & Up & Up

As London races to the end of the 10s, it is a city in transition. What was once a place within human reach has soared ever upwards. Until recently vertical growth was contained to the City of London and Canary Wharf in the Docklands. At present some 435 buildings of over 20 storeys are in the pipeline – double the amount of just two years before – and most are in East London, the Greenwich Peninsula and the South Bank. Only time will tell how the city responds. Keeping pace with the rising skyline are property prices, which continue to increase at eye-watering rates. Indeed, London is now the world's most expensive city in which to buy a property, with the average price of a one-bedroom apartment now a whopping £1.1 million in des res (for 'desirable residence') Kensington and Chelsea. Conditions for poorer Londoners, meanwhile, were brought into sharp focus by a 2017 fire in West London's Grenfell Tower, which killed at least 79 people, mainly council tenants.

Out the Door

Arguably the topic of the moment is Brexit, the UK's departure from the EU, which was approved by the electorate in a June 2016 referendum and is scheduled to take effect in April 2019. The referendum was approved by a 52% to 48% margin nationwide, revealing a divide between London (which voted to remain by 60% to 40%) and many other parts of the country.

Negotiations are likely to be protracted, and there are important issues to consider, the economy and Britain's role on the world stage among them. Many Londoners worry about the city losing its edge on multiculturalism (270 nationalities speaking some 300 different languages). Will the 'new European' labourers, dentists and financiers, many of whom came here with their families when the EU welcomed 10 new member-nations in 2004, be forced to return to a place that is no longer home? Will all those wonderful pop-up restaurants and markets serving everything from Taiwanese pork bao to vegan falafel continue to, well, pop up if foreign influence declines? In the global capital that London has become, that's a growing concern.

All Change

The 'leave' vote in the Brexit referendum appeared to surprise both camps. Theresa May replaced David Cameron as prime minister and, after less than a year in office, called a snap election that looked likely to deliver a parliament dominated by the Conservatives. But an unexpectedly strong Labour performance resulted in a hung parliament, with no overall majority, leaving May a weakened figure.

Brexit's wheels are now turning, but many of its changes will take a long time to solidify and the effect on visitors in the next few years will probably – currency fluctuations aside – be limited.

Closer to home, the mayor of London, Boris Johnson, left office after two terms to join May's Cabinet as foreign secretary. Less than impressed by Boris (he's always been one of those first-name politicians) in his second term, the capital rejected his party's candidate, Zac Goldsmith, in favour of Sadiq Khan, a Labour MP who was born in Tooting in South London to a working-class British Pakistani family and is a practising Muslim, making him the world's first elected leader of that faith in any Western city. His performance after just a year in office has been well-received overall, notably his response to the 2017 terrorist attacks in London and Manchester.

Way to Go

Some of the best news coming out of London involves transport. Crossrail, now officially named the Elizabeth Line, an ambitious and somewhat controversial over- and underground transport system that will stretch for 73 miles east and west and through central London, links London Liverpool St and Shenfield to the east. The Paddington to Heathrow branch in the west opens in May 2018. The new line will increase central London rail capacity by 10% and bring an extra 1.5 million people to within 45 minutes of central London. Even better news is the start of the so-called Night Tube, with the Victoria and Jubilee lines, plus most of the Piccadilly, Central and Northern lines, running all night at the weekend. The Overground and the District, Metropolitan, Circle and Hammersmith and City lines as well as the DLR are all expected to follow suit in the next few years.

population per sq km

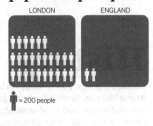

LONDON ENGLAND

≈ 200 people

if London were 100 people

45 would be white British
15 would be non-British
18 would be British Asian
13 would be black British
9 would be mixed British or Other

belief systems
(% of population)

58 Christian
26 Other
8 Muslim
4 Hindu
2 Jewish
1 Buddhist

History

London's history is a long, turbulent narrative spanning more than two millennia. Along the way there have been good times (the arrival of the Romans, with their wine, law and order, and road-building skills, the expansion of London as the capital of an empire) and bad times (plagues, the Great Fire of 1666, the Blitz bombing of WWII). But even when on its knees, London has always been able to get up and move on, constantly re-inventing itself.

Londinium

London was settled by the Romans, and the area, particularly the City of London, has been inhabited continuously ever since. As a result, archaeologists have had to dig deep to discover the city's past, relying more often than not on redevelopment such as the Crossrail high-frequency railway line to allow excavations.

But the Romans were not the first on the block. The Celts had arrived in Britain sometime in the 4th century BC and settled around a ford in the Thames. The river was twice as wide as it is today and probably served as a barrier separating tribal groups.

When the Romans first visited in the 1st century BC, they traded with the Celts. In AD 43, an invasion force led by Emperor Claudius established the port of Londinium, the first real settlement at what is now London, and used it as a springboard to subdue Celtic strongholds. They constructed a wooden bridge across the Thames near today's London Bridge, and this became the focal point for a network of roads fanning out around the region.

The settlement's development as a trading centre was interrupted in AD 60 or 61 when an army led by Boudicca, queen of the Celtic Iceni tribe based in East Anglia, exacted violent retribution on the Romans, who had attacked her kingdom, flogged her and raped her daughters. The Iceni overran Camulodunum (now Colchester in Essex), which had become the capital of Roman Britannia, and then turned on Londinium, massacring its inhabitants and razing the settlement before the Romans defeated them.

They say that if you dig deep enough in the City you'll find a layer of rubble and soft red ash dating from the great conflagration brought about by Boudicca's attack on Roman Londinium.

TIMELINE

55–54 BC	AD 43	47–50
Roman Emperor Julius Caesar makes a fast-paced and badly planned visit to Britain and returns empty-handed – though the Senate declares a celebration that lasts 20 days.	The Romans invade Britain, led by Emperor Claudius; they mix with the local Celtic tribespeople and will stay for almost four centuries.	A defensive fort at Londinium is built. The name Londinium was probably taken from a Celtic place name (a common Roman practice) but there is no evidence as to what it actually means.

The Romans rebuilt Londinium around Cornhill, the highest elevation north of the bridge, between AD 80 and 90. About a century later they wrapped a defensive wall some 2.7m thick and 6m high around it. Towers were added to strengthen it, and the original gates – Aldgate, Ludgate, Newgate and Bishopsgate – are remembered as place names even today in London. By then Londinium, a centre for business and trade but not a fully fledged *colonia* (settlement), was an imposing city with a massive basilica, an amphitheatre, a forum and a governor's palace.

By the middle of the 3rd century, Londinium was home to some 30,000 people of various ethnic groups, with temples dedicated to a large number of cults. When Emperor Constantine converted to Christianity in 312, the fledgling religion became the empire's – and London's – official cult, seeing off its rival, Mithraism.

In the 4th century, the Roman Empire in Britain began to decline, with increasing attacks by the Picts and Scotti in the north, and the Saxons, Germanic tribes originating from north of the Rhine, in the southeast. In 410, when the embattled Emperor Honorius refused them military aid, the Romans abandoned Britain, and Londinium was reduced to a sparsely populated backwater.

Lundenwic

What happened to Londinium after the Roman withdrawal is still the subject of much historical debate. While there is no written record of the town from 457 to 604, most historians now think that Romano-Britons continued to live here even as Saxon settlers established farmsteads and small villages in the area.

Lundenwic (or 'London settlement') was established outside the city walls due west of Londinium and around present-day Aldwych and Charing Cross as a Saxon trade settlement. By the early 7th century the Saxons had been converted to Christianity by the pope's emissary Augustine. Lundenwic was an episcopate and the first St Paul's Cathedral was established at the top of Ludgate Hill.

This infant trading community grew in importance and attracted the attention of the Vikings in Denmark. They attacked in 842 and again nine years later, burning Lundenwic to the ground. Under the leadership of King Alfred the Great of Wessex, the Saxon population fought back, driving the Danes out in 886.

Saxon London grew into a prosperous and well-organised town divided into 20 wards, each with its own alderman, and resident colonies of German merchants and French vintners. But attacks by the Danes continued apace, and the Saxon leadership was weakening; in 1016

Historical Reads

London: The Biography (Peter Ackroyd)

London: A History in Maps (Peter Barber)

A Traveller's History of London (Richard Tames)

London: The Illustrated History (John Clark & Cathy Ross)

Nightwalking: A Nocturnal History of London (Matt Beaumont)

122	190–225	410	597
Emperor Hadrian pays a visit to Londinium and many impressive municipal buildings are constructed. Roman London reaches its peak, with temples, bathhouses, a fortress and a port.	London Wall is constructed around Londinium after outsiders breach Hadrian's Wall to the north. The wall encloses an area of just 132 hectares and is 6m high.	Emperor Honorius decrees that the colony of Britannia should take care of its own defences, effectively ending the Roman presence in Londinium.	Ethelbert, the first English monarch to convert to Christianity, welcomes St Augustine and his 40 missionaries to Canterbury, ensuring that city's religious supremacy.

Londoners were forced to accept the Danish leader Knut (Canute) as king of England.

With the death of Knut's brutal son Harthacanute in 1042, the throne passed to the Saxon Edward the Confessor, who went on to found an abbey and palace at Westminster. When Edward moved his court to Westminster, a division of the city's labour began that would continue to our day: the port (or City) became the trading and mercantile centre of London, with Westminster its seat of justice and administration.

The Normans

The year 1066 marks the real birth of England as a unified nation-state. After the death of Edward the Confessor in 1066, a dispute over who would take the English throne spelled disaster for the Saxon kings. Harold Godwinson, the Earl of Wessex, was anointed successor by Edward on his deathbed, but this enraged William, the Duke of Normandy, who claimed that Edward had promised him the throne. William mounted a massive invasion of England from France and on 14 October defeated Harold at the Battle of Hastings, before marching on London to claim his prize. The newly dubbed 'William the Conqueror' was crowned king of England in the new Westminster Abbey on 25 December 1066, ensuring the Norman conquest was complete.

William distrusted the 'vast and fierce populace' of London, and to overwhelm and intimidate his new subjects (as well as protect himself from them), he built 10 castles within a day's march of each other, including the White Tower, the core of the Tower of London, and Windsor Castle. Cleverly, he kept the prosperous merchants on side by confirming the City's independence in exchange for taxes. London, counting 15,000 people, would soon become the principal town of England.

Medieval London

The last of the Norman kings, the ineffectual Stephen, died in 1154, and the throne passed to Henry II of the powerful House of Plantagenet, which would rule England for the next two and a half centuries. Henry's successors were happy to let the City of London keep its independence as long as its merchants continued to finance their wars and building projects. When Richard I (known as 'the Lionheart'), a king who spent a mere six months of his life in England, needed funds for his crusade to the Holy Land, he recognised the city as a self-governing commune in return for cash.

A city built on trade and commerce, London would always guard its independence fiercely, as Richard's successor, King John, learned the hard way. In 1215 John was forced to cede power to his barons, and to

The winds of change were still blowing a quarter of a century after the Norman Conquest when the Great London Tornado of 1091 swept through town, destroying much of the original church of St Mary-le-Bow, the wooden London Bridge and countless houses.

c 600	604	842	886
The Saxon trade settlement of Lundenwic (literally 'London settlement') is formed to the west of the Roman site of Londinium.	The first Christian cathedral dedicated to St Paul is built on Ludgate Hill, the site of the current cathedral; fashioned from wood, it burns down in 675 and is rebuilt in stone a decade later.	Vikings attack and burn London to the ground; a period of great struggle between the kingdoms of Wessex and the Danes begins for control of the Thames.	King Alfred the Great, first king of all England, reclaims London for the Saxons and founds a new settlement within the walls of the old Roman town.

curb his arbitrary demands for pay-offs from the City. Among those pressing him to put his seal to the landmark Magna Carta, which effectively diluted royal power, was the by-then powerful lord mayor of the City of London; the first holder of this office, Henry Fitz Aylwin, had taken office just a quarter-century before.

Fire was a constant hazard in the cramped and narrow houses and lanes of 14th-century London, but disease caused by unsanitary living conditions and impure drinking water from the Thames was the greatest threat. In 1348 rats on ships from Europe brought the Black Death, a bubonic plague that wiped out almost half the population of about 80,000 over the next year and a half.

With their numbers down, there was growing unrest among labourers, for whom violence became a way of life, and rioting was commonplace. In 1381, miscalculating – or just disregarding – the mood of the nation, the young Richard II tried to impose a poll tax on everyone in the realm. Tens of thousands of peasants, led by the soldier Wat Tyler and the prelates Jack Straw and John Ball, marched in protest on London. The Archbishop of Canterbury, Simon Sudbury, was dragged from the Tower and beheaded, several ministers were murdered and many buildings were razed before the Peasants' Revolt ran its course and its leaders executed.

London gained wealth and stature under the Houses of Lancaster and York in the 15th century, but their struggle for ascendancy led to the catastrophic Wars of the Roses. The century's greatest episode of political intrigue occurred during this time: in 1483 the 12-year-old Edward V of the House of York reigned for only two months before vanishing with his younger brother into the Tower of London, never to be seen again. Whether or not their uncle, Richard III – who became the next king – murdered the boys has been the subject of much conjecture over the centuries (Shakespeare would have us believe he did the evil deed). In 1674, workers found a chest containing the skeletons of two children near the White Tower, which were assumed to be the princes' remains, and they were reburied in Westminster Abbey.

Richard III didn't have long to enjoy the hot seat: he was killed in 1485 at the Battle of Bosworth by Henry Tudor, who as Henry VII became the first monarch of the Tudor Dynasty. In September 2012, Richard's remains, confirmed by rigorous DNA tests, were excavated beneath a car park in central Leicester. They were ceremonially laid to rest in that city's cathedral in March 2015.

The first stone London Bridge was completed in 1209 although it was frequently too crowded to cross, and most people traversed the river on a small boat called a wherry. The current bridge dates from 1972.

HISTORY MEDIEVAL LONDON

1016	1066	1078	1097
The Danes return to London and Knut is crowned king of England, ushering in two decades of relative peace.	Following his decisive victory over King Harold at the Battle of Hastings, William, Duke of Normandy (aka William the Conqueror), is crowned king in Westminster Abbey.	William builds 10 castles within a day's march of London (including the White Tower and Windsor), first in earth and timber and then in stone.	William Rufus, son of William the Conqueror, commences the construction of Westminster Hall. The hall, possibly the largest in Europe at the time, is completed in two years.

The House of Tudor

Though the House of Tudor lasted less than 120 years and three generations, it is the best-known English dynasty. London became one of the largest and most important cities in Europe under its kings and queens, the Americas were discovered and colonised, and world trade thrived.

Henry's son and successor, Henry VIII, was the most extravagant of the clan, instructing new palaces to be built at Whitehall and St James's, and bullying his lord chancellor, Cardinal Thomas Wolsey, into giving him Hampton Court.

Henry's life was dominated by the need to produce a male heir, which indirectly led to his split with the Roman Catholic Church. This occurred in 1534 after the Pope refused to annul his marriage to Catherine of Aragon, who had borne him only a daughter after 24 years of marriage. Turning his back on Rome, he made himself the supreme head of the church in England and married Anne Boleyn, the second of his six wives. He 'dissolved' (abolished) London's monasteries, seized the church's vast wealth and property, and smashed ecclesiastical culture. Many of the religious houses disappeared, leaving only their names in such areas as Whitefriars, Blackfriars and Greyfriars (after the colour of the robes worn by Carmelite, Dominican and Franciscan monks).

Despite his penchant for settling differences with the axe (two of his six wives and Wolsey's replacement as lord chancellor, Thomas More, were beheaded, along with 32 other leaders and up to 72,000 others) and his persecution of both Catholics and fellow Protestants who didn't toe the line, Henry VIII remained a popular monarch until his death in 1547. The reign of Mary I, his daughter with Catherine of Aragon, saw a brief return to Catholicism, during which time the queen sanctioned

Hidden London (http://hidden-london.com) explores and exposes London's obscure attractions, curiosities, districts and localities to the light of day, seasoned with some fascinating historical nuggets and details.

WHAT'S IN THE NAME?

Many of London's street names, especially in the City, recall the goods that were traded there: Poultry, Cornhill, Sea Coal Lane, Milk and Bread Sts and the more cryptic Friday St, where you bought fish for that day of fasting. Other meanings are not so obvious. The '-wich' or '-wych' ending in names like Greenwich, Aldwych and Dulwich come from the Saxon word *wic*, meaning 'settlement'. *Ea* or *ey* is an old word for 'island' or 'marsh'; thus Chelsea (Island of Shale), Bermondsey (Bermond's Island), Battersea (Peter's Island) and Hackney (Haca's Marsh). In Old English *ceap* meant 'market'; hence Eastcheap is where the common people shopped, while Cheapside (originally Westcheap) was reserved for the royal household. 'Borough' comes from *burg*, Old English for 'fort' or 'town'. And the odd names East Ham and West Ham come from the Old English *hamm* or 'hem'; they were just bigger enclosed (or 'hemmed-in') settlements than the more standard hamlets.

1170	1176	1215	1290
Archbishop of Canterbury Thomas Becket, born in Ironmongers Lane and known as Thomas of London in his lifetime, is murdered by four of Henry II's knights.	London Bridge is built in stone for the first time with a chapel in the centre dedicated to St Thomas Becket, although most people still cross the river by boat.	King John signs the Magna Carta (literally 'Great Charter'), an agreement with England's barons forming the basis of constitutional law in England.	King Edward I issues an edict expelling all Jews from England; the banishment will remain in effect until Oliver Cromwell comes to power more than 360 years later.

the burning to death of 200 Protestants at Smithfield and earned herself the nickname 'Bloody Mary'. By the time Elizabeth I, Henry VIII's daughter by Anne Boleyn, took the throne, Catholicism was a waning force, and hundreds of people who dared to suggest otherwise were carted off to the gallows at Tyburn near today's Marble Arch.

Elizabethan London

The 45-year reign (1558–1603) of Elizabeth I is still looked upon as a 'golden age' of English history, and it was just as significant for London. During these four and a half decades, English literature reached new and still unbeaten heights, and religious tolerance gradually became accepted doctrine, although Catholics and some Protestants still faced persecution. England became a naval superpower, having defeated the Spanish Armada in 1588, and the city established itself as the premier world trade market with the opening of the Royal Exchange by Elizabeth in 1571.

London was blooming economically and physically: in the second half of the 16th century the population doubled to 200,000. The first recorded map of London was published in 1558, and John Stow produced *A Survey of London,* the first history of the city, in 1598.

This was also the golden era of English drama, and the works of William Shakespeare, Christopher Marlowe and Ben Jonson packed new playhouses, such as the Rose (built in 1587) and the Globe (1599). Both were in Southwark, a notoriously ribald place at the time, teeming with 'stews' (vapour baths but brothels in reality) and bawdy taverns. Most importantly, they were outside the jurisdiction of the City, which frowned upon such pursuits and even banned theatre.

When Elizabeth died without an heir in 1603, she was succeeded by her second cousin, who was crowned James I. Although the son of the Catholic Mary, Queen of Scots (not to be confused with Elizabeth's half-sister Mary), whom Elizabeth had actually put to death for supposedly plotting against her, James was slow to improve conditions for England's Catholics and drew their wrath. He narrowly escaped death when the alleged plot by Guy Fawkes and his co-conspirators to blow up the Houses of Parliament on 5 November 1605 was uncovered. The discovery of the audacious plan is commemorated on this date each year with bonfires and fireworks.

The Civil Wars & Restoration

When James I's son, Charles I, came to the throne in 1625, his intransigent personality and total belief in the 'divine right of kings' set the monarchy on a collision course with an increasingly confident parlia-

In order to raise money to build ships and develop England's ports, Elizabeth I held the world's first national lottery in 1567, with an unheard-of top prize of £5000. Tickets cost 10 shillings and the draw took place next to Old St Paul's Cathedral.

1348	1455	1476	1558
Rats on ships from Europe bring the so-called Black Death, a bubonic plague that wipes out half the city's population in a year and returns several times until 1375.	The Wars of the Roses between two houses of the Plantagenet Dynasty – Lancaster (red rose) and York (white rose) – erupts and rages for more than three decades.	William Caxton, a prominent merchant from Kent, establishes his press at Westminster, printing more than 90 volumes of works by the likes of Geoffrey Chaucer and the poet John Gower.	The first detailed map of London is commissioned by a group of German merchants; a golden age of peace, art and literature begins as Queen Elizabeth I takes the throne.

ment at Westminster and a City of London tiring of extortionate taxes. The crunch came when Charles tried to arrest five antagonistic members of parliament, who fled to the City. By 1642 the country had slid into civil war.

The Puritans (extremist Protestants) and the city's expanding merchant class threw their support behind Oliver Cromwell, leader of the Parliamentarians (or Roundheads), who battled the Royalist troops (the Cavaliers). London firmly backed the Roundheads, and Charles I was defeated in 1646, although a Second Civil War (1648–49) and a Third Civil War (1649–51) continued to wreak havoc on what had been a stable and prosperous nation.

Charles I was beheaded for treason outside Banqueting House in Whitehall on 30 January 1649, famously asking for a second shirt on the cold morning of his execution so as not to shiver and appear cowardly. Cromwell ruled the country as a quasi-republic for 11 years, during which time Charles' son, Charles II, continued fighting for the restoration of the monarchy. During this period Cromwell banned theatre, dancing, Christmas and just about anything remotely fun.

After Cromwell's death in 1658, parliament decided that the royals weren't so bad after all, refused to recognise the authority of Cromwell's successor, his son Richard, and restored the exiled Charles II to the throne in 1660.

Plague & Fire

Crowded, filthy London had suffered from recurrent outbreaks of bubonic plague since the 14th century, but nothing had prepared it for the Great Plague of 1665, which dwarfed all previous outbreaks.

As the plague spread, families affected were forced to stay inside for 40 days' quarantine, until the victim had either recovered or died. Previously crowded streets were deserted, churches and markets were closed, and an eerie silence descended. To make matters worse, the mayor believed that dogs and cats were the spreaders of the plague and ordered them all killed, thus ridding the disease-carrying rats of their natural predators. By the time the winter cold arrested the epidemic, an estimated 100,000 people had perished, their corpses collected and thrown into vast 'plague pits'.

The plague finally began to wane in November 1665. But Londoners scarcely had a year to recover before another disaster struck. The city had for centuries been prone to fire, as nearly all buildings were constructed from wood and roofed with thatch, but the mother of all blazes broke out on 2 September 1666 in a bakery in Pudding Lane near London Bridge.

1599	1605	1613	1649
The Globe opens in Southwark, alongside other London theatres such as the Rose and the Swan; most of Shakespeare's plays written after 1599 are staged here, including *Macbeth* and *Hamlet*.	A Catholic plot to blow up James I by hiding gunpowder under the House of Commons is foiled; four of the alleged plotters, including Guy Fawkes, are executed the following year.	The Globe theatre catches fire and burns to the ground; it is rebuilt the following year but closed by the Puritans and demolished in 1642.	King Charles I is executed at Whitehall at the height of the English Civil Wars, between Royalists (or Cavaliers) and Parliamentarians (or Roundheads).

It didn't seem like much to begin with – the mayor himself dismissed it as 'something a woman might piss out' before going back to bed – but the unusual autumn heat combined with rising winds meant the fire raged out of control for four days, reducing 80% of London to ash. Only eight people died (officially at least), but most of medieval London was obliterated. The fire finally stopped at Pye Corner in Smithfield, on the very edge of London, not before destroying 89 churches, including St Paul's Cathedral, and more than 13,000 houses, leaving tens of thousands of people homeless.

Wren's London

The inferno created a blank canvas upon which master architect Christopher Wren could build his 51 magnificent new churches and a cathedral. Wren's plan for rebuilding the entire city – much of it on a grid pattern – was deemed too expensive, and many landlords opposed it; the familiar pattern of streets that had grown up over the centuries since the time of the Romans quickly reappeared. However, new laws stipulated that brick and stone designs should replace the old timber-framed, overhanging Tudor houses and that many roads be widened. The fire accelerated the movement of the wealthy away from the City and into what is now the West End.

By way of memorialising the blaze – and rebuilding of London – the Monument, designed by Wren, was erected in 1677 near the site of the fire's outbreak. At the time, the 61m-tall column was by far the highest structure in the city, visible from everywhere in the capital.

In 1685 some 1500 Huguenot (Protestant) refugees arrived in London, fleeing persecution in Catholic France; another 3500 would follow. Mainly artisans, many began manufacturing luxury goods such as silks and silverware in and around Spitalfields and Clerkenwell, which were already populated with Irish, Jewish and Italian immigrants and artisans. London was fast becoming one of the world's most cosmopolitan places.

The Glorious – ie bloodless – Revolution in 1688 brought the Dutch King William of Orange to the English throne after the Catholic James II had fled to France. King William III and Queen Mary II, who ruled jointly, relocated from Whitehall Palace to a new palace in Kensington Gardens and, in order to raise finances for the war with France, established the Bank of England in 1694.

London's growth continued unabated, and by 1700 it was Europe's largest city, with some 600,000 people. The influx of foreign workers brought expansion to the east and south, while those who could afford it headed to the more salubrious environs of the north and west.

For superb city views from London's most iconic piece of ecclesiastical architecture, climb the 528 stairs (no lift) to the Golden Gallery in the dome of Sir Christopher Wren's opus magnum: three-centuries-old St Paul's Cathedral.

The crowning glory of the 'Great Rebuilding', Wren's St Paul's Cathedral opened in 1711 during the reign of the last Stuart monarch, Queen Anne. A masterpiece of English baroque architecture, it remains one of the city's most prominent and beautiful landmarks.

Georgian London

Queen Anne died in 1714 without leaving an heir (despite 17 conceptions). Although there were some 50 Catholic relatives with stronger claims to the throne, a search was immediately launched to find a Protestant relative, since the 1701 Act of Settlement forbade Roman Catholics becoming monarch. Eventually George of Hanover, a great-grandson of James I, arrived from Germany and was crowned King of England, though he never learned to speak English.

Robert Walpole's Whig Party controlled parliament during much of George I's reign and, as 'First Lord of the Treasury', effectively became Britain's first prime minister. He was presented with 10 Downing St, which remains the official residence of the prime minister today.

London grew at a phenomenal pace during this time, and measures were taken to make the city more accessible. The Roman wall surrounding the City of London was torn down, and a second span over the Thames, Westminster Bridge, opened in 1750.

Georgian London saw a great creative surge in music, art and architecture. Court composer George Frederick Handel wrote *Water Music* (1717) and *Messiah* (1741) after settling here at age 27, and in 1755 Dr Johnson published the first English-language dictionary. William Hogarth, Thomas Gainsborough and Joshua Reynolds produced some of their finest paintings and engravings, and many of London's most elegant buildings, streets and squares were erected or laid out by architects such as John Soane, his pupil Robert Smirke, and the prolific John Nash.

All the while, though, London was becoming ever more segregated and lawless. Indeed, King George II himself was relieved of 'purse, watch and buckles' during a stroll through Kensington Gardens. This was Hogarth's London, in which the wealthy built fine mansions in attractive squares and gathered in fashionable new coffee houses while the poor huddled together in appalling slums and drowned their sorrows with cheap gin. To curb rising crime, two magistrates, including the writer Henry Fielding, established the Bow Street Runners in 1749. This voluntary group was effectively a forerunner to the Metropolitan Police Force, which would be established in 1829.

In 1780 parliament proposed to lift the law preventing Catholics buying or inheriting property. One MP, Lord George Gordon, led a 'No Pop-

For trivia, little-known facts and endless specialist information on the history of the East End and its personalities, head to East London History (www.eastlondon-history.com).

1707	1711	1759	1812
The first-ever sitting of the parliament of the Kingdom of Great Britain occurs in London as the Act of Union brings England and Scotland together under one parliament.	Sir Christopher Wren's masterpiece St Paul's Cathedral is officially completed, 45 years after Old St Paul's Cathedral was gutted by the Great Fire.	The British Museum opens to the public for the first time, housed in Montagu House in Bloomsbury and levying no admission fee to all 'studious and curious persons'.	Charles Dickens, Victorian England's greatest novelist, is born in Portsmouth; many of his novels would portray London in all its Victorian squalor.

ery' demonstration that turned into the so-called Gordon Riots. A mob of 30,000 went on a rampage, attacking Irish labourers and burning prisons, 'Papishe dens' (chapels) and several law courts. As many as 850 people died during five days of rioting.

As George III, forever remembered as the king who lost the American colonies, slid into dementia towards the end of the 18th century, his son, the Prince Regent (the future George IV), set up an alternative and considerably more fashionable court at Carlton House in Pall Mall. By this time London's population had mushroomed to just under a million.

Victorian London

In 1837 George IV's 18-year-old niece, Victoria, ascended the throne. During her long reign London would become the nerve centre of the largest and richest empire the world had ever known, covering a quarter of the globe's surface and ruling over more than 500 million people.

New docks in East London were built to facilitate the booming trade with the colonies, and railways began to fan out from the capital. The world's first underground railway opened between Paddington and Farringdon in 1863 and was such a success that other lines quickly followed. Many of London's most famous buildings and landmarks were built at this time, including what is now officially named Elizabeth Tower but popularly known as Big Ben (1859), the Royal Albert Hall (1871) and the iconic Tower Bridge (1894).

The city, however, heaved under the burden of its vast size, and in 1858 London was in the grip of the 'Great Stink', when the population explosion so overtook the city's sanitation facilities that raw sewage seeped in through the floorboards of wealthy merchants' houses and the Houses of Parliament were draped with sheets soaked in lime chloride to allay the stench from the river. Leading engineer Joseph Bazalgette tackled the problem by creating an underground network of sewers in the late 1850s.

At the same time, intellectual achievement in the arts and sciences was enormous. The greatest chronicler of the Victorian age was Charles Dickens, whose *Oliver Twist* (1837) and other works explored the themes of poverty, hopelessness and squalor among the working classes. In 1859 Charles Darwin published his seminal and immensely controversial *On the Origin of Species* here, in which he outlined the theory of evolution.

Some of Britain's most capable prime ministers served during Victoria's 64-year reign, most notably William Gladstone (four terms between 1868 and 1894) and Benjamin Disraeli (who served in 1868 and again from 1874 to 1880). And with the creation of the London County

You may worry about today's vehicle emissions, but at the end of the 19th century 1000 tonnes of horse manure would fall on the streets of London daily. Crossing sweepers, often young boys, made meagre earnings clearing a path for pedestrians.

1838	1843	1851	1878
The coronation of Queen Victoria at Westminster Abbey ushers in a new era for London; the British capital becomes the economic centre of the world.	Connecting Rotherhithe and Wapping, Marc Isambard Brunel opens his Thames Tunnel, the first tunnel to be constructed under a navigable river.	The Great Exhibition, the brainchild of Victoria's consort, Albert, who would die a decade later, opens to great fanfare in the purpose-built Crystal Palace in Hyde Park.	London's first electric lights are installed in Billingsgate Fish Market, using 'Yablochkov candles' (arc lamps).

Council (LCC) in 1889, the capital had its first-ever directly elected government.

Waves of immigrants, from Irish and Jews to Chinese and Indian sepoys, arrived in London during the 19th century, when the population exploded from one million to well over six million people. This breakneck expansion was not beneficial to all – inner-city slums housed the poor in atrocious conditions of disease and overcrowding, while the affluent expanded to leafy suburbs.

Queen Victoria (of 'We are not amused' fame) is often seen as a dour, humourless old curmudgeon, but was in reality an intelligent, progressive and passionate woman. While her beloved husband and consort, Prince Albert, died prematurely of typhoid in 1861, she lived on to celebrate her Diamond Jubilee in 1897 and died four years later at the age of 81. Her reign is considered the climax of British world supremacy.

For an upfront view of WWI and its unspeakable devastation, visit the state-of-the-art First World War Galleries (www.iwm. org.uk/exhibitions/ iwm-london/first-world-war-galleries) at the Imperial War Museum.

From Empire to World War

Victoria's self-indulgent son Edward, the Prince of Wales, was already 60 by the time he was crowned Edward VII in 1901. London's belle époque was marked with the introduction of the first motorised double-decker buses in 1904 on the Peckham to Oxford Circus route, which replaced the horse-drawn versions that had plodded their trade since 1829. And a touch of glamour came in the form of luxury hotels, such as the Ritz in 1906, and department stores, such as Selfridges, in 1909. The first London Olympics were held at White City Stadium in 1908.

What became known as the Great War (or WWI) broke out in August 1914, and the first German bombs fell from zeppelins near the Guildhall a year later, killing 39 people. In all, some 670 Londoners were killed by bombs (half the national total of civilian casualties) and another 2000 were wounded.

The Interwar Years

After the war ended in 1918, London's population continued to rise, reaching nearly 7.5 million in 1921. The LCC busied itself clearing slums and building new housing estates, while the suburbs spread further into the countryside.

Unemployment rose steadily, and in May 1926 a wage dispute in the coal industry escalated into a nine-day general strike, in which so many workers downed tools that London virtually ground to a halt. The army was called in to maintain order and to keep the buses and the Underground running, but the stage was set for more than half a century of industrial strife.

1884	1901	1926	1936
Greenwich Mean Time is established, making Greenwich Observatory the centre of world time, according to which all clocks around the globe are set.	Queen Victoria dies after reigning 63 years and 217 days – the longest reign in British history until Elizabeth II broke that record in September 2015.	London all but closes down for nine days during the General Strike, with little violence and ultimately almost no impact on trade-union activity or industrial relations.	The 'Year of Three Kings': George VI ascends the throne following the death of his father, George V, and abdication of his brother, Edward VIII, who gave up his throne for love.

Intellectually the 1920s were the heyday of the Bloomsbury Group, which counted writers Virginia Woolf and EM Forster and the economist John Maynard Keynes in its ranks. The spotlight shifted westwards to Fitzrovia in the following decade, when George Orwell and Dylan Thomas raised glasses with contemporaries at the Fitzroy Tavern on Charlotte St. Cinema, TV and radio arrived: the BBC aired its first radio broadcast from the roof of Marconi House on the Strand in 1922, and the first TV program from Alexandra Palace 14 years later.

The monarchy took a knock when Edward VIII abdicated in 1936 to marry a woman who was not only twice divorced but - egad! - an American. The same year Oswald Mosley attempted to lead the black-shirted British Union of Fascists on an anti-Jewish march through the East End but was repelled by a mob of around half a million at the famous Battle of Cable St.

WWII & the Blitz

Prime Minister Neville Chamberlain's policy of appeasing Adolf Hitler during the 1930s eventually proved misguided as the Führer's appetite for expansion appeared insatiable. When Germany invaded Poland on 1 September 1939, Britain declared war, having signed a mutual-assistance pact with that nation a few days before. WWII had begun.

The first year of the war was one of anxious waiting for London. Some 600,000 women and children had been evacuated to the countryside from London and the Battle of Britain raged elsewhere, primarily around Royal Air Force bases in England, but no bombs fell to disturb the blackout in the capital. On 7 September 1940 that all came to a devastating end when the Luftwaffe, the German Air Force, dropped hundreds of bombs on the East End, killing 430 people.

The Blitz (from the German *'Blitzkrieg'* or 'lightning war') lasted for 57 nights, and then continued intermittently until mid-May 1941. Some Underground stations were turned into giant bomb shelters, although one bomb rolled down the escalator at Bank station and exploded on the platform, killing more than 100 people. Londoners responded with resilience and stoicism. To the great admiration and respect of the people, the King and Queen refused to leave London during the bombing (their daughters Elizabeth and Margaret remained at Windsor). Buckingham Palace took a direct hit during a bombing raid early in the campaign, famously prompting Queen Elizabeth (the present monarch's late mother) to pronounce that 'Now I can look the East End in the face'. Winston Churchill, prime minister from 1940, orchestrated much of Britain's war strategy from the subterranean Cabinet War Rooms

The night of 29/30 December 1940 has been called the 'Second Great Fire of London', when German bombers dropped more than 24,000 high-explosive bombs and 100,000 incendiary devices on London in a few hours, starting 1500 fires raging across the City and up to Islington.

1940–41	1945	1951	1952
London is devastated by the Blitz, although miraculously St Paul's Cathedral and the Tower of London escape the bombing largely unscathed.	Big Ben is illuminated again in April and full street lighting restored six months after the Blackout is downgraded to a dim-out over London; 'Victory in Europe' is declared in May.	King George VI opens the Festival of Britain, marking the centenary of the Great Exhibition and aiming to lift the national mood after the destruction of WWII.	London is brought to a virtual standstill for four days in December by a thick pea-souper smog that smothers and chokes the city and leaves up to 4000 people dead.

at Whitehall, and it was from here that he made several of his stirring wartime speeches.

London's spirit was tested again in June 1944, when Germany launched pilotless V-1 bombers (known as doodlebugs) over East London. By the time Nazi Germany capitulated in May 1945, up to a third of the East End and the City had been flattened, almost 30,000 Londoners killed and a further 50,000 seriously wounded.

Postwar London & the '60s

Once the Victory in Europe (VE) celebrations had come to a close, the nation began to assess the war's appalling toll and to rebuild. The years of austerity had begun, with rationing of essential items and the building of high-rise residences on bomb sites in areas like Pimlico and the East End to solve the chronic housing problem. To help boost morale, London hosted the 1948 Olympics (dubbed 'the austerity Games') and the Festival of Britain in 1951.

The gloom returned, quite literally, on 6 December 1952 in the form of the Great Smog. A lethal blend of fog, smoke and pollution descended, and some 4000 people died of respiratory disorders. This prompted the promulgation of the Clean Air Act of 1956, which introduced zones to central London where only smokeless fuels could be burned.

The current queen was crowned Elizabeth II in 1953 following the death of her much-loved father King George VI the year before. Rationing of most goods ended in 1954, 14 years after it had begun.

Immigrants from around the world – particularly from the former colonies – flocked to London, where a dwindling population had led to labour shortages. However, despite being officially encouraged to come, new immigrants weren't always welcomed on the streets, as was proved in the Notting Hill race riots of 1958.

Some economic prosperity returned in the late 1950s, and Prime Minister Harold Macmillan told Britons they'd 'never had it so good'. London became the place to be during the 1960s, when the bottled-up creative energy of the postwar era was spectacularly uncorked. London found itself the epicentre of cool in fashion and music: the streets were awash with colour and vitality, the iconic Mini car (1959) and skirt became British icons, and the Jaguar E-type (1961) was launched to adoring crowds.

Social norms underwent a revolution: the introduction of the contraceptive pill, the partial decriminalisation of homosexuality, and the popularisation of drugs such as marijuana and LSD through the hippy movement created an unprecedented permissive and liberal climate. Popular music in the mid-to-late 1960s became increasingly linked with

For an idea of the scale of the devastation brought about by the Blitz on London, visit the website of the Bomb Sight project (http://bombsight. org), which has mapped the WWII bomb census between October 1940 and June 1941 for the first time.

1953	1956	1959	1966
Queen Elizabeth II's coronation is held at Westminster Abbey, the first major event to be broadcast live around the world on TV.	Red Routemaster double-decker buses make their first appearance in London and soon become a city icon.	The Notting Hill Carnival is launched by Claudia Jones to promote better race relations following the riots of 1958 when white and Afro-Caribbean communities clashed.	England beat Germany to win the World Cup at Wembley – possibly the greatest day in the history of British sport and one seared into the consciousness of every schoolboy.

drug use, political activism and a counter-cultural mindset. The Beatles recording at Abbey Road and the Rolling Stones performing free in front of half a million people in Hyde Park were seminal moments. Carnaby St and the King's Rd were the most fashionable places on earth, and pop-culture figures from Twiggy and David Bailey to Marianne Faithfull and Christine Keeler became the faces of the new era.

The Punk Era

London returned to the doldrums in the harsh economic climate of the 1970s. The city's once-important docks never recovered from the loss of empire, the changing needs of modern container ships and poor labour relations, and disappeared altogether between 1968 and 1981. Shipping moved 25 miles east to Tilbury, and the Docklands declined to a point of decay, until they were rediscovered by property developers a decade later. In 1973 a bomb went off at the Old Bailey (the Central Criminal Court), signalling the arrival of the Irish Republican Army (IRA) in London and its campaign for a united Ireland.

Post-1960s music became more formulaic as glam rock ruled, despite the blossoming of London legends Marc Bolan and David Bowie. Economic stagnation, cynicism and the superficial limits of disco and glam rock spawned a novel London aesthetic: punk. Largely white, energetic, abrasive and fast, punk transformed popular music and fashion in one stroke as teenagers traded in denim bell-bottoms for black drainpipes, and long hair for spiked Mohicans. The late 1970s were exhilarating times for London youth as punk opened the door for new wave, a punchy mod revival and the indulgent new romantics.

Meanwhile, torpor had set into Britain's body politic. Seen as weak and in thrall to the all-powerful trade unions, the brief and unremarkable Labour premiership of James Callaghan (1976–79) was marked by crippling strikes in the late 1970s, most significantly the 'Winter of Discontent' of 1978–79 when Leicester Sq became a rubbish tip after waste-collection workers walked off the job.

For a fascinating review of the social, musical and cultural history of 20th-century London, take a look at Another Nickel in the Machine (www. nickelinthemachine. com), a blog covering everything from suffragettes and Charlie Chaplin's homecoming to vintage Bowie.

The Thatcher Years

In 1979 the Conservative leader Margaret Thatcher became the UK's first female prime minister. In power for all of the 1980s and embarking on an unprecedented program of privatisation, Margaret Thatcher – aka the 'Iron Lady' – is arguably the most significant of Britain's postwar leaders. While her critics decry her approach to social justice and the large gulf that developed between the haves and have nots during her time in power, her defenders point to the massive modernisation of

1979	1981	1984	1987
Margaret Thatcher is elected prime minister. Her policies will transform Britain beyond recognition – part vital modernisation, part radical right-wing social policy.	Brixton sees the worst race riots in London's history; Lord Scarman, delivering his report on the events, puts the blame squarely on 'racial disadvantage that is a fact of British life'.	The Thames Barrier, designed to protect London from flooding during high tides and storm surges, is officially opened by the Queen.	A fire, probably started by a dropped match or cigarette, at King's Cross Underground station causes the deaths of 31 people.

Britain's infrastructure (until then in the grip of trade unions) and the vast wealth creation her policies generated.

In the beginning, her monetarist policy sent unemployment skyrocketing; an inquiry following the Brixton riots of 1981 found that an astonishing 55% of men aged under 19 in that part of London were jobless. Meanwhile the Greater London Council (GLC), under the leadership of 'Red' Ken Livingstone, proved to be a thorn in Thatcher's side. County Hall, which faces the Houses of Parliament across the Thames, was hung with a giant banner recording the number of unemployed in the capital and goading the prime minister to do something about it. Thatcher responded in 1986 by abolishing the GLC, leaving London the only European capital without a unified central government.

While poorer Londoners suffered under Thatcher's significant trimming back of the welfare state, things had rarely looked better for the business community. Riding a wave of confidence partly engendered by the deregulation of the stock exchange in 1986 (the so-called Big Bang), London underwent explosive economic growth. Property developers proved to be only marginally more discriminating than the Luftwaffe, though some outstanding modern structures, including the Lloyd's of London building, went up.

Like previous booms, the one of the late 1980s proved unsustainable. As unemployment started to rise again and people found themselves living in houses worth much less than they had paid for them, Thatcher introduced a flat-rate poll tax. Protests around the country culminated in a 1990 march on Trafalgar Sq that ended in a fully fledged riot. Thatcher's subsequent resignation after losing a confidence vote in Parliament brought to an end this divisive era. Her successor, the former Chancellor of the Exchequer, John Major, employed a far more collective form of government.

In 1992, to the amazement of most Londoners, the Conservatives were elected for a fourth successive term in government, without the inspiring leadership of Thatcher. The economy went into a tailspin shortly after, and the IRA detonated two huge bombs, one in the City in 1992 and another in the Docklands four years later. The writing was on the wall for the Conservatives, as the Labour Party re-emerged with a new face.

Blair's Britain

Desperate to return to power after almost two decades in opposition, the Labour Party selected the telegenic Tony Blair to lead it. The May 1997 general election overwhelmingly returned a Labour government to power, but it was a much changed 'New Labour' party, one that had

The Iron Lady (2011) starring Meryl Streep remains a very watchable biopic of the late Margaret Thatcher. It seamlessly traces the former prime minister's life and career from politically astute grocer's daughter to grieving widow suffering from dementia. Thatcher died two years after the film's release.

1990	1997	2003	2005
Britain erupts in civil unrest, culminating in the poll tax riots in Trafalgar Sq; the deeply unpopular tax ultimately proves to be Thatcher's undoing and she resigns in November.	Labour sweeps to victory after almost two decades of Conservative government. Tony Blair's centrist 'New Labour' party wins a majority of 179 in the House of Commons.	London's congestion charge is introduced by Livingstone, a scheme that sees traffic volume reduced by 10% in its first decade.	A day after London is awarded the 2012 Olympics, 52 people are killed by Islamic terrorists in a series of suicide bombings on London's transport network on 7 July.

shed most of its socialist credo and supported a market economy, privatisation and integration with Europe.

Most importantly for London, Labour recognised the legitimate demand the city had for local government, and created the London Assembly and the post of mayor. Former leader of the GLC Ken Livingstone stood as an independent candidate and won handily. Livingstone introduced a successful congestion charge to limit road traffic in central London and sought to bring London's backward public transport network into the 21st century.

London's resurgence as a great world city seemed to be going from strength to strength, culminating in its selection in July 2005 to host the Olympic Games in 2012. London's buoyant mood was, however, shattered the very next morning when extremist Muslim terrorists detonated a series of bombs on the city's public transport network, killing 52 people. Triumph turned to terror, followed quickly by anger and then defiance. Just two weeks later the attempted detonation of several more bombs on London's public transport system sent the city into a state of severe unease, which culminated in the tragic shooting by the Metropolitan Police of an innocent Brazilian electrician, Jean Charles de Menezes, mistaken for one of the failed bombers.

Enter Boris

Ken Livingstone's campaign to get a third term as London mayor in 2008 was fatally undermined when the Conservative Party fielded maverick MP and popular TV personality Boris Johnson as its candidate. Even more of a populist than Livingstone, Eton-educated Johnson, portrayed by the media as a gaffe-prone toff, actually proved to be a deft political operator and surprised everyone by sailing past Livingstone to become the first Conservative mayor ever of London.

Johnson was popularised in the media as an almost eccentric, oddball figure, with his wild mop of blond hair, shapeless suits and in-your-face eagerness. It was a persona Londoners warmed to. He disagreed with Livingstone on many issues, but continued to support several of his predecessor's policies, including the congestion charge and the expansion of bicycle lanes. A keen cyclist himself, Boris is forever associated with the bicycle-hire scheme sponsored by Barclays, now underwritten by Santander Bank and nicknamed 'Boris Bikes' (though Livingstone proposed it first). Johnson pledged to replace Livingstone's unloved 'bendy buses' with remodelled Routemasters, which were introduced on some routes in 2012.

Johnson's first mayoral term coincided with London's transformation for the 2012 Olympic Games. Neglected areas of the recession-hit

The Millennium Dome on the Greenwich Peninsula failed to impress when it opened in 2000. Designed by Richard Rogers and sometimes mockingly referred to as the Millennium Tent, the dome eventually triumphed when rebranded as the O2 in 2007. It is now one of the most successful live-entertainment venues in the world.

2010	2011	2012	2013
Labour is defeated in the general elections, which results in a hung Parliament and a Conservative–Liberal Democrat coalition government with David Cameron as prime minister.	A demonstration against alleged police brutality in Tottenham on 6 August turns into a riot and a spree of mass looting that spreads to numerous boroughs and towns across the UK.	Boris Johnson narrowly beats Ken Livingstone to win his second mayoral election; London hosts the 2012 Olympics and Paralympics.	The Shard, at 310m (1016ft) the tallest building in the EU, opens to the public; MPs vote in favour of legalising gay marriage.

city were showered with investment and a vast building program in East London took shape. The era also saw a transferral of government power from the lacklustre Labour Party under Gordon Brown's leadership to a Conservative-Liberal Democrat coalition government with fellow Etonian David Cameron as prime minister and Nick Clegg as deputy prime minister.

London's Year

The year 2012 promised to be London's year, and few people – at home or abroad – were disappointed.

A four-day holiday in June marked the Queen's Diamond Jubilee – the 60th anniversary of her ascension to the throne. As celebratory and joyous as the Jubilee was, it was but a prelude to *the* London event of the year: the all-singin', all-dancin' Olympics and Paralympics that welcomed some 15,000 athletes competing in almost 50 sports for 800 medals. Over the course of 29 days there were many expected highs (Britain took 65 Olympic and 120 Paralympic medals, to rank third in each games) and some surprising ones (London's transport system did not just cope but excelled).

But nothing came close to Danny Boyle's Olympics Opening Ceremony in which the world was treated to an extravagant potted history of London and the UK, football superstar David Beckham drove the Olympic Torch down the Thames and into the Olympic Park in a high-speed boat, and James Bond (in the form of Daniel Craig) jumped out of a helicopter into the Olympic Stadium accompanied by none other than Her Majesty, 'the Queen'. Dear reader, we're still laughing and cheering.

Survival of the Fittest

Since the Olympics, both the nation and the city have changed leadership (Theresa May replacing David Cameron as prime minister, Sadiq Khan taking over as mayor from Boris Johnson), scores of new highrise buildings have transformed the London skyline, most notably on the South Bank, and an increase in property rates has seen many independent high-street businesses close. Countless construction sites throughout London have reduced traffic to a crawl and the price of a pint has reached £5. Still, pop-ups of everything from shops selling vintage clothing and restaurants dishing up the most exotic of cuisines continue to open at the speed of summer lightning, the West End opens even more exhilarating shows – both home-grown and imported – each season, much of the Underground now runs all night at weekends, and national museums remain free of charge to one and all. What effect Brexit will have on this great city's future remains to be seen.

2014	2015	2016	2017
The southern half of the Olympic site opens to the public as Queen Elizabeth Olympic Park, followed by the Aquatics Centre, Velodrome and ArcelorMittal Orbit.	The Conservatives defeat Labour in the general election, emerging with a narrow majority and abandoning their coalition government with the Liberal Democrats.	Sadiq Khan is elected London's mayor, the first Muslim to hold such a position in a major Western capital; UK electorate votes 52% to 48% to leave the EU, now known as 'Brexit'.	The Conservative Party scrapes home in a closer-than-expected national election and Theresa May forms a new government.

Architecture

Unlike certain other cities, London has never been methodically planned. Instead, it has developed in an almost haphazard fashion. As a result, London retains architectural reminders from every period of its long history, but they are often hidden: part of a Roman wall enclosed in the lobby of a modern building near St Paul's Cathedral, say, or a galleried coaching inn from the Restoration in a courtyard off Borough High St. As you'll soon discover, this is a city for explorers.

Above: The Shard (p166)

Laying the Foundations

London's architectural roots lie within the walled Roman settlement of Londinium, established in AD 43 on the northern banks of the River Thames where the City of London is located. Few Roman traces survive outside museums, though a Temple of Mithras (or Mithraeum), built in AD 240 and excavated in 1954, has moved to the eastern end of Queen Victoria St in the City following completion of the Bloomberg headquarters at Walbrook Sq. Stretches of the Roman wall remain as foundations to a medieval wall outside Tower Hill tube station and in a few sections below Bastion Highwalk, next to the Museum of London.

> The London Festival of Architecture is an annual month-long event in June celebrating the capital's buildings with a range of events, walks, talks, tours and debates.

The Saxons, who moved into the area after the decline of the Roman Empire, found Londinium too small, all but ignored what the Romans had left behind and built their communities further up the Thames. Excavations carried out during renovations at the Royal Opera House in the late 1990s uncovered extensive traces of the Saxon settlement of Lundenwic, including some houses of wattle and daub. All Hallows-by-the-Tower, northwest of the Tower of London, shelters an important archway, the walls of a 7th-century Saxon church and a Roman pavement. St Bride's, Fleet St, has a similar pavement.

With the arrival of William the Conqueror in 1066, the country received its first example of Norman architecture with the White Tower, the sturdy keep at the heart of the Tower of London. The church of St Bartholomew-the-Great at Smithfield also has Norman arches and columns supporting its nave. The west door and elaborately moulded porch at Temple Church (shared by Inner and Middle Temple), the undercroft at Westminster Abbey and the crypt at St-Mary-le-Bow are other outstanding examples of Norman architecture.

Medieval London

Enlarged and refurbished in the 13th and 14th centuries by 'builder king' Henry III and his son, Edward I, or 'Longshanks' (think *Braveheart*), Westminster Abbey is a splendid reminder of the work of master masons in the Middle Ages. Perhaps the finest surviving medieval church in the city is the 13th-century church of St Ethelburga-the-Virgin near Liverpool St station, heavily restored after Irish Republican Army (IRA) bombings in 1993. The 15th-century Church of St Olave, northwest of Tower Hill, is one of the City's few remaining Gothic parish churches, while the crypt at the largely restored Church of St Etheldreda, north of Holborn Circus, dates from about 1250. Southwark Cathedral includes some remnants from the 12th and 13th centuries.

Secular medieval buildings are even scarcer than ecclesiastical ones, although the ragstone Jewel Tower, opposite the Houses of Parliament, dates from 1365, and much of the Tower of London goes back to the Middle Ages. Staple Inn in Holborn dates from 1378, but the half-timbered shopfront facade (1589) is mostly Elizabethan, and heavily restored in the mid-20th century after WWII bombing. Westminster Hall was originally built in 1199; the hammerbeam roof came 300 years later. The great Medieval Hall (1479) at Eltham Palace also has a splendid hammer-beam roof, as does St George's Hall in Windsor Castle, rebuilt after a fire in 1992.

A Trinity of Architects

The finest London architect of the first half of the 17th century was Inigo Jones (1573–1652), who spent a year and a half in Italy and became a convert to the Renaissance-style architecture of Andrea Palladio. His *chefs d'œuvre* include Banqueting House (1622) in Whitehall and Queen's House (1635) in Greenwich. Often overlooked is his much plainer church of St Paul's in Covent Garden, which Jones designed in the early 1630s.

The greatest architect to leave his mark on London was Christopher Wren (1632–1723), responsible for St Paul's Cathedral (1711). Wren oversaw the building (or rebuilding) of more than 50 churches, many replacing medieval churches lost in the Great Fire, as well as the Royal Hospital Chelsea (1692) and the Old Royal Naval College, begun in 1694 at Greenwich. His English baroque buildings and churches are taller and lighter than their medieval predecessors, with graceful steeples taking the place of solid square medieval towers.

Nicholas Hawksmoor (1661–1736) was a pupil of Wren and worked with him on several churches before going on to design his own masterpieces. The restored Christ Church (1729) in Spitalfields, St George's Bloomsbury (1731), St Anne's, Limehouse (1725), and St George-in-the-East (1726) at Wapping are among the finest of his half-dozen churches in London.

Georgian Manners

Among the greatest exponents of classicism (or neo-Palladianism) was Scotsman Robert Adam (1728–92), whose surviving work in London includes Kenwood House (1779) on Hampstead Heath and some of the interiors of Apsley House (1778) at Hyde Park Corner.

Adam's fame has been eclipsed by that of John Nash (1752–1835), whose contribution to London's architecture can almost compare to that of Christopher Wren. Nash was responsible for the layout of Regent's Park and its surrounding elegant crescents. To give London a 'spine', he created Regent St as an axis from the new Regent's Park south to St James's Park. This grand project also involved the formation of Trafalgar Sq, and the development of the Mall and the western end of the Strand. Nash refashioned the old Buckingham House into Buckingham Palace (1830) for George IV.

Nash's contemporary John Soane (1753–1837) was the architect of the Bank of England, completed in 1833 (though much of his work was lost during the bank's rebuilding by Herbert Baker between 1925 and 1939), as well as the Dulwich Picture Gallery (1814). Robert Smirke (1780–1867) designed the British Museum in 1823; it's one of the finest expressions of the so-called Greek Revivalist style.

A 'Gothick' Rethink

In the 19th century the highly decorative neo-Gothic style, also known as Victorian High Gothic or 'Gothick', became all the vogue. Champions were the architects George Gilbert Scott (1811–78), Alfred Waterhouse (1830–1905) and Augustus Pugin (1812–52). Scott was responsible for the elaborate Albert Memorial (1872) in Kensington Gardens and the Midland Grand Hotel (1872), now fully restored as the St Pancras Renaissance Hotel. Waterhouse designed the flamboyant Natural History Museum (1881), while Pugin worked from 1840 with the designer Charles Barry (1795–1860) on the Houses of Parliament after the Palace of Westminster burned down in 1834. The last great neo-Gothic public building to go up in London was the Royal Courts of Justice (1882), designed by George Edmund Street.

The emphasis on the artisanship and materials required to create these elaborate neo-Gothic buildings led to the formation of the Arts and Crafts movement, of which William Morris (1834–96) was the leading exponent. Morris' work can be seen in the Green Dining Room of the Victoria & Albert Museum; at his Red House in Bexleyheath; at the

Charles Dickens referred to the Church of St Olave as 'St Ghastly Grim' because of the macabre ornamentation of skulls above the entrance.

William Morris Gallery in Walthamstow; and in the recently reopened Emery Walker's House in Hammersmith.

Flirting with Modernism

Relatively few notable public buildings emerged from the first 15 years of the 20th century, apart from Admiralty Arch (1910), which was done in the Edwardian baroque style of Aston Webb (1849–1930), who also designed the Queen Victoria Memorial (1911) in front of Buckingham Palace. County Hall, designed by Ralph Knott in 1909, was not completed until 1922. More modern imagination is evident in commercial design: for example, the superb Art Nouveau design of Michelin House on Fulham Rd, dating from 1911.

In the period between the two world wars, English architecture was barely more creative, though Edwin 'Ned' Lutyens (1869–1944) designed the Cenotaph (1920) in Whitehall as well as the impressive Britannic House (1927 – now with modern additions and called Alphabeta – in Moorgate, and the Midland Bank Building (1924) on Poultry in the City – now the Ned hotel and restaurant complex. Displaying the same amount of Edwardian optimism is the former Port of London Authority (1922) designed by Edwin Cooper and now an apartment block and hotel.

Designed by US architect Harvey Wiley Corbett (1873–1954), Bush House, at the southern end of Kingsway and until recently the home of the BBC World Service, was built between 1923 and 1935. It's now part of King's College London. The black-and-chrome curves of the Daily Express Building (1932, Ellis Clarke with Owen Williams) at 120 Fleet St are a splendid example of art-deco grace. Two other art-deco classics are St Olaf House, an office block on Tooley St and fronting the Thames, designed by HS Goodhart-Rendel in 1928, and 55 Broadway (1929), a listed block above St James's tube station designed by Charles Holden and headquarters of London Underground until 2015.

Postwar Reconstruction

Hitler's bombs during WWII wrought the worst destruction on London since the Great Fire of 1666, and the immediate postwar problem was a chronic housing shortage. Low-cost developments and ugly high-rise housing were thrown up on bomb sites and many of these blocks still scar London's horizon today.

The Royal Festival Hall, designed by Robert Matthew (1906–75) and J Leslie Martin (1908–99) for the 1951 Festival of Britain, attracted as many bouquets as brickbats when it opened as London's first major public building in the modernist style. Even today, hardly anyone seems to have a good word to say about the neighbouring National Theatre, a brutalist structure by Denys Lasdun (1914–2001), which was begun in 1966 and finished a decade later.

The 1960s saw the ascendancy of the workaday glass-and-concrete high-rises exemplified by the mostly unloved Centre Point (1967) by Richard Seifert (1910–2001). But the once-vilified modernist tower has now been given a Grade II listing by English Heritage, meaning that it cannot be altered for the most part. The 1964 BT Tower, formerly known as the Post Office Tower and designed by Eric Bedford (1909–2001), has also received the same listed status.

Little building was undertaken in the 1970s apart from roads, and the recession of the late 1980s and early 1990s brought much development and speculation to a standstill. Helping to polarise traditionalists and modernists still further was Prince Charles, who described a proposed (but never built) extension to the National Gallery as being

The famous art-nouveau stained glass of Michelin House (p189) was removed for storage at the start of WWII, but subsequently vanished. The existing glass is a reproduction, based on photographs. The hunt for the original apparently continues.

London's smallest house – a metre wide at its narrowest point – is 10 Hyde Park Pl, now part of Tyburn Convent. Despite being such a small target, it was damaged by a German bomb during WWII.

OPEN HOUSE LONDON

If you want to see the inside of buildings whose doors are normally shut tight, visit London on the third weekend in September. That's when the charity Open House London (p417) arranges for owners of some 850 private and public buildings to let the public in free of charge. Major buildings (eg the Gherkin, City Hall, Lloyd's of London, Royal Courts of Justice, BT Tower) have participated in the past; the full program becomes available in August. Maggie's Culture Crawl (www.maggiescentres.org/culturecrawl), a 15-mile architectural night walking tour for charity, wends its way through the city over the same weekend. Open City (p417) offers architect-led tours year-round.

like 'a monstrous carbuncle on the face of an elegant and much loved friend'.

Epstein & 55 Broadway

Situated above St James's Park Underground station, 55 Broadway was highly controversial when it opened in 1929, not the least for its pair of sculptures *Day* and *Night* by Jacob Epstein. The generous anatomy of the figures caused an outcry and Epstein had to snip 4cm from the penis of the smaller figure *Day*.

Postmodernism Lands

London's contemporary architecture was born in the City and the revitalised Docklands in the mid-1980s. The City's centrepiece was the 1986 Lloyd's of London Building, Richard Rogers' 'inside-out' chef d'oeuvre of ducts, pipes, glass and stainless steel. Taking pride of place in the Docklands was Cesar Pelli's 244m-high One Canada Sq (1991), commonly known as Canary Wharf and easily visible from central London. But London's very first postmodern building (designed in the late 1980s by James Stirling but not completed till 1998) is considered to be No 1 Poultry, a playful shiplike City landmark faced with yellow and pink limestone. The graceful British Library (Colin St John Wilson, 1998), with its warm red-brick exterior, Asian-like touches and wonderfully bright interior, initially met a very hostile reception but has now become a popular landmark.

At the end of the 1990s, attention turned to public buildings, including several new landmarks. From the disused Bankside Power Station (Giles Gilbert Scott, 1947–63), the Tate Modern (Herzog & de Meuron, 1999) was refashioned as an art gallery that scooped international architecture's most prestigious prize, the Pritzker. The stunning Millennium Bridge (Norman Foster and Anthony Caro, 2000), the first new bridge to cross the Thames in central London since Tower Bridge went up in 1894, is much loved and much used. Even the white-elephant Millennium Dome (Richard Rogers), the class dunce of 2000, won a new lease of life as the O2 and is now the world's most successful entertainment venue.

Given its somewhat foreboding appurtenance (it is very black), the Daily Express building was nicknamed 'the Black Lubyanka' by the satirical magazine *Private Eye* in reference to KGB headquarters in Moscow.

Today & Tomorrow

Early in the millennium such structures as the 2002 glass 'egg' (some Londoners see a testicle) of City Hall and the ever-popular, ever-present 2003-built 30 St Mary Axe – or 'the Gherkin' – gave the city the confidence to continue planning more heady buildings.

By the middle of the Noughties, London's biggest urban development project ever was under way: the 200-hectare

30 St Mary Axe (The Gherkin; p152)

Olympic Park in the Lea River Valley near Stratford, where most of the events of the 2012 Summer Olympics and Paralympics would take place. But the park would offer few architectural surprises, with the exception of the late Zaha Hadid's stunning Aquatics Centre and the ArcelorMittal Orbit, a zany 115m-tall public work of art with viewing platforms designed by the sculptor Anish Kapoor and likened to a shisha, or water pipe, by then-Mayor Boris Johnson. It now functions as a massive slide.

Although the 2008 recession undermined for several years what was the most ambitious building program in London since WWII, an improved economic climate at the start of the following decade saw those buildings under construction completed and 'holes in the ground' filled in with the start of new structures.

BROKEN GLASS & RAZOR SHARP

Londoners have a predilection for nicknaming new towers – whether built or planned – and many of them go on to replace the original name. Here are some of the popular ones, inspired, of course, by the building's shape and form:

Cheese Grater (p152) Opening in mid-2014, the recession-delayed 48-storey, 225m-tall Leadenhall Building in the form of a stepped wedge faces architect Richard Rogers' other icon, the Lloyd's of London building.

The Gherkin (p152) The 180m-tall bullet-shaped tower that seems to pop up at every turn has also been known as the Swiss Re Tower (after its first major tenants), Cockfosters (after its architect, Norman Foster), the exotic (or erotic) pickle, the suppository etc. Its official name merely reflect its address: 30 St Mary Axe.

The Shard (p166) This needlelike 87-storey tower by Italian architect Renzo Piano (who originally dismissed tall buildings as 'statements of arrogance') is one mother of a splinter you wouldn't want to tussle with. Views from the top floors are awesome. The Shard is now its real name.

Stealth Bomber (p157) French architect Jean Nouvel's office block and shopping mall next to St Paul's was built to bring new life to the City, especially at the weekend. Its nickname, only occasionally used, comes from its distinctive low-slung design. It's officially called One New Change.

Walkie Talkie (p146) This 37-storey, 160m-tall tower bulges in and bulges out, vaguely resembling an old-fashioned walkie-talkie. It's probably the least popular new building from the outside as it dominates the skyline, but the popular Sky Garden cafe and restaurants at the top have given it a new lease of life.

Razor (Strata; 8 Walworth Rd, SE1; ⊖Elephant & Castle) This 43-storey, turbine-topped tower (officially the Strata building), rising 148m over Elephant & Castle in South London, (sort of) resembles an electric razor. It's one of the tallest residential buildings in London.

Trellis (1 Undershaft, Bishopsgate) Reaching completion at press time, the 305m-tall 1 Undershaft will be the City of London's tallest building and the second tallest in Western Europe. It's already being called the Trellis for its external crosshatch bracing.

Topped out in 2010 were the 230m-tall Heron Tower in the City, then London's third-tallest building, and the very distinctive Strata (150m) south of the river with three wind turbines embedded in its roof. But nothing could compare with the so-called Shard, at 310m the EU's tallest building, completed in 2012. The glass-clad upturned icicle, dramatically poking into Borough skies and visible from across London, houses offices, apartments, a five-star hotel, restaurants and, on the 72nd floor, London's highest public viewing gallery. Not as high but twice as pleasant are the restaurants and cafe-bar in the junglelike Sky Garden on levels 35 to 37 of 20 Fenchurch St, better known as the 'Walkie Talkie'.

Economic recovery in the middle of the 21st century's second decade and the rise in population largely through immigration sparked a building boom unseen since the reconstruction of London after WWII. In the City, 1 Undershaft will match the Shard for height – the maximum currently permissible – and become the tallest in the Square Mile at 73 floors. South London, in particular, is or will soon be one giant building site, especially around Blackfriars (52-storey 1 Blackfriars, Ian Simpson), Vauxhall (49-storey Vauxhall Square, Allies & Morrison) and Nine Elms (twin-towered One Nine Elms, Kohn Pedersen Fox).

For a good look at how London's built environment looks and will look in the future visit New London Architecture (p96) (and don't miss the ever-updated scale model).

Literary London

For more than six centuries, London has been the setting for works of prose and poetry. Indeed, the capital has been the inspiration for the masterful imaginations of such eminent wordsmiths as Chaucer, Shakespeare, Defoe, Dickens, Thackeray, Wells, Orwell, Conrad, Eliot, Greene and Woolf – though not all were native to the city (or even British, for that matter).

Literary London until 1900

It's hard to reconcile the bawdy portrayal of London in Geoffrey Chaucer's *Canterbury Tales* with Charles Dickens' bleak hellhole in *Oliver Twist,* let alone Daniel Defoe's plague-ravaged metropolis in *Journal of the Plague Year* with Zadie Smith's multiethnic romp *White Teeth.* Ever-changing, yet somehow eerily consistent, London has left its mark on some of the most influential writing in the English language.

Chaucerian London

The first literary reference to London appears in Chaucer's *Canterbury Tales,* written between 1387 and 1400: the 29 pilgrims of the tale (plus narrator) gather for their trip to Canterbury at the Tabard Inn in Talbot Yard, Southwark, and agree to share stories on the way there and back. The inn burned down in 1676; a blue plaque marks the site of the building next to the popular George Inn (p172) pub today.

Shakespeare's London

Born in Warwickshire, William Shakespeare spent most of his life as an actor and playwright in London around the turn of the 17th century. He trod the boards of several theatres in Shoreditch and Southwark, and wrote his greatest tragedies, including *Hamlet, Othello, Macbeth* and *King Lear,* for the original Globe theatre (now reconstructed as Shakespeare's Globe) on the South Bank. Although London was his home for most of his life, Shakespeare set nearly all his plays in foreign or imaginary lands. Only *Henry IV: Parts I & II* include a London setting – a tavern called the Boar's Head in Eastcheap.

Built in 1567, the half-timbered Old Curiosity Shop (13–14 Portsmouth St, WC2) may have been the inspiration for Charles Dickens' eponymous novel. His close friend and biographer, John Forster, did live at nearby 57–58 Lincoln's Inn Fields.

Defoe & 18th-Century London

Daniel Defoe might be classified as the first true London writer, both living in and writing about the city during the early 18th century. He is most famous for his novels *Robinson Crusoe* (1719–20) and *Moll Flanders* (1722), which he wrote while living in Church St in Stoke Newington. Defoe's *Journal of the Plague Year* is his most absorbing account of London life, documenting the horrors of the Great Plague during the summer and autumn of 1665, when the author was just five years old.

Dickensian & 19th-Century London

Two early-19th-century Romantic poets drew inspiration from London. John Keats, born above a Moorgate public house in 1795, wrote 'Ode to a Nightingale' while living in Hampstead in 1819 and 'Ode on a Grecian Urn' reportedly after viewing the Parthenon frieze in the British Museum the same year. William Wordsworth discovered inspiration for the poem 'Upon Westminster Bridge' while visiting London in 1802.

Charles Dickens was the quintessential London author. When his father was interned at Marshalsea Prison in Southwark for not paying his debts, the 12-year-old Charles was forced to fend for himself on the streets. That grim period provided a font of experiences on which to draw for his writing. His novels most closely associated with London are *Oliver Twist*, with its gang of Clerkenwell thieves led by Fagin, and *Little Dorrit*, whose heroine was born in the Marshalsea Prison. The house in Bloomsbury where Dickens wrote *Oliver Twist* and two other novels now houses the Charles Dickens Museum (p96).

Sir Arthur Conan Doyle (1858–1930) portrayed a very different London, with his pipe-smoking, cocaine-injecting sleuth, Sherlock Holmes, coming to exemplify a cool and unflappable Englishness. Letters to the mythical hero and his admiring friend, Dr Watson, still arrive at 221b Baker St, where there's a somewhat disappointing museum (p107) to the Victorian detective.

London at the end of the 19th century appears in many books, particularly those of Somerset Maugham. His first novel, *Liza of Lambeth*, was based on his experiences as an intern in the slums of South London, while *Of Human Bondage* provides a portrait of late-Victorian London.

Modern Literary London

American Writers & London

Among Americans who lived in and wrote about London at the turn of the 20th century, Henry James stands supreme with his *Daisy Miller* and *The Europeans*. *The People of the Abyss*, by socialist writer Jack London, is a sensitive portrait of poverty and despair in the East End. St Louis-born TS Eliot moved to London in 1915, where he published his poem 'The Love Song of J Alfred Prufrock' almost immediately and moved on to his groundbreaking epic 'The Waste Land', in which London is portrayed as an 'unreal city'.

Interwar Developments

Between the world wars, PG Wodehouse depicted London high life with his hilarious lampooning of the English upper classes in the Jeeves stories. Quentin Crisp, the self-proclaimed 'stately homo of England', provided the flipside, recounting in his ribald and witty memoir *The Naked Civil Servant* (not published until 1968) what it was like to be openly gay in sexually repressed prewar London. George Orwell's experience of living as a beggar and manual labourer in London's East End coloured his book *Down and Out in Paris and London* (1933).

Top Literary Sites

Shakespeare's Globe

Charles Dickens Museum

Keats House

Carlyle's House

Sherlock Holmes Museum

British Library

The sternly modernist Senate House (1937) on Malet St in Bloomsbury contained offices of the Ministry of Information, where George Orwell worked during WWII. It is thought to have been the inspiration for the Ministry of Truth in his classic dystopian 1949 novel *Nineteen Eighty-Four*.

LITERARY BLUE PLAQUES

The very first of London's blue plaques was put up in 1867, identifying the birthplace of the poet Lord Byron at 24 Holles St, W1, off Cavendish Sq. Since then a large percentage – some 25% of the 900-odd in place – have honoured writers and poets. These include everything from the offices of publisher Faber & Faber at 24 Russell Sq, where TS Eliot worked, to the Primrose Hill residence of Irish poet and playwright WB Yeats at 23 Fitzroy Rd, NW1 (where, incidentally, the US poet Sylvia Plath committed suicide in 1963).

Postwar Literary London

Literary Pubs

George Inn
(South Bank)

Museum Tavern
(West End)

French House
(West End)

Prospect of
Whitby
(East London)

Dove (West
London)

Fitzroy Tavern
(West End)

The End of the Affair, Graham Greene's novel chronicling a passionate and doomed romance, takes place in and around Clapham Common just after WWII, while Elizabeth Bowen's *The Heat of the Day* is a sensitive, if melodramatic, account of living through the Blitz.

Colin MacInnes described the bohemian, multicultural world of 1950s Notting Hill in *Absolute Beginners,* while Doris Lessing captured the political mood of 1960s London in *The Four-Gated City,* the last of her five-book *Children of Violence* series. Lessing also provided some of the funniest and most vicious portrayals of 1990s London in *London Observed.* Nick Hornby, nostalgic about his days as a young football fan in *Fever Pitch* and obsessive about vinyl in *High Fidelity,* found himself the voice of a generation.

Hanif Kureishi explored London from the perspective of ethnic minorities before it became fashionable, specifically young Pakistanis. His best-known novels include *The Black Album* and *The Buddha of Suburbia.* He also wrote the screenplay for the groundbreaking film *My Beautiful Laundrette.* Author and playwright Caryl Phillips won plaudits for his description of the Caribbean immigrant's experience in *The Final Passage,* while Timothy Mo's *Sour Sweet* is a poignant and funny account of a Chinese family in the 1960s trying to adjust to English life.

The decades leading up to the turn of the third millennium were great ones for British literature, bringing a dazzling new generation of writers to the fore: Martin Amis *(Money, London Fields),* Julian Barnes *(Metroland, Talking it Over),* Ian McEwan *(Enduring Love, Atonement),* Salman Rushdie *(Midnight's Children, The Satanic Verses),* AS Byatt *(Possession, Angels & Insects)* and Alan Hollinghurst *(The Swimming Pool Library, The Line of Beauty).*

Millennial London

Helen Fielding's *Bridget Jones's Diary* and its sequels, *Bridget Jones: The Edge of Reason* and the much later *Bridget Jones: Mad About the Boy,* launched the 'chick lit' genre, one that transcended the travails of a young single Londoner to become a worldwide phenomenon. Enfant terrible and incisive social commentator Will Self's *Grey Area* is a superb collection of short stories focusing on skewed and surreal aspects of the city. *The Book of Dave* is his hilarious, surreal story of a bitter, present-day London cabbie burying a book of his observations, which are later discovered and regarded as scripture by the people on the island of Ham. Britain in the distant future is an archipelago due to rising sea levels.

A larger-than-life statue of John Betjeman gazing up in wonder above the departures hall at St Pancras International Station recalls the former poet laureate's campaign in the 1960s to save the Victorian High Gothic structure.

Peter Ackroyd names the city as the love of his life. *London: the Biography* is his inexhaustible paean to the capital, while *The Clerkenwell Tales* brings to life the 14th-century London of Chaucer. His more recent *The Canterbury Tales: A Retelling* renders Chaucer's timeless tales in lucid, compelling modern English. *Thames: Sacred River* is Ackroyd's fine monument to the muck, magic and mystery of the river through history.

Iain Sinclair is the bard of Hackney, who, like Ackroyd, has spent his life obsessed with and fascinated by the capital. His acclaimed and ambitious *London Orbital,* a journey on foot around the M25, London's mammoth motorway bypass, is required London reading, while *Rodinsky's Room,* coauthored with Rachel Lichtenstein, recounts the true story of a Jewish mystic-hermit whose room on Princelet St in Spitalfields is opened up after nearly two decades. *Hackney, That Rose-Red Empire* is an exploration of what was once one of London's most notorious boroughs and is now increasingly trendy.

LITERARY READINGS, TALKS & EVENTS

To catch established and budding authors, attend the **Book Slam** (www.bookslam.com; admission £10) – 'London's leading literary shindig' – usually held every other month at various clubs and venues around London. Guests have included Dave Eggers, Will Self, Paul Beatty and PJ Harvey, and the event features readings, poetry, comedy and even live music. Check the website for dates, times and venues.

Covent Garden's Poetry Café (p127) is a favourite for lovers of verse, with almost daily readings and performances by established poets, open-mic evenings and writing workshops.

Both the British Library (p246) and the Institute of Contemporary Arts (p100) have excellent talks and lectures monthly, with well-known writers from all spectrums.

Bookshops, particularly Waterstones (Map p444; ☑020-7636 1577; www.waterstones.com; 82 Gower St, WC1; ◷9.30am-9pm Mon-Fri, to 8pm Sat, noon-6pm Sun; ⊜Euston Sq), Foyles (p130) and the London Review Bookshop (p129), often stage readings and talks. Some major authors also now appear at the Southbank Centre (p168). Many such events are organised on an ad-hoc basis, so keep an eye on the listings in the freebie *Time Out* or any of the weekend newspaper supplements, including the *Guide* distributed with the *Guardian* newspaper on Saturday.

Current Scene

Home to most of the UK's major publishers and its best bookshops, London remains a vibrant place for writers and readers alike. But the frustrating predominance of several powerful corporations within publishing can occasionally limit pioneering writing. It is often left to smaller houses to discover and groom new and as yet unproven writing talent.

This state of affairs has, however, stimulated an exciting literary fringe, which, although tiny, is very active and passionate about good writing. London still has many small presses where quality and innovation are prized over public relations skills, and events kick off in bookshops and in the back rooms of pubs throughout the week.

Back in the mainstream, the big guns of the 1980s, such as Martin Amis, Ian McEwan, Salman Rushdie and Julian Barnes, are still going strong, although new voices have broken through in the last decade, including Monica Ali, who brought the East End to life in *Brick Lane;* Zadie Smith, whose most recent novel *Swing Time* (2016) recounts the tale of two mixed-race girls from North London; and Elif Shafak, whose *Honour* tells of how traditional practices shatter and transform the lives of Turkish immigrants in 1970s East London. Jake Arnott's *The Long Firm* is an intelligent Soho-based gangster yarn.

'Rediscovered' author Howard Jacobson, variously called the 'Jewish Jane Austen' and the 'English Philip Roth', won the Man Booker Prize in 2010 for *The Finkler Question,* the first time the prestigious award had gone to a comic novel in a quarter-century. Literary titan and huge commercial success Hilary Mantel, author of *Wolf Hall,* won the same award for her historical novel *Bring up the Bodies* two years later.

Every bookshop in town has a London section, where you will find many of these titles and lots more.

Theatre & Dance

London has more theatrical history than almost anywhere else in the world, and it's still being made nightly on the stages of the West End, the South Bank and the vast London fringe. No visit to the city is complete without taking in a show, and just walking among the theatre-bound throngs in the evening in the West End is an electrifying experience. If dance is on your list, take your pick from the capital's various and varied world-class companies.

Above: Edward Watson
and Lauren Cuthbertson
of the Royal Ballet (p128)
perform at the O2 Arena
(p305)

Theatre

Elizabethan Period

Very little is known about London theatre before the Elizabethan period, when a series of 'playhouses', including the Globe, were built in Shoreditch and on the south bank of the Thames. Although the playwrights of the time – Shakespeare, his great rival Ben Jonson *(Volpone, The Alchemist)* and Christopher Marlowe *(Doctor Faustus, Edward II)* – are now considered timeless intellectual geniuses, theatre was then a raucous popular entertainment, where the crowd drank and heckled the actors. The Puritans responded by shutting the playhouses down at the start of the Civil War in 1642.

Restoration

Three years after the return of the monarchy in 1660, the first famous Drury Lane theatre was built and the period of 'Restoration theatre' began under the patronage of the rakish King Charles II. Borrowing influences from Italian and French theatre, Restoration theatre incorporated drama (such as John Dryden's *All For Love,* 1677) and comedy. The first female actors appeared (in Elizabethan times men played female roles), and Charles II is recorded as having had an ongoing affair with at least one, Nell Gwyn.

Victorian Period

Despite the success of John Gay's *The Beggar's Opera* (1728), Oliver Goldsmith's farce *She Stoops to Conquer* (1773) and Richard Sheridan's *The Rivals* and *The School for Scandal* (1777) at Drury Lane, popular music halls replaced serious theatre under the Victorians. Light comic operetta, as defined by Gilbert and Sullivan *(HMS Pinafore, The Pirates of Penzance, The Mikado)*, was all the rage. A sea change only arose with the emergence at the end of the 19th century of such compelling playwrights as Oscar Wilde *(An Ideal Husband, The Importance of Being Earnest)* and George Bernard Shaw *(Pygmalion, The Apple Cart)*.

The 20th Century

In their footsteps appeared such comic wits as Noël Coward *(Private Lives, Brief Encounter)* and earnest dramatists like Terence Rattigan *(The Winslow Boy, The Browning Version)* and JB Priestley *(An Inspector Calls)*. However, it wasn't until the 1950s and 1960s that English drama yet again experienced such a fertile period as it had in the Elizabethan era.

Perfectly encapsulating the social upheaval of the time, John Osborne's *Look Back in Anger* at the Royal Court Theatre in 1956 heralded

If innovation and change are too much for you, drop by St Martin's Theatre, where the same production of *The Mousetrap* has been running since 1952. Or there's the monolithic musicals that show no sign of letting up anytime soon: *Phantom of the Opera, Lion King, Les Miserables, Mamma Mia!* et al.

THEATRE & DANCE THEATRE

SHAKESPEAREAN OFFERINGS

Shakespeare's legacy is generously honoured on the city's stages, most notably by the Royal Shakespeare Company (RSC) and at the Globe theatre. The RSC stages one or two of the bard's plays in London annually, although it has no London home. (Its productions are based in Stratford-upon-Avon and usually transfer to the capital later in their run.)

Shakespeare's Globe (p162) on the South Bank attempts to re-create an Elizabethan open-air theatre experience. Its indoor **Sam Wanamaker Playhouse**, which opened in 2014, is a unique place to savour Shakespeare's words, with an intimate candlelit atmosphere. Shakespeare's plays remain at the core of the Globe's programming, but other classic and contemporary plays do get a look-in from time to time.

CHILDREN'S THEATRE

If you've got junior culture vultures in tow, make sure to scan the theatre listings for kid-friendly West End smashes such as *Matilda the Musical* and *Charlie and the Chocolate Factory*, both of which are adaptations of books by Roald Dahl. It's also worth checking out what's on at the Little Angel Theatre (www.littleangeltheatre.com) in Islington, which specialises in puppetry, and the Unicorn Theatre (www.unicorntheatre.com) in Southwark, which stages productions for infants, children and young adults.

a rash of new writing, including Harold Pinter's *The Homecoming,* Joe Orton's *Loot,* Tom Stoppard's *Rosencrantz and Guildenstern are Dead* and Alan Ayckbourn's *How the Other Half Loves.* During the same period, many of today's leading theatre companies were formed, including the National Theatre.

Though somewhat eclipsed by the National Theatre, today's Royal Court Theatre (p199) retains a fine tradition of new writing. In the past decade, it has nurtured such talented playwrights as Jez Butterworth *(Jerusalem, Ferryman),* Caryl Churchill *(Seven Jewish Children – A Play for Gaza),* Ayub Khan-Din *(East Is East),* Conor McPherson *(The Weir, Shining City)* and Joe Penhall *(Dumb Show).*

Consult London's *Time Out* for weekly theatrical listings and *Tkts* for the best-priced tickets.

Today's Scene

London remains a thrilling place for theatre-lovers. Nowhere else, with the possible exception of New York, offers such a diversity of high-quality drama, first-rate musical theatre and such a sizzling fringe. Whether it's Hollywood A-listers gracing tiny stages and earning Equity minimum wage for their efforts or lavish West End musicals, London remains an undisputed theatrical world leader and innovator.

While the West End's 'Theatreland' gets most of the attention, some of London's hottest theatre tickets are for a trio of innovative venues south of the river: the National Theatre, the Old Vic and the Young Vic. Former National Theatre director Sir Nicholas Hytner's new 900-seat Bridge Theatre, which opened beside Tower Bridge in Borough in 2017, will soon be added to this list. Other innovative off-West End theatres include the Royal Court Theatre in Chelsea, the Bush Theatre in Shepherd's Bush and the Hampstead Theatre. Many successful off-West End plays eventually make their way to the West End for a longer theatrical run.

Even if you've heard that a hot new play is completely sold out for months ahead, its often possible to secure a ticket via standby lists and the like. Check individual theatre websites.

In recent years, the mainstream West End has re-established its credentials, with extraordinary hits by the likes of Donmar Warehouse, while the smarter end of the fringe continues to shine with risky, controversial and newsworthy productions.

Big names can often be seen treading Theatreland's hallowed boards – think Bradley Cooper playing *The Elephant Man* at the Haymarket Theatre Royal; Helen Mirren and then Kristen Scott Thomas playing the Queen in *The Audience* at the Apollo Shaftesbury; Imelda Staunton belting it out in *Gypsy* at the Savoy Theatre or being both witty and malicious in *Who's Afraid of Virginia Woolf?* at the Harold Pinter Theatre; or David Tennant being filthy in *Don Juan in Soho* at Wyndham's Theatre.

There's something for all dramatic tastes in London, from contemporary political satire to creative reworking of old classics, and all shades in between. Recent productions that have won critical acclaim include the children's musical *Matilda,* the adaptation of Mark Haddon's novel *The Curious Incident of the Dog in the Night-Time,* Sam Mendes' version of *Charlie and the Chocolate Factory,* James Graham's political drama *This House,* and JK Rowling's latest money-minter, *Harry Potter and the Cursed Child.*

Dance

Whether contemporary, classical or crossover, London will have the right moves for you. As one of the world's great dance capitals, London's artistic environment has long created and attracted talented choreographers with both the inspiration and aspiration to fashion innovative productions.

London's most celebrated choreographer is award-winning Sir Matthew Bourne – *Play Without Words, Edward Scissorhands, Dorian Gray, Oliver!, Cinderella,* an all-male *Swan Lake* – who has been repeatedly showered with praise for his reworking of classics. Another leading London-based talent is Wayne McGregor, who worked as movement director on *Harry Potter and the Goblet of Fire* and is a Professor of Choreography at the acclaimed Trinity Laban Conservatoire of Music and Dance in Greenwich.

The Place (p127) in Bloomsbury was the original birthplace of modern British dance and is the home of the edgy Richard Alston Dance Company. Sadler's Wells (p219) – the birthplace of English classical ballet in the 19th century – continues to deliver exciting programming covering many styles of dance. Its roster of 16 'associate artists' include such luminaries as Matthew Bourne, Russell Maliphant, Sidi Larbi Cherkaoui, Wayne McGregor, Crystal Pite, Nitin Sawhney, Christopher Wheeldon, Sylvie Guillem, Kate Prince and Hofesh Shechter.

Covent Garden's Royal Opera House is the impressive home of London's leading classical-dance troupe, the world-famous Royal Ballet (p128). The company largely sticks to the traditional – *Giselle, Romeo and Juliet, Sleeping Beauty* – but more contemporary influences occasionally seep into productions.

One of the world's best companies, the **English National Ballet** (☑020-7581 1245; www.ballet.org.uk), is a touring ballet company. You may be fortunate enough to catch it at one of its various venues in London – principally at the London Coliseum.

For more cutting-edge work, the innovative Rambert Dance Company (p175) is the UK's foremost contemporary dance troupe. It is arguably the most creative force in UK dance and is now conveniently located in purpose-built premises in Upper Ground directly behind the National Theatre.

Another important venue for experimental dance is the Barbican in the City, which is particularly good at presenting new works exploring the crossover of dance, theatre and music.

London's Best Theatres

Shakespeare's Globe (The South Bank)

National Theatre (The South Bank)

Old Vic (The South Bank)

Donmar Warehouse (The West End)

Royal Court Theatre (Kensington & Hyde Park)

Young Vic (The South Bank)

THEATRE & DANCE DANCE

Art & Fashion

When it comes to both visual art and fashion, London has traditionally been overshadowed by other European capitals. Yet many of history's greatest artists have spent time in London, including such notables as Monet, Van Gogh and Whistler, and in terms of contemporary art and cutting-edge street fashion, there's a compelling argument for putting London at the very top of the European pack.

Art

Holbein to Turner

Above Runway show, London Fashion Week

It wasn't until the rule of the Tudors that art began to take off in London. The German Hans Holbein the Younger (1497–1543) was court painter to Henry VIII, and one of his finest works, *The Ambassadors* (1533), hangs in the National Gallery. A batch of great portrait artists worked at court during the 17th century, the best being Anthony van Dyck (1599–1641), who painted the *Equestrian Portrait of Charles I* (1638), also in the National Gallery. Charles I was a keen collector of art and it was during his reign that the Raphael Cartoons (1515), now in the Victoria & Albert Museum, came to London.

Local artists began to emerge in the 18th century, including portrait and landscape painter Thomas Gainsborough (1727–88); William Hogarth (1697–1764), whose much-reproduced social commentary *A Rake's Progress* (1733) hangs in Sir John Soane's Museum; and poet, engraver and watercolourist William Blake (1757–1827). A superior visual artist to Blake, John Constable (1776–1837) studied the clouds and skies above Hampstead Heath, sketching hundreds of scenes that he'd later match with subjects in his landscapes.

JMW Turner (1775–1851), equally at home with oils and watercolours, represented the pinnacle of 19th-century British art. Through innovative use of colour and gradations of light, he created a new atmosphere that seemed to capture the wonder, sublimity and terror of nature. His later works, including *The Fighting Temeraire* (1839), *Snow Storm: Steam-Boat off a Harbour's Mouth* (1842), *Peace – Burial at Sea* (1842) and *Rain, Steam and Speed – the Great Western Railway* (1844), now in the Tate Britain and the National Gallery, were increasingly abstract, and although widely vilified at the time, later inspired the Impressionist works of Claude Monet.

The Pre-Raphaelites to Hockney

The brief but splendid flowering of the pre-Raphaelite Brotherhood (1848–54) took its inspiration from the Romantic poets, abandoning the pastel-coloured rusticity of the day in favour of big, bright and intense depictions of medieval legends and female beauty. The movement's main proponents were William Holman Hunt, John Everett Millais and Dante Gabriel Rossetti; artists Edward Burne-Jones and Ford Madox Brown were also strongly associated with the pre-Raphaelites. Works by all can be found at Tate Britain, with highlights being Millais' *Mariana* (1851) and *Ophelia* (1851-2), Rossetti's *Ecce Ancilla Domini!* (The Annunciation, 1850), John William Waterhouse's *The Lady of Shalott* (1888) and William Holman Hunt's *The Awakening Conscience* (1853).

In the early 20th century, cubism and futurism helped generate the short-lived Vorticists, a modernist group of London artists and poets, led by the dapper Wyndham Lewis (1882–1957), that sought to capture dynamism in artistic form. Sculptors Henry Moore (1898–1986) and Barbara Hepworth (1903–75) both typified the modernist movement in British sculpture. You can see examples of their work in the gardens of Kenwood House in Hampstead Heath.

After WWII, art transformed yet again. In 1945 the tortured, Irish-born painter Francis Bacon (1909–92) caused a stir when he exhibited his contorted *Three Studies for Figures at the Base of a Crucifixion* – now on display at the Tate Britain – and afterwards continued to spook the art world with his repulsive yet mesmerising visions. Also at the Tate Britain is Bacon's *Triptych – August 1972*, painted in the aftermath of his lover George Dyer's suicide.

The late art critic Robert Hughes once eulogised Bacon's contemporary, Lucian Freud (1922–2011), as 'the greatest living realist painter'. Freud's early work was often surrealist, but from the 1950s the bohemian Freud exclusively focused on pale, muted portraits – often nudes, and frequently of friends and family (although he also painted the Queen).

Also prominent in the 1950s was painter and collage artist Richard Hamilton (1922–2011), whose work includes the cover design of the

London's Greatest Artworks

....

Fighting Temeraire, by JMW Turner (1839, National Gallery)

....

A Bar at the Folies-Bergère, by Edouard Manet (1882, Courtauld Gallery)

....

Sunflowers, by Vincent Van Gogh (1888, National Gallery)

....

Three Studies for Figures at the Base of a Crucifixion, by Francis Bacon (1944, Tate Britain)

....

Metamorphosis of Narcissus, by Salvador Dalí (1937, Tate Modern)

....

The Seagram Murals, by Mark Rothko (1958, Tate Modern)

....

Self-Portrait with Two Circles, by Rembrandt (1665, Kenwood House)

The Ambassadors by Hans Holbein the Younger

Popular practical art classes are given at the Dulwich Picture Gallery and other museums and galleries around London.

Beatles' self-titled 1968 album (the legendary *White Album*). London in the swinging '60s was perfectly encapsulated by pop art, its vocabulary best articulated by David Hockney, born in 1937 and still very active today. Hockney gained a reputation as one of the leading pop artists (although he rejected the label) through his early use of magazine-style images, but after a move to California, his work became increasingly naturalistic. Two of his most famous works are the Tate-owned *Mr and Mrs Clark and Percy* (1971) and *A Bigger Splash* (1974).

Gilbert & George were quintessential English conceptual artists of the 1960s. The Spitalfields odd couple are still at the heart of the British art world, having now become a part of the establishment.

Brit Art

Despite its incredibly rich collections, Britain had never led, dominated or even really participated in a particular artistic epoch or style as Paris had in the 1920s or New York in the 1950s. That all changed in the twilight of the 20th century, when 1990s London became the beating heart of the art world.

Brit Art sprang from a show called *Freeze,* which was staged in a Docklands warehouse in 1988, organised by artist and showman Damien Hirst and largely featuring his fellow graduates from Goldsmiths' College. Influenced by pop culture and punk, this loose movement was soon catapulted to notoriety by the advertising guru Charles Saatchi, who bought an extraordinary number of works and came to dominate the scene.

Brit Art was brash, decadent, ironic, easy to grasp and eminently marketable. Hirst chipped in with a cow sliced into sections and preserved in formaldehyde; flies buzzed around another cow's head and

The Fighting Temeraire by JMW Turner

were zapped in his early work *A Thousand Years*. Chris Ofili provoked with *The Holy Virgin Mary,* a painting of the black Madonna made partly with elephant excrement; brothers Jake and Dinos Chapman produced mannequins of children with genitalia on their heads; and Marcus Harvey created a portrait of notorious child-killer Myra Hindley, made entirely with children's handprints, whose value skyrocketed when it was repeatedly vandalised by the public.

The areas of Shoreditch, Hoxton, Spitalfields and Whitechapel – where many artists lived, worked and hung out – became the epicentre of the movement, and a rash of galleries moved in. For the 10 years or so that it rode a wave of publicity, the defining characteristics of Brit Art were notoriety and shock value. Its two biggest names, Damien Hirst and Tracey Emin, inevitably became celebrities.

Some critics argued the hugely hyped movement was the product of a cultural vacuum, an example of the emperor's new clothes, with people afraid to criticise the works for fear they'd look stupid. Others praised its freshness and ingenuity.

Beyond Brit Art

On the fringes of Brit Art are a lot of less-stellar but equally inspiring artists exploring other directions. A highlight is Richard Wilson's memorable installation *20:50* (1987) – a room filled waist-high with recycled oil. Entering down the walkway, you feel as if you've just been shot out into space. In Douglas Gordon's most famous work, *24 Hour Psycho* (1993), the Scottish video artist slowed Alfred Hitchcock's masterpiece so much it was stripped of its narrative and viewed more like a moving sculpture. Gary Hume first came to prominence with his *Doors* series:

Since 1999 the Fourth Plinth Commission has offered a platform in Trafalgar Sq for novel, and frequently controversial, works by contemporary artists.

full-size paintings of hospital doors, which can be seen as powerful allegorical descriptions of despair – or just perfect reproductions of doors.

Today London counts some 1500 galleries, and its art scene is one of the world's biggest, with an international reach that rivals traditional hubs such as New York and Paris. Most of the established galleries are in districts like Mayfair but for more cutting-edge work head for Hackney in East London and Bermondsey south of the river.

The biggest date on the art calendar is the controversial Turner Prize at the Tate Britain. Any British visual artist under the age of 50 is eligible to enter, although there is a strong preference for conceptual art.

Fashion

The British fashion industry has always been about younger, directional and more left-field designs. London fashion focuses on streetwear and the 'wow' factor, with a few old reliables keeping the frame in place and mingling with hot new designers, who are often unpolished through inexperience, but bursting with talent and creativity. As a result, London is exciting in a global sense and nobody with an interest in street fashion will be disappointed.

London has weathered a tough decade economically since 2008 and its status as an international fashion centre suffered for it, but the city has returned to the heart of the fashion universe, boasting a bright new firmament of young stars.

London's Who's Who

The biggest names in London fashion are internationally famous and need little introduction. They include punk maven Vivienne Westwood, menswear designer Paul Smith and ethical fashionista Stella McCartney, who has transcended the connection to her famous father (former Beatle, Sir Paul) to become world famous in her own right. Making a

LONDON ARTISTS TODAY

London continues to generate talent across a range of artistic media, keeping critics on their toes. These are some of the biggest-name artists working in contemporary London:

Antony Gormley This sculptor is best known for the 22m-high *Angel of the North*, beside the A1 trunk road near Gateshead in northern England. In London, look for his *Planets* outside the British Library (p246), *Quantum Cloud* below the Emirates Air Line (p416) in the Docklands, and *Room* above the entrance of the Beaumont Hotel (p346).

Anish Kapoor An Indian-born sculptor working in London since the 1970s. His ArcelorMittal Orbit (p23) towers over Queen Elizabeth Olympic Park.

Marc Quinn *Self* is a sculpture of the artist's head made from his own frozen blood, which Quinn recasts every five years. It is owned by (though not always on display at) the National Portrait Gallery (p91).

Chantal Joffe This London-based artist is well known for her naive, expressionist large-scale portraits of women and children.

Phoebe Collings-James Mixed media artist works across painting, sculpture and video addressing sexuality, violence and desire in a deeply physical way.

Banksy The anonymous street artist whose work is a worldwide phenomenon probably hails from Bristol, but you'll find many of his most famous works on London's streets.

Shopfronts, Old Bond Street (p129)

splash on both sides of the Atlantic is the eponymous label of one Victoria Beckham, erstwhile Spice Girl and wife of ex-footballer David.

Other big international names include Christopher Bailey (chief creative and CEO at Burberry), Sarah Burton (royal wedding dress designer and creative director at Alexander McQueen) and Phoebe Philo (creative director at Céline).

With his witty designs and eclectic references, St Martin's graduate Giles Deacon took London fashion by storm with his own label, GILES. Gareth Pugh is also someone to look out for, another St Martin's alumnus who took the underground club fashions of Shoreditch and transposed them for the shop floor. Other designers making a buzz are Erdem Moralıoğlu, Henry Holland, Jonathan Saunders and Christopher Kane.

London Fashion Abroad

The influence of London's designers continues to spread well beyond the capital. The 'British Fashion Pack' still work at, or run, many of the major Continental fashion houses. Houses such as Alexander McQueen retain design studios in London, and several British designers have recently joined US houses, including Luella Bartley to Calvin Klein, who hopes to combine her trademark London cool with the American brand's minimal aesthetic.

Fame & Celebrity

London fashion appears eccentric when compared to the classic feel of the major Parisian and Milanese houses or the cool street-cred of New York designers, and this spirit was best exemplified by Isabella Blow. This legendary stylist discovered Alexander McQueen, Stella Tennant

The high point on the London fashion calendar is London Fashion Week (www. londonfashionweek. co.uk), held in February and September each year at various venues throughout the city including Somerset House.

Models in runway show, London Fashion Week

and Sophie Dahl (among many others) during her career at *Vogue* and *Tatler*. Blow sadly committed suicide in 2007. A further shock for the industry was the tragic suicide of Alexander McQueen in 2010 at the age of 40.

British fashion's 'bad girl' Kate Moss has been in and out of the news since the start of her career – for both her sense of style and Top Shop clothes line and her off-runway antics. The fashion world thrives on notoriety but John Galliano's much-publicised arrest in 2011 for an anti-Semitic diatribe against a couple in a Paris cafe was a nadir for Dior's chief designer, who was consequently dropped by the fashion house. He has since joined Maison Margiela. Despite these tragic losses and moments of scandal, London retains all the innovative ingredients for exhilarating developments in fashion, today and tomorrow.

The Music Scene

Drawing upon a deep reservoir of talent, London's modern music scene is one of the city's greatest sources of artistic power and is a magnet for bands and hopefuls from all musical hemispheres. Periodically a world leader in musical fashion and innovative soundscapes, London blends its homegrown talent with a continuous influx of styles and cultures, keeping currents flowing and inspiration percolating.

The Swinging '60s

At around the same time that The Beatles were laying down their first recordings with George Martin at Abbey Road Studios in St John's Wood, a group of London lads were appearing on stage together for the first time at the Marquee Club in Oxford St. An R&B band with frequent trajectories into blues and rock and roll, the Rolling Stones quickly set up as a more rough-edged counterpoint to the cleaner, boys-next-door image of Liverpool's Fab Four.

In the musical explosion that followed, there was one band that chronicled London life like no other. Hailing from Muswell Hill in North London, the Kinks started out with a garage R&B sound not dissimilar to that of the Stones, but eventually began to incorporate elements of the Victorian music hall tradition into their music while liberally seeding their lyrics with London place names (eg '*Waterloo Sunset*').

The Who, from West London, attracted attention to their brand of gritty rock by smashing guitars on stage, propelling TVs from hotel windows and driving cars into swimming pools. Struggling to be heard above the din was inspirational mod band the Small Faces, formed in 1965 in East London.

Seattle-born Jimi Hendrix came to London and took guitar playing to unseen heights before tragically dying in a flat in the Samarkand Hotel in Notting Hill in 1970. In some ways, the swinging '60s ended in July 1969 when the Stones famously staged their free concert in Hyde Park in front of more than 250,000 adoring fans.

'60s songs

'*Play with Fire*' (The Rolling Stones)

'*Eight Miles High*' (The Byrds)

'*The London Boys*' (David Bowie)

'*Waterloo Sunset*' (The Kinks)

'*Sunny Goodge Street*' (Donovan)

The '70s

A local band called Tyrannosaurus Rex had enjoyed moderate success throughout the '60s. In 1970 they changed their name to T.Rex, frontman Marc Bolan donned a bit of glitter and the world's first 'glam' band had arrived. Glam rock encouraged the youth of uptight Britain to be whatever they wanted to be. Baritone-voiced Brixton boy David Jones (aka David Bowie) then altered the rock landscape with his astonishing *The Rise and Fall of Ziggy Stardust and the Spiders from Mars* in 1972, one of the decade's seminal albums. Genre-spanning Roxy Music blended art rock and synth pop into a sophisticated glam sound.

Back at the rock face, a little band called Led Zeppelin (formed in 1968) were busy cultivating the roots of heavy metal. Two years later Zanzibar-born Farok Bulsara, by then known as Freddie Mercury, led Queen to become one of the greatest rock-and-roll stars of all time. British-American band Fleetwood Mac left blues for pop rock and stormed the charts in the US as well as in Britain; their landmark *Rumours* became the eighth-highest-selling album in history.

The unexpected arrival of punk kicked in the complacent commercial-rock edifice of the mid-'70s. Few saw it coming but none could miss it. The Sex Pistols were the most notorious of a wave of bands that began pogoing around London in 1976.

The Clash, also Londoners, harnessed the raw anger of the time into a collar-grabbing brand of political protest that would see them outlast their peers, treading the fine line between angry punks and great songwriters. The disillusioned generation finally had a plan and a leader in frontman Joe Strummer; *London Calling* is a spirited call to arms.

Punk cleared the air and into the oxygen-rich atmosphere swarmed a gaggle of late '70s acts. The Damned sought out an innovative niche as goth punk pioneers. The Jam deftly vaulted the abyss between punk and mod revivalism (lead singer and 'Modfather' Paul Weller followed up with a hugely successful solo career after sophisti-pop hits with the Style Council) and Madness put the nutty sound on the London map. New Wave and the New Romantics quickly shimmied into the fast-changing music scene ushering in the '80s.

'80s Songs

'Driving in My Car'
(Madness)

'Electric Avenue'
(Eddy Grant)

'West End Girls'
(Pet Shop Boys)

'London Girl'
(The Pogues)

'London'
(The Smiths)

The '80s

Guitars disappeared, swiftly replaced by keyboard synthesisers and drum machines. Fashion and image became indivisible from music. Thin ties, winklepickers, Velcro-fastening white sneakers, spandex, densely pleated trousers and heavy make-up dazzled at every turn. Hair was big. Overpriced, oversexed and way overdone, '80s London was a roll call of hair-gelled pop: Spandau Ballet, Culture Club, Bananarama and Wham!. Wham!'s Georgios Panayiotou changed his name to George Michael and gained massive success as a solo artist.

While the late '80s brought blond boy band Bros and the starlets of the Stock Aitken Waterman hit factory (including Londoners Mel & Kim and Samantha Fox), relief had already been assured from up north with the arrival of the Smiths and their alternative rock innovations. In the closing years of the decade, fellow Mancunians the Stone Roses and the Happy Mondays devised a new sound that had grown out of the recent acid-house raves. Dance exploded in 1988's summer of love, with Soul II Soul, dilated pupils and a stage set for rave anthems such as the KLF's mighty 'What Time is Love?'. A generation was gripped by dance music and a new lexicon ruled: techno, electronica, hip hop, garage, house and trance.

'90s Songs

'Piccadilly Palare'
(Morrissey)

*'Black Boys
on Mopeds'*
(Sinéad O'Connor)

'Parklife' (Blur)

'Mile End' (Pulp)

'Babylon'
(David Gray)

Britpop

The early 1990s saw the explosion of yet another new scene: Britpop, a genre broadly defined as a punky take on The Beatles. A high-profile battle between two of the biggest bands, Blur from London and Oasis from Manchester, drew a line in the musical sand.

Weighing in on the London side were the brilliant Suede and Elastica, not to mention Sheffield defectors to the capital, Pulp (with their irrepressible lead man, Jarvis Cocker). Skirting around the edges, doing their own thing, were Radiohead from Oxford.

But other musical styles were cooking. London's Asian community made a big splash in the early 21st century, with Talvin Singh and Nitin Sawhney fusing dance with traditional Indian music, and Asian Dub Foundation bringing their unique brand of a mix of rapcore, dub, dancehall and ragga, and political comment to an ever-widening audience.

Arguably the most worldwide fame in this period was taken by the London-based boy and girl bands Take That, All Saints, East 17 and the

LONDON'S MUSICAL TIMELINE

➤ 1967 'Waterloo Sunset' (The Kinks) Unimpeachable classic from the '60s.

➤ 1978 '(I Don't Want to Go to) Chelsea' (Elvis Costello) Punchy Costello from the early years.

➤ 1978 'Hong Kong Garden' (Siouxsie and the Banshees) Stirring goth-punk ode to a Chinese takeaway in Chislehurst High St.

➤ 1978 'Baker Street' (Gerry Rafferty) With an iconic and roof-raising saxophone riff.

➤ 1979 'London Calling' (The Clash) Raw and potent punk anthem.

➤ 1984 'West End Girls' (Pet Shop Boys) Smooth and glossy first chart success from the British pop duo.

➤ 1989 'Twenty-Four Minutes from Tulse Hill' (Carter the Unstoppable Sex Machine) SW2 finds fame in this throbbing indie track.

➤ 1993 'Buddha of Suburbia' (David Bowie) One of the Thin White Duke's most sublime songs.

➤ 2004 'Round Here' (George Michael) Moving song drawing on the singer's recollections of his first day at school.

➤ 2006 'LDN' (Lily Allen) Catchy ska-beat hit from the London popster.

➤ 2007 'Hometown Glory' (Adele) Exquisite celebration of West Norwood from the Tottenham-born songster.

➤ 2007 'London Town' (Kano) London rapper on his hometown.

➤ 2008 'Warwick Avenue' (Duffy) The beautiful voice of this Welsh starlet puts Warwick Ave tube station on the musical map.

➤ 2011 'The City' (Ed Sheeran) Dubstep-folkie Sheeran has a cynic's eye for the joys and trials of London.

➤ 2013 'Goin' Crazy' (Dizzee Rascal & Robbie Williams) Rascal and Williams meet up in Dalston on souped-up mobility scooters.

➤ 2013 'My Name is London Town' (Reg Meuross) Sweeping, bittersweet take on the capital recorded at Abbey Road Studios.

➤ 2015 'River Lea' (Adele) Much-lauded singer's paean to the river flowing through her North London stomping grounds.

Spice Girls. Their enduring popularity is reflected in the reunions of some of these bands decades later and the Spice Girls' appearance in the London Olympics closing ceremony in 2012, which cemented them as an inherent part of British music culture.

As Britpop ebbed in the late '90s, other currents were flowing into town, and drum 'n' bass and electronica found an anthem-packed sound with DJs such as Goldie and London band Faithless seeing in the millennium.

The Noughties

London band Coldplay – melodic rockers led by falsetto front man Chris Martin – first made a big splash in the UK at the dawn of the new millennium, before finding international fame. After seven best-selling studio albums, their position as one of the world's biggest rock bands appears unshakeable.

Just as the Strokes did in the US, Pete Doherty and Carl Barât of the Libertines renewed interest in punky guitar music following its post-Britpop malaise. Their 2002 debut single 'What a Waster' created a huge splash and their first album *Up The Bracket* went platinum. Doherty went on to form Babyshambles and Barât released albums with Dirty Pretty Things and The Jackals.

Noughties Songs

'Tied Up Too Tight' (Hard-Fi)

'Me & Mr Jones' (Amy Winehouse)

'LDN' (Lily Allen)

'Warwick Avenue' (Duffy)

'Dirtee Cash' (Dizzee Rascal)

A MUSICAL JOURNEY THROUGH LONDON

Zebra crossing on Abbey Rd, St John's Wood The Beatles' most famous album cover.

23 Heddon St, Soho Where the cover for *Ziggy Stardust* was photographed.

23 Brook St, Soho Former home to composers Handel and Hendrix.

St Martin's College, Mayfair First Sex Pistols gig.

Tree on Queen's Ride, Barnes Where Marc Bolan died as a passenger in a Mini in 1977.

94 Baker Street, Marylebone Site of the original headquarters (1967) of the Beatles' Apple Corporation, including Apple Records and the short-lived Apple Boutique.

3 Savile Row, Mayfair Site of the last Beatles performance on the roof of the Apple building in January 1969.

Fronted by eponymous Alison, Goldfrapp brought a seductive and sensual electronica to the fore on the albums *Black Cherry* and *Supernature,* before abruptly departing in a mystical pastoral-folk direction on the band's much-applauded *Seventh Tree* (2008).

The decade also saw the rise of grime and its successor genre, dubstep – two indigenous London musical forms born in the East End out of a fusion of hip hop, drum 'n' bass and UK garage. Dizzee Rascal and Kano are the best-known rappers working in the genre.

Other London talents from the 2000s that won both awards and enormous success on both sides of the Atlantic include the bellowing Florence and the Machine, quirky West London singer-songwriter Lily Allen and the extraordinary but tragic Southgate chanteuse Amy Winehouse, who died in 2011 at age 27.

London Music Today

While it's never really lost its position at the top rung of popular music creativity, the London sound is once again riding a wave of international commercial success.

2010s Songs

'The City' (Ed Sheeran)

'Under the Westway' (Blur)

'Ill Manors' (Plan B)

'Dirty Boys' (David Bowie)

'River Lea' (Adele)

Tottenham-born soulster-songwriter Adele's clean sweep at the 2017 Grammys, including both Album (*25*) and Song of the Year ('Hello') cemented her success of six years earlier when she spent 10 weeks at number one in the US album charts with *21* (2011) and won Album of the Year at the 2012 Grammys. Other Londoners at the helm of the new British invasion of the US include indie folk-rock ensemble Mumford & Sons, rapper Tinie Tempah and angel-faced soul singer Sam Smith, who took out four Grammys in 2015 for his debut *In the Lonely Hour*.

Meanwhile London band The xx have been busy creating their own genre of stripped-back electronic pop, Brixton-based Jessie Ware has won the hearts of soul and electro-loving audiences worldwide, and the ethereal singer James Blake won critical acclaim for his soulful post-dubstep sound.

Other London-born or -based talent to keep an ear out for are Mercury Prize–winning Skepta, probably the hottest grime artist of the moment; soul soloist Michael Kiwanuka; alternative singer-songwriter Bat for Lashes (AKA Natasha Khan); and London Grammar, whose music mixes melancholy guitar with soaring vocals and plaintive lyrics.

Film & Media

The UK punches well above its weight in its standing on the international film scene, but London is far from the glittering hub of the film industry that it might be, despite notable celluloid triumphs. Nonetheless, the city forms the backdrop to a riveting array of films. The nation's media sphere has had its share of crises in recent years but there's still a wide variety of newspapers and magazines filling the shelves of London newsagencies.

London & Film

The Local Cinematic Industry

Despite frequent originality and creative novelty, British films can be hit and miss, certainly at the box office. Commercial triumphs have been Oscar-winners *The King's Speech* (2010) and *The Queen* (2006), and further back the classics *Four Weddings and a Funeral* (1994) and *Shakespeare in Love* (1998). Unfortunately, a frustrating inconsistency persists, despite the disproportionate influence of Britons in Hollywood.

Film fans nostalgically dwell on the golden – but honestly rather brief – era of Ealing comedies, when the West London–based Ealing Studios turned out a steady stream of hits. Between 1947 and 1955 (after which the studios were sold to the BBC), it produced enduring classics such as *Passport to Pimlico, Kind Hearts and Coronets, Whisky Galore, The Man in the White Suit, The Lavender Hill Mob* and *The Ladykillers*. This was also the time of legendary film-makers Michael Powell and Emeric Pressburger, the men behind *The Life and Death of Colonel Blimp* and *The Red Shoes*.

Today the industry finds itself habitually stuck in a deep groove of romantic comedies, costume dramas and gangster pics, while setting periodic benchmarks for horror. Producers, directors and actors complain about a lack of adventurousness in those holding the purse strings, while film investors claim there are not enough scripts worth backing.

Recently, however, there has been a run of notable British films based on real events, including the Stephen Hawking biopic *The Theory of Everything* (2014); the Alan Turing biopic *The Imitation Game* (2014); *Pride* (2014), which tells the true story of gay activists supporting striking miners in the 1980s; *Legend* (2015), another film celebrating the identical twin gangsters Reggie and Ronnie Kray; and *Lady in the Van* (2015), based on Alan Bennett's play about a transient women who lives in a van in his Camden Town driveway for 15 years.

Where Brits are at the very top of the world is in the field of acting, with British stars taking out numerous Oscars in recent years, including Eddie Redmayne, Dame Helen Mirren, Sir Daniel Day-Lewis, Colin Firth, Kate Winslet, Mark Rylance, Christian Bale, Julianne Moore, Tilda Swinton and Rachel Weisz. Other notable names include Dame Judi Dench, Dame Maggie Smith, Sir Ian McKellen, Benedict Cumberbatch, Ewan McGregor, Ralph Fiennes, Jude Law, Liam Neeson, Hugh Laurie, Keira Knightley, Emily Watson and Catherine Zeta-Jones.

If you're interested in James Bond, especially the various vehicles the superspy drove or was pursued by in his many films, head for the Bond in Motion exhibition at the London Film Museum.

Well-known British directors include Steve McQueen (*12 Years a Slave*), Tom Hooper (*The King's Speech*), Danny Boyle (*Slumdog Millionaire*), Ridley Scott (*Blade Runner, Alien, Thelma & Louise, Gladiator, Black Hawk Down*), Sam Mendes (*American Beauty*), Stephen Frears (*Dirty Pretty Things, The Queen*) and Mike Leigh (*Another Year, Vera Drake*).

London on the Screen

Outdoor cinema is rolled out in London in the warmer months at Summer Screen at Somerset House (p107), where films projected on the city's largest screen can be enjoyed in a sublime setting.

From the impressions of an interwar Harley St in *The King's Speech* (2010) to the seedy South Kensington and Earl's Court of Roman Polanski's *Repulsion* (1965), London remains a hugely popular location to make films. That most die-hard of New Yorkers, Woody Allen, has made four films – *Match Point, Scoop, Cassandra's Dream* and *You Will Meet a Tall Dark Stranger* – in the capital since 2005.

The city's blend of historic and modern architecture works massively to its advantage: Ang Lee's *Sense and Sensibility* (1995) retreated to historic Greenwich for its wonderful parkland and neoclassical architecture. Merchant Ivory's costume drama *Howard's End* (1992) and the biopic *Chaplin* (1992) feature the neo-Gothic St Pancras Station, while David Lynch's *The Elephant Man* (1980) took advantage of the moody atmosphere around the then-undeveloped Shad Thames. *Withnail & I* (1987) remains a quintessential classic of offbeat British comedy, partly set in Camden. Camden also features prominently in spy romp *Kingsman: The Secret Service* (2014), as does Savile Row and Kennington's Black Prince pub.

London also serves as an effective backdrop to the horror genre and dystopian cinema. Battersea Power Station and then-derelict Shoreditch and Docklands provided background for Michael Radford's adaptation of *1984* (1984) by George Orwell. Danny Boyle's shocking *28 Days Later* (2002) haunted viewers with images of an entirely deserted central London in its opening sequences, scenes rekindled in the gore-splattered sequel *28 Weeks Later* (2006). Much of Stanley Kubrick's controversial and bleak *A Clockwork Orange* (1971) was filmed in London, while Alfonso Cuarón's *Children of Men* (2006) forged a menacing and desperate vision of a London to come. Further dystopian visions of a totalitarian future London coalesce in James McTeigue's *V for Vendetta* (2005).

Other parts of town to look out for include *Notting Hill* (1999), which put the eponymous West London neighbourhood on the world map; word on the street is that Joel Hopkins' *Hampstead* (2017), starring

BEST CINEMATIC FESTIVALS

A host of London festivals ranging across the film spectrum entertains cinema enthusiasts, from the popcorn crowd to art-house intelligentsia, and various shades in between.

London Film Festival (p58) The highlight of London's many festivals celebrating the silver screen. Held in October.

Raindance Festival (www.raindance.co.uk; ⊘Sep/Oct) Europe's leading independent film-making festival. It's a terrific celebration of independent, nonmainstream cinema from across the globe, screening for 12 days just before the London Film Festival.

Portobello Film Festival (www.portobellofilmfestival.com; ⊘Sep) Features largely independent works by London film-makers and international directors. It's the UK's largest independent film competition, and it's free to attend. Held in September.

BFI Flare: London GLBT Film Festival (www.bfi.org.uk/flare; ⊘Mar) One of the best of its kind with hundreds of gay and lesbian films from around the world shown over a fun fortnight in March at BFI Southbank.

Diane Keaton and Brendan Gleeson, is about to do the same thing for North London. The Dickensian backstreets of Borough feature in such opposites as chick-flick *Bridget Jones's Diary* (2001) and Guy Ritchie's gangster-romp *Lock, Stock and Two Smoking Barrels* (1998). Smithfield conveys a certain bleak glamour in *Closer* (2004) and Brick Lane finds celluloid fame in its namesake drama (2007). Farringdon and other parts of town north of the Thames provide the backdrop to David Cronenberg's ultraviolent *Eastern Promises* (2007), while Crouch End and New Cross Gate are overrun by zombies in the hilarious *Shaun of the Dead* (2004). Ealing makes an appearance outside its famous studios in the coming-of-age film *An Education* (2009).

Mike Newell's moving drama *Soursweet* (1988) follows the travails of a newlywed Hong Kong couple moving to London in the 1960s. Sam Mendes' well-received *Skyfall* puts London into action-packed context in James Bond's spectacular 2012 outing, while awkward British monster movie *Attack the Block* (2011) sees a South London council-estate gang fighting off an alien invasion. British director Terence Davies' critically acclaimed dramatic adaptation of Terence Rattigan's *The Deep Blue Sea* (2011) conjures up a tragic portrait of post-WWII London.

The urban environment's capacity to isolate people in one of the world's most densely populated cities forms the background of Carol Morley's poignant *Dreams of a Life* (2011), a moving examination of the life of Joyce Vincent, a sociable 38-year-old woman whose dead body lay undiscovered for three years in her North London flat.

Media

Television

When it comes to televisual output, London plays with a stronger hand than it does in film: a huge amount of global TV content originates in Britain, from the *Teletubbies* and *Top Gear* to the extraordinary films of the BBC natural history unit, to cutting-edge comedy and drama across the channels – including smash hits such as *Downton Abbey*, *Doctor Who*, *Call the Midwife* and *The Crown*. British TV shows adapted to localised versions garnering huge followings include *Who Wants to Be a Millionaire?*, *The X Factor* and *MasterChef*. There are five free-to-air national TV stations: BBC1, BBC2, ITV1, Channel 4 and Five. Publicly owned broadcaster the BBC has the advantage of being commercial-free.

Radio

As with television, BBC Radio is commercial-free: BBC London (94.9 FM) is largely a talk-fest; Radio 4 (93.5 FM) has news; Radio 2 (88.8 FM) has adult-orientated music and entertainment; and Radio 1 (98.5 FM) has youth-focused pop. Capital FM (95.8 FM) is Radio 1's commercial equivalent. Then there's Xfm (104.9 FM) for indie music, Kiss 100 (100 FM) for dance and Classic FM (100.9 FM) for the high-brow stuff.

Newspapers & Magazines

National newspapers in England and London are almost always financially independent of political parties, although their political leanings are often quite obvious. There are two broad categories of newspapers, most commonly distinguished as broadsheets (or 'qualities') and tabloids (or 'red-tops'). Nowadays the distinction is more about content than format.

Daily Papers

The main London newspaper is the centre-right *Evening Standard,* a free tabloid published between Monday and Friday and handed out around mainline train stations, tube stations and some shops. At the

FILM & MEDIA MEDIA

Set in Poplar in London's East End in the 1950s, the period drama *Call the Midwife* has been the BBC's most successful TV series of recent years since it first aired in 2012, having been sold to almost 200 territories. It's made an international celebrity out of much-loved British comedian Miranda Hart.

Twitter Accounts

@Secret_London – Londoners' secret finds.

@SkintLondon – things to see and do for free or at low cost.

@stephenfry – actor, intellect and fabulous Londoner Stephen Fry is one to follow.

helm as editor is George Osborne, Chancellor of the Exchequer for six years under David Cameron. *Metro* (also published weekdays) is a skimpy morning paper, a rehash of the previous night's *Standard* and designed to be read in 20 minutes.

Readers are extremely loyal to their paper and rarely switch from one to another. Liberal and middle-class, *The Guardian* has excellent reporting, an award-winning website and a progressive agenda. A handy small-format entertainment supplement, the *Guide,* comes with Saturday's paper. The right-wing *Daily Telegraph,* dubbed the 'Torygraph', is the unofficial Conservative party paper; it has exceptionally good foreign news coverage. *The Times* is a stalwart of the British press, despite now being part of Australian mogul Rupert Murdoch's media empire; it's a decent read with a wide range of articles and strong foreign reporting. Not aligned with any political party, *The Independent* is a left-leaning serious-minded (some say earnest) tabloid with a focus on lead stories that other papers ignore. The *Financial Times* is a heavyweight business paper with a weekend edition offering some of the best journalism in Britain.

For sex and scandal over your eggs and bacon, turn to the *Mirror,* a working class and Old Labour tabloid; *The Sun* for the UK's bestseller – a gossip-hungry Tory-leaning tabloid legendary for its sassy headlines; or the lowbrow *Daily Star.* Other tabloid reads include the mid-level *Daily Express* and the centre-right *Daily Mail.*

Sunday Papers

Most dailies have Sunday stablemates, and (predictably) the tabloids have bumper editions of trashy gossip, star-struck adulation, fashion extras and mean-spirited diatribes. *The Observer,* established in 1791, is the oldest Sunday paper and sister of *The Guardian,* with a great Sunday arts supplement called *The New Review.* The *Sunday Telegraph* is as serious and politically blue as its weekly sister paper, while *The Sunday Times* is brimful of fashion and scandal but much of it can be comfortably tossed in the recycling bin upon purchase.

Magazines

An astonishing range of magazines is published and consumed in London, from celebrity gossip to ideological heavyweights.

Political magazines are particularly strong. The satirical *Private Eye* has no political bias and lampoons everyone equally, although anyone in a position of power is preferred. The excellent weekly 'newspaper' *The Economist* cannot be surpassed for international political and business analysis. Claiming to be Britain's oldest running magazine, the right-wing weekly *The Spectator* is worshipped by Tory voters, but its witty articles are often loved by left-wingers too. The *New Statesman* is a stalwart left-wing intellectual news magazine.

A freebie available from tube stations, big museums and galleries, *Time Out* is an entertainment listings guide and great for taking the city's pulse, with strong arts coverage, while the *Big Issue,* sold on the streets by the homeless, is not just an honourable project, but also a decent read.

London loves celebrities and *Heat, Closer* and *OK!* are the most popular purveyors of the genre. US import *Glamour* is the queen of the women's glossies; *Marie Claire, Elle* and *Vogue* are regarded as the thinking-woman's glossies. The thinking-man's glossies include *GQ* and *Esquire.* A slew of style magazines are published here, including *i-D,* an ubercool London fashion and music gospel, and rival *Dazed & Confused.*

London
Websites

Londonist *(www. londonist.com)* 'Things to Do' *section is tops.*

Urban 75 *(www. urban75.net) Outstanding community website.*

London on the Inside *(http:// londontheinside. com) What's so-hot-right-now.*

London Eater *(http://london eater.com) One of the better food blogs.*

Survival Guide

Transport

ARRIVING IN LONDON

Most people arrive in London by air, but an increasing number of visitors coming from Europe let the train take the strain, while buses from across the Continent are a further option.

The city has five airports: Heathrow, which is the largest, to the west; Gatwick to the south; Stansted to the northeast; Luton to the northwest; and London City in the Docklands.

Most trans-Atlantic flights land at Heathrow (average flight time from the US East Coast is between 6½ and 7½ hours, 10 to 11 hours from the West Coast; slightly more on the return).

Visitors from Europe are more likely to arrive at Gatwick, Stansted or Luton (the latter two are used exclusively by low-cost airlines such as easyJet and Ryanair). Most flights to Continental Europe last from one to three hours.

An increasingly popular form of transport is the Eurostar – the Channel Tunnel train – between London and Paris or Brussels. The journey lasts 2¼ hours to Paris and less than two hours to Brussels. Travellers depart from and arrive in the centre of each city.

Flights, cars and tours can be booked online at lonelyplanet.com.

Heathrow Airport

Some 15 miles west of central London, Heathrow Airport (LHR; www.heathrowairport.com) is one of the world's busiest international airports and counts four passenger terminals (numbered 2 to 5), including the revamped Terminal 2. It's Britain's main airport for international flights.

Each terminal has currency-exchange facilities, information counters and accommodation desks.

Left-luggage Facilities are in each terminal and open 5am (5.30am at T4) to 11pm. The charge per item is £6 for up to two hours, £11 for up to 24 hours, up to a maximum of 90 days.

Hotels There are four international-style hotels that can be reached on foot from the terminals, and another 20 or so nearby. The **Hotel Hoppa** (www.nationalexpress.com/wherewego/airports/heathrow-hotel-hoppa.aspx; adult/child £4.50/free) bus links nearby hotels with the airport's terminals, running every 15 to 30 minutes from around 4.30am to midnight.

Train

Three Underground stations on the Piccadilly line serve Heathrow: one for Terminals 2 and 3, another for Terminal 4, and the terminus for Terminal 5. The Underground, commonly referred to as 'the tube', is the cheapest way of getting to Heathrow; paper tickets cost one-way £6, Oyster or Contactless peak/off-peak £5.10/3.10. The journey to central London takes one hour and trains depart every three to nine minutes. Leaving from the airport, it runs from just after 5am to just after midnight (11.28pm Sunday), and heading to the airport it runs from 5.09am to 11.54pm (11pm on Sunday); tube trains run all night Friday and Saturday, with reduced frequency. Buy tickets at the station.

Heathrow Express (www.heathrowexpress.com; oneway/return £22/37; ☎), every 15 minutes, and **Heathrow Connect** (☑0345 604 1515; www.heathrowconnect.com; adult single/open return £10.30/20.70), every 30 minutes, trains link Heathrow with Paddington train station. Heathrow Express trains take a mere 15 minutes to reach Paddington. Trains on each service run from around 5am and between 11pm and midnight.

Bus

National Express (www.nationalexpress.com) Coaches (one-way from £6, 35 to 90 minutes, every 30 minutes to one hour) link the Heathrow Central bus station with London Victoria coach station. The first bus leaves the Heathrow Central bus station (at Terminals 2 and 3) at 4.20am, with the last departure just after 10pm. The first bus leaves Victoria at 3am, the last at around 12.30am.

N9 bus At night, the N9 bus (£1.50, 1¼ hours, every 20 minutes) connects Heathrow Central bus station (and Heathrow Terminal 5) with central London, terminating at Aldwych.

Taxi

A metered black-cab trip to/from central London will cost between £46 and £87 and take 45 minutes to an hour, depending on traffic and your departure point.

Gatwick Airport

Located some 30 miles south of central London, Gatwick (LGW; www.gatwick-airport.com) is smaller than Heathrow and is Britain's number-two airport, mainly for international flights. The North and South Terminals are linked by a 24-hour shuttle train, with the journey time about three minutes.

Left luggage There are left-luggage facilities in both terminals, open 24 hours in the South Terminal and from 6am to 10pm in the North Terminal. The charge is £6/11 per item for 3/24 hours (or part thereof), up to a maximum of 90 days. You can prebook left luggage online (www.gatwick

airport.com/at-the-airport/passenger-services/luggage).

Train

National Rail (www.national-rail.co.uk) has regular train services to/from London Bridge (30 minutes, every 15 to 30 minutes), London King's Cross (55 minutes, every 15 to 30 minutes) and London Victoria (30 minutes, every 10 to 15 minutes). Fares vary depending on the time of travel and the train company, but allow £10 to £20 for a single.

Gatwick Express (www.gatwickexpress.com; one-way/return adult £19.90/35.50, child £9.95/17.75) trains run every 15 minutes from the station near the Gatwick South Terminal to London Victoria. From the airport, there are services between 5.45am and 12.20am. From Victoria, they leave between 5am and 11.30am. The journey takes 30 mintues.

Bus

National Express (www.nationalexpress.com) Coaches run throughout the day from Gatwick to London Victoria coach station (one way from £8). Services depart hourly around the clock. Journey time is between 80 minutes and two hours, depending on traffic.

EasyBus (www.easybus.co.uk) Runs 19-seater minibuses to Gatwick every 15 to 20 minutes on several routes, including

from Earl's Court/West Brompton and Victoria coach station (one way from £1.95). The service runs round the clock. Journey time averages 75 minutes.

Taxi

A metered black-cab trip to/from central London costs around £100 and takes just over an hour. Minicabs are usually cheaper.

Stansted Airport

Stansted (STN; www.stanstedairport.com) is 35 miles northeast of central London in the direction of Cambridge. An international airport, Stansted serves a multitude of mainly European destinations and is served primarily by low-cost carriers such as Ryanair.

Train

Stansted Express (☎0345 600 7245; www.stanstedexpress.com; one-way/return £16.60/28) rail service (45 minutes, every 15 to 30 minutes) links the airport and Liverpool St station. From the airport, the first train leaves at 5.30am, the last at 12.30am. Trains depart Liverpool St station from 3.40am to 11.25pm.

Bus

National Express (www.nationalexpress.com) coaches run around the

---

CLIMATE CHANGE & TRAVEL

Every form of transport that relies on carbon-based fuel generates CO_2, the main cause of human-induced climate change. Modern travel is dependent on aeroplanes, which might use less fuel per kilometre per person than most cars but travel much greater distances. The altitude at which aircraft emit gases (including CO_2) and particles also contributes to their climate change impact. Many websites offer 'carbon calculators' that allow people to estimate the carbon emissions generated by their journey and, for those who wish to do so, to offset the impact of the greenhouse gases emitted with contributions to portfolios of climate-friendly initiatives throughout the world. Lonely Planet offsets the carbon footprint of all staff and author travel.

clock, offering well over 100 services per day.

Airbus A6 (☑0871 781 8181; www.nationalexpress.com; one-way from £10) runs to Victoria coach station (around one hour to 1½ hours, every 20 minutes) via Marble Arch, Paddington, Baker St and Golders Green. **Airbus A7** (☑0871 781 8181; www.nationalexpress.com; one-way from £10) also runs to Victoria coach station (around one hour to 1½ hours, every 20 minutes), via Waterloo and Southwark. **Airbus A8** (☑0871 781 8181; www.nationalexpress.com; one-way from £6) runs to Liverpool St station (one way from £6, 60 to 80 minutes, every 30 minutes), via Bethnal Green, Shoreditch High St and Mile End.

Stansted City Link 767 (☑0330 123 2004; www.stanstedcitylink.com; one-way from £9) runs to London King's Cross every 30 minutes and takes 75 minutes.

Airport Bus Express (www.airportbusexpress.co.uk; one-way from £10) runs every 30 minutes to London Bridge, Victoria coach station, Liverpool Street and Stratford. **EasyBus** (www.easybus.co.uk) runs services to Baker St and Old St tube stations every 15 minutes. The journey (one way from £4.95) takes one hour from Old St, 1¼ hour from Baker St.

Terravision (www.terravision.eu) coaches link Stansted to Liverpool St train station (one way from £9, 55 minutes), King's Cross (from £9, 75 minutes) and Victoria coach station (from £10, two hours) every 20 to 40 minutes between 6am and 1am. Wi-fi on all buses.

Taxi

A metered black cab trip to/from central London costs around £130. Minicabs are cheaper.

Luton Airport

A smallish, single-runway airport 32 miles northwest of London, Luton (LTN) generally caters for cheap charter flights and discount airlines and serves almost 15 million passengers a year. There are chain hotels nearby and the usual range of facilities.

Train

National Rail (www.nationalrail.co.uk) 24-hour services (one way from £14, 26 to 50 minutes, departures every six minutes to one hour) from London St Pancras International to Luton Airport Parkway station, from where an airport shuttle bus (one way/return £2.10/3.40) will take you to the airport in 10 minutes.

Bus

Airbus A1 (www.nationalexpress.com; one-way from £5) runs over 60 times daily to London Victoria coach station (one way from £5), via Portman Square, Baker Street, St John's Wood, Finchley Road and Golders Green. It takes around 1½ hours.

Green Line Bus 757 (☑0344 800 4411; www.greenline.co.uk; one-way/return £10/17) runs to Luton Airport from London Victoria coach station every 30 minutes on a 24-hour service via Marble Arch, Baker Street, Finchley Road and Brent Cross.

Taxi

A metered black-cab trip to/from central London costs about £110.

London City Airport

Its proximity to central London, which is just 6 miles to the west, as well as to the commercial district of the Docklands, means **London**

City Airport (LCY; ☑020-7646 0088; www.londoncityairport.com; Hartmann Rd, E16; ☎; ☒London City Airport) is predominantly a gateway airport for business travellers. You can also now fly to New York from here.

Train

Docklands Light Railway (DLR; www.tfl.gov.uk/dlr) stops at the London City Airport station (one way £2.80 to £3.30). Trains depart every eight to 10 minutes from just after 5.30am to 12.15am Monday to Saturday, and 7am to 11.15pm Sunday. The journey to Bank takes just over 20 minutes.

Taxi

A metered black-cab trip to the City/Oxford St/Earl's Court costs about £25/35/50.

Train

Main national rail routes are served by a variety of private train-operating companies. Tickets are not cheap, but trains between cities are usually quite punctual. Check **National Rail** (www.nationalrail.co.uk) for timetables and fares.

Eurostar (www.eurostar.com) high-speed passenger rail service linking London St Pancras International with Paris, Brussels and Lille. It has up to 19 daily departures. Fares vary greatly, from £29 one way standard class to around £245 one way for a fully flexible business premier ticket (prices based on return journeys). There are deals on Eurostar Snap, with best value fares for those with flexibility around the specific train they travel on.

GETTING AROUND LONDON

The cheapest way to get around London is with an Oyster Card or a UK contactless card (foreign cardholders should check for contactless charges first).

Tube (London Underground) The fastest and most efficient way of getting around town. First/last trains operate from around 5.30am to 12.30am and 24 hours on Friday and Saturday on five lines.

Train The DLR and Overground network are ideal for zooming across more distant parts of the city. Trains run from a number of stations to more distant destinations in and around London.

Bus The London bus network is very extensive and efficient; while bus lanes free up traffic, buses can still be slow going.

Taxis Black cabs are ubiquitous, but not cheap. Available around the clock.

Bicycle Santander Cycles are great for shorter journeys around central London.

Underground, DLR & Overground

The London Underground ('the tube'; 11 colour-coded lines) is part of an integrated-transport system that also includes the Docklands Light Railway (DLR; www.tfl.gov.uk/dlr; a driverless overhead train operating in the eastern part of the city) and Overground network (mostly outside of Zone 1 and sometimes underground). Despite the never-ending upgrades and 'engineering works' requiring weekend closures, it is overall the quickest and easiest way of getting around the city, if not the cheapest.

The first trains operate from around 5.30am Monday to Saturday and 6.45am Sunday. The last trains leave around 12.30am Monday to Saturday and 11.30pm Sunday.

Additionally, selected lines (the Victoria and Jubilee lines, plus most of the Piccadilly, Central and Northern lines) run all night on Friday and Saturday to get revellers home (on what is called the 'Night Tube'), with trains every 10 minutes or so. Fares are off-peak.

During weekend closures, schedules, maps and alternative route suggestions are posted in every station, and staff are at hand to help redirect you.

Some stations, most famously Leicester Sq and Covent Garden, are much closer in reality than they appear on the map.

Fares

→ London is divided into nine concentric fare zones.

→ It will always be cheaper to travel with an Oyster Card or a contactless card than a paper ticket.

→ Children under the age of 11 travel free; 11 to 15 year olds are half-price if registered on an accompanying adult's Oyster Card (register at Zone 1 or Heathrow tube stations).

→ If you're in London for a longer period and plan to travel every day, consider a weekly or even a monthly Travelcard.

→ If you're caught without a valid ticket, you're liable for an on-the-spot fine of £80. If paid within 21 days, the fine is reduced to £40. Inspectors accept no excuses.

Bus

London's ubiquitous red double-decker buses afford great views of the city, but be aware that the going can be slow, thanks to traffic jams and dozens of commuters getting on and off at every stop.

There are excellent bus maps at every stop detailing all routes and destinations served from that particular area (generally a few bus stops within a two- to

TRAVEL FARES

ZONE	CASH SINGLE	OYSTER/CONTACTLESS PEAK SINGLE	OYSTER/CONTACTLESS OFF-PEAK SINGLE	CAP (OYSTER/CONTACTLESS DAY TRAVELCARD)
Zone 1 only	£4.90	£2.40	£2.40	£6.60
Zone 1 & 2	£4.90	£2.90	£2.40	£6.60
Zone 1-3	£4.90	£3.30	£2.80	£7.70
Zone 1-4	£5.90	£3.90	£2.80	£9.50
Zone 1-5	£5.90	£4.70	£3.10	£11.20
Zone 1-6	£6	£5.10	£3.10	£12

OYSTER CARD & CONTACTLESS CARDS

The Oyster Card is a smart card on which you can store credit towards 'prepay' fares, as well as Travelcards valid for periods from a day to a year. Oyster Cards are valid across the entire public transport network in London.

All you need to do when entering a station is touch your card on a reader (which has a yellow circle with the image of an Oyster Card on it) and then touch again on your way out. The system will then deduct the appropriate amount of credit from your card, as necessary. For bus journeys, you only need to touch once upon boarding. Note that some train stations don't have exit turnstiles, so you will need to tap out on the reader before leaving the station; if you forget, you will be hugely overcharged.

The benefit lies in the fact that fares for Oyster Card users are lower than standard ones. If you are making many journeys during the day, you will never pay more than the appropriate Travelcard (peak or off-peak) once the daily 'price cap' has been reached.

Oyster Cards can be bought (£5 refundable deposit required) and topped up at any Underground station, travel information centre or shop displaying the Oyster logo. To get your deposit back along with any remaining credit, simply return your Oyster Card at a ticket booth.

Contactless cards (which do not require chip and pin or a signature) can now be used directly on Oyster Card readers and are subject to the same Oyster fares. The advantage is that you don't have to bother with buying, topping up and then returning an Oyster Card, but foreign visitors should bear in mind the cost of card transactions.

one more bus journey. You must then top up your credit before you can use your Oyster Card again.

Children under 11 travel free; 11 to 15 year olds are half-price if registered on an accompanying adult's Oyster Card (register at Zone 1 or Heathrow tube stations).

Bicycle

Tens of thousands of Londoners cycle to work every day, and it is generally a good way to get around the city, although traffic can be intimidating for less-confident cyclists and it's important to keep your wits about you. The city has tried hard to improve the cycling infrastructure, however, opening new 'cycle super-highways' for commuters and launching **Santander Cycles** (☑0343 222 6666; www.tfl.gov.uk/modes/cycling/santander-cycles), which is particularly useful for visitors.

Transport for London (www.tfl.gov.uk) publishes 14 free maps of London's cycle routes.

Bicycles on Public Transport

Bicycles can be taken on the Overground, DLR and on the Circle, District, Hammersmith and City, and Metropolitan tube lines, except at peak times (7.30am to 9.30am and 4pm to 7pm Monday to Friday). Folding bikes can be taken on any line at any time, however.

Pedicabs

Three-wheeled cycle rickshaws seating two or three passengers have been a regular part of the West End scene for over a decade. They're less than a mode of transport than a gimmick for tourists and the occasional drunk on a Saturday night. Expect to pay from £5 for a short trip; it's worth confirming

three-minute walk, shown on a local map).

Many bus stops have LED displays listing bus arrival times, but downloading a bus app such as London Bus Live Countdown to your smartphone is the most effective way to keep track of when your next bus is due.

Bus services normally operate from 5am to 11.30pm.

Night Bus

➡ More than 50 night-bus routes (prefixed with the letter 'N') run from around 11.30pm to 5am.

➡ There are also another 60 bus routes operating 24 hours; the frequency decreases between 11pm and 5am.

➡ Oxford Circus, Tottenham

Court Rd and Trafalgar Sq are the main hubs for night routes.

➡ Night buses can be infrequent and stop only on request, so remember to ring for your stop.

➡ Don't forget the Night Tube, which runs along five lines for 24 hours on Friday and Saturday, and can either be used as an alternative or in concert with night buses.

Fares

Cash cannot be used on London's buses. Instead you must pay with an Oyster Card, Travelcard or a contactless payment card. Bus fares are a flat £1.50, no matter the distance travelled. If you don't have enough credit on your Oyster Card for a £1.50 bus fare, you can make the rate before you get in as there have been some high-profile incidents of over-charging. Tours of London are also available, from £80 per person for a pub tour. For more information visit www.londonpedicabs.com.

Taxi

Although expensive, taxis can be a very useful way to get about town. Black cab drivers can be hailed on the street and are both generally very honest and extremely knowledgeable: they know precisely where they are going, though they can talk the hind leg off a donkey.

Black Cabs

The black cab is as much a feature of the London cityscape as the red double-decker bus. Licensed black-cab drivers have the 'Knowledge', acquired after rigorous training and a series of exams. They are supposed to know 25,000 streets within a 6-mile radius of Charing Cross/Trafalgar Sq and the 100 most-visited spots of the moment, including clubs and restaurants.

➡ Cabs are available for hire when the yellow sign above the windscreen is lit; just stick your arm out to signal one.

➡ Fares are metered, with the flagfall charge of £2.60 (covering the first 248m during a weekday), rising by increments of 20p for each subsequent 124m.

➡ Fares are more expensive in the evenings and overnight.

➡ You can tip taxi drivers up to 10%, but most Londoners simply round up to the nearest pound.

➡ Apps such as mytaxi (https://uk.mytaxi.com/hailo) use your smartphone's GPS to locate the nearest black cab. You only pay the metered fare.

➡ **ComCab** (☏cash 020-7908 0271; www.comcab-london.

co.uk) operates one of the largest fleets of black cabs in town.

Minicabs

➡ Minicabs, which are licensed, are cheaper (usually) competitors of black cabs.

➡ Unlike black cabs, minicabs cannot legally be hailed on the street; they must be hired by phone or directly from one of the minicab offices (every high street has at least one and most clubs work with a minicab firm to send revellers home safely).

➡ Don't accept unsolicited offers from individuals claiming to be minicab drivers – they are just guys with cars.

➡ Minicabs don't have meters; there's usually a fare set by the dispatcher. Make sure you ask before setting off.

➡ Your hotel or host will be able to recommend a reputable minicab company in the neighbourhood; every Londoner has the number of at least one company. Or phone a large 24-hour operator such as **Addison**

Lee (☏020-7407 9000; www.addisonlee.com).

➡ Apps such as Uber or Kabbee allow you to book a minicab in double-quick time and can save you money.

Boats

Several companies operate along the River Thames; only **Thames Clippers** (www.thamesclippers.com; all zones adult/child £9/4.50) really offers commuter services, however. It's fast, pleasant and you're almost always guaranteed a seat and a view.

Thames Clipper boats run regular services between Embankment, Waterloo (London Eye), Blackfriars, Bankside (Shakespeare's Globe), London Bridge, Tower Bridge, Canary Wharf, Greenwich, North Greenwich and Woolwich piers (all zones adult/child £9/4.50), from 6.55am to around midnight (from 9.29am weekends).

Thames Clipper River Roamer tickets (adult/child £18.50/9.25) give freedom to hop on and hop off boats on most routes all day.

You can get a discount of one-third of the standard fare and off the price of River Roamer tickets if you're a pay-as-you-go Oyster Card holder or Travelcard holder (paper ticket or on Oyster Card). Children under five go free on most boats.

Between April and September, Hampton Court Palace can be reached by boat on the 22-mile route along the Thames from Westminster Pier in central London (via Kew and Richmond). The trip can take up to four hours, depending on the tide. Boats are run by **Westminster Passenger Services Association** (www.wpsa. co.uk; one-way/return adult £17/25, child £8.50/12.50).

The **London Waterbus Company** (☎020-7482 2550; www.londonwaterbus.com; single/return adult £9/14, child £7.50/12; ⊜Warwick Avenue) runs canal boats between Camden Lock and Little Venice.

Car & Motorcycle

As a visitor, it's very unlikely you'll need to drive in London. Much has been done to encourage Londoners to get out of their car and into public transport (or on their bikes) and the same disincentives should keep you firmly off the road: the congestion charge, extortionate parking fees, traffic jams, high price of petrol, fiendishly efficient traffic wardens, wheel clampers, ubiquitous CCTV cameras recording cars parked (even momentarily) on double yellow lines and so on.

Road Rules

➡ Drive on the left side of the road.

➡ Get a copy of the *Highway Code* (www.gov.uk/

highway-code), available at Automobile Association (AA) and Royal Automobile Club (RAC) outlets, as well as some bookshops and tourist offices.

➡ A foreign driving licence is valid in Britain for up to 12 months from the time of your last entry into the country.

➡ If you bring a car from Continental Europe, make sure you're adequately insured.

➡ All drivers and passengers must wear seatbelts, and motorcyclists must wear a helmet.

➡ It is illegal to use a mobile phone to call or text while driving (using a hands-free device to talk on your mobile is permitted).

➡ Pedestrians have right of way at zebra crossings (black and white stripes on the road); allow them to cross.

➡ The speed limit on most urban roads is 30mph, but there are 20mph zones (indicated).

Congestion Charge

London has a **congestion charge** (☎0343 222 2222; www.tfl.gov.uk/roadusers/ congestioncharging) in place to reduce the flow of traffic into its centre.

The congestion-charge zone encompasses Euston Rd and Pentonville Rd to the north, Park Lane to the west, Tower Bridge to the east, and Elephant and Castle and Vauxhall Bridge Rd to the south. As you enter the zone, you will see a large white 'C' in a red circle.

If you enter the zone between 7am and 6pm Monday to Friday (excluding public holidays), you must pay the £11.50 charge (payable in advance or on the day) or £14 on the first charging day after travel to avoid receiving a fine (£130, or £65 if paid within 14 days).

You can pay online or over the phone. For full details visit the website.

Hire

There is no shortage of car-rental agencies in London, including several branches of major brands such as Avis, easyCar and Hertz. Book in advance for the best fares, especially at weekends.

Fines

If you get a parking ticket or your car gets clamped, call the number on the ticket. If the car has been removed, ring the free 24-hour service called **TRACE** (Tow-Away Removal & Clamping Enquiries; ☎0845 206 8602; https:// trace.london; ⊙24hr) to find out where your car has been taken. It will cost you a minimum of £200 to get your vehicle back on the road.

Cable Car

The **Emirates Air Line** (www.emiratesairline.co.uk; 27 Western Gateway, E16; one-way adult/child £4.50/2.30, with Oyster Card £3.40/1.70; ⊙7am-10pm Mon-Fri, 9am-10pm Sat & Sun; ⊠Royal Victoria DLR, ⊜North Greenwich) is a cable car linking the Royal Docks in East London with North Greenwich some 90m above the Thames. The journey is brief, and rather pricey, but the views are stunning.

Tram

South London has a small tram network called **London Tramlink** (☎0343 222 1234; https://tfl.gov.uk/ modes/trams). There are three routes running along 17 miles of track, including Wimbledon to Elmers End via Croydon; Croydon to Beckenham; and Croydon to New Addington. Single tickets cost £2.60 (£1.50 with an Oyster Card).

Walking

You can't beat walking for neighbourhood exploration. There are plenty of bridges across the Thames and a couple of pedestrian tunnels beneath the river too. It's also worth noting that some tube stations can be far closer to each other on the ground than they may appear on the tube map and it can be quicker to walk (eg Covent Garden to Leicester Square).

There are two pedestrian tunnels beneath the River Thames; one at **Greenwich** (Cutty Sark Gardens, SE10; ⊙24hr; ℞DLR Cutty Sark) and one at Woolwich. Both can be an interesting, diverting, free and unusual way of getting between the north and south sides of London.

TOURS

Air Tours

Adventure Balloons
(☑01252 844222; www.adventureballoons.co.uk; Winchfield Park, London Rd, Hartley Wintney, Hampshire RG27; per person £199) Weather permitting, weekday-morning London flights take off shortly after dawn from late April to mid-August. The flight lasts one hour, but allow four to six hours, including take-off, landing and recovery. See the website for meeting points.

Boat Tours

Crown River Cruises
(☑020-7936 2033; www.crownrivercruise.co.uk; adult/child one way £9.90/4.95, return £13.15/6.58; ⊙11am-6.30pm late May-early Sep, to 5pm Apr, May, Sep & Oct, to 3pm Nov-Mar) Vessels travel east from Westminster Pier to St Katharine's Pier near the Tower of London and back,

calling at Embankment, Festival and Bankside piers. You can travel just one way, make the return trip or use the boat as a hop-on, hop-off service to visit sights on the way. Tours depart half-hourly late May to early September, and every 40 minutes the rest of the year. Vessels are equipped with a multilingual commentary system, enabling passengers to use their smartphone to access an audio commentary in up to six languages (without using data).

Bus Tours

Big Bus Tours (☑020-7808 6753; www.bigbustours.com; adult/child £30/12.50; ⊙every 20min 8.30am-6pm Apr-Sep, to 5pm Oct & Mar, to 4.30pm Nov-Feb) Informative commentaries in 12 languages. The ticket includes a free river cruise with City Cruises and three thematic walking tours (Royal London, film locations, mysteries). Good online booking discounts available. Onboard wi-fi. The ticket is valid for 24 hours; for an extra £8 (£5 for children), you can upgrade to a 48-hour ticket.

Original Tour (www.theoriginaltour.com; adult/child £30/15; ⊙8.30am-8.30pm) A 24-hour hop-on, hop-off bus service with a river cruise thrown in, as well as three themed walks: Changing of the Guard, Rock 'n' Roll and Jack the Ripper. Buses run every five to 20 minutes; you can buy tickets on the bus or online. There's also a 48-hour ticket available (adult/child £40/19), with an extended river cruise.

Specialist Tours

Guide London (Association of Professional Tourist Guides; ☑020-7611 2545; www.

guidelondon.org.uk; half-/full day £160/272) Hire a prestigious Blue Badge Tourist Guide, know-it-all guides who have studied for two years and passed a dozen written and practical exams to do their job. They can tell you stories behind the sights that you'd only hear from them or whisk you on a themed tour – from royalty and The Beatles to parks and shopping. Go by car, public transport, bike or on foot. For private tours by car, driver guides typically charge £365 for a half-day and £525 for a full day.

Alternative London (www.alternativeldn.com) Aiming to avoid the obvious and hackneyed, these cycling and walking tours cover themes such as street art, ethnic food and craft beer, mainly around the East End.

Open House London (☑020-7383 2131; www.openhouselondon.org.uk) Along with the annual free Open House London weekend event during the third week of September, when some 750 to 800 buildings are open to the public, this architectural charity also sponsors talks with architectural tours to various areas of London held by sister organisation Open City (☑020-3006 7008; www.open-city.org.uk; tours £24.50-35.50).

Unseen Tours (☑07514 266 774; www.sockmobevents.org.uk; £12) See London from an entirely different angle on one of these award-winning neighbourhood tours led by the London homeless covering Camden Town, Brick Lane, Shoreditch and London Bridge. Sixty per cent of the tour price goes to the guide.

Directory A–Z

Customs Regulations

The UK distinguishes between goods bought duty-free outside the EU and those bought in another EU country, where taxes and duties will have already been paid.

If you exceed your duty-free allowance, you will have to pay tax on the items. For European goods, there is officially no limit to how much you can bring but customs use certain guidelines to distinguish between personal and commercial use.

Import Restrictions

Item	Duty-free
Tobacco	200 cigarettes, 100 cigarillos, 50 cigars or 250g tobacco
Spirits & liqueurs	1L spirit or 2L fortified wine (eg sherry or port)
Beer & wine	16L beer & 4L still wine
Other goods	Up to a value of £390

Discount Cards

London Pass (☏020-7293 0972; www.londonpass. com; 1/2/3/6/10 days £62/85/101/139/169) Worthwhile for visitors who want to take in lots of paid sights in a short time. The pass offers free entry and queue-jumping to all major attractions, and can be adapted to include use of the Underground and buses. Child passes are available too. Check the website for details.

You can download the app to your smartphone or collect your pass from the **London Pass Redemption Desk** (www. londonpass.com; 11a Charing Cross Rd, WC2; h10am-4.30pm; tLeicester Sq), near Leicester Sq.

Historic Royal Palaces (☏020-3166 6000; www. hrp.org.uk; individual/joint membership £50/77, one/two adult family £66/100) If you're a royalty or palace buff, taking out an annual membership allows you to jump the queues and visit the Tower of London, Kensington Palace, Banqueting House, Kew Palace and Hampton Court Palace as often as you like, making you a fair saving. There can be a lengthy wait for membership cards, but temporary cards are issued immediately.

Electricity

Type G
230V/50Hz

Emergency

Emergency & Important Numbers

International dialling code	☏00
London's area code	☏020
Police, fire brigade or ambulance	☏999
Reverse charge/collect calls	☏155

Insurance

Not all holidays are trouble-free and travel insurance for visits to London are very much recommended. Insurance usually covers medical and dental consultation and treatment at private clinics, as well as the cost of any emergency flight, plus loss of baggage and so forth. Worldwide travel insurance is available at www.lonelyplanet.com/travel-insurance. You can buy, extend and claim online anytime – even if you're already on the road.

Legal Matters

Should you face any legal difficulties while in London, visit a branch of the Citizens Advice Bureau (www.citizensadvice.org.uk), or contact your embassy.

Driving Offences

The laws against drink-driving are very strict in the UK and treated seriously. Currently the limit is 80mg of alcohol in 100mL of blood. The safest approach is not to drink anything at all if you're planning to drive.

It is illegal to use a hand-held phone (or similar devices) while driving.

Drugs

Illegal drugs of every type are widely available in London, especially in clubs. Nonetheless, all the usual drug warnings apply. Cannabis was downgraded to a Class C drug in 2004 but reclassified as a Class B drug in 2009 following a government rethink. If you're caught with pot today, you're likely to be arrested. Possession of harder drugs, including heroin and cocaine, is always treated seriously. Searches on entering clubs are common.

Fines

In general you rarely have to pay on the spot for an offence. The exceptions are trains, the tube and buses, where people who can't produce a valid ticket for the journey when asked to by an inspector can be fined there and then. No excuses are accepted, though if you can't pay, you'll be able to register your details (if you have some sort of ID with you) and be sent a fine in the post.

Maps

Lonely Planet's London City Map is available from http://shop.lonelyplanet.com/map. The *London A–Z* series produces a range of excellent maps and hand-held street atlases. Online, www.streetmap.co.uk and Google Maps are comprehensive.

Money

The UK did not adopt the euro and retained the pound sterling (£) as its unit of currency.

One pound sterling is made up of 100 pence (called 'pee', colloquially). Notes come in denominations of £5, £10, £20 and £50, while coins are 1p ('penny'), 2p, 5p, 10p, 20p, 50p, £1 and £2. Loaded with features to thwart counterfeiters, a new dual-metal, hologram-decorated, 12-sided £1 coin entered circulation in 2017.

ATMs

ATMs are everywhere and will generally accept Visa, MasterCard, Cirrus or Maestro cards, as well as more obscure ones. There is almost always a transaction surcharge for cash withdrawals with foreign cards. There are nonbank-run ATMs that charge £1.50 to £2 per transaction. These are normally found inside shops and are particularly expensive for foreign-bank card holders. The ATM generally warns you before you take money out that it will charge you but be vigilant.

Although many London ATMs are largely tamper-proof, always beware of suspicious-looking devices attached to ATMs, including tiny pinhole cameras. If you are unsure about any particular ATM, find another one.

Changing Money

The best place to change money is in any local post-office branch, where no commission is charged.

You can also change money in most high-street banks and some travel agencies, as well as at the numerous bureaux de change throughout the city.

Compare rates and watch for the commission that is not always mentioned very prominently. The trick is to ask how many pounds you'll receive in total before committing – you'll lose nothing by shopping around.

Credit & Debit Cards

Londoners live off their debit cards, which can also be used to get 'cash back' from supermarkets. Card transactions and cash withdrawals are generally subject to additional charges for foreign cardholders; check with your provider.

➡ Credit and debit cards are accepted almost universally in London, from restaurants and bars to shops and even by some taxis.

➡ American Express and Diners Club are far less widely used than Visa and MasterCard.

➡ Contactless cards and payments (which do not require a chip and pin or a signature) are increasingly widespread (watch for the wi-fi-like symbol on cards, shops, taxis, buses, the Underground, rail services and other transport options). Transactions are limited to a maximum of £30.

Exchange Rates

Australia	A$1	£0.60
Canada	C$1	£0.59
Euro	€1	£0.88
Japan	¥100	£0.71
NZ	NZ$1	£0.56
US	US$1	£0.78

For current exchange rates, see www.xe.com.

Tipping

Hotels Pay a porter £1 per bag; gratuity for room staff is at your discretion.

Pubs Not expected unless table service is provided, then £1 for a round of drinks is sufficient. Do not tip at the bar.

Restaurants Service charge often included in the bill. If not, 10% for decent service, up to 15% if exceptional.

Taxis Londoners generally round the fare up to the nearest pound only.

Opening Hours

The following are standard opening hours.

Banks 9am–5pm Monday–Friday

Post offices 9am–5.30pm Monday–Friday and 9am–noon Saturday

Pubs & bars 11am–11pm (many are open later)

Restaurants noon–2.30pm and 6–11pm

Sights 10am–6pm

Shops 9am–7pm Monday–Saturday, noon–6pm Sunday

Post

The Royal Mail (www.royalmail.com) is no longer the humdinger it once was but it is generally very reliable. To find your nearest post office, consult www.postoffice.co.uk/branch-finder.

Postcodes

The unusual London postcode system dates back to WWI. The whole city is divided up into districts denoted by a letter (or letters) and a number. For example, W1, the postcode for Mayfair and Soho, stands for 'West London, district 1'. EC1, on the other hand, stands for 'East Central London, district 1'. The number a district is assigned has nothing to do with its geographic location, but rather its alphabetical listing in that area. For example, in North London N1 and N16 are right next to each other, as are E1 and E14 in East London.

Public Holidays

Most attractions and businesses close for a couple of days over Christmas and sometimes Easter. Places that normally shut on Sunday will probably close on bank holiday Mondays. The transport network shuts down in London on Christmas Day, apart from Santander Cycles. Hotel restaurants are about the only thing you'll find open.

New Year's Day 1 January

Good Friday Late March/April

Easter Monday Late March/April

May Day Holiday First Monday in May

Spring Bank Holiday Last Monday in May

Summer Bank Holiday Last Monday in August

Christmas Day 25 December

Boxing Day 26 December

Taxes & Refunds

Value-added tax (VAT) is a 20% sales tax levied on most goods and services. Restaurants must always include VAT in their prices, but the same requirement does not apply to hotel room prices, so double-check when booking.

It's sometimes possible for visitors to claim a refund of VAT (p420) paid on goods. You're eligible if you live outside the EU and are heading back home, or if you're an EU citizen and are leaving the EU for more than 12 months.

More Information

Not all shops participate in what is called either the VAT Retail Export Scheme or Tax Free Shopping, and different shops will have different minimum purchase conditions (normally around £75 in any one shop). On request, participating shops will give you a special form (VAT 407). This must be presented with the goods and receipts to customs when you depart the country. (VAT-free goods can't be posted or shipped home.) After customs has certified the form, you can sometimes get a refund on the spot, otherwise the form gets sent back to the shop, which then processes your refund (minus an administration or handling fee). This can take up to 10 weeks.

Telephone

British Telecom's famous red phone boxes survive in conservation areas only (notably Westminster). Some people use them as shelter from the rain while using their mobile phones. Some BT phones still accept coins, but most take credit cards. The minimum charge is 60p, for the first 30 minutes of a national call.

Calling London

London's area code is 020, followed by an eight-digit number beginning with 7 (central London), 8 (Greater London) or 3 (nongeographic).

You only need to dial the 020 when you are calling

London from elsewhere in the UK or if you're dialling from a mobile.

To call London from abroad, dial your country's international access code (usually ☑00 but ☑011 in Canada and the USA), then ☑44 (the UK's country code), then 20 (dropping the initial 0), followed by the eight-digit phone number.

International Calls & Rates

International direct dialling (IDD) calls to almost anywhere can be made from nearly all public telephones. Direct dialling is cheaper than making a reverse-charge (collect) call through the international operator.

Many private firms offer cheaper international calls than BT. In such places you phone from a metered booth and then pay the bill. Some internet shops also offer cheap rates for international calls.

International calling cards with stored value (usually £5, £10 or £20) and a PIN, which you can use from any phone by dialling a special access number, are usually the cheapest way to call abroad. These cards are available at most corner shops.

Note that the use of Skype or Whatsapp may be restricted in some hostels because of noise and/or bandwidth issues.

Local & National Call Rates

Local calls are charged by time alone; regional and national calls are charged by both time and distance.

Daytime rates apply from 7am to 7pm Monday to Friday.

The cheap rate applies from 7pm to 7am Monday to Friday and again over the weekend from 7pm Friday to 7am Monday.

Mobile Phones

Buy local SIM cards for European and Australian phones, or a pay-as-you-go phone. Set other phones to international roaming.

MORE INFORMATION

The UK uses the GSM 900 network, which covers Europe, Australia and New Zealand, but is not compatible with CDMA mobile technology used in the US and Japan (although some American and Japanese phones can work on both GSM and CDMA networks).

If you have a GSM phone, check with your service provider about using it in the UK and ask about roaming charges.

It's usually better to buy a local SIM card from any mobile-phone shop, though in order to do that your handset from home must be unlocked.

Time

London is on GMT/UTC; during British Summer Time (BST; late March to late October), London clocks are one hour ahead of GMT/ UTC.

Toilets

Train stations, bus terminals and attractions generally have good facilities, providing also for people with disabilities and those with young children. You'll also find public toilets across the city, some operated by local councils, others automated

and self-cleaning. Most charge 50p. Department stores and museums generally have toilets. It's now an offence to urinate in the streets.

Tourist Information

Visit London (www.visitlondon. com) can fill you in on everything from attractions and events to tours and accommodation. Kiosks are dotted about the city and can also provide maps and brochures; some branches are able to book theatre tickets.

More Information

There aren't a huge number of Visit London tourist information centres in town, but they can be found at several places:

Heathrow Airport (www. visitlondon.com/tag/tourist-information-centre; Terminal 1, 2 & 3 Underground station concourse; ⊘7.30am-8.30pm)

King's Cross St Pancras Station (www.visitlondon.com/ tag/tourist-information-centre; Western Ticket Hall, Euston Rd N1; ⊘8am-6pm)

Liverpool Street Station (www.visitlondon.com/tag/ tourist-information-centre; Liverpool Street Station; ⊘8am-6pm; ⊜Liverpool St)

Piccadilly Circus Underground Station (www. visitlondon.com/tag/tourist-information-centre; Piccadilly

---

PRACTICALITIES

Smoking Forbidden in all enclosed public places. Most pubs have some sort of smoking area outside. Some pubs and restaurants have a no-vaping policy (so check for each establishment); vaping is not allowed on buses, the tube or trains in London.

Weights & Measures The UK uses a confusing mix of metric and imperial systems.

Circus Underground Station; ⊙9.30am-4pm)

Victoria Station (www.visitlondon.com/tag/tourist-information-centre; Victoria Station; ⊙7.15am-9.15pm Mon-Sat, 8.15am-8.15pm Sun; ⊖Victoria)

Travellers with Disabilities

For travellers with access needs, London is a frustrating mix of user-friendliness and head-in-the-sand disinterest. New hotels and modern tourist attractions are legally required to be accessible to people in wheelchairs, but many historic buildings, B&Bs and guesthouses are in older buildings, which are hard or prohibitively expensive to adapt. Similarly, visitors with vision, hearing or cognitive impairments will find their needs met in a piecemeal fashion.

The good news is that as a result of hosting the 2012 Olympics and Paralympics, and thanks to a forward-looking tourist board in VisitEngland, things are improving all the time.

Resources

Various websites offer useful information.

VisitLondon (www.visitlondon.com/traveller-information/essential-information/accessible-london) The tourist board's accessible travel page has useful links and information on accessible shops, hotels and toilets.

Accessible London (http://www.disabledgo.com/accessible-london-visit-london) Professionally audited guide, produced by DisabledGo, to access in the city.

Transport for London (www.tfl.gov.uk/transport-accessibility/) All the information you'll need to get around London on public transport, including 'how to' videos and a live Twitter feed keeping you up to date on transport access issues such as out-of-order lifts.

Accessible Travel Online Resources (http://shop.lonelyplanet.com/world/accessible-travel-online-resources-2017) Lonely Planet's guide offers many more useful links to get the best out of your visit to London.

Several organisations have a UK-wide remit.

Action on Hearing Loss (☏0808 808 0123, textphone 0808 808 9000; www.actiononhearingloss.org.uk) This is the main organisation working with deaf and hard of hearing people in the UK. Many ticket offices and banks are fitted with hearing loops to help the hearing-impaired; look for the ear symbol.

Disability Rights UK (☏020-7250 8181; www.disabilityrightsuk.org; ground fl, CAN Mezzanine, 49-51 East Rd, N1; ⊖Old Street) Umbrella organisation for voluntary groups for people with disabilities. Many wheelchair-accessible toilets can be opened only with a special Royal Association of Disability & Rehabilitation (Radar) key, which can be obtained via the website or from tourist offices for £5.40.

Royal National Institute for the Blind (☏0303-23 9999; www.rnib.org.uk; 105 Judd St, WC1; ⊙9.30am-5pm Mon-Fri; ⊖King's Cross) The UK's main charitable institution for people with sight loss.

Transport

➡ Around a quarter of tube stations, half of overground stations, most piers, all tram stops, the Emirates Air Line (cable car) and all DLR stations have step-free access. However, even if your starting and destination tube stations have step-free access, stations where you interchange may not and there is always the dreaded gap between train and platform to mind – careful planning and notification of a staff member are recommended before you board a train.

➡ Buses are a much better bet: all can be lowered to street level when they stop and wheelchair users travel free. A recent court case has confirmed that wheelchair users have priority use of the wheelchair space over pram (stroller) users, and bus drivers should back you up if a buggy is blocking the space.

➡ All black cabs are wheelchair-accessible, but power wheelchair users should note that the space is tight and sometimes headroom is insufficient. This should improve as a new fleet of more accessible black cabs is phased in over the next couple of years.

➡ Guide dogs are universally welcome on public transport and in hotels, restaurants, attractions etc.

➡ Throughout the capital pavements are generally in good repair, pedestrian crossings relatively frequent and well placed, and kerb cuts sufficient not to leave you stranded. The further you get from the centre of London, the more likely it is that you'll have the occasional issue with a missing kerb cut.

Visas

Not required for Australian, Canadian, New Zealand and US visitors, as well as several other nations, for stays of up to six months.

Entry & Exit Formalities

UK immigration authorities are stringent and methodical, so queues can get long at passport control, especially at Heathrow Airport.

More Information

Immigration to the UK is becoming tougher, particularly for those seeking to work or study. The exit of the UK from the EU will take several years, but the process has commenced and entry requirements for EU nationals may change. Make sure you check the website of the UK Border Agency (www.gov.uk/check-uk-visa) or with your local British embassy or consulate for the most up-to-date information.

VISA EXTENSIONS

Tourist visas can be extended as long as the total time spent in the UK is less than six months, or in clear emergencies (eg an accident, death of a relative). Contact the **UK Visas & Immigration Contact Centre** (☑0300 123 2241, text 0800 389 8289; ⊙9am-4.45pm Mon-Thu, to 4.30pm Fri) for details.

Women Travellers

Female visitors to London are unlikely to have many problems, provided they take the usual big-city precautions. Don't get into an Underground carriage with no one else in it or with just one or two men. And if you feel unsafe, you should take a taxi or licensed minicab.

Apart from the occasional wolf whistle and unwelcome body contact on the tube, women will find male Londoners reasonably enlightened. Going into pubs alone may not always be a comfortable experience, though it is in no way out of the ordinary.

Behind the Scenes

SEND US YOUR FEEDBACK

We love to hear from travellers – your comments keep us on our toes and help make our books better. Our well-travelled team reads every word on what you loved or loathed about this book. Although we cannot reply individually to your submissions, we always guarantee that your feedback goes straight to the appropriate authors, in time for the next edition. Each person who sends us information is thanked in the next edition – the most useful submissions are rewarded with a selection of digital PDF chapters.

Visit **lonelyplanet.com/contact** to submit your updates and suggestions or to ask for help. Our award-winning website also features inspirational travel stories, news and discussions.

Note: We may edit, reproduce and incorporate your comments in Lonely Planet products such as guidebooks, websites and digital products, so let us know if you don't want your comments reproduced or your name acknowledged. For a copy of our privacy policy visit lonelyplanet.com/privacy.

WRITER THANKS

Damian Harper

Many thanks to Ann Harper, Jasmin Tonge, Kevin and Maki Fallows, Rosemary Hadow, Lily Greensmith, Antonia Mavromatidou, Arabella Sneddon, Bill Moran, Jim Peake, my ever-helpful co-authors, and a big debt of gratitude again to Daisy, Tim and Emma.

Peter Dragicevich

Researching in London is always a joy, due in large part to the company of a great bunch of friends and London-based Lonely Planet writers and editors. Particular thanks go to Kurt Crommelin, Rob Carpenter, Tim Benzie, Paul Joseph, Marcus O'Donnell, Suzannah and Oliver de Montfort, Damian Harper, Emilie Filou, Steve Fallon, Tasmin Waby, Brana Vladisavljevic, Anna Tyler and James Smart for your company and encouragement.

Steve Fallon

Many thanks to fellow authors Emilie Filou, Damian Harper and Peter Dragicevich for their advice and suggestions along the way. Fellow Blue Badge Tourist Guides – too many to name – were also of great help, especially Lia Lalli. As always, I'd like to state my admiration, gratitude and great love for my partner, Michael Rothschild, especially in this year when wedding bells will peal.

Emilie Filou

Big thanks to my friends Catherine, Philippe, Kathleen and Nikki who came along during research and made it so enjoyable. Thanks also to my co-writers Steve, Damian and Peter for all the destination sharing. And finally, thank you to my wonderful husband, Adolfo, for joining me when possible, and our one-and-only Miss Dynamite, aka Sasha, for reminding me that life is all about simple pleasures.

ACKNOWLEDGEMENTS

Climate map data adapted from Peel MC, Finlayson BL & McMahon TA (2007) 'Updated World Map of the Köppen-Geiger Climate Classification', Hydrology and Earth System Sciences, 11, 163344.

Cover photograph: Traditional uniform of a guard outside St James's Palace, Julian Love / AWL ©

THIS BOOK

This 11th edition of Lonely Planet's *London* guidebook was researched and written by Damian Harper, Peter Dragicevich, Steve Fallon and Emilie Filou. This guidebook was produced by the following:

Destination Editor
James Smart

Product Editor Shona Gray

Senior Cartographer
Mark Griffiths

Book Designers Mazzy Prinsep, Wibowo Rusli

Assisting Editors Janet Austin, Katie Connolly, Pete Cruttenden, Gabby Innes, Susan Paterson, Monique

Perrin, Fionn Twomey, Simon Williamson

Cover Researcher
Naomi Parker

Illustrators Javier Zarracina, Michael Weldon

Thanks to Imogen Bannister, Hannah Cartmel, Will Jones, Martin Heng, Indra Kilfoyle, Rodrigo Macedo, Ryan Mak, Kirsten Rawlings, Kathryn Rowan, Tony Wheeler

Index

See also separate subindexes for:

✕ **EATING P429**

🍷 **DRINKING & NIGHTLIFE P431**

☆ **ENTERTAINMENT P432**

🛍 **SHOPPING P433**

🏃 **SPORTS & ACTIVITIES P434**

🛏 **SLEEPING P434**

✕ EATING

Sights 000
Map Pages **000**
Photo Pages **000**

London Maps

Map Legend

Sights

- Beach
- Bird Sanctuary
- Buddhist
- Castle/Palace
- Christian
- Confucian
- Hindu
- Islamic
- Jain
- Jewish
- Monument
- Museum/Gallery/Historic Building
- Ruin
- Shinto
- Sikh
- Taoist
- Winery/Vineyard
- Zoo/Wildlife Sanctuary
- Other Sight

Activities, Courses & Tours

- Bodysurfing
- Diving
- Canoeing/Kayaking
- Course/Tour
- Sento Hot Baths/Onsen
- Skiing
- Snorkelling
- Surfing
- Swimming/Pool
- Walking
- Windsurfing
- Other Activity

Sleeping

- Sleeping
- Camping
- Hut/Shelter

Eating

- Eating

Drinking & Nightlife

- Drinking & Nightlife
- Cafe

Entertainment

- Entertainment

Shopping

- Shopping

Information

- Bank
- Embassy/Consulate
- Hospital/Medical
- Internet
- Police
- Post Office
- Telephone
- Toilet
- Tourist Information
- Other Information

Geographic

- Beach
- Gate
- Hut/Shelter
- Lighthouse
- Lookout
- Mountain/Volcano
- Oasis
- Park
- Pass
- Picnic Area
- Waterfall

Population

- Capital (National)
- Capital (State/Province)
- City/Large Town
- Town/Village

Transport

- Airport
- BART station
- Border crossing
- Boston T/Tunnelbana/ T-bane station
- Bus
- Cable car/Funicular
- Cycling
- Ferry
- Metro/MRT station
- Monorail
- Parking
- Petrol station
- Subway/S-Bahn/Subte/ Skytrain/S-train station
- Taxi
- Train station/Railway/LRT
- Tram
- Tube Station
- Underground/U-Bahn station
- Other Transport

Routes

- Tollway
- Freeway
- Primary
- Secondary
- Tertiary
- Lane
- Unsealed road
- Road under construction
- Plaza/Mall
- Steps
- Tunnel
- Pedestrian overpass
- Walking Tour
- Walking Tour detour
- Path/Walking Trail

Boundaries

- International
- State/Province
- Disputed
- Regional/Suburb
- Marine Park
- Cliff
- Wall

Hydrography

- River, Creek
- Intermittent River
- Canal
- Water
- Dry/Salt/Intermittent Lake
- Reef

Areas

- Airport/Runway
- Beach/Desert
- Cemetery (Christian)
- Cemetery (Other)
- Glacier
- Mudflat
- Park/Forest
- Sight (Building)
- Sportsground
- Swamp/Mangrove

Note: Not all symbols displayed above appear on the maps in this eBook

436

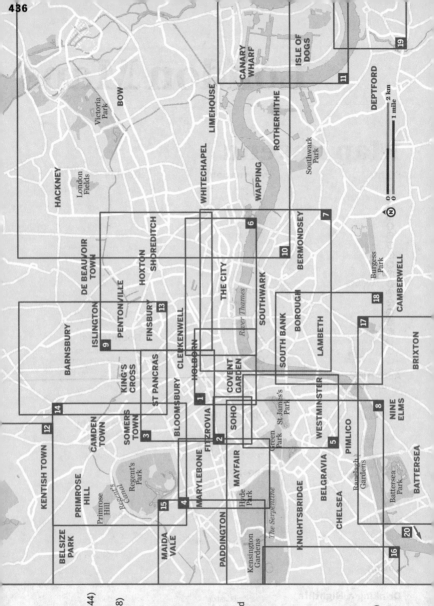

MAP INDEX

Key on p437

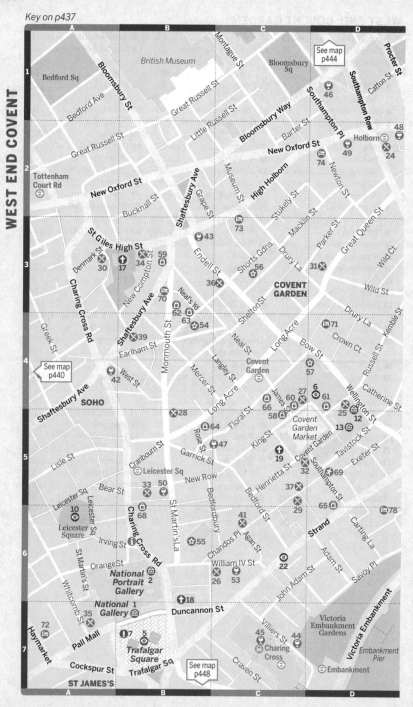

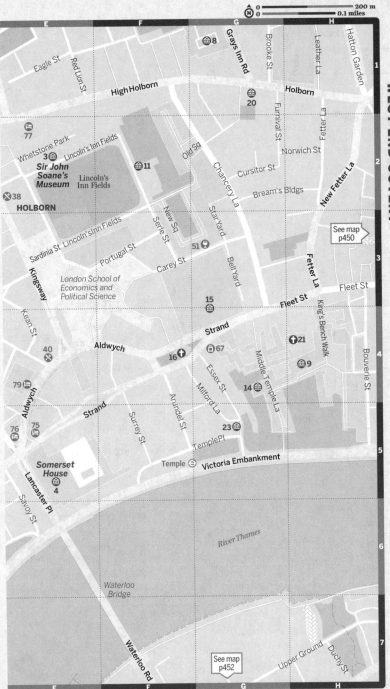

0   200 m
0   0.1 miles

E   **F**   **G**   **H**

8

Grays Inn Rd

Brooke St

Leather La

Hatton Garden

Eagle St

Red Lion St

High Holborn

Holborn

20

Furnival St

Fetter La

77

Whetstone Park

3   Lincoln's Inn Fields

Old Sq

Norwich St

New Fetter La

Sir John
Soane's
Museum

11

Lincoln's
Inn Fields

Chancery La

Cursitor St

Bream's Bldgs

38

HOLBORN

New Sq

Star Yard

See map
p450

Sardinia St   Lincoln's Inn Fields

Serle St

Portugal St

Carey St

Bell Yard

Fetter La

Fleet St

Kingsway

London School of
Economics and
Political Science

15

Fleet St

King's Bench Walk

Kean St

Strand

21

40

Aldwych

16   67

9

Bouverie St

79

Aldwych

Essex St

Middle Temple La

14

76   75

Strand

Surrey St

Arundel St

Milford La

23

Aldwych

Temple Pl

Somerset
House

4

Temple   Victoria Embankment

Lancaster Pl

Savoy St

River Thames

E   **F**   **G**   **H**

Waterloo
Bridge

Waterloo Rd

See map
p452

Upper Ground

Duchy St

6

7

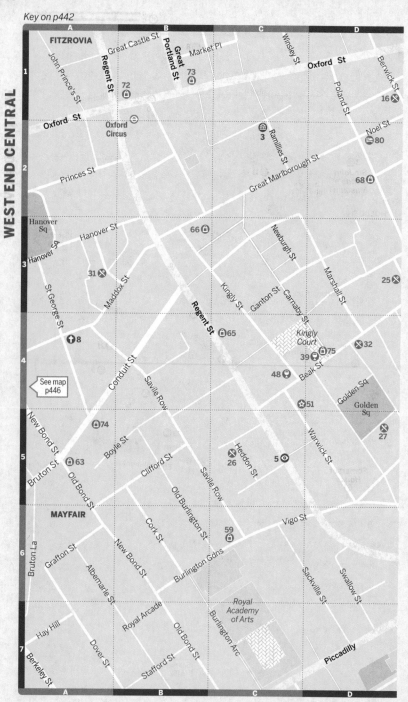

WEST END CENTRAL

FITZROVIA

MAYFAIR

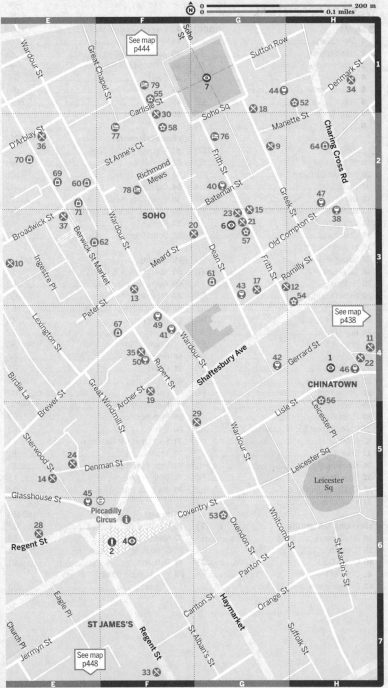

WEST END: CENTRAL *Map on p440*

WEST END CENTRAL

WEST END BLOOMSBURY *Map on p444*

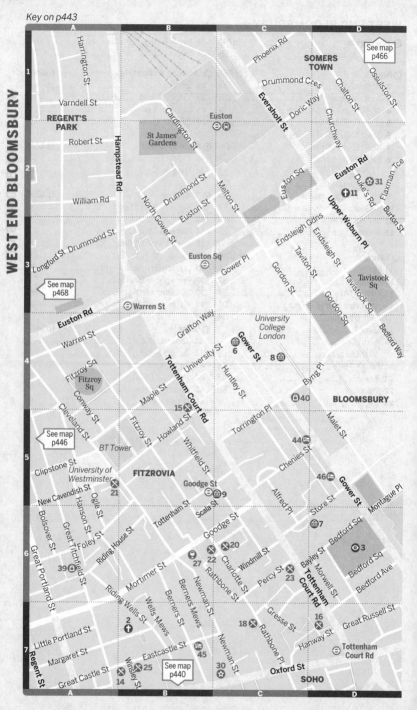

WEST END BLOOMSBURY

REGENT'S PARK

SOMERS TOWN

EUSTON

FITZROVIA

BLOOMSBURY

SOHO

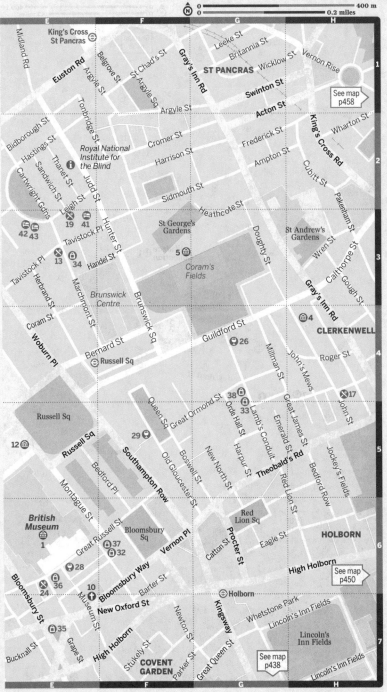

King's Cross
St Pancras

Midland Rd

Euston Rd

Belgrove St

Argyle St

St Chad's St

Grays's Inn Rd

ST PANCRAS

Leeke St

Britannia St

Wicklow St

Vernon Rise

Swinton St

See map
p458

Acton St

Argyle Sq

Tonbridge St

Argyle St

Cromer St

Frederick St

King's Cross Rd

Wharton St

Bidborough St

Hastings St

Royal National
Institute for
the Blind

Judd St

Harrison St

Ampton St

Cubitt St

Pakenham St

Thanet St

Sandwich St

Cartwright Gdns

Leigh St

Sidmouth St

Heathcote St

Doughty St

St Andrew's
Gardens

Wren St

Calthorpe St

Gough St

42 43

19 41

St George's
Gardens

5

13 34

Tavistock Pl

Handel St

Hunter St

Coram's
Fields

Tavistock Pl

Herbrand St

Marchmont St

Brunswick
Centre

Brunswick Sq

Guildford St

26

Gray's Inn Rd

CLERKENWELL

4

Coram St

Bernard St

Millman St

John's Mews

Roger St

Woburn Pl

Russell Sq

Russell Sq

Russell Sq

Bedford Pl

Southampton Row

29

Queen Sq

Great Ormond St

38

33

Orde Hall St

Lamb's Conduit St

Great James St

Emerald St

Theobald's Rd

17

John St

Jockey's Fields

12

Montague St

Bedford Pl

Old Gloucester St

Boswell St

New North St

Harpur St

Red Lion St

Bedford Row

British
Museum

1

Great Russell St

Bloomsbury
Sq

Vernon Pl

Red
Lion Sq

Procter St

Eagle St

HOLBORN

37 32

Catton St

High Holborn

See map
p450

28

Bloomsbury Way

Barter St

24 36

10

Museum St

New Oxford St

Holborn

Whetstone Park

Lincoln's Inn Fields

35

Bloomsbury St

High Holborn

Grape St

Bucknall St

COVENT
GARDEN

Stukely St

Newton St

Parker St

Kingsway

Great Queen St

Whetstone Park

Lincoln's
Inn Fields

See map
p438

Lincoln's Inn Fields

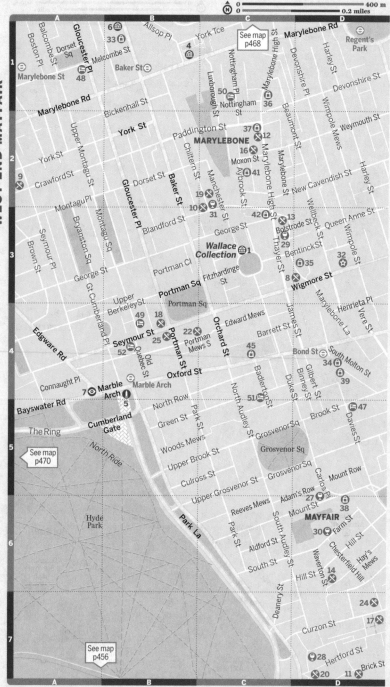

WEST END MAYFAIR

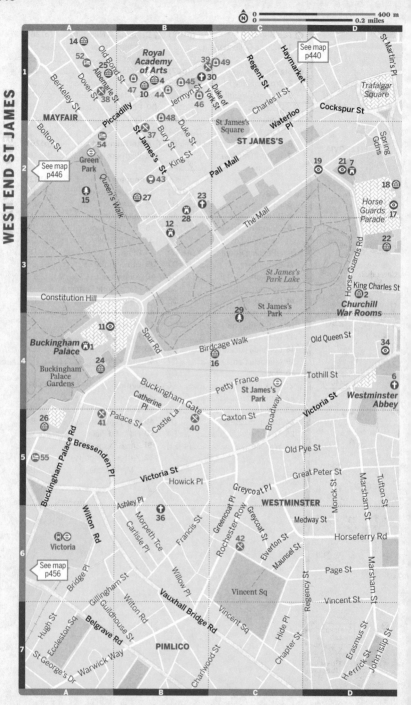

WEST END ST JAMES

See map p438
See map p452

CITY

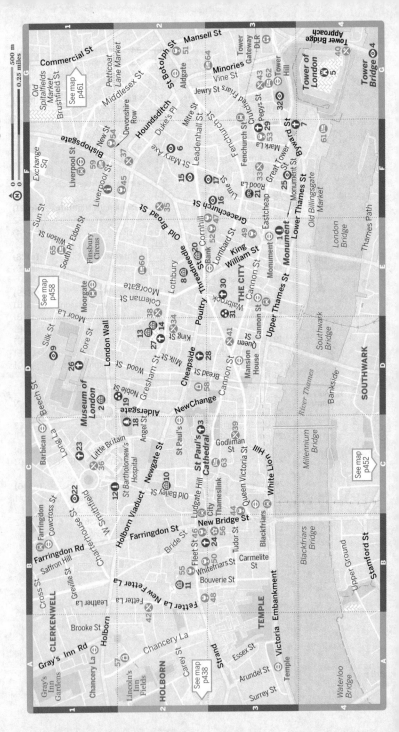

THE CITY

Key on p454

SOUTHBANK

HOLBORN

High Holborn
Holborn

Lincoln's
Inn Fields

Kingsway

Chancery La

New Fetter La

Farringdon St

Newgate St

St Paul's

Fleet St

**COVENT
GARDEN**

Aldwych

Fleet St

Fleet St

City
Thameslink

St Paul's
Cathedral

Arundel St

Bouverie St

Tudor St

Queen Victoria St

See map
p438

Strand

Temple

TEMPLE

Victoria Embankment

Blackfriars

White Lion

Hill

River Thames

Blackfriars
Bridge

●20

Waterloo
Bridge

Bankside Pier;
Tate Boat

13●

64

45

*Shakespeare's
Globe* 4

Park St

Festival
Pier

65

56

21

Upper Ground

Stamford St

**Tate
Modern** 7

SOUTHWARK

58

Waterloo Rd

Whittlesey St

68

Southwark St

*Southbank
Centre*

60

5

16

59

Cornwall Rd

Hatfields St

69

Great Guildford St

*Hungerford
Bridge*

66

55

72

Theed St
24 50

Roupell St

Southwark

Union St

*London
Eye Pier*

32

Waterloo
East

27

The Cut

38

67

3

*London
Eye*

Waterloo Rd

Waterloo

62

29

Great Suffolk St

19

York Rd

57

BOROUGH

10

2

Webber St

Blackfriars Rd

Southwark Bridge Rd

*London
Dungeon*

Belvedere Rd

54

Lower Marsh

Baylis Rd

Waterloo Rd

36

*Westminster
Bridge*

73

47

See map
p448

Westminster Bridge Rd

Lambeth North

Borough Rd

Lambeth Palace Rd

Carlisle La

Hercules Rd

London Rd

St George's Rd

Newington Causeway

*Archbishop's
Park*

**Elephant
& Castle**

*Lambeth
Bridge*

Lambeth Rd

LAMBETH

Kennington Rd

Brook Dr

Oswin St

Newport St

Newington Butts

Hampton St

See map
p476

See map
p450

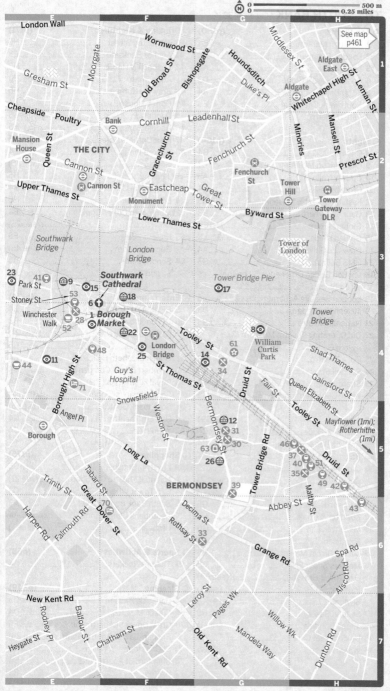

See map
p461

0   500 m
0   0.25 miles

London Wall

Wormwood St

Moorgate

Old Broad St

Bishopsgate

Houndsditch

Middlesex St

Duke's Pl

Aldgate
East

Aldgate

Whitechapel High St

Leman St

Gresham St

Cheapside

Poultry

Bank

Cornhill

Leadenhall St

Minories

Mansell St

Prescot St

Mansion
House

Queen St

THE CITY

Cannon St

Gracechurch St

Fenchurch St

Fenchurch
St

Tower
Hill

Cannon St

Eastcheap

Great
Tower St

Tower
Gateway
DLR

Upper Thames St

Monument

Lower Thames St

Byward St

Southwark
Bridge

London
Bridge

Tower of
London

23

Park St

41

9

15

Southwark
Cathedral

Tower Bridge Pier

17

Tower
Bridge

Stoney St

53

6

18

1

Winchester
Walk

28

Borough
Market

52

22

Tooley St

8

Shad Thames

48

25

London
Bridge

61

William
Curtis
Park

44

11

Guy's
Hospital

St Thomas St

14

34

Druid St

Fair St

Gainsford St

Queen Elizabeth St

71

Snowsfields

Weston St

Bermondsey St

Tooley St

Mayflower (1mi);
Rotherhithe
(1mi)

Angel Pl

12

31

46

Borough

Long La

63

30

37

Druid St

51

26

40

35

49

42

BERMONDSEY

39

Tower Bridge Rd

Maltby St

43

Trinity St

Tabard St

Great Dover St

70

Decima St

Abbey St

Harper Rd

Falmouth Rd

Rothsay St

33

Grange Rd

Spa Rd

Ascot Rd

New Kent Rd

Heygate St

Rodney Pl

Balfour St

Chatham St

Leroy St

Pages Wlk

Old Kent Rd

Willow Wk

Mandela Way

Dunton Rd

THE SOUTH BANK *Map on p452*

HYDE PARK *Map on p456*

⊚ Top Sights (p178)
1 Apsley House F3
2 Hyde Park D2
3 Kensington Palace A3
4 Natural History
   Museum C4
5 Science Museum C4
6 Victoria & Albert
   Museum C4

⊚ Sights (p187)
7 Albert Memorial B3
8 Brompton Oratory C4
9 Carlyle's House D7
10 Chelsea Old Church C7
11 Chelsea Physic
   Garden E7
12 Diana, Princess of
   Wales Memorial
   Fountain C2
13 Diana, Princess of
   Wales Memorial
   Playground A2
   Elfin Oak .... (see 13)
14 Holocaust Memorial
   Garden E3
15 Italian Gardens C1
16 Kensington Gardens A2
17 King's Road D6
18 Michelin House D5
19 National Army
   Museum E6
20 Peter Pan Statue C2
21 Rose Garden E3
22 Royal Albert Hall B3
23 Royal College of
   Music Museum B4
24 Royal Hospital
   Chelsea E6
25 Saatchi Gallery E5
   Sensational
   Butterflies .... (see 4)
26 Serpentine Gallery C3
27 Serpentine Lake D2
28 Serpentine Sackler
   Gallery C2
29 Speakers' Corner E1

30 The Arch C2
31 Wellington Arch F3
   Wildlife
   Photographer of
   the Year .... (see 4)

✕ Eating (p192)
32 Bar Boulud E3
33 Comptoir Libanais C5
34 Daquise C5
35 Daylesford Organic F5
36 Dinner by Heston
   Blumenthal E3
37 Five Fields E5
38 Gordon Ramsay E7
39 Hunan F6
40 Kazan G5
41 Launceston Place A4
42 L'Eto D4
   Magazine .... (see 28)
43 Medlar C7
44 Min Jiang A3
45 Ognisko C4
46 Orangery A2
47 Painted Heron C7
48 Pimlico Fresh G5
49 Rabbit D6
50 Rib Room E4
51 Tom's Kitchen D6
   V&A Cafe .... (see 6)
52 Zuma D3

○ Drinking & Nightlife (p198)
53 Anglesea Arms C6
54 Buddha Bar D3
55 Drayton Arms B6
56 Phene D7
57 Queen's Arms B4
58 Tomtom Coffee
   House F5

○ Entertainment (p198)
59 Cadogan Hall E5
60 Ciné Lumière C5
61 Pheasantry D6
   Royal Albert Hall .. (see 22)
62 Royal Court Theatre E5

○ Shopping (p199)
63 British Red Cross C7
   Conran Shop .... (see 18)
64 Harrods D4
65 Harvey Nichols E3
66 Jo Loves F5
67 John Sandoe Books E5
68 Limelight Movie Art C7
69 Penhaligon's D6
70 Peter Harrington C6
71 Peter Jones E5
72 Pickett E5
73 Rippon Cheese G5
74 T2 .... E5

○ Sports & Activities (p201)
75 Hyde Park Tennis &
   Sports Centre C3
76 Pure Gym C5
   Royal Albert
   Hall Grand
   Tour .... (see 22)
77 Serpentine
   Boathouse D2
78 Serpentine Lido C3
   Serpentine
   SolarShuttle
   Boat .... (see 77)
79 Winter Wonderland E2

○ Sleeping (p350)
80 37 Trevor Square D3
81 Ampersand Hotel C5
82 Artist Residence G5
83 Aster House C5
84 Astor Hyde Park B3
85 Beaufort House D4
86 Blakes B6
87 Cherry Court Hotel G5
88 Gore B4
89 Knightsbridge
   Hotel D4
90 Lanesborough F3
91 Levin Hotel D4
92 Lime Tree Hotel F5
93 Meininger B5
94 Number Sixteen C5

KENSINGTON & HYDE PARK

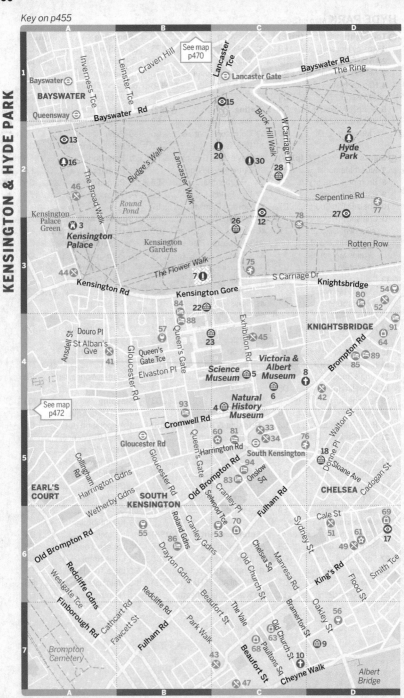

KENSINGTON & HYDE PARK

See map p470

See map p472

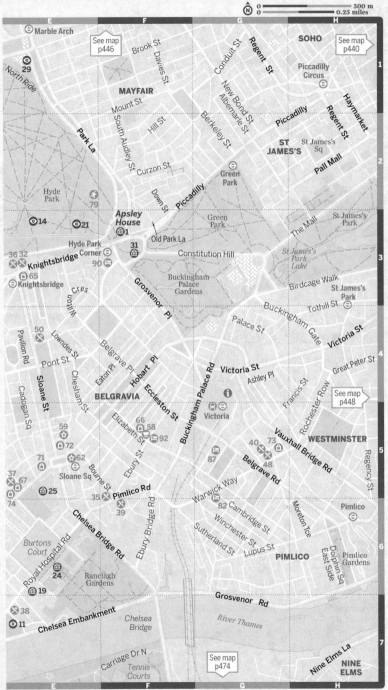

0 — 500 m
0 — 0.25 miles

Marble Arch

See map
p446

29

North Ride

MAYFAIR

Brook St

Davies St

Conduit St

Regent St

SOHO

Piccadilly
Circus

See map
p440

New Bond St

Albemarle St

Park La

Mount St

South Audley St

Hill St

Berkeley St

Curzon St

Piccadilly

Haymarket

Regent St

ST
JAMES'S

St James's
Sq

Pall Mall

Hyde
Park

79

14   21

Down St

Piccadilly

Green
Park

Green Park

The Mall

St James's
Park

Apsley
House

1

Old Park La

Constitution Hill

St James's
Park
Lake

36 32

Knightsbridge

65

Knightsbridge

Hyde Park
Corner

90

31

Buckingham
Palace
Gardens

Birdcage Walk

Buckingham Gate

Tothill St

St James's
Park

Grosvenor Pl

Palace St

Victoria St

50

Wilton Cres

Belgrave Pl

Hobart Pl

Eccleston St

Buckingham Palace Rd

Victoria St

Ashley Pl

Francis St

Rochester Row

Great Peter St

See map
p448

Pavilion Rd

Lowndes St

Pont St

Chesham St

Eaton Pl

BELGRAVIA

Elizabeth St

Victoria

Sloane St

Cadogan Sq

59

66 58

92

40 73

Vauxhall Bridge Rd

WESTMINSTER

72

71

62

87

48

Belgrave Rd

Regency St

37
67

Sloane Sq

25

35

Bourne St

Ebury St

Pimlico Rd

39

Ebury Bridge Rd

Warwick Way

82 Cambridge St

Winchester St

Lupus St

Moreton Tce

Pimlico

Pimlico

74

Chelsea Bridge Rd

Royal Hospital Rd

Burtons
Court

24

Ranelagh
Gardens

Sutherland St

PIMLICO

Dolphin Sq
East Side

Pimlico
Gardens

19

38

11

Chelsea Embankment

Chelsea
Bridge

River Thames

Grosvenor Rd

Carriage Dr N

Tennis
Courts

See map
p474

Nine Elms La

NINE
ELMS

CLERKENWELL, SHOREDITCH & SPITALFIELDS

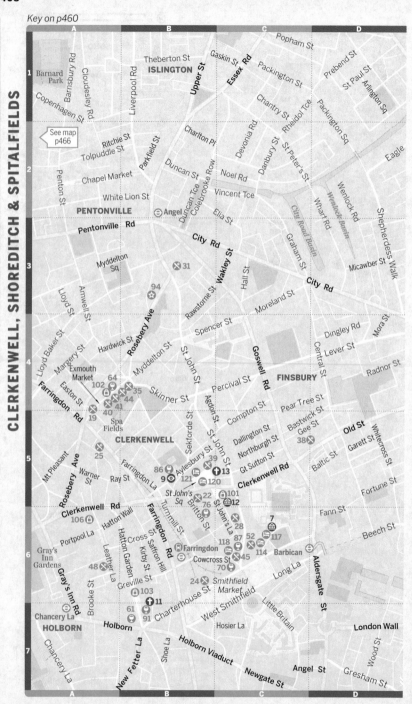

CLERKENWELL. SHOREDITCH & SPITALFIELDS *Map on p458*

EAST LONDON *Map on p462*

Key on p461

EAST LONDON

HOMERTON

Clifden Rd

Glyn Rd

Kenworthy Rd

Downs Park Rd

Clarence Rd

DALSTON

Hackney
Downs

Dalston
Kingsland

Ridley Rd

Dalston La

Homerton High St

Homerton

21

24

Morning La

Hackney
Central

107

108

105 **52**

97

11

Reading La

Chatham Pl

Cassland Rd

Graham Rd

Ball's Pond
Rd

116

Dalston
Junction

Forest Rd

Richmond Rd

49

113

HACKNEY

London
Fields

Well St

Victoria Park Rd

82

**DE BEAUVOIR
TOWN**

Downham
Rd

41

Middleton Rd

Albion Dr

13

48

77

Well St

Laurston Rd

44

84

31

BOW

Haggerston

35

Broadway
Market

40

67

104

43

Victoria Park Rd

Grove Rd

Old Ford Rd

60

Dunston Rd

45

71

32

36

Regent's Canal

Roman Rd

HAGGERSTON

53

Cambridge
Heath

Old Ford Rd

87

10

61

118

51

Columbia Rd

85

88

47

**BETHNAL
GREEN**

30

Hoxton

37

106

55

Cambridge
Heath Rd

See map
p458

6

Gosset St

64

Bethnal
Green

Old St

Bethnal Green Rd

66

42

Bethnal
Green

Grove Rd

Shoreditch
High St

Cheshire
St

103

Vallance Rd

Brick La

Stepney
Green

Mile End Rd

15

Mile
End

Commercial St

WHITECHAPEL

Whitechapel

4

29

96 **114**

Stepney Green

**MILE
END**

Mile
End
Park

18

**Whitechapel
Gallery**

76

Whitechapel
Rd

100

Stepney Way

STEPNEY

Liverpool St

69

63

59

Liverpool St

Middlesex St

62

1

33 **117**

8 **28**

New Rd

Belgrave St

LIMEHOUSE

81

Bishopsgate

Aldgate

Ale St

Mansell St

Ellen St

Cannon St Rd

Commercial Rd

91

Commercial
Limehouse
DLR

See map
p450

38

119

Shadwell
DLR

22

Narrow St

73

Fenchurch St

**Tower
Gateway
DLR**

101

Cable St

5

The Highway

Rotherhithe
Tunnel

Tower
Hill

East Smithfield

Ensign St

WAPPING

Wapping
Wall

83

Salter Rd

26

23

**Tower
Bridge**

Wapping High St

Wapping

River Thames

ROTHERHITHE

Tooley St

58

90

65

78

Rotherhithe

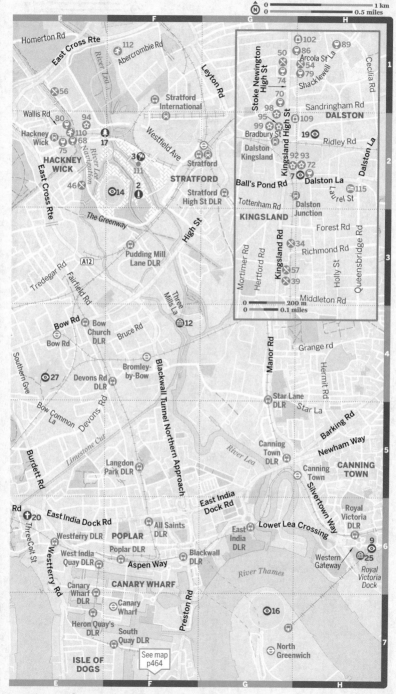

EAST LONDON

Homerton Rd
East Cross Rte
112
Abercrombie Rd
Leyton Rd

102
50
Arcola St
54
79
89
Shacklewell La
Cecilia Rd

Stratford
International
Westfield Ave

Stoke Newington High St
70
98
95
99
74
Bradbury St
Kingsland High St
109
DALSTON
Sandringham Rd
19
Ridley Rd
Dalston La

Wallis Rd
80
94
Hackney
Wick
75
110
68
17
HACKNEY
WICK
East Cross Rte
46
14
3
111
2
STRATFORD
Stratford
Stratford High St DLR

Dalston
Kingsland
92 93
72
7
Dalston La
115
Laurel St

Ball's Pond Rd
Tottenham Rd
KINGSLAND
Dalston
Junction
Forest Rd
Queensbridge Rd
Holly St

The Greenway
Pudding Mill
Lane DLR
A12
High St
Three Mills La

Tredegar Rd
Fairfield Rd

Mortimer Rd
Hertford Rd
Kingsland Rd
34
57
39
Richmond Rd
Middleton Rd

Bow Rd
Bow
Church
DLR
Bow Rd
Bruce Rd
12
Grange rd

27
Devons Rd
DLR
Bromley-
by-Bow
Manor Rd

Southern Gve
Bow Common La
Devons Rd
Blackwall Tunnel Northern Approach
Limestone Cut

Star Lane
DLR
Star La
Barking Rd
Newham Way
Hermit Rd

Burdett Rd
Langdon
Park DLR
River Lea
Canning
Town
DLR
Canning
Town
CANNING
TOWN

Silvertown Way
Royal
Victoria
DLR
9
25

Rd
20
East India Dock Rd
Westferry DLR
POPLAR
All Saints
DLR
East India Dock Rd
East
India
DLR
Lower Lea Crossing
Western
Gateway
Royal
Victoria
Dock

ThreeColt St
Westferry Rd
West India
Quay DLR
Poplar DLR
Aspen Way
Blackwall
DLR
Preston Rd
River Thames

Canary Wharf
DLR
CANARY WHARF
Canary
Wharf

Heron Quay's
DLR
South
Quay DLR
ISLE OF
DOGS
See map
p464
16
North
Greenwich

DOCKLANDS

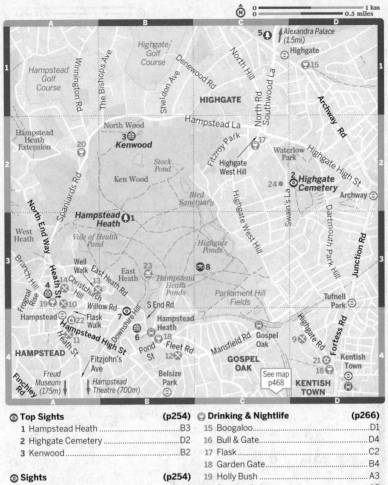

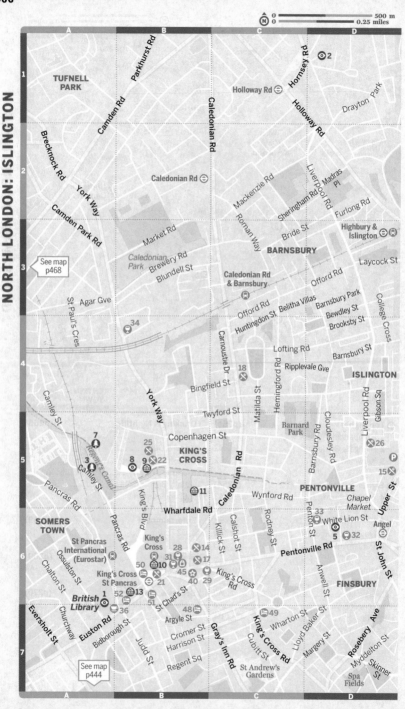

0 500 m
0 0.25 miles
N

TUFNELL PARK

Parkhurst Rd

Camden Rd

Hornsey Rd

2

Holloway Rd ⊖

Holloway Rd

Drayton Park

Caledonian Rd

Brecknock Rd

York Way

Camden Park Rd

Caledonian Rd ⊖

Mackenzie Rd

Liverpool Rd

Madras Pl

Sheringham Rd

Furlong Rd

Roman Way

Bride St

Highbury & Islington ⊖

BARNSBURY

See map p468

Market Rd

Caledonian Park

Brewery Rd

Blundell St

Caledonian Rd & Barnsbury

Offord Rd

Laycock St

Agar Gve

St Paul's Cres

Offord Rd

Huntingdon St

Belitha Villas

Barnsbury Park

Bewdley St

Brooksby St

College Cross

34

Carnoustie Dr

Lofting Rd

Barnsbury St

ISLINGTON

Hemingford Rd

Ripplevale Gve

18

Matilda St

Liverpool Rd

Gibson Sq

Bingfield St

Barnard Park

Cloudesley Rd

26

York Way

Twyford St

Barnsbury Rd

15

Copenhagen St

Camley St

25

KING'S CROSS

Caledonian Rd

PENTONVILLE

P

8

9

22

Pancras Rd

11

Wynford Rd

Upper St

Chapel Market

Penton St

33

White Lion St

Angel

5

32

Wharfdale Rd

Calshot St

Rodney St

Pentonville Rd

SOMERS TOWN

St Pancras International (Eurostar)

Osulston St

Chalton St

Pancras Rd

King's Cross

28

14

31

17

Killick St

King's Cross Rd

Anwell St

FINSBURY

St John St

50

10

King's Cross St Pancras

45

40

29

21

British Library

1

52

13

36

St Chad's St

51

48

Wharton St

49

St Chad's St

Argyle St

Cromer St

Harrison St

Gray's Inn Rd

Cubitt St

King's Cross Rd

Lloyd Baker St

Margery St

Rosebery Ave

Eversholt St

Churchway

Euston Rd

Bidborough St

Judd St

Regent Sq

St Andrew's Gardens

Myddelton St

Skinner St

Spa Fields

See map p444

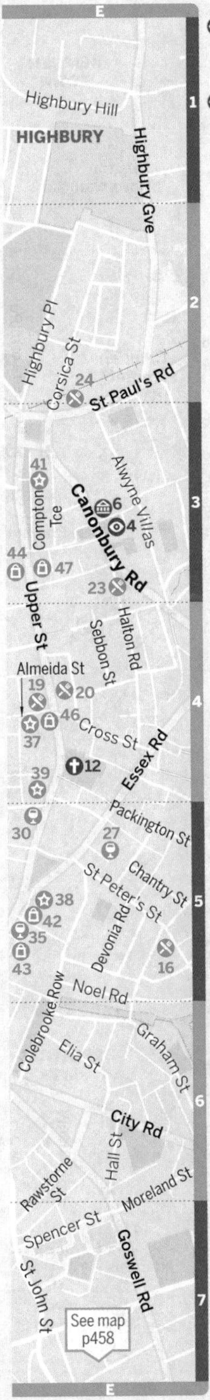

E
Highbury Hill
HIGHBURY
Highbury Gve
Highbury Pl
Corsica St
24
St Paul's Rd
41
Compton Tce
Canonbury Rd
6
4
Alwyne Villas
44
47
23
Upper St
Halton Rd
Sebbon St
Almeida St
19
20
46
37
Cross St
Essex Rd
39
12
30
Packington St
27
Chantry St
St Peter's St
38
42
35
43
Devonia Rd
16
Colebrooke Row
Noel Rd
Elia St
Graham St
City Rd
Hall St
Rawstorne St
Moreland St
Spencer St
Goswell Rd
St John St
See map p458
E
1
2
3
4
5
6
7

Top Sights (p246)

1 British Library........................A6

Sights (p249)

2 Arsenal Emirates Stadium...............................D1
3 Camley Street Natural Park A5
4 Canonbury Square E3
5 Crystal Maze........................ D6
6 Estorick Collection of Modern Italian Art E3
7 Gasholder Park A5
8 Granary Square.....................B5
9 House of Illustration B5
10 King's Cross Station............ B6
11 London Canal Museum B5
12 St Mary's Church.................E4
13 St Pancras Station & Hotel B6

Eating (p258)

14 Addis................................... B6
Caravan..........................(see 8)
15 Chilango D5
16 Duke of Cambridge...............E5
17 Foodilic B6
Grain Store ....(see 8)
18 Iberia.................................... C4
Karpo .... (see 51)
King's Library Café.............................(see 1)
Kipferl ....(see 43)
19 Le Mercury.............................E4
20 Ottolenghi E4
21 Real Food Market................ B6
22 Ruby Violet.............................B5
23 Smokehouse...........................E3
24 Trullo E2
25 Waitrose King's Cross B5
26 Yipin China............................D5

Drinking & Nightlife (p264)

27 69 Colebrooke Row.............. E5
28 Bar Pepito..............................B6
29 Big Chill House......................B6
Booking Office Bar & Restaurant................(see 52)
British Library Coffee Shop ....(see 1)
30 Bull.. E5
31 Camino...................................B6
32 Castle D6
33 Craft Beer Co D6
Drink, Shop & Do .... (see 45)
34 Egg LDN B4
35 Elk in the Woods E5
36 Origin Coffee Roasters A7

Entertainment (p267)

37 Almeida E4
38 Angel Comedy...................... E5
39 King's Head Theatre............. E4
40 Scala.......................................B6
41 Union Chapel......................... E3

Shopping (p269)

42 Annie's Vintage Costume & Textiles........................... E5
43 Camden Passage Market.... E5
Fortnum & Mason........(see 13)
44 Gill Wing E3
Harry Potter Shop at Platform 9¾............. (see 10)
45 Housmans B6
46 Mary's Living & Giving Shop E4
47 Sampler E3

Sleeping (p354)

48 Clink261 ....B7
49 Clink78 ....C7
50 Great Northern Hotel...........B6
51 Megaro..................................B6
52 St Pancras Renaissance London Hotel.......................B6

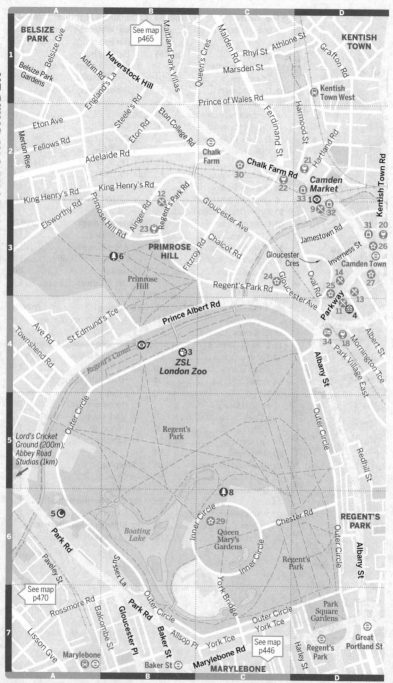

NORTH LONDON: CAMDEN

NOTTING HILL & WEST LONDON

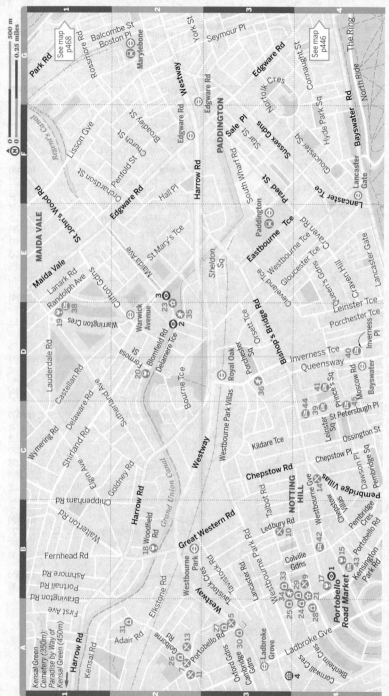

500 m
0.25 miles

See map p468

See map p446

Kensal Green
Cemetery (350m);
Paradise by Way of
Kensal Green (450m)

NOTTING HILL & WEST LONDON

WEST LONDON: SHEPHERDS BUSH

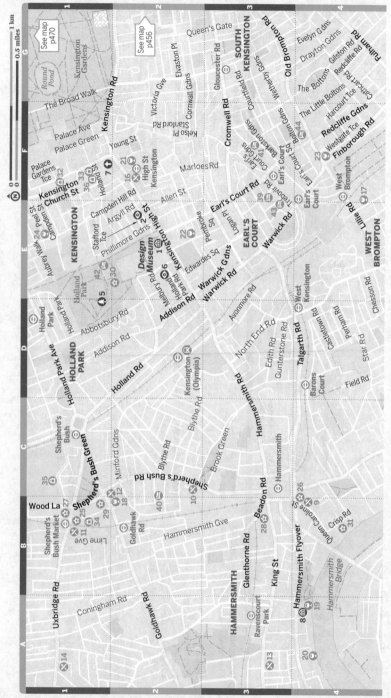

0   0.5 miles
0   1 km

See map p470

See map p456

WEST LONDON: SHEPHERDS BUSH

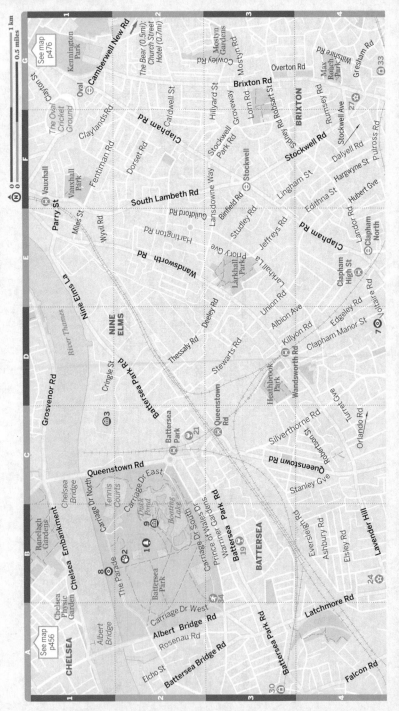

SOUTH LONDON: BRIXTON

See map p476

1 km
0.5 miles

CHELSEA

See map p456

G

Kennington Park

The Bear (0.5mi);
Church Street
Hotel (0.7mi);

Mostyn Gardens

Cowley Rd

Overton Rd

Max Roach Park

Gresham Rd

Wiltshire Rd

33

Oval

Camberwell New Rd

Brixton Rd

Brixton

Rumsey Rd

27

F

The Oval Cricket Ground

Claylands Rd

Clapham Rd

Caldwell St

Hillyard St

Stockwell Park Rd

Groveway

Lorn Rd

Sidney Rd

Robsart St

Stockwell Rd

Stockwell Ave

Dalyell Rd

Hargwyne St

Pulross Rd

Vauxhall

Vauxhall Park

Fentiman Rd

Dorset Rd

Stockwell

Lingham St

Edithna St

Landor Rd

Hubert Gve

E

Parry St

Miles St

Wyvil Rd

South Lambeth Rd

Guildford Rd

Wandsworth Rd

Hartington Rd

Lansdowne Way

Binfield Rd

Studley Rd

Jeffreys Rd

Clapham Rd

Clapham North

Clapham High St

Voltaire Rd

D

River Thames

Nine Elms La

NINE ELMS

Cringle St

Battersea Park Rd

Thessaly Rd

Larkhall Park

Priory Gve

Larkhall La

Deeley Rd

Stewarts Rd

Union Rd

Albion Ave

Killyon Rd

Wandsworth Rd

Edgeley Rd

Clapham Manor St

7

C

Grosvenor Rd

3

Battersea Park

21

Queenstown Rd

Heathbrook Park

Silverthorne Rd

Roberson St

Queenstown Rd

Turret Gve

Orlando Rd

B

Ranelagh Gardens

Chelsea Bridge

Chelsea Embankment

Queenstown Rd

Carriage Dr North

Tennis Courts

Carriage Dr East

Duck Pond

Boating Lake

9

Prince of Wales Gardens

Carriage Dr South

Warriner Gardens

Battersea Park Rd

Battersea

19

BATTERSEA

Stanley Gve

Eversleigh Rd

Ashbury Rd

Elsley Rd

Lavender Hill

24

A

Chelsea Physic Garden

Albert Bridge

2

8

The Parade

Battersea Park

1

Carriage Dr West

Albert Bridge Rd

Rosenau Rd

Elcho St

Battersea Bridge Rd

34

Battersea Park Rd

Battersea Bridge Rd

Latchmore Rd

Falcon Rd

30

SOUTH LONDON: BRIXTON

SOUTH LONDON

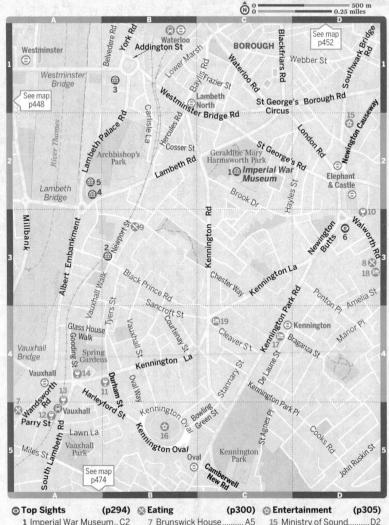

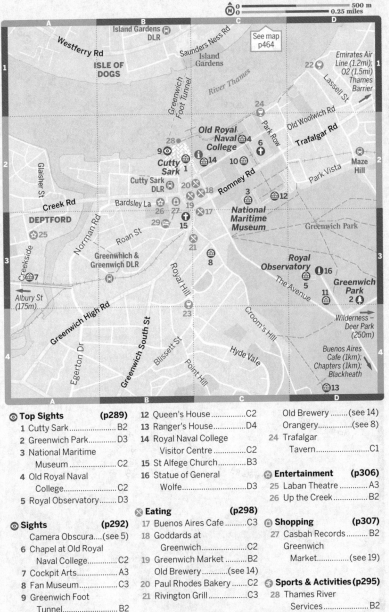

RICHMOND

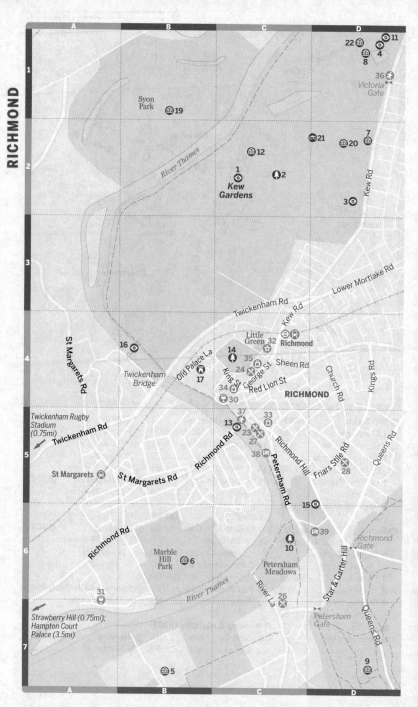

0   500 m
0   0.25 miles

Kew Palace (800m); Orangery (800m)

City Barge (1mi)

29
25
Kew Gardens

Mortlake Rd

Chiswick House (1mi); Hogarth's House (1.2mi)

Sandycombe Rd

Fulham Cemetery

Lower Richmond Rd

Orange Pekoe; White Hart (0.75mi)

Clifford Ave

North Sheen

Manor Rd

Sheen Rd

Barnes (2mi); London Wetland Centre (2mi); Putney (2.5mi); Wimbledon (6mi)

Richmond & East Sheen Cemetery

Sawyer's Hill

18

Richmond Park

Isabella Plantation (1.2mi)

OUR STORY

A beat-up old car, a few dollars in the pocket and a sense of adventure. In 1972 that's all Tony and Maureen Wheeler needed for the trip of a lifetime – across Europe and Asia overland to Australia. It took several months, and at the end – broke but inspired – they sat at their kitchen table writing and stapling together their first travel guide, *Across Asia on the Cheap*. Within a week they'd sold 1500 copies. Lonely Planet was born.

Today, Lonely Planet has offices in Franklin, London, Melbourne, Oakland, Dublin, Beijing and Delhi, with more than 600 staff and writers. We share Tony's belief that 'a great guidebook should do three things: inform, educate and amuse'.

OUR WRITERS

Damian Harper

Notting Hill & West London, Richmond, Kew & Hampton Court, Greenwich & South London, Kensington & Hyde Park, Survival Guide Born off the Strand within earshot of Bow Bells (favourable wind permitting), Damian grew up in Notting Hill way before it was discovered by Hollywood. A onetime Shakespeare and Company bookseller and radio presenter, Damian has been authoring guidebooks for Lonely Planet since the 1990s, and is a member of the British Guild of Travel Writers. He lives in South London with his wife and two kids, frequently returning to China (his second home). You can find out more at www.damianharper.com.

Peter Dragicevich

The City, East London, Survival Guide, Plan Your Trip After a successful career in niche newspaper and magazine publishing, both in his native New Zealand and in Australia, Peter finally gave into Kiwi wanderlust, giving up staff jobs to chase his diverse roots around much of Europe. Over the last decade he's written literally dozens of guidebooks for Lonely Planet on an oddly disparate collection of countries, all of which he's come to love. He once again calls Auckland, New Zealand his home – although his current nomadic existence means he's often elsewhere.

Steve Fallon

The West End, Plan Your Trip & Understand After 15 full years living in the centre of the known universe – East London – Steve cockney-rhymes in his sleep, eats jellied eel for brekkie, drinks lager by the bucketful and dances round the occasional handbag. As always, for this edition of London he did everything the hard/fun way: walking the walks, seeing the sights, taking (some) advice from friends, colleagues and the odd taxi driver and digesting everything in sight. Steve is a qualified London Blue Badge Tourist Guide (www.steveslondon.com).

Emilie Filou

The South Bank, Clerkenwell, Shoreditch & Spitalfields, Hampstead & North London, Day Trips & Plan Your Trip Emilie Filou is a freelance journalist specialising in business and development issues, with a particular interest in Africa. Born in France, Emilie is now based in London, UK, from where she makes regular trips to Africa. Her work has appeared in publications such as *The Economist*, *The Guardian*, the BBC, the *Africa Report* and the *Christian Science Monitor*. She has contributed to some 20 Lonely Planet guides including France, Provence, London, West Africa, Madagascar and Tunisia. You can find out more on www.emiliefilou.com

Published by Lonely Planet Global Limited
CRN 554153
11th edition – February 2018
ISBN 978 1 78657352 0
© Lonely Planet 2018   Photographs © as indicated 2018
10 9 8 7 6 5 4 3 2 1
Printed in Singapore